Jolly Fellows

GENDER RELATIONS IN THE AMERICAN EXPERIENCE

Joan E. Cashin and Ronald G. Walters, *Series Editors*

Jolly Fellows

Male Milieus in Nineteenth-Century America

RICHARD STOTT

The Johns Hopkins University Press
Baltimore

© 2009 The Johns Hopkins University Press

All rights reserved. Published 2009
Printed in the United States of America on acid-free paper
2 4 6 8 9 7 5 3 1

The Johns Hopkins University Press
2715 North Charles Street
Baltimore, Maryland 21218-4363
www.press.jhu.edu

Library of Congress Cataloging-in-Publication Data
Stott, Richard Briggs.
Jolly fellows : male milieus in nineteenth-century America / Richard Stott.
p. cm.
Includes bibliographical references and index.
ISBN-13: 978-0-8018-9137-3 (hardcover : alk. paper)
ISBN-10: 0-8018-9137-X (hardcover : alk. paper)
1. Men—United States—History—19th century. 2. Men—Psychology—History—19th century. 3. Masculinity—United States—History—19th century. 4. Violence in men—United States. I. Title.
HQ1090.3.S76 2009
305.38'96920907309034—dc22 2008044003

A catalog record for this book is available from the British Library.

Special discounts are available for bulk purchases of this book. For more information, please contact Special Sales at 410-516-6936 or specialsales@press.jhu.edu.

The Johns Hopkins University Press uses environmentally friendly book materials, including recycled text paper that is composed of at least 30 percent post-consumer waste, whenever possible. All of our book papers are acid-free, and our jackets and covers are printed on paper with recycled content.

Contents

Jolly Fellows

Introduction

"Why have men quit fighting?" wondered newspaperman Arch Bristow. He knew, from his local history research and even from his own earliest memories, that men in the nineteenth century had once brawled constantly—in barrooms, at dances, circuses, baseball games, even camp meetings. "In every town and village in the country there were wicked, brutal fights." Each locality had its bullies, men who "would rather fight than eat," and the battles between them attracted intense popular interest. Then the fighting stopped. Bristow wondered why. Decreased drinking was perhaps part of the answer. He sensed, however, that something more profound was at work. There must be, he was certain, "some larger, finer reason why fighting has gone out of style." What that reason might be, however, Bristow could not discern.[1]

This is a study of masculine spaces in nineteenth-century America that seeks to discover both why men fought and why they stopped fighting. The brawls that left such a deep impression on Bristow and others were part of a distinctive male comportment that consisted of not just fighting but also heavy drinking, gambling and playing pranks. Men who engaged in such behavior were called "jolly fellows." Although the jolly fellows were a subset of the male population, whenever men, especially young men, gathered in milieus that were all male or where women were rare, such conduct could occur. Such behavior was tolerated, even condoned, by men who were not themselves drinkers, fighters, or gamblers. Both whites and blacks engaged in jolly fellowship. Such comportment was not unique to nineteenth-century America; it was found in colonial times and had equivalents in Europe as well.

In the first half of the nineteenth century, the religious revivals known as the Second Great Awakening and the growth of the middle class brought new standards of respectability that stigmatized this traditional deportment and ended the tolerance that had accompanied it. The temperance movement played a crucial role in reforming male conduct. The sight of men reeling around drunk or locked in bloody combat faded away. Bristow was only one of many observers who believed they had witnessed a momentous change in male behavior. It was, one writer believed, nothing less than a "moral revolution."[2] Respectability, however, did not completely kill jolly fellowship. Economic development and migration patterns created demographic concentrations of young men in which unruly masculine behavior was preserved. In certain city neighborhoods and in the West, jolly fellowship not only persisted but, for a time, flourished.

The decline of jolly fellowship took decades to occur. In some communities the alteration in comportment seemed to have taken place within a few years; in others it took much longer. One locality might be transformed while in a nearby settlement jolly fellows still held high carnival. There was a regional pattern. Reform began in the East and gradually spread south and west. The 1820s and the 1830s seemed to have been the critical era in the Northeast, but in some places more orderly male conduct was apparent in the first decade of the century while the reformation bypassed others until the 1850s. In some locales in the South, jolly men did not begin to abandon their traditional rowdy lifestyle until the 1870s or even later. Unrestrained drinking, fighting, and gambling lasted longest in the West; in the 1880s and 1890s male locales in the region strongly resembled disorderly eastern communities during the early part of the century.

Men drinking, fighting, gambling, and playing dumb jokes? Yes, men in groups can be pretty crude. Boys will be boys. Taken for granted. One of the aims of this study is to cease taking such behavior for granted and to scrutinize and analyze it. Where did it originate? Was it natural, biological? Why drinking, fighting, gambling, and pranks? And then what happened to jolly fellowship? If investigating the origin and meaning of jolly fellowship is central to this study, so too is explaining its decline. Why did such conduct become the target of censure and then ebb? Once, the way for men to settle an argument was to fight it out—the barroom brawl was an American institution. Onlookers would exhort combatants to greater effort. This would be almost unimaginable by the twentieth century, and if an altercation did start, bystanders likely would quickly halt it. Why have men quit fighting?[3]

Part of the story of jolly fellowship and its waning is connected to changing concepts of what it meant to be a man. Conceptions of manhood and masculinity in the past are elusive and were continually evolving. Assessing the relationship of jolly fellowship to such ideas is especially challenging. Drinking, fighting, and gambling are activities that have been traditionally associated with men, and it seems probable that there were men who felt that being jolly fellows made them real men. But what "man" signified varied in different settings, and for most men, even for most jolly fellows, it seems that the idea that men would have a disorderly deportment was only part of a complex of assumptions about how men should behave. Such views were always changing, and in the middle decades of the nineteenth century a divergent view of manhood won increasing allegiance. Jolly fellowship was turned on its head: not drinking, not fighting, and not gambling made a man. This was not a new idea—moralists had long lauded male constraint. This subdued manhood, whose strongest advocates were found among evangelical Christians and the emerging middle class, was to have a powerful influence on American society and culture.[4]

The "moral revolution" that marginalized jolly fellowship seemed to many people at the time something close to a change in human nature. They groped to understand its cause. Some believed that such a transformation in mental attitudes was simply beyond explanation—"a change began to come over the minds of the people" was the way one observer put it. Others saw the hand of God in it. The transformation of male character seemed so thoroughgoing as to be miraculous; men had seen the light and were abandoning the barroom and gaming table for home and the Christian life. Some connected it to the spread of market values: men were voluntarily relinquishing their traditional practices because a sober and temperate middle-class lifestyle was economically attractive. There were also skeptics who doubted that men had really changed much at all. Their behavior had become more sedate, but had underlying attitudes really altered? Men unpersuaded of the benefits of personal reform had been compelled to conform, these skeptics believed, by employers and the law. Refinement was only skin deep; a jolly heart continued to beat.[5]

The reformation of male comportment created social and cultural reverberations that lasted into the twentieth century. Those who believed that fundamental attitudes had changed less than behavior had a point. Many men chafed at, in a constantly repeated phrase, "the restraints of society" and retained a deep-seated fascination for jolly fellowship. They may not have drank themselves or fought or gambled, but they had not stopped thinking about drinking, fighting, and gambling. Women had played an important role in temperance and the moral reform movements of the period, and for many men, milieus where women were scarce were an invitation to jolly behavior. American "progress," the growth of cities and westward expansion, was, paradoxically, fortifying traditional disorderly comportment by creating urban neighborhoods and mining and cattle towns that were heavily male. The most significant such enclave was the Bowery in New York City, where jolly fellowship emerged as a counterculture. Once, drinking, fighting, gambling, and playing pranks seemed ordinary male behavior; it was simply the way men were. But after it had been stigmatized by reformers, jolly conduct became a repudiation of respectability and emerged as a critical cultural reference point. It now sent a message and thus could be wielded for a cultural purpose. Compared with articulate, restrained manhood, jolly fellowship had few spokesmen. Few publicly argued that men should get drunk and get into fights. But if it had few open defenders, unruly male demeanor found many celebrators in popular culture. As New York City consolidated its dominance in American cultural production in the mid-nineteenth century, minstrelsy, vaudeville theater, dime novels, and early comic strips reworked jolly motifs. In the second half of the century, "sporting men," gamblers and prizefighters who were in essence professional jolly fellows, became popular heroes to many men.[6]

Central to comprehending jolly fellowship's social and cultural significance is its link to the American West, a connection that began with the California gold rush in 1849. Part of the event's appeal was that the Pacific Coast was perceived as being beyond respectability, a place where eastern rules, that is, women's rules, no longer applied, and men had an opportunity to drink and gamble without restraint. New York migrants turned San Francisco into a "New New York" and began a back-and-forth movement of jolly men. The interplay between these two cities lasted into the twentieth century and strengthened jolly fellowship's cultural influence. The West's mining and cattle towns of the 1870s and 1880s were among the last enduring male enclaves, and part of the fascination with "the Wild West" stems from the popular perception that such places preserved a traditional male outlook, an archaic code that had become unacceptable elsewhere. As the last redoubt from respectability, the West played an important role in the American imagination. Although marginalized, jolly conduct did not disappear, and it continued to have a powerful influence on American culture.[7]

In the last decades of the nineteenth century, a concern arose that reformers and moralists had done their work too well—American men were becoming too tame. The object of worry was mainly the urban, middle-class white male, who, it was claimed, had become too soft to meet the challenges of a competitive market economy and rival races and lacked the energy to extend America's world role.

The "instinct of pugnacity" had been stifled; men were "overcivilized," placid in comportment, sober, polite. Men needed to remasculinize themselves. Self-control, it was now thought, was well enough established that men ought to be able to find ways to reinvigorate their manly character without lapsing into full-fledged jolly fellowship. Boxing and football, with their controlled violence, were encouraged because they cultivated manliness in both participants and spectators.[8]

Central to this story of jolly fellowship and its cultural influence are pranks, what Edmund Wilson labeled "the tradition of the crippling practical joke." There is an exuberantly playful quality in much of nineteenth-century American culture and society. It was an age of puns, parodies, quips, hoaxes—and practical jokes. "Crippling" is the key word; true jolly fellows took pleasure in others' pain. The mischievous could turn violent in a flash. The "humor" of their pranks came from humiliating and physically hurting others. Laxatives were put in food, saddles unbuckled, faces of men passed out drunk painted black. Writes historian Robert Darnton, "Laughter does not echo unambiguously across the ages. When it reaches us from the distant past, it makes us sense the gap between our ancestors and ourselves."[9]

Constance Rourke in *American Humor* (1931) proclaimed that "humor has been a fashioning instrument in America, cleaving its way through national life." D. H. Lawrence's *Studies in Classic American Literature* (1923) famously declared that "the essential American soul is hard, isolate, stoic and a killer." It might seem that they are affirming contradictory principles as fundamental to the American experience, but both were in a sense correct. Rourke's jester and Lawrence's killer were united in the tradition of the crippling practical joke. This cruel comedy began to infiltrate American literature and theater and became a central trope of nineteenth-century American popular culture. In books and on stage, people were disgraced, beaten, strangled, set on fire, and blown to bits, all in the name of comedy. This violent humor sustained a potent influence into the twentieth century.[10]

People who lived through the era of the jolly fellows and the "moral revolution" were aware of the significance of the change they were witnessing. I have tried as much as possible to capture the everyday experience of men and women as they grappled with the social and cultural transformations of the nineteenth century. Their probing analysis in diaries, reminiscences, and memoirs provided a guide for my investigation. Yet to write this history so "close to the ground" brings with it certain risks. Fighters, gamblers, and jokers were objects of a popular fascination that shaded into folklore, and there is little doubt that exploits became amplified in the retelling. In his autobiography, Samuel Goodrich, author of the popular

Peter Parley children's books, described Matthew Olmstead, a regular at Keeler's tavern in Ridgefield, Connecticut, who had "a turn for practical jokes." Goodrich noted, however, that "a great many of these were told of him, to which, perhaps, he had no historical claim." So thoroughgoing seemed the transformation of male comportment that there is a hyperbolic quality to many accounts: once fighting was the national pastime; now men are as gentle as lambs. In some ways the literal truth of these stories may be less significant than the way they attest to the singular importance many in the nineteenth century attached to these changes: they are literally the stuff of legend. Nevertheless, fiction and fact are not the same, and I have tried to evaluate these accounts as carefully as I can, weighing the context and their inherent plausibility.[11]

Much of this is a story of village and small-town America, as the great majority of Americans lived in the countryside in the nineteenth-century United States. In 1820 only 7 percent of the population lived in places with more than twenty-five hundred people; even in 1880 only 28 percent resided in such locales.[12] But cities also are key. With their large working-class and immigrant populations, they proved less responsive to moral reform; in such places revivals fizzled and temperance stalled. One city in particular is critical to the story—New York. It was a crucible in which jolly fellowship was refined into a counterculture and the place from which jolly themes flowed into American culture and society. Its Bowery neighborhood became inscribed in the popular imagination as the citadel of jolly fellows and the antithesis of respectability.

Most of the men and women mentioned in this book are white, but blacks play a key role in this story. There is considerable evidence that there were black men who were drawn to jolly conduct, and, as white disorderly comportment came under scrutiny and condemnation, blacks emerged as symbols of the lost world of male unruliness. Minstrel show blacks were uninhibited and joyous—they drank, fought, gambled, and joked. The tremendous popularity of this new form of entertainment suggests how jolly fellowship still fascinated many men. In the second half of the century African American sporting men, mostly gamblers and prizefighters, swaggered through black neighborhoods of cities, providing African American folklore with some of its most colorful and notorious characters and renewing the white stereotype of the happy-go-lucky, yet at the same time violent, black man.

This is a story about men but also about women. Jolly fellowship was, with a few notable exceptions, for men only. Women had little reason to be committed to the raucous old social order and took a key role in the religious awakenings and temperance reform that marginalized jolly conduct, and men eventually came to accept women's superior virtue. The mere presence of "respectable" women generally caused men to exercise restraint in their behavior, and the absence of such women seemed to many men a sanction for jolly conduct. True all-male locales were relatively rare: some barrooms were, the army was, and sometimes ships were. More common were settings where the number of women was so few that men could plausibly envision themselves as being in an environment that was all male. Even in all-male locales women were present in men's minds. But still, demography, the actual physical presence or absence of women, was critical.

The jolly fellows' world was one in which drinking whiskey was considered necessary for good health, political arguments were settled with fists, hundreds of dollars hung on the result of a cockfight, and putting an emetic in someone's drink was a hilarious joke. A critical part of this story is to recapture this lost world and the outlook behind it. "That old vanished America," Mark Twain called it, where men drank and swaggered around, "hands under coat-tails, hats tilted over left eye, spoiling for a fight."[13] The quest begins in the jolly fellows' native habitat, the forum for their drinking, fighting, and joking: the tavern.

CHAPTER ONE

The Tavern Crowd

"In nearly every New-England village at the time of which I write," P. T. Barnum remembered of the 1820s, "there could be found from six to twenty social, jolly, story telling, joke playing wags and wits, regular originals, who would get together at the tavern or store, and spend their evenings and stormy afternoons in relating anecdotes, describing their various adventures, playing off practical jokes upon each other, and engaging in every project out of which a little fun could be extracted by village wits whose ideas were usually sharpened at brief intervals by a 'treat,' otherwise known as a glass of Santa Cruz rum, old Holland gin, or Jamaica spirits."[1] Such groups and such behavior were common in antebellum America among men in both villages and cities.

Barnum's adjective "jolly" was the term commonly used to designate such conduct, especially in the phrase "jolly fellows." "Scamper down to the tavern in the village, and tell the jolly fellows there that Ethan Brand has come back," the lime burner tells his son in the Hawthorne tale. Pennsylvania plasterer William Otter "got into company with several jolly fellows" in John Amich's tavern in Hanover in 1835, while a Virginia peddler took "a Cordial cup of Stings" with a "jolly company" at the Stone Tavern in Charlottesville, Virginia. The phrase "good fellows" had a similar meaning. One emigrant guidebook warned against the traditional practice in American drinking establishments of treating "'good fellows' to a drink" when meeting, and "receiving treats from *good fellows* in return."[2]

Men congregated in many places: in taverns and groceries, on the drill field during militia musters, in town squares on election day, in college dormitories, artisans' shops, boardinghouses, firehouses, army barracks, on board ship, in logging camps and mining towns. Some of these settings, such as dormitories and barracks, were places where men lived; others, such as taverns, were where they gathered regularly. Militia musters and election days, on the other hand, occurred only sporadically. Despite the diversity of these milieus, men in them typically displayed a similar comportment, a distinctive nexus of values. When men assembled in all-male or mostly male gatherings, whether white or black, whether in the East or the West, whether in an urban or rural environment, this characteristic conduct could appear. Still, although the behavior was similar, it was not identical—there were geographical, class, and racial differences in jolly fellowship. But they were variations on a theme. This chapter investigates the theme, focusing on taverns and general stores—but also looking briefly at other places where jolly conduct was found—to suggest the similarity of behavior in diverse male locales. Chapter 1 is basically descriptive, cataloging the behavior that defined jolly fellowship. Chapter 2 is analytical, emphasizing the variations and the social and cultural meaning of these male gatherings.

Taverns and groceries were the locations most closely associated with jolly fellows. Such gathering places had existed long before the American Revolution, but these locales, and the men who frequented them, attracted increasing scrutiny beginning in the late eighteenth century. There was a widespread conviction that the war and service in the American army during the Revolution had stimulated drinking, gambling, and unruly behavior in general. "Public morals, in various, respects, and in almost all possible ways, deteriorated," minister Robert Baird lamented. Some of this concern reflected little more than longing for a lost golden age of deference and propriety, but the Continental Army, like most armies, was not a place where refinement and piety flourished. Many soldiers conceded that military service had changed their moral attitudes. Men received a daily liquor ration in the army, and it was alleged that formerly abstemious men developed a taste for alcohol. Gambling was common, and there were reports the Sabbath was not kept strictly and that soldiers drank and frolicked on the Lord's Day.[3]

From all over the new nation after the war came word of male disorder. In Portland, Maine, heavy-drinking veterans came "to exert a marked influence on the entire community," temperance crusader Neal Dow believed. A historian of Spencer, Massachusetts, condemned the continental army as "a school for the vices." When the veterans returned to Spencer, "tavern-haunting, drinking, gambling, fighting, and all the concomitants of idleness, were rife in the community." South Carolinian congressman and author William J. Grayson remembered in his reminiscences that "during my boyhood [in Charleston] many men of the revolution were still alive. They were a jovial and somewhat rough race . . . addicted to deep drinking, hard swearing and practical joking."[4]

"A RENDEZVOUS FOR THE GATHERING OF CONGENIAL SPIRITS"

Postrevolutionary concern about disorderly behavior focused attention on taverns. Taverns in this era served several functions. They provided accommodations for travelers, of course. Public events such as auctions and elections took place there. In backwoods regions, trials, theatrical performances, and even church services were held in taverns. In a heavy-drinking age, the major role of most taverns was selling liquor. Men seeking refreshment usually did not have to search very hard—taverns were everywhere. New York City had nearly eleven hundred licensed taverns for its population of 60,515 in 1800, while Steubenville, Ohio, in 1821 had two banks, twenty-seven shops and sixteen taverns. Major highways were lined with them: the Lancaster Pike had sixty-one on the sixty-six-miles between Philadelphia and Lancaster in 1810. Fr. Simon Bruté described the western Maryland village of Emmitsburg with a population of around seven hundred in 1823 as containing "4 principales taverns—et peut-être 7 à 8 tippling shops."[5]

Taverns were only the most formal drinking places in the early republic. Groceries combined, in the words of a New York newspaper, "the several dignities of store, tavern and post-office." General stores sold flour, coal, dry goods, and other articles. But in many groceries, sales of alcoholic beverages exceeded that of all other items. Much of the rum and whiskey purchased was to be taken home or to work, but many groceries had benches for those preferring to consume their purchase on the premises. A resident of Waldoboro, Maine, recounted how, in the early 1800s, all four groceries "were licensed to sell liquor and have it drunk on the premises. Such places were not merely retail establishments, but loafing and lounging centers on stormy days and the evenings." Thomas Eaton in 1814 depicted in verse groceries in New York City as centers of vice: "And now a jolly set of tars, / Just in from sea, come hopping in, / And order each a glass of gin; / Then seat them by the counter's side, / Regardless what effects betide."[6]

Business in most drinking places was slow until late afternoon; from then until eight or nine o'clock at night was the busiest time. Weekends saw brisk sales. By the 1830s, workers in towns and cities usually had Saturday afternoon and Sunday off, and urban taverns and groceries were packed. The pattern was even more pronounced in the countryside. Farmers would come into town on Saturday to trade, as would "all who thirsted after drink, fun, frolic or fighting," pioneer Kentucky physician Daniel Drake remembered. In Iowa in the 1850s, general stores often stayed open Saturday until midnight to accommodate customers. The arrival of the mail, holidays, court days, election days, and militia musters all saw brisk business.[7]

Most taverns and stores only served whites. (I discuss drinking places catering to blacks separately.) Women certainly were part of the tavern scene. The tavern keeper's wife and daughters appear frequently in accounts of tavern life, cleaning, cooking, and serving food. Women attended dances and public events there, and taverns on major roads would have female travelers among their guests. Some large taverns even had a special women's room, removed from the tumult of male drinkers. But except on highways, travelers were rare; the main business for taverns was their regular customers, and these seem to have been virtually all male. Margaret Van Horn Dwight, the niece of Timothy Dwight, the famed cleric, was revolted at the taverns she had to stay at during her trip from New Haven to Ohio. Too many places, she concluded, were like Phelps's tavern outside Harrisburg, Pennsylvania, full of "drunken, profane wretches." She was mortified at tavern brawls and cockfights and spent most of her time in her room. In one harrowing episode, a drunk wagoner came "crawling on hands & knees" into her room in the middle of the night. Taverns, she concluded, were no place for a lady.[8]

The regulars, men who came in several times a week, usually numbering from four to twelve, set a drinking place's tone. Wadham's grocery in Plymouth in Luzerne County, Pennsylvania, was, "like other stores at the time"—a "rendezvous for the gathering of congenial spirits in the evenings." Isaac Weld, a British traveler, found a set of men "drinking spirits or playing cards, if not engaged at the [billiard] table," in virtually every Virginia tavern in 1796. The proprietor of a Missouri grocery complained in 1825 of "a set of troublesome animals called loungers, who are in the daily habit of calling at my store, and there sitting hour after hour."[9]

Tavern keepers and owners of general stores were often themselves men with a taste for jolly fellowship, and they helped create the ambience. The colonial period had seen a considerable number of women licensed to keep taverns, many of them widows of tavern proprietors, but their numbers declined in the late eighteenth century, and by the nineteenth century the great majority of keepers were men. A number of tavern keepers were Revolutionary War veterans. Many were men with a proclivity for jolly fellowship, such as Samuel Toms, the "rare genius" who kept a merry tippling house in Charlottesville, Virginia, or Charles Wilson the "famed joker" of Oconomowoc, Wisconsin. Plasterer William Otter went from tavern haunting to tavern owning in Emmitsburg, Maryland. In his

1835 autobiography Otter portrays himself and other tavern keepers as not merely tolerating drunken frolics, gambling, and fighting but actively abetting them.[10]

Liquor was the tavern's key attraction. Alcohol use was routine and heavy: adult yearly consumption was seven gallons per person in the 1820s and 1830s. People drank in cities, in villages, and on the frontier. "Spirituous liquors" were consumed at home, in workshops, and in fields. Accounts of the period testify to its universality. "Whiskey was considered a necessary article of life . . . as was bread or meat," reformer Henry Clark Wright recalled of his youth in Hartwick, New York. Alcohol was considered salutary for physical well-being, not to drink unhealthy. Ministers openly drank. Business agreements were sealed with a drink. Masters and journeymen would imbibe together in the shop. Heavy labor demanded alcohol, no house could be built or field harvested without it. One southern plantation owner justified providing a barrel of whiskey to his slaves as "a wholesome corrective to the vast quantity of water" that cotton picking demanded. It was a holiday tradition in schools for the master to cheer his students with alcohol. On New Year's Day 1818, a teacher in Cooper County, Missouri, for instance, treated the "boys of the school . . . to a keg of whiskey."[11]

Some European observers were convinced that even though Americans consumed more alcohol than people in the Old World, drunkenness was rarer. "To meet them . . . labouring under the effects of liquor is a rare occurrence," one English emigrant wrote. Some Americans agreed: Samuel McGill related that in Williamsburg County, South Carolina, in the 1830s, "people very generally drank freely of liquors, both at home and in company, yet it was a rare thing to see a drunken man." Although drinking binges were common among men who did not have regular access to liquor, such as seamen or lumbermen, it may well be that drinking simply to get drunk was less frequent than in the Old World, leading to the European perception of American restraint. With such a high routine intake, however, intoxication often occurred. The elaborate taxonomy of inebriation that existed in this period suggests the ubiquity of heavy drinking. The Rev. Mason Weems disgustedly listed these slang terms, in more or less ascending order: "boozy," "groggy," "blue," "damp," "tipsy," "fuddled," "haily gaily," "how came you so," "half shaved," "swipy," "has got a drop in his eye," "has got his wet sheet abroad," "cut in the craw," "high up to picking cotton," "a little on his staggers," "quite capsized," "snug under the table with the dogs," and "stuck to the floor without holding on."[12]

"SOMETIMES THEY WILL GET TO FIGHTING"

Many men no doubt hung out in taverns solely to consume alcohol, but drinking was the jolly fellows' least distinctive habit in a hard-drinking age. It would have seemed peculiar if men in the early nineteenth century had gathered without "a glass of Santa Cruz rum" or two or three. With drinking came fighting, gambling, and playing pranks. Men battled constantly both as individuals and in gangs, and taverns and stores were a locus of the brawling. No public gathering could occur "without the absolute certainty of having at least one fight," recalled one Pennsylvanian. John Morris, who grew up in Marietta, Ohio, believed "Americans have always been a fighting people" and "a Fourth of July, St. Patrick's Day, a general muster, or even a camp-meeting, that passed without the average amount of fighting . . . was a thing unheard of." South Carolinian William Grayson recalled an era when "every public day was a day of drinking disorder and fighting throughout the country."[13]

Fighting was a way of life. Usually fighting is associated with the brutal brawlers of the South and the frontier, but men in the East clashed as well. In Adams, Massachusetts, a tavern keeper's daughter remembered watching a drunken fight in the 1790s between two men who tore off each other's clothes. John Heckewelder, a Moravian minister, stopped at Thomas King's tavern in western Pennsylvania in 1786 and was horrified to discover the "people of the neighborhood were all come drunk from a *vendue*." He recorded in his diary that they "had one fight after another," and two of the brawlers ended up with "blood running down all over them." There was no shortage of truculent men in the Old Northwest. Newell Leroy Sims, a pioneering rural sociologist, discovered in his research on the history of Angola in northeastern Indiana that in early days "a fight could be seen most any day on the public square. Dances usually ended in a 'free for all.' Political discussions were settled by fist fights." An old resident remembered that, in Brownsville, Illinois, in the 1820s and 1830s, there were often half a dozen arguments each day that turned into fights. Southerners were extraordinarily belligerent. The diary of free black Natchez barber William Johnson chronicled with loving precision the public brawls in that city in the 1830s and 1840s. "Old La Vine and a little Frenchmen by the name of Surie has a Street fight. . . . Surie made La Vienne back clear Back from Mr Murchersons store to his own," Johnson recorded on 4 June 1836. "All sorts of fights at the City Hotell to night," reads another entry. "Mr. Geo Pulling and Thom Munce. Mr. Munce got whipped and there [were] several other fights." Court days and muster days in Pike County, Georgia, were fighting days. Men would take off their coats and "enter a ring to settle a quarrel," and then, it was said, "in twenty minutes, perhaps, there would be as many fights going on."[14]

Motives for fighting were various and complex. It was an accepted and commonplace way for men to settle disagreements. The regulars in Reynolds's tavern, in Kingston, Rhode Island, "will get drunk and quarrel amongst themselves; and sometimes they will get to fighting." Once a dispute began the public nature of drinking places made it hard to back down. Tavern protocol called for going outside to settle matters. Passing through Bayardstown, Pennsylvania, in 1818, James Flint recorded that "three fights have taken place this afternoon. . . . They originated from private quarrels in taverns. The combatants sallied from them to the street, where the battles were fought." When wood sawyer George Haydock got into a dispute in a New Jersey tavern, "as was customary, all hands adjourned out doors for a regular fight." But there were also many brawls inside taverns. In New York City, tavern fights that ended with the tavern trashed were a popular tradition. William Otter relates that one evening while playing billiards for drinks with his fellow gang members at John McDermot's New York City grocery in 1804, "we began to quarrel amongst ourselves." When McDermot tried to break it up, "we took the hint and let him have it." They knocked McDermot down, and he "received the hearty kicks of every one who could get foot on him. Some of the spare hands fell upon the negroes who were employed by him to shock oysters, and drove them into the cooking room, and beat them, poor d——ls[,] into a jelly."[15]

Politics was another common cause of fights, or at least a convenient excuse for them. In Newport, Rhode Island, both the Republicans and Federalists each selected a supporter "whose boxing qualities were well known [and] . . . fresh fights continued until dark." During the 1792 campaign in Kingston, New York, Clintonians poured out of a tavern where they had gathered and stormed a Federalist procession. A "severe and bloody" club battle ensued. William Dean Howells remembered that there were always election day fights between Whigs and Democrats in Ohio. Two men strode into Lyon's grocery in Pine Mountain, Georgia, one afternoon in the early 1850s and "swore they could whip any Democrat in town," recounted Edward Isham, a notorious ruffian whose seventeen-page "Confession" chronicles his participation in thirty-nine fights. Isham grabbed a shovel handle and in a wild brawl "the candles were knocked down and we fought for a long time in the dark" before one of the Whigs was seriously hurt and the other ran out the back door.[16]

Samuel Wood and Sons, "Drinking Scene," 1813. In *Engravings Used by, or Available to, the Wood Publishing Firm to Illustrate Their Books* (New York, 1820). Collection of the New-York Historical Society, New York City.

Arguments were not the only cause of physical combat. For many, fighting was a pleasurable recreation, and men purposely gathered to battle. Virtually every hamlet had at least one noted brawler, and "set fights" between them and combatants from other communities were eagerly anticipated. "Each city, town and village had its bullies, who were esteemed . . . in proportion to their prowess," John Morris explained. In some communities wrestling was the favored form of combat. In New Hampshire "at all the public gatherings at an early period, the most prominent amusement was wrestling, and there was always a champion in these games in every community." Henry Jenkins "for the plain" fought against Ira Bagley representing "Paddock Village" in front of a St. Johnsbury, Vermont, tavern by lantern light one Saturday evening in the 1790s. The line between a wrestling match and a no-holds-barred brawl was often faint. In Warren County, Pennsylvania, one man recalled, wrestling "was a rough game without any well defined rules." The same was true elsewhere. Abraham Lincoln's celebrated 1831 battle with Jack Armstrong, leader of the rowdy "Clary's Grove Boys," started as a wrestling contest. ("Boys" was a flexible term in this period encompassing males into their twenties.) It became a rough-and-tumble fight when the future president, according to William Herndon, infuriated by Armstrong's foul tactics, "fairly lifted the great bully by the throat and shook him like a rag." Many wrestling matches ended in free-for-alls. In Ohio, each winner "is generally attacked by a fresh man and a pitched battle between a single pair often ends in a battle royal, where all present are engaged."[17]

In parts of the Midwest and in the South, rough-and-tumble fighting was the preferred form of combat. In these affairs almost everything was allowed—wrestling, punching, choking, kicking, biting, even eye gouging—unless the combatants specifically agreed to prohibit them. North Carolina brawlers were celebrated eye gougers—"a North Carolinian cannot salute you without putting his finger in your eye," gibed an Augusta, Georgia, newspaper. The struggle continued until one fighter declared "enough." These contests made a powerful impression on men who witnessed them. In "them Days, this Was Fashionable to Gouge Out Eyes & Bite ears of[f]," remembered Ebenezer Stedman of 1820s Tennessee. He saw one fight where a man "Bit [Mort] Prices Ear & Spit it on the Ground." On Saturdays in Keokuk, Iowa, in the 1830s, "a rough set of men," "honest" but "wild," rode in "to have a good time" and "test the manhood" of "neighborhood bullies" in brawls. In Paris, Kentucky, "fellows would come in from the outskirts," and "go up and down the street seeking a fight, and not be satisfied to leave town without first having one," an old settler remembered.[18]

Fights between gangs of men were common, not just in cities but also in the countryside. Neighborhood bands of brawling young men were a familiar feature of urban life. Gang fights were a way of life in New York City. In the 1840s the Northern Liberties suburb of Philadelphia "used to be in agitation almost every Saturday night by the regular clans of 'rough and tumble' fighting between the ship-carpenters from Kensington and the butchers from Spring Garden," John F. Watson related. Smaller cities as well saw gang fights. In Newport, Rhode Island, there were four gangs, and to solicit a brawl it was only necessary to sing this insulting ditty:

The up-town bullies,
The over-the point brats,
The down-town gentlemen
And the long wharf rats.

Those singing substituted their quarter in the "gentlemen" line. "The greatest rivalry existed" between the salt-making settlement of Salina, New York, and the adjacent canal town of Syracuse in the 1820s. Henry Borgadus's Mansion House was the gathering place for the Syracuse forces, and there were "hard-fought sternly contested . . . free fights every time the residents of either town crossed the boundary line."[19]

Villages and rural areas also had a powerful heritage of collective fighting. Independence Day was a traditional day of drinking and brawling, and on 4 July 1824, the "forces of Vernon [New Hampshire] sent word that they would be at the Checkered House to 'whip all Hinsdale.'" Capt. John Burnett, it was said, knocked down the leader of the Vernon forces with one punch and sent them packing. "Uptown" and "downtown" gangs fought in Plymouth, Pennsylvania, in the 1840s, and on occasion both contingents would unite against the Welsh Hill neighborhood in a "general battle." On the National Road, young men living along the road brawled with those living in the countryside. Stephen Logan remembered how in the 1830s in Menard County, Illinois, "gangs of country bullies used to meet" at groceries "to fight one another. One was from Lick Creek and the other from Spring Creek." Collective brawling generally seems less common in the South, but in east Tennessee when men from the north and south sides of Bay's Mountain met, "sometimes there would be twenty couples fighting at one time," an observer reported.[20]

"ON EVERYTHING BETTING WAS PRESENT"

Gambling was closely associated with the tavern and grocery regulars. Men in this era wagered eagerly and openly. Gambling games in New York City taverns, an English immigrant discovered, included "cards, dice, checquers, or draughts, dominoes, bagatelle, the old English game of shovel-board" as well as billiards and bowling. The most popular gambling game from the end of the American Revolution until after the Civil War, when it was eclipsed by poker, was faro, a banking game in which men wagered on the order cards would be drawn in. It "almost may be styled the national game," believed self-proclaimed reformed gambler J. H. Green. Horse racing, bullbaiting, cockfighting, dogfighting, and human fighting were also popular subjects for tavern gambling. In many places, as in Martinsburg, Virginia, "on everything betting was present." The regulars in Stephenson's tavern in Dauphin County, Pennsylvania, wagered on whether one of their companions was able to ride a wild horse. (He could.) Men in a tavern in Delafield, Wisconsin, placed money on whether the cook could kill and dress a chicken and have it in the pot in three minutes. (He did.)[21]

Even in staid New England wagering was widespread. Gambling was illegal almost everywhere, but unlike in most places, authorities in the region made a serious effort to enforce the law. Betting nevertheless continued. A Sturbridge writer recounted that in the early decades of the century "a very great portion of our public houses . . . had their recesses for gamblers." An 1860 history of Montpelier, Vermont, noted that "gambling was a common practice" there early in the nineteenth century. Horse racing and shooting matches were especially popular. A Peterborough, New Hampshire, historian denounced a "worthless set of vagabonds" who gathered at the general store in the late 1700s to drink, gamble, and race horses.[22]

Men in the South and West loved to gamble. When Isaac Weld arrived in Richmond in 1796, "I had scarcely alighted from my horse at the tavern when the landlord," who had tables for faro, hazard (a dice game), and billiards, "came to ask what game I was most partial to." "Many times I have been forced to proceed much farther in a day than I have wished, in order to avoid the scenes of rioting and quarreling I have met with at the taverns." In Manchester, South Carolina, in the first decade of the nineteenth century, "some of the villagers and neighbors met *every day* at a store, where the card table was brought out into the piazza soon after breakfast, and gambling went on until night." Timothy Flint in *Recollections of the Last Ten Years in the Valley of the Mississippi* (1826) concluded that drinking and gambling were "the prevailing vices of the west." When traveler Alexander Pratt entered "Uncle Abe" Nichols's tavern in Mineral Point, Wisconsin, in 1837, he observed that "in one corner of the room" there was "a faro bank" and in another corner "a Roulette [wheel]" and that in yet another corner "sat a party engaged in playing cards."[23]

Billiards, cockfights, and horse races were all favorite objects of tavern gambling. Weld found billiard tables in virtually every Virginia tavern he visited, and when Benjamin Henry Latrobe stopped at the tiny village of Hanover Town, Virginia, in 1797, he discovered that "the whole town is assembled every evening at the billiard room." At the turn of the century billiards was probably more popular in the South than anywhere else, but it quickly became a tavern favorite throughout the country. In Vincennes, Indiana, it was not unusual in 1813 for thirty games a day to be played in Christian Gaetner's tavern. In New York, billiards exploded in popularity in the 1820s, and by the next decade the city had hundreds of tables that one could find in establishments ranging from ornate billiard salons to groceries.[24]

Cockfighting was a favorite tavern pastime from upstate New York—Buffalo was famed for its fighting birds—to Louisiana. Taverns throughout the country held cockfights on Christmas, Shrove Tuesday, and Easter Monday. Harman's tav-

Benjamin Latrobe, “Billiards in Hanover Town, Virginia,” 1797. Benjamin Latrobe papers, The Maryland Historical Society, Baltimore.

ern in Pittsboro, North Carolina, held a three-day “main” of twenty-one matches for $10 a match in 1806. Good’s tavern in Westmoreland County, Pennsylvania, held a two-day main on 26 and 27 December 1819. In major cities taverns had specially built cockpits and regularly scheduled fights. Sometimes several gamecocks would be matched together in a “battle royal.” Breeders took immense pride in the beauty of their birds, but wagering was the main interest for most men, a nerve-wracking experience because a losing bird could suddenly strike a single fatal blow with his sharp steel spurs.[25]

Horse racing, like cockfighting and billiards, seemed to attract only limited interest apart from wagering. There were tracks in some cities where owners could race their steeds—Richmond had three early in the century. In most areas, however, racing was done on streets or on a stretch of open road. These short races became known in the South as “quarter races” because their usual length was one-quarter of a mile. They were remarkably informal: men would gather at taverns and general stores to have a drink, brag about their horses, place their bets, and race. Matches were held on Race Street in Philadelphia, while steeds in Baton Rouge galloped down Third Street. Virtually every observer of American horse racing commented on the drinking and fighting that accompanied the racing. "A considerable gathering of people" congregated at the store in the hamlet of Mocksville, North Carolina, one Sunday in 1825 to watch the races. "Too much whiskey had been drunk," and one rider lost control of his horse and was thrown against a tree and killed.[26]

"A CLASS OF MEN WHO WERE PECULIARLY ADDICTED TO PRACTICAL JOKES"

No activity was more closely associated with the tavern and store crowd than practical joking. In an age of pranks, "rigs," "saws," "sells," "set ups" and "bodily wit," the jolly fellows took the lead. The regulars at Davis's tavern in Concord, Massachusetts, planned and executed "practical unkind jokes," related physician Edward Jarvis. The village of Kingston, Rhode Island, became nicknamed "Little Rest," because, so one story goes, Reynolds's tavern there was the "headquarters of a class of men who were peculiarly addicted to practical jokes[,] . . . giving their victims little rest." In Lewis County, New York, it was the practice "for the male portion of the community to meet . . . in little informal gatherings at taverns." High among their amusements were "tricks and pranks," some "genuinely spontaneous, spur-of-the-moment affairs," others "carefully planned . . . in the tiniest details." Concluded Charlestonian William Grayson, "boisterous practical joking, like . . . drinking[,] was in character with the manners of the age."[27]

Just as every community had its renowned fighters, each had its celebrated pranksters. Lawyer Thomas Heald was the leader of the jolly jokesters in Concord, Massachusetts, while Elisha Gardiner led the pranksters in South Kingston, Rhode Island. Bowman Shepler was a terror in Fallowfield, Pennsylvania, "in the way of mischief and tricks." Shiloh True was "the trickiest trickster of them all" in early Hickman County, Tennessee. Attorney Alexander Randall was "the leader in all 'sells,' fun, practical jokes, and hilarity" in Waukesha, Wisconsin.[28]

Pranks were diverse. Some were gentle, others cruel, some spontaneous, others meticulously prepared. Many "saws" were as relatively mild as dispatching someone on a fool's errand. Invitations were extended for nonexistent husking bees at unsuspecting farmers' homes—the more remote the better. The "snipe hunt," in which the supposed hunters tell the victim that they will flush the birds to him but then go back to the tavern, leaving the dupe holding the bag, became part of American folklore. Grocery regulars in Catskill, New York, put eggs in a man's hat. Peddler James Guild stopped to take a drink at a tavern near "Canasherog," New York, where a "gang of about 20 were drinking and carousing." Guild wrote in his diary that he "ris up from my chair" to discover that "they had pinned papers and rags on me so that they hung almost to the ground," which generated "a terrible laugh alover the room." Putting large objects on top of roofs was popular sport—one teamster who stopped at the Albert Tavern in Blue Ball, Pennsylvania, found his wagon on top of a barn the next morning. (Blue Ball, like several other Pennsylvania communities, including King of Prussia and Bird in Hand, was named after the local tavern.) Switching shopkeepers' signs was a perennial favorite. After an evening of drinking, a "posse" of men in Alexandria, Virginia, cut some "wild capers" that included stealing a sign that read "Cakes and Beer for Sale Here" and putting it over a minister's door.[29]

The "good fellows" in Reynolds's tavern in Kingston, Rhode Island, were dubbed "the Hornet's Nest" in the early 1800s because of their pranks and unruly behavior. Some of their "sells" were as simple as pouring a bucket of water on someone. The Hornet's Nest, however, was also capable of elaborate ruses that required careful preparation, as the gullible Charles Comstock learned after he moved to Kingston in 1802. "Being at Joseph Reynolds' tavern," Comstock wrote in an 1806 pamphlet, he was introduced by local farmer Elisha Gardiner to "a stranger," one "Col. Cook" from New London, and "Col. Cook" began inquiring about buying mules. And cats. Cook planned, he said, to ship the mules and cats to two West Indian islands. Because all the felines on the islands had perished, cats "would fetch a great price." Comstock actually began collecting cats before someone finally clued him in that Gardiner was the leading prankster of the Hornet's Nest, that "the man that Elisha Gardiner had recommended to be Colonel Cook of New-London, was Cook the hatter," and that "it was all a joke." Comstock wrote in a tone of wounded outrage, hoping in that way to expose the unchristian, unscrupulous behavior of the Hornet's Nest.[30]

There were also pranks that Barnum called "rather severe tricks" that involved actual physical suffering. "The practical jokes of the times were sometimes mischievous and sometimes worse," recalled South Carolinian William Grayson. Jolly fellows in Concord, Massachusetts, one night tied a long rope between the fetlock of a horse and the hitching post. The owner came out and started off, the horse "reached the end of the rope, he fell, and both rider and animal were somewhat injured." Adding laxatives or emetics to food and drink of unsuspecting victims and enjoying the subsequent effects was considered amusing. Seth Wyman had an argument with some of the regulars in a tavern near Augusta, Maine, so "in a mad prank contrived over the brandy flagon," he and a companion put emetic tartar in the tavern's pail of drinking water and blocked the doors shut. They exulted in the sound of vomiting, the cries of "we're poisoned, oh!" and the pitiful pleas for help; it was, they said, "sweet music to our ears." In Milwaukee

Lewis Miller was a carpenter who lived most of his life in the area around York, Pennsylvania. In the 1850s Miller made a series of drawings of scenes from everyday life. This building, writes Miller, is "the Old Market House in York 1804. One night Some young man and boys had Some Sport the putting a wagon on top of the market house. The[y] got it up After taking it apart, piece by piece." Collection of the York County Heritage Trust, York, Penn.

in 1837, a journeyman working on a new house annoyed his roommates by coming to bed late. So as a "practical joke," they wedged over the door not the classic bucket of water but "tin-ware, a shovel, fireplace tongs and other metal objects." The journeyman opened the door "with a jerk that brought about eighty pounds of old iron down upon him, with the noise like the dumping of a load of stone." As might be guessed, in many of these pranks both victim and victimizer had been drinking.[31]

Just as the jolly fellows enjoyed seeing human victims of pranks suffer, they also took delight in vicious "jokes" on animals. Cruelty to animals was certainly not unique to the tavern crowd, but it was characteristic. William Otter was a plasterer who lived in New York City, Pennsylvania, and Emmitsburg, Maryland, and a self-proclaimed "jolly fellow." Known as "Big Bill" because of his six-four height, he brags in his 1835 autobiography about his brawls, mean-spirited pranks, and torture of animals. A tavern near Lititz, Pennsylvania, kept "a very large baboon chained to the sign-post." Otter and his companions decided to "have some sport" with the beast, and so, recounted Otter, "I let him have a splash of lime from my [plasterer's] brush bip into his eyes, which burnt the poor devil equal to fire, it made him raving[.] . . . And in his fit he danced about like though he were mad." The jolly fellows in Davis's tavern in Concord, Massachusetts, were said to have tossed a kitten into a boiling pot on the fire. "Uncle Jim" Ruppert in Rockport, Illinois, the story goes, liked to give a dog a piece of meat tied to a string. After the dog swallowed it, Ruppert jerked it out. "Turpentining" cats and dogs by applying the liquid to their private parts was also popular with the store crowd. Another favorite was to take a rag soaked with turpentine, tie it to the dog's tail, ignite it, and watch the "antics."[32]

Taverns were sites of bull, bear, and badger baitings, in which the animals were attacked by dogs. Wagering was clearly a large part of the attraction, but there was also relish in torment. The Robinson Crusoe tavern on the edge of Philadelphia was the place to see bears and bulls baited in the late eighteenth and early nineteenth centuries. Forsyth's tavern in Paris, Kentucky, in 1814 advertised in the town's newspaper that a "HE BEAR will be turned loose and five dogs will be entered every half hour to fight him." Henry Fearon, an Englishman sent to investigate American conditions by a group of potential English emigrants, saw a notice in New Orleans for an exhibition that featured a battle between a tiger and a bear. "If the Tiger is not vanquished in this fight with the Bear," spectators were promised, "he will be sent alone against the last Bull, and if the latter conquers all his enemies, several pieces of fire-works will be placed on his back, which will provide a very entertaining amusement."[33]

Time and again, accounts of the tavern and grocery crowd detailed drinking, fighting, gambling, and pranks. Of course not every imbiber was a gambler, nor every practical joker a fighter, but these activities correlated closely and appear routinely in accounts of male sprees. The Kinderhook, New York, tavern regulars "spent the evening, til probably mid-night, in drinking, gambling, cockfighting, horse-racing, or perhaps fighting among themselves." A Baptist preacher in Missouri in 1811 came on a "turkey shoot," a common tavern entertainment in which contestants fired at a tethered live turkey. By evening participants were "pretty well inebriated. . . . Some would be quarreling, some fighting, some swearing, some playing tricks, such as knocking off each other's hats, and cutting bridles and saddles." Among the Manchester, South Carolina, store crowd "drinking

Lewis Miller, "1806, Panther Beat on the Common York Borough." The panther, "belonging to Robert Smith, . . . [is] fast with a Chain to the post." Collection of the York County Heritage Trust, York, Penn.

freely was their regular habit week after week, varied by quarter races, feats of strength and activity, and an occasional fist fight."[34]

Drinking, fighting, gambling, pranks, and animal cruelty come up most often in accounts of men gathered at taverns and groceries, but the regulars were linked with a wide range of other sorts of disorderly conduct. Many viewed the tavern as a center of irreligion. Keeping Sunday holy was taken very seriously by clerics, who saw it as a principal battleground in the struggle against secularism. The tavern crowd routinely transgressed the New England practice of beginning the Sabbath at sundown Saturday evening—indeed, that was the tavern's busiest time. In Waldoboro, Maine, "the whole of lower Friendship Road would trek to the village on Saturday nights. . . . Each [man] had his own favorite hangout where cronies would gather." The jolly fellows in the East and the more settled areas of the Old Northwest, however, seem to have been more restrained on Sunday than on Saturday. The "joke-playing wags and wits" that Barnum remembered in Bethel kept the Sabbath. Daniel Drake recalled the sharp contrast in early Kentucky between the drunken and unruly Saturday behavior and the relative decorum of Sunday. The Sabbath seems to have been kept less rigorously in the Deep South. Sunday in early nineteenth-century Charleston was, in Grayson's words, "a day of . . . drinking and fighting."[35]

The tavern regulars were also charged with blasphemy and profanity. Charles Comstock alleged that he heard one member of the Hornet's Nest proclaim "God was a whore-master, the Virgin Mary was a whore, and that Christ was a bastard." When the young Heman Bangs, later a noted minister, went to work in a tavern near Fairfield, Connecticut, in 1810, he was horrified to discover the Sabbath desecrated by drinking, cursing men without "any pretensions to piety." Margaret Van Horn Dwight was disgusted at "the profane and vulgar" songs she heard being sung in one tavern in western Pennsylvania. Profanity may have been characteristic of jolly fellows, but it was certainly not limited to them. European visitors commented on its universality among men of all classes and regions in the United States. Sir Charles Augustus Murray, who found much to admire in America on his 1834–36 visit, was repelled by the constant swearing of even well-bred men.[36]

The tavern's critics accused the regulars of sexual licentiousness. Most jolly fellows were married, but wives are very rarely referred to in accounts by and about jolly men, and their marital relations remain largely a mystery. Charles Comstock noted that the Reynolds's tavern crowd engaged in what "they term squaw hunting, hunting black rats; and when they say that they have ketched a black rat, their meaning is that they have had to do with a squaw." Physician Cornelius Larison described "the grand old times" at Put's Old Tavern in rural New Jersey early in the nineteenth century and claimed that he treated "several old gamesters" for maladies that were incurred by the "frequent intercourse with as such congregated there." There were taverns and grog shops, especially in cities, where prostitutes gathered to meet male clients. Even more alarming to reformers were places like the Star House on Reade Street in New York City, where, according to one newspaper, men "lie with beasts in the shape of men." For the most part, however, evidence about jolly fellows and sex is meager. Writers of diaries, autobiographies, and reminiscences felt more comfortable recounting rollicking episodes of drinking, fighting, and gambling than sexual affairs.[37]

Sexual independence among both men and women seems to have increased in the late eighteenth century. Informal marriage, "self-divorce" and premarital pregnancy all apparently grew in the 1790s, the era during which an alleged decline in public morality exposed the tavern crowd to reproach. Republican freedom seemed to open new possibilities in many aspects of life, and the Revolutionary Army veterans who were alleged to be so prominent among tavern regulars may have brought looser sexual attitudes back to their communities after their service. So were the jolly fellows in the vanguard of sexual liberation? Or did they, as their partaking in "squaw hunting" indicates, merely perpetuate conventional patterns of male sexual exploitation of women? The behavior of rowdy young men in New York in the first half of the nineteenth century suggests the latter. Gangs of drunken men stormed houses of prostitution, making, as the *New York Post* explained, the "demolition of houses of ill-fame the ostensible object of their disorderly practices." "Ostensible" suggests that these attacks were actually more of a male spree than an effort to curb prostitution. Plasterer William Otter recounts his participation in one such attack in his autobiography. He and his roughneck pals descended on a "notorious" dance hall for "the express purpose of raising a row and we were gratified to our heart's content." These rampages often ended with prostitutes beaten and raped. Jolly culture in cities in the early and mid-nineteenth century was associated with sexual aggression. It seems less likely, however ("squaw hunting" to the contrary), that this was the case in villages. In a period when brawling, gambling, and nasty pranks were publicly tolerated to a surprising degree, there seems to have been less sympathy for libertinism, which had the potential to be devastatingly destabilizing in small towns where face-to-face relationships were the rule. Many of the rural tavern crowd, as chapter 2 shows, were men of high reputation, and most were married. Village jolly fellows could even act to enforce traditional attitudes. Men from Cilley's tavern in Goffstown, New Hampshire, were instigators in the first decade of the nineteenth century of "rough music," a charivari, the traditional European method of censuring those violating village norms. After Seth Wyman was suspected of having an affair with a married woman, the regulars followed him "throughout the day with hoots and shouts."[38]

"ALL WAS LET LOOSE"

Although taverns and groceries were the central focus of jolly fellowship, it could appear almost anywhere men gathered in groups. Three such other milieus were the militia, colleges, and workplaces. Their diversity is striking. Men went to work daily and could go to a tavern regularly if they wished; militia training only happened once or twice a year. Frequenting a tavern was a conscious decision, but adult men were required by law to attend militia musters. Villages were the site of most militia musters, but many artisans' shops were in cities. Those who labored in manufactories were skilled or semiskilled workers, while college students tended to be drawn from "the better sorts."

Militia training day is an example of periodic jolly fellowship as opposed to the routine gatherings of the tavern crowd. Most states in the early 1800s required all white males aged eighteen to forty-five to muster with their rifles for militia drill. Training days were "acknowledged holidays" in Henderson County, Kentucky, and almost everywhere else. Typically, the drill field would be lined with wagons and booths selling "cider, . . . ginger cakes, apples, whisky and all the other *et cetera* of the camp." Field days usually started relatively sedately, but the steady drinking of the soldiers often eventually led to disorder. In Concord, Massachusetts, "the military companies all had toddy carried out to them in pails" to refresh them. A barrel of liquor was set outside Hosford's tavern in Franklin County, New York, and the men marched by to take their "grog in turn as a matter of course." Things became increasingly uproarious. "The carnival at Rome or the ancient *Saturnalia* of the Romans in their height of reveling would be tame and insipid when placed in juxtaposition with such an occasion," asserted Edward L. Starling of muster day in Kentucky. Fighting started. In Lincoln County, Maine, "the irritable would become angry, and strip off their coats; and then a cry would be raised, 'A fight, a fight.'" One onlooker at a 1833 muster in Ithaca, New York, reported that it was "excellent sport for bruizers, black eyes, bloody noses, broken ribs and shins." There was practical joking. In Old Palestine, Missouri, in 1841 an officer "imbibed pretty freely" and got into a fistfight with a civilian. The men decided to have some fun with their superior and got a "a pretended constable" to serve the officer with a realistic-looking indictment for attempted murder.[39]

Militia service seemed increasingly unnecessary as the likelihood of foreign war and Indian attack faded. Even in the South where the militia was regarded as essential for suppressing slave insurrections, it became an excuse for frolicking. The day took on a carnivalesque quality. Men in the nineteenth century delighted in disguising their faces and bodies and burlesqued the proceedings by painting their faces and dressing up in fantastic outfits, making it a sort of giant practical joke on the officers and spectators. It became "largely farcical and not infrequently characterized by buffoonery and horse-play" in Franklin County, New York. Some of the militia in Burlington, New Jersey, in 1835 constituted themselves into the "Watermelon Army"; some painted "their faces like indians" while "others wore clowns' caps and striped pants, and carried immense wooden swords and great wooden pistols." A group calling themselves "the Quizzicals" turned the musters in Henderson County, Kentucky, into a travesty in 1847. Too drunk to actually march, the mummers staggered around the field behind the regular militia, "uniforms and false faces absolutely hideous," blowing tin horns. Dubbed "Fantasticals" or "Calithumpians," these burlesque organizations spread throughout the nation. The increasing disorderliness that accompanied the musters led most states in the 1840s to abolish compulsory militia training.[40]

Like the militia, colleges had a reputation for tumult. Students had been renowned since medieval times for turbulence, and American scholars did their part to uphold the tradition. Drinking, gambling, brawls, wild pranks, and even riots were more or less routine. Maintaining discipline became the primary objective of college officials, but, even so, success often eluded them. Many institutions were short of students and were reluctant to expel even the rowdiest. Drinking and gambling were almost universal. "You will find your student at the tavern . . . [or] the gaming-table" was the prevailing sentiment in Boston. The sight of drunken collegians reeling about was so familiar that publicly inebriated students usually were not punished unless they combined drinking with some other misbehavior, such as at Middlebury College in 1810, where four students having "indulged themselves to excess, did strip themselves on the public bridge," or at the University of North Carolina, where three drunken students in 1818 began "tumultuously shouting on the streets of the village, breaking into a kitchen, [and] beating a Negro." Gambling was routine. At the University of Virginia, Saturday, Sunday, and Monday nights were gambling nights. One collegian in 1826 was said to have lost $250 in a dormitory known to be a "gambling hell." Some southern students even brought their gamecocks with them to school.[41]

Both fighting between individuals and brawls between classes were features of college life. Fistfights were so common authorities paid no attention. At North Carolina only students' clashes with knives or guns attracted notice—Hyder Davie was "reprimanded" by the trustees for stabbing another student in an affray. The future historian of the Spanish conquest of Mexico, William Prescott, was passing the dining hall at Harvard in 1813 when "rude frolicking among the undergraduates" caught his attention. He turned his head, and a large piece of hard bread knocked him to the floor and partially blinded him. Sometimes fights escalated into full-scale riots. Yale was one of the most disorderly campuses. In 1823 students blew up the chapel with gunpowder. In the 1840s "at least one pitched fight a year took place between the classmen and the 'townies.'" Hundreds took part in these battles between undergraduates and New Haven residents, who were sometimes aided by sailors. The 1841, 1854, and 1858 brawls were especially intense. In the 1841 melee between students and volunteer firemen—themselves one of the most combative groups of the era—the Yalies routed the watchmen with bricks, stormed the firehouse, cut the fire hoses, smashed the engine, and scattered the fragments in the college yard.[42]

College pranks were the stuff of legend. Stealing the bell from the chapel was an enduring favorite, as was leading animals into classrooms or dormitories. A bogus announcement of the cancellation of classes was another traditional joke. Stink bombs were a perennial. Hobart College students, including one disguised as a minister, went to an off-campus revival service. Hobart was an Episcopal college, a denomination that believed in an educated clergy, and the pranksters did not want to miss a chance to mock a less scholarly and presumably less genteel revivalist minister. The prankster stood up after the sermon, read a passage from the Greek New Testament, and solemnly asked the evangelist for his exegesis. When the preacher professed bewilderment, "all was let loose," future Cornell president Andrew Dixon White remembered. Another Hobart student put asafetida in the stove while others threw buckshot against the windows "making a most appalling din." At North Carolina a prankster picked a quarrel with a fellow student and challenged him to a duel. Unknown to the victim, the guns were loaded with blanks. When the shots were fired, the victim's adversary fell "dead," bathed in fake blood. Other pranks were even rougher. At Harvard's commencement in 1791 a practical joker put an emetic in the breakfast water and more than one hundred students fell sick with cramps and vomiting. At North Carolina, "a trick played on a professor" by students was putting a charge of gunpowder under his chair and igniting it.[43]

The workshops of antebellum America confirm how deeply rooted such disorderly attitudes were among men. It was obviously in the interest of the employer to keep his workplace orderly, and workers were disciplined or fired for misbehavior. Most employees themselves recognized that it was to their economic advantage to keep the workshop functioning smoothly. Yet despite this disciplined attitude, jolly fellowship slipped in. Workplace drinking was open and heavy. Henry Clarke Wright worked as an apprentice hatter from 1814 to 1817 in Norwich, New York, and "three times a day . . . I went to a whiskey shop to get whiskey for the journeymen. There was not a day, rain or shine, foul or fair, holy days or unholy days which I did not repair with a bottle to the shop." One carpenter in the shipyards along the East River in New York City in the 1830s was considered by a coworker as a relatively sober man since "on working days Abe never drank more than ten times."[44]

Fighting was common. Workers were expert in badinage and usually the appropriate rejoinder to an insult was a witty reply. However, as iron founder Henry Brokmeyer learned, "There are days when personal collisions, hand-to-hand fights . . . will result from the same causes which some other day will be . . . turned into an idle jest." Among Lynn, Massachusetts, shoemakers, "scuffles" often took place in their tiny "ten foot" shops; in one such shop, an apprentice annoyed by the overbearing attitude of a journeyman pulled the "jour" off his stool and choked him. Bosses were not above such belligerence: in the Andrus bookbindery in Hartford, Connecticut, in the mid-1830s, the foreman and a journeyman got into a prolonged, vicious fight; they "knocked each other, scratched and pulled hair." The workers "followed them around all the time to see fair play," a delighted apprentice recorded. Papermaker James Campbell eventually had to give up his dream of becoming a master because he was not big enough to intimidate journeymen.[45]

Workplace pranks were an established part of the artisanal world. Henry Folsom was taken on as a new apprentice in the Norwich hat shop where Wright worked. "Scarcely had he entered the shop, before his sensitiveness to jokes was made manifest," and he became "daily and hourly the victim of some practical joke" by the other employees. In other shops, tools were glued or nailed down, buckets of water poured over workers, laxatives put in food. Gambling went on. Lynn shoemakers loved to "troll the stick." The stick's sides were numbered one to four and each man had three throws or "trolls"; the one with the highest total would win. Usually the loser had to pay for the next round of drinks. Workers recounted practical jokes and fights that had stayed in their memory; most days surely passed without such excitement. These accounts, however, do make clear that jolly behavior was part of male workshop life.[46]

"NEGROES LIKE THEIR MASTERS WILL GET DRUNK"

Most whites were convinced that black Americans shared the jolly fellows' love of drinking, gambling, fighting, and pranks. "The character of negroes is a tolerably correct index to that of the white population in which they reside," believed the Rev. John Mason Peck. Slaves and free blacks, he felt, could hardly be expected to be any more principled than their white masters and employers. This was Peck's explanation of why the free blacks of St. Louis gathered in the 1820s on a square near Main Street "in the pleasant afternoons of the Sabbath to dance, drink and fight."[47]

African Americans were generally not welcome in respectable taverns. On the National Road, black and white wagoners stopped at the same taverns but ate at separate tables. It was illegal to sell liquor to slaves, and against the law in southern states for free blacks to vend alcohol. African Americans both free and slave, however, usually had little trouble getting liquor—drink was so deeply woven into the fabric of American society that it was virtually impossible to keep it out of their hands. Blacks could patronize unlicensed grog shops kept by free blacks. Or buy from a white grocer. In the Philadelphia neighborhood of Moyamensing, "there were numerous petty shops" that supplied blacks with rum, complained the 1849 *Statistical Inquiry into the Condition of the People of Color of the City and Districts of Philadelphia*. In Wilmington, North Carolina, white bartenders commonly sold "three cent drinks" to blacks "on the wink." "There are a good many groceries" on Broadway alone, complained a Louisville judge in 1858, "where negro slaves can obtain liquor," despite a "very stringent" Kentucky law. Since African American customers in most states could not testify in court against a white man, there was little risk.[48]

On plantations, one former slave recalled to a Works Progress Administration interviewer, "niggers didn't drink much whiskey fo' the war, dey only got whiskey when de white folk give it to 'em." Slaves may have consumed less alcohol than whites, but consume it they did. As in the North, harvesters, of course, were supplied with spirits. Slaves were liberally provided with liquor on Christmas and Independence Day and sometimes on Sunday as well. "Negroes like their masters will get drunk," concluded one Bostonian after watching the Christmas revelry on a South Carolina plantation. Frederick Douglass, a staunch temperance man, saw these blowouts as "conductors or safety valves" that helped drain the "explosive elements" from the rigors of bondage. Having alcohol provided by a master was only one way for slaves to obtain it. "De niggers git hold of some likker somehow," recalled an Arkansas ex-slave. Some brewed their own beer. Large plantations often had stills, so, one slave recalled, some masters would sell whiskey to slaves who paid for it from the money they "earned by over work." Others purchased it illicitly.[49]

As with whites, fighting and gambling accompanied the drinking. Put's Old Tavern in western New Jersey was kept for a time by Sylvia Dubois, a free black, and "blacks and whites alike partook in the pastimes" and drank, gambled, and fought together. "Blacks in slavery did not hesitate to fight each other," Edward L. Ayers discovered in his study of southern crime. Henry Bibb, a former Kentucky slave, remembered that on Sundays slaves "would resort to the woods in large numbers . . . to gamble, fight, get drunk and break the Sabbath." Dubois described how in Hunterdon County, New Jersey, "negroes quarreled and fought and pounded each other, and bit each other's ears off, and then pounded each other's noses down." On training day when blacks had rum, "you'd hear 'em yell more than a mile. And when they got into a fight, you'd hear 'em yell more than five miles." William Grayson, who recounts white male disorder in his autobiography, found Charleston blacks equally unruly. On Sunday, "the negroes from the country assembled in town and broils were common among them." Bibb described the rough-and-tumble fights between plantation champions. After the bets were laid down, "a ring or circle [was] formed to fight in" by spectators, slave and white, and the contestants chose seconds. The masters acted as referees and stopped the fight when a combatant was in danger of getting seriously hurt. Bibb attributed slaves' involvement in these spectacles to the "want of moral instruction" on the part of planters. He believed masters, themselves drinkers, fighters, and gamblers, brought slaves down to their level. G. W. Offley, a free black Maryland preacher, defended his role in teaching others "the art of wrestling, boxing and fighting," explaining that "I was trying to be respectable by doing like the rich."[50]

Gambling seems to have been as popular among black men as among whites. Policy—privately conducted lotteries—was very popular among both races in cities. There were estimated to be two hundred policy shops in Philadelphia in 1847, many catering to African Americans. Slaves, free blacks, and whites gambled together with dice and cards at southern grogshops. William Attamore recorded in his diary the horse-racing scene outside Pendelton's tavern in New Bern, North Carolina. There were "Negroes eagerly betting . . . a quart of Rum, a drink of Grog &c., as well as gentlemen betting high." James Thomas was nostalgic about the "many old time blacks [who] were genuine sports" in Nashville. "Horse racing [and] cock fighting were the most exciting for them," and they brought their gamecocks to the woods at the "back of the racetrack" to fight. "Cards and Chuck o luck [hazard] also came in for a large share of attention."[51]

The trickster played a major role in black culture. Although folkloric European pranksters like Robin Goodfellow and Till Eulenspiegel did not cross the Atlantic, African American folklore contains a number of animal and human tricksters—of which Brer Rabbit is only the most famous—with clear African antecedents. Typically, Rabbit outwits Bear and Fox, showing that the weak can, through guile, triumph over the strong, which, of course, had significance for a people in bondage. Black folklore also celebrated stories of slaves who were able to trick their masters into giving them some desirable thing, such as food, or into not doing something undesirable, such as punishing them. But the tales also display, argues Lawrence W. Levine in his study of black folklore, the true mentality of the prankster—pleasure at the pain and humiliation of others. There is a didactic character to many tales, but in others there is no goal to the trickster's deception beyond the psychological pleasure in hurting others without fear of retribution. In one tale, Rabbit comes across Alligator's nest, and "didn' he jes scratch the aigs for pure meaness an' leave 'em layin' around to spile."[52]

Although the trickster played a key role in African American culture, pranks by blacks on blacks do not seem to have been as common as practical jokes among whites. "Snipe hunts," one of the classic pranks among whites, was also practiced by blacks. Most tricks, however, were aimed not at fellow slaves but at masters. Such mischief persuaded many whites that slaves were the cleverest of tricksters. Combined with black drinking, fighting, gambling, and alleged sensuality, the mischief whites associated with blacks would help make African Americans in the eyes of many whites by the 1830s and 1840s the embodiment of jolly values. At a time in which restrained conceptions of manhood were gaining ground, blacks symbolized uninhibited pleasure. Minstrel shows picked up this theme, and it was to remain a standard motif in white popular culture for the rest of the century.[53]

Not all men, of course, were jolly fellows. Rather they formed, as chapter 2 illustrates, a distinct subset of the male population. Disorderly male comportment was, however, very widespread, especially when men gathered in groups. In other chapters, I show that when men set foot on steamboats the drinking began, and before long fighting, gambling, and pranks followed. Jolly fellowship flourished among soldiers in the Mexican War, during the Pennsylvania oil rush, in lumber towns, and in western mining and cattle towns. Not every man in these environments drank, fought, and gambled, of course, nor was every drinker a brawler, nor every gambler a prankster. There were significant geographical and racial variations in the jolly pattern. But they were variations on a pattern, a pattern that, time after time, appeared when men congregated. Drinking, fighting, gambling, and practical jokes became watchwords in descriptions of nineteenth-century male gatherings. What was the connection? And where did jolly fellowship originate? Why was it so attractive? The next chapter suggests that it was not unique to America. Underlying it was a sensibility that was very old—a sensibility that combined compassion and cruelty in ways that were to have a powerful influence on nineteenth-century American culture.

CHAPTER TWO

Jolly Fellowship

"What for a Man are you?" demanded Joseph Blakemore of John Everet. Blakemore was in the Coach and Horses Tavern in London in 1731 "playing a Game of Skettles with one Thomas Bennesfield, and there happen'd to be a Dispute about the Game, on account of a Bett." When onlookers, including Everet, said that Bennesfield had won, Blakemore furiously turned on Everet, asking whether he was a man or not. "A Man, or Piece of a Man as well as you," Everet replied. "And upon this," Blakemore struck Everet "upon the Breast, and made him stagger; and several Blows were struck on both Sides," according to the summary of Blakemore's trial. Everet was thrown down, as he was getting up, Blakemore "struck him a Blow on the Side of the Head." Everet collapsed and died.[1]

Despite the perception of increased male disorder in late eighteenth-century America, the Revolution did not create jolly fellowship. It had been common among men, especially groups of men, for several centuries in both America and Europe. This chapter examines the meaning of jolly fellowship by first looking more closely at the tavern regulars. What was their social background, their age, politics, religion? Chapter 1 describes the behavior that defined jolly fellowship, whereas this chapter considers the class, racial, and geographical variations among disorderly men. It also examines the way others regarded jolly fellows. Their conduct generated complex responses that reveal a surprising tolerance for their frolics. The European antecedents of jolly fellowship suggest how deep seated these attitudes were. The most difficult question to answer is why men took enjoyment in such comportment. What was the pleasure in heavy drinking, fighting, gambling, and rough practical jokes? Some saw jolly conduct as proof of mankind's innate sinfulness. Others were convinced that its genesis was biological—it was simply men's nature to drink and carouse. Men who engaged in jolly behavior did so because of certain conceptions they had of manliness and honor, but that is only part of the explanation. There is a deep-seated aggression, physical and mental, that, at times, challenges rational explanation.

"THE GENIAL SPIRITS OF THE VILLAGE"

Jolly fellowship might be usefully conceptualized in terms of concentric circles. At the center were, of course, the tavern and grocery regulars who gathered daily or several times a week. A larger circle would be men who were not tavern regulars but who would occasionally join them in jolly behavior. The largest circle is men—and women—who did not take part in the tavern crowd's sprees but shared at least some of their attitudes and tolerated, even enjoyed, their capers.

Tavern regulars were separated by race. Blacks sometimes worked at taverns as cooks and hostlers, but they were rarely part of the tavern crowd. In Kinderhook, New York, "it was the custom for white men" only to congregate in the town's taverns. Most white patrons would not tolerate African Americans, and few tavern keepers could bear the dishonor of a white man waiting on a black person. There were interracial "groggeries" in cities and groceries where blacks congregated to drink. As temperance spread, the tavern crowd that had once been viewed with bemused toleration was increasingly seen as a threat to the moral order of the community. The jolly regulars were shunned by respectable men and women; they were not as scorned as African Americans, of course, but their ostracism possibly opened the way to greater interaction among fellow outcasts and to more interracial drinking. At Put's Old Tavern, well off the beaten path in rural Hunterdon County, New Jersey, "color was but little regarded" in the 1840s, Cornelius Larison recalled. Local blacks and whites and "gamesters" from New York and Philadelphia came to wager on cockfights, wrestling matches, and prizefights and men of both races could be found "drinking and talking, laughing and shouting." Such places, however, seem to have been the exception, not the rule. Generally white jolly fellows shared the racial attitudes of most Americans, and blacks were much more likely to be targeted with violence and practical jokes than treated to a drink.[2]

Women likewise virtually never seem to be among the tavern's regular customers. Women certainly enjoyed liquor, but they mainly drank in private. There are, however, examples of women exhibiting certifiably jolly conduct. In early St.

Johnsbury, Vermont, Sally Tute, sure of her riding skill, leaped on a horse, "called for a stimulant and challenged any man of the crowd to overtake her" in a race. "Mistress Hess" and "Mistress Fornsch" battled in the street in York, Pennsylvania, in 1803. In the first decade of the century, women in Richmond wagered on the card game loo, and, it was said, sometimes fights resulted. For the most part, however, the record of jolly conduct among women is silent—it was generally an activity for men. William Otter probably spoke for most male tavern regulars in expressing his scorn for jolly women. He joked of his own alcoholic intake—"we had drank as much as we wanted, and more too"—yet when he encountered a tipsy woman he was shocked, pronouncing it "a weakness which is utterly unsufferable in the female."[3]

Who were the jolly fellows? Here a clear rural-urban difference emerges. In villages the regulars were diverse in social rank. Some were well off, others men of average wealth. Col. A. D. Williams's store in the upstate New York hamlet of Unadilla in the 1840s was "a rendezvous . . . for the genial spirits of the village including the Colonel himself." Williams, who was born in rural Otsego County in 1802, was married, and he was elected colonel in the county militia in 1831. By 1850 he owned $8,500 in real property, an above-average assessment. Two doctors were among this "coterie of fun-loving men": John Colwell, a well-known local physician, born in 1794, a bachelor, "sharp, quick-witted and very sarcastic," who boarded in Kingsley's Hotel and owned no property, and Gaius Halsey, the author of the reminiscences that provide most of the information on Williams's store. Halsey was born in 1819 and later became a politician. The group also included three artisans—Bennett Woodruff, a married blacksmith with $1,300 in real property, Benjamin Ayers, a hatter born in 1806 who owned $3,500 in real estate, and Rufus Mead, a mason. The wealthiest regular was A. B. Watson, a married banker born in 1800 with two servants and property worth $11,250, making him among the best off men in the region.[4]

The village regulars were not riffraff. Elisha Gardiner, the leader of the Hornet's Nest in Kingston, Rhode Island, was a reputable farmer "at one time doing a great business," according to the Gardiner family genealogy. Bernhardt Gilbert was the tavern keeper at the Spread Eagle Tavern in Gettysburg, Pennsylvania, and in 1818 he helped concoct one of William Otter's wildest sprees in which Otter got into a fencing match with a local doctor using canes and later "bepissed" in his face. Gilbert was one of the richest men in town, owning more than $8,507 worth of property. Whenever "a monstrous practical joke was perpetrated" in Waukesha, Wisconsin, "it was always charged to 'Aleck' Randall and his friends." Randall was a married man in his thirties and a successful lawyer.

The pattern seems similar in the South. A North Carolina newspaper denounced "*gentleman farmers*, who rise at eight and breakfast at nine o'clock; ride out into the fields and ask a few questions of the overseer, and then repair to some customary place of resort, whether a tavern, or a store at some cross-roads." It was still possible in this era to be both a tavern habitué and a respectable member of the community.[5]

Still, despite the presence of well-off individuals among the jolly fellows, many tavern regulars were obscure men. The village tavern was a institution that encompassed, and perhaps united, men of diverse social standing. One of Otter's most regular partners in pranks, "one of the wonders of the world," was Caleb Bailes, an Abbottstown, Pennsylvania, mason, a man of average wealth, not prominent in local records. "Cook the hatter," apparently a journeyman, was the "Col. Cook" of the Hornet's Nest prank on Charles Comstock. Drovers as well as planters according to Daniel R. Hundley, frequented the southern country tavern,. Nevertheless, even with such diversity, there seem to have been comparatively few ordinary farmers among the regulars. Taverns were usually located in villages, and most farmers came to town once a week, so most regulars lived in the village or nearby. Farmers were likely well represented in the second concentric circle of men who would engage in jolly behavior occasionally.[6]

If men involved in agriculture seem underrepresented among tavern habitués, men in politics and the legal system were heavily overrepresented. William Otter became mayor of Emmitsburg, Maryland; Elisha Gardiner was deputy sheriff of Washington County, Rhode Island; Bernhardt Gilbert, Otter's partner in pranks, served as Adams County sheriff in the 1820s; and Aleck Randall in Waukesha became governor of Wisconsin during the Civil War. Politicians met and mobilized support in taverns and stores. In some localities each party had its own hangout. The Democrats in Indianapolis gathered at the Mansion House in the 1830s, the Whigs across the street at Washington Hall. Davenport's store in Plymouth, Pennsylvania, "was Democratic headquarters, and there in the evening would assemble the patriots of the neighborhood who would line up on the counters, spit tobacco juice, swap stories and discuss politics." Most drinking places, however, were politically neutral, and at them, supporters of the two parties could enjoy debating the issues of the day.[7]

Before the 1830s there does not seem to have been any clear political orientation to jolly fellowship. There were both jolly Republicans and Federalists. With the growth of the temperance movement, however, Democrats seem to have become more prevalent among the tavern and grocery crowd than Whigs. The Whig party never officially endorsed temperance, but it often nominated protemperance men, and members of antidrink organizations were considerably more likely to be Whigs than Democrats. To jolly fellows, the "government is best which governs least" philosophy of the Democrats was likely more appealing than the reform-minded moralism of their rivals. Whigs certainly thought so. "Loafers from around the grog-shop" was Horace Greeley's surly assessment of the voters that defeated Henry Clay in 1844.[8]

Not only were politicians among the tavern's loyal patrons; so too were men involved in the legal system. In an era of traveling circuit courts, lawyers were known for conviviality, and they, along with judges, bailiffs, and clerks, appear routinely in accounts of the escapades of the regulars. Thomas Heald, the leader of the raucous regulars at Davis's tavern, was a prominent Concord lawyer, and the law occupies a large place in the sprees of even jolly fellows who were not lawyers. Sham lawsuits were one common prank. In the fall of 1803 Charles Comstock, the Hornet's Nest's favorite victim, went to Providence on business. "When I returned home, I found seven copies of writs, and one pair of my oxen carried away." When Comstock complained about this baseless legal action, they replied "they were in jest: for that is part of their sort of wit." False suits for debts were also a favorite prank of Wisconsin tavern jokers.[9]

The jolly fellows' fascination with the law and the legal process found expression in the mock trial. A traditional European male ritual, the mock trial could be staged wherever men congregated in nineteenth-century America, in taverns, fire companies, steamboats, in western mining towns and even in state legislatures. Bob Smith's House of Commons tavern in New York City held such trials, complete with wigs, as a regular entertainment for the customers. The volunteer firemen of Hook and Ladder Company Number Three in New York City in 1835 "summoned up a jury for a mock trial, to try a man for falling asleep in club house, found guilty and fined a pot of beer," printer Thomas Chamberlain recorded in his diary. "The boys" in Licking County, Ohio, staged a sham trial of their comrades who pulled down an abandoned schoolhouse. So many jolly fellows were associated with courts and law enforcement that sometimes they were able to make a mock trial appear to be a real one. James S. Buck, in his jolly *Pioneer History of Milwaukee* (1876–86), tells the story of a sham lawsuit in early Milwaukee that was gotten up to settle a dispute between Egbert "Limpy" Smith and Frederick Wingfield, which stemmed from gossip the tavern crowd had started as a joke. Asa Kinney, a real justice of the peace, presided. The whiskey jug was passed freely, and Smith and Wingfield were drunk by the time the proceeding started. At the conclusion of the trial the two men were instructed to embrace, "'AND NOW,'" ordered the "judge," "'let the Sheriff embrace the court!'"

John Haight, the plaintiff's lawyer, who was not in on the joke and who had been promised forty acres of land if he won the case, "sprang to his feet, 'By God! it's all a d——d sell.'"[10]

Mock trials usually were contrived for the amusement of those taking part rather than to chasten someone. They may have served some of the same purposes as debating societies: to provide a forum for young men to practice the skills of argument and public speaking. This would be especially true for men interested in the law and politics, as many regulars were. The male ritual may also have helped define the playful nature of jolly fellowship. Participating in an enterprise that required the involvement of a number of men could have given those taking part a sense of unity and distinctiveness.

The religious views of the tavern crowd, like their social ranking, were diverse. Critics accused them of indifference to divine matters. Charles Comstock censured the Hornet's Nest: "As to their religion, part of it is Rum, some of them are Nothingarians, some of them Universalists, a few of them Friends, and some of them are Baptists, but most of them are Nothingarians." Like the population generally, many jolly fellows were unchurched. There were also, however, many others who were churchgoers. The Williams's store gathering in Unadilla was largely made up of Episcopalians, several of whom were quite active in church affairs. Aleck Randall, the Waukesha joker, was a Presbyterian. These regulars saw no contradiction between a jolly life and a Christian life. None of the Ten Commandments, after all, mentioned drinking, fighting, gambling, or playing pranks. Barnum describes Bethel, Connecticut, as a pious Presbyterian village in the 1820s despite all the drinking, practical joking, horse racing, and general hilarity that went on; indeed the clergyman sometimes even joined in the pranks. This easygoing attitude began to disappear in the 1820s and 1830s as religious revivals and the temperance movement surged. Sedate demeanor became a prerequisite in many denominations for being a good Christian.[11]

The regulars in a village tavern typically varied in wealth, age, political affiliation, and religious outlook. In cities, however, where class lines were more sharply drawn, there were different drinking places for different social groups. In New York in the 1830s workers drank in groceries and "three cent" houses, while "more respectable people" congregated in "six cent" houses. And, increasingly, new standards of gentility meant more respectable men shunned drinking places altogether. There were certainly jolly white-collar men in cities. Newspaperman Thomas Nichols visited a rowdy Buffalo tavern in 1837 whose customers included not only sailors and canalers but also "some of the wilder young clerks." But generally urban grocery and tavern regulars seem more likely to have been manual workers and also to have been younger than village patrons. William Otter engaged in jolly fellowship with men who occupied a wide variety of social positions in Adams County, Pennsylvania, but his comrades in New York City and Philadelphia were solely apprentices and journeymen. John Lane, Big Bill Otter's "particular croney" in New York, was an obscure baker whose name never appeared in a city directory. The great majority of men arrested in New York City tavern brawls were manual workers, most under age thirty.[12]

Although evidence exists that enables one to generalize about tavern and grocery regulars, it is more difficult to find information about the second circle of men, those who joined in jolly sprees and frolics only occasionally. In Kingston, Rhode Island, according to Comstock, "There are some young men who live there, who are not in full communion with the hornet's nest cunning, although they are sometimes drawn in; for bad company bears a great sway upon the youth." In Bethel too, men who were not part of the store crowd sometimes joined in their pranks. In rural areas this fringe group likely included men who lived too far from a tavern or store to hang out there regularly. On Saturday they could come to town, repair to their favorite spot to drink, gamble, fight, and joke away the day. Jacob Drafts in Lexington, South Carolina, lived quietly on his farm most of the time, but when he came to town he spent his day drinking, "bragging, blackguarding and sometimes fighting." He then returned home until the jolly craving overcame him again.[13]

The largest circle was men (and women) who rarely, if ever, engaged in jolly behavior but who were not necessarily hostile to the jolly fellows or repulsed by their conduct. Tavern regulars had their critics (discussed in chapter 3), but most people, it seemed, tolerated, even condoned, the jolly fellows' escapades. In part this was because such comportment was accepted as inevitable and unchangeable: it was men's nature. But this tolerance went beyond resigned acceptance—there is considerable evidence that the frolics, fights, and pranks were intriguing, even alluring, to many people who themselves would not participate in them. Edward Jarvis explained that "the moral sense of the [Concord] community did not approve" but neither "did it effectively condemn" the village's tavern roisters, and it considered tales of their exploits "as proper means of entertaining their friends or others." Sources of entertainment were scant compared to later in the nineteenth century, and boozers, brawlers, and bettors provided lively topics of discussion. The jolly fellows' romps did more than add zest to local gossip. Many men and women regarded their antics not just with interest, but with relish. Concordians who would not themselves join in the drink-fueled "waywardnesses" of Thomas Heald and his cohorts "found amusement in relating them to their families and neighbors," Jarvis observed.[14]

Being drunk occasionally was considered "proof of spirit." In St. Johnsbury, Vermont, related Samuel Graves, "It was counted a good joke for an honest man to lose his way home of an evening, or mistake his neighbor's home for his own." When former Mississippi governor George Poindexter, "somewhat fuddled" after an evening at the Mansion House Bar in Natchez in 1836, opened what he thought was the door to his room and plunged twenty feet onto the sidewalk, he became the talk of the town. Tales of drunken revelry were considered appropriate even for children. A Philadelphia publisher in 1815 published a series of nursery rhymes that included "Pug's Visit to Mr. Punch." A bored Punch (as in Punch and Judy) and his wife decide to "send for [their] friend Pug" and to "make [themselves] jolly" by cracking "a good bottle or two." Pug comes immediately,

For he always was ready to kick up a row,
So they eat Mr. Punches tarts, jellies and pies,
And they all got as tipsey as David's old sow,
Too drunk to walk home on the carpet Pug roll'd.[15]

It was not just the tavern and grocery regulars who were interested in fighting; the allure was widespread. In Marietta, Ohio, in the 1830s, John Morris remembered, the "educated portion of the people," who would never themselves fight, "did not consider it beneath them to be the aiders and abettors of rowdyism." Morris believed that the fights between local "gladiators" in the antebellum period were to most people "as interesting and exciting as were those which took place in the arena of ancient Rome to its people." Matches between champions were eagerly anticipated almost everywhere and were a topic of village discussion and wagering. Jonas Heinrich Gudehus, a German immigrant who traveled through Pennsylvania in 1822 and 1823, discovered that before "a frolic or vendue begins there is especially much talk about who wants to fight at the same, for that is their chief pleasure. . . . One always hears people say: . . . 'Haven't you heard who's going to fight at the frolic?'" Whether drunken brawls or "set fights," battles would immediately attract large and enthusiastic crowds. So intense was the desire of spectators to see the fighting in Williamston, North Carolina, "that they would often climb up on each other's shoulders." When anticipated battles failed to "come off," there was dejection. "A very Poor Court, no fighting or Gouging, very few Drunken people," a disappointed peddler recorded in his diary of his visit to Liberty, Virginia, in 1807. Rather than trying to prevent battles, onlookers let men fight it out, and once the confrontation started they often exhorted belligerents to greater effort. In Union, Maine, when a battle began, the crowd "would run and gather round the ring, to give the combatants room and see that they had fair play." In Martin County, North Carolina, should anyone try to halt the fight or interfere, another spectator would "spring upon the interloper" and stop him, often leading to another brawl." In the celebrated fracas on the floor of the House of Representatives in 1798 between Matthew Lyon of Vermont and Roger Griswold of Connecticut (one of a number of fights in legislative bodies in this era), shouts of "Part them, part them," were immediately countered by cries of "Don't."[16]

Pranks likewise had a wide appeal. Papermaker Ebenezer Stedman recalled in his handwritten reminiscences of the 1820s how in Lexington, Kentucky, "the talk amounght the people . . . was, 'Well what is Hostutters last prank?' " referring to Frank Hostutter, the town's most celebrated practical joker. His "tricks & Pranks [were] Enjoyed By Evry Body that day in Lexington." Though women rarely participated in jolly sprees, they joined in finding the antics of the regulars amusing. A Connecticut peddler had a special bean in his snuffbox that imparted, he believed, a much improved flavor. P. T. Barnum tells the story that his grandfather, Phineas Taylor, a legendary joker, one day borrowed the bean, telling the peddler that he wanted to see if it would improve the flavor of his own snuff. Taylor then whittled a piece of wood, dyed it to look like the original bean, and returned it to the peddler. Taylor then "acquainted nearly all the town with the joke." The next time the peddler passed through Danbury "nearly every man, woman and child begged for a pinch of snuff," praised its taste, and questioned the owner about the special qualities of the bean, questions he happily and proudly answered. The joke was eventually revealed and the peddler never forgave Taylor "to the day of his death."[17]

Popular tolerance is illustrated by the almost complete lack of legal sanctions for jolly conduct; men involved had little reason to fear arrest. The law was clear. Drunkenness, fighting, gambling, and malicious mischief were illegal and had been so since colonial times. But carousing men received wide latitude from authorities. This was in part, no doubt, because judges, justices of peace, and sheriffs often were themselves jolly fellows. But the lack of effective legal sanctions cannot be attributed just to the influence of jolly officials. There is considerable evidence of a widespread, though not universal, view that disorderly male behavior was not criminal, no matter what the laws said.

Habitual drunkards faced arrest, but men inebriated on a spree seemed to have received little in the way of punishment from either public opinion or the law.

Professional gamblers faced prosecution even in the South, but only in Massachusetts and Connecticut were private bettors in any real danger of arrest. Fights between men were "personal difficulties," not breaches of law. Henry Fearon witnessed a tavern brawl in New Orleans and noted that such things "are an everyday occurrence; and it is not often they are taken cognizance of by the police." Even when someone was seriously hurt, or even killed, in a fight, the perpetrator was rarely punished unless weapons had been used. He was simply unlucky—with thousands of punches thrown in hundreds of fights, a few will prove crippling or fatal.[18]

Free-for-alls and even minor riots were an accepted part of urban life. Tavern disturbances, such as the general fight in McDermot's grocery in New York City that involved William Otter and his mates, was only a minor cause for concern. Both the public and legal authorities believed it inevitable that groups of young men would let off a little steam from time to time. Indeed, many deemed such spontaneous brawls beneficial because they made major riots less likely. Only purposeful disorders, those in which the participants had a goal beyond mere mayhem, alarmed authorities. Violent holiday roistering was a tradition, and a crowd of men in New York on New Year's Day 1822 "went forth . . . displacing signs, knocking down the watchmen," firing pistols, and pelting any women they came across with snowballs. They were eventually arrested, but, according to the sheriff, the magistrate "in consideration of the day discharged them all, with suitable admonitions, and without requesting any fees."[19]

This leniency suggests the extent to which jolly fellowship was accepted. The tavern crowd in villages and towns were by no means outcasts; they often included members of the local elite. Although the regulars were viewed as a distinct subset of the male population, many other men occasionally engaged in jolly behavior, and many more men and even women were intrigued by it. The drinking, fighting, gambling, and pranks of the tavern regulars were not isolated phenomena: their actions found sympathetic resonance with others.

"TIS NO FESTIVAL UNLESS THERE BE SOME FIGHTINGS"

The disorderly conduct of men in groups in the early republic was nothing new. The American Revolution stimulated male disorder, but it did not create it. In colonial New England, taverns were centers of male sociability, and most had their band of regulars. When magistrate Samuel Sewell went to Wallis's tavern in Boston in 1714 to halt the "disorders" there, the group of men drinking "refus'd to go away. Said they were there to drink the Queen's health, and they had many other Healths to drink. Call'd for more drink; drank to me." In a Wenham, Massachusetts, tavern in 1681 the tavern keeper's daughter promised Thomas Abby, already in his cups, "that she would give him a quart of wine if he could whip" John Hutton. Abby "fell upon" Hutton and wrestled him to the floor and proclaimed himself "the best man in the land." Gang fights in Boston were a tradition on Guy Fawkes Day, known in America as Pope's Day. "Champions of both ends of the town engage each other in battle under the denominations of North and South End," recorded an eyewitness to the traditional brawl in 1764. On the evening of 5 November "the two parties met near the Mill Bridge where they fought with clubs, brickbats for half an hour, when those of the South End gained victory. . . . In the fray, many were much bruised and wounded in their heads and arms, some dangerously." Cards, dice, bowling, and shuffleboard were "virtually universal in Bay Colony taverns," according to Richard Gildrie in his study of Puritan comportment. Cotton Mather denounced not only tavern fighting and gambling but the "*Horse-play*" of the customers.[20]

Outside New England, taverns seem to have been even rowdier. A Philadelphia grand jury denounced "whites in their tumultuous resorts . . . [who] most Daringly . . . swear, Curse Lye Abuse and often fight." As in the nineteenth century, onlookers were shocked by the "Kicking, Scratching, Biting, Throttling, Gouging [and] Dismembering" that characterized Southern combat and the way enthusiastic spectators urged on participants. In a notorious 1766 incident, two friends, Robert Routlidge and Col. John Chiswell were drinking in Mosby's tavern in Prince Edward County, Virginia. They had words, Chiswell tried to smash a toddy bowl over Routlidge's head, then threw furniture at him, and finally fatally stabbed him. One traveler had hardly alighted from his carriage on election day at Hanover Court House, Virginia, when a fight began "between two very unwieldy, fat men, foaming and puffing like two furies." Gambling was openly engaged in. Richardson's tavern outside of the City of Brotherly Love on the Germantown road was the site of the most famous cockfighting match in colonial America. In March 1770, James Delancey brought his birds down from New York to fight those of Timothy Matlack. The cockfight ended in a human fight. Southern taverns were sites of incessant wagering on both cockfights and horse races among other events. Militia days, court days, and election days were traditional scenes of disorder.[21]

Groups of men, especially young men, displayed similar conduct both in early modern England and continental Europe. English taverns and beer houses were centers of conviviality in both city and village, and men spent a considerable amount of time and money there. Wagering was a normal part of tavern recreation in an age when men carried dice with them as a matter of course. Enterprising English tavern keepers sponsored horse races, boxing and wrestling matches, cockfights, and bullbaitings. Fights, even small riots, were a part of daily life. At a bullbaiting in Chester in 1619, "a contention fell out betwixt the butchers and the bakers of the citye." They "fell to blows" and "a brawle" commenced.[22]

"The 'habit of fighting from boyhood' was deeply ingrained in English culture," J. Carter Wood discovered in his study of English violence. "A fair fight," complete with seconds, was the traditional English way for men to settle disputes or merely to determine who was the better man. As in America, market days and holidays were especially violent, and the English saying was "tis no festival unless there be some fightings." Boxing and wrestling matches were traditional entertainments. The practice in the north of England of "up and down" fighting in which no holds were barred led to occasional fatalities. Collective combat was equally common. Witney, Oxfordshire, had an annual brawl on Guy Fawkes Day between the "up-town and down-town boys." During Christmas season in London it was customary for men from St. Anne's parish to battle St. Giles's parish with sticks. Shrove Tuesday in London and other English cities in the sixteenth and seventeenth centuries was not only a day of cockfighting but of brawling, wrecking bawdy houses, and rioting. Battles sometimes ended with crowds coursing through the streets, breaking windows and creating bedlam. Violence could whirl into brutal pranks: in London passersby were rolled in barrels; in Bayton, Worcestershire, drunken villagers would drag "timber in the night time into the highways . . . , [and] pull up men's pales and stiles and rails and cause general havoc."[23]

Male English disorder was part of a broad European pattern. In Augsburg, Germany, tavern brawls were an almost daily occurrence. Minor riots "arising haphazardly for a variety of reasons" were a routine part of Paris life, historian Thomas Brennan discovered. Men would pour out of taverns, cabarets, and workshops and join the battle. Fairs in France, like those in England, could flare into violence—the battle cry when the fighting started was the village name; all townsmen were expected to rally to the cause. The *compagnons*—the clandestine French brotherhoods of young journeymen that were separate from the occupation-based guilds—were notably unruly. Their weapon of choice was the stout cane each carried, and when they met members of rival brotherhoods, they were "led to fight by rage and unparalleled fury so as to kill one another." These fierce brawls continued into the nineteenth century. Gambling was an integral part of tavern life—in French medieval taverns, the dice game hazard, still popular in nineteenth-century America, was a great favorite. Practical jokes were popular tavern pastimes. A German favorite was hiding a man's hat and refusing to return it until the victim bought a round of drinks. Drinkers who had fallen asleep or passed out were "the victims of countless tricks" in France.[24]

In seventeenth- and eighteenth-century Venice, neighborhood groups fought for command of bridges over the canals. Arranged in advance, the *Guerre di pugni* (the War of the Fists) began with individual fights on the bridges between champions, and then the general brawl began. The rival bands, often numbering in the hundreds, pushed and threw each other into the canals, where the fighting continued. When they gained control of a bridge, the winning fighters and the victorious neighborhood earned immense honor. Given the ubiquity of fighting in Europe, the reputation of the Irish as the Old World's eagerest brawlers is indeed impressive. Much of this renown was based on the huge fights between village-based gangs that occurred in eighteenth- and nineteenth-century Ireland. In what were known as "faction fights," gangs with names like the "Pudding Lane Boys" and "Black Hens" would battle in village streets with cudgels, often for several hours. There seems to have been no discernable motive other than what one observer described as "the agreeable recreation of fighting." Lives were sometimes lost, but, he explained, "they are lost in pleasant fighting—they are the consequences of the sport."[25]

Sociologist Norbert Elias has argued that European society underwent a "civilizing process" whereby spontaneous, impulsive individual attitudes gave way in the seventeenth and eighteenth centuries to a reflective and restrained personality structure. In Freudian terms, the superego became stronger. Elias believed that this process could be seen in many areas of social life, including sexual behavior and table manners. And in interpersonal violence. Homicides are an indicator of the overall level of violence and provide a way of comparing the European and American experience. Homicide rates in early modern Europe vary widely across space and time, but the overall picture seems clear: lives often came to violent ends. Lawrence Stone's conclusion that in medieval and early modern England most killings were a result of "drunken bar-room brawls or village quarrels" seems applicable to Europe generally. The usual agents in these deadly melees were bladed weapons or staffs, both widely carried. The European homicide rate was generally high, in the range of twenty to forty killings per one hundred thousand people per year in the late medieval period. (For purposes of comparison, in the United States in 2000 it was five and a half per one hundred thousand.) In some places it was even higher—in sixteenth-century Amsterdam it was forty-seven, higher than any rate ever recorded for New York City. The European homicide rate in the seventeenth and eighteenth centuries sharply dropped, as Elias's

Irish faction fight. From the title page of William Carleton's *The Battle of the Factions, and Other Tales of Ireland* (Philadelphia, 1845).

model predicts. The primary reason for the decline, according to criminologist Manuel Eisner, "seems to have been . . . a decrease in male-to-male fights." By the end of the eighteenth century the rate in London was in the range of two per one hundred thousand.[26]

American homicide rates before the nineteenth century have not been extensively studied, but Randolph Roth puts the seventeenth-century New England rate at seven to nine per one hundred thousand (slightly higher than England in this period), dropping to one to two in the next century. Eric Monkkonen's statistics on New York City in the late eighteenth and early nineteenth centuries show rates in the range of five to ten. Rates in both the South and West vary considerably but were higher—in some places much higher. Although American men often fought, it was usually with fists—and sometimes feet and teeth—but outside the South rarely with guns and knives. The sectional difference is clear. New England was the least violent and deadly region. Men in New England battled, but probably less frequently and certainly less brutally than anywhere else in the country; fatalities were virtually unknown. The combat of choice in northern New England, "collar-and-elbow" wrestling, so named from the starting position, was tamer than fist fighting or no-holds-barred wrestling; you only had to throw your opponent down to win. Weapons in male combat were almost unheard of in the region. Charles Woodman was stunned when his antagonist in an 1827 tavern brawl in New Haven pulled a knife and stabbed him in the hip.[27]

The South was a different story. Battles were often brutal, rough-and-tumble eye-gouging, biting affairs in which the loser was literally defaced. Southerners were also much more apt to resort to weapons. William Johnson's Natchez diary recounts fights with chairs, iron bars, umbrellas, shovels, hatchets, sword canes, whips, bowie knives, dirks, and pistols. Although only a tiny minority of southern fights were, in the language of the day, "shooting affrays" or "stabbing affrays," they were clearly much more common than elsewhere. White southerners were more likely to carry weapons and to use them. Edward Isham got into a fight outside Chattanooga with "a fellow named Moore." He "had a revolver and rock and I had a little pocket pistol." It was "a desperate fight" that ended when Isham, after his gun failed to fire, pistol whipped his adversary. In an 1837 Natchez fight with "a Dr Reigna," "Mr Rogers of Manchester" fired at him with a revolver, and then, recorded William Johnson, knocked Reigna down, pulled a knife, and "stabbed him clear through the body and screwed it around in his Dead body."[28]

"A GENEROUS PARCEL OF ROWDIES"

What are we to make of such conduct, widespread among men in not only the American but the European past as well? Was it simply a fragmentary collection of attitudes and acts, or was there some underlying outlook, perhaps even an ethic? "Ethic" is surely too strong; it is very doubtful there was a consistent motive behind jolly conduct in all times and all places. Yet, it does seem that there was more to it than simply random notions and escapades. There clearly was a pattern to jolly demeanor, perhaps even a meaning, and the rest of this chapter tries to suggest some of the causes and purposes of disorderly male conduct. Such an effort requires moving at times beyond the evidence to make interpretations and suppositions about the motivation for the behavior I've been describing. A few cases draw on evidence from male domains I discuss in other chapters in the book. The following analysis is necessarily speculative. It hopes to recover some plausible explanations of the attitudes that underlie jolly fellowship, though such explanations cannot be certain or complete. And in so doing, the analysis aims to help one comprehend the importance of this distinctive comportment not just in the antebellum period but in other places and times where men engaged in similar conduct.

It was taken for granted that many men simply could not restrain themselves from drinking, fighting, gambling, and playing pranks, even if they had wanted to. Jolly male conduct was viewed as spontaneous, even involuntary. Among gamblers it was axiomatic that "no man can resist cards and brandy." It is striking how often such behavior is described in terms that make it seem like a natural force. Fights broke out and swept over bystanders like a storm. In Williamston, North Carolina, when a battle would start one man would jump in, and "then another and another would go in until the battle would wax fierce and general." Yale students visiting a Wild West show were described as "overcome" by rowdyism. Similar language described pranks. The young Isaac T. Hopper, for example, often "felt the spirit of mischief too strong to be resisted." Henry Brokmeyer, who had once worked in a St. Louis foundry, remembered that "days would pass without a word being heard beyond the ordinary civilities." Then suddenly one day an urge to frolic would overpower the shop, and the men would erupt into "regular field days of banter . . . with a lively sprinkling of blackguarding thrown in gratis. . . . How these days come, what causes them, no one can tell." Drinking was surely part of the reason for this impetuous conduct. Perhaps some of the attraction of such conduct was that it opened a space in which one could exercise less self-restraint and engage in pleasurable activities without hesitation or compunction. Drinking, however, does not necessarily lead to impulsive or rowdy conduct in all times and places. The influence of alcohol on human behavior is complex and socially variable. In future decades American men drank heavily without getting into fights. It may be that drinking was more a justification or rationale for disorderly comportment than a cause.[29]

Emotions were expressed physically. When angry, men fought, when sad, they cried, when happy, they embraced. Men had words, brawled, made up, and were friends again. Just as a man could get mad at someone and punch him in the face, he could with equal passion fall on a favorite male companion with kisses. Many nineteenth-century men were as unreserved in expressing fondness for other men as they were in displaying animosity; both were part of the same impulsive emotional pattern. Male friendships were often intense. George Birmingham, a Buffalo bookbinder, wrote to New York cabinetmaker Henry Price, "I shall never forget you, and I can always bring you to mind when I think of your kindness, I think of you every day." It was not simply that men used sentimental language to express friendship. Affection was more than a matter of words; it was also physical. Men kissed, hugged, held hands. On court day in Williamston, North Carolina, men would drink, then battle in rough-and-tumble fights, and then "towards the close of the day the *boys* would become 'unco happy,' and be seen walking about shaking hands, hugging each other in the most affectionate manner, and making vows of eternal friendship." In Georgetown, Kentucky, two veterans of the Battle of Lundy's Lane encountered one another for the first time in years. "They clinched And such hugging & kissing. . . . Then they held each other By the hand & Surveyed their Looks," Ebenezer Stedman recounted. The men then began drinking and "commenced Singing War Songs." Two bosom companions in early Milwaukee had a falling out, as male friends so often did in this period, and a dinner was arranged to effect a reconciliation. "To strengthen their brotherly love," they ate off each other's plates "and finally wound up with a kiss." Displays of emotion and even physical affection were not unmanly.[30]

Such behavior was considered normal and usually occasioned little comment. It was common for men to be photographed with their arms around each other. Men could be much more open in avowing affection for and in touching other men than they could be with women because it was believed there was nothing erotic about men's love for other men. Such comradeship was explicitly defined in opposition to sexual love. A letter writer to the *New York Clipper* explained the attachment volunteer firemen felt for each other; it was "so fond, so devoted, nothing [could] alter it, *nothing [could] surpass it.*" But this love was sublime precisely because it was "so divested of passions[,] . . . so disconnected with selfish sensuality." In male relations with women it seemed a slippery slope from touching to kissing to intercourse. There seems to have been the implicit conviction that the ultimate purpose of a man's relationship with a woman was sexual and thus required close monitoring. There was little such concern in relationships between men, so physical expressions of male devotion, such as holding hands, were not viewed as a prelude to depravity. Just the opposite. Men holding hands represented an unaffectedly forthright conjunction of kindred spirits.[31]

Because men focused so much emotional attention on each other, it seemed as if they had an ability to "see" other men with exceptional acuity: faces and bodies were scrutinized and remembered. In a period during which most Americans lived in villages and farms, other people seemed to have occupied a larger part of human experience than today. Few traveled very far, and for most men and women their frame of reference was their neighbors. The occasional stranger never failed to attract intense interest. Letters, diaries, and reminiscences, some written many years later, contain detailed, often eloquent descriptions of other men's physical appearance, more detailed, often, than their portrayals of women.

James Buck his *Pioneer History of Milwaukee,* writing almost forty years after the fact, describes early male settlers with "coarse and shaggy hair," "dark eyes," "arms of great length," and "short thick ears." The precise physical descriptions by whites of whites stands in contrast to the often vague white word portraits of the faces and bodies of people of color. It seems as if whites could see little beyond blackness. Perhaps many were like the traveling salesman in Owen Wister's *The Virginian,* who claimed he could recall every face he had ever seen—"can't lose one off my memory." But he added, "white men, that is. Can't do nothing with niggers or Chinese."[32]

Conduct-of-life literature warned that "true character" could not be judged by appearance, but there remained a widespread conviction in this era that people could, indeed should, be judged by their looks. A well-built or good-looking man was likely a superior person, a puny or ugly one inferior. Men ceaselessly sized up other men. Height and weight were carefully assessed and shoulders, chests, and arms scrutinized and evaluated, eyes, noses, and mouths studied and judged. Large men and men with powerful physiques received attention and honor. There was "an unfeigned admiration of the powerful man" in antebellum Oneida County, New York, James M. Williams discovered. Bullies were not esteemed, but "physical power" mattered; it was taken for granted that the strong would dominate the weak. Power at this level was direct and personal. In an era when only men could vote, politics was a masculine endeavor, and big men often prevailed. Nineteenth-century ward bosses in New York City were brawny men, while elected officials in Oneida County were typically "great big men." Handsome men also were honored. Leaders among groups of men were routinely singled out for their looks, their "finely chiseled features," or their "honest, open face." Unattractive men were scorned. William Baumgartner in early Milwaukee was unusually ugly, so "his very presence caused a chill wherever he went," James Buck remembered. Physical oddities were openly noted and became the subject of ridicule. John Stone in Concord "walked with a jerk, so he was called *Hop Stone* and jeered on account of this peculiarity." Perhaps this is part of the reason why men were fascinated with disguise in this era. Painted faces and fantastic costumes liberated men from the tyranny of their natural face and body, creating a sort of momentary equality in masquerade.[33]

Tavern regulars had a reputation for charity. Poor men and women were often treated either by the tavern keeper or the regulars to free meals, and those who were sick and had no other place to go were taken care of without charge. It was said of Yankee Lewis's tavern outside Kalamazoo that "no man was allowed to go away from his house hungry." Benevolence in this era was not entirely disinterested. The attitude, John M. Williams discovered, was "You help me and I'll help you." Chance played a central role in life, and few could dare live as individualists, as Caroline Kirkland discovered in Michigan, given that a stray spark or sudden illness could "throw you entirely upon the kindness of your humblest neighbor[.] If I treat Mrs. Timson with neglect to-day, can I with any face borrow her broom to-morrow?" Nor was aid automatic. Paton Yoder discovered that race, nationality, and social status all were factors in a person's decision to help. Blacks, as a rule, had no claim on white compassion. At times charity seemed almost whimsical—one person would be profusely helped, another seemingly similar person turned away, perhaps ridiculed, for reasons difficult to discern. However, even in an era when mutuality was a way of life, the tavern crowd retained a powerful reputation for generosity. Such compassion was, by later standards, direct and personal. The Clary's Grove Boys in Illinois were as openhanded as they were wild. "They were a terror to the entire region," wrote William Herndon, "yet place before them a poor man who needed their aid, . . . a widow, an orphaned child, and they melted into sympathy and charity at once. . . . There never was a more generous parcel of rowdies."[34]

While treating some with compassion, the tavern crowd could turn ruthlessly on others. Blacks and Indians, the Irish, cripples, lunatics, weaklings and drunken men were open to humiliation and assault. Animals were also beyond the frame of moral reference. All were fair game. Blacks, of course, were routinely targets of violence. "Having always a propensity for fun," Big Bill Otter and his pals in Philadelphia were presented in 1807 with "an opportunity . . . to give loose to, and gratify it." With the approval of white neighbors they stormed a black church and beat up the congregation; "they kept on until nearly the whole of the darkies were stretched out," Otter boasted. "No particular regard was paid to sex, they levelled them indiscriminately." It is well known that violence against blacks by whites was widespread, and so the point requires little elaboration.[35]

The Irish also faced attacks. There was, however, a difference. The violence against blacks was rougher, deadlier, and motivated more by racial hatred than anything else—they were more often than not assaults, not fights. William Otter's autobiography relates attacks *on* blacks but fights *with* Irishmen. On Christmas Day, 1806, in New York, Otter and some of his companions came on a brawl between sailors and Irish that turned into a riot that "kept both sides fighting all that night." The confrontation with the Irish was certainly inspired by ethnic and religious enmity, but it is also possible to discern in it a devotion to fighting so characteristic of this period. The Irish had battled among themselves in Ireland and continued their faction fighting on the other side of the Atlantic. They were not reluctant brawlers and neither were Americans. Elias Pym Fordham, an English visitor in 1816, was struck by the similarity: "When intoxicated . . . [Pennsylvanians] sometimes fight most furiously. In this they resemble the Lower Irish." The coming of significant numbers of Irish helped unite American brawlers. Instead of one end of town fighting the other, how much more exciting it was for native-born men from both ends of town to combine to battle the Irish, as happened in Lockport, New York, on 24 December 1822.[36]

Other races, outsiders, and those without power faced perpetual rough jokes, tricks, and frauds from the jolly fellows. There was always an element of aggression in jolly joking, and "pranks" against those whose victimization attracted little sympathy were often brutal, even deadly. In the Hudson River town of Catskill, New York, "a set of wild and reckless young fellows, spoiling for sport, concluded it would be fine amusement to pitch "SONCE," a "spruce and rather consequential darkey," off the dock, "compensating him for each immersion by a glass of rum." Eventually they got Sonce so drunk that he drowned, which James D. Pinckney, author of an 1862 reminiscence, found comical, since "it seemed a puzzle how the water got into him when he was chock full already." Catskill carousers also targeted a feeble-minded man; cats were thrown through his window, and they "used levers to move his house off the foundation." Gambler Robert Bailey in his autobiography tells the story of an elaborate prank in which a Virginia physician tricked a pharmacist's black helper into eating excrement to cure him of his idea of becoming a doctor. The boy was "reconciled to his situation." Edwin Scott's reminiscence of life in Columbia, South Carolina, in the 1820s and 1830s describes practical jokes on those perceived as community outsiders. Pranksters hung a "stuffed Paddy" on Terence O'Hanlon's door, a common trick on St. Patrick's Day. "Some wags" persuaded Jewish storekeeper Sammy Lopez that he could be elected mayor and convinced him to campaign vigorously; his humiliation at the polls on election day was a fine joke. In Milwaukee, Native Americans were the victims of nasty pranks. Firecrackers were tied to one Indian's blanket, and the explosions so startled him that he jumped up and to the delight of onlookers landed in the mud and "spoilt all his good clothes."[37]

Why did so many men engage in jolly conduct, drinking, fighting, and gambling? Why did their responses to others swing capriciously from empathy to animosity? Why did they act so openly and impulsively? To many in the first half of the nineteenth century, it hardly needed explanation—it was simply human nature or, more precisely, men's nature. Traveling geologist G. W. Featherstonhaugh's explanation of the uproarious conduct he witnessed in Little Rock in the 1830s was that he was viewing "the animal man before religion and education have made him a rational being." Savage male fighting could be understood only by reference to the natural world. An English visitor to North Carolina was shocked to see men butting heads—a popular method of fighting in some locales—"as practiced in battle between bulls, rams and goats." The men who engaged in this behavior sometimes themselves used animal metaphors. Herndon describes Abraham Lincoln, age sixteen, after his triumph in a fight over William Grigsby, waving a whiskey bottle over his head and swearing "he was the big buck of the lick. . . . If anyone doubts it . . . he only has to come and whet his horns." From the "animal man" perspective the constant fighting could be interpreted as a way of establishing a male pecking order. In Scott County, Tennessee, the best fighter was the cock of the walk: "The victor would leap on a stump crowing and flapping his arms." Equally animalistic seemed the howling that often broke out among men in groups. In Rochester, New York, in 1828 men stood outside a theater "hooting, howling, shouting, shrieking." Soldiers on shipboard on their way to fight in Mexico in 1846 began "hooting, hissing, and hallooing . . . [in] imitations of wild beasts and domestic animals." Christmas was a common time for men to howl. In Philadelphia on 24 December 1833 "men and boys howled as if possessed by the demons of disorder."[38]

Are men fighting and howling "the animal man" in action? Could biology play a role in such comportment? "Is there a deep structure of manhood?" asks anthropologist David D. Gilmore in his cross-cultural study of masculinity. He finds "intriguing similarities" in men's behavior among societies that otherwise exhibit little in common. Hormones, of course, can affect human behavior, and men as a whole are more aggressive than women because of testosterone. Male fighting is widespread in a range of different cultures—in the Truk Islands, for example, brawling and unrestrained drinking made one a real man. Yet Gilmore also points out that the influence of testosterone on comportment seems relatively modest, and there are cultures, most famously the Semai of Malaya, in which men are submissive and pacific. Jolly fellowship clearly is not universal. Gilmore, however, acknowledges that, across cultures, assertive masculinity seems more common. Is there a deep structure of manhood? He can only conclude "maybe." And if research in evolutionary psychology were to determine that such male behavior had a foundation in human biology and change Gilmore's "maybe" into a "probably," what would that really prove? It would be significant, but jolly male behavior, which seemed so "natural" to people in the early nineteenth century was regarded by the end of the century as unnatural. Manhood by then had come to be equated with self-control—men who did not get drunk, gamble, punch, and kiss other men were normal. Restraint was second nature. However "natural" the grounds for this behavior, men in groups, can—and as chapter 3 suggests—do control their behavior when they want to.[39]

Other observers believed the explanation was not so much biological as ethical. Men were, as Charles Francis Adams put it in describing the drinking and attendant disorder in eighteenth-century Massachusetts towns, in "the earlier stages of moral development." Minister Horace Bushnell attributed the impulsive, indiscriminate generosity of so many men to their living in "a childlike age." Society had matured, but men's attitudes remained that of boys. There is something puerile in jolly behavior: the impetuosity, the fighting, the bullying, the fascination with vomiting and other bodily functions, the crude and often silly jokes, the thoughtless cruelty to animals. Can human culture be childish in the way that individual humans are? Do cultures grow up? Norbert Elias has argued that central to the history of Western societies since the Middle Ages is a pattern whereby conduct once appropriate and routine for adults becomes restricted to children. In the course of the civilizing process, men and women learn to behave peacefully and with bodily restraint. What was once human behavior becomes "childlike" behavior. It may be that one of the reasons terms like "youth" and "boy" were imprecisely defined in the nineteenth century was that the variation in the comportment of children and adults was less distinct than it later became.[40]

Male behavior was indeed often impulsive and violent, but approaching jolly fellowship from the perspective of "the animal man" or childishness yields complexities and contradictions. Fighting among men was not simply natural but embedded in social convention. Rough-and-tumble fights had rules. Combatants settled in advance what tactics would be permitted. "Whatever terms are specified," an English traveler discovered, "they never infringe [their agreement]." In Hookstown, Pennsylvania, fighters were not allowed to bite until first blood had been drawn—to do otherwise was "dishonorable." Jonas Gudehus provided a fascinating account of fighting in Pennsylvania in the 1820s. Men with a grudge against each other would drink together at an auction or other public gathering and begin insulting each other "as though they were joking," then scuffle, "still to be viewed as joking until some rough boxes on the ear or kicks." (Note the close connection Gudehus describes between comedy and violence; this is a common phenomenon in this era.) Then comes the challenge. "Would you like to fight?" "Ei, I think so." "Ei, I think so too." They then drink "quietly a good glass of rum," which seems to serve as a kind of sanction for the fight. They take off their jackets, hats, and scarves and "grab each other at the chest to check first who stands the surest." Only after that does the actual fighting begin. They furiously "hit, kick, scratch and bite" until some one yells "Enough," which instantly ends the battle.

Head butting contests, which could seem so wild and animalistic to observers, were often arranged in advance and followed a conventional procedure. Combatants did not charge each other like rams but butted "in the usual manner," that is, by holding each other's ears. Jolly fellows' behavior was not completely uncontrolled. They stopped drinking before getting drunk and often would stop gambling before they had lost all their money. Many of their pranks required extensive calculation and preparation. Jolly fellowship cannot be reduced simply to natural or adolescent behavior. It seems best regarded as a constructed comportment with equivalents, if not roots, in the European past.[41]

"DAMN YOU, ARE YOU A MAN?"

What was the allure of this behavior? Why were so many men spontaneously drawn to jolly conduct? In part, what accounts for jolly fellows' joy is simply that they were engaging in what was then and what is still today defined as pleasurable activity. Drinking and gambling certainly have proved gratifying in a very large number of cultures over a very long period. It is easy for us to understand the happiness men might have felt sitting around the tavern fire quaffing rum with friends, joking and discussing issues of the day. Or the pleasure they might have taken in lining up an easy shot at the last ball in billiards with money on the line. Nor is it hard to see why the Hornet's Nest was so gleeful when Charles Comstock swallowed the cat story. But other aspects are less easy to understand. What is the allure in gouging someone's eye, dosing unsuspecting victims with harsh purgatives, and tormenting animals?

What played a significant motivating role in much of this behavior was a view of what it meant to be a man. In the early and mid-nineteenth century, there were shifting and competing views about manhood, and manliness could be secured and enhanced in different ways. Many in the nineteenth century equated manhood with self-control, with mastery over impulse. Such men found fulfillment in home, work, and religion. By the middle of the nineteenth century, restrained manhood had achieved the status of a coherent outlook and wielded considerable discursive power. The jolly fellows' views of what made a man are harder to pin down. There were hundreds of conduct-of-life books aimed at young men praising self-controlled manhood, but jolly comportment had few overt defenders—there were very few authors writing that men should get drunk, should fight, should gamble. Even antitemperance writers emphasized their abhorrence of excessive alcohol consumption. Jolly fellowship lacked a vocabulary; it was a matter as much of actions and gestures as words. There was some common ground with restrained manhood. William Otter's sense of what made him a man was complex—his six-four body, his drinking, fighting, and practical jokes were crucial, but perhaps even more important was his capacity for hard work.[42]

Generally jolly fellows were less willing to restrain their aggression. Manliness, they thought, ought to be examined and displayed in public in the company of other men. Drinking and gambling were manly endeavors, but fighting was perhaps the most primal means by which male honor could be enhanced. Blakemore's question to Everet at the Coach and Horse Tavern, "What for a Man are you?" was a challenge to fight, recognized as such. Phrases like "Are you a man?" or "I am your man" were in America, as in Europe, an invitation to combat. An argument in 1811 New York City between a drunken passerby and a wood sawyer escalated into a fight with the words, "Damn you, are you a man? If you are a man walk out in the street." "May the better man win" was much more than a figure of speech. "Chaw his lip or you'll never be a man" was the advice of a Florida father to his son on how to fight. "Mr. McClure" and "Col. Sanders," recorded William Johnson in his diary, had an argument in a Natchez court. As they exited the courtroom, "Mr. McClure Knocked him Down and Jumped on to him and was gouging Him in an instant." So "many Persons was Surprised to find McClure So much of a man" that a banquet was held in his honor. As John Morris explained, men were "esteemed . . . in proportion to their prowess in 'free fights.'" A brawler could lose favor when defeated. When pugilist Dan Rice whipped "Devil Jack" in a Bayardstown, Pennsylvania, tavern brawl, "the bully . . . lost prestige" and his friends "of the lower element" deserted him.[43]

If a winner gained honor, a defeated fighter did not always lose respect. What was unmanly was refusing to fight or failing to put up a good fight. Such a person would be called a coward, which was among the most debasing insults any man could receive. Although efforts were made to insure competitive matchups, it was understood that some men were simply bigger and stronger than others, so pride could often be maintained in a hard-fought loss. "The defeated" in Scott County, Tennessee, were "not considered disgraced if [they] put up a good fight." Wiley Britton, who was beaten up in several fights while working as a teamster on the Sante Fe trail, discovered "that a man who makes a good fight in defense of his rights wins the respect of his associates" even when he is defeated. If honor was gained only in victory, men would be sharply divided into winners and losers; defining honor simply as putting up a hard fight was a broad definition that may have helped reinforce jolly male solidarity.[44]

There was a difference between North and South. Male honor in the North was more often corporate, male honor in the South more individual. There were, of course, many one-on-one battles outside the South. But in the North and Midwest bands of men representing a village or neighborhood brawled, an activity that appears to have been less common in the South. Northern honor followed the European pattern more closely. Not only was Southern reputation more solitary, but the stakes were higher. The slave system made southern white men extremely sensitive to social status and determined to protect it. You could not submit to another. With stakes so high, southern combatants were more likely to resort to weapons to defend their honor, and thus injuries and deaths in fights were more common. The duel was the epitome of the southern stress on reputation. There were "affairs of honor" in the North—James Watson Webb, the pugnacious editor of the *New York Commercial Advertiser*, issued challenges and fought duels in a manner that would not have been out of place for a truculent South Carolina planter. But he was an exception; dueling was far more common south of the Mason-Dixon Line. It was limited mainly to elite southerners and helped confirm their social status; challenges by men deemed ordinary were contemptuously dismissed. The duel was a way for southern gentlemen to maintain their elite position by settling quarrels without taking part in the rough-and-tumble brawls that common southerners engaged in. In reality, however, southern elite men seemed to have dueled in addition to, rather than instead of, fighting. When their blood was up, southern men went at each other, regardless of their social status. William Johnson recorded many street brawls in Natchez that leading citizens of the town, including doctors and lawyers, participated in.[45]

The Southern cult of honor permeated even the world of slaves. Planter Robert Wright, a former Maryland governor, put so much stress on personal honor that he told not only his sons but even his bondsmen not to brook any indignities—he commanded his slaves "not to take an insult from any rich man's domestic slaves under any consideration," remembered G. W. Offley, a free black minister. French count Francis de Castelnau recalled watching a street brawl in Tallahassee, Florida, in the late 1830s between planters in which accompanying slaves joined in on their master's side. On Christmas Eve, 1858, in legendarily violent Edgefield County, South Carolina, two slaves argued over a twenty-five-cent debt; when one asserted "he was as good a man" as his adversary, a fight broke out that ended in a fatal stabbing.[46]

A successful prank could also enhance a man's repute. Successfully carrying out a sharp practical joke brought prestige; by the same token, being duped in a prank meant a loss of honor, at least temporarily, as jokers would remind victims of their humiliation. Actor Dan Rice "hoaxed," in his words, the citizens of Rock Island, Illinois, by collecting admission for a comic performance and then absconding without giving a show. Rather than going to the authorities and charging Rice with fraud, the spectators instead scurried home to avoid losing face by being observed having been hoodwinked by Rice's "joke." A victim could complain or even attack a joker, but then he would be "a bad sport." The appropriate thing for the butt of a joke to do, an Illinois lawyer explained, was to "console his irritated feeling with the reflection that he would get his revenge on some future occasion." Among jolly fellows there was reciprocity to pranks. Today's victim might be tomorrow's perpetrator. The circular nature of practical joking may have also contributed to a feeling of unity among jolly fellows.[47]

Honor in fighting and pulling off pranks could be shared. But manhood also often was enhanced at the expense of others. The jolly fellows believed that it was their prerogative to bully and humiliate men who were puny, dimwitted, of different races, or otherwise misfits or outcasts. By attacking and denigrating marginal groups the jolly fellows helped enforce the social order by maintaining a boundary between themselves and outcasts. Publicizing and strengthening widely accepted social divisions helped clearly to mark the ambit of the community and allowed those within it to feel a camaraderie with each other and an empathy for one another. Male peer groups served a similar function in Europe, where the charivari targeted individuals who violated village norms. In a multiethnic and multiracial American society, this function may have been of greater importance than in Europe. The jolly fellows were publicly tolerated in part because their targets were often those whose mistreatment elicited little sympathy. There may also have been a tacit public understanding that the jolly fellows' conduct helped enforce the boundaries of the recognized community.[48]

The boundary-maintaining function was also satisfied by the use of nicknames, which were almost universal wherever men assembled in both Europe and America. Nicknaming practices are complicated; they may serve several functions and meanings can vary by the context in which they are used. To have a nickname established one as an insider, and the nature of the nickname suggested one's status in the circle of men. A "little coterie of persons" in Medfield, Massachusetts, gave each other exalted nicknames that were used more often than their real names. The storekeeper was "Emperor," the tavern keeper "Alderman." There was also a "Pope," "Count," and "Marshal Ney." John Janney remembered in Loudon County, Virginia, in the 1820s a "Squire Tommy," a "Long Tommy" and a "Bacon Fat Sammy," among many others. It was the custom in early Keokuk, Iowa, "to select for every character of any special note in the place, some *soubriquet* or nickname," an old-timer explained. Timothy R. Mahoney discovered a remarkable 106 nicknames among the early settlers there. Many names referred to physical appearance, as if a man's essence was embodied in his face and physique. Egbert Herring Smith in Milwaukee walked with a halting gait, and so he was "Limpy." "Big-bellied Sam" resided in Loudon County. In Keokuk were a "Cock-eye," "Bow Legs," and "Peg Leg."[49]

The jolly fellows' behavior did more than simply stigmatize outsiders. It unified insiders. Charles Fenno Hoffman, a writer who visited the Old Northwest and upper South in 1833 was astonished at the combination of benevolence and brutality he witnessed. People were extraordinarily hospitable "to the white stranger, but having no place in their system of doing good for the unfriended Indian," whose life "does not weigh a feather." Westerners, he concluded, must have "two consciences—one for the white and one for the red man." There was a puzzling juxtaposition of heartless and humane in the conduct of jolly fellows and in that of many other Americans as well. Examples of generosity toward fellow native-born whites contrast with instances of viciousness toward African Americans, Indians, and other marginal groups. Perhaps this is not contradictory; perhaps there is, in a way, only one conscience. Communities are defined in part by who they exclude, and the very clear-cut ethnic, racial, and other barriers that the jolly fellows helped sustain may have strengthened the connectedness of those inside the boundary. Impulsive, instinctive benevolence may have been possible, in part, because the line was so distinct between who merited community sympathy and who did not. Perhaps charity among fellow whites was strong not despite their contempt toward people of color but because of it—the price paid for community kindliness was intolerance. They were two sides of a coin.[50]

"PLEASURE AT THE PRICE OF MISERY TO OTHERS"

The regulars did not behave as they did simply to delineate the social border of the recognized community and strengthen white sympathy and solidarity. At an even more profound level, they seem to have taken a deep and intense psychological satisfaction in inflicting pain, both mental and physical. "The desire to make fun of others—the weak, the odd, the unfortunate—was common," Jarvis remembered. People of color, disfigured persons, simpletons were prime targets. But any person vulnerable in any way could be a victim. One of the most characteristic activities of the tavern crowd was darkening the faces of men passed out drunk, to humiliate them by making them literally black men. "Wags" in Kingston, Rhode Island, it was said, intentionally got a man dead drunk so they could make up his face "in the most fantastic style." Charles Fenno Hoffman came across one such victim in Tazewell, Tennessee. He spotted a man beside himself in fury: "I caught sight of his face by the moonlight, and discovered that he had undergone a very common piece of western waggery, having his face blackened when overcome by liquor." Drinkers in Georgia would recover to find their faces blackened, pant legs cut off, hair cut off, hats and shoes taken. Amos Banks, the leading joker of Lexington, South Carolina, victimized men dead drunk. "As one lay in the street," he would hire some of the boys "to black his face and cover him with an empty crate loaded down with heavy weights, which, when he woke up prevented his escape from the cage without help, or he would scatter corn around the prostrate body and call the hogs to root and roll it over and over."[51]

There is no suggestion in these accounts that "niggering" persons was intended to shame them into shunning future excessive drinking; perpetrators like Amos Banks were themselves hard-drinking men in a hard-drinking age. The victims were not necessarily adversaries of the blackeners. Some victims were socially marginal men, but in other cases they were simply in the wrong place at the wrong time. Sometimes they were even friends of pranksters; they had just left themselves unprotected and were thus fair game. The motive seems to have been the visceral pleasure of power over another, the pleasure derived from inflicting humiliation and pain without remorse or fear of retribution. The joy was achieving mastery over the helpless, making them, as happened to Kentucky victims, "for months the laughing Stock" of the community. This is very similar to the strain in black folklore that Lawrence Levine detected—the humiliation and injury of others for its own sake. It is not so much the cleverness of the prank but the suffering of the victim that afforded the most pleasure. John M. Roberts, an Ohio schoolteacher, recounted that when Addison Cornwell got drunk in 1853 "a set of harpies" from the village "fell upon him & tore his clothes, blackened his face, & hauled him around the turnpike." Such men, Roberts believed, were "ever ready to pounce on a poor, weak individual who is unable to help himself." By drinking themselves insensible, the victims made themselves vulnerable, temporarily placing themselves in the same category blacks and Indians were in permanently.[52]

Many other men besides Roberts's "set of harpies" derived pleasure from others' suffering. William Otter's autobiography recounts many examples of his cruelty, often in fond detail. Otter might seem mentally disturbed, but others routinely accompanied him in his sadistic escapades, such as when Big Bill drowned a friend's dog "for a piece of sport." Eventually it becomes clear that Otter expected readers, like his confederates, to join him in finding these vicious rampages enjoyable. Not just enjoyable but comical. One night in Gettysburg on a "spree," Otter pulled the ladder out from under a journeyman chair maker named James Doogan, who was using it to climb up to visit his girlfriend. "Poor Jim . . . had a very hard fall, [and] he came crawling on his hands and knees toward me, making his way homewards as well as he could, every yard or two he would mutter the words O Lord, which tickled me most prodigiously, I almost killed myself laughing at him."[53]

To Otter, Doogan's suffering was hilarious, and others shared his malicious sense of humor. Frank Hostutter, the celebrated practical joker of Lexington, Kentucky, put a slab of tobacco in the soup at White's tavern, remembered Ebenezer Stedman. "Old Feaster" commenced vomiting and others quickly followed. "First one woold Puke, then the other, then all together." One regular was certain he was poisoned and "was Goin to Die & Hell wod Be his portion." Stedman concludes: "Frank got the Prais on all hands of Playing the Best Joke of the Season & people did enjoy a good Joke in them days." Commentators on humor from Hobbes through the mid-nineteenth century took it for granted that the comical was cruel.[54]

Just as men could take pleasure in the pain of other humans, they savored the agony of animals. William McLaren recalled with delight how a favorite amusement in early Illinois "was to round up a chip-monk, rabbit, or a snake, and make him take refuge in a burning log-heap, and watch him squirm and fry." At times the killing of animals exploded into a paroxysm of slaughter. In a "circle hunt," hunters drove animals before them into the center of an ever-contracting circle, where they were massacred. In one such hunt near Waverly, New York, in 1818, as the men approached the center "the excitement increased to rashness and recklessness." The hunters were so beside themselves in Dionysian bloodlust that "they shot in every direction" and ended shooting each other as well as animals. The slaughter of passenger pigeons in James Fenimore Cooper's *The Pioneers* (1823) is another example. Virtually the entire village, man, woman, and child, joined in using guns, bows and arrows, and even poles to knock the birds out of the air. A cannon loaded with bird shot was used. Fluttering, dying pigeons covered the ground, but "none pretended to collect the game." As the killing frenzy wound down, an abashed Judge Temple reflects that he "has purchased pleasure at the price of misery to others."[55]

Sometimes this pleasure seemed to come from the sheer anarchic delight in destruction and obliteration, in creating chaos out of order. A balloon ascension was scheduled to take place at Philadelphia's Vauxhall Garden on 8 September 1819 at five-fifteen in the afternoon. Eight hundred paid the $1 admission fee to the garden, and the surrounding streets, fields, and lots were jammed with an estimated thirty thousand onlookers. The wind was unfavorable and the bag slow to inflate. At six, the throng, said to have been drinking steadily, went berserk.

They tore down the fence around the garden and swarmed in. The money box was pillaged, the balloon ripped to shreds, and the balloonist's equipment demolished. The mob then "attacked the bars, drank the liquor, [and] broke the bottles and glasses." The rioters then "commenced work on the pavilion," recounted J. Thomas Scharf and Thompson Wescott in their 1884 history of Philadelphia. By eight the building was plundered and trashed. They then set it on fire and "in a short time the pavilion was in ashes." The rioters "completed their work by destroying the shrubbery and shade trees of the garden," *Niles' Weekly Register* reported. At the University of Georgia, a "young mob" of students, according to the school's historian W. Merton Coulter, wreaked havoc in 1830, pulling down fences, tearing up corn, blocking roads, breaking the railings off the bridge, and stealing wagons and pushing them into the creek. Boatmen on the Ohio, Mississippi, and other major rivers were notoriously unruly in the first decades of the century. They drank and fought, and then, reported an observer, for no apparent reason other than a joy in devastation, they would go wild, "breaking furniture, demolishing bars and taverns, and pull[ing] down fences, sheds and signs."[56]

Bill Buford, an American magazine editor living in England in the 1980s, fraternized with a gang of Manchester United football hooligans and went with them to an international match in Turin, an episode described in his book *Among the Thugs* (1991). After an 1984 game, the Manchester supporters, accompanied by Buford, went on a rampage, smashing shop windows, overturning cars, and beating up Italian fans. Buford recounts with amazement how profoundly appealing he found the senseless destruction and how enjoyable inflicting pain on others was. "I would have assumed, if I had thought to think about it, that the violence would be exciting, . . . but the pure elemental pleasure was of an intensity that was unlike anything I had foreseen or experienced before." That men derived emotional satisfaction from cruelty and mayhem does not mean that the jolly fellows' violence and degrading pranks did not also serve calculated and rational ends. As this chapter and other chapters make clear, they very often did. But it does offer the suggestion that beneath even the most considered violence there may be a deep-seated craving to hurt and humiliate others. Yet the ambit of human behavior was wide. Men who inflicted pain on their vulnerable fellow men for their own pleasure could just as spontaneously give openhanded help to others. Examples of extraordinary brutality stand beside examples of great generosity.[57]

Jolly fellowship was not unique to the antebellum United States. Similar conduct could be found in both colonial America and seventeenth- and eighteenth-century Europe. Such behavior required no explanation; it was just the way men were. The strong ruled the weak, the clever dominated the dull. Jolly attitudes reverberated with many who did not themselves join the drinking, fighting, and gambling, and usually the frolics of the tavern and grocery crowd received only mild reproach, if not tacit approval. Yet this traditional male behavior came under powerful scrutiny in America beginning in the second and third decades of the nineteenth century. What once was natural now required explanation, what once was unobjectionable was now censured. This process would reshape the moral order of American society.

CHAPTER THREE

Reform

"About the year 1825, a change began to come over the minds of the people" of Concord, Massachusetts, remembered Edward Jarvis, a physician and local historian. "It was produced, in some measure, by the temperance advocates. But, in greater part, it was a moral and intellectual epidemic—one of those silent unrecognized changes in public opinion that creep over a community, [when citizens] occasionally find their views of things, and the motives of action that had governed them, giving way and other [views and motives] taking their places."[1] Jarvis perceptively summarizes the change in attitudes and behavior that occurred in the first half of the nineteenth century, a transformation that stigmatized jolly fellows and marginalized both their outlook and world.

A surge of moral reform in Concord and elsewhere made jolly fellowship the antipode of respectability. There were, of course, many restrained and sober men before this period of reform and certainly many rowdy ones afterward. There was, however, a clear contemporary perception of a profound shift in male comportment in the first half of the nineteenth century. Some antebellum moralists affirmed a golden age of virtue that had existed in an idealized past, a period that few of them could actually remember. But within living memory of people in the mid-nineteenth century there was widespread agreement with Jarvis of a turn toward sober and more restrained living. The boisterous impetuosity that characterized jolly fellowship gave way to more self-controlled behavior. George Davis expressed delight in his 1856 history of Sturbridge and Southbridge, Massachusetts, that "a blessed change has succeeded" eradicating drinking and gambling among respectable men. Ohioan John Morris, writing in 1873, similarly believed that "the morals and social condition of the people of these United States have undergone a remarkable change. . . . Rampant rowdyism and drunkenness is not nearly so prevalent." Once drunken fights marked every holiday, but now the "'glorious fourth,' and St. Patrick's day pass[ed] off quietly," brawling firemen disappeared, even election days were usually tranquil. In Cobb County, Georgia, "a change of sentiment came over the people," and temperance societies were organized that reduced drinking and disorder. Writer Samuel Goodrich bristled at the idea of a "degeneracy from the Revolutionary standard of public virtue." In a conversation in the 1850s with William Grayson, he asked Grayson to compare the "manners and morals" of present-day Charleston with that of sixty years earlier. Grayson answered immediately that "the improvement of the present times over the past was incalculable." Once, every Sunday and holiday was marked by drinking and fighting, but now "the riotous sensuality of the old times had disappeared." Goodrich explained that he "had put the same question to a great number of persons, in every part of the country, and had received the same reply everywhere, . . . the good, wise virtuous old times were to be found in the imagination only."[2]

Jarvis confidently asserted that in Concord, "about the year 1825, a change began to come over the minds of the people," but few others were able to match Dr. Jarvis's chronological exactitude. The table in appendix A is compiled from first-person accounts in reminiscences, autobiographies, and local histories in which the author refers to a significant decrease in male disorder. The information is intended only to give a very general sense of timing. The changes were rarely complete or unilinear. In some villages the change took place within a few years; in others it was gradual, spanning two decades. Several authors refer to an initial dramatic decrease in disorder in the wake of revivals or temperance enthusiasm, then a resurgence in jolly behavior as the initial reform impulse faded. Henry Clarke Wright, later a noted reformer, remembered the 1817 revivals as having a transforming impact on the upstate New York village of Norwich, noting that "nothing else was talked of." All "amusements among young people were abandoned." Yet Clarke later explains that after several weeks the excitement ebbed and that it was not until around 1828 that daily drinking of liquor halted.[3]

It is possible to perceive a pattern whereby moral improvement occurred first in the East and then spread to the West and South, but there are striking exceptions. That moral reform was well underway in both the East and Old Northwest regions by the 1820s and 1830s is clear, but the timing is less clear in the South. Jolly fellowship had nowhere been jollier, and the battle lines had never been more clearly drawn. Grayson dates the beginning of "the Change in Society" in

Charleston to 1803 when there began "a great awakening" of religion that diminished "deep drinking, hard swearing and practical joking." In Henderson County, Kentucky, religious revivals in the first decade of the nineteenth century, according to its historian Edmund L. Starling, checked the "looseness" that had previously reigned in the area and brought virtue and respectability. Yet there were other places in the South where there seems to have been no real decline in disorderly demeanor until decades later. Ted Ownby in his book *Subduing Satan* (1990) shows that despite the progress of moral reform with its emphasis on self-control, jolly behavior survived in some places into the late nineteenth century and even into the early twentieth century. Heavy drinking, gambling, and fighting continued. Court days and holidays were still tumultuous. Cockfighting and dog fighting remained common. In many cities and much of the Trans-Mississippi West, like the South, enclaves that sustained traditionally rowdy male behavior persevered.[4]

Reform in personal conduct had made significant national headway by the 1840s, even in the South. Observers were often able to date, at least loosely, the onset of improved male conduct in their own communities. There was, however, no agreement as to why it had happened. Most believed that a decrease in drinking had been the crucial element. Here the timing can be determined relatively precisely: William Rorabaugh's statistics show a steep decline in per capita adult alcohol consumption from an estimated 7.1 gallons in 1830 to 1.8 in 1845. Moralists saw drinking as the critical factor in loosening self-control and stimulating sinful behavior such as gambling, swearing, and Sabbath breaking. The founding of a temperance society signaled Concord's "change . . . over the minds of the people." Jarvis accepts that a decline in drinking was central in reforming behavior, but he sees it merely as a manifestation of a deeper change in outlook. Heavy consumption of alcohol had been the rule in Concord since its founding. The real question for Jarvis, as for others who reflected on it, was why in 1825 did people *want* to have a temperance society? Why after generations in which drunken brawls and wild pranks were taken for granted did Concordians begin to reject such behavior?[5]

Jarvis saw "a moral and intellectual epidemic" that profoundly transformed mental attitudes. There was simply no longer any desire to do such things—jolly fellowship became unappealing, the prospect of a sober, pious life more enticing. To Jarvis this shift was essentially voluntary: "Men came, themselves, to their natural fullness of power . . . [and] gradually and imperceptibly found their reasons for drinking losing power over them." Jarvis's use of "men" in this sentence is significant. He, like many others, saw male jolly conduct as the linchpin of social disorder, and much of the reform discourse was aimed specifically at men. In Jarvis's view, men were drawn to a staid and subdued, and presumably more affluent, lifestyle. There was coercion involved, but, Jarvis argued, it was not sinister; it took the form of enlisting the influence of public authorities to achieve the widely held aspiration of an orderly community. Jarvis grounds his change-in-mentality interpretation in a secular framework, but religious commentators focused on the metamorphosis in personality that followed spiritual conversion. Christian attitudes infused American society, and men and women born again during revivals had their lives dramatically altered.[6]

Not everyone was convinced that male character actually had been transformed. Behavior had changed, but had underlying attitudes? Many men still found drinking, fighting, and gambling alluring, but the social, economic and psychological costs were now too high to indulge in them. John Habermehl, who spent much of his life as a boatman on the Mississippi, agreed that male conduct had altered. "The outer surface of men becomes more refined," Habermehl conceded. Men's true nature, however, remained unaltered, because "religion is generally located in the upper story." "Desire was held under restraint," but "the lumber remains the same." Refinement was just a crust over a jolly filling. Habermehl maintained an essentially Hobbesian view of human nature: men's passions can only be controlled by force, spearheaded in this case by churchmen, the middle class, and women for their own ends. Behind self-control was social control. The "natural inclination" to carouse endured, but it was now "kept in check by the moral force of public opinion" and the law.[7]

As public attitudes changed, the indulgence of earlier days diminished, and those who refused to adapt paid a cost for disorder. In an era in which the vast majority of Americans lived on farms and villages where life was governed by face-to-face relationships, the waning acceptance of jolly fellowship had a powerful impact on behavior. Drinkers, fighters, and gamblers were singled out and ostracized, their marriage prospects were clouded, and their chances for economic success dimmed. Many came under psychological duress. Respectable neighbors constantly pointed out the immoral nature of jolly fellowship to make reprobates feel guilty about their roistering. Such things were not just wrong; they were sinful. Legal coercion certainly played a role. Arrests for "crimes against public order" increased. John Morris, himself a former professional gambler, saw the significance of law enforcement in the shift away from disorder. In the 1830s, he noted, there were no police "worthy of the name, even in large cities." Once ignored, drunkenness, assault, gambling, and disorderly conduct could, by midcentury, result in arrest. There is no doubt that decorum was, as Habermehl argued, often forced on unwilling men. However, the rest of this chapter suggests that drawing a line between self-governance and governance by others is often difficult, and interpretations that emphasize social control do not capture the breadth and depth of religious awakenings and other personal reforms of the period.[8]

Although Morris accepted the importance of compulsion in reforming male character, he was convinced that even more significant was a transformation in public attitudes. True, police forces were larger and better trained and organized, "but if the people had not learned to appreciate good order, the police would be powerless." Formerly, Morris remembered, "people enjoyed a fight, and so far from assisting any lawful authority to prevent or break up a disturbance, would actually hinder them in their discharge of duty." In the 1870s when Morris was writing, onlookers often stopped brawls before the police arrived. There had been regulations virtually everywhere on the books for decades against public drunkenness, gambling, and fighting, but without popular support such laws proved unenforceable. "No law can stand in a government like ours," a Rhode Island reformer explained, "unless it is in unison with public opinion. . . . The powerful voice of public opinion will blow it away like chaff before the wind." Liquor regulation could be effectively implemented only where temperance enjoyed a large measure of public approval. Mississippi, for example, had passed an ordinance in 1839 to curb drinking by prohibiting sales of distilled liquor in amounts less than a gallon. However, in Warren County there was little sentiment in its favor, and the grand jury blandly pronounced the act "in advance of public opinion" and refused to issue indictments.[9]

Jolly fellowship went back centuries and was central to the temperament of too many men and too widespread to be repressed by anything short of overpowering force. Norbert Elias, in outlining his theory of the "civilizing process," has argued that in Europe a pivotal factor promoting decorum was the formation of centralized governments that monopolized violence. In the United Sates the national, state, and local governments did not have—nor did most people want them to have—the sort of authority it would have taken to suppress jolly fellowship. The Ann Arbor *Michigan Sate Journal* explained in 1836 that American liberty made it necessary that order not be based on compulsion: the French have "an iron government . . . to keep the passions of men within bounds. We have to govern ourselves." It was taken for granted that sovereignty was too weak to effectively curb disorder without a change in attitude.[10]

All of these factors—a shift in outlook, social pressure, better law enforcement—played a role in the transformation of male behavior. Many men no doubt were truly remade, but the persistence of a jolly strain in American culture throughout the century suggests that many still found jolly values alluring. In other chapters, I show that disorderly comportment still held a deep fascination for large numbers of men who no longer themselves drank, fought, or played pranks or perhaps even consciously wanted to.

Why did this change occur? The first half of the nineteenth century witnessed a social and cultural transformation: the development of the factory system, the rapid advance of commercial agriculture, the growth of cities, the creation of an urban middle class, railroads, the spread of newspapers, books, and magazines, the rise of the common school and the emergence of mass political parties. Traditional gender roles were recast. There was an upsurge of religion. Nineteenth-century commentators listed multiple reasons for improvement in manners and conduct. Some pointed to better education. Others argued for the significance of improved transport and communication, which eroded parochialism and gave a greater exposure to the outside world. Most observers, however, focused on the spread of market values and the religious revivals of the era, and they, like later historians, puzzled over the connection between them.[11]

"IT IS BETTER THAT EACH SHOULD DO HIS OWN WORK"

Some commentators saw economic changes as the primary cause of the reformation in male comportment. As canals and railroads were built, small towns found their local economies increasingly integrated into national and even global markets. Farms became capitalist enterprises. Local artisans faced the hazards of competing over a wide geographical area. The increase in personal wealth in the first half of the nineteenth century was erratic and halted by the 1837 depression, but overall, the evidence suggests that probably more people benefited than not from the growth of capitalism. There were now opportunities for men and even women to make money in new ways. In the eighteenth and early nineteenth centuries, wealth seemed to many largely a matter of luck, a gamble. Many were unpersuaded that steady work guided by foresight, calculation, and self-control would be rewarded; life was too unpredictable. It was almost impossible to save enough to be safe. The path to security lay less in individual initiative than in cooperating with friends and neighbors to weave a web of reciprocal obligations. Individualism was perilous, and accumulating social, not economic, capital seemed the safest course. Because "people had less means of affecting their purpose within themselves" in Concord, according to Jarvis, "mutual sympathy and cooperation" were needed. Life was often precarious and interdependence was a simple fact, understood as such.[12]

With economic growth, individualism began to seem possible, even desirable. Some men embraced autonomy; others found it forced on them by capitalist development. The reciprocal assistance that was so characteristic of American eighteenth-century and early nineteenth-century rural and small-town life eroded. After a fire burned down a village store in the Hudson Valley in 1803, the *Hudson Bee* praised the way "neighbors . . . intend to volunteer their services" to rebuild it. When a tannery burned in 1828, the *Catskill Recorder* viewed coolly efforts to solicit donations for reconstruction, explaining that "we are opposed to the practice of assisting by public subscription those who sustain losses by fire," and it criticized the tannery owners for not having insurance. Jarvis thought that Concordians were "no less kind, sympathetic and generous than their fathers," but most believed "that it is better that each should do his own work." "You help me" was no longer automatically followed by "I'll help you." Immigrants from the Old World were unpleasantly surprised to learn that in America when you asked for aid, the answer often was, as one German put it, "Help youself." Sympathy toward others certainly did not disappear—it may not have even diminished—but it did change. Compassion, like all feelings, now should be controlled. "Sympathy," the *New Englander* explained in 1858, "should be feeling, but regulated feeling, the action of the heart guided by purest reason." Charity became less direct and impulsive; more deliberate and broader but more diffuse. The period that saw the rise of universal benevolence seems to have witnessed the decay of spontaneous personal benevolence.[13]

Sharp fluctuations characterized the American economy in the first half of the century, but more and more men became convinced that success lay in their own hands; with diligence and prudence they could make their own way in the world. Jarvis, a pioneer in psychiatry and medical statistics, described the change. In early nineteenth-century Concord, the typical farmer in the area "produced little more than was sufficient for the year's sustenance and often fell short of that." Then "habits of labor changed." All over New England littered, slovenly farmyards were cleaned up. Houses were painted, animals fenced in. Horses replaced oxen. Agricultural societies were formed. Farmers planted new crops and adopted better varieties of old ones to take advantage of the growing Boston market. People labored more steadily and systematically. The reward was "more return for the cultivation of his labor," Jarvis remembered. The diet improved: more meat was eaten, wheat bread replaced rye, and items like coffee became widely available. Consumer goods once possessed only by the wealthy now were within the reach of ordinary people. Carpets, pianos, and easy chairs appeared in homes. Clothing got better.[14]

There was now a greater incentive for orderly conduct. Self-control, sobriety, and industry seemed a more realistic path to achievement than it earlier had. The vision of personal economic and social independence must have been captivating for many. You could be your own man. These changes and growing individualism, some observers believed, curtailed jolly behavior. Rev. Joseph Doddridge watched the economic development of the frontier regions of western Maryland and Virginia in the last decades of the eighteenth and early nineteenth century. Though a minister himself, he put more emphasis on the civilizing effects of economic growth than on religion in improving character. He recalled when drinking and fighting were routine throughout the area. The introduction of commerce, Doddridge believed, gave "a new current to public feeling and individual pursuit." A higher standard of living brought improved deportment. "Had the hunting shirt, mocasson and leggins continued to be the dress of our men, had the noggin, the trencher and the wooden bowl continued to be the furniture of our houses, our progress towards science and civilization would be much slower." With material progress, Doddridge explained, people abandoned their rough material objects and manners for "that of civilized man"; they were transformed and "assumed a new character, a new line of life." Doddridge noticed areas that had been bypassed by these developments when he was writing in 1824. In these places "the costumes, cabins, and in some measure the household furniture of their ancestors are still in use. The people of these districts are far behind their neighbors in every valuable endowment of human nature." They were lazy. Schools and churches were rare and intemperance common.[15]

It is noteworthy how often improved dress was cited as a critical factor in reformed demeanor. In an era in which appearance was seen as a key to character, clothes helped to make the man. A slovenly appearance symbolized slovenly attitudes. As with the more orderly farmyards, personal neatness symbolized the rewards brought by individual application. Where once homespun was a sign of republican virtue, by the nineteenth century it was a mark of demoralizing listlessness. In Illinois, Thomas Ford remembered, linsey-woolsey shirts and buckskin britches were replaced by cloth coats and wool hats around 1830. Women began to wear shoes. "With the pride of dress came ambition, industry, the desire for knowledge, and love of decency." The writer Alfred Henry Lewis noted the same phenomenon in New York City. When a worker began to wear a suit off the job, he became mild mannered. "He must," Lewis explained, "live up to his costume. He must be polite, courteous, a gentlemen of dignity. And he must not fight." For these writers higher living standards were the cause, not the result, of improved personal decorum. It was, however, likely the process was more complex. As new opportunities opened, men took advantage of them through more regular and industrious exertion, which in turn paid economic benefits.[16]

These benefits were not equally distributed. For economic winners, and for those who hoped to become winners, refinement became a way to distance themselves from the losers. Decorum was part the story of middle-class formation. Gentility was associated not just with higher living standards—a pianoforte and étagère in the parlor, silver spoons, and broadcloth suits—but also with a specific comportment. Although there were certainly boisterous wealthy men and refined poor men, economic success was increasingly associated with a code of social conduct. "The culmination of a genteel lifestyle," Richard Bushman has written, "was a genteel person." Restrained, disciplined, well mannered. Not a jolly fellow. Fighting was uncouth and laughing at others impolite. "Raillery," exposing someone to "Shame and Contempt," Henry Fielding warned in his classic essay on manners, is not "consistent with Good-Breeding" and marked one as a boor.[17]

"A GREAT AWAKENING OF RELIGIOUS SENTIMENT AMONG THE PEOPLE"

Although some commentators cited the increase in living standards as crucial in reducing jolly behavior, most suggested religion played a more important role. "Prayer meetings and songs of praise have killed off and stilled forever the sound of midnight revelry and debauchery," John Bolton O'Neall and John A. Chapman argued in their history of Newberry County, South Carolina. The timing of the improvement in comportment corresponds loosely to that of the religious revivals later labeled the Second Great Awakening. The perceived moral decline that followed the Revolution was especially worrisome in light of the widespread view that republics were fragile and could succeed only where virtue prevailed among citizens—virtue, many clerics believed, that could be sustained only through the Christian religion. The late eighteenth century witnessed the beginning of a vast effort to save souls. The 1790s saw numerous revivals in both North and South; the well-publicized 1801 Cane Ridge revival in Bourbon County, Kentucky, for example, converted hundreds of whites and blacks. The period 1815–18 again saw religious awakenings throughout the country. The preaching of Charles Finney in upstate New York marked the onset of another wave of religious excitement in the 1820s and 1830s. Revivals waned in the 1840s in the East, but the South saw many awakenings and thousands of converts during this time. In 1857 and 1858 there were revivals in New York, Philadelphia, and other cities.[18]

The revivals had their most visible and spectacular manifestation in outdoor gatherings like Cane Ridge, but their impact on comportment seems limited. Camp meetings were a source of entertainment; for many, they were a welcome break from the monotony of daily life on the farm or small town—in short, a spree. English immigrant clothier William Brown, traveling west in the early 1840s came on a Methodist camp meeting fifteen miles outside of Cleveland. The great majority "were enjoying themselves comfortably with smoking, drinking, or chewing tobacco, chatting with the women or talking politics with the men." The disorder that routinely arose when men congregated was a regular feature of such gatherings. Ohio schoolteacher John M. Roberts, a Universalist who attended an open air revival only "to study human nature," noted the circus atmosphere and wrote in his diary that he saw "more gamblers than preachers, more whiskey than religion, more swearing than praying, more drunkenness than psalms, more fighting than kissing."[19]

Most awakenings did not take place at camp meetings but occurred within churches, and institutional religion seems more likely to have been able to influence daily lives than dramatic but sporadic events like outdoor revivals. Such church-based awakenings were diverse: some, like some of the early Finney revivals, were marked by intense emotionalism in which whole villages were caught up. Most—such as the decorous awakening in Wilmington, North Carolina, in 1816 where "at no time [was there] an overwhelming, sweeping revival, but almost every week some were converted to God"—were less impassioned. Afterward, the churches incorporated and instructed the converts.[20]

The 1817 Norwich, New York, revival suggests both the complexity and the significance of the religious excitement that swept through America in this period. Settled in 1788, Norwich was the seat of Chenango County, New York. Joshua Bradley, who compiled an account of American revivals, likely exaggerated when he claimed that the village was "notorious for vice and almost every species of wickedness." It was not, however, a very spiritual community: an agent from the Missionary Society of Connecticut reported in 1814 that "very few of the settlers were religious people." There had been a few revivals in New England and elsewhere in 1815, but a killing frost in June 1816 and the attendant distress spurred a wave of awakenings. In Norwich, according to Henry Clarke Wright, then a twenty-year-old apprentice hatter, the preaching of John Truair, invited from nearby Sherburne by the Congregational church to spend "a few weeks among them as an evangelist," triggered the revival. Wright remembered the handsome Truair as "thoroughly versed in the art of moving the feelings, and producing an excitement in society." The reading of an account of the recent awakening in

Lenox, Massachusetts, created a sensation in Truair's congregation, according to Bradley. Who among them would be saved? Who would be damned? Prayer meetings multiplied, Wright remembered, and "praying and singing were more frequent and energetic; exhortations and appeals to the unconverted were more earnest."[21]

"A certain class of youths" in the village decided to try to halt the awakening by holding a New Year's party to greet 1817. The best hall in town was rented, a famous fiddler hired. Wright listened as Truair, from the pulpit, denounced the celebration as an "atheistical design . . . to 'drive the Lord away from Norwich'" and announced a prayer meeting for the same time. It was, Bradley recounted, "emphatically a sealing time." The inhabitants "were called upon to act decisively. . . . They halted between two opinions . . . on one hand they were solicited by their evil propensities to go and enjoy the pleasures of mirth . . . [;] on the other they were impressed by the Spirit of God to turn from vanity." Some who went to the party "were so much affected and so greatly distressed, . . . they left the ball-room and sought relief in tears." Wright explained that "when it was known how signally the ball had failed, the remark was usually made, that the dancers had found the Lord too strong for them." "From this time," reported Bradley, "the work became general. . . . Business was in great measure suspended. Religious meetings were attended almost every day of the week." Two Universalists were converted, as were several village leaders.[22]

To devout Christians like Wright the issue was a momentous one—eternal salvation. He began fervently praying for his rebirth. Suddenly and dramatically "as I thus lay brooding over my condition, there was an instantaneous revolution in my feelings; from deep anguish, I passed to great joy." Later Wright came to reject the idea that "religion was a thing to be hunted for and found" and concluded revivals were the work of man, not God. At the time, however, he was convinced that "I was then and there made a Christian." He wrote a letter to his family in Hartwick, New York, to warn them: "You are," he stated, "in a state of rebellion against the Almighty." All were in danger of damnation. "I invite you—I entreat you—I pray you—I beg you—I warn you—to prepare yourselves to stand before the awful Judge. . . . Come, now, my brothers and friends, and let us give glory to God. Amen." All over Norwich, Bradley reported, the converted went "with trembling and affectionate concern . . . to their ungodly friends, who were distinguished for profligacy and infidelity, and conversed with them about Jesus Christ, the Savior of sinners." Eventually, the enthusiasm waned, and men and women went back to work. But the fruits of the revival were significant: the Congregational church added sixty new members, the Baptist church one hundred. Each built a new building within the year. "This village which was once the strong hold of satan," Bradley believed, was now a Christian community.[23]

To Bradley the cause of religious revivals was simple: God was working among the people. Others, including many Christians wary of religious enthusiasm, agreed with Wright that they were largely an emotional response to clerical manipulation. Historians also have tended to focus on secular causes of the awakenings. According to some scholars, the religious resurgence was the work of a Protestant clerical establishment that, buffeted by growing egalitarianism and religious disestablishment, looked to the awakenings to restore their languishing authority. Others have seen the revivals as promoted by businessmen to create a tractable and orderly labor force in the period of early industrialization. The increasing attention that evangelists paid to personal probity is consistent with such an argument.[24]

The relationship between the economic changes of the early nineteenth century and the period's religious revivals is complex and not completely clear. There likely were places where religious enthusiasm was affiliated with a clerical attempt to maintain power or with the spread of market values. Certainly businessmen encouraged the awakenings. Finney's "Western revivals" in upstate New York in the 1820s and the great 1830–31 Rochester revival, historians have argued, were connected to the rapid economic and social changes taking place in the wake of the building of the Erie Canal. However, the duration of revivals over a period of decades and their wide geographical range makes it difficult to use such examples to formulate a general explanation. To the degree to which we accept the waves of revivals known as the Second Great Awakening as a single event, then they began in the late eighteenth century in the rural, agricultural, slave South, not in the urbanizing, industrializing Northeast. From this broader perspective, the religious zeal of the period seems to make more sense viewed as one of the recurrent bursts of Christian fervor that have marked American religious history.[25]

"ORDER IS HEAVEN'S FIRST LAW"

Why, if so many observers are correct, did religious enthusiasm translate into such a dramatic change in comportment? Unbridled conduct had long been denounced as incompatible with piety, and church edicts condemned disorderly behavior. The Methodists' "Rule of the United Society" (1743) explicitly prohibited intemperance and fighting. But most Christians before the nineteenth century did not see a serious contradiction between moderate drinking, gambling, and voluntary fighting and a devout life. Ministers imbibed and sometimes even wrestled and played pranks. The Second Great Awakening was distinctive in its connecting conversion and comportment—religious enthusiasm became more closely tied to rigorous standards of daily life. Many Protestant denominations in the early nineteenth century became more outspoken and relentless in condemning "licentiousness," which in this period meant not just sexual impropriety but a whole constellation of disorderly behavior, including drinking, fighting, gambling, Sabbath breaking, swearing, and theater going. Much of the censure was aimed at specifically male behavior, but women too were admonished to avoid alcohol, gossip, dancing, and undue familiarity with men. Church courts began to enforce rules against such sinful conduct more vigorously. Rowdiness was now incompatible with Christian existence; in historian Donald G. Mathews's phrase, piety became coupled with propriety. "*Order* and *discipline*," Mathews discovered, "were probably the most universally applicable words which Evangelicals used to describe the Christian life." Alexander Pope's dictum that "Order is heaven's first law" was cited by Presbyterian minister John Todd to specify how Christians should make their way in the world.[26]

Churchmen involved in the revivals were convinced that their impact on conduct was nothing short of miraculous. The Great Revival in the first decade of the century was said to have had a profound effect on the South. A cleric reported in 1805 that formerly when men got together in Bath County, Virginia, "drinking, swearing, horse-racing, fighting, and such like practices were common among them—But now . . . you seldom see one pursuing any of these practices." David Ramsay concluded in his history of South Carolina that "great good has resulted" from Methodist activities. This "is evident to all who are acquainted with the state of the country before and since they commenced their evangelism in Carolina. Drunkards have become sober and orderly—bruisers, bullies and blackguards, meek, inoffensive and peaceable."[27]

The religious press brimmed with accounts of a marvelous metamorphosis in behavior. Many of the accounts focused specifically on male conduct. After an 1820 awakening in Provincetown, Massachusetts, men returning from sea were amazed when they walked the streets "to hear no swearing, to see no fighting" and shocked that "the place of carnal mirth was not to be found." Finney's preaching in Utica "made 'new creatures' of gamblers, and drunkards, and swearers, and Sabbath-breakers." In the rough Wisconsin lead mining region, Rev. John Lewis reported in the *Home Missionary*, that formerly groceries had been crowded every day of the week. "Intemperance was very general, gambling almost universal . . . [and] fighting, often very severe, was common." In the spring of 1845 Lewis began protracted meetings. "The holy spirit was evidently present." A temperance society formed. "Fighting is much more rare. A physician told me a few days since that it is now a rare thing for him to be called upon to bind up a broken head. In short we are becoming quite a moral, respectable community."[28]

Male milieus associated with jolly behavior were redeemed. Militia training day in Irasburgh, Vermont, had traditionally been "given up to drinking and rioting." There had been "a general revival of religion" in Vermont in 1827, and "much anxiety rested upon the mind of Christians" that the customary militia revelry would impede the movement. The officers proposed an opening prayer: "The Company was formed into a hollow square, and two deacons offered up their heartfelt prayers," to the astonishment of onlookers. The review continued "with much solemnity," and the afternoon "was turned into a religious meeting at the courthouse." This June training "was the day of New Birth of *16 individuals*," according to the anonymous author of an 1856 local history. Many colleges were also caught up in the religious excitement. There were forty-one separate revivals at New England colleges alone between 1811 and 1840. After an 1812 awakening at Williams College, it was reported that "various petty mischief and tricks which had been so common before, entirely disappeared." At Amherst "a revival in 1831 immediately changed . . . the whole aspect of the College. Many of the most thoughtless & Immoral young men here, have submitted themselves to Jesus Christ." Even workplaces were converted. One minister described how in a cotton textile factory in Whitestown, New York, during the Western Revival of 1826, employees, many in tears, "knelt in prayer around the machinery" and pledged themselves to Christ.[29]

Such descriptions cannot be taken at face value. Many accounts were written more to kindle and sustain religious fervor than provide a factual report of conversions. Even some clerics admitted that nearly miraculous stories of triumphs were exaggerated. Baptist preacher Wilson Thompson was told that after an awakening in Cincinnati in the 1820s, "the very air in the city seemed changed" and that the entire community was enveloped in Christian gravity. When he visited the Queen City, the disappointed Thompson discovered that, as he rather suspected, things were much the same as before. But if accounts were often inflated, there is no question that the awakenings brought thousands into churches. William McLoughlin Jr. estimates that between 1800 and 1835 the proportion of Americans who were members of Protestant churches grew from 7 percent to 12 percent, a significant increase. This also means, of course, that 88 percent were not members of Protestant churches. Many were Protestants who attended church services but were not admitted members. Others included Catholics, freethinkers, and those simply unconcerned about religion.[30]

Women played a central role in revivals and the subsequent reform movements, of which temperance was the most crucial in the reform of male comportment. Before the revivals women had been more likely to join churches than men and less likely to drop out. As in the First Great Awakening, most of those converted during the Second were women. A sample of new members during the 1799–1801 revival in Connecticut determined that 70 percent were women. In Baltimore about two-thirds of the converts in the 1820s revivals were female, about equal to their percentage in churches before that. Even in the 1857–58 urban awakening, the famed "Businessmen's Revival," which was said by many churchmen to have been marked by an increase in male religious enthusiasm, 60 percent of converts in New York City were women. In Oneida County, New York, and elsewhere, much of the organizational infrastructure for the awakenings was provided by women through local tract and Bible societies. Also as in the First Great Awakening, many of the converts, male as well as female, were young, the children of church members. Many others were former members; relatively few seemed to be without prior church connections.[31]

Which raises an obvious question: how many of the men doing the drinking, fighting, gambling, and "petty mischief and tricks," all said to have declined so dramatically, actually were among the converted? How many jolly fellows were reborn as Christian comrades? Some were. William Grayson relates that a key to the 1803 Charleston revival was the conversion of the wealthy Robert Barnwell, one of the leaders of the town's coterie of boisterous Revolutionary War veterans said to be "addicted to deep drinking, hard swearing and practical joking." Barnwell became "an active and devout member of the church." Storekeeper Hermon Camp kept whiskey in his Trumansburg, New York, shop and freely treated his customers. Converted during an 1831 awakening, he became, literally a new man, according to an 1890 history of the village. This formerly "light-hearted, open-handed, freethinking man became an austere and uncompromising Calvinist." He joined the temperance movement and "abandoned the sale of liquor and began to war against its use and sale which he fought to his dying day."[32]

The majority of the tavern crowd no doubt remained, like most Americans, unconverted, and many were active opponents of revivals. Jolly fellows were surely among the "camp rowdies" that constantly attempted to disrupt religious meetings. Methodist preacher Peter Cartwright denounced them as "doggery-haunting renegades of the towns and villages around." Most were probably attracted by the socializing and drinking that occurred at camp meetings, but others may have been drawn by contempt for a movement that they saw, correctly, as threatening their lifestyle. Often the opponents would pitch their tents a few hundred yards away from the religious gathering, and the rowdy camp and the revival camp would survey each other like rival armies. Different harassing tactics were used. The rowdies would ride around yelling. Opponents, according to Cartwright, would sometimes hover in adjacent woods "to bark like dogs, to howl like wolves, to hoot like owls." On one occasion they infiltrated the worshipers and "pretended to get religion, and jumped and shouted at a fearful rate." Sometimes men attempted to break up revival services in churches. Baptist evangelist Jacob Knapp's sermons excoriating drinking and gambling generated a fury. In Rochester a mob packed the pews, Knapp claimed, and drowned him out and later systematically broke the church's windows.[33]

Clerical accounts of a dramatic reformation of morals were overdrawn: only a relatively small percentage of the population was converted and most of those were women, and resistance was widespread. Yet many observers, even some hostile to awakenings, acknowledged that the era's religious enthusiasm had diminished disorder. William Grayson understood that many converts were "swayed by sympathy" rather than principle and that many others were "crafty self-seekers" who viewed a profession of faith as in their interest. After a few months most new members became backsliders. Still, Grayson remained convinced that the awakenings had produced "ample, genuine invaluable fruits . . . [with] manifest advantage . . . to the moral condition of the people." But could the relatively small number of true converts really have such a significant impact? Many thought the answer was "yes" because even men and women who themselves were unmoved by the religious enthusiasm became more orderly. Revivals were said to have a ripple effect, and nonconverts, perhaps from the shame they felt when they compared themselves to their sanctified neighbors or perhaps simply from politeness, altered their behavior. The *Pittsburgh Gazette* thought that "human nature is insensibly actuated by . . . secret springs and touches" and that the presence of dignified, reverent inhabitants "restrains the disorderly in the streets where he walks or the neighbourhood where he lives." In Bath County, Virginia, after an 1805 revival, even "those who make no pretension to religion, still appear under great restraint."[34]

Hoosier Village, published in 1912 by pioneering rural sociologist Newell Leroy Sims, presents a unique and perceptive account of a revival's influence. *Hoosier Village* is a community study of "Aton," obviously Angola, Indiana, an isolated town in the northeast corner of the state that had been bypassed by antebellum moral reformation. The change in deportment occurred mostly in the 1860s, late enough for Sims to interview people who experienced it. Thus his account is worth examining in detail. In the 1850s, "impulsive action" was still the rule. Drunks reeled through the streets and "fights occurred with great frequency." Dances and political discussions often ended in brawls. Card and billiard playing were rampant. A religious awakening began in 1867 among the Disciples of Christ and spread to other denominations. "All classes seem to have been equally susceptible to its influence." Church membership shot up. "There is a feeling that 'you have to go to church,' and 'one must join the church for everybody does.'" Those who did not attend services came under intense pressure. The church "folks kept dinging away at me until I got tired" and joined, grumbled one man. Sims himself "felt the force of this custom."[35]

Churchgoers achieved a critical mass that allowed them to influence the entire village. The church "rigidly enforced its moral standards" until it became "the leading factor in forming the social type of the group," and "through constant repetition in season and out of season," these moral standards "crystalized into a customary way of life." Guilt was crucial. The constant emphasis on probity subjected people to mental stress by making them uneasy about their unrighteousness. "Their badness goads their consciences." Eventually the strain became too much, and people succumbed, recognizing they simply would be happier being respectable. Legal coercion also played a significant role in implementing the new standard of conduct: arrests for intoxication and assault shot up. But even more influential, Sims believed, was the informal coercion of public opinion. "Gossip plays the part of an invisible policeman, keeping watch over every individual, prying into domestic circles, thrusting himself into places of business, patrolling every street and alley[,] . . . inspiring fear and controlling conduct." Churchgoers had a sympathetic and personal concern for the state of others' souls, but their methods of ensuring salvation included duress. Anyone who even considered using "liquor as a beverage" was ostracized. Not just drinkers, but gamblers, women who were "flirty," and alleged transgressors of any sort risked becoming community outcasts.[36]

The change in attitude was profound. "An evolution has taken place in the type of individual dominant in the community." People before and after Angola's moral reformation represented "two vastly different social moulds." In an earlier era

> the typical man was a fighter; . . . he was self-indulgent, ready to drink and gratify his passions in excess; he was aggressive, inclined to regard right as

> might, and rather impulsive in his actions. The present social environment produces as the prevailing type the austere, dogmatic Puritanic individual, who is a champion of denial, a believer in fair play and justice, a devotee of religion and reform movements.

Sims summarizes the change in terms of ideal types, but he is aware that reality is more complicated: "Only in a rough way can the two periods be defined; since the transition from one to the other, like all other social changes, has been gradual." Although Sims may underestimate the role of personal religious commitment, he captures the significance of the change and suggests the mechanisms by which the evolution in emotional patterns advanced.[37]

"SUCCESS OF TEMPERANCE REFORMATION [IS] VITAL TO THE INTEREST OF TRUE RELIGION"

The revivals had instigated the moral awakening of American society, but they were not, by themselves, enough. A wide variety of changes would be needed to transform America into a righteous nation. The goal was not simply pious and sedate Christians but a pious and sedate American society. It would thus be necessary to coax—or, if required, compel—others to modify their sinful behavior. Lyman Beecher was perhaps more than anyone responsible for pushing nineteenth-century Protestantism in a more censorious direction. A Connecticut Congregational minister and dynamic preacher, Beecher was sympathetic to religious awakenings, even as he criticized the emotional excesses of the Finney revivals. Like many others, he was dismayed by the immorality that he saw flourishing in the early republic, and his sermons condemning Sabbath breaking, profanity, intemperance, gambling, dueling, and slavery were published and widely circulated.[38]

In *A Reformation of Morals Practicable and Indispensable* (1814), "practicable" is a key word. It signaled Beecher's comprehension that many people believed that, however desirable, eradicating long-standing transgressions like drinking was impossible. Alcohol, after all, had been part of daily life for generations. But he argued, American Christians must try. Here the revivals played a critical role. In *A Reformation of Morals* Beecher asserted that the recent awakening of religion showed that the spirit of God was moving in the land and that the time was ripe for an all-out offensive against any and all immorality. Change was feasible—thousands had been converted and brought into churches. Now was the time for the godly to mobilize to eradicate sin.[39]

Beecher questioned whether, despite the many glowing claims, awakenings by themselves could transform America into a morally healthy nation. What was needed were institutions to further advance moral improvement. The vehicle Beecher proposed was "local voluntary associations of the wise and the good to aid the civil magistrate in the execution of laws." This was a traditional strategy, first employed in England after the Glorious Revolution and sporadically used in eighteenth-century America. Beecher understood that public authorities in the United States lacked the strength to enforce propriety on the unwilling, but with the aid of a Christian public mobilized through voluntary organizations, success might be achieved. Beecher believed that "in a free government moral suasion and coercion must be united." He hoped such associations would shame miscreants into decorous conduct. But there was also a role for compulsion—the necessary laws were on the books, but "laws unexecuted are worse than nothing." Christians must probe for iniquity and report it to public authorities.[40]

To implement this program, Beecher in 1813 had helped form the Connecticut Society for the Suppression of Vice and Promotion of Good Morals. The vision of an American society characterized by godly concord proved powerfully attractive. Beecher's initial concern had been with New England, but moral societies sprung up all over the nation—in New York, New Jersey, Pennsylvania, Ohio, Illinois, Kentucky, North Carolina, and Alabama. The Andover (Massachusetts) South Parish Society for the Reformation of Morals was created in 1819 to "discountenance immorality, particularly Sabbath-breaking, intemperance and profanity." Some groups, like the Schenectady, New York, Society for the Promotion of Good Morals, formed in 1814, proposed only "to faithfully and affectionately counsel and admonish" those who practiced intemperance, profanity, and Sabbath breaking. The New Jersey society, however, vowed to employ "the full effect of the laws of the state against vice and immorality, by aiding civil authorities" in punishing drunkards, blasphemers, and horse racers.[41]

At first simply one aspect of a broad campaign to improve humanity, decreasing alcohol consumption emerged as the central focus of the personal reform effort. Beecher increasingly emphasized how drinking was the root cause of much of the sinful behavior he condemned. Alcohol was the key that unlocked jolly fellowship: it loosened self-governance and thus led to fighting, gambling, swearing, and other disorder. The Congregational *Christian Spectator* in 1819 labeled intemperance "that parent of almost all other vices in our country." To Rev. Lebbeus Armstrong, a pioneer temperance organizer, alcohol became "the curse of all curses." To reformed drinker James Campbell, drink was nothing less than "the cause of all human misery." The temperance movement helped consolidate the reform in comportment that resulted from revivals and helped ensure it would endure. Jolly fellows could disregard the religious enthusiasm of the period, though at their peril. The goal of the temperance movement, however, especially after the shift to prohibition in the 1840s, aimed to close the taverns and put an end to the regulars and their world. Temperance became the touchstone of the reformers' vast project of human betterment, an issue of intense conflict, central to the reformation of male character. To growing numbers of people, according to Kentucky physician Daniel Drake, "the village church and the village tavern did in fact represent two great opposing principles: good & evil,—the spirit and the flesh. One might have been taken as the symbol of Heaven—the other of Hell!"[42]

The antidrink movement gained ground in the 1820s, and by 1833 the American Temperance Society claimed it had one million members affiliated with local chapters. The earliest organizations battled only excessive drinking, but the logic of their arguments about the immense dangers of alcohol caused the United States Temperance Union (the American Temperance Society's successor) to condemn "all [substances] that will intoxicate," including beer and wine. Teetotalism led to bitter controversy, but eventually it came to dominate the movement. In 1840 six artisans in a Baltimore tavern formed the Washington Temperance Society. Earlier organizations had been religiously oriented; the more secular Washingtonians, on the other hand, appealed to artisans and workers and attracted hundreds of thousands of adherents. The fraternal and semisecret Sons of Temperance was started in New York City in 1842 and by 1851 was said to have a membership of a quarter of a million. But it was becoming obvious that for all the pledges not to touch alcohol, drinking continued throughout the country. This failure led to a turn away from voluntary teetotalism toward legal prohibition. In 1851, Maine, after a tenacious campaign by Neal Dow, president of the Maine Temperance Union, passed a law that effectively banned sales of liquor in the state and in the 1850s twelve more states in the East and Midwest followed suit.[43]

Temperance was strongest in the East but received support everywhere in the country. Although there were fewer societies in the more rural South, voluntary abstinence was strong there as well. The Virginia Temperance Society was founded in 1826 and by 1835 had thirty-five thousand members. The Sons of Temperance had half its membership in southern states; in Alabama it was estimated in 1849 that the organization had enrolled between fifteen to twenty thousand men, one quarter of the state's white male population. Even in the Louisiana backcountry, the cause was said to be "spreading like wildfire" in 1842: "From every direction we hear of the organization of temperance societies, and of the redemption of many confirmed topers." In the Old Northwest, the movement

J. W. Barber, "The Grog Shop," from "The Drunkard's Progress; or, The Direct Road to Poverty, Wretchedness and Ruin" (New Haven, 1826). Underneath this picture is a list of evils associated with the grog shop: "Bad Company, Profaneness, Cursing and Swearing, Quarreling & Fighting, Gambling, Obscenity, Ridicule and Hatred of Religion, The Gate of Hell." An American Time Capsule: Three Centuries of Broadsides and Other Printed Ephemera, http://lcweb2.loc.gov/ammem/rbpehtml, Library of Congress, Rare Book and Special Collections Division.

started slowly but quickly burgeoned. In Cincinnati eight thousand men took the Washingtonian pledge in 1841. Midwestern states were among the strongest supporters of a Maine law, and in Michigan seventy thousand residents signed petitions in a successful 1855 prohibition campaign.[44]

The role of women was pivotal. Insulated from the tumult of business and politics, women, it was argued, were particularly virtuous and thus able to provide moral instruction to men. Was it not obvious, Sara Josepha Hale asked, that the wife was "the heart of humanity, as her husband was the head?" "WOMAN," Hale explained, is "God's appointed agent of *morality*, the teacher and inspirer of those feelings and sentiments which are the virtues of humanity." The majority in many churches and more likely than men to be converted in revivals, women were vigorously involved in antebellum benevolent and reform movements. "Feminine influence," in the absence of strong government, became for many moralists, both men and women, the key to reforming male character. The advice literature of the period urged men to seek the company of virtuous women, who would restrain misguided behavior, and men themselves came to accept women's superior virtue. The mere presence of women, as other chapters in this book show, was often enough to make men behave, and women's absence seemed to many men a license for jolly fellowship.[45]

The American Temperance Society encouraged women to work through their families and churches to counter the influence of alcohol. Both the Washingtonians and the Sons of Temperance had large female auxiliaries. Women who joined these societies signed the pledge and engaged in benevolent acts. Part of their effort was to halt female drinking. But equally significant, "feminine influence" was viewed as critical in converting men to the cause. Women encouraged, even pressured, men to sign the pledge and ensured that those who signed kept their word. "Teetotal or No Husband" read a banner in a precession of the Worcester Daughters of Temperance; in Vermont temperate women were urged "to kiss the lips of Temperance men to ascertain whether they keep their pledges" not to drink.[46]

Women's support of temperance is obviously consistent with their support of moral reform in general. But for women, temperance was far from the abstract issue that was world peace or prison reform, or even, outside the South, slavery. They knew, often from personal experience, the demoralization that drink could bring wives and families. For them, the gleaming vision of a sober, orderly America was especially attractive. When "a change began to come over the minds of the people," women had less reason to be attached to the old order than men did. What did jolly fellowship have to offer them, except the occasional entertaining story of the antics of the tavern regulars? It was for men only; men went to the tavern and the grocery to drink and carouse while women stayed home. One wonders what went through the minds of the wives of jolly fellows as they spent their evenings, and their money, in taverns.[47]

The breadth of the movement was striking. There were young men's temperance societies, workers' societies, sailors' societies, Catholic societies, black societies. College students founded antidrink societies. There were temperate volunteer militia and fire companies. In Pittsburgh, in 1843 the Blues militia joined the Washingtonians en masse and signed the pledge. There was a strong African American temperance movement in both cities and southern states. Even some slaves championed temperance—one Virginia planter claimed "that a large portion of my slaves have given up use of spirits." A whole temperance culture emerged with temperance books and newspapers, temperance songs, temperance dramas, temperance canal boats, temperance livery stables, temperance hotels, temperance groceries, and even temperance taverns.[48]

The most famous temperance novel, *Ten-Nights in a Bar-Room*, published in 1854, illustrates how high the stakes seemed. Written by veteran author Timothy Shay Arthur, it was intended as a brief for the Maine law. Only a minor best seller when first published, its strong sales during the rest of the century, often to anti-drink groups who distributed it free, made it a publishing phenomenon. Equally popular was the 1858 stage adaptation that for the remainder of the century was second in number of performances only to *Uncle Tom's Cabin* on rural circuits. *Ten-Nights in a Bar-Room* is set in the Sheaf and Sickle, a newly opened tavern in the previously upright village of Cedarville. As the narrator visits Cedarville over the years, he chronicles the community's progressive degradation. It is the tavern, more than alcohol itself, which is the origin of Cedarville's corruption; its masculine bonhomie lures men out of the home and into drink. The regulars rule the Sheaf and Sickle under the tutelage of tavern keeper Sam Slade and eventually come to dominate the village. Slade on stage was one of the great villains in nineteenth-century theater, an insinuating, cowardly, callous man.[49]

The Sheaf and Sickle works its malign influence on Cedarville. As in *Uncle Tom's Cabin*—published two years earlier—the worst evil is the destruction of families. Like Stowe, Arthur assumes women have a key role to play in moral redemption: there are virtually no female drinkers in *Ten Nights in a Bar-Room*, and women try to halt men's drinking. In the book and play's most famous scene, Mary, the daughter of inebriate Joe Morgan, a once-respectable farmer, comes into the tavern to plead with him to return home. In many stage versions Mary appealed to her father by singing Henry Clay Work's temperance ballad, "Father, Dear Father, Come Home with Me Now." A drunken Slade throws a glass at Joe but hits Mary, and she dies a noble, lingering Little Eva-like death. But even female influence is not enough—only men themselves can bring about the needed reformation. Cedarville's decline continues. "Neglect, decay and dilapidation were visible, let the eye fall where it would." The inhabitants become "derationalized through drink," coarser, more profane, slovenly, savage. Clothing is old and torn. Men gamble. Fights break out. Cedarville is regressing to what America had been before "the change in society." The Sheaf and Sickle, in short, has done nothing less than reverse human progress. Finally, after Slade is killed by his drunken son, the men of Cedarville demolish the Sheaf and Sickle and prohibit the sale of liquor. Men regain control of their lives from the dominion of drink.[50]

Alcohol was a way of life and to abandon it totally was a decision of momentous significance. In Wilbraham, Massachusetts, in 1827, an interdenominational group met and drew up a temperance pledge. Some came forward and signed, "but others hesitated: to resolve not to use ardent spirits themselves, nor permit it to be used in their homes, seemed so much like entering into a new world, and adopting new modes of life, that they hardly knew what to say or do." As long as temperance focused on voluntary abstinence and moral suasion, controversy was sharp but restrained. When, however, temperance supporters began to endorse local options that allowed communities to ban liquor sales and later to push for statewide prohibition, open, bitter conflict broke out. "There is no neutrality in this warfare," warned the *Temperance Recorder.* "If you drink none, you are for us, if you drink any, you are against us." The balance of power varied widely from town to town, and the reluctance of established political parties to become involved contributed to the fluid nature of the situation. In each place, there was usually a coterie of jolly fellows and a growing number of temperance men and women but also many who equivocated. There were nondrinkers outraged by the bullying nature of some temperance campaigns. There were drinkers who suspected that prohibition was good for society, even though they personally enjoyed alcohol. In many places the conflict was intense and prolonged.[51]

The first inhabitants to stop consuming alcohol were met with incredulity and ridicule. On New Year's Day 1824, thirteen-year-old Horace Greeley announced his decision to stop drinking distilled liquor. Indignant Westhaven, Vermont, neighbors seized him at a sheep washing, held him down, and poured alcohol into him: "The liquor was turned into my mouth, and some of it forced down my throat." The young M. M. "Brick" Pomeroy remembered that when he refused to take a drink with his fellow employees in a Corning, New York, print shop in the 1830s, he was "jeered, ridiculed, sneered at and laughed at for being a milksop." To give up drinking seemed like surrendering one's manhood. But as the movement gained adherents, it was drinkers who found themselves disdained. Temperance opponents reacted with the violence and pranks that were so characteristic of jolly fellowship. During a temperance meeting in 1831 in Orleans County, New York, "there came a sleigh load of men . . . [who] took a bottle from their pockets and went to drinking &c" and "tried to force spirits down one of the members." The house of a leading prohibitionist in Providence, Rhode Island, was blown up in 1838. An Illinois minister who preached in favor of a Maine law, had a mob throw eggs, rocks, and firecrackers at his house and then march around it "barking like dogs [and] howling like wolves." In Tallahassee, Florida, an 1833 meeting to organize a temperance society was packed by "the rabble" who unanimously supported a total abstinence provision and then voted to add one absurd amendment after another to the organization's constitution.[52]

One repeated battleground was Independence Day. Traditionally a time of heavy drinking and fighting, temperance supporters claimed the holiday for their own. Alcohol-free July 4th celebrations were organized all over the nation. The Pittsburgh *Spirit of Liberty* reported in 1842 that in western Pennsylvania, the "friends of temperance seem to have quite a monopoly of the celebration of the Fourth." Not quite everywhere, however. In Muncy, Pennsylvania, when the local temperance society announced an Independence Day observance, another announcement shortly appeared for a celebration for "citizens who are *not members of the temperance society*." Both groups made elaborate preparations. On July 4, 1842, "the temperance folks," recalled one participant at the alcoholic fete, "were tempering their glowing patriotism with cooling draughts of lemonade," while their antagonists "were arousing their love of country to a much *louder* pitch with copious portions of 'inspiring John Barleycorn.'" There were patriotic speeches and fifty toasts, including denunciations of temperance and abolitionism. Writing decades later, the narrator explained that he was leaving out of his account certain incidents that would dismay contemporary readers. "Times have changed," he concluded, "and we cannot judge them by the standard of to-day."[53]

Slowly temperance forces gained ground. Although drinkers put up a strong fight, they increasingly found themselves on the defensive. In Washington County, Ohio, the district attorney, a staunch Presbyterian, was a strong temperance man who used every legal tool at his disposal to harass those who continued to imbibe. He held the post for years, "notwithstanding the efforts of the 'jolly boys' at every election, to out him from office," John Morris mournfully remembered. By 1845 per capita adult alcohol consumption was down to 1.8 gallons, one-fourth of what it had been fifteen years earlier. Once hospitality demanded every visitor be offered a drink. In the Western Reserve region of Ohio by the 1830s, when visitors called, any liquor was hidden immediately, unless the host "wished to insult" guests, "in which case, the first thing he [did was] to set the whiskey-bottle before them." Many groceries had stopped selling liquor altogether. In Martinsburg, Pennsylvania, in 1854 only one of three stores sold alcohol and that one stopped by the end of the year. Horace Greeley claimed that by the 1860s in many villages it was impossible to buy liquor and that tipplers could fill their jug only by sending it to the city.[54]

Teetotalers were optimistic that temperance by itself would reform American society and bring about an orderly nation, but reformers did not ignore other moral improvements. There were antigambling campaigns in a number of places, mostly in the South and West, and regular antigambling societies in cities such as New York. Students at Dartmouth College in New Hampshire and Transylvania College in Kentucky created organizations to eradicate wagering. In some places reformers lobbied for new antigambling laws; in others they urged that existing laws be enforced. The 1851 New York State Act for the More Effective Suppression of Gambling, drawn up on advice from J. H. Green, a reformed gambler, not only instructed district attorneys, sheriffs, and police to enforce the law but made them subject to arrest if they did not.[55]

The playing of cruel practical jokes began to wane. Although vicious pranks faced little public criticism until the last thirty years of the nineteenth century, the *Memphis Appeal* in 1844 detected a change in popular attitudes. "Instances of practical joking seem to have become more rare, and the relish for this species of amusement less keen, than in former times." Was it the *Appeal* wondered, because "of the advancement of arts and sciences" and railroads, "which by adding a variety and extension to business and pleasure, scarcely allow a man time to be idle, to stay in one place long enough 'to get the blues' or to devise the 'ways and means' by which to expel them?" Or was it because "the bump of benevolence, or philanthropy, in the human cranium has . . . become enlarged?" Nowadays people believed that the pain to the victim "nine times overbalances the amount of enjoyment derived by the adverse party." Whatever the cause, "one thing is certain; there is evidently a decline in practical joking."[56]

"DRIVEN INTO A CORNER"

The day when it was possible to live a drinking, brawling, prank-playing life and remain a highly regarded member of the community was passing. "True manliness" meant self-control. Timothy Shay Arthur in *Advice to Young Men on Their Duties and Conduct in Life* (1847) advised that "a modest deportment is that which best becomes a young man." His "inward disorders" must be "subdued and brought under the control of good principles." The sentiment was not new; moralists had been praising self-governance since the eighteenth century, and this standard of demeanor continued to gain influence. Similarly, male honor was enhanced not by fighting but by refusing to fight. In an 1843 book for teenage boys titled *Conquest or Self-Conquest; or, Which Makes the Hero?* young Frederic is goaded into battling the school bully Arthur Macon, who proceeds to break Frederic's arm. When Frederic's arm heals he wants to retaliate, but after a talk with his father, Frederic comes to understand that honor is achieved not by conquering others but by conquering one's passions. He decides he would show "more courage in not fighting Arthur Macon than in fighting him." This wins the respect of the other boys, and he becomes, as the title of the chapter puts it, "A Champion though No Fighter." Frederic joins the navy where his refusal to drink and gamble awes his fellow sailors, and eventually he becomes a hero in the War of 1812. Restrained manhood was developing into a powerful and increasingly articulate and coherent discourse in sharp contrast to discursively inchoate jolly fellowship.[57]

Sobriety was now a "credential of character." Anyone with ambition had to at least appear to live a sedate and temperate lifestyle. This was especially true among the small but growing middle class. Adventurers by this time did not appear suited to what had become a more rationalized economy—a gambling temperament was less likely of reward. It now took, in an oft-repeated phrase of the period, a "system" to succeed. "Form habits of SYSTEM, in everything," John Todd advised. "System" meant taking a steady and methodical approach to work, keeping good records, and maintaining tidy arrangement of offices and workshops. It also meant cultivating an orderly personal disposition. The advice literature of the period agreed that the desire for wealth must never take precedence over living a moral life. But aggressive impulses, which no longer could be physically externalized by respectable men, could honorably be channeled into getting ahead in business. Here revivals and the personal reforms of the period intersected with capitalist development. Often only abstainers were hired for responsible jobs. "Other things equal," a member of the Sons of Temperance boasted, a pledged applicant "has an advantage of place and occupation over an unpledged applicant." Those whose habits were not abstemious and orderly had trouble getting financial backing. The Mercantile Agency credit reports routinely commented on drinking habits and deportment. "Likes to drink too much" and "leads a sporting life" stigmatized one businessman, "too fond of a spree" another. After examining credit agency ratings for his history of Kingston, New York, Stuart Blumin discovered that "there *is* a fairly close correspondence between 'good habits' and the fortunes of men." Those whose personal qualities were judged satisfactory generally succeeded; those of "questionable habits," on the other hand, like Eugene Best, a member of a rowdy "Bumble Bee Boys" gang, failed to prosper. Jolly fellows' chances for securing wealth were shrinking. The social location of jolly fellowship that once cut across class lines was now becoming associated with the lower and working class, and well-to-do men who engaged in disorderly behavior were consciously crossing a class boundary.[58]

Also significant, especially in villages and small towns, was the companionship of women. Women embraced the reform and temperance movements, and their influence was considerable. Henry C. Noble, a young Unadilla, New York, bachelor learned just how committed women were to the era's reform efforts when he and others attempted to hold a cotillion in 1831, apparently in an attempt to counteract the spiritual effect of the great Rochester revival. They discovered, however, that they "can get but few ladies to go. Many of them have got a kind of religious scruple about the matter." Churches and benevolent organizations, along with the ubiquitous singing societies and the increasingly rare husking bees, became the main places, perhaps in some villages, the only places, to meet women. Respectable young women now insisted on morally correct suitors. "Teetotal or No Husband" was more than just a slogan, as English immigrant jewelry maker Henry Walter learned.[59]

After his first wife's death in New York City, Walter drifted around the East before finally settling down in New Britain, Connecticut, in 1845, age thirty-two. While there he was introduced to "one of the nicest Girls in New Britain" by a friend, who urged him "to try and get her." The friend arranged a meeting, and they became acquainted, but Walter discovered that "though she might be pleased with me, She would not from principle marry me." Walter soon learned why: she had received letters denouncing him as a reformer's nightmare. One message, he learned, claimed he "was seen coming from a certain house disguised with liquor. Another I was playing cards, still another I was profane. . . . And the last point was, That she . . . could not mate herself with one who was an Unbeliever." Walter pleaded innocent to all charges, but although no dissolute atheist, he seems, in truth, not to have been very devout or have much interest in personal reform. Walter began regularly attending church and won over her mother, who was convinced that anyone who paid such close attention to dull sermons could not merely be feigning interest. With her encouragement, he resumed his efforts, and this time was successful. Now married, Walter continued to attend church, largely it seems to please his wife, who he conceded was "the Christian head of the family." To what seems to be his own astonishment, during a service in August 1851, he was saved. "I was . . . a new creation. . . . Everything seemed changed. I wanted to speak to everyone I met about the Saviour I had found, or rather who had found me." This formerly footloose man was now a "home loving And home sharing individual" and, like his wife, "a Strong, fervent, earnest Christian."[60]

The claims of Sara Hale and other didactic writers about the importance of "feminine influence" were in Walter's case no exaggeration. Only by altering his lifestyle to conform to the ideal of the pious, temperate man could he marry the woman he loved. Walter was genuinely transformed, but many others found themselves forced to live up to the ideal of the devout, sober, self-controlled man that employers, young women, and respectable society demanded. There is little doubt that such conforming to expectations led to hypocrisy. Many men likely took a drink as soon as they got out of town. Horace Greeley believed that large numbers of men were forced "to maintain an exterior decency which would once have exposed them to ridicule" and that they gratified interior appetites in anonymous cities. "Men away from home" was a nineteenth-century expression for jolly behavior, implying both male hypocrisy and the likelihood that men would carouse when separated from women, family, church, and community. In cities or areas bypassed by reform, men continued to drink and gamble without reserve. Big Bill Otter never became Sweet William. Living in western Maryland and later Baltimore, he persisted in his hard-drinking, hard-fighting, prank-playing lifestyle with little restraint.[61]

A great many men, however, in the mid-nineteenth century were neither Walters nor Otters nor conscious hypocrites—they were caught in the transition between an age when male revelry was customary and an age in which manly respectability was the standard. The diary of Edward Carpenter, a cabinetmaker in Greenfield in western Massachusetts, suggests the complicated response to the demands of restrained deportment. Carpenter was a backer of the moral reform movements of the day and a reader of self-improvement literature. A temperance supporter, he subscribed to a Washingtonian newspaper and was disappointed when "the Rum party" prevailed in local elections. Yet he continued to drink "small beer." Carpenter "took a hand of High low jack & the game" but explained that it was "just for amusement for I never played for money." He was one of the town's mechanics who organized a boycott of the riotous Mansion House Tavern and voted to suppress, by force if need be, the nightly disturbances caused by "a lot of rowdies." Yet he enjoyed local brawls, and he eagerly came out to the street to watch a battle "between a saucy fellow named White & a chap by the name of Rundel. White got some hard knocks & I was glad of it." Carpenter was well versed in the moral reform agenda of the period and believed that he himself, the community, and the nation would benefit from it. Greenville had not yet been caught up in the absolutism that characterized reforms such as temperance, and

Carpenter seems to have felt that indulging in minor vices did not compromise his general commitment to ethical improvement.[62]

John M. Roberts, a schoolteacher in Madison County in central Ohio, was equally ambivalent. Roberts was fascinated with the drinkers, fighters, and gamblers of the vicinity, yet he maintained his distance from them. He enjoyed associating with the German American Long brothers, "a jovial, ranting [trio of] old bachelors . . . fond of fun and whiskey. They are of the old school of men." Yet despite his love of such company, Roberts remained ambivalent about their jolly lifestyle and felt guilty after his own sprees. After revelry with a "jovial, rollicking set of chaps that take things easy and good natured as the law will allow," Roberts was troubled that he was "getting to be almost too well acquainted. I am not in favor of getting to[o], as I think that familiarity breeds contempt." For all his drinking, Roberts favored Ohio's Maine law, perhaps feeling that it would help him govern his own jolly tendencies and maintain his self-control.[63]

Men like Carpenter and Roberts were between two worlds. There were surely Carpenters and Roberts in every community, as well as born-again Walters and rowdy Otters. More Walters, surely, in Connecticut and more Otters in Maryland, but for all the individual and regional variations the trend was clear—the "old school of men" was dwindling, jolly fellowship was fading. Public places like the tavern and street were shunned by respectable men; the home became the place to demonstrate honor and manhood. The temper of the times had changed. Reformers in St. Johnsbury, Vermont, boasted that "gambling, drinking and profanity, which once were our disgrace," are now "forsaken or driven into a corner." Disorderly comportment still fascinated large numbers of men, but fewer and fewer followed an unruly lifestyle.[64]

Jolly fellowship was a male comportment with connections to conduct in the European past, and the slow shift toward more rational and self-controlled conduct, Norbert Elias's "civilizing process," had been going on for at least two hundred years. America, with the possible exception of the South, was never as reckless and violent as Europe had been. Although Indians were routinely victims of deadly violence, the eighteenth-century homicide rate among whites in the United States appears to have been relatively low. However, what seemed reserved to one generation could seem unrefined to the next. "Violence" is a relative concept. As Emmanuel Leroy Ladurie suggests in his discussion of the betterment of conduct in seventeenth- and eighteenth-century Languedoc, a tavern brawl *is* restrained compared to a jacquerie. Pranks were a tamer form of aggression than a physical attack. American society in the late eighteenth century was still, in comparison to later periods, marked by a great deal of casual disorder and violence. In a long-term trend toward refinement, the 1820s, 1830s, and 1840s might be seen as a reforming spurt, marking, perhaps, a final consolidating phase of the civilizing process.[65]

"LARGE CITIES AND THINLY SETTLED PLACES ARE THE *EXTREMES* OF SOCIAL LIFE"

This "moral revolution," as one cleric dubbed it, begun by the revivals and continued by temperance and other benevolent movements, would, reformers hoped, usher in a new age of Christian virtue not only in America but throughout the world. Overall progress was being made. There was widespread satisfaction by the 1840s that in most villages behavior was better, though there was still room for improvement. But reformers were increasingly aware that America encompassed domains where personal regeneration seemed to have stalled. The growing confidence about rural and small-town life allowed moralists to turn their eyes to those areas where reform was much less impressive, most prominently cities and the West.[66]

William Alcott, editor of the *Moral Reformer*, observed that "large cities and thinly settled places are the *extremes* of social life. Here, of course, vice will be found in its worst form." Only in small, established communities, where "every body knows every body and feels an interest in every body," had revivals really flourished, Calvin Colton believed. In urban areas and in the West the march of personal reform had been slower, and drinking, gambling, and fighting persisted. Alcott's view of a "middle landscape" of morality was widely shared: villages were bulwarks of rectitude in contrast to cities and the frontier where disorder still thrived.[67]

The moral danger of city life was, of course, a staple of Anglo-American discourse, and, although the early nineteenth century saw the appearance of a cogent defense of urbanity, prorural sentiments remained strong. William Cowper's axiom that "God made the country and man made the town" was widely quoted. Many religious tracts and reform novels of the period contrasted the virtuous village with the evil city. The problem was, as the usually urbane *Knickerbocker* magazine explained, "great cities are not, to the mass of inhabitants, favorable to the growth of virtue . . . [and] few have the moral power to resist its influence." The anonymity of urban life freed men and women from communal restraint. Migrants, warned the *Evangelist and Religious Review*, all too often were "swayed into the broad road of destruction by the immediate and powerful influence of the city." Popular novels of the period like George Lippard's *The Quaker City*

(1845) portrayed cities as stygian worlds of wickedness. Home missionary societies turned their attention to urban areas, especially New York, Boston, and Philadelphia, built churches, established Sunday schools, and made visitations to slum areas.[68]

The frontier was also cause for concern. Congregational cleric Timothy Dwight was disheartened by the settlements he visited on the New England frontier in Vermont and Maine. "A considerable proportion" of this population, he explained, "will, almost of course, consist of roving, disorderly, vicious men." This was not, in Dwight's view, such a bad thing. The frontier functioned as a safety valve, siphoning off unruly men from Connecticut, making the Land of Steady Habits all the steadier. However, as Americans pressed west, farther and farther from the Atlantic seaboard, farther and farther from New England, clerical concern grew. Lyman Beecher was convinced that the "religious and political destiny of our nation is to be decided in the West," where, clerics worried, disorder, infidelity, and Catholicism reigned. In the East, James L. Batchelder, explained, the "principles and actions of citizens . . . who make no pretensions to piety, are guided and restrained" by the "pure principles of the Bible." But "a different state of things prevails in the West. There Christianity floats on the bosom of troubled waters, like the Ark, tempest tossed." Western ministers like Peter Cartwright disputed descriptions of their region as a moral swamp, but eastern reformers remained troubled. There was a concerted effort in the 1830s—motivated by both sincere concern and denominational rivalry—to bring the Gospel to the Ohio-Mississippi Valley. Led by the American Missionary Society, the campaign was strongly supported by the American Temperance Society, the American Bible Society, and the American Sunday-School Union.[69]

There was, as reformers perceived, a clear correspondence between "the extremes of social life," the frontier and city. American "progress"—the growth of cities and westward expansion—was, paradoxically, fortifying traditional male comportment. Both cities and the West, as will be seen, contained male domains, and in both, jolly behavior not only endured but thrived. Such sites emerged as redoubts in an increasingly temperate and restrained America. In such places, and especially in New York City, jolly fellowship became concentrated and distilled into a counterculture. The preservation, indeed intensification, of jolly fellowship in these locales was to have significant implications for American culture and society.

CHAPTER FOUR

New York

"A great city," explained Horace Greeley speaking of New York, "derives its subsistence and its profits from ministrations, . . . not only to the real needs of the surrounding country, but to its baser appetites, its vices as well; and, as the country becomes less and less tolerant of immoral indulgences and vicious aberrations, the gains of cities therefrom, and their consequent interest therein, must steadily increase." Greeley was proposing a connection between the moral reformation of the 1820s and 1830s—a "great though silent change . . . in public sentiment," he called it—and the strength of disorderly conduct in urban areas in later decades. Cities, of course, were home to many refined residents and neighborhoods, but reformers were convinced that like the frontier, few, if any, major cities as a whole had reached the level of sobriety and uprightness of the small towns. Clerics and moralists continued to regard urbanites as an obstacle to their project of moral improvement. And with reason.[1]

Defenders of jolly fellowship rejoiced that cities were, as former boatman John Habermehl explained, simply too large and too diverse for "the religious people" to ever wipe out "resorts for worldly pleasure." John Morris agreed. "Puritanism" was, he conceded, powerful, but "the unruly spirits of the land, more especially in our large cities and many important towns in the Southern and Western states[,] revolted against their arbitrary and despotic acts, and prevented them from being enforced." Cities remained places where men could still drink, fight, and gamble, much as they had done for centuries. But jolly fellowship did not just go on as it had in urban areas. It was transformed.[2]

Critical to this transformation was the role of what sociologist Robert Park, examining early twentieth-century American cities, called "moral regions," or "vice districts." He defined a moral region as a neighborhood, or even a whole section of the city, "in which a divergent moral code prevails, because it is a region in which the people who inhabit it are dominated . . . by a passion or some interest" such as gambling. "In the process of imposing its discipline upon the individual," Park explained, "in making over the individual in accordance with the accepted community model, much is suppressed." Every large city develops milieus "in which vagrant and suppressed impulses, passions, and ideals emancipate themselves from the dominant social order." In such a place a man can "purge himself . . . of these wild and suppressed impulses."[3]

Moral regions—"immoral regions" would perhaps be a better term—began to appear in American cities in the 1830s and 1840s at the same time that revivals and temperance were peaking, and such districts continued to flourish until the end of the century. Neighborhoods dominated by saloons, gambling halls, billiard parlors, brothels, and vaudeville theaters arose. Their size and significance varied: in "wide open" cities such as late nineteenth-century Chicago, an entire district was given over to such activity. In other locations, such as in Boston, the moral region might be only a few blocks of a single street. Virtually every major city developed one. By the 1850s there was the Black Sea in Boston, the Bowery in New York, South Street in the Moyamensing neighborhood of Philadelphia, the Sands in Chicago, and Murrell's Row in Atlanta. By the 1890s there was the Potomac Quarter in Detroit, Hell's Half Acre in Fort Worth, the Soudan in Sioux City, Bucktown in Davenport, Whitechapel in Des Moines, Little Cheyenne in Chicago, Little Chicago in Cheyenne, Commercial Street in Salt Lake City, the Tenderloin in Seattle, Whitechapel in Portland, the Stingaree in San Diego, and the Barbary Coast in San Francisco.

Greeley believed that unreformed men from reformed villages fueled urban disorder: "Thousands who formerly gratified their baser appetites without disguise or shame now feel constrained, not to 'leave undone' but to 'keep unknown' by hieing to some great city . . . and there balance a year's compelled decorum by a week's unrestrained debauchery." Jolly fellowship, John Habermehl agreed, retained an appeal and periodic urban binges were a way of life for many rural men. In sober and sedate villages such men were, Habermehl believed, like horses "tied to a post, pawing and champing the bit under restraint." Cities gave them "a little elbow room"; men "under the pressure of steam can without let or hindrances lift the safety valve to ease up." "Men away from home" would drink, gamble, and wench and then return to their settled, temperate lives. Habermehl seems to think that without the railroad and the ease of travel to cities it brought, men stifled by small-town life might eventually have exploded and carried out some sort of violent mutiny against "the religious people." There were also some rural tavern regulars who permanently moved to cities where there was no reason to even pretend to be abstemious and orderly—in the cities they could continue to live as jolly fellows. The rowdy plasterer William Otter moved from Emmitsburg, Maryland, to Baltimore in 1851 and opened a saloon.[4]

Cities have always accommodated a diversity of lifestyles, and Greeley and Habermehl called attention to the difficulty many men from the countryside had in accommodating themselves to the new social order. But jolly fellowship in cities was spurred not only by men on a bender and rural refugees. Writing in a more urban age, Park believed that moral regions catered mostly to city dwellers. He seems to have had middle-class men in mind; their "suppressed impulses" could find release in vice districts, and they could continue to lead respectable bourgeois lives. Cities also had large numbers of working-class immigrants who had not been exposed in their native lands to Protestant virtues like temperance and bodily restraint and seemed slow to embrace them in America, despite the best efforts of employers and reformers. All of these groups combined to ensure that jolly behavior continued in cities even as it faded in the countryside.[5]

New York had the earliest and largest urban moral region. The area around the Bowery became lodged in popular imagination as the symbol of indulgent, impious New York. The contribution of visitors on a binge was no doubt substantial, but local residents were surely the primary consumers. New York City had always had plenty of disorder—the presence of large numbers of sailors, who were notorious drinkers and fighters, guaranteed it. The growth of New York's vice district, like those in other cities, was likely spurred by the moral reform campaigns of the 1820s and 1830s, but its size and strength was much enhanced by changes in Manhattan's population and geography. The explosive growth of urban areas in this era separated residents not only by class but by age and sex. Because of selective migration from Europe and from the American countryside, New York, like most cities, had an unusually large population of young men. An astonishing 35 percent of the male population in 1850 was between ages fifteen and thirty, and there were more men in that age group than there were in the group over the age of thirty. The many bachelors in New York and elsewhere helped fuel jolly fellowship throughout the nineteenth century. Most unmarried men, whether American, Irish or German, were boarders, and, as Walt Whitman observed, there were "whole neighborhoods of Boarding-houses" in the lower wards of Manhattan.[6]

Most boardinghouses were male establishments. Many did not accept women.

Wherever men congregated in groups in this era, jolly fellowship could emerge, and boardinghouses were no exception. Many boardinghouse keepers endured the drunken revelry of residents as an inevitable "sowing the necessary wild oats." Thomas Butler Gunn in his comic 1857 account of boardinghouse life, *The Physiology of New York Boarding-Houses*, describes "the boisterous animal indulgences" in a boardinghouse inhabited mainly by medical students as little short of uproarious: "They got up boxing-matches in garrets, [and] danced infernal dances accompanied with shrieks and howlings." Drinking was heavy, and "frequent brawls ensued." Surely few places were this wild, but many were lively. Practical jokes were a boardinghouse way of life. A dwelling occupied largely by shipbuilders was "a headquarters of considerable jocularity," where the boarders "one night went out on a festive expedition . . . changing sign-boards in modern college fashion." Almost everywhere, pious boarders were a favorite target of pranksters. Boardinghouses were so associated with merriment that boardinghouse humor became a recognized genre in the nineteenth century, both in printed works and on stage.[7]

Boardinghouses were key to the vast scale of New York's moral region. The common room of most houses was too small to accommodate all residents in the evenings so, an immigrant's guidebook explained, a boarder "has very little choice left him in the matter. He must go to a tavern or drinking-house, or theaters or other places of amusement." In the evenings men poured into the saloons, theaters, and gambling houses of the city's lower wards. Statistical correlations of single young men, boardinghouses, saloons, and lower-ward location (see appendix B) suggest that by 1855 the whole area below Canal Street had evolved a distinctive demographic and social profile. The lower wards, symbolized in the Bowery, became the antithesis of sober respectability; the Bowery itself became the metaphor for the high-spirited, manly ambience of the lower wards and even for the indulgent cosmopolitanism of New York City itself. The Bowery caught the popular imagination, but the city's disorderly district was far larger than a single street. Sporting saloons and theaters lined Park Row across from City Hall Park and lower Broadway. The main gambling houses were west of Broadway on Barclay Street and Park Place, while the city's prostitution centered even further west along Church Street.[8]

Yet the Bowery was special. Alvin F. Harlow, the street's great chronicler, dates the emergence of a distinctive Bowery scene to the late 1820s. It flourished until almost the end of the century. Just about everyone agreed the Bowery was wondrous. Writer Cornelius Mathews in 1853 found it "the greatest street on the continent, the most characteristic, the most American, the most peculiar." Junius

Henri Browne wrote in his 1869 book *The Great Metropolis* that it was "a city in itself." To the *National Police Gazette,* which extensively covered the lower-ward for its readers, it was "another city." The Bowery was the major shopping street for residents of the working-class area that later would become known as the Lower East Side, but it was "the Bowery after dark," the recreational Bowery, that made the street notorious. It was renowned for its "drinking and gambling houses, its poultry-raffling shops, . . . its 'crack' ice-cream saloons," and its dance halls and theaters, *Tribune* reporter George Foster explained to readers eager to know more about the infamous neighborhood. At night, especially on Saturday night, the Bowery thronged with revelers. The crowd was part of the show: the vibrant cavalcade of humanity that assembled on the Bowery—"a grand parade ground," Foster called it—was as much a part of the Bowery experience as the saloons and theaters.[9]

Given the large number of men in nearby neighborhoods, it is not surprising that the Bowery was, as social reformer Francis McLean was later to call it, "a man's street." Or, more precisely, a white man's street. Many vice districts were interracial, but the Bowery was unusual in its faint black presence. The theater audiences were mostly white men, and many of the saloons and gambling halls were for white male patrons only. Although most customers were men from nearby working-class neighborhoods, its attractions also lured middle-class New Yorkers and visitors from outside the city, for whom an expedition to the legendary street was a must. Noting that "men set the tone," Christine Stansell has also called attention to the white working-class women who were a part of the Bowery scene, promenading in their bright dresses and shawls. With so many bachelors in the area, it is not surprising that less respectable women were also present. The street was virtually unique among vice districts in having relatively few brothels actually located on or near it (most were to the west), but many prostitutes cruised the Bowery, and they were often found in the infamous third tier of its theaters.[10]

The saloons, theaters, and street scene were not the only things that made the Bowery distinctive—there was a character to the street, a spirit. Mathews noted that "in personal deportment, the Bowery people are perfectly independent—every man for himself. . . . They are as near to a primitive state as people in a great city can be, their original traits pretty much as they come from the hand of nature." Mathews may have been referring in part to the many workers in the crowd, oblivious to middle-class decorum. Yet Mathews may have also been suggesting that the Bowery was a place where the rules that governed the rest of society seemed suspended or at least loosened (with the obvious exception of racial attitudes), where nonconformity flourished, and where standards of behavior were more lenient. The more fastidious attire that accompanied reformed male demeanor, for instance, was not required on the Bowery. "You needn't trouble yourself to put on a coat when you go into the street[.] . . . [N]o one will cut you for that breach of etiquette."[11]

"The old Bowery was a street of carnival," one reporter remembered. It had a reputation for rowdiness and as a site of male revelry, pranks, and brawling. A famous early incident that helped shape the street's unrestrained reputation occurred on New Year's Day, a traditional day for male mayhem, in 1828. It began as a giant charivari. A large crowd of men, said to number four thousand, gathered on the Bowery in the evening with "cracked kettles, drums, rattles, horns, &c." They then "commenced their orgy," remembered Gabriel Furman. They pelted a tavern with lime and flour until it was white, then seized a Conestoga wagon and started down the Bowery. They routed the watchmen "in the genuine thwak '*um*' style," Furman recalled, and then began a frenzied, anarchic spree of destruction that groups of men in this period sometimes engaged in. Signs were torn down and barrels, carts, carriages, or anything else in their way was smashed. This seemingly mindless havoc then gave way to more focused, if no less pleasurable, violence. The mob demolished all the windows, doors, and seats of an African American church and attacked all the blacks they came on. They continued downtown, running riot, finally ending up at the Battery. In the future Bowery sprees would be less tumultuous, but the street would long be associated with revelry and brawling. Although male fighting was on the wane in most places, on the Bowery, Junius Henri Browne discovered in the 1860s, "fighting is always a proposal to be received, and is generally welcome to someone within the sound of your voice." By stigmatizing jolly conduct, the crusade for moral reform and self-improvement had given it an important symbolic significance. A geographic area given over to drinking, gambling, fighting, and theaters was now by definition the antithesis of respectability.[12]

The peculiar demographic and residential patterns of the lower wards made the Bowery America's largest and most significant urban moral region. No other city came even close until the 1880s, when Chicago's burgeoning vice district challenged it. But virtually every urban area had, by the end of the Civil War, its neighborhood of theaters, gambling halls, saloons, and brothels. Philadelphia lacked a boardinghouse district, so the demographic impetus was weaker there than in New York. Still, although its vice districts were never quite as lusty as Manhattan's, they were significant nonetheless. Because of the hostility of Quakers to the stage, several theaters had been built on South Street, which was outside the city until a 1854 consolidation. The street neighborhood became "a haven for those who shunned orthodox customs" made up of a jumble of saloons, cheap theaters, used-clothing shops, groceries, dance halls, and gambling, billiard, and prostitution houses. In marked contrast with the overwhelmingly white Bowery scene, there was a strong black presence in "Moya," and racial clashes were frequent.[13]

Chicago's vice districts eventually came to eclipse the Bowery. The first moral region to arise was the Sands along Lake Michigan just north of the city, but Chicago mayor "Long John" Wentworth took advantage of an 1857 dogfight that lured the gamblers and saloon keepers outside of town and demolished the gambling houses and bordellos. Then, in 1861, when the Civil War halted traffic on the Mississippi, unemployed riverboat gamblers converged on Chicago and established Gambler's Row on Randolph Street, also known as "the Hair-trigger Block," which became the city's next gambling center. Dubbed the "Wickedest City in the United States" by the war's end, vice in Chicago continued to flourish after 1865. More than in New York, visitors propelled Chicago's disorderly district. The city's role as a railroad hub allowed it to draw patrons from all over the central United States, a vast hinterland of men looking for drink, gambling, sex, and excitement. "Chicago was 'wide open,'" one newspaperman remembered. "It was not far removed from a western mining camp." By the 1870s there were twenty "first-class" gambling halls and dozens of less elegant ones in Chicago. "The Store," as it was jokingly called, the luxurious downtown casino run by famed gambler Mike McDonald, became one of the most celebrated gambling palaces in the country. Satan's Mile developed on the South Side in the 1880s, centered around the Levee, and became the city's—and eventually the nation's—most infamous vice region. The Levee's "resorts"—whorehouses—were the chief attraction, but in the diversity of its entertainments, it equaled its New York counterpart. One Chicagoan recalled its "drug stores, blacksmith shops, oyster bars, barrel house saloons, sailor's free and easies, livery stables, gambling joints, dance halls, Chinese laundries, pawn shops, flop houses, basement barber shops, tintype galleries[,] . . . penny arcades, fake auctions, shooting galleries and newsstands selling obscene books." Although the Bowery was the first and most culturally significant moral region, it was far from the only one.[14]

"I'M A B'HOY AND I'M IN FOR A MUSS"

Part of the reason the Bowery caught the popular interest was the fascination with the denizens who animated it. In the 1840s the press began to focus attention on a seemingly novel breed of young men known as "b'hoys," who were rowdy in comportment and rough in language. This discourse about b'hoys reveals much about how jolly fellowship was being both preserved and reshaped in urbanizing America. The b'hoys' hallmark was fighting. B'hoys were not found everywhere but were limited to the "large cities and thinly settled places" that had so concerned reformer William Alcott, places where jolly fellowship was flourishing. The Bowery b'hoy was the most celebrated specimen of the type, but there were b'hoys in other cities and on the frontier as well. Philadelphia was noted for the toughness of their b'hoys. "I'm a b'hoy in the Spring Garden style, . . . I'm a b'hoy and I'm in for a muss" (a fight) went a song of the day. Baltimore had b'hoys—"I'm one of the *b'hoys*—an out and out Fell's Pinter," declares a character in William T. Thompson's *Major Jones' Sketches of Travel* (1843). B'hoys were also found in the West. In 1847 a western traveler referred to "the *sans ceremonie* peculiar to the 'b'hoys' of the frontier." On his way to California during the gold rush, Ohioan Peter Decker encountered "Capt. Goodhue one of the 'B'hoys' . . . , a 'Mountain Man.'" The b'hoy was not unique to the Bowery, but they were so common there that they became identified with the locality.[15]

"Bowery *Boys*" were not new; they had been around since the eighteenth century. Gangs composed of young men had been an established feature of city life since the eighteenth century, and New York had "Bowery Boys," "Broadway Boys," and "Boys" from virtually every neighborhood. But "Bowery *B'hoys*" were something more than gang members; they represented a lifestyle. The word can be traced to an English farce called *Beulah Spa; or, The Two B'hoys* (1833) that opened at the Bowery Theater in 1834 and featured unruly, impertinent teenage brothers. The play was a hit, and "b'hoy" passed into the language as the byword for disorderly young men, especially those who loved to brawl. The Bowery B'hoy exploded into national consciousness in 1848 both on stage and in literature. Benjamin Baker's comic theater sketch about a brawling volunteer fireman named Mose proved sensationally popular. Baker quickly expanded it into a full-length hit play, *A Glance at New York* (1848). George Foster's series "New York in Slices," which featured b'hoys, ran in the *New York Tribune* for three months in 1848, and in 1849 it was published as a book.[16]

The plot of *A Glance at New York*, which details the efforts of a volunteer fireman named Mose to save an upstate greenhorn from city sharpers, was hackneyed, but actor Frank Chanfrau's true-to-life performance made the play a triumph. Mose's distinctive appearance immediately marked him as a b'hoy—wide suspenders, polished boots, a cigar clenched in his teeth, and, the b'hoys' emblem, "soaplocked" hair, greased down, long in front of the ears and short in back. Mose came from a long line of disorderly male characters in novels and plays, yet he also represented a new urban type emerging in working-class neighborhoods east of the Bowery. He is a native-born worker, a butcher by trade; he is, Moses says of himself, "a little raw." Both butchers and firemen had a reputation for fighting, and the fame of prizefighter Tom Hyer, a former meat cutter, had indelibly connected butchering and brawling in the public mind. Mose's love of a good fight—a "muss"—is his most conspicuous characteristic: "If I don't have a muss soon, I'll spile." One scene ends with this stage direction: "*Mose upsets bench and pitches into Jake—General row, stove upset, &c.*" Despite his unruliness, Mose is a sympathetic character. He is a brave volunteer fireman and a loyal friend to his chum Syksey, and he treats his girlfriend, Lize, respectfully. Mose explains that "the fire-boys may be a little rough outside, but they're all right here. [Touches breast.]"[17]

The play became, in the words of George C. D. Odell, the great chronicler of the New York theater, "one of the greatest successes ever known in the history of the New York stage." Genteel critics such as William K. Northall were disgusted at this "unmitigated conglomeration of vulgarity and illiteracy," but they admitted that audiences loved it, and Northall noted that "nothing was heard, sung or talked about but Mose." A newspaper exclaimed that "it is now impossible to talk or write of life in New York without a Mose." *A Glance at New York* was only the first of a series of Mose plays; it was followed by such works as *New York as It Is* (1848), *Mose in California* (1849), *A Glance at Philadelphia* (1848), *Mose in a Muss* (1849), *Mose in France* (1851), and *Mose's Visit to the Arab Girls* (1848). Mose was something of an urban Davy Crockett, popular not just in New York but all over the country: Chanfrau may have played the role four thousand times. Twelve-year-old William Dean Howells in Martin's Ferry, Ohio, adored Mose and even dreamed of playing the role himself one day.[18]

The fascination with b'hoys was further fueled by George Foster's urban sketches for the *New York Tribune*. *New York by Gas-Light* (1850), a collection that dealt extensively with b'hoys and their female counterpart "g'hals," was a tremendous success, selling over two hundred thousand copies, making it one of the era's best sellers. Edward Z. C. Judson, who used the pen name "Ned Buntline," wrote Mose and Lize into his *The Mysteries and Miseries of New York* (1848), which he followed with *The B'hoys of New York* (1850). Their popularity made Buntline's literary reputation. As they publicized the b'hoy, Foster and other writers struggled to gauge this seemingly novel urban type. It was generally agreed that most b'hoys were manual workers, but writer Cornelius Mathews was convinced that the b'hoy was not simply the representative of a social class, noting that b'hoys are found "sprinkled in every company, less rarely, it is true, as you

Playbill from the Chatham Theatre, 1848, listing Frank Chanfrau as Mose in *New York as It Is*. Mose is watching a dance contest among blacks in Catherine Market. The Harvard Theatre Collection, Houghton Library.

ascend the social scale." Northall agreed, describing the city's b'hoys as extending "from the complete rowdy . . . to the intelligent young mechanic, who only seeks an occasional 'lark.'" The g'hal was also most often working class, and with her bright dress and urban slang, she too became a fixture of metropolitan sketches in the late 1840s.[19]

George Foster's groundbreaking urban journalism in the *Tribune* did much to establish the uniqueness of New York life in American consciousness. Foster not only heightened public awareness of the b'hoy but also provided the most detailed analysis of him. Foster reports how, like a naturalist, he ventured into saloons and firehouses in the Bowery region to observe the b'hoy in his native habitat. Foster helped develop the "sunshine and shadow" approach that dominated writing about American cities for most of the nineteenth century, and his New York was a city of contrasts. Three geographical areas of New York symbolized the city's three social groups: Broadway exemplified the elite and the Five Points neighborhood represented the degraded, mostly immigrant, poor. Standing between these extremes and mediating them was the Bowery, the locus of "the American b'hoy, and g'hal."[20]

Although most b'hoys were manual workers, b'hoyishness, Foster believed, did not really originate on the job. Rather it was a deliberate choice, a comportment forged in public performance on the street. Foster's report on the b'hoy is mixed. Their sociability led to excessive drinking, "the worst feature in the character of the b'hoy." The b'hoy's bellicosity was his trademark. They were fighting constantly among themselves and with others. "A good strong 'muss' is the only safety-valve through which can escape their immense exuberance of animal spirits," explained Foster. But they brawl more often in fun than in anger: "A fight is a capital joke, and a crown is cracked as though it might be a conundrum." The b'hoy is a great humorist. "His strongest passion seems fun," according to Foster, and "he revels in a spirit of broad coarse humor, sparing nothing in its way, and finding its delight in hard knocks as well as droll conceits." B'hoys are loyal friends, "good, unselfish frolicsome creatures," "brave [but] easily led astray." The g'hal is described less precisely—Foster notes that "the g'hal is as independent in her tastes and habits" as the b'hoy himself but spends most space describing her flamboyant dress.[21]

There had been many rowdy young men in cities, towns, and villages for decades, and soaplocked hair had been worn since the 1830s. Why did the image of the Bowery b'hoy impose itself so powerfully in national culture in the 1840s? The answer has in part to do with New York's ascent to dominance in American publishing at the same time the Bowery milieu was developing. Magazines and

"The B'hoys," *Rural Repository*, 11 March 1848. This picture accompanied an article on b'hoys reprinted from the *New York Sunday Mercury*.

weekly editions of the city's daily newspapers were read throughout the country and confirmed the city's preeminence in cultural production. But it was not just a question of supply; there was also demand. Certainly, much of the media curiosity with Bowery b'hoys was the result of the very rapid growth of cities in this era, and debate about b'hoys was part of a larger discourse about the prospects and perils of urban life. Yet for all the novelty of large cities in American culture, the b'hoy was intriguingly familiar. With his disorderly behavior the b'hoy no doubt reminded many readers and theatergoers of the rowdy regulars of the tavern crowd. The b'hoy was the antithesis of the sober and restrained male that was becoming the ideal in the wake of religious revivals and temperance. He was really only an urban jolly fellow—a drinker, fighter, and joker. The new urban type was, paradoxically, an old rural type. And, for that matter, an old urban type as well. Two decades earlier such disorderly comportment probably would have attracted little notice, but now as temperance and the cult of self-control spread, the conduct of the b'hoy fascinated Americans. The g'hal, unlike the b'hoy, seems genuinely new and to have been limited to New York City. The g'hal never seems to have quite caught the popular imagination like the b'hoy. Readers, perhaps, could more easily identify with the b'hoy, who offered a traditional image of masculinity, than they could with the less familiar and more unsettling g'hal.[22]

"THE HEADQUARTERS OF THE SPORTING FRATERNITY"

Until the 1820s and 1830s, jolly fellowship was widely tolerated even though it diverged from mainstream values in various ways. But with what Greeley called the "great though silent change . . . in public sentiment," traditional male values and activities came under fire. Cities, most especially New York City, not only kept jolly values alive but concentrated and intensified them and began to adapt them to an urbanizing society. New York's lower wards became a cultural crucible refining jolly fellowship into something close to a counterculture. No longer could respectable men openly drink, fight, and gamble. These activities, nevertheless, remained profoundly appealing for many, and new urban institutions and male roles emerged that allowed men to participate in them in new ways. Like so much else in antebellum America, jolly fellowship became commercialized and professionalized. The era in which fighting and gambling ceased to be an ordinary part of daily life for most men saw the advent of prizefighting and gambling houses as well as the rise of the "sporting man," a gambler-politician who was a sort of professional jolly fellow. What were once informal, spontaneous activities carried on by men everywhere now could be occupations for experts, and the appeal of pugilism could be satisfied by reading accounts of battles between professional fighters.

Boxing became nationally popular in the 1840s. Early pugilists were mostly men who had achieved success as local bullies in set fights; instead of fighting just for honor, they now fought for stakes. A New York butcher named Jacob Hyer in his later years claimed he fought the first American prizefight in 1816 with an English sailor. Although prizefighting was illegal, and early boxers faced prosecution for assault, other fights followed in the 1820s, and in the mid-1830s New York emerged as the undisputed center of American pugilism. The development in Manhattan of big-time gambling helped fighters in raising stakes for matches, and extensive coverage by the *New York Herald* and the sporting press consolidated the city's predominance in the sport.[23]

"In the year 1840 the fighting spirit took a sudden start," the *New York Herald* recalled. This upsurge coincided with the arrival in the United States of James "Yankee" Sullivan, who was to become the country's first professional prizefighter. Born in 1813 near Cork, Sullivan (one of his many aliases; his real name was apparently James Ambrose) was a petty criminal and prizefighter. Convicted of burglary, he was transported to the penal colony at Botany Bay in Australia. Sullivan eventually worked his way to America and then back to England—hence the nickname "Yankee"—where he resumed his fighting career. "Sully" returned to the United States in 1841, and his knowledge of prizefighting gained in England led to a rapid refinement of the sport in America. His career stumbled, however, when he helped promote an 1842 match in which his protégé Chris Lilly killed Tom McCoy. The death sent Sullivan into prison and prizefighting into eclipse until the late 1840s.[24]

Sullivan's expertise permitted him to easily vanquish early opponents, and distraught native-born Americans began to "cast their eyes about the pugilistic circle to find a man capable of holding up the honor of the Stars and Stripes against the encroachments of the Green Flag of the Emerald Isle." Their hopes came to focus on Jacob Hyer's son Thomas. The much-anticipated Sullivan-Hyer showdown took place in 1849 for a huge stake of $10,000. Dodging legal authorities by sailing around Chesapeake Bay, on 7 February Hyer and Sullivan landed on the Eastern Shore accompanied by about two hundred friends and fans. Along with a few nearby residents, they were the only people to actually see the contest. It was remarkable that prizefighting was able to attain great popularity even though before 1860 probably only a total of a few thousand people in America had ever seen a match. In a short, intense bout, Hyer was victorious, making him a national hero. The clash raised popular interest to an extraordinary level, where it would remain, with the exception of a post–Civil War lull, for the rest of the century. Professional fighting spread to Philadelphia in the late 1840s and to New Orleans and San Francisco in the next decade.[25]

It is almost impossible to overstate how much interest major prizefights attracted in the nineteenth century and how famous top prizefighters were. It was a journalistic commonplace that a championship match would sell more newspapers than any other event, including a presidential election. The public enthusiasm over the Yankee Sullivan–Thomas Hyer bout in 1849 illustrates how the sport captivated Americans. In New York, the *Herald* believed, the excitement rivaled that of the Mexican War, noting that "throughout the city . . . excitement" was "tremendous" as word spread that the fight was imminent and that nothing "has been heard or talked about for several days past but the fight." Crowds swarmed outside newspaper buildings, and taverns and saloons were jammed as New Yorkers awaited word of the outcome. In Philadelphia it was the same story. The *Public Ledger* reported that the fight "was almost the sole topic of conversation in our streets, and caused hundreds to congregate in the vicinity of newspaper offices for the purposes of obtaining particulars" of the outcome. Taverns in Baltimore were jammed with men "in feverish anxiety," and rumors in the street were "as thick as blackberries," the *Sun* reported. In San Francisco, throngs met every ship from eastern ports in the early summer of 1849. A passenger on the *Leonore* that arrived in San Francisco harbor in July vividly remembered the scene in a poem:

We knew they longed to meet us,
To hear the news from home
Of fathers, mothers, sisters
They'd left, so far to roam
. . . .
And now their greeting voices
Across the sea rang clear,
Who won the fight, who won the fight?
I'll bet it was Tom Hyer.

No! Yankee Sullivan's the boy,
Another crowd would cry,
How many rounds, how many rounds?
He'd lick his man or die.[26]

The popular interest in prizefighting peaked with the 1860 battle between American John C. Heenan and the English champion Thomas Sayers. Born in Troy, New York, Heenan went to California during the gold rush. After briefly working in Benicia as a blacksmith—thus to be forever dubbed "the Benicia Boy"—he returned to New York City in 1857 to make his career as a professional fighter. Reports that his match with Sayers was finalized caused a sensation throughout the country. "Never in the history of nations," Thomas Bigelow Paine remembered, "has there been a sporting event that even approached it in public importance." Newspapers printed article after article. Heenan's departure for

England was a major public event; there were stories from the training camps of both men and speculation on the organizers' plans to elude the police. Tension rose as the entire nation awaited word of the outcome. On 28 April 1860 the news arrived that the forty-two-round fight had been ended by the crowd pushing into the ring, preventing, Americans believed, Heenan's impending victory. Interest reached an almost hysterical level according to the *New York Clipper*:

> The Charleston Convention was almost forgotten. Scarcely any work outside of the newspaper world was done on that day. On Saturday night the city went wild with enthusiasm. . . . The fight, and the heroic conduct of both Heenan and Sayers[,] was the topic of conversation at the family fireside, in the markets, stores and everywhere. Go where we might, it was nothing but fight talk. Fight here, fight there and fight everywhere.

Even genteel publications gave the match huge play—*Harper's Weekly* denounced the "bloody, brutal and blackguard prize-fight in England" but ran a two-page illustration of it. Heenan became a national hero. When English war correspondent William Howard Russell arrived in 1861 to cover the Civil War, he was amazed to discover that Americans seemed more interested in rehashing Heenan-Sayers than discussing the impending conflict between the states.[27]

Part of prizefighting's appeal was as symbolic ethnic and national competition. The notion that a contest was between two individuals, one of whom happened to be an Irish immigrant or an Englishman and the other of whom happened to be a native-born American, was incomprehensible to most nineteenth-century men. Yankee Sullivan *was* Ireland. The Heenan-Sayers fight was America versus England, part of an intense sporting rivalry between the two nations that also included the 1851 victory by the yacht *America*.[28]

The main reason, however, for prizefighting's tremendous appeal was simply that fighting remained fascinating to many men. Indeed, the sport's role as symbolic national and ethnic competition may have been as much a justification for interest in boxing as a cause of its popularity. The all-Irish Yankee Sullivan–John Morrissey battle in 1853 attracted almost as much interest as the Sullivan-Hyer fight. The public fighting tradition, waning but still vibrant in many places, was the foundation of the sport's appeal. Most prizefighters had begun fighting in neighborhood brawls. John Heenan had led the West Troy boys in their battles with Troy gangs in the early 1840s. And prizefighters often battled outside the ring—most seem to have liked to fight. The Thomas Hyer–Yankee Sullivan prizefight had its origin in a confrontation between the two at a drinking house at the corner of Park Place and Broadway, where they happened to run into each other.

Neither man could back down without a humiliating loss of honor, and the furious barroom melee left Sullivan bloodied. "It is scarcely possible to describe the excitement this event occasioned. . . . For five or six days nothing else was talked of in all circles," a biography of Sullivan related. "Broadway swarmed with crowds which concentrated from all quarters to catch a glance, while parading from one drinking house to another, of the man who had whipped Yankee Sullivan." Rough-and-tumble champions still could receive great acclaim: New York's Bill Poole was considered by many the greatest fighting man in the city in the 1850s—better than Hyer, better than Heenan—even though he never fought a prizefight. Yet, though it was built on a popular fighting tradition, its supporters argued that boxing actually contributed to the waning of individual male fighting. *The American Fistiana* (1849), an early history of the sport, claimed that rather than stimulating brawling as critics alleged, prizefighting's prominence actually had a "marked influence in the repression of all kinds of rowdyism." Prizefights aided men in controlling their bellicose propensities by allowing them to vicariously participate in matches between professionals. Instead of fighting themselves, men could read the round-by-round, blow-by-blow accounts of bouts that newspapers provided.[29]

The "sporting saloon," a distinctive nineteenth-century institution, exemplified the popular fascination with pugilists. Boxing was illegal in most places, and matches were staged more or less clandestinely, so income from fighting was meager. Prizefighters therefore opened saloons where their celebrity would attract customers eager to rub elbows with a fighting man. It was a jolly fellow's delight: your work was to lounge around the bar. Yankee Sullivan's Sawdust House in New York City in the 1840s was among the earliest sporting houses. Sullivan's place was said by the *Clipper* to have been "continually thronged with supporters of all classes" hoping to meet the great man and perhaps even get to spar with him. "Park Row and the Bowery teemed with 'sporting houses,'" prizefighter Owen Kildare remembered. Sporting saloons spread to Boston, Philadelphia, and other cities. A typical sporting saloon had a bar, a ring for boxing exhibitions, billiard tables, and tables for faro and other card games. Some houses had pits where dogs and gamecocks could fight and where badgers and other animals were baited. (Virtually all major prizefighters owned fighting dogs.) Gribben's sporting "hostelrie" on the Bowery, for instance, had a sparring room and files of past issues of the *Spirit of the Times*, an American sporting and horse-racing paper. Most were elaborately decorated with *objects sportif*—Gribben's featured a gallery of prints of famous past and present prizefighters. The decorations of another "celebrated Sporting-house in New York" included two stuffed fighting dogs that had been preserved after they killed each other in competition. Many establishments employed what the press called "pretty waiter girls," who were, if the price was right, available for sex.[30]

Like prizefighting, gambling became institutionalized. A passion for gambling once had been fulfilled by wagering at cards or billiards in taverns; now men could indulge their fancy in gambling houses and billiard parlors run especially for that purpose. The first gambling halls in America seem to have appeared in New Orleans in the 1820s or perhaps even earlier. A crackdown by authorities in 1835 curbed New Orleans wagering, and Manhattan eclipsed the Crescent City as America's principal gambling center. Pat Herne and Henry Colton opened the earliest "first-class" casinos in the city in the 1830s, and others followed in the 1840s. An exposé of gaming in the 1850s announced that "the city of New York is the great headquarters of the gamblers in this country." The rules set by the city's gaming establishment came to be followed nationwide. Park Place, Barclay, and Vesey streets west of Broadway emerged as the center of New York first-class gambling. These fancy establishments had elegantly furnished salons for faro and roulette and smaller rooms where poker and other card games were played. Most set out a lavish free banquet for patrons. Bettors at such places included members of the city's elite, businessmen visiting the city, and "rich young rakes and spendthrifts" as well as professional gamblers. Second-class and third-class houses opened all over the lower wards where less well-heeled customers could "buck the tiger," that is, play faro, in the slang of the day. In such places players were said to be bilked with stacked dealing boxes. By 1867 one magazine claimed that there was "scarcely a street without a gambling-house" in New York.[31]

The first billiard saloon in the city opened on Park Row in the 1820s, and by the 1840s there were a number of large, ornate billiard parlors in the lower wards. The most famous of these fancy billiards establishments was on Ann Street, and it became one of "the headquarters of the sporting fraternity." By the 1850s admission was charged to watch games between top players, and the matches were covered by the press. Billiard competitions soon were dominated by professionals, most famously Michael Phelan from Troy, who became the sport's first star.[32]

Other cities soon followed New York's lead in developing institutionalized gambling. It was estimated there were twenty gambling "hells" in Boston in 1833, and in 1844 Lyman Brittain brought first-class gambling to the city. New York gambler Joe Hall opened an elegant casino in Philadelphia in 1853, but first-class houses never flourished there the way they did in other cities. Gambler John Morris believed that wagering in the City of Brotherly Love "was under the control of the rowdy element" who ran the second- and third-class houses

"Free and Easy at Country McCleester's, in Doyer Street," *New York Clipper*, 29 January 1859. This sporting saloon, operated by prizefighter John "Country" McCleester, was one of the best known in the country. Note the pictures of a dogfight, prizefight, and racehorse on the wall. English in origin, the "Free and Easy" was a fascinating nineteenth-century male ritual. According to a 17 March 1860 article in the *New York Leader*, traditionally the participants gathered at the tavern or saloon on Wednesday and Saturday nights. The "president" then called the meeting to order and a vice president was elected. Drinks were served. It was the president's prerogative to begin the first song, which, by custom in New York City, was "Old Domestic Drama." Then came a toast such as "luck in a bag and shake it out as you want it." They alternated between toasts and songs the rest of the evening. Jerome Robbins Dance Division, The New York Public Library for the Performing Arts, Astor, Lenox, and Tilden Foundations.

and used strong-arm tactics to demand such large payoffs that genteel gambling houses found it hard to make a profit. Washington, D.C., with its concentrations of politicians—"men away from home"—had a particularly large and vigorous vice district. Edward Pendleton's House of Fortune on Pennsylvania Avenue was one of the nation's earliest fashionable houses and among the most famous. Although elegant casinos like the House of Fortune attracted widespread public attention, only four of Washington's seventeen major gambling houses were labeled first class. By the end of the Civil War there were said to be one hundred gambling houses and hundreds of professional gamblers in the nation's capital. In New Orleans the 1835 crackdown proved only a temporary hindrance, and by the 1840s gambling was thriving again. Herbert Asbury cites an estimate that there were five hundred gambling places in the city, including thirteen first-class houses. San Francisco, with a population of approximately forty-thousand in 1852, had forty-six gambling houses.[33]

"A COMBINATION OF GAMBLER, HORSEMAN AND POLITICIAN"

In the 1840s the first New York lower-ward luminaries emerged. These celebrity b'hoys, or "sporting men" as they came to be called, embodied qualities that other men, and not just men with a taste for a jolly lifestyle, found intriguing. They were living a male fantasy of a life of drinking and gambling. Many continued the jolly fellows' tradition by getting involved in politics. In essence they were a kind of professional jolly fellow and as such became New York legends. There had always been an element of performance in jolly fellowship—the village bully strutting down the street—and these men presented themselves to the public as the epitome of jolly existence. As New York consolidated its dominance of cultural production, some became nationally famous. The turbulent careers of Mike Walsh, Isaiah Rynders, and Thomas Hyer suggest how the Bowery milieu was becoming a counterculture in which men who embraced jolly fellowship could not only live but thrive. In later years their lives and the New York of the 1840s took on the aura of a kind of foundation myth for the postbellum sporting fraternity.

Politician-editor Mike Walsh was one of the most colorful personalities of his era. Born near Cork, Ireland, in 1810, he emigrated to New York where he apprenticed as a printer and "ran" with volunteer fire company Number Thirty-four, the renowned Howard Hose. He soon attracted notice. Part of his appeal was good looks. He had, according to the *New York Ledger*, a "handsome[,] . . . open, honest face, and a fine intellectual looking head." Walsh worked for several newspapers and became well known as the owner and editor of the vituperative *Subterranean* between 1843 and 1847. Walsh was a Democrat, but he shrewdly steered his own course around the myriad city and state party factions, most of the time remaining independent of Tammany. His popularity among workingmen and his gang of followers, organized in 1840 as the Spartan Association, gave him enough influence to win election to the state assembly in 1846 and in 1852 to the House of Representatives. After his return to New York, he was "more or less connected to the city press" until his 1859 death.[34]

Walsh's political accomplishments, however, do little to suggest why he became so celebrated—and so reviled. His brilliant oratory as the angry champion of the city's workingmen was part of the reason for his fame. Walsh's rhetoric was a peculiar mixture of republican attacks on luxury and growing social inequality combined with boisterous, profane vilification of those whom he felt were not true friends of the workingman, which seemed to include at one time or another just about everyone not named Mike Walsh. One main target was the "jugglers, wire pullers and office beggars of Tammany Hall"—"Boys! Look out for them!" His invective was personal and relentless: city recorder Frederick Talmadge was described as a "beastly and polluted old vagabond," while *New York Sun* editor Moses Beach was "a lecherous lover of black wenches" (Walsh threw racial slurs around freely). Walsh's arrests and trials for libel provided him ongoing publicity. When he was released from prison after an 1844 conviction, fifty thousand (or so he claimed) of "the subterranean populace of New York" gathered in City Hall Park to greet him.[35]

Walsh's renown was based in part on his unquestioned devotion to the city's workingmen, in part on his superheated oratory, and in part on his carefully crafted reputation as one of the jolliest fellows in the city. Walsh portrayed himself and the Spartans as real men, men who used their hands at work and were not afraid to use their fists in politics. "You have *men* to contend with here!" he bellowed at Tammany hecklers in an 1841 political meeting. Walsh's opponents were, he suggested, less virile than the Spartans. A favorite rhetorical technique was to focus on their diet: they were "milk and water men," "walking vegetables," "fish-blooded calves who live on bran and water." Walsh and his gang, in contrast, were meat-eating, liquor-drinking, hot-blooded men. The combativeness was not just rhetorical. The Spartan Association had in its ranks a number of fighting men, including at one point boxers Yankee Sullivan and John "Country" McCleester, and Walsh's roughnecks tried, sometimes with success, to bully and brawl their way to victory in party caucuses and even elections. In an 1842 local election, the Spartans attacked men distributing ballots for a Sixth Ward candidate they opposed. Walsh, despite his Irish heritage, considered himself a "true American," and the fight escalated into a full-scale riot between the Spartans and Irish.[36]

Walsh was not ashamed of his reputation for frolicking and fighting; indeed, he emphasized it—the b'hoyish persona was part of his appeal. Mike—not Michael—bragged of his own alcoholic intake in the *Subterranean*. Not only did he lead the Spartan Association in its political brawls, but, despite being a small man, he also engaged in some well-publicized personal fistfights, including one in Washington with James Lindsay Seward, a Georgia congressman. He enhanced his bellicose image by associating with prizefighters and was one of the referees at the 1842 Yankee Sullivan–Thomas Secor fight. Much was made of Walsh's friendship with prizefighter Thomas Hyer. Walsh often drank with Hyer at the Hone House on Broadway opposite City Hall Park, and Walsh was among the small group of men who actually witnessed Hyer's Eastern Shore prizefight with Yankee Sullivan in 1849. Like his pugilist friends, he was an avid gamecock fighter. Rumors connecting Walsh with Kate Ridgely, a "dashing looking woman" who was one of the city's best-known prostitutes, enhanced his virile image.[37]

Walsh never shied away from writing about himself and sometimes recounted his nocturnal rambles for the edification of *Subterranean* readers. An 1846 column entitled "A Glorious Time" relates how he began one evening by going to a Bowery saloon where he fell in with "Country," presumably boxer John McCleester, and three other men. They went on to another drinking place where "all the boys were in perfect ecstasies at seeing me." After an evening drinking and singing on the Bowery, Walsh made his way at dawn to Red Hook in Brooklyn to witness a rough-and-tumble fight, staged "merely to settle a dispute." After enjoying the "nineteen well-contested rounds," he returned to the city, stopping first at the Saracen's Head Tavern in Dey Street and then a Chatham Street saloon before finally making his way back to the Bowery. Walsh's critique of the emerging industrial economy seems in part motivated by his sense that the sober, businesslike ethos of the age was suffocating the traditional egalitarian, tavern-based lifestyle he so loved. Walsh strongly defended male jolly revelry from criticism by clerics and temperance advocates.[38]

It was Walsh's status as the most tireless and original practical joker of his era that cinched his reputation as one of New York's jolliest fellows. There were other celebrated pranksters in the city, such as Blaisus "Blaze" More, the legendary fire department joker who once hired a man to whitewash the marble city hall. Despite such competition the *New York Leader* proclaimed that "Mike Walsh was in eminent degree the best practical joker of his time." The *New York Times* in its

1859 obituary noted that Walsh "was exceedingly fond of practical jokes, and was accustomed to indulge this propensity in this respect on all occasions, whether in legislative halls or drinking saloons." Walsh's most celebrated prank, and among the most famous American pranks of the century, was the "Frank McLoughlin sell," which, the *Leader* declared, kept New York "in a fever of excitement for nearly a week." When McLoughlin, a noted sporting man, returned to New York from the California gold rush, Walsh went around to saloons spreading the word that McLoughlin had "many letters and presents to the boys in New York from old acquaintances in California," recalled James Fairfax McLaughlin. Walsh directed them to Kelly's saloon in Bayard Street where he said McLoughlin awaited them. Before they arrived there, Walsh told the bartender to tell them McLoughlin was at the Ivy Green on Elm Street; "from the Ivy Green," they were directed "to the Carlton House, from the Carlton House to the Franklin House and so on." The *Leader* claimed that at one time five thousand men were engaged in this wild goose chase through the lower wards.[39]

Walsh's jolly reputation was a significant part of his appeal. After he died in 1859 at age forty-four, some newspapers suggested his short life exemplified the evils of alcohol. A broadside ballad quickly appeared defending Walsh's character. To the tune of the traditional drinking song "Rosin the Bow," the lyrics noted the press reports that Mike "indulged in sthrong dhrink":

Well, fhot if he did? don't yees know-o-o
That a dhrop always dhrives away woe,
An I'm shure a small taste av the craythur
Would keep out the cowld here also.

The *Leader* in 1860 ran a series called "Anecdotes of Mike Walsh" that recounted his most famous practical jokes. For instance, he had once sent a message to the city coroner that "Col. Owl of New Orleans has died." When the coroner arrived he found a stuffed owl in bed. In later years the *Clipper* and even *Harper's New Monthly Magazine* printed tales of Walsh's pranks, which suggests that some better remembered him as a jolly fellow than as a working-class tribune.[40]

The careers of Isaiah Rynders and Thomas Hyer demonstrate that in the lower wards it was not only possible to live a jolly lifestyle but to make a living doing so. Walsh's political rival Isaiah Rynders was one of New York's first sporting men, a term with a quite specific meaning in nineteenth-century America. A "sporting man," explained the *New York Tribune*, was "a combination of gambler, horseman and politician—prominent among whom were 'Tom' Hyer, 'Bill' Poole, [and] 'Yankee' Sullivan." *Police Gazette* writer Edward Van Every designated the sporting element as made up of "'shoulder-hitters' [pugilists], dog-fighters, gamblers, actors and politicians." Billiard players could be sporting men. Pimps and confidence men could also be "sports," as they were also called. Members of the theatrical profession, especially minstrels, likewise could be sports. In an era when respectable people condemned the theater, stage performers often identified with gamblers and pugilists as fellow outcasts and associated with the sporting fraternity.[41]

Both the term "sporting man" and the type originated in the early 1840s and by the 1860s were found in every major city. There were professional gamblers early in the century, mostly in the South. But before the 1840s most gambling men, "blacklegs" as they were called, were nomads, traveling from town to town with their gambling paraphernalia and running games in taverns or rented houses. As the "moral revolution" swept the countryside, gamblers filtered into urban areas and settled down. Many jolly fellows had been involved in law enforcement or had held political office, and sporting men extended this heritage. Virtually all sports had a connection to politics, usually as Democrats. Some, like Rynders, were basically professional politicians, while others like Yankee Sullivan lent their support in other ways, most characteristically by providing muscle in caucuses and on election day. Many owned saloons where they and their cohorts, like the tavern crowd before them, spent their time.[42]

Isaiah Rynders was born in 1804 near Troy, New York. In the jolly fellow tradition, every sporting man needed a nickname, and Rynders's was "Captain," owing to his having briefly been the skipper of a Hudson River sloop. "A lithe, dark handsome man" with "a prominent nose and piercing black eyes," Rynders headed west and was said to have been a faro dealer on a Mississippi riverboat. He killed a rival gambler, so the story goes, in Natchez in an 1832 duel with bowie knives and fled to South Carolina where he became the superintendent of a racing stable. Rynders returned to New York in 1840 with a stake from his pursuits in the South and, as the *New York Times* explained, "established himself as a 'sporting man,' and at the same time became identified with Tammany Hall and began to take an active part in politics."[43]

Rynders, according to the *Clipper*, had "a strong love for the card-room and the race-track." Rynders let it be known that he carried a bowie knife, and he engaged in some well-publicized fistfights that enhanced his combative reputation. The Captain eventually purchased a farm in New Jersey where he raised trotting horses that he raced at New York–area tracks. Rynders's opened a saloon, the Arena, adjacent to the Park Theater on Park Row across from City Hall Park. It became the hangout "of many of the leading sporting men of the metropolis," the

Clipper remembered, and a popular rendezvous for "actors, gamblers, pugilists and the like." Rynders also seems to have profited from connections to brothels in the city, using his political leverage to protect them.[44]

Rynders's power burgeoned. An energetic speaker, he used rhetoric that "suited the bhoys exactly," the *Herald* remembered. Like his archrival in the turbulent world of lower-ward politics, Mike Walsh, the Captain mixed Biblical and Shakespearean quotations with invective: "'Boys, I want to tell you that L— is a damned liar,' or 'M— is a notorious scoundrel who wants to get into office to rob you.'" The establishment of the Empire Club, a Democratic political association "first organized principally among sporting men" in 1844, was his most significant accomplishment. Rynders was "as practical and persistent as Walsh was the reverse," wrote reporter Matthew P. Breen, and, the *Leader* explained, the new group "threw the Spartan Band entirely into the shade." At its height, Rynders's organization was, according to the *Herald*, "the strongest political club in the country." Rynders once admitted to journalist Thomas L. Nichols "that we have a good many sporting men and fighting men" in the Empire Club, but he claimed, "that is the worst you can say of us." Whigs and abolitionists, however, did say worse things about the Captain and his club. Rynders, along with Walsh, was one of the first to understand how brute force could be a recipe for political success in the turbulent world of nineteenth-century urban politics.[45]

Election-day brawling had a long Anglo-American tradition, but Rynders used it more systematically to consolidate power than anyone had before. With contingents of prizefighters that included at various times Thomas Hyer, Yankee Sullivan, Chris Lilly, John McCleester, and Charles "Dutch Charley" Duane as well as fire company sluggers like David Scannell, the Empire Club battled to victory in ward-nominating caucuses and disrupted Whig gatherings and rallies. The club's members attacked the "Grand Clay parade" in 1844, and when Yankee Sullivan grabbed the reins of Cornelius Vanderbilt's horse, it was said that the Commodore jumped off and thrashed him. In national politics Rynders aligned with the southern wing of the Democratic Party. If he hated anyone "more than a Whig it was an Abolitionist," reported the *Times*, and he and his supporters delighted in breaking up abolition and Free Soil meetings. Rynders was rewarded by Tammany for his strong-arm tactics in its support. He was made a weigher in the Customs House, and in 1857 Buchanan appointed him United States marshal for the New York district, a top patronage office. Though his authority fell short of later-day politicos like William Tweed and "Honest John" Kelly, Rynders was perhaps New York City's first political boss. The Captain was a friend of actor Edwin Forrest, and Rynders achieved something close to national infamy in 1848 when he allied with fellow sporting man Edward Z. C. Judson—the writer "Ned Buntline"—to incite the demonstrations against Forrest's English rival Charles C. Macready. The result was the Astor Place Riot in which twenty-three were killed. Rynders's gambling and racing background, his popular saloon, his association with pugilists, his truculent reputation, his staunch Democratic politics, and his hard-hitting rhetoric were all part of his manly appeal to Empire Club members and all part of what men in general admired about the Captain.[46]

Prizefighters were an important part of the sporting fraternity, and Thomas Hyer's nickname, "the Chief," suggests his exalted position in the city's sporting world. Son of pioneer prizefighter Jacob Hyer, Tom was raised in the rowdy world of butchers and gangs. His original vocation as a meat cutter is significant. In medieval times, butchers, by violating the traditional taboo against shedding blood, placed themselves, like barber-surgeons, on the margin of social acceptability. Butchers in New York remained a group apart—they were regarded the jolliest, most violent, most racist segment of the city's working class, and it was almost inevitable that b'hoys would be depicted as butchers as often as they were. Butchers were renowned as drinkers even in a heavy-drinking age: alcohol was said to counteract the malign effects of dead meat, and meat cutters from each market had their taverns where they would gather after work. Butchers were noted pranksters. Thomas F. De Voe, himself a former butcher, recalled that Catherine Street Market's butchers included "several 'regular jokers,' full of life and fun, and fun they would have, sometimes at considerable expense." Ernest Keyser, who did the largest business of any butcher in the city from his Washington Market stalls in the 1830s, was famed for his practical jokes. He became something of a legend, and in city slang someone who "kill[ed] for Keyser" (that is, slaughtered beef for Keyser) was a working-class rowdy.[47]

Butchers seemed to revel in blood; it was their vocation and their avocation. Mose, the butcher-hero of the play *A Glance at New York*, brandished this sanguinary symbolism: "Mose: 'What! Yer don't know where de slaughterhouse is yet? Well, drive up Christie Street till you smell blood and dere stop.'" Meat cutters shed blood every day in the markets and seemed less hesitant than other men to shed blood outside it. They were notorious in their love of blood sports, especially dogfighting and bullbaiting. And butchers loved to brawl. They were far more often involved in both collective and individual violence than any other occupational group in the city; it was the hallmark of their subculture. Meat cutters took part in tavern riots, joined antiabolition mobs, attacked wardens trying to round up stray hogs, and were found among theater rioters.[48]

Although Tom Hyer's stint at the Centre Street Market was brief, he was always identified in the public mind as a butcher. Hyer was arrested five times for rioting as a young man. Violence against women seems to have been another part of the butchers' subculture, and in one rampage in 1836, the seventeen-year-old Hyer was part of a gang that demolished a grocery store, attacked three brothels, and raped a prostitute. He was convicted of sexual assault but served only a short sentence. Hyer was clearly a very rough customer, but his 1879 biographer put the best face he could on Tom's ferocious nature, noting that Hyer "was born with a love of fight, whether man, dog or game fowl," alluding to the fact that Hyer was also a dedicated fighter of gamecocks and dogs. Hyer first gained fame in the prize ring in 1841, upholding native honor with his victory over Country McCleester. His 1849 victory over Yankee Sullivan made him America's first athletic star.[49]

Just as Hyer's rise probably helped pave the way for the Mose plays, so the success of the Mose plays probably contributed to the view of Hyer as not just a great fighter but the embodiment of assertive white working-class manliness. Hyer's good looks and fine physique contributed to his towering status. Prizefighters became the gold standard in male beauty, and their bodies were described with loving precision in the press. Yankee Sullivan's torso, the *New York Whip* rhapsodized, had a "symmetry and beauty that we have seldom, if ever seen equaled." Hyer became something of a sex symbol, admired more, it seems, by men than by women. Stories about Hyer consistently described his gorgeous face and magnificent physique; he was "one of the finest looking men of modern times," raved the *Clipper.* Accounts resorted to classical allusions to praise his appearance—Hyer was "the American Achilles"; he was "slim-waisted, beautifully modeled and had the features of a roman senator." Having a fine build was almost essential not only for boxers but for any luminary in the lower-ward sporting and political world. Isaiah Rynders "had good shoulders and was physically powerful." The youthful William Tweed "possessed the physique of a young gladiator," and Tammany chieftain Honest John Kelly had "the thews and sinews of a young Hercules."[50]

People clamored for a glimpse of the Chief. The honor of being the best fighter not just in the neighborhood or village but in the entire country was immense. When the hero walked down Broadway, passersby stopped dead, and "their gaze would follow this tall, commanding figure until it disappeared from view," his friend Dutch Charley Duane remembered. Like many sporting men, Hyer went into the saloon business and opened a barroom next to the Bowery Theater that was "for some time, literally coining money." Men of "all climes and creeds flocked for the privilege of gazing upon Hyer," *Police Gazette* reporter Theodore "The" Allen recalled. Hyer capitalized on his renown by giving sparring exhibitions and even going on stage. When he appeared at the Bowery Theater, hundreds were

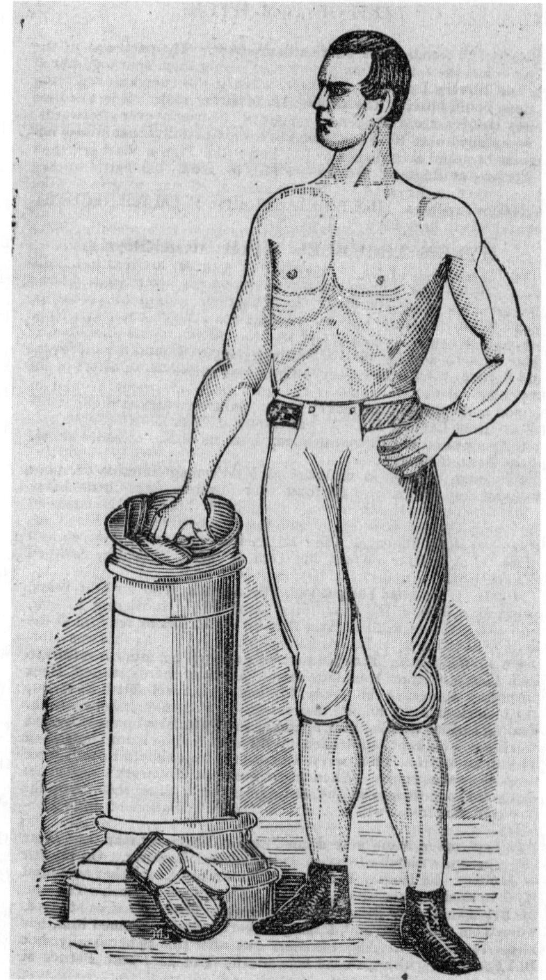

"Tom Hyer in Ring Costume," c. 1850. Hyer was considered one of the handsomest men of the age. In *Life and Battles of Tom Hyer,* comp. Ed. James (New York, 1879). Beinecke Rare Book and Manuscript Library, Yale University.

said to have been turned away. He went on tour, performing in Albany and elsewhere. With his fame and appearance, Hyer was positioned to become a force in city politics. He became one of the many pugilists in the Empire Club, but after a falling out with Rynders, the Chief left the Captain's organization and became part of a loose gang of native-born butchers and other "muscular men" clustered around Washington Market butcher and prizefighter "Boss" William Harrington. Known as the Unionists or the Union Club, these pro-Whig sluggers congregated in a saloon on the other side of the Park Theater from Rynders's Arena and battled the Empire Club on election day. Often urged to run for office—it was widely believed that a seat in Congress was Hyer's for the asking—he always refused.[51]

Hyer, like many other pugilists, went to gold-rush California, and when he returned he found his reputation as best fighting man in the city no longer secure. One challenger was John Morrissey, a swaggering Irish-born tough who came down from Troy in 1848 to make his mark in the New York fighting fraternity. Morrissey's Hibernian background and overbearing manner quickly antagonized Hyer. Police broke up a rough-and-tumble fight between the two, but, despite constant rumors of an impending match, a prizefight was never arranged. There was, in addition, Bill Poole, a native-born competitor, also a former butcher. Despite being handicapped by a small body, Poole was a tremendous fighter. Openly ambitious, he hoped to use his brawling ability to make his mark. He was too scrawny to match Hyer or any good boxer in the ring, but in rough-and-tumble fights "Butcher Bill" was unbeatable; his great quickness enabled him to throw down a rival and "easily keep him there until he cried 'enough,'" Allen wrote in the *Police Gazette*.[52]

Poole turned his attention to provoking the hot-headed Morrissey. After a confrontation in a barroom in July 1854, Morrissey agreed to a set fight. The battle, the most famous rough-and-tumble match in the city's history, took place on the Amos Street Dock for $50 a side. It was short and brutal. Poole was able to throw Morrissey, "and then went at him with fists and feet . . . , gouging out his right eye . . . , [and] cutting head, face, ears," according to the *Tribune*'s breathless account, and Morrissey was forced to submit. The followers of the two men then engaged in a wild free-for-all. Poole's victory over a champion prizefighter created a sensation. A broadside ballad immediately feted the winner: "Oh! Billy Poole! Oh Billy Poole! You are a tip top scholar. / For by the rule of Hyer's school, you made the champion 'holler.'"[53]

Hyer found himself increasingly surpassed in popular esteem. The sociable, handsome Poole, with his "finely chiseled" face and "full and manly" chest, was the man of the hour. Poole quit butchering and became a sporting man, opening a barroom on the Bowery where "men of all stripes and callings from all over the country" came hoping to meet the hero. Like other sporting men, Poole became involved in politics. In origin the Poole-Morrissey rivalry does not really seem to have been political or ethnic—the *Clipper* believed that the real issue was simply who was "the biggest ram in the pen"—but as the Know-Nothings skyrocketed to prominence, Butcher Bill saw his chance and claimed leadership as the head of nativist brawlers. When an antagonist sneered to Poole, "Aren't you a pretty

American?" he proudly proclaimed, "Yes I am—I am their standard bearer." After increasingly bitter clashes between the two men's supporters, Butcher Bill ran into Morrissey in the elegant Stanwix Hall barroom on Broadway on the evening of 24 February 1855. The confrontation was broken up but later that night, Poole returned to Stanwix Hall, a fight broke out, and in the melee a Morrissey supporter shot Poole in the chest, severely wounding him.[54]

The shooting created a furor. Poole with his Amos Dock victory had become "generally known to the great mass of the people," reported the *New York Times*, and as he lingered near death the scene outside his Christopher Street home "resembled a market place or camp. By day it was crowded with people . . . and at night parties of [Greenwich] villagers camped about a watch-fire." Poole died on 8 March; his last words allegedly were "I die a True American." (According to Charles Haswell, the word on the street was that his last words were a distinctly less elevated "By —, boys, I'm a goner!") Butcher Bill was a martyr, and his funeral was a maelstrom of nativist passion. It was, according to the *Herald*, "one of the most extraordinary demonstrations ever made in a Christian country." An estimated crowd of eighty thousand lined Broadway to watch the funeral procession. A weeping Tom Hyer was one of the pallbearers.[55]

The arrival in 1857 from San Francisco of yet another handsome native-born fighter, John C. Heenan, completed Hyer's eclipse. Retired from prizefighting, Hyer worked as a saloon keeper and later a celebrity faro dealer in a gambling house. Always a heavy drinker, Hyer's health was by this time in decline, and his once magnificent face and body deteriorated until he was "a perfect wreck of his former self." As his looks faded, his friends and supporters fell away. Hyer died in 1864 at age forty-five, but he continued to be honored among men, and his portrait could be found in saloons throughout the city into the next century.[56]

"A GLORIOUS TIME"

Walsh, Rynders, and Hyer personified the lower-ward moral region of New York City as it emerged in the 1840s. They acted out a swaggering manliness that surpassed anything of the jolly fellows. The tavern had been a male domain, but the New York sporting world was much more so. In Mike Walsh's account of his midnight rambles in "A Glorious Time" all twelve people named are men. The only women mentioned are several at Red Hook who watched the rough-and-tumble fight. One might dismiss "A Glorious Time" as fiction, but the coroner's inquest after Walsh's death similarly tells a virtually all-male story. On Wednesday, 17 March 1859, Walsh began drinking at five-thirty in the afternoon in a Fifteenth

Ward saloon with a sporting man named Billy Mulligan. Walsh then went on to a hotel saloon where he shared drinks with several other men before finally ending up around eleven at his favorite watering hole, the Hone House at Broadway and Park Place. There he met Tom Hyer and several other men and continued to drink heavily until two in the morning. The testimony makes it clear that such evening barhopping was his customary routine. While walking home Walsh collapsed and died, apparently from a heart attack. The inquest after Poole's shooting reveals a similar picture; the action was played out mainly in saloons, and all twenty-two witnesses who testified or gave affidavits were men.[57]

In the lower-ward world, jolly fellowship became more emphatic and ostentatious, the drinking heavier, and the fighting more violent than among the tavern crowd. It was a masculine world but not a bachelor world. The large number of unmarried men in the lower wards fueled the Bowery scene, but Walsh, Rynders, and Hyer were all married. It comes as something of a surprise in the inquest into Walsh's death when his wife, Catherine, is called to testify. It turns out Walsh lived with his wife and two children on West Twenty-first Street. Poole had a wife and young child when he died. Their position as husbands and fathers did not deter them from spending their evenings and often their days drinking with other men in saloons. What did Catherine Walsh think night after night as her husband came home drunk at two or three o'clock in the morning? The record is silent. Mike himself seems rarely to have mentioned Catherine—there is virtually no information on her.[58]

The brawny world of the lower wards marginalized respectable women, but this was, for many men, part of its attraction. Cities remained places where they could still be men and live a traditional two-fisted jolly life. As rural and small town America became more tranquil and monotonous, the disorderly city, the evil city, stood out all the more. New York City emerged as the most powerful redoubt from respectability, and the Bowery b'hoy captured the popular imagination as symbol of unfettered urban life. Sporting men appeared who seemed to live as full-time jolly fellows, drinking, gambling, and fighting. They too became objects of public curiosity, not just in New York but throughout the country. Jolly fellowship was professionalized and amplified into something close to a counterculture in New York's lower wards in the 1840s and 1850s. In future decades, "sporting society" would only increase in scope and cultural significance.

For some men the Bowery region was attractive, a place where they could conduct their lives according to their own wishes. For others it was an evil place, the antithesis of Protestant, middle-class propriety. For all it was a place of fascination. In 1849, at the height of the Bowery b'hoy mania, another masculine domain materialized on the Pacific Coast that immediately exercised a similar allure and repulsion, even more alluring and more repelling: gold-rush California. The city's newspapers, which had done so much to publicize the Bowery and the b'hoy, now turned to promoting "the California adventure." The two moral regions were to become connected by more than unruly behavior. Many New York gamblers, prizefighters, and sporting men went west, establishing a link between eastern urban vice districts and the frontier that would last until the end of the century.

CHAPTER FIVE

The Gold Rush

On 26 December 1849, Kimball Webster, a twenty-one-year-old gold hunter from Pelham, New Hampshire, began his journey up the Sacramento River to the mining regions. Webster had known the boat's captain, Thomas D. Bonner, back in New Hampshire as an agent and lecturer for the Washington Temperance Society. Thus Webster was surprised when Bonner "topped one of the whiskey barrels [on board] and commenced drinking the contents. At first he drank a little, and after a short time he took a little more, and he continued to take a little quite often and said he could not live in California without it, . . . but that if he should return to his home in the East, he would again be as strong an advocate of temperance as formerly."[1]

Webster and Bonner were two of the more than eighty-five thousand non-Indian men in California in 1849 and 1850. For a few years after the discovery of gold, California was a moral region like the Bowery, but on a much grander scale. As Webster's account suggests, many of those involved in the gold rush perceived the West Coast as "outside" society, out of bounds, a place where traditional social rules, eastern rules, were suspended, even inverted. "Here in California we *have* to do such things," according to a disgusted Sarah Royce, was the common excuse for male conduct in the Golden State. The California gold rush was to prove a key episode in the evolution of jolly fellowship. By allowing men to satisfy their jolly desires, albeit temporarily, it may have helped accommodate them to a later life of staid respectability. Yet at the same time, the rush energized the emerging sporting counterculture. It also generated a deep network of connections between

New York and California that was to have a significant influence on American cultural production.[2]

"THEY ACT LIKE FREED PRISONERS"

Long before the gold rush, moral reformers had worried about the West. One problem was the kind of men going to the frontier. It seemed men with a taste for disorder were heading west as well as to cities. Too many migrants seemed like those in 1831 Indiana who, an agent of the American Bible Society claimed, had "left civilized and religious society for the simple purpose of getting out of its restraints." These were the same sort of rolling stones Timothy Dwight had found in Vermont and Maine. Even more worrisome was that many who left the East intending to remain pious and sober were, in the absence of settled society, unable to do so. Sustaining male propriety in areas with few churches and ministers and relatively small numbers of white women proved difficult. An American Tract Society correspondent could only conclude that men somehow were transformed when they crossed the Appalachians. A dismayed missionary to the Western Reserve region of Ohio discovered many formerly devout men from Connecticut but was shocked to see that "now they act[ed] like freed prisoners" and had abandoned all restraints of religion. They were freed from preachers, freed from women, freed from teetotalers. They were free to drink, to fight, and to gamble—to be jolly fellows.[3]

The ceding of Alta California to the United States at the end of the Mexican-American War, of course, made the gold rush possible. And the war was to foreshadow the rush in the type of men who would partake in it, their motives, and the comportment they displayed. The conduct of the American soldiers in the war made clear to observers that once men were removed from regular communities—once men became "men away from home"—there was a strong possibility that jolly fellowship would reemerge. Reasons for enlisting in the war were complex. In an era in which even the humblest tavern had a flag on the wall, American patriotism played an important role. Many of those who volunteered were Democrats who supported Polk and manifest destiny. One can even see territorial expansion itself as a manly act, and jolly fellows were no doubt well represented among the enlistees. The central reason for taking part seems, however, to have been a yearning for manly camaraderie and, in the words of the *New York Tribune*, "a spirit of romance and adventure." Volunteers in Indiana, the newspaper reported, looked upon military service as "a fine frolic." No doubt the desire to escape the tedium of daily life has played a part in may wars in inducing men to join the army. The incentive may have been especially important in the Mexican-American War because the personal moral reforms of the previous thirty years had for many men robbed everyday existence of some of its zest.[4]

From the start of the war there were reports of drunken and riotous conduct. A puzzled *Niles' National Register* informed its readers that "the public journals from the vicinity or routes taken by the volunteers, bring to us, we are sorry to say, innumerable proofs of . . . disgraceful rowdyism among the volunteers." Brawling among the men was routine: one Pennsylvania regiment spent its last night in Pittsburgh "drinking, fighting, and walking and yelling around the streets." John R. Kenly served as an officer in the Baltimore and Washington Battalion, "a wild, frolicsome reckless set, full of fun and hard to keep in camp," that was banished from the District of Columbia to a fort on the Potomac for its disorderly conduct. A Louisville paper lamented the "riotous and rowdy disposition manifested by the citizen soldiery" in that city, which culminated in a "disgraceful row" between "volunteers and citizens" in which a local man was nearly beaten to death.[5]

The behavior at sea of the volunteers was even more disorderly. Men on board ship, whether at sea or on a river, routinely lapsed into unruliness in mid-nineteenth-century America. In Kenly's battalion, "from the first hour they came on board, until the present time, by day and night . . . , *gambling* has been going on under every shape and device skill can suggest." There was "almost continual fighting in the hold," including one "pretty general free fight . . . which was difficult to quell." Before leaving for Texas, the Second New York Regiment was presented with Bibles, which most of the men promptly threw overboard, and the voyage was spent in near mutiny with the volunteers fighting, drinking, and howling. The journey of the First New York Regiment to California was equally chaotic. On the ship *Susan Drew* the officers completely lost control. "Half the men are drunk, I can do nothing with them," moaned a lieutenant. Soldiers were constantly fighting among themselves. When some of the men were sent to a guardhouse constructed on the ship's deck, the rest of the enlisted men liberated them, tore down the guardhouse, and threw the pieces overboard, singing, to the minstrel favorite "Old Dan Tucker": "Get out of the way you old guardhouse (repeat) / For you shan't stay on the *Susan Drew*." When the men went ashore in Rio, "they played a great many pranks on the Brazilians."[6]

Capt. Franklin Smith of Ohio pondered the unruly behavior of the soldiers. Most, he was convinced were "honorable men" at home, but service in the army had somehow imbued them with "a strange sort of morality." Their military service, the volunteers knew, was temporary, so many seemed to see it as a transient release from ordinary existence. Once away from wives and family, in the company only of other men, their comportment became increasingly unrestrained. The rowdiness continued in Texas and Mexico. In camp near the mouth of the Rio Grande, a dispute between men of the Baltimore and Washington Battalion and the First Ohio Regiment over who caught a catfish escalated into a "fearful riot" in July 1846. In camp outside Matamoros, one soldier was killed in an alcohol-fueled "general melee" that began between two companies of the First Georgia and later involved Illinois volunteers. Despite the tumult of camp life, the volunteers were usually orderly and disciplined in combat, where their belligerence proved an asset.[7]

In January 1848, one week before the signing of the Treaty of Guadalupe-Hidalgo formally ended the war, gold was discovered on the American River in California. By early 1849 there were reports from all over the nation of men preparing to head to California. Moralists smelled trouble—the track record of men in the West was not encouraging. A minister on his way to California confirmed their fears. He met some upright men journeying to the goldfields, but many were "adventurers, with no local attachments, ready for anything." "Lowest in the list" were "a few gamblers, and one of *pugilistic* notoriety." New England clerics, who had always questioned whether godliness could exist outside their region, were certain it could not survive three thousand miles away on the Pacific shore. A Bangor, Maine, pastor warned that California could become a "great slaughter-house of character and souls."[8]

The gold rush, critics believed, would arouse greed, to the detriment of spirituality and stability. But the California fervor was especially threatening because of the scarcity of women. *Graham's American Monthly Magazine* warned that without "female restraint, their tender charities, and gentle generosities and affections, and noble self sacrifices, which knit the bands of society together and render man human, . . . there [will] cause to be let loose all the savage passions and instincts of our natures," and California will become "a second Pandemonium." The gold rush and the resulting tumult threatened devout, family-oriented society. "The real Eldorado . . . IS AT HOME—AROUND OUR OWN HEARTH-STONE," pronounced *Graham's.* As it became obvious that didactic and clerical resistance was having little effect in preventing the rush, *Godey's Magazine and Lady's Book* urged that female teachers be sent to California, and Protestant denominations extended their missionary activity to the Pacific to try and prevent God-fearing men there from forsaking their faith.[9]

There were also voices urging men west. While the Whig press, troubled about the potentially destabilizing social effects of territorial expansion, was measured in its enthusiasm for the rush, Democratic newspapers promoted it. Hyperbolic articles described huge lumps of gold sitting on the ground for the taking. Among the shrillest voices was the *New York Herald*—"Ho! For California" headed its daily column of gold-rush news. It became clear that many were listening. Although it is impossible to estimate the number with any exactitude, perhaps as many as two hundred thousand men went to California between 1849 and 1852. And not only from America; "a heterogeneous mass from all parts of the world" came both by sea—around the horn or across Panama—and by land on the Overland Trail. Mexico, England, Germany, China, France, Australia, and Chile were well represented.[10]

Ethnically the miners were diverse, but in one respect those who came to the West Coast were remarkably uniform—they were overwhelmingly male. California's population in the 1850 census was 85,000. (Indians were not enumerated, but were estimated to number 150,000.) Ninety-three percent of the non-Indian population were men; 66,000 were males ages twenty to forty (71 percent). Three-quarters were American born. There were 962 blacks. In the mining regions, women were even rarer: Calaveras County in 1850 had 16,537 men and 265 women. The gold rush was thus very different from the pioneer experience in Oregon and other states settled by families, which had a large female population almost from the beginning. Women were present in California, certainly, in the minds of the miners and were discursively on hand in the letters from mothers and wives. And "respectable women" could be found even in remote mining camps, but their numbers were so small that men could plausibly imagine California as a land without women. In this sense, California in the 1850s was a "masculine space," and most women there shared with Eliza W. Farnham "a universal feeling of being sadly out of place."[11]

The young miners were of diverse social background. The "adventurers," as the press labeled them, were, in an oft-repeated phrase, "of all classes of men." Scottish wanderer and artist J. D. Borthwick remembered in his book *Three Years in California* (1857) that the miners included "professional men, labourers, sailors, farmers, mechanics and numbers of long, gaunt Western men with guns as long as themselves." There were prim New Englanders, b'hoys from New York, southern gentlemen and "Pikers" from Missouri. The *New York Herald* agreed that "all classes of our citizens" were involved but noted that "the expenses of the journey restrict[ed] the adventurers in some measure." The number of unskilled workers among those journeying west was indeed small. Passenger lists of ships heading for California from American ports show that the majority were skilled and semiskilled manual workers. There were also large contingents of nonmanual workers and farmers. The overland route was cheaper, and those coming that way likely included many farmers, the largest occupational group in the United States.[12]

The great majority of the men involved hoped, of course, to discover gold. The ancient attraction of the precious metal was immensely powerful, and, for all the newspaper hyperbole, the gold was there: between 1849 and 1855, $300 million worth was extracted from California. But a desire for gold was only the beginning of a complex decision to head west. Visions of fabulous wealth usually were not by themselves enough to get men to take part, and hundreds of thousands of men stayed home. Some who went west saw themselves as more or less forced into going. They had debts, needed money, and saw the gold rush as their chance. Those in real economic distress, however, seemed to have been a relatively small minority; the American economy was booming in the late 1840s and early 1850s, and most who were truly needy could not afford the trip. Other young men saw the gold rush as an opportunity to get away from vexing parental authority or from an unhappy or tedious marriage. For some it was a chance to test their manhood in novel and dangerous surroundings. But it was those men who dreamed of riches and who also had a taste for speculation, adventure, and living on their own with other men that most often went west. For those with an appetite for gambling, the rush was especially appealing, since striking gold was almost completely a matter of luck. "The whole mining system in California was one great gambling, or perhaps better—lottery transaction," explained Louise A. K. S. Clappe who wrote under the name "Dame Shirley."[13]

Many forty-niners agreed, that the gold was only part of the story. Charles D. Ferguson, who was seventeen when he left for California in 1850, explained that "it was not the gold alone, but an awakening of a strong desire for adventure which pervaded my spirit." For many, perhaps most, that the gold rush was a male adventure, a spree, was part of its attraction. Nineteen-year-old Georgian Thomas Wylly, in a reminiscence written fifty years later, confessed "that I believe the prospect of adventure weighed more forcibly with us than any idea of gold in California." For thousands of young men, the adventure aspect was an essential part of the appeal as is suggested by the fact that men continued to migrate to California through 1852, long after reports had made it clear that deposits that could be mined by individuals were exhausted.[14]

Women frequently tried to prevent husbands, sons, and brothers from becoming forty-niners. Before the gold rush, women had generally been far less enthusiastic about settling in the West than men, and the California venture was usually met with female skepticism. Many wives and mothers believed that men who participated in the gold rush were abandoning their duty to their families. The men insisted that they were not journeying west to take part in some irresponsible adventure, but that they were going on a quest for wealth to benefit their parents, wives, and children. Female opposition often proved futile. Kentuckian William H. Crosby wrote to his sister that he was aware that both she and their mother were opposed "to this course of mine But still I go."[15]

As reports of the unrestrained nature of California life spread east, some went to California specifically to lead a disorderly life. "I . . . started on this trip because I had become tired of society and its restraints," wrote twenty-six year-old Illinois physician Charles A. Kirkpatrick in his diary. "I determined therefore . . . to try for a while the life of liberty and unrestrained indulgence, the future will show the result." Kirkpatrick seems to have been as good as his word, spending his first Sunday in the mining region "forgetting the Sabbath" by playing cards. The tavern crowd was certainly represented. Gauis Halsey and Rufus Mead, two of "the coterie of fun-loving men" who gathered at Col. Williams's store in Unadilla, New York, went to California in 1849. Many accounts note the large number of lawyers, a group famous for its high jinks, among the forty-niners. The most striking connection between jolly fellowship at home and participation in the gold rush was established by the migration, which I discuss at the end of this chapter, of hundreds of Bowery types from New York City to California. That such men might go west is not surprising, but what is surprising is how even men who went intending to remain pious and abstemious were unable to resist the lure of jolly fellowship in the Golden State.[16]

"THE CALIFORNIA POX"

Only a minority of "argonauts," as the press dubbed them, went west specifically to sample jolly fellowship. But many others, even many men who hoped to remain devout and sober, found, as they headed west by boat or wagon, the appeal of jovial conduct becoming increasingly powerful. Despite the best efforts of reformers in the preceding decades, a deep-seated affection for jolly fellowship remained, and in the absence churches, "respectable women," and organized communities, it quickly reasserted itself. The trip to California introduced men to all-male living, and even before they got to the "diggings," the "strange sort of morality" that Capt. Franklin Smith had noted among the Mexican War volunteers began to take hold. Benjamin Butler Harris, a twenty-six-year-old lawyer, took the southern route through Texas to the goldfields in 1849. "When we left civilized men, about 1/3 of our party appeared pious—several making noisy prayers every night." But by the time they reached the Rio Grande, "all profession of sanctity had disappeared. . . . 'Old Negro Dick' was the only one of us whose religion lived through the voyage." Shipboard life seemed equally corrosive of propriety. Baptist minister Benjamin Brierly, the chaplain of the ship *Duxbury* bound from Boston to San Francisco, preached a sermon in June 1849 that urged men to relax their religious scruples: "There was a great deal of religion that had better be left this side of the Cape [Horn], as it would only prove a curse. . . . [T]he less of it one had the better—it wouldn't pay for transportation to California." The passengers' drinking, uproarious behavior, and mean-spirited practical jokes on the voyage suggest that Brierly may simply have been facing reality in directing the men to loosen their morals.[17]

Some men leaped at the opportunity to shed the trappings of respectability and drink whiskey out the jug and went west specifically to live a "life of liberty and unrestrained indulgence." For others, however, the story was more complex. Young "men away from home"—thousands of miles away from home—with few white women and few churches did indeed find the appeal of jolly fellowship irresistible, but such jolly fellowship was not as morally menacing as it might seem. In their own minds, many adventurers remained respectable even as they drank, gambled, and swore because, as far as they were concerned, traditional eastern moral rules simply did not apply to California. "Here in California we *have* to do such things." Jolly behavior was temporary—an essential, if pleasurable, accommodation to western conditions. As one adventurer explained to San Francisco preacher William Taylor, "I knew I couldn't carry my religion with me through California, so when I left home in Missouri, I hung my religious cloak on my gate until I should return." It was widely accepted that while men were in California most would not, could not, remain steadfast in their faith; "the California Pox" one minister called it.[18]

Miners viewed California as a land where white women were so few as to be inconsequential, and female scarcity was repeatedly cited as the main cause of waning religiosity and the profane boisterousness of California life. As moralists had foreseen, on their own, without women, many men proved incapable of pious and refined behavior. Explained C. W. Haskins, a forty-niner from New Bedford, Massachusetts, "it is very seldom that any of us are enabled to see the effect of the *absence* of women so practically illustrated as it was in the mines." ("Mines" was California shorthand for the mining regions of the Sierra Nevada.) Gold-rush California "showed conclusively that man, when alone, and deprived of that influence which the presence of woman only can produce, would in a short time degenerate into a savage and barbarous state." In San Francisco, explained a twenty-four-year-old doctor, "all the restrictive influence of fair women is lost, and the ungoverned tempers of men run wild." Miners, on the rare occasions they encountered "respectable women," usually treated them politely and refrained from rowdiness and swearing, but prostitutes and women of color were not treated as nicely.[19]

Both miners and their critics often wrote as if the disorder, "the second Pandemonium," was the almost automatic result of men removed from civilizing influences and the presence of women. It also, however, was a result of specific historical circumstances. There was no California state government at all until the fall of 1849, and more broadly the tumult reflected the limited power of the American government in this period. Gold rushes in other countries were far calmer. The Australian gold rush in 1851 was, in comparison to California, remarkably tranquil. *Household Words*, Charles Dickens's magazine, boasted that "the contrast is very great between the orderly behaviour at the goldfields in Australia, and the disorders of California." The cause, *Household Words* believed, was the Englishman's intrinsic love of order. Perhaps so, but probably more significant was that British authorities in Australia set up and maintained an effective police presence in the mining region. In Australia, miners (some of whom came directly from California) and liquor sellers were required to have licenses, and the region was closely controlled with a ratio of one policeman for every fifty-six miners. The boisterous comportment that was so noticeable in California was evident in Australia but far more subdued. In the 1897 Klondike gold rush, the contrast between the chaos in the Alaskan debarkation port of Skagway and the calmness in the Canadian goldfields maintained by the Royal Canadian Mounted Police was similarly striking. Although everyone realized the necessity of organizing a California government, most observers argued that ultimately order could not be brought to the Golden State through law enforcement but only through a moral transformation of men wrought by religion and women.[20]

Not every man in California, of course, ran wild. There were miners, *Harper's Weekly* was pleased to report, "who have brought with them and maintained the New England propriety of conduct." Such men remained godly and walked the straight and narrow. But even those remaining righteous teetotalers admitted experiencing strong, almost overwhelming, temptations. William Swain came from western New York with a target of finding $10,000 in gold to help his family, and he vowed to return home immediately after obtaining it. Swain was well aware of the allure of California life, noting in a letter to his mother that "temperance men are disregardful of their solemn pledge, and Sons of Temperance of their secret oaths of abstinence." But Swain claims he was not such a man, attending church regularly and shunning saloons and gambling halls while diligently, though unsuccessfully, searching for gold.[21]

Some men adopted a few mildly jolly traits, perhaps concerned that total refusal to drink and gamble would risk social ostracism. It may also be that they were trying to somehow inoculate themselves against complete licentiousness by sinning in moderation. Hinton R. Helper—who four years later was to create a national furor with his antislavery book, *The Impending Crisis*—wanted one Sunday in 1853 to go to a bear-and-bull fight, California's distinctive contribution to blood sports. But "how could I reconcile the instructions of a pious mother with an inclination so much at variance with divine command?" "I made up my mind to go, and went. Anxious, however, to diminish the sin as much as possible, I determined to hear a sermon first, and then go to the bull-fight afterwards."[22]

Twenty-two-year-old Nathan Blanchard, a miner on the Bear River, recorded his struggle between revelry and respectability in his diary. He was ever aware of the temptations of California life and was disappointed, although not surprised, to learn his old friend William Butterfield had fallen "into the evil fashions of the country." Blanchard and Butterfield had both been members of the Sons of Temperance back in Maine, but Butterfield was now not only drinking but selling liquor and had fallen "into the evil habit of swearing." Blanchard struggled to avoid Butterfield's fate. "I have been in the habit for a few months of playing cards. . . . —And every time I feel it to be wrong. . . . God, if I have ever lived near to thee I must have strayed off some way." Four months later he swore off cards, but three months after that he was back playing and wagering. Blanchard accepted that it was extremely difficult for men in California to keep such pledges: "I dare not say I *will*, for instance, play no more billiards, but with Gods assistance I will hope to."[23]

As men left their homes and set out across the prairie or sailed out of New York harbor into the Atlantic, they left behind a familiar world of family and relations, of farm, shop, and factory. As they landed in San Francisco and headed up into the mountains and found mining settlements with names like Hangtown, Whiskey Creek, and Rough and Ready and encountered miners from France, Australia, Mexico, and China, it confirmed that they were in surroundings far different from what most of them had previously known. They soon discovered that with fifty-eight thousand miners in California by 1850, the odds were heavily against a major gold strike. Yet most extracted enough to pay their living expenses, and they continued to hope for a lucky find while enjoying the scenery and, for many, the jolly miners' lifestyle.

"MUCH DRINKING AND FIGHTING . . . GAMBLING ETC. THIS CONSTITUTES CALIFORNIA LIFE"

The Pacific Coast was geographically and racially unlike anything the adventurers had ever known. But culturally, there was something familiar. There was an atavistic quality to white American male life in California—the routine drinking, the gambling, the practical jokes, and the fighting resembled pretemperence, premoral reform America of years past. Only, California was jollier and wilder than the East or South had ever been—it was as if jolly fellowship had become concentrated in locations like the Bowery and California and thus become that much more potent. On an adventure without women, men could live more or less as they pleased. And the way they pleased was almost the reverse of what most people in "the states," as Californians referred to the rest of the country, considered respectable.

The improvement in dress that had accompanied the betterment in male demeanor was discarded. J. D. Borthwick, who considered the gold rush a social movement, noted the transformation in attire. "Almost every man, after a short residence in California, became changed to a certain extent in his outward appearance." Miners in California were often literally unrecognizable as their former selves. Some may even have consciously played the role of the disheveled California miner. On the Stanislaus River, English adventurer William Ryan encountered an acquaintance from New York City, Frederick Whittle, who

> I certainly should not have known again, from the change that had taken place in him, from the gentlemanly young fellow to the rough miner. His face . . . was half-covered with a huge shaggy beard flowing down nearly to his waist. He wore a short, green-baize jacket, buckskin breeches, leather leggings, and a wide-brimmed hat; his neck enwrapped in a dirty red handkerchief, and altogether presenting, in his entire person, an appearance so different from the spruce exterior with which my memory was familiar, that it was no wonder I remained for some time doubtful of his identity.

As on the Bowery, standards of dress loosened. In the mining regions even merchants and public officials wore flannel shirts, overalls, and boots, and "a well-dressed man was looked on with suspicion." Stovepipe hats were "jammed down . . . 'just for fun you know,'" C. W. Haskins remembered. When men did dress up, it was not in business clothes but in flamboyant attire. Borthwick described men displaying bright silk scarves over their shoulders and hats decorated with feathers, flowers, and squirrel tails. Men braided their beards in whimsical ways. One miner with very long hair tied it under his chin with a bow.[24]

Another element of the gold-rush transformation was taking a fresh name. Some adventurers decided even before leaving for the West on their new appellations, as if they recognized both the importance of separating themselves from their former existence and the necessity of a nickname in a masculine realm like California. Indianan John Doble and his friends "settled on the names that we each should [be] known and called by" in New York City before they even set sail. In the mining regions, Haskins remembered, "it was the habit, or custom rather, in the early days to give to each man a certain nickname by which he was usually known, his real name being, as a rule, unknown or even unasked for." Actually, it seems most men's real names were known, but Haskins is correct that many went by nicknames. Haskins's friends included "French Flat Pete," "Texas Jack," "Old Pike," "Big Yank," and "Scotty." George Hunter from Ohio was known as "Buckeye"; Canadian argonaut Pringle Shaw's acquaintances included a miner whose "name was unknown, but we called him Sawbones; for he was an M.D."[25]

There were certainly devout men in the mines, but for many, spirituality, which often had withered on the passage to California, altogether vanished. Argonauts almost always commented on California Sundays. Most mining activity ceased—but it was not a day of religious devotion for most miners. Churches were few and poorly attended, and, according to Hinton R. Helper, "the Sabbath in California" was "kept, when kept at all, as a day of hilarity and bacchanalian sports . . . horse-racing, cock-fighting, cony-hunting, card-playing, theatrical performances, . . . duels and prize-fights." Men of God despaired at the situation. William Taylor, a San Francisco minister who went on a preaching tour through the mines, claimed he traveled a week before meeting "a good Christian man." Religious observances that were attempted sometimes turned into frolics. Charles Kirkpatrick described a Sunday service on the Mokelumne River led by a "Capt. Lupton," a graduate of West Point. "The meeting began with his treating the company." Lupton himself was imbibing heavily, and "during the sermon . . . he could not stand with out leaning against a post." Some miners were not just indifferent but actively hostile to religion. One group of men near Downieville in 1851 "organized a club[,] . . . one of whose resolutions was *to treat to a dose of mud any clergyman who should chance to come upon the [sand]bar*" they were mining by throwing him into the river.[26]

Preachers who themselves became infected with "the California Pox" and joined in the revel were a gold-rush legend. "Religion had been forgotten, even by its ministers," believed James H. Carson, a former soldier in the Mexican War.

Jolly fellowship seemed so irresistible on the Pacific shore that even missionaries sent out from the East specifically to stem California infidelity could not resist. Phineas Blunt, a miner from New York City, saw that "many who leave the States who were men of Good Morals loose their Consciences. Here Ministers of the Gospel who came here have been . . . Brandy Drinkers & Gamblers." Twenty-six-year-old Peter Decker recorded in his diary that "Episcopalian Preacher sent here from New Jersey as a Missionary is now gambling, swearing & drinking, so says Capt. Moore. A Methodist Preacher this Summer peddled Monte cards on Nelson Creek." Another minister turned gambler explained to one miner that his fall from grace was due to his being "away from the society he had been used to."[27]

If religion waned, drinking waxed. Alcohol was the linchpin of jolly behavior and temperance the hallmark of its rejection. In a period in which alcohol consumption was declining in the states, its pervasiveness in California stunned visitors. Drinking seemed virtually mandatory. "Men steeped their souls in liquor," remembered Hubert Howe Bancroft who had come to San Francisco in 1852 and devoted his later life to writing and supervising the writing of dozens of volumes of California and western history. "If hot they drank to get cool, if cold to get warm, if wet to get dry, if dry . . . to keep out the cold." English traveler Frank Marryat discovered that "drinking is carried on to an incredible extent." The tradition of sealing business agreements with a drink was revived. In California "no trade could be without a preliminary washing down," one San Franciscan explained. Everyone was a manual worker in the mines, and the traditional association of liquor with physical labor was resurrected. "Work and hard drinking with many went hand in hand," asserted Bancroft. Binge drinking on holidays reappeared. At Rich Bar in 1851, drinking began on Christmas evening, according to Dame Shirley, and lasted four days, at which point "men were lying in drunken heaps" in the barrooms. The men then "commenced an unearthly howling;—some barked like dogs, some roared like bulls, others hissed like serpents and geese. Many were too far gone to imitate anything but their own animalized selves." After that the revelry diminished "from sheer exhaustion."[28]

Other manifestations of jolly fellowship in the East—fighting, gambling, pranks, and blood sports—were all immensely popular in California. Their potency suggests both the close connection between these pastimes and the powerful attraction they retained. "Much drinking and Fighting . . . Gambling etc. This constitutes California life," wrote Massachusetts miner Alonzo Hubbard in his journal. Brawling was routine. At Rich Bar, Dame Shirley explained, "we have had innumerable fights during the summer with the usual amount of broken heads, collar bones, stabs, etc." Rather than break up brawls, onlookers urged on the combatants: "Give 'em room—let 'em go," reported a disgusted Alonzo Delano. "'Give it to him, Pete,' . . . 'tap his claret; by ——, he's done it—smashed his nose flat.'" As had once been customary in the states, fights broke out for no apparent reason, washing over men like a sudden storm. Benjamin Butler Harris attended a mass meeting in Yorktown to nominate men for the California state legislature. After the senate nomination was completed two sailors began friendly sparring, and almost instantly "the entire crowd, chairman excepted, peacemakers included began brawling."

> A 1/2 acre of ground had men striking at nearest heads—friends pumelling friends or foes. What gouging, kicking—tumbling, squirming, piling—rolling downhill not knowing or heeding what they hit. It was Donny Brook Fair many times magnified. At length by tacit understanding the tumult ceased—then quietly resuming seats the convention serenely proceeded to nominate the two Assemblymen, then placidly dispersed. Never before or since have I known men to fight for the love of fighting.[29]

Fatal affrays and duels were common. Men often carried guns and knives, and clashes could quickly turn violent. A miner wintering in Sonora in the racially diverse "Southern Mines" complained that "people here are continually fighting and shooting at each other, and they do not care who they kill, for they shoot at each other when hundreds are standing all around them." White American miners shared their nation's racial attitudes and usually regarded people of color with suspicion and hostility. Even by gold-rush standards Sonora was exceptionally violent—there were nineteen killings between October 1850 and August 1851, a homicide rate that John Boessnecker calculates as an astonishing 503 per 100,000. No other place was that deadly, but shooting and stabbing affrays were common everywhere from San Francisco to tiny mining camps. Not all violence was interracial. Among whites after a few drinks, a wrong word or gesture could result in a clash with weapons. The deadly violence in California seems closer to the southern than northern pattern as does the California penchant for dueling. Nothing exemplified more the archaic quality of gold-rush life than the duel. The practice had virtually disappeared in the East by the 1850s and had begun to fade even in the South, but in the Golden State the desire to preserve male honor was so potent, Bancroft remembered, that an "insult could be washed out but by blood alone." Eighteen-fifty-four saw "a mania for duels. Editors fought. Lawyers, judges, shoulder-strikers, doctors, loafers fought." The most talked about affair of honor that year was a wheel-and-fire duel with rifles at forty paces—Achilles Kewen turned and put a bullet through the heart of his antagonist.[30]

The adventurers were men predisposed to take a chance, to make a bet, and miners gambled ardently everywhere. "I pronounce that no where in the world is gambling carried on so openly & to the extent it is in Cal[.] In these towns it is grander, but in the mines in some old tent it is steeper," concluded James Warren Wood. In the goldfields, recounted an adventurer, "no matter how staid and sober they had been . . . the air of the mining camp upset all their sobriety . . . [and] they all became accomplished gamblers." *The Annals of San Francisco* (1855) noted that wagering in that city "was *the* amusement—*the* grand occupation of many classes—apparently the life and soul of the place." A deck of cards was called a "California prayer-book," and Sunday was the casinos' busiest day of the week.[31]

Betting on blood sports such as cockfights, dogfights, and bullfights was especially popular. Adventurers, however, refer most often and most enthusiastically to the Golden State's addition to blood sports, the bear-and-bull fight. When Borthwick arrived in Mokelumne Hill in the spring of 1852, he was greeted by a poster for a match, jokingly presented as an allegory of the Mexican-American War, between "the celebrated Bull-killing Bear, GENERAL SCOTT," and a wild young bull "of the Spanish breed." The bull's horns, the poster emphasized, are "*not sawed off to prevent accidents.*" On Sunday, Borthwick "found myself walking up towards the arena," he recalled. A large and festive crowd of Americans and Mexicans had gathered, and they were drinking and socializing. The grizzly quickly grabbed the bull's snout and hung on, chewing the bull's "nose and lips into a mass of bloody shreds" to "shouts of delight from the excited spectators." With the bear winning, the promoter addressed the crowd and announced that for $200 he would let in another bull and let all three fight it out to the death. The money was raised, the new bull sent in, but even two bulls were unable to make much headway against the grizzly, so the event was halted and the two bulls shot to put them out of their misery.[32]

"It was customary, also, among many of the miners to play all kinds of practical jokes upon each other," remembered Haskins. Pranks had begun to fade from daily life in the states, but in California the practice revived. "Miners of the early days never passed up an opportunity to play a joke on a fellow miner," wrote William T. Russell, a resident of El Dorado County. One prank he remembered was painting a miner's gray horse black and enjoying the owner's consternation as he searched for it. "Tricks to bring the uninitiated into ridicule and make them 'treat'" were a favorite. Mock trials were one such common "trick": Rich Bar had a mock vigilance committee that hauled men before it, tried them "on some amusing charge," and then sentenced them to "treat the crowd" to drinks. Other jokes were rough. "All those young men delighted in pranks that involved a measure of danger," one miner recalled. Sham duels and shootings with blanks were a California speciality. "The only explanation that can be offered" for such buffoonery, newspaperman Matthew Gilbert Upton thought, was that "the argonauts of '49 believed that they were engaged in a . . . frolic rather than in the business of founding an American state."[33]

There was a strikingly childish aspect to some of this reawakened jolly fellowship—miners often referred to themselves as "the boys" and engaged in children's games. Warren Sadler, a married adventurer from Lockport, New York, returned to his San Francisco boardinghouse one day to find the residents having a water fight; another time he found them "carrying on like a pack of wild boys. Dean plays the Bear and Boardman had a lasso, said he was the master of the ring, so he would lasso Dean &c." On Mokelumne Hill in 1851 the miners played an uproarious game of follow the leader. The leader, for example, would shoot at a shop sign, and then everyone else would take a shot at it as they ran by. There was a spontaneous, impetuous character to such behavior, by turns beguiling and reckless.[34]

This impulsiveness could result in a show of instant compassion or sudden cruelty toward others. The range of male behavior seems even wider in California than in the states; affection seemed stronger, repulsion more forceful. Men expressed their love for one another. Miners hugged and kissed. Gustavus Swansey, a married man with children who came to San Francisco after a dispute with his Boston parents, kept a journal chronicling his fondness for William Sitton, "the man I love better than all other men." Miners generally worked in groups in an isolated and dangerous environment, and this seems to have intensified fraternity. John de Laittre believed that in the absence of women "men would associate more closely." It was, he explained, "an almost unheard of thing" for companions to desert each other, "and if in trouble, [they] would cling closer together." This contributed to the white egalitarianism that observers believed was so characteristic of California. When one of Louise Clappe's mining neighbors at Rich Bar on the Feather River came to borrow a teaspoon for a party, she suggested he take them all. "'Oh, no,'" was the response, "that would be too much luxury. My guests . . . would think I was getting aristocratic, and putting on airs. One is enough; they can pass it around."[35]

This male camaraderie is exemplified in the generosity of miners. William M'Collum, a physician from Lockport, New York, asked "how do people live who are sick and out of money in California? They get along better than the unfortunate and destitute anywhere else in the world. There is a fellow-feeling there, a spirit of active, practical benevolence." "Fellow feeling" was, as in the states, bounded by race and ethnicity, but among whites, Edward McIlhany discovered, "a man scarcely ever suffered for the want of something to eat or a help in business or in charity." Miners drinking at the Kossuth House in Shasta City in 1853 during the Trinity River rush instantly walked out when the proprietor refused to board the destitute and frostbitten eighteen-year-old George Hunter unless he paid in advance. A miner named Jack Moore took Hunter to another hotel where Moore and the owner split Hunter's bill.[36]

This powerful white benevolence was accompanied by brutality toward people of color. The boundary between those who merited white compassion and those who did not was drawn with extraordinary sharpness; the "two consciences"—a compassionate one for whites, often a merciless one for other races—was often starkly evident. Were they connected? Was white solidarity stronger because the line excluding outsiders was drawn so unambiguously? Stories of exceptional solicitude to fellow white miners in diaries and reminiscences are interspersed with accounts of savagery to outsiders. The exclusionism of the forty-niners was complex. Occasionally native-born Americans opposed all other groups in the mines including French and German immigrants, but usually it seems to have been the color line that mattered most. Blacks in the mining regions, as almost everywhere else in nineteenth-century America, were treated as inferiors. Boardinghouses served African Americans only after all the whites were finished eating. Borthwick, however, was surprised they were served at all and felt that "in the mines the Americans seemed to exhibit more tolerance of negro blood than is usual in the States." There were even more alien people to contend with.[37]

There was some confusion among American miners about what race Latin Americans were, but most considered them nonwhite: "half-civilized black men," one neighbor explained to Dame Shirley. Mexicans, in Pringle Shaw's opinion, were "filthy, ignorant, lazy and vicious." When a Mexican, or "greaser" in miners' parlance, killed an American in a brawl at Rich Bar in July 1852, the white miners went wild: "Drive every foreigner off the river! Don't let one of those murderous devils remain," the mob shouted, according to Dame Shirley. They quickly tracked down the slayer and lynched him. The other Mexicans on the river were expelled by the local vigilance committee and "beaten like dogs." Chileans were equally despised. The "D——d Copper Hides," exhorted the leader of white miners on the Calaveras River in December 1849, "should be driven from our Digging," according to miner John Hovey, who thoroughly agreed. Although the Chilean miners had been there first, they were forced out, precipitating a violent confrontation the press dubbed "the Chilean War." In the struggle a Chilean and two Americans were killed. In retaliation, the Americans took the Chileans involved into custody, executed three by firing squad and cut off the ears of three others. Chinese miners were targets of similar prejudice and were immediately driven off any river or creek white miners thought would yield a profit.[38]

Though some white miners were sympathetic to Native Americans, most viewed them as subhuman. "Between the Digger Indians and the grizzly bear," James H. Carson explained, "there is but a slight difference existing, which amounts to the bear being brave . . . otherwise they live on the same food and their habits are similar." ("Digger" was the miners' derisive label for any one of the numerous Indian tribes found in the mining regions.) "Partly man and partly beast," agreed Charles Ross Parke. Warren Russell discovered that miners from the West "have such a hatred for Indians that many of them would shoot one on sight." Whenever a miner was killed, a horse was stolen, or food robbed and there was no clear suspect, Indians were blamed. If the guilty Indian could not be discovered, white custom allowed men to take revenge on any Native American they could find. J. M. Letts met a miner on the American River who was searching for his stolen horse and swearing he "would shoot the first red-skin he met," though Letts was sure the horse was stolen by a white miner. Massacres of Indians were rare but did happen. "A party of armed white men," reported the *Alta California* in 1849, attacked a group of Indians working for a white miner. One Indian working on his knees was immediately killed. Another was wounded and ran a short distance and tried to hide, but he was discovered, "and his brains were beaten out with rocks and stones." The others fled but were surrounded and fourteen of them killed.[39]

"A NEW NEW YORK"

Where jolly attitudes had once been widespread in America, by the 1850s they predominated only in masculine milieus like California and the Bowery. From the very beginning of the gold rush, California exercised a profound fascination on men in New York's lower wards. The Pacific Coast was perceived as a similar refuge from respectability as the Bowery, but it was larger, manlier, jollier, and much more lucrative. The two milieus became connected both socially and culturally, and the bonds between New York and California were to remain intact until the end of the century. This articulation of disorderly locales East and West strengthened both and helped give greater coherence to the emerging jolly sporting subculture.

The timing of the gold rush was critical in forging this cultural connection. The discovery of gold took place in 1848, which was the "Mose Moment" in New

York, the year that both George Foster's "New York in Slices" began running in the *New York Tribune* with its sketches of b'hoys and the theatrical hit *A Glance at New York* with its hero named Mose, the Bowery B'hoy, began playing on stage. The forty-niners loved Mose. The play may even have prepared adventurers for the jolly side of California life. Its popularity also may have contributed to the theatricality of the rush; the flamboyant miners' costumes, the ostentatious jolly fellowship. Unadillan Gaius Halsey in New York City waiting to sail for California in 1849 witnessed the performance "'Mose trying to go to California.' . . . It was exceedingly amusing. 'Mose' the leading character, was so strikingly like one of our company we dubbed him 'Mose' and he is still known by that name by old members of that company." The Mose plays, especially *Mose in California* in which he searches for gold and "lams" Indians, were favorites of California theatergoers. In the spring of 1850 the *Alta California* ran a series of "Letters from Mose" in which the famed b'hoy recounted his adventures with Lize in San Francisco. Actor Frank Chanfrau, forever typecast as Mose, played the role in California in 1851. Miner Joseph Warren Wood read Ned Buntline's novel of Mose and Lize, *The Mysteries and Miseries of New York,* in his cabin on the Tuolumne River.[40]

A fascinating document at the Huntington Library in San Marino, California, illustrates the cultural affinity between Bowery and gold rush. The "Petrel" is a handwritten newspaper apparently posted weekly on the ship *Duxbury* bound from Boston to San Francisco in 1849. Started and mostly written by argonaut William De Costa, it humorously chronicled the voyage. Many of the stories are about drinking, fighting, and pranks. The passengers on the *Duxbury* not only displayed a jolly attitude in general but were fascinated by its specific Bowery variant. They portrayed themselves, as Brian Roberts has noted in his analysis of the "Petrel," as "a group of 'b'hoys' on a spree." There are references not just to Mose but also seemingly to lines from *A Glance at New York.* "Well, he didn't do nothing else," the "Petrel" remarks at one point, which is one of Mose's taglines that had entered the vernacular in 1848. A "Petrel" poem includes the line "I thought I'd be running fore I got into a muss," a reworking of Mose's famous exit line at the end of *A Glance at New York:* "I'm goin' to leave you . . . Sykesey's got in a muss." This cultural connection between New York and the West would evolve and strengthen in later years.[41]

The link between Manhattan and gold-rush California was not only cultural: there was also a migration of men, including many from the lower wards, to the Pacific Coast from New York City. The New York–California connection actually originated during the Mexican-American War. The First New York Regiment, commanded by Tammany stalwart Col. Jonathan Stevenson, was to be made up of single men, with the understanding that enlistees would, as the troop's great champion, the *New York Herald*, explained, "go to California, with the intention of remaining" after the war and settling the newly conquered territory. Seven of the ten companies were made up mostly of men from Manhattan. Members of Mike Walsh's Spartan Association formed a company and volunteered, but the enterprise collapsed when Stevenson refused them the traditional militia right of choosing their own officer (i.e., Walsh). A letter to the *Tribune* raised a widespread misgiving about the enterprise. What sort of person would leave home and relations for the wilds of California? Only men "who have grown weary of the tameness of civilized society," adventurers intent on turning around their fortunes, freebooters looking for plunder. Walter Murray of Company A emphasized that the regiment included "steady mechanics of all trades" but admitted there was "a smart sprinkling of the b'hoys." The second mate on one of the ships that took them to California was blunter: "The men of the regiment were a tough lot of fellows[,] . . . three hundred New York Fourth Ward roughs."[42]

Even compared to the uproarious behavior men typically displayed on shipboard, the First New York's journey to California with its men in near mutiny, drinking and fighting, was remarkable, and the disorderly conduct continued on land. One officer from the regiment was cashiered for a drunken rampage during which, among other things, he tried to break down the door of the sutler's store in Los Angeles, shouting as he banged, "I can lick him God damn him." An ex-volunteer, William Landers, committed San Francisco's first recorded homicide in 1847 in an affray that began when Landers barged into a saloon and bellowed that he "could whip any son of a bitch in the house." Men from the regiment continued to fraternize in San Francisco and were apparently at the core of a gang called "the Hounds," also known as, according to Hubert Howe Bancroft, "the 'Boys,' after the fashion of the New York Bowery, where many of them formerly used to sun themselves."[43]

The Hounds first attracted attention in the spring of 1849 by "parading the public streets in fantastic or ridiculous dresses, and by commission of pranks of a character calculated to amuse the community." After marching, they pushed "into saloons . . . and [would] help themselves to what they wanted and refuse to pay" and engaged in street brawls. The Hounds episode suggests how quickly and easily seemingly unplanned jolly disorder could be turned to instrumental purpose. "Under the pretense of mutual defense against the encroachments of foreigners," they began to attack Chileans, Peruvians, Mexicans, and Chinese. Things came to a head on 16 July 1849. The Hounds vowed to "whip and drive every damned Chileno out of the town," and they did so. In a ferocious attack they

H. R. Robinson, "One of the Californian Bo-Hoys Taking Leave of His Gal," 1846. This is a comic look at the chaotic departure of the First New York Regiment for California in October 1846. Several companies rebelled when the cost of their uniforms was deducted from their pay. The regiment's commander, Col. Jonathan Stevenson, a former tailor, is at right. An attempt by the New York sheriff to serve Stevenson with a court order challenging his military authority was forcibly prevented by the soldiers at Stevenson's order. The California History Room, California State Library, Sacramento.

plundered the Chileans' tents and tore them down and savagely beat the men and raped the women.[44]

This coterie of b'hoys from New York who were already in California before the gold rush set the stage for a movement of figures from New York's sporting subculture to San Francisco. They quickly discovered the City by the Bay's similarity to Manhattan's lower wards. Both were dominated by young men living in boardinghouses, and, as in New York, because "homes were scarce," *The Annals of San Francisco* explained, "numerous places of amusement" flourished. "An exodus, or transmigration" of sporting men from Manhattan to San Francisco occurred, reported *Wilkes' Spirit of the Times.* Pugilists, gamblers, strong-arm politicians, billiard players, minstrels, and volunteer fireman all came and helped recreate the Bowery world of sporting saloons, gambling houses, theaters, and bordellos. There was as well a steady migration of more respectable New Yorkers. Philip J. Ethington concluded in his study of San Francisco public life that "the Capital City of the 'Wild West,'" was really a 'New New York.'"[45]

David C. Broderick was the central figure in this exodus from the Bowery. A stonecutter, he became a volunteer fireman in the renowned West Side Howard Engine Company, and, with the commanding physique developed in his trade, he quickly achieved notice by battling "the bravest fighters and hardest hitters of companies that antagonized his own." He fraternized at the Ivy Green Tavern or at the Comet Saloon with the lower-ward elite, including Yankee Sullivan, Tom Hyer, Mike Walsh, and Walsh's coeditor on the *Subterranean*, George Wilkes. Broderick's pugilistic skills and "an instinctive fondness for excitement and rough play" made him a hero in the city's firehouses and saloons, but he was much more than a b'hoy. He was well mannered and, although self-educated, widely read in Shakespeare and English poetry. Walsh was Broderick's political hero. Broderick was one of the founding members of Walsh's Spartan Association and named his own saloon the Subterranean in tribute to his friend. Like Walsh he championed the rights of workingmen, and like Walsh, he retained a personal base of support even when he cooperated with Tammany.[46]

Openly ambitious, Broderick rose quickly in the New York Democratic Party, and in 1846 at age twenty-six he became the West Side Democratic nominee for Congress. "The b'hoys," warned the *Tribune*, "intend to vote five or six times for Broderick." He was so personally popular that even though he was an Irish-American running in a predominantly native-born district, he was favored to defeat Whig candidate Frederic Talmadge. But "the more aristocratic portion of Tammany Hall" ran a candidate that split the Democratic vote, and Broderick was defeated. Crushed by the loss and the expense of the campaign, Broderick largely

Edward Hooper, "The Hounds." The members of the gang are attacking Chileans and other Latin Americans in San Francisco on July 16, 1849. In Frank Soulé, John H. Gihon, and James Nisbet, *The Annals of San Francisco* (New York, 1865).

withdrew from party politics. Urged by acquaintance Col. Jonathan Stevenson, the commander of the New York regiment disbanded in California, to come west, Broderick left for California in April 1849 in a group of seven men, including his friend Sixth Ward alderman Frederic Kohler, who became one of Broderick's key political supporters in San Francisco.[47]

Mose welcomed "ders David Broderick and Fred Kohler" in the *Alta California.* According to George Wilkes, Broderick became "a NEW MAN" in the West. Employed by Stevenson in a private gold mint, Broderick threw himself into California's amorphous politics. As in New York, he used the volunteer fire company to gain backers. The Empire Hose, of which he became foreman, contained many ex–New Yorkers and was his early base of political support. It is doubtful that Broderick ever developed an organization that was as tightly controlled as his critics alleged, but a group of men mainly from Manhattan worked together to advance their political careers, and Broderick was the acknowledged leader of this group. Broderick's supporters and political style were linked so closely to New York that the *Alta* dubbed him "the chief of the Bowery bhoys."[48]

One of Broderick's most devoted adherents as he was building up "the Tammany Democracy," as his organization was sometimes called, was Thomas Maguire. A brawling hack driver, Maguire was an active Empire Club shoulder hitter and later became the proprietor of the popular Star House on Reade Street. When Broderick arrived in San Francisco he found Maguire running a gambling saloon and trying to set himself up as a theatrical entrepreneur. Broderick moved in with Maguire, and they roomed together for almost five years, during which time Maguire aided in the forging of Broderick's political organization, and Broderick helped Maguire, who eventually would reign over a western theatrical empire, succeed as a theater owner.[49]

Another ex–New Yorker in the Broderick wing of the San Francisco Democracy was Billy Mulligan. "A prince among the political roughs of the day," he was perhaps the most colorful sporting man of the era. Irish-born, a cooper by trade, he weighed only 118 pounds but was an extraordinary rough-and-tumble fighter—in 1853 when a drunken ex-member of Stevenson's regiment insulted Broderick, Mulligan headbutted the offender senseless. It is hard to separate fact from legend with Mulligan, but it seems in 1847 he fled from a New York burglary charge to Texas and fought in the Mexican-American War. He then worked his way to California and settled in San Francisco in 1851, hooking up with Broderick. Despite several well-publicized barroom affrays, he became deputy city treasurer and later prison warden.[50]

Other prominent New Yorkers with lower-ward connections who came to San Francisco included Malachi Fallon, a saloon owner and fire company brawler; the powerfully built David Scannell, another fire company slugger and saloon keeper, known as a "choice spirit," who had a daily eye opener of whiskey and absinthe; and Dutch Charley Duane. Duane had been a prominent rough-and-tumble fighter in New York and ally of Poole and Hyer. "A splendid animal, of powerful frame and physique," Bret Harte recalled, Duane arrived in San Francisco in 1850, and by 1852, after seven arrests for brawling, he was notorious. A Whig in New York, apparently his geographical loyalties outweighed his political ones, and allied himself with Broderick and his supporters, who quashed the fighting indictments. Fallon was appointed chief of police after the Hounds riot, perhaps on the premise that it took a New York rough to tame New York roughs. Scannell became city sheriff and Duane fire chief in 1853.[51]

Virtually every major boxer in the United States went to California in the years between 1850 and 1852, and many of them lent a strong arm to Broderick. Yankee Sullivan, Chris Lilly, Tom Hyer, John Morrissey, and John C. Heenan all went. "Champions," *The American Fistiana* remembered, "were as plentiful in California about those days as earwigs in a sunflower." Prizefighters recognized that they would be luminaries in manly California and hoped to make easy money, either by battling for large stakes or by capitalizing on their fame in the saloon business as they had back in New York City. Enos Christman, a San Francisco printer, recorded in his journal in February 1850 that "'Yankee' Sullivan, the notorious pugilist, arrived here in the last steamer and now constitutes a bright star in this constellation." Sullivan returned to New York but went back to California again in 1854. Chris Lilly, the Yankee Sullivan–trained fighter who had killed Tom McCoy in the ring in 1842, had studied strong-arm politics from the master as a member of Rynders's Empire Club. A "beautifully formed" man "with a small waist and well-rounded chest," Lilly came to San Francisco where he supported himself by pimping, "sporting generally," and strong-arm politics. John Morrissey also came to California in 1850 where he "soon found lots of acquaintances [he] had known in New York." He ran a faro bank and fought his first prizefight in California in 1852 against English fighter George Thompson. Hyer fell ill shortly after arriving in California and quickly returned to New York. John C. Heenan was only seventeen when he arrived in 1851 and worked as a blacksmith in Benicia. He did not fight any prizefights in the Golden State, but as a "young giant in strength and stature," he was "in demand during . . . rough election times."[52]

Perhaps the most significant ex–New Yorker to come west to join Broderick was George Wilkes. Born in 1819 in New York City, Wilkes came to public attention in 1841 by publishing a scandal sheet called the *New York Sunday Flash* that focused on the city's prostitutes and brought him an obscenity conviction. An energetic and talented polemicist, Wilkes, together with his friend Mike Walsh, started the *Subterranean* in 1843. After a falling out with Walsh (later mended), Wilkes quit the *Subterranean* and became the founding coeditor of the sensationalistic *National Police Gazette* in 1845. A jaunty, elegantly dressed man, Wilkes became a well-known figure in New York. After repeated urgings from Broderick, in 1852 Wilkes sold the *Gazette* and went to California to join his friend as speech writer and advisor.[53]

Broderick attracted more respectable backers as well. He gained political and financial support from ex–New Yorkers Jonathan Stevenson and Frederick Kohler as well as from prominent non–New Yorkers, including banking and real estate leaders. Broderick's political rise was extraordinary. The Democratic Party, as in New York City, was the dominant party in California. Although party loyalties were less fixed there than in the states, California was "Democratic by nature," the *Pacific News* believed. Most of the adventurers seem to have been Democrats back East and remained loyal to that party in the West. The appeal of living in an unfettered, secular society was likely more attractive to Democrats than Whigs. Broderick was appointed to fill out an unexpired term in the California state senate, and by 1851 he was president of the senate. In 1852, after failing to get the U.S. Senate nomination, he became lieutenant governor. He was by then one of the most powerful politicians in the state and a recognized kingmaker.[54]

During Broderick's dazzling ascent, the Tammany-style Democratic organization in San Francisco that supported him became the target of increasingly heated complaints. The political successes of men like Mulligan, Scannell, Fallon, and Duane convinced many that law enforcement and fire protection in the city were in the hands of a bunch of thugs. Repeat voting, ballot-box stuffing and strong-arm tactics may have been politics as usual back in New York City, but to opponents unused to what one called "N.Y. 6th Ward Irish" methods they were outrageous. Indignation was building, and when newspaper editor James King, who had railed in print against "the dark fiend . . . David C. Broderick," was killed in a 9 May 1856 street affray with ex–New Yorker James P. Casey, a vigilance committee was formed. Casey was lynched, and "political ruffians" from New York became the scapegoats for San Francisco's corruption and disorder. Broderick ignored a request to appear before the vigilantes and left for the state's interior to garner support for another Senate bid, too powerful politically to be directly challenged. The vigilantes had demanded Sheriff David Scannell's resignation, but he saved his job by cooperating and handing over Casey to the vigilance committee to be hanged. The committee voted to banish Thomas Maguire, but eventually allowed him to stay in California. Other members of San Francisco's "Tammany Democracy" were not so fortunate. Mulligan, Lilly, and Duane were among the men jailed by the committee, sentenced to exile, and put on outbound ships. Yankee Sullivan, the man who had made prizefighting a major sport in the United States, was arrested by the committee, confessed to vote buying and ballot box stuffing, and on 31 May 1856, committed suicide in detention by slashing his arm.[55]

Broderick was chosen United States senator by the California legislature in January 1857. Eight years after he had left, he returned in triumph to New York in February on his way to Washington to take his seat as the youngest member of the Senate. He had been associated with the often pro-South Hunker faction in New York Democratic politics, but Senator David Broderick, the western "NEW MAN," became a foe of slaveholders—he opposed both the state's fugitive slave law and a law forbidding free blacks from settling in the state. Broderick's stance led to a bitter struggle with the prosouthern "Chivalry" faction of the California Democratic party. After an extraordinarily vituperative 1859 election, Broderick received a challenge to meet on the field of honor from Chivalry loyalist David S. Terry, the chief justice of the California Supreme Court. Broderick had already spurned one challenge to a duel and to refuse another might diminish his reputation in the manly world of California politics. Pistols at ten paces was the agreement. The men met outside San Mateo on 13 September 1859. Broderick fired first and missed. Terry's shot hit Broderick in the chest; three days later he was dead. The shooting created a national sensation, and Broderick was eulogized as having been martyred by Southerners for his support of Free Soil.[56]

Broderick's death weakened the New York–San Francisco political connection, but it did not end Manhattan's links to the West. Virtually all of those who left or were expelled from San Francisco by the vigilantes returned to New York where they continued to socialize. When Mike Walsh died in 1859, the inquest revealed that his drinking companions that night included Billy Mulligan, Tom Hyer, and George Wilkes, all ex-Californians. Wilkes left early to have dinner with Broderick, who was then in town on a visit. Some of those banished, such as Dutch Charley Duane, returned to San Francisco permanently after the vigilantes had disbanded; others like Mulligan, circulated among New York, San Francisco, and other western cities. New Yorkers continued to go west, and San Franciscans without previous New York connections filtered into Manhattan's lower wards. This countermovement from California east furthered the bond between the West and the Bowery.[57]

The gold rush did more than establish a link between the moral regions of cities and the West. The argonauts felt free to reject the tenets of bourgeois conventionality not only because of the absence of white women and churches but also because their California sojourn was temporary. As soon as "men made up their minds to settle permanently in the country," the Rev. William Taylor noticed, "their conduct underwent a great change for the better." Most of those involved understood that the day would come when they would return to their settled existence in the states. Horace Greeley thought that rural men went to cities "to balance a year's compelled decorum by a week's unrestrained debauchery." If a week on the Bowery could compensate for a year of pious and sober behavior, what would a year in California do? Balance it for a lifetime? California lived on in the memory of former miners as something close to paradise, a place that had afforded them a charmed season of youth, jolly fellowship, and few responsibilities. One forty-niner wrote of his "fascination in the memories of that time . . .

[and] intense longing for such days again, . . . I feel a pang, almost a *pain*, at the thought that I shall never see their like again." Perhaps the careful gold-rush diaries that so many men kept were to help them vicariously relive their once in a lifetime adventure. For the returnees, indulging their unruly impulses during the gold rush may have helped reconcile them to their more sedate later lives in the field, workshop, and office and thus have facilitated the embrace of the values they temporarily abandoned.[58]

It is possible that the rush thus served a significant function in consolidating the transformation in male comportment that had begun earlier in the century. Yet, there were also men who returned east with their disorderly appetites only whetted by the West Coast experience. Miner Richard Hale was convinced that "it is an easy matter to make a Yankee into a Californian, but it is no easy matter to change him back again." Such men, recalled ex-gambler J. H. Green, "came back imbued with the habits and principles of a gamester" and continued to wager and carouse for the rest of their lives. As the rush ended, sporting men fanned out from California and help to create jolly enclaves around the country where former forty-niners and others could indulge their taste for gaming. Gambler John Morris estimated that the rush created two thousand new professional gamblers in two years. The California excitement thus gave a significant boost to the sporting subculture that had its genesis in New York in the 1830s and 1840s. The gold rush may have had the paradoxical effect of both dampening and spurring jolly behavior.[59]

The forty-niners manifested comportment and values that were not solely found on the Pacific Coast even as they raised them to new heights. The rush suggests linkages and divisions in nineteenth-century American society that complicate such traditional dichotomies as East/West, urban/rural, and working class/middle class. Where jolly attitudes had once been widespread in America, by the 1850s they predominated only in moral regions like the lower wards of New York City and in western masculine milieus. These masculine bastions were to have a significant influence on shaping an American popular culture that exalted jolly fellowship in print and on stage even as it faded in taverns and streets.

CHAPTER SIX

Cultural Connections

"At the present moment," wrote James K. Kennard Jr. in the *Knickerbocker* magazine in 1845, "a certain ubiquitous person seems to be in the way of the whole people of these United States simultaneously . . . and any one may hear him told, a hundred times a day, to, 'Get out ob de way, Old Dan Tucker!'" The phrase was from a popular minstrel song, and Kennard was celebrating the incredible popularity of blackface performances. He recognized both that minstrelsy performed by white men pretending to be black was something novel and that it was distinctively American, and, tongue in cheek, he hailed minstrels as "our national poets."[1] Jolly fellowship found few defenders arguing openly that men should drink heavily, fight, and gamble, but it found many celebrators in popular culture. In the lower wards of New York—a refuge from respectability—minstrels and writers rubbed elbows with sporting and other jolly men. This convergence proved culturally fruitful as New York City spawned the blackface minstrel show and helped shape a new style of American fiction that later scholars were to label "southwestern literature." Both were, in part, discourses about masculine disorder, and both were to prove popular with men throughout the country.

By making jolly fellowship disreputable, the crusade for moral reform and self-improvement gave it a significance it had not had in the early part of the nineteenth century. No longer was it simply the way men behaved; it was now also an overt rejection of gentility, a repudiation of a whole cluster of middle-class values. There was now a meaning to mayhem, to borrow a phrase from Elliott Gorn, and so it could be employed with cultural purpose, manipulated, wielded.

Representations of jolly behavior in earlier decades when men routinely drank, fought, and played practical jokes had limited symbolic significance. Now jolly fellowship's cultural meaning was explored and exploited. Although the tavern crowd no doubt found such literary and stage portrayals fascinating, likely more significant as cultural consumers were men who had learned to control their own behavior but still found disorderly conduct fascinating. Fighting, drinking, gambling, and pranks had waned, but jolly fellows were not forgotten. In the Kingston, Rhode Island, region, wild tales of jolly forebears at Runnels's tavern in the early 1800s circulated until the 1870s, while stories of William Otter's escapades were passed down in southern Pennsylvania for decades after his death. Literary and theatrical depictions of jolly behavior may have helped men tame their own rowdy longings by allowing them to partake vicariously in such conduct. The two "extremes of social life" that reformer William Alcott worried about—the city and the frontier—were locations where jolly fellowship remained potent, and in the 1830s and 1840s creative artists in each milieu drew on jolly perspectives to make distinctive contributions to American culture.[2]

Pivotal to both the minstrel show and western literature was what Edmund Wilson labeled "the tradition of the crippling practical joke," which became one of the most significant American cultural motifs of the era. P. T. Barnum's autobiography offers what is both an explanation and a justification for his own use of pranks in his career as an entrepreneur, and more generally, for the cultural significance pranks came to have in this era. The opening paragraph of *The Life of P. T. Barnum: Written by Himself* (1855) tells the story of how his grandfather Phineas Taylor had willed him a five-acre parcel of land near Bethel, Connecticut, known as Ivy Island. As Barnum was growing up, hardly a week went past without someone speaking of his "precious patrimony"—his mother reminded him of his "immense possessions," and his grandfather never failed to note that Ivy Island made Barnum "the richest child in town." Finally, when he became twelve years old the time arrived for him to visit his magnificent legacy. "I scarcely slept for three days, so great was my joy . . . to look upon the promised land." Finally the great moment arrived and after fording a stream and pushing through the underbrush, he laid eyes on his domain. It turned out the fabled place was an inaccessible, worthless bog of "stunted ivies and a few straggling trees. . . . The truth rushed upon me. I had been made a fool of by all our neighborhood." For years afterward relatives and friends asked him what he thought of his inheritance.[3]

Barnum places the Ivy Island prank front and center in his life's story. By doing so he suggests that if in his later career as a showman he might have hoodwinked people, he was only doing what generations of men, including the "story telling, joke playing wags and wits" in Bethel's tavern, had done before. He was simply bringing the folk tradition of practical joking up to date, polishing and reworking it to fit an urban, commercial society. The language of pranks, after all, was the language of the market—perpetrators "sold" a prank to the victim who "bought" it. Barnum in his autobiography insists that in 1835 when he presented Joice Heth as George Washington's 161-year-old nanny, he did so in good faith. When, however, during their visit to Boston, people appeared too credulous, accepting without question that Heth was indeed the first president's nanny, Barnum anonymously promoted doubts about her authenticity in the city's newspapers. Was she a humbug or not? From this perspective was not Heth a kind of slick practical joke carried out for financial rather than psychological gain, the audience rendered spectators rather than participants?[4]

Barnum's hoaxes were in the spirit of the age. Newspapers in the nineteenth century routinely printed phony stories, duping gullible readers who believed them and delighting those clever enough to see the joke. The *New York Sun* printed the most famous of such tales in 1835, purporting to be an account of the development of a very powerful new telescope by John Herschel, a real astronomer. When turned on the moon the telescope discovered vast crystal mountains, beaver-like creatures who walked on two legs, and the winged "vespertilio-homo, or man-bat; . . . innocent and happy creatures, notwithstanding that some of their amusements would but ill comport with our terrestrial notions of decorum." The *Sun* was also the paper that in 1844 printed Edgar Allan Poe's famous hoax describing a transatlantic balloon flight. Even as late as 1860 the *New York Leader* presented the "startling revelation" that Albert Hicks, who had committed an infamous murder at sea and was hanged by Isaiah Rynders in his capacity as New York marshal (actually true), had been resuscitated by "an electro-chemical bath," was living in Poughkeepsie, and would shortly provide the paper with an article "describing the sensation of being dead." By 1860 the journalistic hoaxing tradition was fading in the East, but it remained alive and well in western newspapers until the 1880s.[5]

"A NEW VEIN OF LITERATURE . . . HAS BEEN OPENED IN THIS COUNTRY"

The newspaper *Spirit of the Times,* which was to hone literary pranks into a genre, was America's first sports newspaper, and it was to prove central in the creation of a cultural space where Americans continued to honor the values of masculine disorder and violence. Founded in 1831 by William T. Porter, a New

England editor and horse-racing enthusiast, the early success of *Spirit of the Times* was in large part the result of the professionalization of horse racing. Once men had tested their steeds on local roads, but increasingly matches were conducted on specially built tracks with horses ridden by paid jockeys. The Union Race Course, the country's finest, had opened on Long Island in 1821, and it became the site of a series of well-publicized stakes matches between northern and southern horses. The Boston-Fashion match race in 1842, the most famous of these intersectional contests, brought horse racing to unparalleled popularity and made the *Spirit* a national success. Yet the subject matter of the *Spirit* was much broader than racing. Porter promised to devote his paper not just to the turf but also to "the Ring, the Angler, the Hunter—News, Literature, Fashion, Taste, the Drama, and Scenes of Real Life." The *Spirit* carried hunting and fishing articles, stories on rowing and other minor sports, New York City items, theater reviews, and humorous fiction. To maintain a genteel tone, Porter abandoned his early coverage of prizefights and cockfights.[6]

Both the *Spirit* and the six-four Porter, nicknamed "the Tall Son of York," were closely connected to the sporting fraternity of the city's lower wards. The *Spirit* building was on Barclay Street, the center of New York gambling in the 1840s and just across Broadway from the sporting saloons on Park Row. The *Spirit* writers' favorite hangout was Frank Monteverde's fancy billiard and bowling saloon, nearby on Barclay Street, which became a rendezvous for the city's literary and sporting elite in the late 1830s and 1840s. Porter held court there surrounded by a "crowd of 'smilers' [drinkers] who followed in the wake of York's Tall Son," the *New York Leader* remembered. "The patrons . . . were decidedly fast men." The diverse crowd that made up the "Barclay Street Guards," as the regulars were called, included not only *Spirit* writers such as Thomas Bangs Thorpe and Albert Pike but also the poet and wit Fitz-Greene Halleck, influential editors Lewis Gaylord Clark and Nathaniel P. Willis, urban journalist George Foster, and the painter Henry Inman. Edgar Allan Poe and Herman Melville were said to pay the occasional visit. These literary men rubbed elbows with sporting men, including Pat Herne, perhaps the most famous gambler of the era.[7]

The early *Spirit* vaunted its urbanity and its pages reflected the boisterous lower wards. But from the beginning most of its subscribers were from the South and West, where horse racing was a passion. There, as is New York City, the progress of moral reform had been slow. There had began to develop powerful networks of connection, both socially and culturally, between New York and the South and the West. This intersection of the early New York sporting scene and rural jolly fellowship proved artistically fertile, and an outpouring of violent, comic fiction, set on the frontier, became the most distinctive feature of Porter's paper. This style of humor did not originate with the *Spirit.* Stories surrounding Congressman David Crockett, a Tennessee Jacksonian turned Whig, were the genesis of this literature. James Kirke Paulding's 1831 play *The Lion of the West* (also called *The Kentuckian; or, A Trip to New York*) featured a character clearly based on Crockett, Nimrod Wildfire, who was a frontier boaster: "My father can whip the best man in old Kaintuck, and I can whip my father. When I'm good natured I weigh about a hundred and seventy, but when I'm mad, I weigh a *ton.*"[8]

A series of comic almanacs published in New York, Boston, Philadelphia, Baltimore, and Nashville between 1835 and 1856 made Crockett a folkloric figure. The almanacs relate his ludicrous adventures in the backwoods world with his sidekick Ben Hardin and his sometimes-antagonist, the legendary flatboatman Mike Fink. The almanacs' frontier is a grotesque environment of gigantic animals and gnarled, disfigured humans, a world without religion or sentimentality. The almanac Crockett is the archetypal backwoods roarer: an intrepid hunter, hard drinker, savage rough-and-tumble fighter, and unrestrained trickster. "Thar'll be no fun till I cum," promised Crockett. The almanacs were among the earliest print representations of the characteristic comic-violent strain in jolly fellowship. They recount many uproarious jokes and brutal fights and pioneered what would become a popular cultural motif for the rest of the century, the killing and mutilation of people of color for humorous effect. In *Crockett's Yaller Flower Almanac* (1836), he boasted he could "swaller a nigger whole without choking." In another tale Crockett headbutts an Indian in half, then grinds another into "injun gravy with my foot, and spread it over" the first Indian "and made a dinner for me and my dog. It was superlicious."[9]

The year the first Crockett almanacs appeared, 1835, also saw the publication of Augustus Baldwin Longstreet's rustic comedy of manners, *Georgia Scenes.* A Yale-educated lawyer and judge who later became president of Emory College and the University of Mississippi, Longstreet originally wrote these sketches for Georgia newspapers. Claiming the stories were based on "fanciful *combinations* of real incidents and characters," Longstreet humorously depicted Georgia life in tales set around horse trades and races, militia musters, rough-and-tumble brawls, shooting matches, dances, and gander pulls. The collection of his stories was a hit in both the North and South, selling more than eight thousand copies. Longstreet's success spawned imitators, and such dialect tales developed into a distinctive literary genre.[10]

Georgia Scenes' success encouraged Porter to print some regional sketches, and the 1840s saw a torrent of them in the *Spirit.* Porter collected a coterie of able contributors, mostly from the South and West. Among the best known were Thomas Bangs Thorpe—a native New Yorker then living Louisiana—whose story "The Big Bear of Arkansas" was among the most celebrated humorous pieces of the era; Alabaman Johnson Jones Hooper, whose *Adventures of Captain Simon Suggs* (1845) was dedicated to Porter; Henry Clay Lewis, a Louisiana physician; and Tennessean George Washington Harris, creator of the *Sut Lovingood* tales. The humorous pieces by these and other writers quickly became the *Spirit*'s most popular feature. Despite a high subscription price of ten dollars a year, the circulation of the twelve-page weekly grew rapidly, and in the mid-1840s circulation may have reached forty thousand. The popularity of the *Spirit* tales encouraged western newspapers, most prominently the *New Orleans Picayune* and the *St. Louis Reveille*, to publish works in a similar vein.[11]

In his 1858 obituary for the Tall Son of York, George Wilkes, having returned to New York and become *Spirit* coeditor, maintained that Porter had created "an American literature, . . . fresh, crisp, vigorous, elastic . . . , full of force, readiness, actuality and point." Porter himself, in his preface to *The Big Bear of Arkansas and Other Tales* (1845), a collection of *Spirit* stories, boasted that "a new vein of literature, as original as it is inexhaustible in its source, has been opened in this country." This "new vein of literature" owed much to old veins of literature. Picaresque novels, such as those of Henry Fielding and Tobias Smollett, were an influence on the *Spirit*'s humorists, and the colorful, eccentric characters that inhabit their universe owed a good deal to Dickens. Yet Wilkes was right to emphasize their freshness. At a time when much American fiction was tame and formulaic, the *Spirit* directed readers' attention to a wild and brutal element in American life.[12]

There is considerable similarity in milieu and mood in these tales. Most are set in newly settled areas of the South or border states, and the characters usually speak in dialect, the hallmark of American regional fiction. In their use of the popular vernacular, these tales set the stage for Mark Twain and later writers. *Spirit* tales set outside the South or West were lackluster, and only with the Mose plays beginning in 1848 was roistering southwestern-style humor successfully transplanted to an urban milieu. This was a literature written by white males for white male readers—in only a handful of *Spirit* stories are women central characters, children are rare, and blacks usually appear only on the margins, often as the victims of white jokes. Protagonists include frontiersmen, tavern and grocery regulars, boatmen, doctors and lawyers. Disorderly white male behavior is central to the works of the southern humorists. Liquor flows freely. Men gamble, and horse races, cockfights, and dogfights are typical story settings. What Norris W.

Yates calls "jovial brutality" characterizes the tales—savage brawls are a recurring theme, and there is remorseless cruelty to animals.[13]

The prank, argued Constance Rourke in her book *American Humor* (1931), is the key motif of these tales. Central to these stories were "vast practical jokes, pranks played on ministers and camp meetings, and on settled and respectable people generally. . . . Grotesquerie and irreverence made up their center." The *Spirit* writers who were part of the "Barclay Street Guards" were in real life noted pranksters, and their love of joking infused their writing. The *Spirit of the Times* in the 1840s printed dozens of anecdotes and stories about practical jokes, most very much in the jolly-fellow mode. Typical titles indicate the focus: "Results of a Practical Joke," "Reminiscences of a Philadelphia Joker," "Practical Jokes and Bad Liquor," "A Young Practical Joker." Porter furthered the jolly ambiance by occasionally printing a burlesque newspaper, *The Trumpet Blast of Freedom* inside the *Spirit*. Printed in "Buncombe," it is full of in-jokes and parodied the *Spirit* and other New York newspapers with mock accounts of horse races, outlandish advertisements, and lampoons of serious literary men such as Cornelius Mathews and James Watson Webb.[14]

The cruel humor of the jolly fellows echoes through *Spirit* fiction. "There are some made to *saw*, others to be sawed, and in fact, of these two classes are the world composed," explained one sketch. Humor and violence are inextricably linked together in these tales. Before leaving home, Johnson Jones Hooper's Simon Suggs puts gunpowder in his mother's pipe, carefully covering it with tobacco, hoping "to blow the old woman within a foot and a half of kingdom come." In the *Spirit*'s "An April Fool Trick," set in Louisiana, the host at a banquet serves the guests a dessert pudding laced with sawdust and soap. Vomiting quickly follows, and the perpetrator watches his guests' misery, "splitting his sides with laughter." In William Thompson's "The Duel," the tavern crowd eggs the terrified Major Jones into an affair of honor. Everyone but Jones knows that the seconds have loaded the guns with blanks. Jones fires and his "wounded" antagonist drops, and, seemingly writhing in pain, asks the horrified Jones to approach him before he dies as "the boys" revel in Jones's anguish.[15]

This fiction at first glance might seem to be simply a celebration of jolly conduct—of drinking, fighting, gambling, and practical joking. But as scholar Kenneth Lynn emphasizes, there is also a countertext of disapproval. Tales in the *Spirit* mode are typically told by what Lynn calls "the Self-controlled Gentleman," who remains a detached narrator and writes in a calm and polished style that contrasts sharply to the uproarious events recounted and the coarse dialect of the characters. Noting that most of the southern humorists were Whigs, this

"Self-controlled Gentleman," Lynn argues, represents the Whig ideal. Though the *Spirit* was nonpolitical, Porter was himself a Whig, as were Thorpe, Hooper, and Longstreet. Human progress, the stories implied, touching on a favorite Whig theme, hinged of necessity on individual self-control; only by exercising self-control could men hope to avoid the natural tendency to self-indulgence and its attendant disorganization.[16]

Mississippi lawyer Joseph G. Baldwin's "How the Times Served the Virginians" in his collection *The Flush Times of Mississippi and Alabama: A Series of Sketches* (1853)—a classic of the genre—suggests the Whig concern with self-governance. Baldwin depicts the speculative boom of the 1830s as a "reign of humbug and wholesale insanity" in which "calculations of prudence" were ignored and "riot and coarse debauchery filled up the vacant hours." Groceries were "in full blast in those days, no village having less than a half-dozen all busy all the time," and Alabama and Mississippi swarmed with hustlers, shyster lawyers, quack doctors, crooked gamblers, and confidence men. It was an age of "vulgarity—ignorance—fussy and arrogant pretension—unmitigated rowdyism—bullying insolence," unrestrained by religion, public opinion, or law. It would be mistaken, however, to see these tales simply as parables on the evils of male dissipation. The reaction of the *Spirit* writers to the raucous lost world they depict is more complex than merely glorification of self-control. The more violent stories may been intended to help male readers spurn jolly activities. By enjoying these tales of ferocious fights, drunken revels, and sharp pranks, disorderly impulses might remain fantasies. It would, however, be mistaken to focus too much on the didactic character of these tales. The southwestern writers considered themselves humorists and were writing to entertain, and the genre's popularity depends to a considerable degree on a yearning for unfettered male comportment of earlier days. While the self-controlled gentleman keeps his distance from the events and often condemns the rowdy proceedings, there is no question that he finds them amusing and captivating and assumes readers will as well. There is, throughout the entire genre, a powerful undercurrent of nostalgia for male revelry. What is most striking in the stories is not the often perfunctory denunciations of disorder or praise of moral progress, but the exhilaration of living in such a time, the sheer, uninhibited joy of drinking, gambling, fighting, and joking to a man's heart's content. The esteem for masculine escapades is palpable—beneath the amused disdain is a robust undercurrent of affection.[17]

These stories are fully comprehensible only in the context of the vanishing world of jolly fellowship. Critical to comprehending the significance of these stories is that they were set mostly in the past. Rowdy comportment could be admired at a distance since it no longer seemed an imminent peril to self-controlled individualism. Longstreet boasted, as did other southwestern authors, that his literature was drawn from real life, and scholars have agreed, echoing Constance Rourke that "character and custom in small sections of the Southwest were portrayed with such close and ready detail as to provide something of a record of the time and place." But the time depicted is usually not the 1840s or 1850s when the stories were written; it is an earlier America, an America before moral reformation began to undercut white masculine disorder. Longstreet's "Georgia Theatrics," in *Georgia Scenes*, locates the action in 1809 in the "Dark Corner" of Lincoln County, so called "from the moral darkness which reigned over that portion of the county at the time of which I am speaking." Longstreet adds, however, that since then the county has seen "instances of the most wonderful transitions, from vice and folly to virtue and holiness, which have ever, perhaps been witnessed." William T. Thompson sets the stories in *Major Jones' Scenes in Georgia* (1843), some of which were published in the *Spirit*, in the fictional town of Pineville, "before the temperance society was organized . . . when Pineville was 'another sort of place.'" Joseph Baldwin's *The Flush Times of Mississippi and Alabama* is set in "the old times," that "halcyon period, . . . that golden era" before the frolic was ended by the Specie Circular and the Panic of 1837. Those *Spirit* stories not set in the past were set west of the Mississippi River—stories from the 1840s usually were set in Missouri and Arkansas and those from the 1850s in California. Other contemporary stories are set in masculine milieus such as steamboats, courtrooms, colleges, and the military.[18]

Baldwin's brilliant depiction of Seargent S. Prentiss in *The Flush Times of Mississippi and Alabama* suggests southwestern writers' attachment to the lost world of raucous male camaraderie. Prentiss was a real Mississippi Whig lawyer who was elected to Congress in 1837 but was never seated because of a dispute over the legitimacy of his special election. A minor politician and lawyer, Prentiss attained towering stature as the embodiment of southern jolly fellowship. He became a hero to southern men owing to his combination of good looks, intelligence, and eloquence that thrilled listeners with its "manliness of tone." Baldwin clearly situates Prentiss in the context of the past: he "was a type of his times," a representative "of the wilder and more impetuous part" of Mississippi's young male population in the 1830s and 1840s. Prentiss's impressive physique garnered him instant regard: he was "large and uncommonly athletic and muscular; his arms and chest well-formed; . . . his head large, and a model of classical proportions and noble contour." His personality, however, was to Baldwin, even more magnificent. To know Prentiss was to love him. Always cheerful, he was forthright and brave, generous and loyal to comrades. He would cosign friends' notes for a loan without even looking at the amount, and "when he treated, it was a mass entertainment." He bet thousands on the turn of a card and won or lost with the same good-humored nonchalance. He once put down his poker hand and went off to fight a duel, "laughing with his friends as to a pic-nic." A fabled prankster, in an oft-repeated tale, Prentiss awakened the owner and tavern guests to hold a mock trial for a bedbug.[19]

Prentiss's flaws, for Baldwin, were those of his age. Baldwin can never bring himself to openly declare what Prentiss seems to have been, a compulsive gambler and alcoholic, mentioning only his pleasure in the "midnight revel and drunken carouse," but Baldwin concedes some flaws in Prentiss's character. He lacked "regular, self-denying, systematic application. . . . Life . . . was a thing to be enjoyed—a bright holiday season—a gala day, to be spent freely and carelessly." His example had a harmful effect on the "mediocrity"; young men who tried to imitate Prentiss but, lacking his brilliant temperament, energy, and intelligence, were doomed to founder. Baldwin, however, ends on a strongly positive note. Despite his ambivalence, he must stand in admiration of such a man, a man whose character contained "so much that is honorable, noble and generous—so much of a manhood whose robust and masculine virtues are set off by wild and lovely graces that attempered and adorned its strength." When Prentiss, sunk in dissolution, died in 1850 at age forty-two, it seemed "that the world had somehow grown commonplace." "Regular, self-denying, systematic application" was becoming the order of the day. Mississippi's full-blooded youth had ended, its humdrum adulthood had commenced.[20]

Henry Clay Lewis and George Washington Harris brought western humor to a pinnacle of fevered intensity. They realized the profoundly subversive, even anarchic, potential of the practical joke. Their stories are often set in the present, and the ambiguity about jolly fellowship that marked the work of Baldwin and others gives way, at times, to open celebration in theirs. Lewis was a Louisiana physician, and his sketches for the *Spirit* in the 1840s were later collected in *Odd Leaves from the Life of a Louisiana Swamp Doctor* (1850). The doctor's name is Madison Tensas, a combination of the names of two rural and isolated Louisiana counties on the Mississippi River. The Mississippi had long been associated with jolly comportment, but this is not the Mississippi of rollicking river towns or steamboat gamblers. The bayou country where Tensas practiced is a remote, atavistic, primitive universe of its own, far removed from the polite world of planters and townsmen. Most of its few inhabitants are loners, misfits, and freaks. The name of Tensas's horse is Chaos, and the love for random disorder is at the heart of Lewis's humor. Violence is humor, tragedy is comedy. There is a relish in dismemberment of bodies, dead and alive, human and animal. Stories recount the torment of women, Irishmen, and blacks under the guise of medical treatment. In "Cupping an Irishman," burning alcohol is poured over the patient. Tensas, in "Stealing a Baby," sneaks the corpse of a black infant out of the morgue to dissect and accidentally drops it on the street. In another tale Tensas slices off the face of a black albino corpse and, as a prank, leaves it where the landlady of his boardinghouse would find it.[21]

Torture of animals is high comedy. In the "Day of Judgement," one of Lewis's most characteristic tales, Tensas is returning from a house call when he stops at a tavern. There he falls in with the regulars; drinking begins in earnest, and by nightfall the group is "prepared for any wild freak or mad adventure." A camp meeting was going on nearby, and Tensas and his friends decide to put a halt to it. (Disrupting religious revivals was a favorite of the *Spirit* humorists.) There seems no particular reason for doing this beyond the pleasure in the distress of others in general and pious Christians in particular that it afforded. It was 1844, the time of William Miller's millennial predictions, and the tavern crowd decide to "personify the fiery consummation which revelation tells us shall terminate the world." Stealing a mule from the tavern stable and carrying horns and burning torches, they creep up to the riverside meeting ground. The pranksters cover the mule with turpentine and tar and ignite it. "Quick as lightening the fire spread over the body of the devoted animal." The mule gives "a scream of terror and anguish," as they chase it toward the gathering. With "with the roaring of the flames, our piercing yells, discordant horns, and the horrible cries of the animals," the blazing charivari causes bedlam among the worshipers. "Prayers and blasphemy" mingled with "the maniacal shouts of the conscience stricken sinners." The story concludes:

> The stream was nearly reached; with ecstasy the poor brute beheld the glistening waters; he sped on with accelerated steps—one more spring, and he would find surcease of anguish 'neath their cooling waves. But he was destined never to reach them; he fell exhausted on the brink, vainly endeavoring, with extended neck, to allay his fiery thirst; as the flame, now bereft of fuel, sent up its last flickering ray, the poor mule, with a low reproachful mourn, expired.

That Lewis's *Odd Leaves*, wrote Kenneth Lynn, "was considered a humorous work is amazing, but true."[22]

The Sut Lovingood tales written in the 1850s by George Washington Harris and set in the Tennessee hills depict a world somewhat similar to Lewis's. Harris,

"Stealing a Nigger Baby." In Henry Clay Lewis (Madison Tensas pseud.), *Odd Leaves from the Life of a Louisiana "Swamp Doctor"* (Philadelphia, 1858).

who wrote as "Sugartail" for the *Spirit of the Times*, was one of the rare Democrats among Porter's contributors. Even more open in his valuation of the jolly worldview than other *Spirit* writers, he offers in his work something of a culmination of the genre. Edmund Wilson, in his discussion of Harris in *Patriotic Gore* (1962), calls *Sut Lovingood: Yarns Spun by a "Nat'ral Born Durn'd Fool"* (1867) "by far the most repellent book of any real literary merit in American literature," memorably describing the ne'er-do-well Sut as "a dreadful half bestial lout, . . . a peasant squatting in his own filth." Wilson argues that central to the Lovingood tales is "the crippling practical joke," and vicious pranks are the focus of many of the most memorable stories. Although there is a strain of class resentment in the tales, the victims are more often powerless than powerful. Harris's racism, like Lewis's, is constantly on display. Victims include not only blacks but Yankees, Irishmen, Jews, preachers, strong-minded women, "stuft up fellers"—anyone, indeed, Sut dislikes or is simply at hand.[23]

F. O. Matthiessen believed that Harris "brings us closer than any other writer to the indigenous and undiluted resources of the American language, to the tastes of the common man himself." But what tastes! A Tennessee Till Eulenspiegel, Sut seems to have no occupation and spends most of his time at the grocery bar taking on "a hed ove steam" and watching for opportunities to raise hell. Lovingood is a fascinating character, by turns self-pitying and belligerent. "I ain't got a soul, nuffin but a whiskey proof gizzard," proclaims Sut. The name "Lovingood" is ironic; despite his best efforts he is no ladies' man. Sut, an uncompromising believer in the depravity of man, is the joker as nihilist, whose merciless pranks shatter any uncertainty about the desperation of the human condition. "Ef ever yu dus anything tu enybody wifout cause, yu hates em allers afterwards, an' sorter wants to hurt him agin." Lovingood elucidates with characteristically earthy metaphors: "When yu sees a littil long laiged lamb a-shaking hits tail an' a-dancin staggerinly onder his mam a-huntin for the tit . . . yer fingers *will* itch tu seize that ar tail, and fling the littil ankshus son ove a mutton over the fence amung the blackberry briars, not tu hurt hit, but jis' tu dispirit hit." Or with a human baby: "Don't yu feel hungary to gin hit' jis' one 'cussion cap slap rite, onto the place what sum day'll fit a saddil . . . to show hit what's atwixt hit an' the grave." People act solely in their self-interest, and anyone who claims not to is either a liar or a fool.[24]

Humor and violence are inextricably bound: in a typical story Sut disrupts a "nigger" camp meeting with a giant stink bomb and a swarm of angry bees. As in Lewis's tales, some of the most memorable episodes in the Lovingood stories involve cruelty to animals. One scholar has described "skinned carcasses or the bloody parts of butchered animals" as one of the recurring motifs in the tales. In one of the most popular stories, which was widely anthologized, Sut feeds a dog a sausage skin filled with gunpowder.

> I hearn a noise like bustin sumthin, an his tail lit atop ove my hat. His head wer way down the hill and hed tuck a death holt outer a root. His fore laigs were fifty feet up the road, a makin runnin moshuns, and his hine ones a straddin ove the fence. His innerds were hanging in links onter the cabin chimney, sept about a

> yard in mam's bussum, and his paunch cum down permiscusly like rain. Es tu the dog hisself, *es a dog*, I never seed him agin.

M. Thomas Inge, who in 1967 edited a collection of the Lovingood tales, expressed wonder that "Sut's famous dog story" was so often reprinted and adds "one is hard put to explain exactly why the nineteenth-century reader found it humorous."[25]

For Lovingood, critic Milton Rickels has explained, "every practical joke is a delight because it is a conspiracy against all order." Sut's delight in bedlam is on flamboyant display in "Frustrating a Funeral." A slave named Caesar "tuck a noshun" he'd spite his master Hunnicutt by dying, "an durned ef he didn't du hit." A doctor wants Caesar's "cackus tu chop up," so he hires Sut to steal the dead body. That night Sut sneaks onto Hunnicutt's farm and finds the body in a slave cabin along with another slave named Major who is dead drunk. Sut decides, for no reason other than to create bedlam, to "swap niggers." He puts Major in the coffin, paints his face with red and whites stripes, and puts "yearlin's ho'ns" on him to make him look like the devil. Harris shares with Lewis the view that black corpses were for whites' amusement, and Sut turns his attention to Caesar. He smears crushed fireflies on him to make him glow, "I then pried open his mouf, an' let his teef shet onto the back ove a live bull-frog," and "pinned a littil live garter-snake by hits middil crosswise his mouf." Sut leaves the corpse standing upright in the corner and then hides to see what happens. A black preacher comes in, spots Caesar, and runs off in terror. The next to come is the owner Hunnicutt. Whites prove as easily frightened as blacks. As Caesar's master spies the corpse, Sut moans, "*yu am* fell from grace" with "Missus Loftin. *Cum wif me.*" Hunnicutt bolts off and continues running, even as Sut yells, "Stop!, I means tu take Missus Loftin *wif yu.*"[26]

The comedy continues. Sut lugs Caesar's corpse to the doctor's office and sets him up in the corner. When the terrified physician lays eyes on him he dashes off and keeps going until he gets to California. Sut carries Caesar's body into the woods and dumps him and returns to Hunnicutt's where he is pleased to learn that "everybody wer skar'd durn ni outen thar wits." The relatives decide they better bury what they think is Caesar immediately, but in the wagon on the way to the graveyard Major awakes from his drunken slumber and emerges from the coffin. "Thuty screams mixed in one . . . an' thar warn't a nigger lef in site afore a stutterin man cud whistil." Major, unaware of his painted face, wanders around producing chaos: "Wimen went head-fust intu the houses, doors slam'd, sash fell [and] cats' tails swell'd." Major eventually washes off the paint, and Sut returns and buries Caesar, but the disorder endures. Sut exults in the pandemonium that only confirms his cynical view of the human race. "The county's ruinated, an' hits haunted yet wif all sorts ove orful haunts; yu ken buy land thar fur a dime an acre, on tick at that."[27]

"SPORTING MEN WERE FOND OF THE MINSTRELS"

In addition to the flowering of southwestern literature, the decade of the 1840s saw the creation of the minstrel show. There were important similarities and connections between the two. Both were entertainments by white men for white men, both often dealt in various and complex ways with jolly fellowship, and both were set in the South. The differences, however, are important. The *Spirit* tales are mostly set in the white backwoods South; minstrelsy, on the other hand, presents an idealized version of the slave South. Southwestern literature eulogized a lost jolly rural past; minstrelsy, by contrast, exuberantly celebrated the jolly urban present. Despite its putative depiction of southern slave life, minstrelsy's origins and outlook were city oriented. In southwestern literature detachment was temporal; stories are set in former times. In minstrelsy the separation was physical; the blackface maintained the distance. And, though most of the southwestern writers were Whigs, the leading minstrels were Democrats, and minstrel songs and sketches often advanced positions congruent with their political views.

Minstrelsy from the start was closely tied to New York City. Theatergoing was a tremendously popular source of urban entertainment in a city where so many young men, especially young working-class men, lived as boarders. New York's many theaters catered to them with minstrel shows and other entertainments geared to men. In an era when virtually every theater had an attached bar, the heavily male audiences were boisterous, and minstrel performances reflected this disorderly urban ambience. The men on stage were also often New Yorkers. "The minstrel performers and song writers and actors were all people from N. Y. or some northern city," remembered James Thomas, himself a minstrel. Thomas D. Rice was the first prominent "Ethiopian delineator." Born in 1808 in New York's waterfront Seventh Ward, Rice had apprenticed as a shipbuilding carpenter and began singing in saloons and working as an extra at the Park Theater. There had been earlier performances in blackface, but Rice's song about a black slave featured a catchy tune and a distinctive dance that made it a hit and Rice a star. The chorus went:

Weel about and turn about
And do jis so,
Eb'ry time I weel about
And jump Jim Crow.

Rice claimed he based "Jim Crow" on a dance by a black livery stable employee he saw in Louisville, but W. T. Lhamon Jr. suggests it is more likely that Rice was inspired by the black dancers and their contests at the Seventh Ward's Catherine Market in the 1820s. Rice was already well known when he opened in New York at the Bowery Theater in 1832, and the song became a national sensation. Rice's landmark performance set off a rage for "plantation melodies" that would continue almost until the end of the century.[28]

If minstrelsy's early roots were in New York, it was also closely tied to the lower-ward milieu, and the close connections between minstrels and the city's sporting fraternity were to prove significant in pushing early minstrelsy in a jolly direction. In a period when theater people were usually scorned by respectable society, minstrels, even more than other stage performers, tended to fraternize with the demiworld of gamblers, sporting men, and their hangers-on that centered on lower Broadway and Park Row. In "ante bellum days sporting men were fond of the minstrels," the *New York Herald* commented in 1875, in explaining the friendship of Dan Bryant—in the 1850s minstrelsy's greatest star—with gamblers and prizefighters. Some minstrels bridged both worlds. Charles White, founder of White's Minstrels and one of minstrelsy's biggest stars, was also a professional gambler who would bring his weekly pay every Saturday night to a Mercer Street saloon and deal a faro game.[29]

Even to other actors, minstrels seemed a breed apart. The minstrel, actor John J. Jennings remarked, "talks differently from other people, acts differently, eats differently." They "always talk[ed] in hyperbole," recalled Ralph Keeler from his days as a blackface performer. The *New York Clipper* believed minstrels "became so accustomed to joking on the stage" that they became jesters off stage as well. They were legendary for their pranks. Dan Bryant and his friend and troupe member Nelse Seymour were the leading spirits in minstrelsy's most famous practical joke at a formal dinner for Philip Lee, the stuffy husband of the famous English actress Adelaide Neilson. Bryant and Seymour suddenly had words, then went at each other, wrestling on the banquet table before pulling pistols and blazing away with blanks. Minstrels wore flashy clothes, large rings, and diamond tie clasps much like sporting men. They were legendary for their generosity, especially to their fellow minstrels, a generosity that was reflected in the elaborate benefit performances the minstrel fraternity staged to raise money for a deceased minstrel's family. The benefit following Dan Bryant's death in 1875 was held in eleven theaters simultaneously and featured virtually every major star in the profession.[30]

There had been individual blackface acts like Rice on stage for two decades, but it was only in the 1840s that minstrel groups skyrocketed to popularity. Ensemble minstrelsy was a tightly organized evening of songs, dances, and comic skits depicting fanciful plantation settings and performed by four or more white men in blackface. The minstrel show began in New York, which remained its greatest stronghold. In the winter of 1842–43 four veteran blackface entertainers met in a Catherine Street boardinghouse and began practicing together. Led by Billy Whitlock, a former *New York Herald* printer turned banjoist, the others were Dan Emmett, an Ohio-born musician-songwriter, and Dick Pelham and Francis Brower, both native New Yorkers. The four gave some performances at the Branch Saloon on the Bowery and at Bartlett's billiard room, a well-known establishment where Tom Hyer later worked. The group then visited the Bowery Theater, as Emmett told the *New York Clipper* years later, to "give one of the proprietors (Uncle Nate Howes) . . . a 'charivari' . . . to 'browbeat' . . . [him] into giving them an engagement, the calculation being that he would succumb in preference to standing the horrible noise." They debuted at the Bowery on 6 February 1843 as the Virginia Serenaders. Their first performance on their own was at the Cornucopia, a Park Row sporting saloon that later became Rynders's Arena. They went on tour as the Virginia Minstrels to rave notices—"they are rare boys—'full of fun' and music," the *Boston Evening Transcript* wrote of their debut in that city. Later in the year they played in London. Other groups followed their ensemble format, most prominently Christy's Minstrels, and within a few years there were ten minstrel theaters in New York.[31]

The person the Virginia Minstrels chose as their agent was George B. Wooldridge. Perhaps no one, with the exceptions of George Wilkes and Isaiah Rynders, was more deeply involved in New York's sporting subculture than Wooldridge. A former butcher and volunteer fireman, in the 1830s he became a tavern keeper and in the early 1840s ran a "dance hall" called the House of Novelty on Chambers Street and later managed other establishments that also were almost surely brothels. In 1841 he became involved in the so-called flash or sporting press, co-editing with sporting man George Wilkes the *New York Sunday Flash*, a scandal sheet. Wooldridge then edited the *New York Whip*, "devoted to the Sports of the Ring, the Turf, and City Life—such as Sprees, Larks, Crim Cons, Seductions, Rapes, &c.—not forgetting to keep a watchful eye on all the Brothels and their frail inhabitants." One of the most active members of Rynders's Empire

Club, Wooldridge in 1844, tired of "one man power," led "fifty Old Sports" into his newly formed Order of Clever Fellows. The Clever Fellows eventually collapsed, and the Captain had the pleasure of seeing Wooldridge and his followers "humbly beg their way back" into the Empire Club. In the middle of all this, Wooldridge—who may well have helped organize the group and even may been at the original Catherine Street gathering—was acting as manager of the Virginia Minstrels and traveled with them to England and elsewhere. In 1859, by then living in Washington where he had a political appointment, Wooldridge began writing a column about past and present sporting men for the Tammany *New York Leader.*[32]

The easy mingling of early minstrelsy with sporting activities is illustrated by the early career of Dan Rice. Born Daniel McLaren in New York's tough Five Points neighborhood of the Sixth Ward, he may have taken the name Rice to try and associate himself with Thomas Rice. Even as a teenager Dan attracted attention with his magnificent physique; he was "as powerful a human machine as any one of his day and generation had seen." An enthusiastic gambler, he was a jockey in horse races in the New York area and elsewhere. Still under twenty, Rice headed West where he worked, so he later claimed, as a Mississippi riverboat gambler. Shortly thereafter he toured with an "educated pig" and performed as a strongman, billing himself the "Young American Hercules." Rice's victory in a rough-and-tumble fight outside of Pittsburgh with "Devil Jack, the Bully of Bayardstown" attracted notice, but Rice was beaten badly in his only prizefight. Rice maintained that he performed at Barnum's Museum in 1841 as "The VIRGINIA NEGRO," and it is certain he later toured as a minstrel with the Ethiopian Serenaders. Eventually, Rice became the first great American circus clown, but at this point in his career it is hard to know what to call him. Gambler? Pugilist? Sporting man? Minstrel?[33]

Though the minstrel show was born in New York City, its popularity soon spread throughout the country. Nowhere was it as popular as in California. Dan Emmett's ballad "Jordan Is a Hard Road to Travel" became the anthem for men heading West, since the Overland Trail was indeed "a hard road to travel." San Francisco, which "for its size and age . . . appeared to surpass New York in theatrical diversions," was the focus of Pacific Coast minstrelsy, but virtually every major mining town, including Marysville, Sonora, and Stockton, California, and Virginia City, Nevada, had theaters where minstrel groups performed. In the mining regions minstrels performed in saloons or even in the open air, and there were amateur performances by the miners themselves. The San Francisco Minstrels, who originated in that city in 1864, became one of the most popular minstrel groups ever. Their rapid-fire combination of puns, parodies, and pratfalls, interspersed with their trademark risqué wisecracks, made the group too uninhibited to be acceptable outside of California—except in New York City. When they arrived in Manhattan in 1865 they were a sensation and continued to play there in their own theater, never touring, until the group disbanded in 1883.[34]

"LIFE IS BUT A SPAN . . . , LIVE AS JOLLY AS YOU CAN"

Minstrel performances were extraordinarily eclectic, a pastiche of artistic forms and styles of music and humor that operated on many levels. The performances involved singing, dancing, instrumental solos, and comedy, and no single factor can explain minstrelsy's broad appeal; it was all of them together. The typical show opened with five or six white male performers in blackface sitting on stage with their musical instruments. There was no real plot—each song, dance, or comic skit was self-contained. There was not even a fixed performance: the mix of dance, banjo instrumentals, ballads, and humor depended in part on the reaction of the raucous audiences of the period, who did not hesitate to make their wishes known. Performances were infused with energy. "They could not stay still for an instant," writes minstrelsy's historian Robert Toll. They darted about the stage, keeping up a steady stream of songs, dances, jokes, puns, and pranks. At its most frenzied, minstrel performances spiraled into howling; "their wild hollering and their bobbing, seemingly compulsive movements charged their entire performances with excitement." The minstrel show was chaos, but controlled chaos. Extensive rehearsal was needed to master the split-second timing the dances and sketches required—minstrelsy was on the margin between mayhem and self-mastery, creating a tension that was part of its attraction.[35]

Although its subject matter was eclectic from the beginning, in the 1840s minstrel groups devoted most attention to allegedly accurate depictions of the songs and dances of happy slaves on southern plantations. By the 1850s minstrelsy broadened to include an increasingly wide range of material that reflected the dynamism of America's booming cities: "*Hi! Hi!! Hi!!! Hi!!!! Dis is de Screamer and it Aint Nuffen Else!*" one songbook proclaimed. Minstrelsy was a passion in major cities, but it was popular almost everywhere. Although many moralists denounced it as crude and vulgar, by the 1850s dozens of blackface troupes toured the country. Minstrel music, explained a writer in *Putnam's Magazine*, "touched a chord in the American heart" and thus became popular with all classes—from farmers to even "merchants and staid professional men." It was, *Putnam's* agreed, America's national entertainment.[36]

Minstrelsy's messages were embedded in dense layers of cultural references and perspectives, and its remarkable complexity was likely part of its appeal. Its attraction was intricate, but central to it was that it was performed by white men pretending to be black. In an era when so much attention was paid to faces and bodies, disguise could have a powerful liberating effect. By giving white men black bodies to play in, minstrelsy provided a highly creative cultural construction. Many scholars have seen the conflicted response of white audiences as central to minstrelsy's power and popularity: they were repulsed by blacks but nevertheless fascinated by them. The blackface distanced audiences, who could thus relish minstrels' free spirits and extravagant antics without identifying completely with them. On one level, they could envy their spontaneity and jolly jests; on another level, they could still feel superior. As multilayered and complex as minstrelsy was, the supposed affinity of real blacks for jolly fellowship—which minstrelsy both drew on and reinforced—was a significant part of its appeal.[37]

Although the high-spirited performers on stage were engaging, minstrels always reminded audiences that they were watching *black* singers, jesters, lovers, drinkers, and brawlers. Time after time songs and sketches emphasized the appearance of African American faces and bodies. Mostly it focused on their repulsive otherness, their blackness, flat noses, large lips, and distinctive hair, usually described as "woolly," making them seem more animal than human. "Yaller gals" could be attractive, but darker women were grotesque. "Lubly Fan" had "lips . . . like de oyster plant, . . . / I try to kiss dem but I cant, / Dey am so berry large." Black men were equally bizarre. The description of "Old Dan Tucker" was typical: "His nose so flat, his face so full, / De top ob his head like a bag ob wool." One of the nineteenth century's strangest racial stereotypes was the belief that blacks had misshapen heels—those of the children of "Dandy Jim from Caroline" "stuck out three feet behind." Minstrel blacks usually were depicted as ignorant and foolish, their talk represented as an ineffectual and pretentious attempt to imitate white speech.[38]

If, as *Putnam's* suggested, minstrelsy "touched a chord in the American heart," it was a heart that still relished jolly fellowship. "Life is but a span . . . , live as jolly as you can," went a song in *The "Guzzlin' Jim" Songster.* Even as blackface performers underlined the repellent physical appearance of blacks, they also presented them as alluring. As white society became more restrained, black stereotypes became, it seemed, even more uninhibited. Many minstrel songs celebrated the jolly behavior that men had so long enjoyed, and this likely contributed to the entertainment's popularity. On stage, African Americans were hypermasculine—exuberant, impulsive, always ready for a drink, a fight, a bet, a woman. Minstrelsy's blacks were constantly laughing. "Gay is the Life of a Colored Man, / He is bound to be happy wherever he can," sang Bryant's Minstrels. "De niggers fight, de niggers play, / Always on a holiday," went one song. Women in minstrel songs were equally a male fantasy, forever encouraging men's affections with winks, smiles, and nods.[39]

Male fighting was a constant topic of early minstrel songs. Thomas Rice's landmark Jim Crow was one bellicose fellow. A black Davy Crockett, he boasted that "I wip my weight in wild cats, / I eat an Alligator." Central to almost all the myriad versions of the song is Jim Crow's victory in a fight over "a Philadelphia nigger" who disparages New York City.

So I knocked down dis Sambo,
And shut up his light,
For I'm jist about as sassy
As if I was half white.

Weel about and turn about
And do jis so,
Eb'ry time I weel about
And jump Jim Crow . . .

And den I go to Orleans,
An feel so full of fight,
Dey put me in de Calaboose,
An keep me dare all night.
Chorus

When I got out I hit a man,
His name I now forgot,
But dare was nothing left
'Sept a little grease spot.
Chorus

In one of the most popular blackface songs from the 1830s, "Tell Me Josey Whar You Bin," Josey gets in a brawl in an oyster cellar where "[a] Nigger hit me wid a stick / And I laid him flat wid a large big brick" and in doing so breaks his antagonist's back.[40]

The first song that the Virginia Minstrels performed in their Catherine Street boardinghouse, according to George Wooldridge, was Dan Emmett's "Old Dan Tucker," a song that went on to become one of their most celebrated numbers and one of the most popular songs of the nineteenth century. The opening verse portrays Dan Tucker as a black disturber of the peace.

I come to town de udder night,
I heard de noise and saw de fight,
De watchman was a runnin' roun,
Cryin' Old Dan Tucker's come to town,
So get out de way! Get out de way! Get out de way!
Old Dan Tucker, your too late to come to supper.

Tucker is a nice old man,
He use to ride our darby ram;
He sent him whizzen down de hill,
If he hadn't got up he'd lay dar still.
So get out de way! . . .

. . . .

Old Dan Tucker and I got drunk,
He fell in de fire an kick up a chunk,
De charcoal got inside he shoe
Lor bless you honey how de ashes flew
So get out de way! . . .[41]

With its dizzying swings between violence and nonsense and its catchy melody, "Old Dan Tucker" became a national sensation. Both C. W. Haskins's shipmates and "the Mob" on the *Petrel* sang it on the way to California. By 1855 it was suggested that "it has been sung, perhaps, oftener than any melody ever written." The song quickly passed into the oral tradition: Cornelius Mathews heard it sung in the early 1850s on a Hudson River steamer by young men from the "East Bowery" on a "water frolic." Tucker was, of course, a black man in the original version, but detached from his minstrel origins, in white folk versions Old Dan becomes a racially indeterminate, perhaps white, hell-raiser. The song eventually passed into the African American folk tradition where Tucker once again became black.[42]

White minstrel audiences enjoyed watching characters portraying blacks batter each other. Sketches routinely ended with stage directions for a "general row." Minstrelsy at times reveled in gore. "The Quack Doctor" featuring Jim Crow and "Dr. Squash" ("Bone Squash" was a stock minstrel character) is reminiscent of Henry Clay Lewis. Sings the doctor,

A doctor I am ob wonderful skill.
I can bleed, I can purge, I can kill;
I can cut a man's leg off—his arm or his head.

When "Julius Caesar" comes in for treatment of an eye injured in a brawl, Dr. Squash gouges it out, and according to the stage directions "holds up the eyeball on the end of his thumb." In the finale the outraged patients gang up on the doctor, forcing him to run the gauntlet, pummeling him as he passes.[43]

Pranks played a crucial role in minstrelsy. Indeed, one could interpret the genre as such as a kind of practical joke carried out on the audience. The sight of white men masquerading as black men and women was in itself comical, a humorous effect that was amplified, perhaps, by the fact that blacks were a traditional target of pranks by the tavern crowd. The humor itself was the pitiless humor of the jolly fellows. "Your grinning minstrel is cruelly sarcastic, and cuts and slashes his best heroes and heroines with cool discrimination," a writer for the *Literary World* explained. In this way, and in others, there is a similarity to southwestern literature. It is impossible to trace the direction of influences between stage and literature, but it seems very likely, given their common connections to the lower-ward world, that they drew upon each other. Farcical militia drills and revivals were popular in both southwestern literature and on the minstrel stage. The *Spirit* in 1855 printed "The Harp of a Thousand Strings" by William P. Brannan, one of numerous burlesque sermons it published. The piece proved one of the most popular and oft-reprinted comic sketches of the era. Minstrelsy routinely presented skits lampooning black exhorters. Dan Emmett wrote and performed forty burlesque sermons with such titles as "Bressed Am Dem Dat 'Spects Nuttin,' Kaze Dey Aint a Gwine to Git Nuttin!"[44]

The history of Bryant's Minstrels illuminates the connections of minstrels to the Bowery milieu, their manipulation of jolly topics, and the thematic similarities between *Spirit*-style literature and minstrelsy. Dan, Jerry, and Neil Bryant (O'Brien was their real last name) were brothers from Troy, New York. Dan, born in 1833, was said to have first appeared on stage as an extra in *A Glance at New York*. He and his brothers went on to hone their skills for a variety of minstrel troupes and opened together as a group in New York in 1857. Dan was an outstanding dancer and skilled banjoist, while Jerry and Neil played the bones and tambourine. All were accomplished comics. Together they were a sensation. "Such a combination of comical talent was never before witnessed in Ethiopian minstrelsy," raved the *Clipper*, adding that "the success of this troupe is certainly without parallel." Hundreds were turned away every night from their Broadway theater. The Bryants were recognized as both the most talented and the most popular minstrel group of the age. With the addition of Dan Emmett (who wrote the song "Dixie" while with the group) they played continuously in New York in their own Broadway theater until the San Francisco Minstrels eclipsed them in popularity the mid-1860s.[45]

The brothers, like many minstrels, were deeply involved in the lower-ward sporting world. The Dexter House near their theater was a "favorite resort for the better class of sporting men and members of the theatrical and minstrel profession" and was the Bryants' favorite hangout. The brothers became friends with Tom Hyer and Pat Herne, the big-time gambler and Monteverde's regular, attending boxing matches and horse races with them. Neil Bryant was a frequent drinking companion of prizefighter John C. Heenan, and Neil became one of the leaders in assembling the financial backers for the Benecia Boy's fight with Englishman Thomas Sayers, while Dan Bryant actually went to England and saw the famed 1860 contest. Both Dan and Neil were avid billiards fans, and Neil later opened a billiards parlor and became a major figure in the sport. The Bryants were also well connected with the New York City Democratic Party. When Dan died in 1875, former New York mayor Oakey Hall (of Tweed Ring infamy) was one of the pallbearers. Organizers and supporters of a series of benefit concerts for his widow included current Democratic mayor William H. Wickham, ex-mayor John T. Hoffman, Jay Gould, and John Morrissey.[46]

Their usual opening song, "We're the Boys of Pleasure," set the tone for the performance: "We're the boys of pleasure, as you shall quickly see, / For we always gib good measure—so happy, light and free." The Bryants were one of the more traditional troupes in terms of performance, but they included a great deal of material that had little to do with either slaves or free blacks but much to do with the contemporary urban scene. "Where Can I Get a Drink?" was their attack on the 1857 New York State Sunday closing law for barrooms. Each performance featured a "comicality" that made little pretense of realism. In July 1860 their finale was "May the Best Man Win," a "laughable burlesque of HEENAN and SAYERS," featuring Jerry as prizefighter Tom Sayers and Dan, just returned from the fight in England, as the Benecia Boy. (On his first night back, Dan received a roar of laughter when he told the audience he had visited England for the "benefit of his health.")[47]

Among their favorite concluding numbers was "Who Struck Billy Patterson?" a song whose popularity reflects both the pugnacious strain in minstrelsy and suggests its affinity with southwestern humor. It is unclear exactly where the phrase "Who struck Billy Patterson?" originated, but an early version of the joke has one Billy Patterson beaten badly in the 1837 Broad Street Riot in Boston between Irishmen and native-born volunteer firemen. A combative friend loudly vowed to take revenge once he found the man who had struck Billy Patterson.

Bryant's Minstrels in "We Ain't Got Time to Tarry." In *Bryant's Power of Music* (New York 1859). Brown University Library.

The attacker was located, but he proved to be a towering, powerful man, so the would-be avenger meekly offered felicitations. The *Spirit of the Times* took the lead in pushing the Billy Patterson fad, printing several stories about "Mr. William Patterson—an individual whose fame is . . . imperishable." The 1840 "Jones' Fight," which recounts a rough-and-tumble battle between a Kentucky militia colonel and Billy Patterson, was among the most popular *Spirit* sketches and was included in Porter's anthology *The Big Bear of Arkansas.* "Who struck Billy Patterson?" became a catchphrase in the 1840s—the boys on the ship *Petrel* on the way to the gold rush asked this weighty question as did the 1849 *Alta California.* Billy Patterson moved into minstrelsy—and became black—when Dan Emmett wrote "Billy Patterson" in 1859 for the Bryants' finale:

> Dar was an old nigg dat got his wid a brick,
> He wasn't knock'd down kaze head too thick
> De first word he said when he was come to,
> O don't hit a-gin for dat will doo!

A later verse explained:

> Dar's one ting sartin and plain to see,
> 'Twas neider "Sayres" nor "Morrisey";
> Dey both told me (or I is a liar),
> 'Twas edier "*Heenan*" or "*Old Tom Hyer.*"[48]

The Bryants were part of the shift in minstrelsy from a stylized genre that represented slave and free blacks to a form of entertainment that made less pretense of being about slaves or even African Americans. Some troupes gave the first part of the performance "in white faces" and only then blacked up.[49] By the 1850s the dialect (at least as reflected in printed minstrel songs and sketches) had softened—often only substituting /d/ for /th/. The pro-Democratic orientation, which despite the political connections of many minstrels had been previously relatively subdued on stage, became more open.

Minstrels constantly changed their persona in performance. The range of perspectives and cultural references was enormous. At one moment blithe and ingratiating, they could suddenly turn violent and menacing. They were sleigh riders dashing through the snow singing "Jingle Bells," then black bullies brawling. They could be slaves celebrating a plantation festival, boatmen singing, Irishmen praising Erin, forty-niners on their way to California. Minstrel blackness became shot through with racial confusion and contradiction. They were, despite the dark faces, stock white characters. What are we to make of "Ill Count McGinnis, a Hibernian darkie"? Or "Sally Black," an African American Piker? Or the black b'hoy, a stock figure in 1850s minstrelsy? The introduction of Pat on stage proved smooth since the stereotypical minstrel Irishman was remarkably similar to the black—he loved to drink and fight. "Ould Ireland's the place for a frolic, / The boys and Girls are frisky," sang the Bryants. In their version of "Finnegan's Wake," Finnegan lived on Walker Street in the Sixth Ward. In the Christy Minstrels' "Conny O'Ryan," the hero "beat St. Patrick at forty-fives [a version of faro] a playing for lager bier." Although, as David Grimsted notes, the frontier roarer was never as popular on stage as in literature, some minstrels did draw on western stereotypes in their combination of comedy and combat. Tony Pastor's "Tuscaloosa Sam" and an antagonist fight all day until all that's left is "two quarts of buttons, two big knives, / Some whiskers and four eyes."[50]

Mose, the pugnacious fireman hero of Benjamin Baker's 1848 A *Glance at New York*, appeared on the minstrel stage. The appropriation was fitting because from the start the high-spirited brawling of Mose in Baker's play seemed so similar to the high-spirited brawling that was associated with blacks. Baker always insisted he chose the name "Mose" randomly, but it was a common black name, one often used for black characters on stage and in literature. In "The Hop of Fashion," the Bryants' version of one of the most popular of all minstrel sketches, ticket taker "Slim Dipsey," played by Dan, tries to prevent a succession of people from sneaking into a dance without paying, including Lady Macbeth, "Hamlet's Ghost," and Mose, played by Neil. The Bryants altered "Wake Up, Jake," a popular song about a locomotive fireman, into "Wake up, Mose," in which the hero is black.

Oh white folks, listen to my song, come listen to my ditty,
I'll tell you 'bout a *color'd chap*, born in de Empire City;
He used to run de machine, he was the engine tender—
Oh, golly! He was something, when he got upon a bender.

Bryant's Minstrels' 1857 "Challenge Dance" sketch was likely inspired by a Catherine Market scene in *New York as It Is.* To further confuse ethnic and racial categories, Dan dressed as a b'hoy and played this scene as "Ill-Count McGinnis," whom the playbill dizzyingly (and punningly?) described as "the Italian refugee from Cork."[51]

"WILD AND ASTOUNDING FORMS"

These comical types frequently focused their attention on lampooning the forces of respectability and the critics of jolly fellowship. The main approach was burlesque, in which references to the quotidian life of the city subverted genteel cultural creation. Using the language of the streets as mocking counterpoint to affectation is probably as old as comedy, and quodlibet, which humorously contrasted popular and pious songs, goes back to medieval times. What was novel in the 1850s was the "moral and cultural epidemic" that created a zealous, self-confident standard of Protestant middle-class propriety that no doubt seemed almost readymade for ridicule. The key source of minstrel parody was "parlor songs" written not for public performance but for respectable families to sing at home, accompanied on that emblem of genteel refinement, the pianoforte. Henry Russell's "Woodman, Spare That Tree" and Henry Bishop's "Home, Sweet, Home" were beloved favorites. Pious heroines dying lingering deaths were a favorite subject. Titles suggest the nature of the genre: "Ring the Bell Softly, There's Crape on the Door," "Only a Withered Rose," "Sunny Days Will Come Again," "Hark! I Hear an Angel Sing."[52]

Minstrels sometimes performed parlor songs, but when they did, they typically juxtaposed them with comic songs. In one of Bryant's songsters, "Put Me in My Little Bed" is followed two pages later by "Lager Beer Sally is Her Name." More characteristic were parodies of such parlor songs. Laughter ruled. Travesties of opera and serious plays had long been popular with minstrels, but with their subversion of parlor songs, a genre so closely connected with the Victorian middle class, the jolly thrust became more pointed; the raucous voice of the lower wards

"Challenge Dance." Dan Bryant as a black Mose. Compare with illustration on page 106. In *Bryant's New Songster* (New York, 1864), Brown University Library.

subverted genteel discourse. A sentimental song like "You'll Remember Me" collided in a pastiche with "The Rat Catcher's Daughter":

Other lips and other hearts,
Their tales of love shall tell,
In language whose—
Father caught rats while she sold sprats.

The didactic "You Never Miss Your Water until Your Well Runs Dry" became "You Never Miss de Lager till de Keg Runs Dry"; "Jenny's Coming o'er the

Green" became "Whiskey in Decanter Clean." Henry Clay Work's famous temperance ballad "Father, Dear Father" was too inviting to be ignored. The original final verse was:

Yes, we are alone—poor Benny is dead,
And gone with the angels of light,
And these were the very last words that he said—
"I want to kiss father good night."

Work's song was parodied by J. W. Lingard with:

Benny is here dead-drunk—Honor bright,
The truth I am telling you now;
And these were the very last words he said:
We'll go on a good drunk tonight.[53]

The jolly travesty of the genteel ballad tradition culminated in the 1860s in what journalist George Wakeman called "grotesque songs." "It is co-ordinate with the language of slang, and it ramifies with a wonderful circulation, all those channels of amusement, patronized more especially by the lower classes of cities. . . . You will find them in 'free and easys,' [and] at negro minstrel halls." Humor and violence merged in "wild and astounding forms." In these songs "there are no stale similes about starry eyes, rosy cheeks, coral teeth and raven hair." The main focus of the songs was, as in so many parlor songs, death—but a very different death from that of the pure, serene parlor song. In grotesque songs the deaths are farcical. Suicide was a favorite demise: one heroine killed herself by swallowing a candlestick, another "poisoned herself with toasted cheese." Blackface songs of the 1860s reveled in such macabre humor. "The Brewer's Daughter" drowned herself in the vat.

I remember the customers praised that week,
The flavor of the porter;
They little knew the cause of that
Was the brewer's only daughter.

Compared to southwestern tales where a more realistic, bloody violence mixed with comedy, in minstrelsy, violence tended to be more hyperbolic and nonsensical. There is a less menacing, even cartoonish, quality to grotesque songs. This stylized comic violence of minstrelsy would pass into the vaudeville and comic strips of the later nineteenth century.[54]

Alexander Saxton has called attention to "the dual relationship of city and frontier" in the nineteenth century. Saxton points out that men in the United States were not randomly distributed: in both "East and West, the male population was concentrated in factories, boardinghouses, construction and mining camps."[55] In these realms jolly fellowship not only persisted but flourished, and link were forged between these disorderly domains. Men began moving from New York's lower wards to San Francisco and the West. Cultural connections emerged between minstrelsy and southwestern literature. The crusade for moral reform had redefined jolly fellowship—it was now no longer simply the way some men behaved but an explicit repudiation of gentility. These forms of cultural production became spaces where Americans commemorated the values of masculine disorder and violence even as mainstream society embraced restrained male conduct. The cultural vitality of jolly fellowship was thus preserved, even extended.

The popularity of southwestern fiction and minstrelsy suggests how potent interest in jolly fellowship remained, even as fewer and fewer followed a jolly lifestyle. But there were still locations where men could live a disorderly life if they chose, and not only in large cities. In the East there were lumber, canal, and oil-rush towns where rowdy behavior continued. After the Civil War, however, most masculine milieus were found in "the Wild West," where mining and cattle towns became legendary for their drinking, gambling, fighting, and joking. As respectability advanced, these western locales stood out all the more and attracted an intense popular interest that was to insure the Wild West a central place in American folklore and culture. Among these masculine realms, East and West, circulated sporting men, the combination of gambler, fighter, politician, and celebrity that had emerged in New York City in the 1840s. Turning jolly comportment into a vocation, sporting men became, as bearers of the jolly standard in increasingly sedate surroundings, objects of intense public interest and even admiration.

CHAPTER SEVEN

Wild East and Wild West

"Guess you haven't seen much as rough as this afore?" was the question that greeted English newspaperman John White as soon as he entered a Julesburg, Colorado, gambling saloon in 1867. Julesburg was one of what *Harper's Magazine* dubbed "air towns," the temporary termini of the transcontinental railroads that were among the most disorderly places in the West. White replied that it really seemed no worse than some neighborhoods of Paris or London. "My friend, however, would not abate the claim of the town to be 'the very roughest place out.'" Perhaps the patrons did not look more despicable than European rowdies, but "he took refuge in their being more dangerous." The indignant questioner refused to let the matter drop, demanding to know "do they shout as much in such places there?"[1]

Jolly fellowship continued to flourish in masculine domains, East and West, until the end of the nineteenth century. As moral reformation proceeded, such locales became increasingly conspicuous. The most celebrated jolly enclaves were the western mining, railroad, and cattle towns such as Deadwood, Cheyenne, and Dodge City in the last thirty years of the nineteenth century. Much of the allure of the Wild West both in the nineteenth century and today is the recognition that in such places a traditional male outlook persisted and an archaic code of conduct was still followed that had become outmoded elsewhere. Yet, though the significance of this region in American tradition is well established, there were unruly locales located east of the Mississippi. Heavily male lumber towns in Maine and Michigan were almost as wild as cattle towns. The Pennsylvania oil rush in the late 1860s was said to be as turbulent as any of the western mineral rushes. To recover the Wild East and its similarities and differences from the West helps one comprehend the persistence and significance of jolly conduct in the last five decades of the nineteenth century.

Jolly behavior could still appear spontaneously wherever men, especially young men, gathered, whether in boardinghouse districts of cities, eastern lumber towns, or western cattle and mining towns. Yet the American West was distinctive. A coterie of men specifically attracted by jolly values flocked there, refugees from the tameness of middle class life. Many had never quite felt at home in settled society and longed for turmoil, for revelry, and like Robert Service's "Men That Don't Fit In," would "roam the world at will" looking for exhilaration.[2] Many consciously embraced their status as misfits and mavericks and, like the man White met in Julesburg, were proud to live in places where middle-class respectability was a faint rumor. Their presence made post–Civil War western male concentrations especially uproarious. This mix of men carried on the jolly tradition at that same that they altered it. The characteristic combination of compassion and cruelty was magnified in the region, the sympathy seemingly more tender, the brutality more inhumane.

"ANOTHER CALIFORNIA"

By the 1870s virtually every large eastern city had its vice district of saloons, gambling halls, and whorehouses. In addition to these well-known urban locales, there were also a small number of eastern towns and villages where disorderly comportment had survived. Most of these were relatively isolated settings, places where the dominant industry employed a workforce that was predominantly young and male, such as in timber, canals, or drilling for oil.

The earliest major lumber towns were in Maine and New Hampshire. By the late 1850s and 1860s eastern logging supremacy waned as the region's forests were depleted, and many loggers left for more promising realms in Michigan and later Wisconsin. Most of the lumbermen were young men—in their twenties or thirties—and most viewed the work as temporary (the occupation widely was regarded as too physically demanding to follow into middle age). Logging was hard, dangerous work undertaken in remote locales, and it is likely that many of the men who pursued it did so only when no other work was available. Yet the loggers' reputation for unruly behavior was so well known that many lumbermen must have had a at least a tolerance for jolly conduct, if not an actual affinity. After belief in the old idea that hard physical labor was impossible without liquor waned, most lumber camps prohibited or at least limited consumption of alcohol. When the season was over and the logs were floated down river at spring runoff, the men and their wages headed for town and for the lumbermen's customary "blowout." Sociologist Walter Wyckoff, who investigated working-class life disguised as a day laborer in the 1890s, believed that loggers preserved their financial, psychic, and physical energy for this huge explosion. After being without alcohol, women, or excitement, lumbermen would go on a short, frenzied debauch, making up in a week for the jolly recreation they had missed. "Who gives us pay for one big drunk, / When we hit Bangor slam kerplunk— / John Ross and Cyrus Hughes," sang Maine lumbermen, naming two major bosses.[3]

Loggers indeed hit the lumbering towns "slam kerplunk." In Milltown on the St. Croix River near Calais, Maine, wrote John S. Springer in *Forest Life and Forest Trees: Comprising Winter Camp Life among the Loggers, and Wild-Wood Adventure* (1851), "loggers would arrest passers-by, take them by force, bring them into . . . [the] grog shop and baptize them by pouring a quart of rum over their heads." This kept up until the rum "was running in brooks over the floor." The "more distinguished the candidate, the more hearty the fun," Springer added. In Bangor—Maine's principal lumbering center—Haymarket Square was lined with saloons, gambling houses, and bordellos. Loggers fought street brawls there with sailors on the ships that came up the Penobscot River. There was even a short-lived vigilante movement to rid Bangor of prostitutes and sporting men. Lumbermen who came down the Kennebec River in the spring would assemble in a body and march to the Bowdoin campus for the traditional annual "Yager" fights with students.[4]

The Michigan lumber towns of the 1870s and 1880s were believed even more disorderly than those of Maine. The loggers' sometimes began their springtime fun by trashing the trains that took them out of the woods. They descended on the logging towns' vice districts, of which the Catacombs in Bay City, a block of interconnected buildings, was probably the most notorious. Muskegon, with a resident population of about six thousand in 1870, had sixty saloons, even though Michigan was, in theory, a dry state. The Canterbury, Muskegon's infamous dance hall, was the site of prizefights, cockfights, and dogfights, and, it was said, "all forms" of perversion. It was taken for granted that men could not resist jolly fellowship in such an atmosphere, and so it would not been shocking to learn that even the permanent residents of these places were sometimes caught up in the roistering. Lawyer John Moore was surprised that in an era when temperance was so powerful, "everybody drank" in Saginaw. The "leading figures of those days, able dignified, honored . . . , drank freely and enjoyed the conviviality of the times."[5]

With drinking came fighting. Recalled Saginaw policeman Parker Owen, "most of all they [lumbermen] loved to fight," and "if their wasn't an invitation for a fight they'd issue one themselves—always with plenty of takers." Many loggers were proud of their fistic prowess, and the best rough-and-tumble fighters of the 1870s and 1880s, such as "Silver Jack" Driscoll, became legends. (Nicknames among lumbermen were almost universal—Wyckoff befriended "Karl the Swede" and "Long-nosed Harry" in his lumber camp.) Towns struggled to contain the brawls and riots. The village of Seney, Michigan, "literally swarmed with fighting loggers," Dr. John P. Bohn, remembered. The custom in Seney was that when a fighter was down, his standing opponent would grind his boot cleats into him. On Christmas Day, 1890, Bohn recalled, "I worked all day and night treating the fighters who could find their way to my office following the red trail on the snow that reddened and broadened as the day wore on." Localities struggled to preserve order. Like Bangor, Saginaw eventually formed a vigilance committee to curb the disorder.[6]

Canal settlements also had a reputation for rowdiness. One Rochester newspaper labeled the Erie Canal the "Big Ditch of Iniquity." It was believed that more than fifteen hundred grog shops lined the canal between the Hudson River and Lake Erie. "Fighting was an every day occurrence," recalled H. P. Marsh, a former canal boat captain known as the "Bully of Black River" for his victory in a battle on that upstate waterway. "There were canal bullies all along the line," and their battles with each other and with boatmen kept many settlements in turmoil. The Side Cut, where the Erie Canal connected with Watervliet and Troy, was especially notorious. It contained twenty-nine saloons within two city blocks, and its emergence in the 1830s made this among America's earliest vice districts. Its reputation continued after the Civil War when it was labeled the "Barbary Coast of the East" for its dissipation. Buffalo, at the other end of the canal, also had a reputation for commotion. Canal Street with its ninety-three saloons and fifteen "dance halls" was called the "Wickedest Street in the World." As the railroad superseded canals, the rowdy renown of most canal towns faded, but Honesdale, Pennsylvania, upheld its notoriety into the 1870s. Honesdale was the western terminus of the Delaware and Hudson Canal, and few holidays went by there without disorder. Hooliganism was chronic; windows were broken, fires set, dogs poisoned, public meetings broken up. Some typical escapades, drawn from 1866: "A gang of rowdies, armed with pistols and clubs held high carnival in our streets"; on a dark evening planks were removed from the sidewalk on the bridge over the canal; a church service was disrupted by "a gang of drunken loafers, who . . . hooted and stomped"; and a railway train was derailed as "a prank."

The pandemonium abated after 1870, but as late as 1874 a sham gunfight with blanks on Main Street sent passersby scurrying.[7]

As disorderly as were the canal and lumber towns, the wildest towns in the East in the post–Civil War period were probably the Pennsylvania oil towns. As in the gold rush, few found riches, but many found revelry. Oil had been discovered in Venango County in 1864, and as long as local men were doing the drilling, things remained fairly sedate. But as word spread, fortune seekers, discharged soldiers, and adventurers descended on sparsely populated northwestern Pennsylvania, and "Petrolia," as the region was dubbed, became, in John W. Forney's words, "another California." Pithole was the first oil boomtown. When a *New York Herald* correspondent visited it in July 1865, it was only a little over a month old and its inhabitants consisted of two thousand white men, eleven white women and a single black person. By the fall its population was sixteen thousand, which included, it was said, four hundred prostitutes. Men in Pithole "appeared to cut loose from all moral restraint," a disgusted S. P. Irvin wrote. They simply "went crazy," agreed John J. McLaurin. As Charles C. Leonard's jocular 1867 *History of Pithole* put it: "The first building in Pithole—a faro bank. . . . The last building in Pithole—a church." Saloons, gambling halls, and variety theaters lined the streets. "Streetfights are common," noted the *Pithole Daily Record*, and prizefighting exhibitions and matches were a regular feature of Pithole life. In September 1866 a ball staged by the town's tiny black population was disrupted when pranksters on the above floor shook pepper through the cracks.[8]

Other towns along Oil Creek were equally disorderly. As in California, law enforcement ranged from ineffective to nonexistent. Nearby Petroleum Centre was felt by some to be even wilder than Pithole; there were "revelers by the hundred . . . fast men and faster women." Two "dead game sports" were said to have shot dice for twelve hours at $1000 a throw. In Titusville, before vigilantes restored order in January 1866, the local newspaper had complained that the town was "literally given over to mob law and rioting." Other hamlets in "Oildom," places with names like Red Hot, Tip Top, and Babylon—which by one report had eight houses and six gambling halls—seem to have been just as wild.[9]

"PANDEMONIUM AFLOAT"

For all the uproariousness of eastern male milieus like Pithole, it was the American West that became a byword for masculine disorder. The Mississippi River and the unruly towns along its banks in the three decades before the Civil War were, in many ways, the beginning of the Wild West. Even before then New Orleans had developed the reputation as being perhaps the most unfettered major city in the United States. "All the inhabitants of this place do nothing but drink and play billiards," one 1821 observer marveled. The Sabbath was nonexistent. The Crescent City was recognized by the 1820s as the wagering capital of the nation. "Gambling houses *throng* the city," Henry Fearon discovered, and the Metairie racetrack was among the nation's most famous. In 1835 the Louisiana legislature banned gambling establishments, but the subsequent crackdown only drove New Orleans wagering underground, and by the 1850s most of the casinos were back in full swing and were formally legalized in 1869. One observer in 1881 counted eighty-eight major gambling halls in the city. Prostitution was a recognized New Orleans institution, legal until the end of the nineteenth century. The French Quarter became the city's best-known vice district, alive with bordellos, saloons, gambling houses, and dance halls. Blood sports like cockfighting, bearbaiting, and even bullfighting went on with little hindrance. New Orleans was the only southern city with a vibrant prizefighting tradition, and many important championship fights—including James J. Corbett's famed knockout of John L. Sullivan in 1892—were held there or in the vicinity.[10]

Vicksburg, Mississippi, is about 160 miles up the Mississippi from New Orleans, and during Vicksburg's boom years of the 1830s "adventurous spirits of every description" flocked to the city. Fifty faro banks were said to be in operation in the Kangaroo, the town's vice district, which was, according to H. S. Fulkerson, "the great firmament of gamblers." Sporting men so dominated Vicksburg that "the better class stood in awe of them." In 1835 a pugilist-gambler, under the "potent spirit of old rye," disrupted the town's Independence Day banquet and punched one of the speakers. His timing was bad. Newspaper reports had alleged that one John Murrell, the "Great Western Land Pirate," had organized southern gamblers into a conspiracy to incite a slave insurrection on Christmas Day 1835 and, in the subsequent chaos, to plunder the South. Panicked and outraged Vicksburgians forced the offending gambler out of town and took dramatic action to reclaim their city from "desperadoes." A mob of citizens entered the gambling houses and began smashing faro tables and other gambling apparatus when, suddenly, shots were fired and a Vicksburg doctor fell, fatally wounded. The building was stormed, and five gamblers inside were seized and immediately lynched, an event that later sporting men invested with an almost mythical significance in the founding history of their fraternity.[11]

Other Mississippi towns were equally disorderly. Natchez's Under-the-Hill district along the river was infamous. Even in Spanish times this area had been noted for dissipation. Henry Ker, who visited it in 1816, claimed "every house is a grocery, containing gambling, music, and fornicators." Some riverboats would lay over specifically "for the sake of the passengers having a *spree*," according to the reminiscences of actor Joe Cowell. William Johnson, the black barber who left a fascinating diary of Natchez life in the 1830s and 1840s, chronicled the drinking, gambling, fighting, pranks, and revelry throughout the town. Virtually all major river cities had vice districts. Memphis was a notably tough town with a large boardinghouse population where heavy drinking and gambling led to so many brawls that it acquired the nickname "Bloody Memphis." The St. Louis waterfront shared many of the characteristics of other Mississippi river towns. "The Sabbath never crossed and never will cross the Mississippi" was the boast of men there according to the Rev. Mason Peck, who visited the town in 1818. "At least" half the population, the shocked Peck claimed, were "infidels" given up to "profane revelry."[12]

The steamboats on the river were worlds unto themselves with "a distinctive life and folkways," in historian Louis Hunter's words. Like gold-rush California, the riverboat was a place out of bounds where normal rules of social constraint and propriety were suspended. Men who worked on the river were noted for their wildness, and many passengers, although only temporarily part of river society, delighted in the boisterous atmosphere. The length of time that the riverboat flourished and the large number of men who either boarded or worked on one created what approached being a jolly world. The Mississippi steamboat, like the Bowery, became a recognized symbol of an alternative existence.[13]

Even before steamboats, flatboatmen and keelboatmen on the Mississippi and its tributaries captured the public imagination in a rowdy age as just about the rowdiest group of men in the country. They were, one observer believed, "driven by a wild and restless spirit . . . unwilling to submit to the restraints of society." Many reveled in their reputation for unruliness. Most did not intend to make it a permanent occupation and welcomed the chance to bask in the mystique of the boisterous boatman before settling down. As in the gold rush "every body was 'Jack' or something else. . . . No one cared for ones true name" afloat. The work, especially poling upstream, was extremely hard, though no doubt mitigated by the three daily rations of liquor most boats provided. When they docked, the crews unwound with a spree. Their love of fighting was "an appetite, and like pressing hunger, had to be appeased," remembered Southwestern humorist Thomas Bangs Thorpe. "Playing severe practical jokes upon one another" was another favorite pastime, Thorpe recalled. George Brown and his crewmates played "all kinds of jokes and pranks." Among their rough "amusements" was "sweeping the streets," explained S. Wilkeson. This was done "with a long rope extended across the street." The men on each end "moved forward quickly, "tripping up and capsizing whatever happened to be within the scope of the rope. Men, women, and children, horses, cars and cattle were overturned."[14]

The most renowned flatboatman on the river was the legendary Mike Fink. It is almost impossible to separate facts from folklore about Fink. Born around 1770, he worked mostly on the river, where he was said to have developed a magnificent physique that added "the symmetry of an Apollo to the limbs of a Hercules." He soon gained a reputation as a legendary western roarer and hard drinker (he chugged down a gallon of whiskey a day, it was said) as well as notoriety as an unbeatable rough-and-tumble fighter, headbutter, and relentless practical joker. The first story about him appeared in 1828. He also appeared in some of the Crockett almanacs and later in the *Spirit of the Times* and the sporting newspaper *New York Clipper.* Fink's most celebrated "prank" was of the kind that "makes us sense the gap between our time and theirs," in Robert Darnton's words. One day Fink noticed a black boy on shore with an uncommonly large heel. In Timothy Flint's retelling, "the unshapely foot offended Mike's eye, and outraged his idea of symmetry so much, that he determined to correct it. He took aim with his rifle . . . and actually shot it away. The boy fell, crying murder, and badly wounded."[15]

Steamboats inherited some of the men and much of the atmosphere of the flatboats. Mississippi steamboats were much more than simply vessels moving men and goods from one location to another. Mark Twain, himself a riverboat pilot for two years, revealed in the *Adventures of Huckleberry Finn* that he understood how men on the Mississippi were literally adrift from social convention. Usually authorities on shore made little effort to govern what happened on the river. The captain was monarch: "Steamboat officers did what was good in their own sight, with none to molest or make them afraid," explained John Morris. As with flatboats, many of those who worked on steamboats did so because the lifestyle was appealing to them. "River men, like other people, did not all think alike," recalled John Habermehl, himself a former boatman, but generally they "were really a jolly set of 'fellers,' as the saying goes." One of the most commented on features of life afloat was the close socializing of black and white deckhands, who drank and gambled together.[16]

Before riverboats with staterooms began to be built in the 1850s, there was a partitioned chamber for women in the rear of the main cabin. Men essentially had the run of the rest of the boat. Temporarily detached from ordinary society, with only a faint female presence, ships took on the ambiance often found in masculine enclaves. G. W. Featherstonhaugh witnessed a group of "*gentlemen*" board at Vicksburg who almost instantly began "gambling, drinking, smoking and blaspheming." It became, in Featherstonhaugh's words, "pandemonium afloat," and he gloomily concluded that the passengers "had escaped the restraints which society imposed . . . and seemed determined to exhaust all the extravagances that brutality and profanity are capable of." Habermehl believed that, before railroads allowed men easy access to urban vice districts, some men went on boat trips specifically for the jolly experience. Women and ministers regarded a steamboat voyage as an ordeal to be survived. Preachers were sometimes invited to spend the day in the female chamber. Recalled John Morris, you could hear "in the ladies' cabin a group of the godly praying and singing psalms," while the main cabin resounded with "the loud laughter of the jolly carousers around the drinking bar" mixing with the voices of the poker players and the clinking of chips. Even Peter Cartwright, the robust western minister who spent much of his life denying a tale that he had bested Mike Fink in a brawl, was taken aback on his 1827 steamboat trip from St. Louis to Pittsburgh. "The jolly set" he met appalled him: atheists, Universalists, "profane swearers, drunkards, gamblers, fiddlers and dancers." Missionaries attempted to convert crewman, but, as in California, it proved almost impossible: "We cannot be religious while we are boatmen," explained one.[17]

Many male passengers took off their topcoats as soon as they boarded a steamboat and spent the rest of their voyage in shirtsleeves. Most then headed for the bar. "The scene of drinking and gambling had no intermission," Thomas Hamilton discovered; it continued day and night and even on Sunday, the axiom being "on steamboats there is no Sunday." Ships' captains discouraged fighting, but most would have "rather see[n] a fellow fight than take an insult," explained riverboat gambler George Devol, who himself boasted of having been in "more fights in the cabin and bar of steamboats than any other man in the country."[18]

Mississippi riverboats were notorious for their gambling. Even men who never played on shore were drawn into games on the river. Steamboats were, of course, the domain of the legendary riverboat gambler, men such as George Devol, who in his entertaining book *Forty Years a Gambler on the Mississippi* declared himself "more at home on any of the Mississippi steamboats" than on land. The river is critical in the history of American gambling, and poker apparently began to eclipse faro as the nation's most popular gambling game on the Mississippi. In addition to the professional gamblers, there were sometimes also, according to the *New York Clipper*, "contra-gamesters" on board. Camouflaged as ordinary passengers, the contra-gamesters would attempt to scout out the sharpers and dupe them at poker. Melville's *The Confidence-Man*, in which during a steamboat voyage both the confidence man and his opponents appear in disguise, is obviously allegorical but perhaps not as far fetched as might be imagined.[19]

"The Unexpected Encounter." A drinking contest in a steamboat bar. In T. B. Thorpe, "Reminiscences of the Mississippi," *Harper's New Monthly Magazine* 12 (1856).

The autonomy of life on the Mississippi enabled the mock trial to reach its zenith. Anyone who has traveled much on western steamboats, actor Sol Smith asserted, "has witnessed the proceedings of the self-constituted courts on boiler-decks." In the early days, the "Court of Uncommon Pleas," as such judicial bodies were called on the river, seemed to have usually tried real crimes such as theft, but by the 1840s, they often were simply masculine entertainments. Typically, a chosen victim was someone alleged to have committed a breach of male protocol. On the river, as in California, many temperance men felt that their pledges were temporarily suspended, and in one trial witnessed by Smith, a teetotaler was accused of drinking whiskey from "a j-u-g." Devol presided over the trial of a man accused of stealing chickens. After hearing evidence the jury returned dabbing their eyes with handkerchiefs, "as if they had been crying over the awful verdict they were about to render." Devol's sentence was that the defendant had to return the chickens and pay a fine of six bottles of wine and be imprisoned in the barroom until the penalty was paid.[20]

"ADVENTURERS OF ALL SORTS, READY FOR ANYTHING OR ANY ENTERTAINMENT"

Long before the gold rush, reformers had noted, and lamented, the tendency of men who moved beyond settled society, beyond women and churches, to lapse into jolly behavior. As the frontier pushed beyond the Mississippi, the danger became even more apparent. Jolly fellowship never burned more brightly than in the West. "Fun" took on new meanings. The drinking was heavier, the gambling more frantic, the fighting more desperate, the pranks more vicious. As such the Wild West can be seen as perhaps the zenith of jolly fellowship.

The West caught Americans' imagination as a special place, a distinctive and characteristic chapter in their nation's history. And it has continued to be so viewed, and not only by Americans—men around the world have been captured by the romance of the Wild West. It is a peculiarly male romance. The frontier had long been associated with freedom and license, a province of both promise and menace. It was, I would suggest, the persistence, indeed the amplification, of jolly fellowship in the West that accounts for part of the region's popular mystique. As restraint and sobriety became the convention in the East and South, the contrast between those locales and the less confined West became more apparent and thus more arresting. Like the California gold rush, the post–Civil War West was an atavism, a throwback to an earlier age. It was not an age most men east of the Mississippi necessarily wanted to return to, but it nevertheless fascinated them.

The Wild West was only a part of the American West. The sprawling farming areas on the Great Plains and in California, Oregon, and Washington had a settled population with balanced sex ratios and were almost as orderly as rural areas and small towns in the East. Economic development, however, also generated mining towns that were among the largest localities in the region. Virginia City, Nevada, site of the great Comstock Lode silver strike, may have had twenty-five thousand residents at its height in the 1860s; the population of Deadwood, South Dakota, may have exceeded ten thousand during the 1876 gold rush; there were fourteen thousand living in Leadville, Colorado, in 1880; and Tombstone, Arizona, had almost ten thousand inhabitants during the 1880s. "Cow towns" like Wichita and Dodge City, Kansas, were smaller, but the male population of the cattle towns swelled in the summer when the cowboys arrived with the cattle herds for shipment east. Most of these locations were disproportionately populated by young men. At the height of the Deadwood boom it was estimated that 97 percent of residents were male, the great majority younger than forty. Estelline Bennett, one of the handful of children in the town, never remembered meeting a person older than fifty-five.[21]

A demographic determinism that automatically equates disorder with a tiny female population would, however, be misleading. Compared with gold-rush California, many of these locations attracted a considerable number of women. By 1880, 35 percent of Deadwood's population was female. In Dodge City in 1880, at the height of its fame as the "Wickedest Town in America," 44 percent of the permanent residents were women. Some of these were prostitutes who were a conventional and accepted part of regional life, but many others were "respectable" women. Unlike in Stephen Crane's short story "The Bride Comes to Yellow Sky," where the mere presence of a single genteel woman instantly tames an entire community, in Dodge and elsewhere in the West swaggering manliness endured despite the presence of significant numbers of women. Such places continued to be dominated, as one westerner explained, by "the 'good fellows,' the popular fellows, the generous fellows, the well-known fellows, in short, the boys."[22]

Surely part of the reason a resoundingly masculine culture persisted in such places was that it was a manly kind of man who populated them. The men who lived in them did not represent a random cross section of the male population. In many locales there was a coterie of men that had come specifically to follow a jolly lifestyle. These refugees from respectability included men looking for excitement, alcoholics, gamblers, hotheads, and misfits. A significant number came west on a spree—they planned to spend a year or a few years in the region and then return east. Anne Ellis was surprised to discover how many of the prospectors she met in Bonanza, Colorado, in the 1880s were from "good families and . . . came West for adventure." There were men who didn't fit in like George Kohrs, who wrote in his autobiography of "the natural restlessness of my disposition. . . . I was never content in one place." He spent most of his life roaming about California, Montana, and Nevada. Rougher types came as well. There were outcasts such as the killer of Jesse James, Robert Ford, "the dirty little coward," in the words of the famous ballad, who "ate Jesse's bread, and he slept in Jesse's bed, / And he laid Jesse in his grave." Ford was a pimp and bartender in the mining town of Creede, Colorado, before he himself was shot dead in 1892. The West teemed with professional gamblers and sporting men like Con Orem who owned saloons in Denver and later Virginia City, Montana, and boxed throughout the region. There were confidence men like the legendary Jefferson "Soapy" Smith who ran his "soap game" throughout the region. Smith would attract a crowd on the street by appearing to insert bills from $1 to $100 in the wrappers of bars of soap and place them with other bars in a pile. He then auctioned off the soap bars. Smith, of course, had palmed the bills.[23]

These men who went west were attracted by the region's iniquitous reputation, but many more followed Greeley's famous advice and went simply to seek their fortune. Most worked hard, and many also played hard. As in California, even men intending to remain sedate found jolly fellowship alluring. "It was catching and you could not resist the temptation," cowboy Bill Jones remembered. In Dodge City even ministers would "join in the wild revels." It was not unusual in Cheyenne, the *New York Clipper* reported, to see "a person of professed Puritanical ideas and high toned moral dignity suddenly transformed into a frequenter, perhaps a patron, of dance and gambling houses." A reporter for a Denver paper discovered that "men of decent appearance seen elsewhere, as soon as they reached Leadville, "jibbed, sang low songs, walked openly with painted courtesans . . . and generally gave themselves to what they term 'a time.'" As in the gold rush, the extensive use of nicknames testified to the sense that men in the region were somehow transformed. "The West . . . reserved the right to select a nickname for a man," cowboy historian Philip Ashton Rollins explained, while in the Nevada silver-mining region nicknames were so widespread that "in some instances their true names were never known." Such milieus, like California, seemed places apart, beyond civilization. "Are you bound for America? . . . Give my respects to Uncle Sam," John D. Young was told as he left Denver heading east in 1860.[24]

Whether looking for adventure or seeking their fortune, a large number of those who went West planned eventually to return home. But journalist A. K. McClure discovered that many ended up staying permanently because they came to "love the semi-civilized condition of society." Few men, McClure believed "can content themselves in the East after having spent a year or two in the mines. The conventionalities and restraints of established communities are painful to them, and they long for the freedom of their huts and Western life." Boasted Montana saloon keeper George Herenden in a letter home, "you do not know how to live back East and have fun." There were even women who enjoyed the freedom to live as they pleased. When Libeus Barney arrived in Denver in 1859 he became aware of the large number of women in the city dressed as men—"in gentlemen's attire throughout." One told him "she is not ashamed to say that she prefers the pants to the petticoat."[25]

It was a combustible blend. Early San Antonio was said to be made up of a "motley, mixed up crowd" of "dare-devils," ex-politicians, renegades and "adventurers of all sorts, ready for anything or any entertainment." In Washington, Texas, the "fixed, resident population," John Lockhardt remembered, and the "floaters[,] . . . fond of fun, whiskey and cards," eyed each other with hostility. Some jolly residents would leave as soon as they perceived that their communities were becoming serene. Realizing that "California was settling down to order" and "becoming uncongenial for wild spirits," some former forty-niners headed to Colorado. As Charles White discovered in Julesburg, many men delighted in living in places where disorder seemed the defining value. "There is a class, still a large one," the *Dodge City Globe* reported in 1879, for whom "liv[ing] in 'the wickedest city in the west' is a source of pride. . . . They are not such bad fellows after all, but do not long for a quiet life."[26]

"THE PRIVILEGES OF A RIOTOUS LIBERTY"

There was an atavistic quality to male comportment in western cattle and mining areas: what the East once had been the West now was. Masculine enclaves in the region sustained the jolly way of life almost into the twentieth century. There are obvious continuities with the behavior of the tavern crowd earlier in the century and even in early modern Europe. National liquor consumption was 1.1 gallons of alcohol per person in 1880; in Washoe County, Nevada, where the Comstock Lode and Virginia City were located, it was 3.4 gallons, the national level of the 1820s. But by the 1870s and 1880s disorderly male comportment had assumed a considerably different form in the West from that it had taken in earlier eastern milieus. It seemed intensified, even desperate, as if those involved somehow sensed that this might be jolly fellowship's last fling. The presence in many western enclaves of a coterie of men bent on leading an everlastingly disorderly existence and of misfits and desperadoes as well as the universality of weapons gave jolly fellowship an edge it had not had previously.[27]

As in the California gold rush, male wildness was only lightly constrained by public authority. Law enforcement officials were few and scattered. "There is no law, no jails, no penitentiaries, & no courts in the country," wrote minister Alexander Taylor Rankin of Colorado in 1860. Many of the marshals and sheriffs were sporting men, keeping alive the traditional association of jolly fellowship and politics. "Wild Bill" Hickok, Wyatt Earp, and Bat Masterson were hired on the theory that, as a resident of the cattle town of Caldwell, Kansas, put it, "you must fight the devil with his own man." Sheriffs and marshals were well aware that the cowboys, miners, and others on which these towns depended coveted "the privileges of a riotous liberty" and that their role as peace officers was to keep rowdiness within limits, not eliminate it. Kansas's temperance law and its antigambling laws were not seriously enforced in cattle towns. Even deadly violence was often met with indifference. H. V. Redfield in his pioneering 1880 study of criminology, *Homicide, North and South,* compiled statistics from the 1870s showing that of the 125 men charged with murder in west Texas, only 3 were convicted. There were 45 homicides in Kansas cattle towns between 1870 and 1885, but, aside from one man who was lynched, no one was executed.[28]

Despite the presence of abstainers and moderate drinkers, consumption of alcohol in western boomtowns and regions was heavy and sustained. Arizonian John Cady believed that "the entire fabric of the territory was constructed on liquor." Mrs. M. M. Mathews who lived in Virginia City, Nevada, explained that "all classes drink, high and low." It is not surprising that the saloon occupies such an important role in western lore; many men were single, and they loved alcohol. The drinking patterns themselves were reminiscent of earlier days. Breakfast at one boardinghouse in Dakota City, Nebraska, consisted of donuts and a washbasin full of whiskey. Election days and holidays were occasions for blowouts. One newspaper editor counted fourteen men on the street asleep or passed out drunk on election day in 1878 in Kingman, Kansas. Ann Ellis believed every man in the town of Cañon City, Colorado, got drunk on Christmas Day 1895. "They staggered and stumbled, fought and fell"; the "soberest, most reliable man in town fell by the town pump and was unable to get up."[29]

For all its similarity with earlier jolly fellowship, however, much of the drinking seems almost frantic, less exuberant, more tawdry. The diary of "a celebrated old pisser named George Hand," a Tucson saloon keeper is, night after night, full of men drunk, men fighting drunk, vomiting drunk, hallucinating drunk, passed out drunk. "Lots of the boys are drunk today. Pat O'Meara got tight, fell down and someone stepped on his nose. Overstreet hit a Mexican and the Mexican hit Harrison with a rock and cut his head," Hand recorded in 1875. "Every one drunk, me also. I nearly got broke up wrestling and fooling around. Got a black eye, skinned nose and my leg nearly broke. Went to bed early," reads another typical entry. Much of the time when Hand is sober he has a hangover or he is nursing injuries received in a fall or fight or both. Jolly fellowship for some seemed to have become a kind of performance, living up to the stereotype of the wild westerner.[30]

As usual, heavy drinking was accompanied by fighting. Despite the centrality of the gunfighter in western lore, most fights were with fists—and occasionally feet and teeth. Some brawls were extremely brutal. The *Boise News* reported that one 1864 melee left men "with fractured skulls, some with bunged eyes and swollen faces. . . . Puddles of blood were distributed over so large a district that it was almost impossible to locate the fight." Battles would spontaneously erupt and just as suddenly stop. There were gang fights. Agnes Morley Cleveland remembered one among New Mexican cowboys in the 1890s that began as a food fight with boiled potatoes. The men then divided, the "minority of big fellows against the majority of smaller ones." Not surprisingly, prizefighting was a passion in western mining, cattle, and railroad towns. There was a boxing match in Cheyenne only four months after it was founded in 1867.[31]

Fighting could easily turn deadly. Western individual male violence more closely mimicked the southern pattern of years past than the eastern one. The American West was literally littered with guns. "Andy Johnson has found another revolver on the prairie," recorded Rolf Johnson of Phelps County, Nebraska, in his diary in 1877. "Arms are frequently found on the prairie. John Nelson found a gun one day as he was going home from school." In El Paso, "every citizen, whatever his age and calling, habitually carried a six-shooter at his belt," W. W. Mills remembered. In such places the sound of what western newspapers jokingly liked to call the "festive revolver" was familiar. Men in the region pointed to the danger of Indians as an explanation for why they carried weapons—just as in the South, heightened violence accompanied the presence of people of color. But it also seems many westerners felt that challenges to male honor must be defended with a weapon. The traditional view, which lumbermen and other fighting men in the East continued to uphold, was that only an unarmed "fair fight" was manly. But some westerners disdained fighting with fists. Male honor required protection with deadly force. "If God almighty wanted me to fight like a dog he'd have given me long teeth and claws," one cowboy scoffed. When J. J. Ryan and T. J. Collins got into an argument in 1878 in Martinsburg, Texas, the *Galveston News* reported, "Ryan proposed to fight them without arms. . . . Collins replied that they did not fight that way in Texas. Collins then shot and wounded Ryan." Because so many men went about armed, large, powerful men were no longer so respected and so feared. Billy Snyder, the six-three bully of Payette, Idaho, "a mean hombre," was said to have been shot dead from behind a tree. "God created men," went the western adage, and "Samuel Colt made them equal."[32]

Hollywood-style shootouts on main street decided by who was the quicker draw were virtually unknown, and western historians are quite right to emphasize that killings were not the everyday affairs the legend of the Wild West would suggest. But the homicide rate was extremely high: fifty to one hundred per one hundred thousand in some mining and cattle towns. The most common killings seem to have taken place during affrays between men drinking. In his study of homicides in Arizona, Clare V. McKanna Jr. found that a substantial majority of both victims and perpetrators had consumed alcohol. In a classic example of fatal western violence, Tom McDonald and Alex Nixon were having a friendly drink at the Shamrock Saloon in Bodie, California, in 1879 when they began quarreling. McDonald upped the stakes, claiming he was the better man. Nixon then floored the smaller McDonald with one punch. Rising, McDonald pulled his pistol and asked if Nixon would give him "even chances." "Yes, by God," Nixon replied, drawing his own gun. Both men opened fire; Nixon was hit and died two hours later.[33]

Like drinking and fighting, gambling was a hallmark of life in the West. As in the California gold rush, adventurers, men who liked to take risks, were everywhere. "That's what life on the frontier is, chance," Deadwood newspaper editor "Blondy" McFarland told Estelline Bennett. Virtually every western town had its full complement of sporting men and gambling halls. "You have no idea of the gambling carried on in Auraria [the original settlement of Denver]. They go at it night and day. Sundays and all," William Larimer Jr. wrote to his wife. When Richard Hughes arrived in Deadwood during the Black Hills excitement in 1876 he found that on Main Street "every form of gambling known in America was conducted." The town's fourteen casinos never closed their doors. Leadville in 1879 had 4 churches, 4 banks, 3 restaurants and 131 gambling places. In Dodge City "every saloon in the city has one or more gambling tables. Faro, monte, and the other usual games are dealt openly."[34]

There certainly were western men like Jules Sandoz, brooding on the Niobrara River, who was nicknamed "Old Jules . . . because of his aversion to practical jokes, the current frontier humor." But other westerners liked pranks, and the rougher the better. The jokes, nasty enough among the tavern crowd, became even more malicious. As in the East, favorite victims were those who were deemed vulnerable: newcomers, blacks and Chinese, and drunks. Or even men who were just asleep. Among the "endless practical jokes" carried out by New Mexican cowboys, a favorite was to tie a saddle rope to a sleeping cowboy's bedroll and pull him into the water. "It is very funny, of course, to see a wrathful man emerge from the middle of a pond." In Red Lodge, Montana, "pranks" included tearing up fences, pelting homes with rocks, and disrupting church services. Duels and gunfights with blanks were a perennial favorite. The most perilous prank was probably setting men on fire—the "hotfoot" was the West's contribution to the American practical joking tradition. A Colorado City, Texas newspaper described how local attorney W. W. Schermerhorn, "under the influence" in Memph Elliott's barroom, "had his feet badly burned by some unprincipled party pouring coal oil [kerosene] in his boots and setting fire to them." A man was "inoffensively taking a drink," the *Dodge City Times* reported, at the Alhambra Saloon in 1877, when "some one set fire to the lower extremities of his coat." In Virginia City, Montana, a barroom snoozer was liable to be awakened by having an oil-soaked cork put in his nostril and ignited.[35]

The mock trial flourished in the West. "Cowboys 'lying over' must have diversion, and one of the never tiring amusements . . . is a mock trial," New Mexico cowboy Albert Thompson remembered. "It's sho yous found guilty," black cowboy Henry Pobasco recalled to a WPA interviewer, "'cause de fine am a drink for de bunch." As had been true in the East, real law enforcement authorities often took part in these trials. The West's most famous mock trial was "The Great Landslide Case," described in Mark Twain's *Roughing It* (1872), a comic account based on his western travels and his residence in Carson City and Virginia City, Nevada, from 1861 to 1864. A landslide had carried a cabin down the hillside, so the story goes, and deposited it on top of another cabin. Who owned the surviving cabin? As "a practical joke," the attorney hired by the buried cabin's owner staged an elaborate mock trial with a judge, lawyers, and witnesses who sank the plaintiff's case with increasingly absurd testimony. Twain insisted that it actually happened, but it seems likely the trial was not so much a prank on anyone in particular but rather a burlesque of the mining laws in which all involved were in on the joke.[36]

Men in the West not only spoofed the execution of the law; they also lampooned the making of it in a ritual known as the Third House. These mock legislatures were operating in Illinois in the 1840s, came to California with the gold rush, and by the 1860s had became an established western tradition. The Nevada Third House, a " 'rip-snortin' gymnasium," which appeared in 1862 and lasted into the next century, was the best established. It was composed of lawmakers, lawyers, journalists, and townsmen who burlesqued the processes and results of legislation. The Nevada Third House met at first in saloons and later for a time in the real legislative chamber, where it carried on before a considerable number of spectators. Mark Twain presided as "governor" over one session and wrote an account of it for the *Virginia City Territorial Enterprise*. James Polk Miller, who took part in the Nevada Third House in 1867, summarized the governor's address in his diary: "The main point" was "the donation of two million dollars to the territory of Misselaneum. At the conclusion a motion to print two Million seven hundred thousand copies was lost. Various reports were held and the Committee of Ways and Means . . . was continued, also the committee on Wet Stationary."

Legislators in California would occasionally convene the Third House on the floor of the assembly during recesses, and at times there was confusion over what had been passed by the real house and what by the Third House. When the San Francisco *Alta California* ridiculed a proposed bill in the California legislature that prohibited the birth of illegitimate children, the newspaper quickly received a communication from a member "of the third house" informing it the "resolution was introduced in a spirit of badinage, and was a legislative jeu d'esprit while the house was without a quorum."[37]

"A FRONTIER LIFE STIMULATES ALL THE QUALITIES OF MANHOOD"

The traditional "two consciences" of compassion and cruelty was powerful in the West; never, in fact, was it more apparent. The characteristic kindness and liberality of westerners was appealing. Living in a place with an economy less developed than in the East and a large population of single men, westerners, like earlier generations of Americans, relied on reciprocal generosity. "Mutually dependent on each other," noted A. K. McClure, "they cultivate the highest measure of neighborly kindness." McClure believed that "the whole civilized world does not furnish a more cordial, frank, and hospitable class of citizens." Westerners were proud of their openhandedness. "No city ever contributed more lavishly to the sick and afflicted," wrote Carlyle Channing Davis of Leadville. Edmund F. Hartshorn claimed that in California in the 1880s, doors were left unlocked and that if anyone came along hungry he was welcome to come in and eat. Western saloons often let bummers spend the night inside in cold weather, and sometimes the regulars would help the bartender care for sick strangers. Even men and women generally hostile to wild western society were amazed by the benevolence of people in the region. Mrs. M. M. Mathews was convinced that "no city is so given to vice as Virginia City," Nevada. Yet even she found much to admire: "Men and women are very generous; they will divide their last potato with you, or give their last 'bit' to a charitable cause . . . and would take their chances in getting another."[38]

Western benevolence had strict limits, however, and those viewed as outsiders were treated with contempt and cruelty. "A frontier life stimulates all the qualities of manhood, the true, the good and the bad," the *Dodge Times* explained. Obviously the West had no monopoly on racism, and blacks were certainly dealt with much more violently in the South, but the contrast of western sympathy and ferocity was stark. There were many black cowboys, and blacks were found throughout the region, but they remained outcasts in the eyes of many whites. At breakfast in the Metropolitan Hotel in Cheyenne, Wyoming, in 1879, a black man sat down at the table with a group of cowboys who had just driven a herd of cattle up from Texas. The trail boss, without saying a word, smashed a chair over the black man's head. He was fortunate compared to the African American who dared to ask for service at the Criterion Saloon in Denver and was shot dead by a white customer. The Chinese were regarded by many westerners as subhuman. Fred Hart, editor of the *Austin (Nev.) Reveille*, reflected the prevailing view: "His vices are legion, and comprise, in part, dishonesty, cruelty, filth, idolatry, and opium smoking . . . , to steal [is] his creed, to lie his religion." In 1880 four drunken white toughs in a Denver saloon attacked some Chinese billiard players, and the violence quickly escalated. A white mob formed and beat one Chinese man to death and left the Chinese quarter of the city "gutted as completely as though a cyclone came in one door and passed . . . out the rear," the *Rocky Mountain News* reported.[39]

A. K. McClure, the journalist who judged that "the whole civilized world does not furnish a more cordial, frank, and hospitable class of citizens" than westerners, also related that "ninety-nine out of every hundred Western men believe that the sooner the indians are killed off the better, and they insist it is a humane work to kill them when ever and wherever found." Indian hunting, in fact, was rare, but calls for extermination were more than just rhetoric. Deadwood offered a bounty on Indian heads in 1876, and prospector Jerry Bryan recorded that a Mexican came into town with the severed head of an Indian. "The Greaser was Surrounded and carried through Town. . . . The head was Strung up on a pole and put up at auction and carried around to the places of Busyness." After Indians killed a white settler in southern Idaho in 1864, William T. Ballou, who had taken part in the California gold rush and was prospecting in the area, joined in a punitive expedition. On July 20 the white volunteers got the Indians "into a cañon; . . . & Lord bless your Soul if we did not let them have it. We killed everything that looked like an Indian, dog or anything else; young ones, by George—shot them all. Col. Moore said 'Kill them all, little as well as big; Knits make lice.'" Thirty-five Indians, mostly women and children, were reported to have died. Some infants, it was said, were bashed to death on rocks.[40]

By the 1880s, as civility and moderation triumphed elsewhere in the United States, jolly attitudes had found a home in western masculine locales. Drinking, fighting, and gambling now were an open repudiation of respectability, and many in places like Virginia City, Nevada, Leadville, and Dodge City seemed proud of their reputation for iniquity. Many openly scorned religion. "There is no God west of the Missouri" went the boast. Most cowboys were indifferent to spiritual matters, but many others "were open scoffers" who "devoted considerable thought to the invention of new and ingenious combinations of sacrilegious expressions." Rolf Johnson watched as a missionary attempted to preach on the street in Sidney, Nebraska, as "jeers and jokes met him on every hand." Leadville wallowed in its heathen reputation, and visitors could drop by Charles "Pap" Wyman's famous saloon that featured a large open Bible on a shelf behind the bar or the Little Church Saloon that patrons entered through a mock chapel front.[41]

Jolly fellowship reached something close to a climax in Dodge City, the westernmost of the cattle towns. Dodge, remembered Bill Jones, "was the whole show, a regular three ring circus, with something going on in each ring all the time." Dodge City was to become a byword for violence. Brawls were routine, and there were numerous shooting and stabbing affrays, although homicides were fairly rare. But, in the 1880s, the town's reputation was multifaceted. Known for violence, yes, but also famed for the benevolence of its inhabitants: "So proverbial had the liberality of Dodge City become that it was known for miles up and down the old Santa Fe trail." And, in its heyday, Dodge was almost as renowned for its practical jokes as for its fights and mayhem. Never were violence and comedy more closely connected. "The humor of those wild days," remembered Dodge City merchant Robert Wright, "was often almost as startling and nerve-testing, as its warfare was desperate."[42]

In Dodge "everyone had a practical joke to play upon you," Bill Jones remembered. Whatever prank was pulled off it was attributed to the town's mythical joker "Luke McGlue." In a typical episode, a traveling cigar seller who discovered that several boxes of cigars had vanished was quickly informed that Luke McGlue had taken them to a nearby saloon. The cigar seller went to the saloon and was directed to another one, and so on. In each barroom "everybody was smoking and praising the cigars Luke McGlue had given them, but Luke could not be found." Robert Wright gives a number of examples of Dodge's "startling and nerve-testing humor." Anyone who left himself vulnerable was a potential victim. When two Dodge men discovered Jim Dalton passed out drunk, they put him in a large crate and exhibited him as "the only living specimen of man and brute combined," stirring him up "by vigorously prodding him, in the mid-section, with a broomstick." Blacks were favorite targets of pranks. One saloon kept a large cage of rattlesnakes in the back lot. A "darkey" would be invited to bend over and inspect them and a huge stuffed snake would be draped over his shoulders. Attendees of a masked ball held by the town's minuscule African American community were doused with cayenne pepper. The "day of carnival" that developed spontaneously on September 4, 1876, was Dodge at its most uproarious. So many men were on a

Gambling in a Leadville, Colorado, saloon in the 1880s or 1890s. Denver Public Library, Western History Collection, X-297.

drunken spree, the *Dodge City Globe* explained, that "we cannot mention the pranks of each without overlooking some and causing them to feel slighted." What began as a water fight turned into a huge food fight that ended with a brawl and "one or two gun plays, . . . [which] by reason of lack of execution were not effective." Concluded the *Globe*, "Such is life in the far, far west."[43]

Dodge also seems to have been a byword in animal cruelty. Men there made what seems a genuine breakthrough in animal torment with the discovery of bisulfite of carbon, known in western parlance as "hokey pokey" or "high life," a substance that proved much more agonizing than the traditional turpentine. Robert M. Wright had been one of Dodge's leading businessmen in its cattle days and devoted almost four pages of his reminiscences to hokey pokey. "When applied to any animal with hair . . . it had a wonderful effect[.] . . . [T]he animal just went crazy." It was "a means of great sport among the gang in the early days." Wright's delight in recollecting those days is palpable. Any cowboy in Dodge who boasted of his riding ability risked having his horse hokey pokeyed. "I never did see a man who could retain his seat on doped horse," Wright chortled. In one case, "the gang" hokey pokeyed a trained bear belonging to "two dagoes." The bear howled, ran about and rolled his eyes in agony. When the bear finally calmed down, his trainers, believing him poisoned, frantically rubbed the bear's stomach, to the further amusement of the perpetrators.[44]

Dodge, in Wright's account, was the last frontier town, and his book is pervaded with nostalgia, a sense that Dodge was out of place in an increasingly refined and serene society. That perception only increased popular fascination with Dodge and other such localities. And that fascination did not end when these places became refined or disappeared. (Many western boomtowns were virtual ghost towns by the end of the century.) The Wild West continued to live on in popular culture as a place where men adhered to an older social code.

"HIS NAME IS MOSE, HE RUNS WID DE HOSE"

The connection of the West with that other great center of male disorder, New York City, did not cease with the gold rush. Men from the lower wards continued to travel west. New York and the Bowery milieu fascinated men in western mining and cattle towns, and western jolly fellows and sports began to filter into Manhattan. After the discovery of the Comstock Silver Lode in Nevada in 1859, Virginia City became, as San Francisco had been earlier, a Mecca for New Yorkers; some came via California, others directly from Manhattan. Virginia City's volunteer fire department contained a number of men from the New York fire department, including John Van Buren Perry and Thomas Peasley, the owner of the popular Sazerac Saloon. Both did their best to live up to the Bowery boy persona. Renowned brawlers, they, in the time-honored New York tradition, used fire companies as stepping stones to elective office in the 1860s: Perry to marshal and Peasley to sheriff. In Mark Twain's *Roughing It,* Peasley appears as "Buck Fanshaw," who was described as once having "licked four Greasers in eleven minutes" and who was a hero to the "vast bottom-stratum of society." Fanshaw's friend Scotty, "a stalwart rough" who always joined the weaker side in a fight, is apparently based on Perry. The toughest New Yorker in Virginia City was likely the diminutive roughneck Billy Mulligan. Expelled from San Francisco by the vigilantes in 1856, Mulligan returned to New York, where he was involved in several affrays, including a notorious 1858 attack on a former member of the vigilance committee Mulligan spotted walking down Broadway. He traveled to England in 1860 as one of John C. Heenan's seconds in his renowned prizefight with Thomas Sayers. Later the same year, "William Mulligan, Esq.," as the press sarcastically called him, was sent to prison after pulling a gun on a policeman trying to eject him from John Morrissey's swank gambling house. Out of jail, he drifted back west to Virginia City in 1864, where Mark Twain enrolled him among the town's "long tailed heroes of the revolver."[45]

When Twain visited New York City in 1867 he was immediately struck by the similarity in deportment between the men he had known in Nevada and the audience in the Bowery Theater, who he described as "a wild, lawless, independent lot . . . [who] would make good desperado stuff to stock a new mining camp with." Henry Nash Smith, the pioneer scholar of the literature of the American West, noted "how easily folklore motifs from the slums of New York could become naturalized in the Far West." Although the Mose plays had faded in the East by the Civil War, they continued to thrill and convulse western audiences. The Apollo Theater in Denver in 1861 showed both *A Glance at New York* and *Mose and Lize*; in 1863 in Virginia City, minstrel Jake Wallace sang for an encore,

> In the street you knows, meets one of my foes,
> His name is Mose, he runs wid the hose,
> A quarrel arose, we came to blows,
> He hit me in de nose, and down I goes.

Mose was still being performed in Virginia City in 1871 when newspaperman Alf Doten, a former colleague of Twain's, saw it. Bowery strains swirled through the West. "Wake Up, Jake" was the name of a popular laxative. Alf Doten had a fighting dog he named "Kyzer" after the legendarily unruly Washington Market butcher of the 1830s. When New Mexican cowboys, according to Agnes Cleveland, told tall tales about the Wild West to visitors from the East, the easterners countered with their own stories about a New York City so uproarious that riots preceded every theater performance.[46]

The affinity between the West and the lower-ward milieu of New York is highlighted by the career of sporting man Bartholomew "Bat" Masterson. Just as an earlier generation of rowdies from Manhattan journeyed to California, men from the West with a taste for jolly living began to flow to New York. Born in 1853, Masterson grew up in Illinois and Kansas. He became a buffalo hunter and then an army scout. In a furious 1876 Texas shooting affray of which details are murky, Masterson was wounded and a man and woman killed. Although this may have been the only time Masterson fatally shot anyone, he emerged with the reputation as a ruthless gunman. Masterson's good looks attracted immediate attention. "One of the most perfectly made up men you ever saw," Robert Wright believed. Masterson, who had a convivial manner and penchant for practical jokes, became a popular figure among the saloon crowd in the locales he lived in. He

"Scotty Regulating Matters." Scotty, at right, is in full b'hoy regalia. Note the soaplocks. The object in Scotty's hand is a speaking trumpet used to shout out orders at fires. In Mark Twain, *Roughing It* (Hartford, Conn., 1872).

came to Dodge City in 1876 and was a policeman and saloon keeper before being elected sheriff of Ford County, where Dodge is located. His high-handed and often violent methods, along with his closeness to "the Gang," Dodge's saloon sporting crowd, led to his defeat for reelection in 1879. After a brief stint gambling in Leadville, he followed Wyatt Earp, who had been his deputy in Dodge, and other sporting men to the mining town of Tombstone, Arizona Territory, where he worked in a gambling hall.[47]

Masterson was always an ardent boxing fan. He attended the 1882 Paddy Ryan–John L. Sullivan fight and many of the other heavyweight championship fights of the era, including the 1889 Jake Kilrain–Sullivan fight where he was in Kilrain's corner, having been recruited by Richard J. Fox, the anti-Sullivan editor of the *Police Gazette*, in the hope that Masterson's gunslinging reputation would prevent Sullivan's entourage from making trouble. Masterson, by this time known as the "Boss Gambler of the West," refereed prizefights in the 1880s and in the 1890s moved to Denver and promoted boxing matches throughout Colorado. With his ambitions as a boxing promoter hindered by rival Denver sporting men, and perhaps sensing that the region might be becoming too respectable for his tastes, Masterson left for New York City in 1900.[48]

He quickly hooked up with other transplanted westerners who invigorated Manhattan's sporting scene in the 1890s, most prominently Alfred Henry Lewis, who became Bat's patron. Lewis had meandered around the West as a ranch hand, miner, lawyer, and finally newspaperman and author. His popular novel *Wolfville,* published in 1897, was one of the earliest cowboy novels with pretensions to literary merit. Narrated by the garrulous "Old Cattleman," the stories are set in Tombstone and mix violence, sentiment, and humor, mostly in the form of crude practical jokes. Hired by Hearst's *New York American,* Lewis began writing sketches of the Bowery and lower-ward milieu. His collected New York stories were published as *Confessions of a Detective* in 1906 and *Apaches of New York* in 1912.[49]

With Lewis's aid, Masterson secured a regular boxing column in the *New York Morning Telegraph,* a breezy sporting and theatrical daily. Masterson maintained his reputation as a wild westerner by engaging in some well-publicized fistfights. He was a regular at the Metropole Bar on Broadway and a favorite with the theater and gambling crowd, and with his affable ways he became a honored figure in the New York sporting fraternity. An acquaintance with Theodore Roosevelt led to his appointment as a deputy U.S. marshal for New York, but Bat never matched pioneer sporting man Isaiah Rynders by becoming marshal. Among Masterson's friends was a young baseball and boxing reporter for the *American,* Damon Runyon. From Pueblo, Colorado, Runyon worked as a newspaperman in the mining towns of Trinidad, Colorado, and Denver before coming to New York. A pallbearer at Masterson's funeral in 1921, Runyon later memorialized Bat with the character Sky Masterson in his famous short story "The Idyll of Miss Sarah Brown" (1933), the basis for the musical "Guys and Dolls."[50]

The "dual relationship of city and frontier," in Alexander Saxton's words, is apparent in the careers of men like Masterson, Lewis, and Runyon. The drinking, fighting, gambling, and pranks that had defined jolly fellowship had once been routine among men. But in the second half of the nineteenth century such conduct faded in most of the nation. Yet in the moral regions of large cities and other male-dominated redoubts in the Wild East and Wild West, this older disorderly style remained intact in an altered but still recognizable form. The Second Great Awakening and the temperance movement had made jolly comportment, which once seemed simply how men behaved, into a repudiation of respectability. The persistence of this outlook into the late nineteenth century came to have a significant influence on the American cultural terrain. In masculine milieus, East and West, jolly fellowship was evolving into a counterculture. By preserving disorderly values in the face of growing civility, these enclaves kept alive what could be in the hands of writers like Lewis and Runyon and Mark Twain a kind of resource, which was, if not an alternative to, than at least a contrasting perspective from, that of genteel, middle-class refinement.

These jolly strongholds, especially those in the West, were the focus of a great deal of popular attention, both in the nineteenth century and after. This fascination with the West was not only with places such as Deadwood, Dodge City, and Tombstone but also with the men in them and with one type of man in particular—the sporting man. Sporting men became such significant figures in the history of the region that they have sometimes been considered a distinctively western phenomenon, but the peculiar combination of gambler and politician had originated in New York City in the 1840s and by the 1880s could be found in cities throughout the nation. A sporting subculture with its own institutions and traditions developed. Just as places like the Bowery and Dodge intrigued even refined men, so sporting men like John Morrissey and Bat Masterson with their distinctive appearance, ethos, and customs became national celebrities, their jolly lives a tantalizing rebuke to middle-class respectability.

CHAPTER EIGHT

Sporting Men

"I'm God damn glad I killed the son of a bitch," snarled Jere Dunn as the Chicago police took him into custody. Sprawled dead on the floor was Jim "Cockeyed" Elliott, a Brooklyn prizefighter and a good one, at one time light-heavyweight champion. Dunn, originally from the tough Sixth Ward of New York, was a "well-known sporting character" who had been, among other things, a racehorse trainer and a confidence man. There had been bad blood between the two for some time. Dunn called Elliott "a bag of wind," a "cur," a coward, and a "dunghill." Elliott returned the compliments, labeling Dunn a "dirty dog, a liar, not a sporting man, but a hanger-on and a pimp." On 1 March 1883, Elliott, just returning from a visit to Dodge City, was drinking with some gamblers in the Tivoli Saloon on Dearborn Street, a place "patronized largely by the sporting fraternity and the demi-monde," according to the *Chicago Tribune*'s five-column story on the killing. Dunn walked in, and as soon as the men saw each other they pulled their revolvers and opened fire. The wounded Elliott smashed a chair over Dunn, more shots were fired, and the rivals struggled on the floor until parted by bystanders. Both men had been shot twice, Elliott fatally.[1]

The killing was a national sensation. It was a front-page story throughout the country, attracting even more coverage than the celebrated affray involving sporting men at the O.K. Corral in Tombstone seventeen months earlier. Manhattan gambling men and prizefighters immediately made plans to return Elliott's body to his native city and bury it "with all the honors sporting society should suggest." "Many sporting gentlemen" escorted the body to the Chicago train station, and Frederick Krohne, a well-known "pedestrian" (long-distance walker), accompanied the corpse back to New York. "During the trip thousands of persons requested permission to look at the face of the dead man," according to the *New York Times*. The body was met at Grand Central terminal by a large delegation of "sports." The assembly conveyed the corpse to the home of Elliott's brother-in-law on Canal Street, where "sporting men from the principal cities of the country" journeyed to pay their respects. Long lines of ordinary New Yorkers stood to view the body and thousands had to be turned away. Not since Bill Poole had "the funeral of a sporting man in this city caused so great a demonstration," the *New York Clipper* reported. For hours prior to the start of the funeral procession the five blocks of Canal Street between the Bowery and Centre were completely packed with a turbulent, pushing crowd "of both sexes, of various ages, and composed of nearly all classes of society, . . . attracted mainly by a desire to see the many noted sporting men who were expected to be in attendance." The streets were so jammed that the funeral procession had trouble making its way to the ferry. In Brooklyn, the route was lined with spectators, and an estimated twelve thousand people gathered at Calvary Cemetery to witness the funeral and interment.[2]

The sporting man emerged as a type in New York City in the 1840s. Most were politically influential gamblers and pugilists who fraternized together in the sporting saloons of the lower wards. Among the most prominent early sports were political gang leader Isaiah Rynders, prizefighters Yankee Sullivan and Tom Hyer, gambler Pat Herne, and minstrel Dan Bryant. By the 1850s sporting men could be found in the vice districts of Boston, Philadelphia, and other major cities and even in smaller places such as Troy and Buffalo. There were, by 1880, sports in virtually every city in the nation, large and small, as well as in western mining camps and cattle towns. The total size of "sporting society" is impossible to determine, but in Manhattan there were estimated to be fifteen hundred to three thousand sports in the 1870s and by the next decade five to ten thousand. As the numbers of sporting men expanded, a sporting subculture with its own institutions and traditions emerged.[3]

Elliot's murder and funeral revealed how sporting men by 1883 had come to share a sense of their separateness from ordinary society and of solidarity with each other. Sports saw themselves as having a distinctive code of ethics, different from that of conventional society but, in its own way, no less honorable. The reaction to the killing also illustrates the intense public interest in sporting men and the sporting milieu. The most renowned sports of the day such as John Morrissey, Harry Hill, and Bat Masterson were national celebrities, known from coast to coast, their activities closely chronicled in the press. The popular allure of the sporting fraternity was reflected in the many fictional representations of sports. The extraordinary curiosity about sports and their lives resulted in part from the perception that they were one of the last groups of men left who ostentatiously embraced jolly values. In most areas of the country, jolly fellowship had ebbed, yet nostalgia lingered for the unfettered male comportment of earlier days. Sporting men's perceived adherence to this obsolete demeanor was intriguing, even inspiring. The sporting fraternity became a counterculture, and sports were romanticized as adherents to an archaic mode of conduct and ethics, increasingly out of place in a docile and deliberate modern world.

"WHAT IS COMMONLY KNOWN AS THE 'SPORTING ELEMENT'"

In later years, pre-gold-rush New York City took on many of the aspects of a foundational myth among sporting men, revisited repeatedly in the sporting press. Isaiah Rynders may have been the prototypical sporting man, but prizefighter Yankee Sullivan was the first sporting celebrity, a type that would become quite common in later years, and he helped shape the popular image of the sporting man. With his magnificent body and flamboyant dress—tight pants, green velvet coat, and cluster-diamond pin—Sullivan demanded to be noticed. New York was the sporting capital, and with his string of popular sporting saloons, the flashy Sullivan set the standard. "When not in liquor, a clever sort of man," remembered the *Clipper*, his "opinions concerning the cock-pit, badger baits, and other pleasures of the sporting fraternity was always considered decisive." In an era when "force and muscle exerted great power electing the rulers," in the words of sport J. R. Talbot, pugilists like Sullivan were very useful when the brawling began in party caucuses or at the polls on election day. "Sully" used his popularity, connections with New York's volunteer fire companies, and his talents as a party shoulder hitter to become an influence in the Sixth Ward. The fighting-gambling-politics association that Rynders and Sullivan pioneered was to be routinely replicated by future sports.[4]

Sporting men, or "rounders" and "the fancy" as they were sometimes called, congregated in vice districts of other cities besides New York. "Squire" William McMullen, the son of a grocer, was probably Philadelphia's best-known sport. From his Moyamensing saloon, McMullen organized the Keystone Club in 1850, an Empire Club–style troop of Democratic brawlers that helped elect him alderman. Washington's Edward Pendleton was that city's most famous antebellum gambling man. His Pennsylvania Avenue casino, the House of Fortune, was patronized by some the nation's leading politicians, many of whom were the well-bred Pendleton's personal friends. In Atlanta after the completion of the railroad in 1845, "what is commonly known as the 'sporting element'" surged, related a 1902 history of the city. Gambling, cockfighting, and prostitution were epidemic, and on Saturday nights free fights on Murrell's Row "sometimes assumed the proportions of a riot." Respectable elements organized politically in 1850 into what became known as the "Moral" Party, while sporting men answered by establishing what was dubbed the "Rowdy" or "Disorderly" Party. A brawling mayoral campaign followed and after the Moral Party's victory, "volunteer police" began a crackdown on vice. In New Orleans prizefighter Chris Lilly was the leader of Crescent City's sporting fraternity. Notorious for having killed Thomas McCoy in the ring in 1842, Lilly learned his political skills in New York as a member of Rynders's Empire Club and became a veritable Johnny Appleseed of strong-arm politics. When Lilly came to New Orleans around 1846, he quickly energized the prizefighting scene and introduced "the city's first organized system of ruffianism, for electioneering purposes." Lilly left in 1852 to help David C. Broderick install organized ruffianism in San Francisco, and he remained there until he was expelled by the vigilantes.[5]

The Mexican-American War (1846–48) was a milestone in the history of the sporting fraternity. "When the Mexican War broke out," New York sporting man Edward "Ned" James remembered in the *Clipper*, "many of the old crowd volunteered." The sports who joined seemed mostly to be looking for adventure and plunder, foreseeing, as one account put it, "plenty of whiskey, 'golden Jesuses,' and pretty Mexican gals." Prizefighting came virtually to a halt in 1847–48, the *New York Illustrated News* reported, because the war carried away so many "combative spirits." Prominent sporting men who enlisted included Chris Lilly, John McCleester, Billy Mulligan, and Empire Club brawler and later Broderick loyalist David Scannell. *Wanderings of a Vagabond* (1873), by John Morris, a fascinating, if overdramatized, history of the early sporting community, claims that there were entire regiments made up of gambling men and rowdies: "Boston sent out to Mexico one regiment of her roughs, Philadelphia two, while New York sent one to join the army of General Scott, and another to California. New Orleans sent two six months regiments." This is obviously exaggerated. The New York regiment sent to California that Morris refers to is Stevenson's First New York Volunteers, which, as chapter 5 explains, did enroll a number of sporting men and others "grown weary of the tameness of civilized society" but also included many ordinary mechanics. The Second New York Volunteers, the other New York regiment Morris mentions, seems to have contained only about two hundred lower-

A "first-class" Washington gambling house. The men at the table in front are playing faro. In Edward Winslow Martin, *Behind the Scenes in Washington* (n.p., 1873).

ward types among its eight hundred soldiers. Similarly, the First Pennsylvania Infantry had a reputation for disorder only on account of Company D. Recruited in Philadelphia by Squire McMullen, it was reputed to be mostly made up of "the Rowdy Gang known as the Killers," along with gamblers, shoulder hitters, and volunteer firemen.[6]

Although Morris's account is overstated, it is true that many rounders took part in the war. As sporting men associated with each other, it likely furthered their awareness of being part of a group, of a sporting fraternity. After the war, Mexico continued to occupy a special place among sports. "Sharpers from the United States flocked there in droves," Morris remembered. The "dazzling panorama of Mexican sporting life," as J. Frank "Florry" Kernan put it, was extremely alluring. As stricter standards of propriety made headway in the United States, Mexico's appeal grew, as sports believed men could pursue a jolly lifestyle freely and cheaply there. Gambling and cockfights were conducted openly and on a greater scale than in American cities. Bullfighting was intriguing. For rounders, Mexico symbolized a carefree freedom quite similar to the liberation from middle-class restraint that Mexico was to epitomize for a later counterculture, the beats of the 1950s.[7]

Shortly after the Mexican War ended, the California gold rush brought what

George Wilkes called an "exodus, or transmigration of the 'Fancy'," from New York and other cities. Gamblers, prizefighters, and "the daring and adventurous spirits of the Atlantic states" came to the West Coast. As the gold rush wound down, the next adventure became, for some sports, filibustering. New York, New Orleans, and San Francisco—the three main gambling locales in the country—were also the cities where the filibustering spirit was the strongest. Few sports and others who became filibusters had much interest in promoting freedom and democracy. Most were looking for adventure, and, as one put it, "pillage and plunder." The all-male camaraderie of army life may also have been part of the allure. And, while it would be an exaggeration to say that the sporting fraternity had a foreign policy, filibustering was agreeable to the expansionist Democratic politics of most antebellum sporting men. Sports likely found many other men congenial to their tastes among the ranks. Amy S. Greenberg suggests in her study of filibustering that most who went to Nicaragua were what she calls "martial men" who liked to drink and who "reveled in their physical strength." The tavern and grocery crowd were well represented. Joseph G. Baldwin claimed in *The Flush Times of Alabama and Mississippi* that the reason boisterous young men had been found in such profusion hanging around groceries in the South in the 1830s was that, unlike in the two decades that followed, there were no "Mexican wars and filibusters" to draw them off.[8]

With the 1852 election of Democrat Franklin Pierce, filibustering moved into high gear, focusing on Mexico and Nicaragua. The spirit flamed in New York and New Orleans, "but nowhere," writes Charles H. Brown in his history of the activity, "did it become so easily ignited as in California." The "California gold excitement," explained Hubert Howe Bancroft, "in stirring the lust for roaming and adventure" and "in massing a horde of reckless brawlers" fostered filibustering. Remembered Horace Bell of 1850s California, "to sympathize with filibustering at the time was popular. An actual filibuster was a lion—a hero."[9]

The first California-based filibustering expedition was to Sonora, Mexico, in 1852, led by French ex-miner Raoulx de Raousset-Boulbon. It was a total failure, but it nevertheless inspired others, including William Walker, the man who would become the most vigorous and famous filibuster of the age. Originally from Tennessee, Walker worked as a newspaper editor in San Francisco and later as a lawyer in Marysville, California. With few good prospects in Alta California, he resolved to "liberate" Baja California. He gathered forty-five men, secured a ship, and in November 1853 arrived in lower California and declared himself president. The expedition was a fiasco: Walker and his men soon found themselves desperately short of supplies and were forced to flee back to the United States.[10]

Walker's daring, indeed reckless, scheme captured the imagination of the public, and upon his return to San Francisco he became an idol. Owing to the popular belief in physiognomy, male faces and physiques were carefully evaluated in this era, and Walker, as a commander of men, was especially intently observed. Generally, reviewers of his face and body were disappointed. "We could hardly believe that the little insignificant looking person before us was the [great] man," complained one. Only five-four, there was nothing in Walker's features "to counter balance this serious deficiency in inches," noted a correspondent for the *New Orleans Delta*. His build was scrawny, his hair thin, his nose ordinary, his mouth characterless. There was, however, one outstanding feature: his eyes. They were "deep, intensely brilliant blue-gray . . . , large and intelligent." Everyone who met Walker commented on his eyes, and he was to become known—admiringly to supporters, sarcastically to detractors—as "the Gray-Eyed Man of Destiny."[11]

Now a major public figure in the Golden State, Walker became editor of a pro-David Broderick, Sacramento newspaper. Tried and acquitted of violating the neutrality laws, Walker soon was organizing another filibuster, this one to Nicaragua. A civil war was going on there, and one faction's leaders offered him grants of land in return for recruiting and leading a contingent of Americans to help the insurgents. Moving fast—rival efforts were in the works—Walker organized a new expedition. There were reports of parties of miners descending from the mountains to enlist. Walker's first group of fifty-eight recruits left San Francisco in May 1855.[12]

Walker himself had connections with San Francisco's sporting fraternity, and many California sports were among Walker's followers. Morris claimed that as the gold rush waned, "the great bulk" of California's gamblers "followed the fortunes of Gen. Wm. Walker, in his Nicaraguan expedition, where the climate, bad whiskey, and the bullets of the natives, in a majority of cases closed their careers." In New York the sporting fraternity was feverishly pro-Walker. Isaiah Rynders, Walker's "great friend and admirer," became one of the expedition's leading backers and recruiters. George Wilkes, Mike Walsh, and Tom Hyer were Walker supporters and helped raise funds for supplies. Bryant's Minstrels saluted the Gray-Eyed Man of Destiny with "I'm Off for Nicaragua in de Morning." Walker's New York recruits, according to an American naval commander sent to intercept them, were reputed to be "'shoulder hitters,' 'strikers,' 'bouncers,' 'killers' & the like." The most prominent sporting men who went to Nicaragua to join Walker were Billy Mulligan and Chris Lilly. Mulligan returned, Lilly did not. Expelled from San Francisco by the vigilance committee, Lilly headed to Central America. He opened a monte bank in Grenada that won "about all

William Walker, the "Gray Eyed Man of Destiny." *Harper's Weekly*, 13 October 1860. Library of Congress, Prints and Photographs Division, Washington, D.C.

the ready money of Walker's officers" and then carried supplies from Mexico to Walker by schooner. In 1857 Lilly was captured by Guatemalan authorities and shot as a *filibustero.*[13]

Perhaps as many as half of the five thousand Americans who went to Nicaragua died there, but for all its manifest dangers—perhaps in part because of them—it became, at least for a time, a kind of spree. From the start rowdiness prevailed. The male shipboard environment was, as usual, pandemonium. The group of filibusters that James Carson Jamison traveled with in 1855 pillaged the ship's storeroom, swigged down the liquor, and, in a "drunken orgy," engaged "in the most wanton and riotous acts." On the *Star of the West* the next year, the men "had several quarrels among themselves . . . and one of their officers was severely beaten in the melee." Once the men arrived in Nicaragua, when they were "not actively campaigning . . . there was much merry-making," Jamison remembered. Drinking and fighting were serious problems among both officers and enlisted men, and Jamison was startled to witness "a lively shooting scrap" between a general and colonel in a billiard hall. Gambling was widespread and dueling so routine that it was estimated that an affair of honor was settled virtually every day. Jamison witnessed a mock court martial staged as a practical joke: a soldier who believed the proceedings were genuine was sentenced to hang for stealing gold coins from a dead Nicaraguan soldier. A noose was put around his neck before the sentence was reduced to treating "the court" to a ten-gallon keg of whiskey. As in the Mexican-American War, for all the disorder in camp, the soldiers usually fought bravely. Forced to surrender after the intervention of neighboring Central American states, Walker was returned to the United States, from which he launched further unsuccessful expeditions to Nicaragua before he was captured and executed in September 1860.[14]

Sporting men were active on both sides in the Civil War. Though some northern sports, including Rynders, were Peace Democrats, most backed a war to preserve the union. Southern sports sided with the Confederacy, and it was asserted that in Washington "the entire sporting fraternity . . . leans toward secession." "Better join in boys, rather than loafing on the streets or hanging around barrooms," urged the unionist *Clipper* in a revealing comment on how it perceived its readership. By April 1861 the *Clipper* proudly reported that "many of the 'boys' have already enlisted." According to Morris, "the rowdy element, boiling over with patriotism, formed themselves into several regiments" in New York, and roughs in Philadelphia and Baltimore did the same. Louisville and New Orleans sent contingents of gamblers and shoulder hitters into the Confederate army. Morris believed that so many sporting men enlisted that their political power was permanently weakened in those cities.[15]

The only regiment of rowdies that Morris specifically names is the Eleventh New York, the famed Fire Zouaves. "Composed of fire laddies and other muscular fellows," according to the *Clipper*, its enlistees included prizefighters Mike Trainor, Mike Tagan, and Johnny and Harry Lazarus, the sporting sons of Izzy the "Obese Man" Lazarus, a boxing instructor and owner of the Falstaff, a renowned Jones Street sporting saloon. The Sixth New York, also a Zouave regiment, was raised and led by Billy Wilson, a lightweight prizefighter turned Tammany politician, and was said to have been made up of veterans of Nicaragua, sporting men, and criminals along with ordinary mechanics, clerks, and others. Billy Mulligan, with "several fellows of his own kidney," formed the Empire City Cavalry Regiment before Mulligan's checkered past led the army to dismiss him. Philadelphia sporting man and Mexican War veteran William McMullen enlisted eighty-four members of the Moyamensing Hose in an independent battalion that, with McMullen as captain, was incorporated into the First Pennsylvania Volunteers. Some sports, like McMullen, returned home as soon as their enlistments expired, while others, like Trainor and Harry Lazarus, spent most of the war in the Union army. The *Clipper* regularly ran features with such titles as "Musclemen in the Army" that reported on "sporting lads from this and other cities" in an attempt to persuade the public to regard sporting society more positively. Southern sports enlisted as well. William Howard Russell, the English war correspondent, in the spring of 1861 visited the camp outside of New Orleans of the Perrit Guards, "a company of *professional gamblers*, 112 strong." Russell was impressed with their "imperturbability of demeanor," even though they were considered "pariahs of American civilization." He might have been less impressed with Wilson's Louisiana Rangers, another contingent of New Orleans sporting men. At the outbreak of war, "some of the gamblers in New Orleans," recalled member George Devol, "got up a cavalry company." It paraded around the city, but when the union army approached in 1862, the men buried their uniforms and fled.[16]

The soldiers themselves seem to have been notably less rowdy than in the Mexican War. The earlier conflict was for many volunteers a foreign adventure with the prospect of plunder. The Civil War was different. Many of the soldiers were not eager to serve; they had been drafted or had enlisted to avoid the draft. The conflict seemed far more serious: the country was divided, and casualties were extremely heavy. It was no spree. The comparative serenity of the troops when off duty may also reflect the progress in reforming male comportment in the years between the wars. There was, to be sure, still plenty of jolly behavior. "'Pay day—most of the boys drunk' . . . appears so often in soldiers' letters and diaries as to become monotonous," historian Bell Wiley observed. Gambling went on almost incessantly, and the dice game hazard, more commonly called chuck-a-luck in this period, was so popular among soldiers it became known as "the army game." "So strong was the fascination which the vice of gambling cast over the men, that they risked their lives," Mason Long remembered, throwing dice "while the bullets were flying thick and fast about us." Yet, such rollicking comportment was muted in comparison with the Mexican War. As the war dragged on, and the dead and wounded mounted, jolly behavior seemed to decline even more.[17]

The Civil War, however, did give a significant boost to gambling and thus to the sporting fraternity. Just as reformers in the 1780s and 1790s had been concerned that soldiers had become accustomed to drinking and wagering in the Revolutionary Army, moralists after the Civil War believed military service had resulted in a loosening of moral restraint. No doubt many of the men who gambled in the military never placed a bet again, but, as with the gold rush, others found the experience stimulated an appetite for wagering. Mason Long, an Ohio farm boy, was an inveterate gambler in the army, and after the war, he became a sporting man. Morris concluded that "during the rebellion, gambling increased all over the country, and at least ten times as many faro-banks as before flourished." The war created, Morris was convinced, at a minimum, fifteen hundred new professional gamblers. The Washington police chief estimated that at the war's end there were 500 sporting men in that city, 1 for every 218 adult inhabitants.[18]

"KEPT IN PRACTICALLY EVERY SALOON IN THE COUNTRY"

The twenty-five year period following Appomattox was the golden age of the sporting man. The war, the development of western mining and cattle towns, and the establishment of new eastern gambling resorts such as Saratoga and Long Branch, New Jersey, created fresh opportunities. The sporting fraternity continued to coalesce, as rounders from different cities became acquainted at major prizefights and horse races. Just before the war, the *New York Tribune* had noted the "gathering of the clans" in Buffalo for the 1858 John Morrissey–John C. Heenan fight. "Nearly every sporting man of notoriety" was present, the newspaper reported, some coming from as far away as New Orleans.[19]

The sporting press did much to further the development of the sporting community through its relentless publicity. William T. Porter's *Spirit of the Times*, founded in 1831, provided very thorough coverage of horse racing but paid little attention to prizefighting or gambling or to those who made a vocation of such pursuits. The *National Police Gazette*, begun in 1846 by George Wilkes, initially focused almost solely on crime stories. The first true sporting publication was the *New York Clipper*, founded in 1853. The *New York Herald* had recognized the popular appeal of news about prizefighting and the rowdy side of city life, and the *Herald*'s "Uncle Joe" Elliott, probably the first sports reporter in the nation, helped make boxing a national passion in the 1850s. Frank Queen, the *Clipper*'s founding editor, saw a place for a weekly sports journal. The *Clipper* thoroughly covered all sports, including cockfighting and dogfighting. It chronicled sporting men and sporting saloons and provided extensive theater coverage. It generally presented itself as an objective journal that simply reported on such events, but Queen's editorials provided an oblique, qualified defense of jolly fellowship, making it one of the few public voices defending traditional male disorderly behavior. Queen attracted an able set of journalists. Boxing correspondent Ned James was said to know "all the American fighters from Freeman the Giant to Riley the Mouse." Henry Chadwick covered baseball, and his *Clipper* writings did much to popularize the new sport and codify its rules. The paper was must reading for sports and others interested in the sporting subculture, and Queen became a celebrity in his own right. The *New York Leader* described him as "the pet of all the free-and-easy sporting men about town. . . . Frank is at all times a welcome guest and, in sporting houses, is certain to be welcomed by three cheers."[20]

Important to the postwar sporting upturn was the return of prizefighting to its previous glory. The activity had been crucial to the early growth of the sporting fraternity, but after the fervor of the Heenan-Sayers fight in 1860 boxing had gone into a steep decline. Police repression, rumors of fixes—one involving Heenan himself—and the lack of attractive fighters all contributed. "The prize ring is fast losing its prestige," the *Clipper* worried in 1870.[21]

Richard J. Fox's purchase of the *National Police Gazette* and the rise of heavyweight fighter John L. Sullivan once again made boxing the most popular sport in the United States. Fox took over the nearly bankrupt paper in 1878 and immediately expanded prizefighting coverage, systematized weight divisions, and created jewel-studded belts for the champions in the various weight classes. The *New York Times* estimated that Fox disbursed over $1 million in prizes. The breakthrough came in 1880 when the *Gazette*—billing itself the "Leading Prize Ring Authority in America"—helped generate tremendous popular interest for a heavyweight fight between Joe Goss, a past English champion, and American Paddy Ryan, a former Erie Canal locktender from Troy who first made a name for himself brawling with canal boatmen. The June 1880 fight issue, Edward Van Every claimed, sold four hundred thousand copies, and "from then on the *Police Gazette* came into tremendous vogue."[22]

The spectacular rise of John L. Sullivan helped make the *Gazette* a national institution. The "Boston Strong Boy" was the first heavyweight skillful and powerful enough to routinely knock out opponents with a blow to the jaw. His arrival in New York in 1881 electrified the city's sporting fraternity, and Sullivan propelled prizefighting back into the national spotlight. Interest in fighting in part revived because many men, including men who would not dream of fighting themselves, still regarded a fistic clash the truest test of manhood. Ryan, after his 1882 defeat by Sullivan, told the press that "the Boston Boy . . . is a better man than I am." The *Clipper* believed that Sullivan's prominence proved that people "still admire figure and worship physique." Sullivan's jolly lifestyle enhanced his charisma. He made little pretense of middle-class respectability. John L.'s natural conviviality made him a regular in saloons and sporting houses, and his legendary drinking sprees and his brawls outside the ring were widely reported. By the mid-1880s the Strong Boy was one of the best-known men in the country. "Excepting General Grant, no American has received such ovations," one newspaper claimed. His exploits were described, praised, and denounced.[23]

Sullivan's fame elevated both boxing and the *Police Gazette* to new heights. Fox's paper, however, covered more than boxing. It gave considerable attention to the sporting fraternity, running profiles of noted sporting men and stories about sporting life in columns by Samuel Mackeever ("Paul Prowler") and Theodore "the" Allen, owner of the popular Bal Mabille sporting saloon in Manhattan. Most reporting focused on New York City, and tales of Yankee Sullivan, Heenan and Poole and other sports of the 1840s and 1850s were a staple. The *Gazette* described sports and sporting life in other cities as well, emphasizing the extent and diversity of the sporting scene throughout the country. Crime remained a *Gazette* favorite and it relished scandals—especially about preachers, which it ran under headlines such as "Ministerial Misconduct" and "Clerical Capers." It was not only words that made Fox's publication notoriously popular. It was also pictures. Every issue was full of lurid drawings: voluptuous burlesque stars, Long Branch "bathing belles," well-muscled prizefighters, baseball players, gruesome train wrecks, lynching victims, brawling college students, fighting dogs. The pictures were accompanied by a punchy, one- or two-paragraph story with eye-grabbing captions such as "Burnt to a Crisp" or "She Chopped His Head Off."[24]

By the mid-1880s the *Police Gazette* had a regular weekly circulation of 150,000, and the presses in its imposing headquarters in lower Manhattan could turn out several hundred thousand copies for a major fight. Printed on its trademark pink paper, it was found wherever men gathered, and "its files were kept in practically every saloon in the country," sportswriter Edward Van Every remembered. The *Gazette*'s success led to the establishment of numerous local sporting publications, including the *Boston Sporting World*, the *Chicago Sporting Life*, the *Chicago Sporting Gazette*, the *Illustrated Sporting West*, and the *California Police Gazette*. At a time in which the swaggering male comportment of the first few decades of the century was being domesticated, the *Gazette* and its numerous imitators remained unashamedly reading material for men. Although it usually did not editorialize about the events it covered, the very nature of the enterprise made it a champion of jolly values. Fox's publication appealed not just to the saloon crowd but surely also to men who themselves no longer got drunk, gambled, or fought and yet savored reading about those who did. They were spectators of jolly life in its pages.[25]

"THE FRATERNITY HAS A CODE OF ITS OWN"

The massive convergence of sports on Louisiana for the 1882 John L. Sullivan–Paddy Ryan fight showed the sporting fraternity at its peak. New York "and the principal cities were depleted of their representative sportsmen," reported the *Police Gazette* which seemed almost as interested in the sports who attended as the fight itself. Rounders from all over the country headed for New Orleans. On 28 January a special train carrying "an immense throng of New York sporting men," as well as actors and "quite a number of boys from the best social clubs in the city," left for New Orleans. There were also chartered trains from Boston and Troy, as well as large delegations of sports from many other cities. The *Gazette* listed the famous sporting men who were there, including Harry Hill from New York, Squire McMullen from Philadelphia, "King" Mike McDonald from Chicago, and Bat Masterson from Colorado. Once in New Orleans, sports greeted old friends and began "seeing the town and talking fight and canvassing the prospects of their favorites." On the day of the fight, sporting saloons in New York, Boston, and other cities were jammed, and, the *Clipper* reported, "around the bulletin boards at newspaper offices expectant sports gathered" to await word of the fight, which ended with a spectacular ninth-round knockout by John L.[26]

Sports were well aware of the popular interest—they knew they were watched, hated, and envied. The sporting life, in comparison to jolly fellowship, seems at times to have been as much a matter of performance as comportment. They were living a male fantasy and wanted others to appreciate it. This theatrical persona would shape popular representations of the sporting man, who would in turn be shaped by them. Sports had an image to live up to. They believed that they were a special group of men, separate from mainstream society. Sporting pursuits, such as gambling, prizefighting, and pimping (an increasingly significant sporting activity), were illegal, and sports knew it was imperative for them to cooperate to survive. There were, to be sure, rivalries among sporting men, as the dispute between Elliott and Dunn starkly illustrates. But they often united to achieve mutual ends. A famous example of sporting unity was the 1883 "Dodge City War," when a coterie of western sports led by Bat Masterson and Wyatt Earp converged on Kansas to support saloon keeper, gambler, and fellow member of the fraternity, Luke Short, in a dispute with Dodge authorities.[27]

The sporting men's sense of solidarity was reflected in their adoption of nicknames, a practice that forged a link between them and the jolly tavern crowd in the early part of the century. From Captain Isaiah Rynders on down a nickname was evidence of one's admittance to the fraternity. Virtually all prizefighters had monikers: James Sullivan was "Yankee," "Sully," or "Ginger," Tom Hyer was the "Chief," John McCleester was "Country," Heenan "the Benicia Boy," Morrissey "Old Smoke," and John L. Sullivan the "Boston Strong Boy." Among sporting men could be found Orville "Awful" Gardiner, "Sir" Price McGrath, "O Bill!"

Dance, "Sitting Bull" Bush, and John Coffee, the "Shrewdest of the Shrewd." Western sports included "Mysterious Dave" Mather, "Rowdy Joe" Lowe and Ellis "Lucky" Baldwin, who built the first Santa Anita racetrack. Oneida, New York, sporting man Harry Dodge was known as "Dupely," short for "duplicate," from his no doubt useful fighting technique of punching and kicking simultaneously.[28]

The postbellum sporting fraternity had their sporting saloons, their sporting newspapers, and even sporting retailers. "Sporting Men, Buy Your Goods of a Sporting Man," urged the Sporting Men's Emporium on Liberty Street in New York City, which sold boxing prints, dealing boxes for faro, poker chips, dice, and marked cards. Rounders had their own style of dress. John Hess, a German American prizefighter known as the "Clapping Lion," recorded in his autobiography that after a big win at faro "[I] proceeded to equip myself in the costume of a professional sporting man." Earlier sports favored the flashy outfits pioneered by Yankee Sullivan, but by the 1880s most dressed in a plain black suit with a gold watch chain, diamond stickpin, and top hat. Baltimore's preeminent sport, Robert "Doc" Slater, wore clothes that were "always of a fashionable but subdued cut and style."[29]

Sporting men believed what bound them together was not just occupation, common history, nicknames, and dress. They believed they shared a collective outlook. "Sporting men are, in a certain sense, detached from the outside world," former gambler Mason Long explained. Wagering and fighting had ceased to be ordinary, everyday activities in most places but had become the purview of specialists in cities and masculine milieus. Sporting men thus might be considered professional jolly fellows. Most sports were not simply purveyors of jolly amusement; they also led jolly lives. Their perceived affinity for this older male emotional style, once so familiar, now set sports apart. They ostentatiously personified values that many scorned but that some still found exhilarating and many others intriguing. Accounts of sporting men highlighted this archaic connection; words such as "chivalrous" often appeared in press reports. They were, in an oft-used phrase, "knights of the green cloth."[30]

The "sporting fraternity" was, as the name suggests, mostly male. In Deadwood, "gambling was distinctly a masculine indulgence." Estelline Bennett believed there were only two women in the town who "ever even saw gambling action." There is evidence that women were intrigued with the sporting life, in part no doubt because it was, for most, inaccessible. After Edward Pendleton, the Washington gambler, died, the contents of his casino were auctioned off, and women flocked to view the opulent male sanctum. In 1883 the *Police Gazette* ran a series titled "The Female Sports of New York by One of Them," but I suspect the stories are mostly, if not entirely, fiction. There were in the West a small number of women gamblers. The *Clipper* reprinted an 1876 article in the *Kansas City Times* about "a female gambling-house in this city," where women smoked cigars, played faro, and shot billiards with male friends. The West's most famous female gambler was "Poker Alice" Ivers. She dealt poker and faro in Leadville and other mining and cattle towns and was said to have drank her whiskey straight and carried a gun.[31]

The most famous woman associated with sporting life was the actress and poet Adah Isaacs Menken. Born in New Orleans in 1835, in 1859 she married the Benicia Boy, prizefighter John C. Heenan, whose battle the next year with Englishmen Thomas Sayers would make him a national hero. Menken may been the first American to understand that there is no such thing as bad publicity. The revelation that in her ardor to marry the Benicia Boy she had neglected to divorce her first husband led to a scandal that only increased her celebrity. The voluptuous Menken's star continued to rise when she turned an adaptation of Byron's *Mazeppa* into a national sensation. Wearing a flesh colored body stocking, she was tied to the back of a horse that then galloped around the stage. Menken reveled in unconventional behavior. She hobnobbed with sporting men and minstrels; her greatest supporter and confidant over the years was *Clipper* boxing writer Ned James. Menken drank and smoked in public and enjoyed dressing up in men's clothing to go to gambling halls to play faro. In Virginia City, Nevada, in March 1864, she attended a dogfight and even, it was said, laced up the gloves and sparred with three miners in the Sazerac Saloon. This remarkable woman was also, when she was in New York, part of Henry Clapp's bohemian literary crowd that met in Pfaff's Broadway saloon and included Walt Whitman. Clapp was drama critic for the *New York Leader,* the most sporting of the city's dailies. That Clapp wrote for a sporting newspaper taken together with the fact that Menken was part of his bohemian crowd suggests an intriguing connection between sporting and literary countercultures.[32]

The women who appear most often in accounts of sporting society were prostitutes or former prostitutes. When Estelline Bennett remarked that few women in Deadwood had ever seen gambling, she surely meant "respectable women," for the town's gaming parlors teemed with prostitutes. From the 1840s on, there had been close ties between the sporting fraternity and prostitution. The sporting men of Denver, for example, joined madams and prostitutes in 1877 in holding a picnic in a Denver park. By the late nineteenth century, the term "sporting man" had as much a connotation of pimp as gambler. Sports offered political protection to brothels and were rewarded both financially and sexually. Several prominent sporting men were accused of being, at one point or another in their careers, "fancy men," that is pimps, including Isaiah Rynders, George B. Wooldridge, Chris Lilly, George Wilkes, and Billy Mulligan. John Morrissey, according to legend, acquired his nickname "Old Smoke" when he was pushed against a stove by another sport, Tom McCann, in a battle for the affections of Kate Ridgely, a well-known prostitute. John Harrison, who kept a famously "square" gambling house on Park Row in New York, was for a time the consort of Julia Brown, the most renowned courtesan in antebellum America.[33]

Madams and prostitutes often served as the female companions—what the press often referred to as "wives," quotation marks firmly in place—of sporting men. Many sports eventually married; some wedded former prostitutes, others women who seemingly had no connection to the world's oldest profession. Isaiah Rynders was legally wedded, and, in Deadwood, a gambler known as "California Jack" was married to a woman who local inhabitants politely addressed as "Mrs. California Jack." But many others dispensed with the formality of marriage, moving from one cohabitational relationship to another. After Yankee Sullivan died in the custody of the vigilantes, it emerged he had a "wife" in San Francisco and another "wife" in New York. The flexible and informal nature of sports' relationships with women, perhaps another continuity with the jolly fellows, no doubt contributed to the public fascination with the sporting fraternity.[34]

For the most part, however, "sportingdom" was a man's world. Sports spent most of their time in the company of fellow men, many of whom were single. Even among married or cohabitating sporting men, their closest emotional relationships often seem to have been with other men. The era of ardent male friendships was passing, but sporting men remained distinctive in their devotion to male comrades. "Dad" Cunningham was said to be "the only man who could lead Morrissey when [he was] drunk," and the two were close companions for years, as were George Wilkes and David C. Broderick. Wyatt Earp and Doc Holliday were famously friendly. "His whole heart and soul were wrapped up in Wyatt Earp," Bat Masterson later wrote of Holliday.

The friendship of John C. Heenan and James Cusick was particularly strong. Heenan first met Cusick in California, and Cusick traveled with Heenan to England for the Sayers fight. They remained close. In 1873, Heenan, who had divorced Menken and remarried, went to Colorado to recover from a lung ailment. When he failed to improve, he decided to return to California, and Cusick immediately came west to assist in the journey. But on the train Heenan began coughing blood. According to the *Clipper,* "Cusick's arm was around Heenan's neck, and the latter's around Jim's as soon as the hemorrhage began." Heenan literally died in Cusick's arms, and "Jim then laid his loved friend out upon the bed."[35]

The sporting life exemplified "manhood and decency," rounders believed. They were following, Mason Long explained, a vocation "entirely legitimate and honorable."[36] Gamblers and prizefighters felt that they were simply satisfying the demand of those who yearned to partake of traditional male enjoyments. The same could be said for sports' involvement with prostitution. Jolly fellowship, however, was not only their business; for most it was also their pleasure. There were certainly differences in attitudes and comportment among real sports—between, for example, Baltimore's reserved, abstemious Robert "Doc" Slater—one of the country's most renowned gamblers—and the thuggish, profligate Billy Mulligan. But, like their customers, sports relished jolly recreation.

Most loved both alcohol and cards. "My passion for gambling and sporting" was only "second to that for drink," confessed John Hess, who routinely ended up intoxicated each day. Yankee Sullivan, Thomas Hyer, the young John Morrissey, and Ed Chase, Denver's well-known sport, were among the famous sports renowned for hitting the bottle. Similarly, most sporting men loved gambling, and when they won money they often kept on betting until it was gone. J. R. Talbot explained that "what was made at their own table was lost on that of another." Pat Herne, New York's famed gambler, the *New York Tribune* reported, won "not less than half a million dollars" at his New York casino, but he "loved to play for its own sake" and eventually lost his wealth. Sports relied on loans and handouts from other sporting men until they hit a lucky streak and got back in the money.[37]

Sporting men were also fighting men. Like jolly fellows, their moods could change as rapidly as the weather—squalls occurred on sunny days, especially when their honor was at stake. For prizefighters, of course, pugilism was their profession, but most boxers fought at least as many brawls outside the ring as in it, as the barroom confrontations in the 1850s among Hyer, Yankee Sullivan, and Morrissey illustrate. Gamblers, too, were ready for a fight. "I would rather fight than eat," admitted George Devol in *Forty Years a Gambler on the Mississippi*. Welsh-born gambling man R. G. Williams confessed he "was "quick and sudden in a quarrel." When he got angry he started swinging, no matter who the antagonist was. Williams was stabbed by a Chicago sport in one fracas and was almost killed in an election day melee while working for John Morrissey's state senate campaign. Williams was probably lucky. The *Police Gazette* and *Clipper* routinely ran obituaries of sports killed in affrays. In a typical stabbing affray in

1873, Billy Dwyer, a middleweight boxer, was sharing a friendly drink in a San Francisco saloon with John Harrington, "a short card [poker] player generally known by the nickname of 'Happy Jack.'" They got into an argument and came to blows, at which point Harrington pulled his knife and stabbed Dwyer, later explaining "he hit me." Dwyer died within minutes.[38]

Like jolly fellows everywhere, sporting men were famed for their love of pranks. John Chamberlain, who developed Long Branch into a major gambling resort, was renowned for "his inveterate passion for practical jokes." Both Wyatt Earp and Bat Masterson were noted pranksters. Masterson in 1880 helped mastermind one of Dodge's most celebrated practical jokes on a traveling phrenologist and healer of venereal diseases. "Meredith, M. D." gave a lecture, which, following a "fiendish yell from Luke McGlue," "the boys" turned to pandemonium by blazing away at each other with blanks, sending the lecturer scrambling for cover.[39]

Both sporting men and outside observers were convinced that underlying their distinctive deportment was an ethic, perhaps even a worldview. "Their ideas of right and wrong were peculiar, but they had such ideas nonetheless," W. W. Mills remembered of sports he met in El Paso. "The fraternity has a code of its own," Mason Long wrote. At the heart of the sporting code, Long explained, stood three principles. A true sporting man must accept both losing and winning with "imperturbability." Second, he should be "generous and extravagant to an excessive degree," and third, he should "keep his word." These were the hallmarks of noble gamblers in the many fictional portrayals of the period, and it seems they had a basis in reality. Real gamblers may even have felt obliged to live up to their literary counterparts. The sporting ethic certainly did not derive from any religious beliefs—most sports were "hard and cold to spiritual things," discovered D. S. Tuttle, Episcopal bishop of Nevada, who knew a number of Virginia City gamblers. But even Tuttle had to concede that many sports did adhere to Long's ideals.[40]

Like men and women of an earlier generation, chance was a central feature of a gambler's existence. "One Day it's milk and honey, next day hustling round for money, / Every gamblin' man knows, easy comes and easy goes" went a popular song. There were times when Doc Slater, for instance, was worth half a million dollars and " other times when he was practically penniless." That was why it was so senseless, so unseemly, to exult over winning a big pot or "kick" (that is, become angry) after a losing. Today's victor would be tomorrow's loser and vice versa. A true sport left the table "as if nothing ha[d] happened," no matter how much he had won or lost, J. H. Green explained. Winnings were not saved for a future rainy day; life was to be lived in the here and now. "Their habits are extravagant in the extreme," the *New York Times* reported. When rounders were flush, the money typically would be used on a spree of fine liquors, food, and clothes, would be bet on cards or roulette, or would be simply given away. Devol "never had much use for anything" he "could not put in my pocket." It was understood that those who were in the money would help those members of the brotherhood who were broke: benevolence was a essential component of the fraternity. Denver's Ed Chase contributed immense sums to old sports and saloon bums. Many gamblers extended their beneficence to anyone truly in need. "Protestant or Catholic, Jew or Gentile," to all of them John Morrissey gave "with a lavish hand," the *New York Herald* eulogized. And many sports were, as Long contended, legendary for their honesty. Of Slater it was said, according to the *Baltimore Sun*, that "his word was as good as his bond," and his acquaintances declared "they would rather have his unsupported promise than most men's bonds."[41]

Such truthfulness and liberality were, however, strictly circumscribed; the "two consciences" were part of sporting life. Fort Wayne gambler John Sterling was, Long wrote, "a good-natured warm-hearted man, always ready to help the needy or skin a sucker," as if helping the needy and skinning a sucker were essentially identical. Both were getting what they deserved. Sporting men might treat fellow rounders and other men down on their luck with compassion, but those outside the realm of their benevolence, such as suckers or drunks or people of color, were fair game. They could be—indeed, sports believed they should be—victimized by practical jokes or cheating at gambling, which in the eyes of sporting men were more or less the same thing. Cheating and swindling were viewed as a type of prank, "a good joke," in gambler John Morris's words. In his "as told to" autobiography, Frank Tarbeaux, a legendary gambler and con man, entitled the chapter on his confidence scams "The Horse Gyp and Other Pranks." Most gamblers would resort at various times to dishonest methods. Marked cards and fixed faro boxes had been widely available since the 1830s. The chief defense for "sharp practices" was the one offered by the merciless practical joker: a sucker deserved everything he was stupid enough to fall for. "Served him right, if he couldn't protect himself" was the typical attitude according to Morris. George Devol had no sympathy whatsoever for his victims and reveled in the ability of gamblers to disgrace chumps, to make men who think they're so smart "do anything they wanted him to do."[42]

"KNOWN ALL OVER THE COUNTRY"

The postwar heyday of the sporting fraternity was the era of the celebrity sporting man. The lives of sporting men seem to have had a vitality ordinary daily life lacked. As keepers of the flame of jolly fellowship, sports were viewed as members of a kind of counterculture and were thus fascinating figures to many men, dangerous but attractive—indeed, attractive because dangerous. The *Police Gazette* and other sporting journals fed popular interest by providing stories about the sporting life for the education of their "sensation-seeking" readers, and at least one daily newspaper in most major cities diligently reported the doings of the fraternity. Even lesser rounders were locally renowned, and the top sports were among the most famous men in the country. Baltimore's Doc Slater was "known throughout the length and breadth of the land." Chicago sport Mike McDonald's "name was familiar from coast to coast," according to the *Chicago Record-Herald*, while the *Denver Times* called Bat Masterson "the best known man between the Mississippi river and the Pacific Coast." The coverage sporting men received varied from reverent to caustic, but they were unquestionably news.[43]

At the top of the heap was John Morrissey, who became the symbol of this exuberant sporting era. His name was "a household word," his rags-to-riches story "known to every school-boy in the land," J. R. Talbot claimed. The former prizefighter was not only the nation's foremost sporting man; he was also the fraternity's first and only superstar. Morrissey's prominence coincided with the zenith of sporting activity, and his death presaged its decline.[44]

Born in Ireland in 1831, Morrissey came with his parents to America and settled in West Troy, New York. As a teenager the strapping Morrissey became the leader of the "Downtown boys" in their brawls with the "Uptown boys" in the gang fighting that so characterized antebellum life. Morrissey's victories in eight consecutive rough-and-tumble fights made him by age eighteen, according to the *New York Herald*, "the subject of discussion and notoriety in sporting circles in every State in the Union." The Morrissey legend was born the first time he visited New York. As years passed, it would become increasingly hard to separate fact from fiction in the myth of the man.[45]

The story goes that one afternoon in 1849, Morrissey, at that time working as a fireman on a Hudson River steamer, showed up at Isaiah Rynders's saloon on Park Row. Eager to make his mark, Morrissey asked the Captain "whether there were any fighters in the house." Rynders admitted that there just might be a few around. At that point the brawlers in the room, led by Awful Gardiner, pounced

John C. Morrissey. In George W. Walling, *Recollections of a New York Chief of Police* (New York, 1887).

on Morrissey and gave him a thorough beating. Rynders finished off Old Smoke by smashing a spittoon on his head. Morrissey's pluck, however, quickly became the talk of the city's sporting circles, and he stayed in New York, working as a faro dealer. In 1851, Morrissey, along with his companion Dad Cunningham, went to California. Once there, Morrissey began dealing faro and fought his first prizefight, defeating Englishman George Thompson on a foul. Morrissey returned to New York as the "California champion," a man to be reckoned with.[46]

Yankee Sullivan had refused to fight the swaggering Morrissey when both were in San Francisco, but when they were both back in New York in 1853, Sully agreed to a match. Morrissey was billed as "the Irish champion," while Sullivan, in the convoluted allegiances that marked New York's lower-ward world, became the American favorite, backed by Tom Hyer and Bill Poole. Despite Sullivan's clearly superior skill, the battered Morrissey—"a gamer man never lived," Talbot believed—held on; a brawl then broke out at ringside, and when Sullivan joined in, the referee awarded Morrissey the victory. Now famous, Morrissey used his winnings to buy into a New York saloon and to purchase some expensive fighting cocks. The Amos Dock fight with Bill Poole and Butcher Bill's subsequent murder by a Morrissey hanger-on added to Old Smoke's notoriety. His final prizefight was in 1858 with John C. Heenan. Morrissey's eleven-round victory created nationwide excitement and secured his claim as American heavyweight champion.[47]

Until this point, Morrissey seemed just one more prizefighter—a drinking, brawling roughneck. Out of the ring most champion boxers, including Hyer and Heenan, coasted into lives of dissipation as saloon celebrities. Not Morrissey. He was one of a very small number of sporting men who saw his line of work not as a revered lifestyle but as a means to an end. Once he decided never to fight again, he made up his mind to become the wealthiest and most famous gambler of his era. And he did.

Morrissey worked hard to shed his rowdy image. According to Talbot, he pledged to stop drinking until he made his fortune. Morrissey laboriously taught himself to read and polished his manners. His commanding physique had always earned him respect, and with his newfound refinement, he became an acceptable, even congenial, companion for gentlemen. Through study and experience, "he learned to become an expert in all of the various games of cards" and became a partner in a Barclay Street gambling house. In 1864, he, along with several other sporting men, opened a sumptuous casino on West Twenty-fourth Street. Morrissey prospered: the *Herald* estimated his gambling profits to be $700,000 over the next nine years. He began to move in higher social circles, becoming acquainted with Cornelius Vanderbilt, August Belmont, and other moneyed New Yorkers. He was no longer "John Morrissey," the *Clipper* proudly reported, but "*Mister* Morrissey."[48]

Morrissey's crowning achievement was bringing big-time gambling to the popular spa of Saratoga Springs, New York. He had brought gaming apparatus up from Manhattan during the 1861 season and carried on business in a rented house. When he proposed building a racetrack at Saratoga in 1863, his elite connections paid off. Vanderbilt pledged $3,000, and the money was quickly raised. The track was extraordinarily popular from its opening in 1864, and the following year forty-thousand visitors descended on Saratoga Springs for racing week. Morrissey used the racetrack profits to build and furnish the Club House Casino in Saratoga, which the *New York Times* proclaimed as "undoubtedly the finest building devoted to its special purposes in the world." Nothing but the best would do at the Club House: the furnishings were gorgeous, the food the choicest. Morrissey lured the West's most celebrated faro dealer, Hamilton Baker, from Virginia City, Nevada, by offering to pay him a reported monthly salary of $4,500.[49]

As Morrissey's gambling career thrived, he acquired political influence. Old Smoke had worked as a Democratic shoulder hitter in the 1850s, and in the next decade, with his fame and wealth, he carved out a career in politics. In 1866 he was nominated as the Tammany candidate for the House of Representatives from the East Side's Fifth District. The nomination of an ex-prizefighter and current gambler and cockfighter for a seat in Congress played badly outside of Manhattan, but Morrissey won and was reelected in 1868. He declined renomination in 1870. Although often associated with Tammany, "he was always a disturbing spirit in its counsels" and was outspoken in denunciation of its corruption, becoming one of the organizers of the "Young Democracy" movement that opposed "Boss" William Tweed. After Tweed's fall, Morrissey unsuccessfully challenged Honest John Kelly for the leadership of Tammany, but he was victorious in his 1875 campaign for the New York State Senate as an anti-Tammany candidate.[50]

Morrissey was now at the height of his fame. The press, the *New York Clipper* claimed, followed his career "with as much care and truth, probably, as the movements of Gen. Grant." It ran regular stories of Old Smoke's comings and goings under the title "Morrisseyiana." Much of his renown owed, of course, to the popular allure of fighting and gambling. But he was also an American success story, the classic self-made man—*The Irish Boy Who Fought His Way to Fame and Fortune* (1878), as one biography of him was entitled. He was "Governor of the Springs," congressman, and friend and confidant of America's elite. Yes, he was a gambler, but in an era when Wall Street speculators were called "stock gamblers," was he really any different from his friend Vanderbilt? Old Smoke's death in 1878 was mourned by thousands in New York, and the city hall flag was flown at half-mast. The *New York Times* ran a front-page, six-column obituary and followed it up with a glowing editorial. After his death, Morrissey survived as a legend among men, literally a folkloric figure. Researchers in the 1920s discovered at that time two ballads about Morrissey still being sung, "John Morrissey and the Black," and "Morrissey and the Russian Sailor." In the latter ballad, popular in the West, Morrissey triumphantly vanquishes all comers, including Bill Poole and Thomas Sayers as well as the Russian sailor. "He fought his way to fortune, to money and to fame, / He also was a gambler but square he played the game," it concludes.[51]

Second only to Morrissey in sporting renown was Harry Hill. It was Hill's inspiration to create a sporting saloon refined enough that genteel customers could partake of the sporting experience without having to worry about finding themselves in the middle of a free-for-all or being pestered by prostitutes. There were a number of well-known New York sporting houses in the 1870s and 1880s, but Hill's Club House on Houston Street was the most famous. Born in England, Hill came to New York City in 1852. "A good wrestler and very handy with his fists," Hill fought as a middleweight boxer with some success and like so many pugilists opened a saloon. By 1867, when Mark Twain visited Hill's, it was probably the most prominent sporting establishment in the city.[52]

Hill's expanded from a sporting saloon into a sporting theater. Admission was twenty-five cents. Patrons went upstairs to a hall "ablaze with light and heavy with smoke." There was dancing, and there were variety acts, often in blackface, but it was wrestling and boxing, including sparring matches between women, that were Hill's most celebrated attractions. Many of the country's top boxers, both white and black, displayed their talents there, including Hill's friend John L. Sullivan, and Hill held the purse for most of the heavyweight championship fights of the era. Given the drinking and raucous entertainment, it was inevitable that "little disturbances occur more or less frequently," as the *Police Gazette* put it, but Hill's rugged bouncers, mostly ex-boxers, quickly broke up brawls and threw out the combatants. Hill's trademark "pretty waiter girls" seem to have been just that, and prostitutes who worked Hill's understood that they had to be highly discreet or they would be barred. Sporting men were among Hill's customers, of course, but the theater also attracted more respectable men, including, according to Edward Van Every, P. T. Barnum, James Gordon Bennett, and Thomas Edison.[53]

It was visitors to the city, however, who made up the bulk of Hill's patrons. "Strangely," Samuel Mackeever remarked in the *Police Gazette*, "Harry Hill's is more discussed and made more of in the country than anywhere else." Rural and small-town men seem to have found this headquarters of disorderly amusement little short of mesmerizing. A new genre of literature developed that catered to America's fascination with its growing cities and the seamy side of urban life. *The Night Side of New York: A Picture of the Great Metropolis after Nightfall* (1866), Matthew Hale Smith's *Sunshine and Shadow in New York* (1868), Mackeever's *Glimpses of Gotham and City Characters* (1881), James D. McCabe's *New York by Sunshine and Gaslight* (1882) and J. W. Buel's *Metropolitan Life Unveiled: Or the Mysteries and Miseries of America's Great Cities* (1882), all included descriptions of Hill's. It was claimed that *Glimpses of Gotham*, which reprinted Mackeever's *Gazette* articles, including the ones on Hill's, sold more than 175,000 copies. Explained Mackeever:

> There is hardly a young man who comes up to "York," but takes Harry's in. . . . When he gets back to Rushville or Punkton and the gang assemble down at the depot to see the freight train come in, he tells such glowing stories of the place that those of his listeners who have not yet had such a sensational experience dream all night of the account, and never rest until they, too, have gone, and seen, and conquered.

G. W. Averill and Co., Harry Hill's Variety Theatre, 1878. Hill's famous "pretty waiter girls" are at the top, and Hill himself is at the bottom right. Picture Collection, The Branch Libraries, The New York Public Library, Astor, Lenox, and Tilden Foundations.

Hill developed a sporting empire. In addition to the Houston Street theater, he had a thoroughbred horse-breeding farm and "Harry Hill's Pavilion Hotel" on Flushing Bay, which he billed as "one of the finest and best-equipped road houses in the country, with superior facilities for Genuine Sport." Hill even bought a steamboat to run customers from Manhattan to the hotel. His theater closed in 1887, the victim of persistent, if usually short-lived, reform campaigns, losses on the steamboat line, and Hill's legendary largesse.[54]

Virtually every city had its celebrated sporting men. The *Police Gazette* called Chicago's "King" Mike McDonald "the richest gambler in the country," and he was also among the most politically influential. "Gambling king, political boss, and all-round sport," one Chicago newspaper described him as. A former faro dealer, in 1873 McDonald opened his famed four-story casino, The Store, not in one of the city's rambunctious vice districts but downtown at Monroe and Clark streets. The Store "made money hand over fist." As his fortune grew, his clout surged. "His [political] 'machine,' was the first one worthy of that name Chicago had known," the *Chicago Tribune* believed, reaching its apex with the election of Carter Henry Harrison as mayor in 1879. Baltimore's Robert "Doc" Slater was "one of the most noted of the so-called 'sporting fraternity' in the country," the *Baltimore Sun* believed. "A rare good fellow," he prospered running a faro bank, and in 1862, he renovated a building on South Calvert Street into a gambling casino that a correspondent for the *New York World* claimed, likely with some exaggeration, "exceeded in splendor and completeness any of the kind in this country." Some of Doc Slater's profits found their way into politicians' and voters' pockets, and the *Baltimore American* claimed that at one point in the early 1880s Slater "held the Democratic destiny of East Baltimore in his hand." Denver was famed as a wide-open town, and Big Ed Chase was its premier sporting man. In 1864 as a member of Col. John Chivington's Third Colorado Cavalry, Chase participated in the infamous massacre of Cheyenne Indians at Sand Creek in southern Colorado. In the 1870s he ran a series of increasingly impressive gambling houses in Denver that featured celebrity faro dealers like Wyatt Earp and Bat Masterson and rooms for trysts with the pretty waiter girls. Chase's opulent Palace, a combination gambling house-variety theater, had a wagering floor that could accommodate 200 players and a theater with a capacity of 750. "He took an active part in politics," the *Denver Rocky Mountain News*, explained, and he became "a law in the lower wards," eventually being elected alderman.[55]

Black sporting celebrities also appeared in this era. None were as famous as Morrissey or McDonald, to be sure, but they were men who in the cities where they operated were well known among both races. Almost every large city had its black gamblers and prizefighters and its black vice district of sporting saloons, gambling dens, and houses of prostitution. Wagering, especially on the numbers game, had been common among African Americans for decades, but references to black sports were scarce before the Civil War. The war seemed to have boosted betting everywhere, and in 1864 the *Clipper* reported on a large gathering of rounders at Hanft's Myrtle Avenue Park in Brooklyn that was predominantly, though not exclusively, black.[56] The black sporting fraternity surged in the 1870s and 1880s. *Police Gazette* editor Richard Fox promoted black boxing and created medals for "colored" fighters in various weight classes, just as for whites. Like white sporting men, blacks sports dressed nattily, fraternized in saloons, and helped out on election day, though usually for Republicans instead of Democrats.

Although African Americans were barred from white-run casinos, black gambling halls, Morris wrote, "did not show the same spirit of exclusiveness" and "the African and Caucasian could frequently be seen . . . seated side by side" wagering. New York City was clearly preeminent among white sports, but the black gambling community seems more dispersed. Albert "Starlight" Boyd was Cleveland's top black sporting man, while in Detroit William Dotson ran a "notorious resort renowned for its crap games and white clientele." Cincinnati had John the "Fashion Plate" Stovers and John Alexander, known as the "Black Prince," who was admitted to the biggest white games. Like white rounders, black sports got into affrays. In Chicago, "Big Stephen" Alexander, known as the "Prince of Craps," was killed in a gambling house brawl in 1884. Two rival lightweight fighters in Philadelphia in 1894, Walter Edgerton, the "Kentucky Rosebud," and John Henry Johnson bumped into each other in a poolroom. When Edgerton put up his fists, Johnson grabbed a pool cue, and Edgerton shot him in the face. Johnson was not seriously hurt.[57]

Ordinary sporting men could only dream of the riches and fame amassed by the profession's luminaries. For every sporting celebrity there were hundreds of less successful rounders who only rarely made much money. Most lived day to day, getting by on handouts between big wins, and they found themselves in and out of jail on gambling, fighting, or drunkenness charges. Small-time sports had to be ready to do almost anything to make a buck. New York boxer Owen Kildare sparred in the city's dozens of sporting houses, provided muscle on election day, served as a barroom bouncer, and worked as a billiard hustler. But, he proudly noted, he refused to break strikes. Many sports found it necessary to take odd jobs between prizefights and major scores at the gaming table. Malinda Jenkins, who described herself as "married to a sport"—gambler William "Jenky" Jenkins—defined a sport as "a man that makes his livin' by his wits." She recounted, how, at one point, her husband picked hops while she worked as a cook in a lumber camp to support their family. "Full-fledged sport" Charles Spencer Tate, a con man and gambler, remembered in his autobiography the exact date of his sole big win—$1,700 on 7 January 1890. But most of the time he was broke, bumming around the West and taking any work he could get, at one point selling pens door to door. Despite such hardships, it was a life many loved and were reluctant to abandon.[58]

"DIE THE WAY YOU LIVE—ALL OF A SUDDEN"

The scruffy reality of the lives of real sports did little to halt the increasing romanticization of sporting men in the last three decades of the century. The reputation of professional gambling men, "blacklegs," had been low earlier in the century—they were menacing cheats who brought disorder to otherwise respectable and peaceful locales. Robert Bailey had been shunned and persecuted in Virginia in the 1790s and 1800s. John Murrell's alleged 1835 conspiracy of slaves and gamblers to loot the South had a tremendous impact, the scheme ceaselessly rehashed in the early *Police Gazette.* It was in the wake of the Murrell hysteria that a Vicksburg mob lynched five gambling men. Popular literature reflected the low opinion. Harvey Green, the gambler in T. S. Arthur's temperance classic, *Ten Nights in a Bar-Room* (1858), is evil incarnate. Though a neat dresser, Green is "a man of evil passions" with a laugh "so unlike a human laugh that it caused my blood to trickle, for a moment, coolly along my veins."[59]

Gamblers continued to face condemnation from moralizers and reformers, if not for the wagering itself, then for the rowdiness and violence that often accompanied it. After the Civil War, however, a counter theme began to emerge—the noble gambling man. Now that wagering was increasingly confined to certain city neighborhoods and isolated western milieus, gamblers no longer seemed such an imminent threat to community serenity. John Morrissey, an anathema as an Irish thug to refined Americans in the 1850s, now was being lauded for his openhandedness and manly, direct honesty. Virtuous gamblers began to appear in pulp novels like Warren Baer's *Champagne Charlie! or, The "Sports" of New-York* (1868). These novels and stories often have as a hero an honest gambler—typically the handsome, scapegrace son of a wealthy family—who must face down an evil, cheating gambler. In the end, the gambling hero realizes the error of his ways and forsakes the sporting life. Readers, though, were less likely impressed by the hackneyed moral sentiments than by the tempting descriptions of hedonistic pursuits, of the pleasure of a life drinking, gambling, and carousing.

The gallant gambler was permanently enshrined as a literary type in 1869 with the publication in the *Overland Monthly* of Bret Harte's "The Outcasts of Poker Flat." Harte, who was born in 1836, had grown up in New York City and in 1854 went to California. He held a series of jobs, apparently including very briefly mining gig on the Stanislaus River in 1855, an experience that allowed him to claim gold-rush bona fides. Harte eventually found work as a newspaperman. His fictional contributions went unnoticed until "The Luck of Roaring Camp" became a national sensation in 1868. "The Outcasts of Poker Flat" appeared the next year and was almost as successful; it was reprinted in dozens of newspapers, including the *New York Clipper.* The protagonist was "Mr. John Oakhurst, gambler," a "cooly desperate man." One Sunday morning in 1850 Oakhurst became "conscious of a change in . . . moral atmosphere" in Poker Flat. In a "virtuous reaction" against recent thefts and a killing, the settlement had set up a vigilance committee that lynched two men and voted to expel "objectionable characters." Oakhurst, who had won several big pots at poker, was banished along with two prostitutes and "Uncle Billy," a drunkard-thief. On the trail over the mountains, the outcasts camp for the night with young lovers on their way to Poker Flat to be married, the guileless miner Tom Simson and Piney Woods, a "stout, comely damsel" of fifteen. During the night Uncle Billy steals their horses and most of their provisions, leaving the group desperate when they are trapped by a snowstorm the next day. There was little chance anyone could get through the deep snow to alert rescuers, but they finally decide that Tom should try. Oakhurst then strolls away from the camp and does not return. Both prostitutes have hearts of gold and try and comfort Piney, but by the time help arrives all are dead. The rescuers find Oakhurst's body beside his derringer and the deuce of clubs on which he had written his own epitaph: "Struck a streak of bad luck . . . and handed in his checks on the 7th, Dec, 1850."[60]

The handsome and "studiously neat" Oakhurst is an unsentimental man in a sentimental tale. While snowed in, he misses the excitement of the gaming table, but he remains calm and rational, even detached, during the ordeal. "He was too much a gambler to not accept Fate." The hand has been dealt, and he must play it. The name Oakhurst indicates his steadiness and conveys a suggestion of archaic virtue. He is reserved but not indifferent. Harte establishes the essential goodness of his character by relating that at a poker game a few months earlier, the gambler had won $40 from Tom, all of the miner's total stake. After the game, Oakhurst privately returns the money, telling Tom that although he might be a good man, he "can't gamble worth a cent." Oakhurst never considers abandoning the women and trying to make his way down the mountain alone. According to Harte, he "settled himself cooly to the losing game before him." He writes his epitaph on the two of clubs, the low card in the deck, and chooses a manly sudden death, a gambler's death, by bullet. Oakhurst and the prostitutes were "outcasts" from a community that had established its virtue by lynching two people and banishing four people—"the deported wickedness" of Poker Flat—of whom only one, Uncle Billy, is truly evil. One could read "The Outcasts of Poker Flat" as an allegory of western history in which gamblers and prostitutes pass away as "respectability" advances. Harte seems to be asking readers to reflect on the character of this "progress."[61]

Oakhurst appeared in later Harte stories and became the prototype of gambling heroes who would appear in literature for decades. Neatly dressed in black, they were handsome, gentlemanly, honest, and generous. And doomed. Like real sporting men, fictional ones were romanticized as disciples of a style of life that was vanishing from ordinary existence. The literary sport was almost invariably, like Oakhurst, sober and taciturn. He knew his fate. The fictional rounder's background was usually southern; often, he was the son of a formerly wealthy plantation family. Elite southerners in earlier decades certainly loved wagering, and the fictional gambler encompassed the aristocratic ideal. The lost cause of the South became merged with the lost cause of jolly fellowship. For all the romantic haze, the literary portrayals of gamblers often did capture, as Harte did with Oakhurst, the nonchalant way true sporting men accepted victory and defeat, and even, as we shall see, death.[62]

Dime novels picked up the gambler hero. These were cheaply printed stories, formulaic in plot, that were popular with a broad range of readers, including ordinary workers and farmers. Most dime novels are set either in New York City or in western mining towns such as Leadville, Tombstone, and Deadwood, the home of Edward K. Wheeler's "Deadwood Dick," hero of one of the most successful series of the entire genre. Dozens of these tales featured sporting protagonists, and they helped fashion the iconic Wild West hero. Edward Willett, a workhorse for Beadle and Adams, the publisher of the most popular dime novels, created "Flush Fred, the Mississippi Sport," a typically honorable gambler. Flush Fred, who made his debut in 1884, was a sporting man but also "very intelligent and gentlemanly." He was "tall, with the figure of an athlete and the grace of a young Apollo," and, of course, he won his bets "without any real show of joy." He survives affrays, duels, and steamboat explosions while pursuing his calling honestly, vanquishing dishonest gamblers, and helping those in need. Flush Fred was only one of the dozens of sporting heroes in these tales. There was also "Dainty Lance, the Boy Sport," and Ace High, one of Beadle and Adams' numerous sporting heroines who C. E. Tripp popularized in *Ace High the Frisco Detective; or, the Girl Sport's Double Game* (1893). Howard Holmes's Captain Coldgrip, "the Sport Detective," had a puzzling doppelganger in Doc Grip, "the Sporting Detective" by Albert W. Aiken.[63]

The noble gambler appeared in more serious fiction as well. Alfred Henry Lewis's popular *Wolfville* novels, the first of which was published in 1897, featured sport Cherokee Hall, a "person of sensibilities as well as benevolent impulse." The nameless "square gambler" in Stephen Crane's "Blue Hotel" (1899) ruthlessly parts suckers from their money in "Fort Romper," Nebraska, but because of his honesty and delicate choice of victims he was "trusted and admired. People called him a thoroughbred." The stereotype appeared into the twentieth century. Perhaps the best-known fictional portrayal of a sport, and in fact a quite accurate depiction of the sporting scene, is in Edna Ferber's 1926 best seller, *Showboat.* Gaylord Ravenal, "of the Tennessee Ravenals," is handsome and charming, a "picturesque, mysterious and romantic figure," though also impulsive and rather impractical. Ravenal marries Magnolia Hawks, the daughter of a showboat captain, and the couple move to Chicago where Ravenal becomes a full-time sporting man. Their life is a roller coaster: after winning at faro at Mike McDonald's Store, they stay at the Palmer House and eat at the best restaurants; during losing streaks they pawn prized possessions and rent rooms in flophouses.[64]

Hollywood honored the good gambler in many films. Clark Gable played noble gambling men no fewer than three times in four years—Blackie Gallagher in *Manhattan Melodrama* (1934), Blackie Norton, "King of the Barbary Coast," (said to be based on real-life sporting man and wit Wilson Mizner)in *San Francisco* (1936), and Duke Bradley in *Saratoga* (1937). Hatfield, the gambler, in John Ford's *Stagecoach* (1940) is along traditional lines. A southerner, neatly dressed in black, Hatfield is something of an opportunist, but he is courtly in manner and proves dauntless in a crisis. The film *Casablanca* (1942) provides something of an apotheosis of the sporting man. Both the type and the term were archaic by then, but Humphrey Bogart's Rick embodied both the deportment and noble traits that had been associated with fictional gambling heroes since Oakhurst. Rick is reserved and cynical, but this only makes his instinctive decency more striking. The continuity of the stereotype is suggested by the scene in which Rick allows two war refugees from Bulgaria to win at roulette so they can go to America.

This episode mirrors closely a scene in Harte's "The Argonauts of '49," where Oakhurst lets a miner win $3,000 on a fixed deal at poker so he and his wife can return east.[65]

The noble gambler was part of a dying breed of men, not just figuratively but literally. "Life is but a span . . . , live as jolly as you can," the minstrel ballad went, and this might have served as the sporting credo. Life was to be pursued with gusto and enjoyed to the fullest, so at the end there would be no regrets. Clark Gable, playing the virtuous Blackie Gallagher (loosely based on famed real-life gambler Arnold Rothstein) in *Manhattan Melodrama,* insouciantly urges the other prisoners on death row to "die the way you live—all of a sudden," as he himself goes to the electric chair. Gallagher, like Oakhurst, understood that a natural death was not for a true sporting man. Real sports in the face of death could live up to their fictional counterparts. Granville Stuart watched monte player B. F. Jermagin lynched as a horse thief in Hell Gate, Washington territory (later Missoula, Montana), in 1862. The gambler bore his fate with an equanimity that would have done credit to Harte's and Hollywood's gamblers. Jermagin, Stuart recorded in his journal, "seemed to take little interest in the proceedings" of the vigilante court and walked to his death "with a step as firm and countenance as unchanged as if he had been the nearest spectator instead of the principal actor in the tragedy."[66]

Sports understood there was a price to be paid; they were taking chances not only at the gaming table but in their lives. Perhaps this fatalism contributed to their bravery in Mexico and Nicaragua. The bottle claimed many; a bullet claimed many others. Bill Poole dead at age thirty-three, Jim Elliott at thirty-eight, John C. Heenan also at thirty-eight, Chris Lilly at forty-one, John Morrissey at forty-seven, Yankee Sullivan at forty-nine. Characteristically, Billy Mulligan made the most spectacular exit. On 7 July 1865, in a drunken delirium, the forty-five-year-old Mulligan began shooting out the window of his room in the St. Francis Hotel in San Francisco, shouting that the vigilantes were after him. He killed a passerby and then a friend who was trying to convince him to surrender. Finally a police sharpshooter put a bullet through Mulligan's head. The next day, the *Alta California* reported, a hearse took the corpse through the streets to the cemetery, as "six well dressed men . . . with crape upon their arms, walked on either side."[67]

Sporting men by the 1870s were found in all the major cities and throughout the American West, and leading sports were national celebrities. Gradually, the sporting subculture ebbed. Once-booming western mining towns disappeared into oblivion. Uproarious cattle towns became staid farm centers. Wide-open cities saw reform campaigns that closed gambling halls. By the end of the century, there were still sports to be found, but it was clear they were on the losing side, their days numbered. One of the reasons gamblers were romanticized in fiction was because they no longer were so threatening in reality. But as respectability seemed near its triumph, doubts began to be heard, even from reformers. Perhaps it was possible for propriety to go too far, for men to become too tame. The fascination with the noble gambler was to foreshadow how the jolly strain in American culture would wax even as real male disorder waned.

CHAPTER NINE

Continuities and Complexities

"A 'House of Commons,' as it was sometimes called, assembled late in the afternoon or early in the evening either on the veranda or inside the [general] store, depending on the weather" in the 1870s in his hometown of Gurleyville, Connecticut, remembered Wilbur Cross years later. "It was a variable group of men who came in for their mail and sat until somebody said it was time to go home. . . . There was no parliamentary restraint in that Yankee House of Commons." But by the 1880s the men were aging. "The members dwindled to three and four graybeards and then all disappeared from the earth, leaving at last only their memory in the mind of a boy who sat in and listened. . . . With the passing of the graybeards . . . the old social order came to its end."[1]

In the last decades of the nineteenth century, propriety continued to make advances in most places. Even in the South and West raucous male behavior declined. Yet the reformation of male comportment begun in the 1820s remained incomplete. Wide-open cities were becoming less common, but urban areas still played their customary role as refuges from straight-laced village life. More novel was the easing of standards in some small towns. The battle against jolly fellowship had been won, and propriety was magnanimous in victory. Now that self-restraint, not self-indulgence, seemed more normal, the vigilant moral regime that had once seemed necessary to force men into line no longer seemed so essential. Even some reformers wondered if they had gone too far, if men were becoming too domesticated.

As disorderly male comportment declined in reality, representations of it in literature and on stage flourished. The old connection between the comic and cruel endured. American popular culture celebrated violence. African Americans remained targets of white laughter. White jolly fellows, now often represented in the form of the mischievous "bad boy," were an ongoing source of comedy. The jolly strain in American culture proved enduring.

"THE YOUNG MAN WHO DARES TO DRINK LOSES THE ESTEEM OF 'RIGHT-THINKING PEOPLE,' AND IS 'A NOBODY' "

Drinking, gambling, and practical jokes continued to be censured and repressed. Temperance, the issue at the heart of nineteenth-century moral reformation, had been largely eclipsed by abolitionism in the 1850s, but the anti-drink campaign was reenergized by the "women's crusade" of 1873. Beginning in rural Ohio, female "visitation bands" called on saloons, general stores, and drugstores and demanded that they give up the evil trade in liquor. If the owner refused, the women would pray and sing hymns outside, often for days, to force the establishment to cease selling alcohol or close. There seems to have been a significant shift in outlook among moral reformers by this time. Governance of others now seemed to take precedence over self-governance. The two had always been connected, but there was now a sense that white, native-born, Protestant America had been to a considerable degree rehabilitated. In Chicago, crusade leader Eliza Stewart explained, opposition to prohibition was centered among the "lowest, most ignorant class of foreigners." Sober deportment by them could only be achieved through compulsion.[2]

The crusade began in Hillsboro, Ohio, in late 1873 and enjoyed considerable success. In some villages, gangs of men tried to disrupt the protests by drowning out the hymns and prayers with howling and rough music, but usually to little effect. Often men aided the female crusaders. In Grant County, Indiana, in 1874, a saloon keeper who had been instructed to close his barroom "hesitated too long," and a mob hauled him out of town on a rail. By one estimate, seventeen thousand drinking places in Ohio closed down, and much of rural Ohio became completely dry. The Woman's Christian Temperance Union (WCTU) was an offshoot of the crusade. Founded in Cleveland in 1874, it grew to be the largest female voluntary organization in the country. With 150,000 members by the 1890s and chapters in almost every town, the WCTU's sponsorship of temperance lectures, pledge signings, temperance education, and prohibition laws put it at the forefront of the antiliquor campaign in the last two decades of the century.[3]

In 1880 Kansas became the first state since the Civil War to pass a prohibition

O. S. Reinhart, "Women's Crusade against Intemperance." This was a scene in front of a Xenia, Ohio, saloon. In *Harper's Weekly*, 14 March 1874.

law; Iowa followed in 1882, Maine (again) in 1884, and Rhode Island in 1886. Public opinion remained divided, however, and progress was halting; Rhode Island repealed its ban in 1889. But even where statewide prohibition stalled, other methods of curbing drinking succeeded. One technique was to prohibit the selling of alcohol near schools—four miles was the specified distance in Tennessee. High license fees were another method. The most popular was the local option, which enabled municipalities to forbid the sale of alcohol if they wished, thus allowing the battle to be carried out at the community level. By the end of the nineteenth century, in some areas of the country, especially in the Midwest, drinking alcohol seemed to be a thing of the past, a vestige of an earlier, less enlightened age.[4]

Other moral reforms continued apace. Laws against gambling were strengthened and, more importantly, strictly enforced. The 1894 New York State constitution explicitly prohibited all forms of wagering for money. William Travers Jerome, the son of Lawrence Jerome, a member of the high-rolling Belmont clique in the 1860s and 1870s, spurned his father's lifestyle, and as New York City district attorney, he launched an all-out campaign against gambling. The opulent first-class casinos, a feature of New York life since the 1840s, were slowly but inexorably shuttered. Around the same time, authorities upstate were putting Saratoga's gambling palaces and racetrack out of business. Many other states in the 1880s and 1890s passed and implemented new antigambling statutes. By the second decade of the twentieth century, betting on horse racing was legal in only three states. Even in the West the trend was the same. The perception that a territory's chances for statehood were improved by cracking down on gambling strengthened the hand of reformers in that region. Illegal wagering went on (big-time gambler Arnold Rothstein was a celebrated figure of the 1920s), but more effective laws and enforcement made it harder and harder for men openly to place bets.[5]

Practical jokers previously had attracted little public criticism, but they faced mounting censure in the last thirty years of the century. Truly malicious and destructive pranks, the *New York Clipper* noted in 1870, had dwindled. The havoc wreakers of earlier days have been superseded by the "milder type of practical jokers" who cut bed cords and poured water in men's boots. Even mild practical jokers were too much for the *New York Times*. They "show an inconsiderateness and recklessness of giving pain which should win for those who practice them contempt, and where possible, chastisement." But, rejoiced the *Times* in 1873, pranks "are no longer in such vogue as they once were." Only "very young or very uncultivated people still find a primitive delight in . . . poising pails of water over doorways to be tilted upon unsuspecting heads, or sending unwary persons off on wild-goose chases by means of fictitious messages." In 1882 the paper returned to this theme to urge those who pulled violent practical jokes be jailed. Too often in the past, the defense that it was "all in fun" allowed pranksters to go unpunished. Only "one in a thousand . . . is brought before a court for consideration." If they seriously feared the law, practical jokers would have to "revise some of their plans and methods." The *Times* approvingly called attention to a case in which a "jolly fellow"—a waning term—was traveling on a train "in company with other jolly fellows" who bet him "that he did not dare to go through the train and kiss all the ladies." One of the women he forcibly kissed had him arrested and he was fined. In another case in New Jersey, a newly married couple going on their honeymoon were treated to a "'charivari' or 'skimmelton'" with the usual horns, drums and howling. "To heighten the impression" the revelers set off a charge of dynamite that accidentally blew the railroad depot to pieces. They also were successfully prosecuted.[6]

Cruel treatment of animals, which previously attracted scant attention, emerged as a significant issue. The impetus came, according to James Turner in his study of the development of humane attitudes toward animals, from "the outgrowing of a way of thinking and feeling and the emergence of a new, distinctively, modern sensibility." No longer were animals necessarily outside the frame of moral reference. No longer could men inflict pain on animals for pleasure without loss of respectability or fear of arrest. The movement quickly received support from a number of former abolitionists. Women, including Harriet Beecher Stowe and Lydia Maria Child, played a significant role in the campaign for animal protection. The William Lloyd Garrison of the movement was Henry Bergh, son of one of New York City's most prominent shipbuilders, who founded the American Society for the Prevention of Cruelty to Animals (ASPCA) in 1866. Bergh "laid restraining hands on a fundamental evil," *Scribner's* magazine explained in 1879, "that blind and strangely human passion of cruelty" that vents "its cowardly malice on weak humanity and defenseless dumb animals."[7]

Bergh cast his net wide. Abuse of draft horses, maltreatment of circus animals, foxhunting, "swill dairies" in cities where penned cows were fed discarded brewery oats all were targets of the ASPCA. Bull- and bearbaiting had been effectively suppressed by the 1820s, but dogfighting and cockfighting had continued largely unhindered. Bergh received considerable publicity with a crusade that began in 1868 against Christopher "Kit" Burns's Sportsmen's Hall, New York's most famous site of dogfights and competitions in which terriers killed rats. Acting on an ASPCA complaint, the New York police raided the establishment, and Burns, one of the cities best known sporting men, eventually was forced to close. The ASPCA developed widespread support and established chapters in other cities. Bergh was especially concerned about the West, endorsing the view of a Colorado correspondent that "the cruelty to animals in the East . . . seems insignificant to the wholesale barbarity in the West." The ASPCA tried to halt the slaughter of buffalo and attempted to halt a widely publicized bullfight in Dodge City in 1884.[8]

The transformation of male comportment over the course of the century in rural and small-town America was striking. Public opinion combined with the force of law to insure that in many villages, drinkers, gamblers, and fighters were stigmatized and often arrested. By the 1840s and 1850s heavy drinking had marked one a transgressor; by the 1880s and 1890s even a sip of liquor made a man something close to a moral leper. In the Iowa community where humorist George Ade grew up, drinking alcohol "seemed to be about as reprehensible as burning an orphan asylum." A drinker was said to be "without shame and lost to all sense of decency. The godly residents wagged their heads at him and the women and girls avoided him as a wild and dangerous character." Anyone in Angola, Indiana, who would even "think of using liquor as a beverage" would be "talked about" and regarded with disdain. No longer was it enough not to gamble oneself; now respectable men had to avoid even the faintest association with wagering. Sociologist Newell Leroy Sims discovered that in Angola even the most reputable person dared not enter a pool hall, even on business, "lest they say he's drinking or gambling."[9]

This did not mean that everyone had stopped consuming alcohol, of course. Many certainly had, but others, Ade remembered, learned to be discreet about imbibing, buying liquor surreptitiously and drinking at home or going on a binge in an anonymous city. Other drinkers were part of the small coterie of dropouts from decorum, found in almost every village. The nonconformists included not only drinkers and wagerers but almost anyone who displayed unconventional behavior—freethinkers, socialists, "swell dressers," and women who went on unchaperoned dates. Some reveled in their outcast role. The scoffing village atheist was an institution, and there were barroom regulars who, Don Marquis remembered, "took a hangdog delight . . . in being called wicked and thought wicked." The price paid, however, was significant. Once the village elite gathered openly in taverns; now in Angola and many other places, a man "who dares to drink loses the esteem of 'right-thinking people,' and is 'a nobody.'"[10]

There were still some men who gathered at general stores, barbershops, and drugstores. The "House of Commons" convened in Gurleyville, Connecticut, while "John Prien's Standing Army" rendezvoused at Prien's grocery in Columbus, Wisconsin. The men who assembled at Cross's store in Gurleyville in the 1870s illuminate the changes in male conduct from the early years of the century. They discussed religion and politics, told ghost stories, swapped Civil War tales, and traded horses. But the joking was verbal, not practical; men made "what are now called wisecracks," according to Cross. One twentieth-century study of rural society described "store porch humor" as "gentle," an adjective seldom applied to the jests of the antebellum jolly fellows. Cross never mentions gambling or fighting. In contrast to the belligerence of men in former times, occasionally in heated arguments, "eyes flashed and fists doubled up, [but] . . . no blows were ever struck."[11]

In the South, as in the West, the advance of calmer male comportment had been slower. Heavy drinking, gambling, and fighting continued, especially in isolated, rural areas, into the late nineteenth century. In Milton County, Georgia, in the 1870s, "it was not considered a disgrace to get drunk," Walter McElreath recalled. On one election day in the village of Freemansville, "dozens of men were vomiting or lying dead drunk under the trees." During the same decade in Windsor, North Carolina, raucous turkey shoots and bearbaitings remained popular. On Saturday, men gathered in saloons and "presently a dispute would arise . . . [and] everyone . . . would rush to the scene of the battle," according to a fascinated onlooker. Within a few moments the street would be filled with fighters, "a half acre of them, swearing and tearing at each other's clothes, and all about the most trifling incident. . . . To miss a part in a free-for-all fight was considered a sore disappointment."[12]

As in antebellum times, southern fights often turned deadly, especially when male honor was a stake. H. V. Redfield determined in *Homicide, North and South,* a pioneering 1880 investigation of patterns of criminal violence, that "barroom affrays, street fights, and 'personal difficulties' in which weapons were used" were forty times more common in the South than in the North. Only a minority of fracases were interracial. Most combatants were either both white or both black, and Redfield's statistics showed that deadly fracases were more common among whites than blacks. Middle-class blacks often complained about the failure of white police to crack down on black disorder. The cult of honor seemed to have become increasingly important among blacks, and much black violence, like white, involved liquor-fueled altercations between men, a good deal of it centered in black urban vice districts. Because southern whites made few distinctions among blacks, African American brawls discredited the entire race. After a free-for-all at a Memorial Day ceremony in Nashville in 1874, a black newspaper reported that the "better class of colored men" were outraged because "it looks like negroes cannot come together without fighting."[13]

Even in the South, however, there was a discernable tendency toward greater self-control. In largely white Milton County, Georgia, where, in the past, it had not been "considered a disgrace to get drunk," a "remarkable change in sentiment occurred" in the late 1870s, McElreath recalled, and temperance societies were organized. "The drinking of liquor fell under such reprehension" that he could not remember a single case of drunkenness after that in the area. In some places in the South jolly comportment held out until the twentieth century. In Mize, known locally as Sullivan's Hollow, in the piney woods region of Mississippi, nicknames, drinking, gambling, fighting and rough practical jokes endured. The male inhabitants were "scrupulously honest in their business dealings, fiercely loyal to friends, and courageous . . . but they *would* drink whiskey, and they *would* fight." A brawl at a basketball game in 1922 was "the last great fight"—after that disorder ebbed, and Sullivan's Hollow's unruly reputation survived only as legend.[14]

Even in the once Wild West rowdiness diminished. Many of the most uproarious communities vanished. The final western gold rush in Goldfield, Nevada, peaked in 1906, and, as gold and silver deposits were exhausted, the inhabitants of most mining towns drifted away. Tombstone, which may have had a population of as many as 10,000 at its height in the 1880s, by 1900 had only 641 residents. As more and more land came under the plow, cattle drives north from Texas became impossible by the late 1880s, dooming Dodge City and Wichita as cow towns. The West slowly lost its demographic distinctiveness. As male nodes faded and more women moved West, the sex ratio equalized. Overall, almost as many women as men moved into the Rocky Mountain and Pacific states between 1880 and 1900. Colorado, for instance, was 66.5 percent male in 1880, but by 1900 only 54.7 percent of its population were men; Arizona in 1880 was 69.8 percent male, but by 1900 54.8 percent of its residents were men.[15]

The West was becoming like the rest of the country. "The time has come," announced the territorial governor of Arizona, "when more care should be taken in our deportment . . . [than] when our towns and villages were the abodes of men chiefly, or of but few women and children," and he urged the passing of statutes to improve the moral environment, including antigambling laws. As in "the East" (no longer "the states" or "America"), the female population aided probity's cause. California, its unbridled days a thing of the past, passed a local option law in 1887. In some towns, temperance sentiment was as strong as in the Midwest—the barbershop in Calvert, Texas, in the 1880s had an entrance inside to an adjacent saloon so men who wanted a drink could "conceal their patronage." Even the most uproarious places simmered down. A *Harper's Weekly* reporter who visited Leadville, Colorado, in 1888 found it "as steady-going as Salem or Plymouth Rock" with seven churches. "Leadville!" one old-timer joked when questioned about the town's placidity. "No stranger, this ain't Leadville. It's only some infernal Sunday-School town that ain't named yet."[16]

Physical comportment and tastes became more restrained. Photographs of men holding hands and embracing became less common by the end of the century. The American dining habit of grabbing what one wanted at mealtime that so appalled Dickens and other European visitors gave way to refined eating. Men waited their turn to serve themselves. John Habermehl was amused how men once scoffed at dining etiquette as undemocratic, but now "exchange the fork to the right hand after they had cut the meat . . . because it is fashionable." Not only were attitudes and actions becoming more restrained but tastes were also becoming increasingly refined. Men had once taken pride in robust flavors and scents, in drinking whiskey and smoking cigars. When men now drank, their alcoholic beverage of choice was typically quite different from that of their rough-and-ready forebears. Lager beer became popular in New York City just before the Civil

War and by the 1860s and 1870s, the rest of the country was drinking it too. Although total alcohol consumption remained much below the levels of the 1820s, national beer consumption, negligible before the 1850s, rose to eighteen gallons per person in 1885. American-style lager is only 4 percent alcohol. "A man can get drunk" on lager, applauded one beer champion, "but few will." Other habits changed as well. A "seegar," aggressively thrust forward, had been a key part of the iconography of the b'hoy. Cigarettes were at first ridiculed as fit only for women and were considered decadent and "devitalizing" for men. When Richard "Big Dick" Butler, a New York City longshoreman, began smoking cigarettes, his fellow dockworkers taunted him as a "ciggy smoker." Despite these effete associations, in the 1880s "mild smokes" boomed and by the twentieth century were the most popular tobacco product.[17]

Earlier reformers boasted about having driven drinkers, gamblers and fighters " into a corner," and the corners only became fewer. At the turn of the twentieth century, traditional male disorder could be found only in the interstices of American society, in a waning number of ostentatiously masculine settings. "The West Side dockworkers of New York City that Big Dick" Butler's describes sound much like men in the city decades earlier: it is a drinking, brawling, joking, nicknamed-filled world. "A real longshoreman is never so happy as when he is using his fists. . . . If he has a principle to fight for, all the better," Butler explained. Folklorist Richard Dorson discovered a "Lumberjack Code" in the Upper Peninsula of Michigan "that stressed the ability to brawl and the necessity to get insensibly drunk." As recently as the early twentieth century, "belligerent jacks for little reason flailed each other with bruising fists as long as a man could stand."[18]

"EVERY INDIVIDUAL TASTE, EVERY NATURAL APPETITE, WAS BRIDLED WITH CAUTION"

The advance of rectitude seemed so relentless that it appeared to some that joy was being squeezed out of ordinary life. A group of poets and novelists emerged that protested the reign of unbending propriety in the name of personal freedom and happiness. In "The Revolt from the Village," an influential 1921 *Nation* essay, Carl Van Doren critically scrutinized what had become by then a literary genre. Books like Edgar Lee Masters's *Spoon River Anthology*, Sherwood Anderson's *Winesburg, Ohio*, and Sinclair Lewis's *Main Street* exposed what Van Doren called the "pitiless decorum" of small-town life. Although these works differ significantly from each other, they all portray how individual growth is stunted by the prudery, conformity, and mendacity of the midwestern village. Free spirits of every sort were regarded with suspicion: not just drinkers and card and billiard players but also theatergoers, socialists, women who crossed their legs, and anyone who did not attend church—all were targets of censure. Such impossibly high moral standards—"puritanical" in the parlance of the day—led to expansive hypocrisy. Inhabitants struggled to break through the emotional repression to communicate their feelings to others. "Too many inhibitions can distort human spirit into grotesque forms," was Van Doren's summary of these works.[19]

Edgar Lee Masters's *Spoon River Anthology* (1915) suggests how suffocating small-town life might have been for some people. Masters's village of Spoon River is based on Lewistown, the central Illinois village where he grew up. *Spoon River Anthology* consists of a single stanza in verse about each of the men and women who lie buried in the town cemetery. Virtually all the characters and many of the events in the poem are based on real people and incidents that Masters remembered growing up in the 1880s. Lewiston was, as Masters later explained in a magazine article, divided into two groups—the conservatives, largely from New England, Republican, and very moralistic, and a more easy-going and permissive faction who were mostly southern Democrats. "The annual issue with Lewistown was saloons or no saloons," Masters recalled, and the two sides battled bitterly over it. Edgar's father, Hardin Masters, was a "rollicking man" who loved playing poker and "made no bones about the fact" that he "believed in drink in moderation," strolling into barrooms through the front door. Hardin became a leader of the indulgent faction and thus the bane of the dominant conservatives. The conflict between these two groups, and their opposing worldviews, is a central theme of *Spoon River Anthology*. "The eternal struggle," Edgar Lee Masters explained to an interviewer, is between "those who want to enjoy this world and those who want to make a hallway to another one."[20]

In *Spoon River*, Jefferson Howard is modeled on Hardin:

Stealing odd pleasures that cost me prestige,
And reaping evils I had not sown;
Foe of the church and its charnel darkness,
Friend of the human touch of the tavern.

The villains of the poem are the conservative leaders, Thomas Rhodes, and A. D. Blood, apparently both modeled on Hardin's real-life nemesis, Henry Phelps, president of the local bank, village council chairman, and superintendent of the Presbyterian Sunday school. Blood boastfully asks "who closed the saloons and stopped all playing at cards . . . / In many a crusade to purge the people of sin?" When the drunken Oscar Hummel mistakes Blood's house for his own and pounds on the door, Blood bursts out "roaring about the cursed saloon, and the criminals they made," and bludgeons Hummel to death. The conservatives ostracize drinkers, radicals, dancers, divorcees, even attendees of an *H.M.S. Pinafore* performance. The Spoon River Social Purity Club forces Jim Brown to remove a breeding colt from his farm on the edge of town so as not to corrupt public morals.[21]

The poem concludes with the mock-heroic "Spooniad," which recounts events from the 1880s that culminated in a key local election. Throughout the poem, the conservatives' moral standards prove flexible when their own interests are involved, and they hire "Hog-eyed Allen, terror of the hills," to intimidate antiprohibition voters at the polls. Liberal leader Kinsey Keene (also seemingly based on Hardin Masters) recruits Bengal Mike who kills Allen in an epic brawl. But the conservatives win anyway and hire a new town marshal:

> They wanted a terrible man,
> Grim, righteous, strong, courageous,
> And a hater of saloons and drinkers,
> To keep law and order in the village.

Spoon River becomes dry; "the regimen of gloom" has triumphed.[22]

To Masters and other writers critical of small-town life, the decades-long campaign of moral reformation had eradicated not only licentiousness and disorder but almost everything natural, festive, and free. As he walks at night down the deserted main street of Black Hawk, Jim Burden in Willa Cather's *My Ántonia* feels like he is living under tyranny. "People's speech, their voices, their very glances, became furtive and repressed. Every individual taste, every natural appetite, was bridled with caution." Inhabitants had little choice but to conform, become a social outcast, or like the Revolt authors themselves, flee to Chicago or another city.[23]

So much had male conduct changed in the course of the century that there began to emerge a concern that American men had become "overcivilized," a word coined in the late nineteenth century. Perhaps reformers and moralists had done their work too well. The worry here was less about village comportment than about the allegedly enervated urban, middle-class male, and it was a concern that had been aired as early as the 1850s. Raised by women, cooped up in city offices, men became reserved in conduct, sober in mien, polite in manners. American men, critics charged, were growing soft. The passing of the Civil War generation, men forged in battle, added to the unease. Indeed, Victorian culture itself, with its feminized sentimental Protestantism and genteel fiction, seemed to many to be effeminate. Henry Childs Merwin gave expression to these concerns in an 1897 essay in the *Atlantic Monthly* titled "On Being Civilized Too Much." Merwin lamented overeducated, "over-sophisticated and effete" men in whom all natural impulses, all spontaneity, have been stifled. Such men lacked two key primal instincts. Most obviously, they were bereft of "the instinct of pugnacity," which "is or may be weakened by the process of civilization," and he, like a number of others in this era, mourned its passing. Intriguingly, Merwin also was troubled by the more subtle, and perhaps more worrisome, way that instinctual, natural pity was muted by calculating conscientiousness. How many middle-class men actually fit this bloodless stereotype is unclear—the gruff, hardheaded man of business seems an equally prevalent archetype—but the concern was real.[24]

The solution was for middle-class men to remasculinize themselves. In the late nineteenth century, historian John Higham observed, a "new activist mood" began "to challenge the restraint and decorum of the 'Gilded Age.' . . . In many instances, the activists' rhetoric affirmed a continuity with an older, pre-modern culture." No one advocated a return to two-fisted jolly fellowship. But self-control, it was hoped, was firmly established enough that men could find ways to invigorate their manly nature without lapsing into full-fledged disorderly behavior. Athletic activities seemed one key way this might be achieved. Churchmen and reformers had once scorned sports as a diversion from the serious business of life. Slowly, attitudes began to change. "The sage leaders of morality," marveled the *Clipper* in 1879, "have come to look leniently, even admiringly, upon muscle, . . . the barriers of prejudice have been swept away."[25]

Respectable society had once looked askance at pugilism, but in the last decades of the century, fighting began to be viewed more affirmatively by high-minded men. Not bloody, dusty, rough-and-tumble fighting, but scientific boxing and sparring: a restrained fighting. Duffield Osborne sounded the call in "A Defense of Pugilism," published in the *North American Review* in 1880. "Civilization and refinement," Osborne explained, "are excellent things, but they must not be confused with mere womenishness, nor must men learn to faint at the sight of blood as proof of their refinement." He attacked boxing's critics, who, "unmanly themselves," are "caught by such specious watchwords as 'progress,' 'civilization,' and 'refinement.'" The solution was for "thinking men who value their manhood" to "regulate and control pugilism." Reputable men must wrest control of this virile pastime from the unsavory characters who presently dominate it and strictly enforce rules to eliminate its most brutal elements. Once fighting's reputation is restored, a boy can, "as of old," settle "his petty disputes with his fists," and "we shall die leaving men behind us, not a race of eminently respectable female saints." The new, clearly spelled out, Marquis of Queensberry regulations mandating gloves and timed rounds made the sport less gory and seemed to reduce the bedlam that had often accompanied fights. Sparring became a respectable form of exercise. In 1884 the elite New York Athletic Club hired Mike Donovan, a former prizefighter who had fought at Harry Hill's, as an instructor in the manly art of self-defense. Other clubs followed suit, and men of standing began lacing up the gloves.[26]

Another sport that allowed for regulated violence was football. In the late nineteenth century, football was basically a college game played "solely by gentlemen's sons," according to the *Police Gazette.* College officials had never been able to completely suppress undergraduate fighting, and football offered a means, they hoped, of channeling unruliness into an activity that could be controlled and manipulated in ways that would enhance college solidarity and encourage in participants both self-mastery and athletic masculinity. Academic authorities were not at first completely successful. Early football relied heavily on brute force and was often little more than a controlled brawl and, at worst, an uncontrolled brawl when fans joined the battle. John Heisman, who played football at Brown in the late 1880s, remembered how players fought it out one on one: "You didn't stand much of a chance of making the line in those days unless you were a good wrestler and fair boxer." The sport quickly came under attack as unmanageable and dangerous. The *Police Gazette* pointed out the incongruity of men of alleged refinement celebrating football—"It takes real hard rough-and-tumble fighting to satisfy the delicate needs of the upper classes." But others defended football not on the grounds that it was not brutal but because it was. Two Ivy League medical professors championed the sport in the *North American Review* in 1894. People who went to football games and saw players carried off on stretchers did not realize most injuries were minor, and an injury "not severe enough to leave permanent traces is not necessarily an evil but often even a positive good by building manliness," they believed.[27]

Football's most powerful defender was Theodore Roosevelt, the self-proclaimed embodiment of respectable fin-de-siècle manliness. An advocate of the "strenuous life," TR seemed bursting with masculine energy. The word "bully," which except among jolly fellows used to have a negative connotation, was TR's favorite term for something splendid. American men were once sturdy but now had become delicate. In our "perfectly peaceful and commercial civilization," Roosevelt worried, "there is always a danger of laying too little stress upon the more virile virtues," virtues for which "no amount of refinement and learning, of gentleness and culture can possibly atone." The one section of the country where such virtues still survived, he believed, was the West. The primitive condition of the region encouraged "vigorous manliness." TR often visited the West and eventually bought a ranch in southern Dakota. The epigraph for his *Ranch Life and Hunting Trail* (1888), one of three books he wrote about his western experiences, was taken from Robert Browning: "Oh our manhood's prime vigor!" Western life, remote from civilized society, cultivated the fighting virtues. Roosevelt relished stories of shooting affrays and recounted them in some detail. The West remained for Roosevelt, as in the American imagination, a place where red-blooded male vitality and honor still survived, and TR urged that undeveloped areas be preserved in their primitive, uncivilized splendor.[28]

Sports, Roosevelt hoped, could harden the American white middle-class male to face challenges to national greatness, especially in the Darwinian struggle with other races. Weak male bodies needed strengthening, and the era saw a rage for body building. A weight lifter himself, TR also favored more violent sports. He loved boxing and fought as an amateur at Harvard, and when he was governor of New York he sparred with Mike Donovan. John L. Sullivan was an acquaintance and occasional guest at Sagamore Hill. But, Roosevelt believed, "there is no better sport than football." Collegiate football built character, and TR staunchly defended it from critics, "persons who are by nature timid, [and] shrink from the exercise of manly and robust qualities if there is any chance of its being accompanied by physical pain." True, there was a risk of injury, Roosevelt admitted, but that was a small price to pay if colleges turned out "vigorous men" instead of "mollycoddles," and, anyway, football was certainly safer than polo or foxhunting. In 1905, after a highly publicized series of football injuries and deaths and muckraking accounts of "tramp" players who competed for two and even three colleges in a season, Roosevelt convened a White House meeting of college officials and coaches that eventually led to reform of the rules, which included the introduction of the forward pass.[29]

"THE DENIAL OF THE DENIAL OF SELF-INDULGENCE"

Roosevelt and other commentators who lamented that civility had gone too far need not have been so worried. A significant countertrend had already begun that was loosening strict Victorian standards of comportment. Cities, one of "the extremes of social life" that William Alcott had worried about in 1836, had long been the bane of moralists. Urban places were certainly less disorderly than they had been earlier in the century, but they still fell short of the righteous consensus that characterized much of small-town life. Fighting had dramatically diminished. Once tavern brawls and even minor riots had been common; now bystanders intervened and halted fights. Gambling and drinking, however, had not been eliminated. The closing of casinos and gambling halls was eliminating public gambling, but illegal wagering continued. And in most cities, saloons remained open. The fate of the women's crusade of 1873–74 in urban areas suggests the difficulties reformers faced. From the beginning the saloon protesters had been warned that "the praying plan will do well enough for small towns, but when it comes to the large cities . . . —why it's folly to think about it!" Cincinnati, with its three thousand saloons and large German population, greeted the antidrink crusaders with intense and sustained hostility. When women prayed outside of saloons, they were hooted and jeered. Unsympathetic police arrested them for blocking the sidewalk, and the campaign soon fizzled out. Even in villages there were signs that the moral crusade might be beginning to wind down. Growing real incomes, shorter working hours, and new and popular varieties of entertainment made it harder to convince people of the value of self-denial. In midwestern small towns where the triumph of propriety had been relatively recent, stern respectability was still firmly in the saddle, but in villages in the East where decorum had been long established, there was a perceptible easing of standards.[30]

That cities were never as mobilized as the countryside in the campaign against male disorder is an old story. What was new is what was happening in small towns in the East. In Waterville, in Oneida County, New York—the upstate village studied by sociologist James M. Williams in the 1890s—the story was quite different from the one told by revolt-from-the-village authors. The first part of Williams's analysis of Waterville life is familiar enough. A moral reformation transformed the disorderly comportment of the community in the 1840s. The "austere party" came to dominate, and drinking, fighting, and "animal spirits" waned. But then around 1875 a new phase began. "The principle underlying all customs, in the first period, was the denial of self-indulgence. This has changed to the denial of the denial of self-indulgence." Williams argues that this denial of self-denial was due to both the influence of city life and to a rising standard of living. The battle against jolly fellowship had been won, and once won, the exceptionally strict standard of propriety, "the cult of self-control," that had characterized the first period of struggle no longer seemed imperative. Not that self-control was no longer essential; rather it was now internalized. It had become second nature.[31]

The change was played out in Waterville's churches. The Episcopal church, which allowed its members to drink, dance, and play cards, represented the surging "convivial party," according to Williams. The Baptists were the hub of the austere faction. The Episcopalians and the increasingly convivial Presbyterians gained members in the 1880s and 1890s, while the Methodists and Baptists lost them. Where once most of Waterville's leading citizens had embraced rigorous personal constraint, many now cut themselves, and others, some slack. The more relaxed standards were obvious in many areas of village life. Excessive drinking was still shameful, but moderate social drinking was no longer cause for reproach. Leisure became part of everyday life. All-male socializing waned, and heterosocial mingling grew. The Grange began to hold dancing and card parties. An opera house was built and theatergoing boomed. Bowling and roller skating, both condemned by the austere element, became fashionable. "Stock gambling" became unobjectionable. In contrast to the narrow-minded, almost totalitarian, villages depicted by the revolt authors, Waterville was now easygoing.[32]

Waterville's history suggests that, at least in the East, the moral revolution had essentially succeeded. There now was confidence that self-control, not impulsiveness, was normal. Restraint was taken for granted. It seemed that a person could have a glass of beer and not become a drunkard, play a hand of cards and not be transformed into a gambler, go to a boxing match and not become a brawler. There were those who had not become party to this consensus who still needed to be reformed, but for most men and women, the stern, unyielding code of propriety that the moral revolution had brought in its wake now seemed outdated and unnecessary, even rather silly. In Gurleyville, Connecticut, in the 1880s, a new minister who excoriated playing cards as "painted demons" and "hellspots" and later assailed parishioners who had attended a circus was regarded as little short of a madman. Only the forceful intervention of the church elder saved the cleric from being forced to resign. Even in the Midwest, things may have been changing. Edgar Lee Masters depicts Lewistown, Illinois, in *Spoon River* as under the authority of an unyieldingly moralistic regime. Perhaps that had been true in the 1880s, but the 1890s told a different story. In that decade, the liberals became the dominant faction in the village. Hardin Masters, whose fictional persona in the poem is a martyr to the conservatives' intolerance, was elected mayor and reopened the saloons.[33]

The sweeping reform movement that had begun in the early nineteenth century—what Edward Jarvis called a "moral and intellectual epidemic"—had peaked. Reformers believed that more still needed to be done, but there was, in fact, much for them to be proud of. Jolly behavior, which once seemed to be an inherent male trait, now was looked on as deviant. Self-governance was the new standard. The very success of civility allowed it to moderate. People who remembered the raucous "old social order" of former days looked back at the transformation in male comportment with amazement. William Lynch, a railroad engineer, marveled at the alteration in male conduct he had witnessed over the course of his life. In "former times, the first place to go after putting way the train was to the saloon and tank up with booze and play cards, get drunk and fight. But now we hardly ever hear of a railway man getting drunk. They all seem to be sober and perfect gentleman."[34]

"THE MORE OFTEN HE IS BEATEN THE MORE WE LAUGH"

If, as Wilbur Cross believed, the raucous "old social order" had come to an end, the old cultural order proved more enduring. The dimming of jolly fellowship does not seem to have been accompanied by any significant reduction in its cultural significance. The violent humor that characterized the Mose plays, southwestern literature, and minstrelsy continued to hold an important, perhaps even central, place in American popular culture in the late nineteenth and early twentieth centuries. As before, New York City played a key role in this process. The level of violence both in comic literature and popular theater increased to a frenzied level, but mayhem became more stylized, often inflated to levels that clearly moved it into the realm of fantasy.

In the last three decades of the nineteenth century, vaudeville theater had evolved into a tremendously diverse and vital popular entertainment. A vaudeville show consisted of a sequence of acts, ten or fifteen minutes long, featuring singers to trapeze artists, dancers to ventriloquists, magicians to dog acts, and comedians to regurgitators. More women attended the shows than in earlier decades, but audiences still were predominantly male. Comic violence remained a staple. The aggressive strain in vaudeville was general, but increasingly stage violence came to be associated with Irish and African Americans. Many Irish entertainers, male and female, cultivated a combative persona. Among the most popular was Maggie Cline, "the supreme Irish comedienne of the nation," according to the *New York Herald-Tribune.* Said to have gotten her start singing at Harry Hill's sporting theater, she weighed two hundred pounds, and her blaring voice led her to be dubbed the "Brunhilde of the Bowery." Cline had many hits, including "Pitcher of Beer," "Down Went McGinty" and "Choke Him, Casey, Choke Him," but her signature song was "Throw Him Down, McCloskey" (1890). She would stride on stage and announce, "Now ladies and gentleman I will sing the dainty and pathetic little ballad that drove me into the business."

'Twas down at Dan McDevitt's at the corner of the street,
There was to be a prize fight, and both parties were to meet;

> To make all the arrangements, and see ev'rything was right.
> McCloskey and a naygur were to have a finish fight.

The chorus went:

> Throw him down, McCloskey, was to be the battle cry,
> Throw him down, McCloskey, you can lick him if you try;
> And future generations, with wonder and delight,
> Will read on hist'ry's pages of the great McCloskey fight.

The "naygur" does not show up, but "McCracken" agrees to fight, "stand up or rough-and-tumble, if McCloskey didn't bite." The fight goes forty-seven bloody rounds until "McCloskey got a mouthfull of poor McCracken's jowl. / McCracken hollered 'murther,' and his seconds hollered 'foul.'" A free fight breaks out. The song ends by cataloging the carnage, noting that "McCloskey lost an upper lip, McCracken lost an eye." As Cline sang, she shadowboxed. "Throw Him Down, McCloskey" was an smash hit. The *New York Herald-Tribune* recorded in her obituary that she sang the song "not less than 6,000 times, not only for the gallery boys, but for Grover Cleveland, William McKinley and Theodore Roosevelt." Cline was so identified with the song that she tried to drop it from her act, but this only set off "a loud clamor for the classic" from the audience.[35]

Blacks, even more than Irish, were the embodiment of comic violence in vaudeville, continuing a theme begun in minstrelsy. "Coon songs" that comically mocked blacks became hugely popular in the 1880s. Songs caricaturing African Americans had been popular since the 1830s, and coon songs fall squarely within the minstrel tradition, but with their catchy syncopated rhythms they became a fad. May Irwin, a white vaudeville star who had made a specialty of coon songs, achieved a huge hit in 1896 with her "'Bully' Song," also known as "The New Bully" and "The Bully of the Town." The exact genesis of the song is unclear. The flourishing black sporting subculture had provided African American folklore with a panoply of outsized bad men of whom Stagolee was only the most famous, and "The 'Bully' Song" may have begun as a black folk song. In Irwin's version a new brawler shows up in town, and "he's round among de niggers a layin' their bodies down." The narrator, the reigning town bully, boasts "I'm a Tennessee nigger and I don't allow, no red-eyed river roustabout with me to raise a row." He vows to find the new bully and "make him bow." After a long search—the stirring chorus goes "As I walked dat levee round, round, round, round . . . , I'm lookin' for dat bully an' he must be found"—the inevitable confrontation occurs: "When I got through with bully, a doctor and nurse, / Wa'nt no good to dat nigger, so they put him in a hearse." "Dere's only one boss bully, and dat one is me," the song concludes. With its truculent lyrics, similar to those of antebellum minstrel hits about black brawlers such as "Jim Crow" and "Old Dan Tucker," and its infectious tune, "The Bully Song" was a sensation, and like "Old Dan Tucker," it long remained popular in the folk tradition.[36]

Irwin's success sparked a rage for bully songs. The violence was deadlier than in the Irish brawler songs—rather than merely having an eye gouged out, Irwin's new bully is killed. Jim Crow only used his fists; blacks in coon songs, by contrast, were armed. The razor became the hallmark of their alleged propensity for violence—"took along my trusty blade to carve that nigger's bones," Irwin's bully relates. When the sheet music for "The 'Bully' Song" was published in the cartoon supplement to the *New York Journal*, a razor was prominently featured. Even armed with razors or guns, blacks could still be figures of fun. The bully on the cover of Irwin's song is a grotesque caricature of a black urban dandy with colossal lips and prominent heels, standard features of black caricatures for decades, who looks too dopey to be really dangerous. Bully songs reflected and reinforced white fears about murderous black men, yet at the same time they could remain comic since those sliced up and killed were African Americans.[37]

The Irish and blacks took center stage among vaudeville brawlers, but the battling b'hoy was not forgotten. Real b'hoys had long since disappeared from New York streets. Mose too was gone, having departed Manhattan for the West. But belligerent New Yorkers continued to tread the stage. In the 1870s the b'hoy stereotype was brilliantly updated and renewed in the "Dan Mulligan" sketches of Edward "Ned" Harrigan. Harrigan's career suggests the endurance of the New York–San Francisco axis. Born, as was Thomas "Jim Crow" Rice, in New York's waterfront Seventh Ward, Harrigan worked as a ship caulker. In 1867 he left for the Pacific Coast. Harrigan had performed as a minstrel during amateur nights at the Bowery Theater, and, after a short stint caulking in San Francisco, he became a full-time vaudevillian. "In the West," the *New York Times* explained, "he found his mission in life—that of making others laugh."[38]

Teamed with Tony Hart, an outstanding farceur, he returned to New York in 1872. Their breakthrough came in the series of rollicking Mulligan plays that made Harrigan and Hart among the most celebrated theater performers of the era. Featuring such popular songs as "The Mulligan Guards March" and "I Never Drink Behind the Bar (but I Will Take a Mild Cigar)," the act was immediately successful and played to packed houses not only in Manhattan but throughout the country. The plots usually focused on the very Irish Dan Mulligan (played by Harrigan) and his family's relations with their tenement neighbors, especially

Cover of sheet music for May Irwin's "Bully Song." This was included as a Sunday color supplement in William Randolph Hearst's *New York Journal* on 12 April 1896. The Lester S. Levy Collection of Sheet Music, Special Collections, Sheridan Libraries, The Johns Hopkins University.

Dan's German nemesis, Gustav Lochmuller, a butcher. If Lochmuller shared Mose's occupation, it was Mulligan who shared Mose's comportment. A jolly *Clipper*-reading, Fourteenth Ward grocer and saloon keeper, Mulligan was always ready for a drink, fight or practical joke.[39]

Harrigan's plays owed a good deal to minstrelsy. Characters were ethnic and racial caricatures. Blackface roles were important in almost all of Harrigan's sketches. Usually played by Hart or Billy Gray, a veteran of Bryant's Minstrels, Harrigan's "nagurs" talked in the comically pompous speech of the minstrel stage and were prone to pull razors. A recurrent motif was the rivalry between Mulligan's Irish volunteer militia company, the Mulligan Guards, and the black Skidmore Guards. In the *Mulligan Guard Ball* (1891), the formal dances of both the Mulligan Guards and Skidmore Guards are by mistake booked at the same hall at the same time. A free-for-all ensues. Eventually the Skidmores are prevailed on to take an upstairs room, but in the climax the floor collapses, spilling them down onto the Mulligan Guards. The "coons came down in chunks," and the icewagon had "to take ten of 'em to de hospital."[40]

The *Mulligan Guard Ball* is not unusual in its uproarious climax. "Melee" and "general melee" were two of Harrigan's favorite stage directions. Blowing up things was a jolly-fellow favorite, and Harrigan made explosions something of a trademark. *The Major* (1881) ends with the protagonist getting drunk and accidentally dropping his cigar in a fireworks factory. "Explosion[.] . . . Fireworks seen through the windows of factory[,] . . . the front of the factory sinks through the stage and the debris of the roof crashes." In a scene that recalls the dismemberment of blacks in Henry Clay Lewis's stories, African Americans conveniently sitting on the roof of the factory are blown to bits. The stage directions call for "heads, limbs, and bodies . . . seen by audience descending from the sky," presumably to howls of laughter. So mangled are the remains that a surviving black remarks that "you couldn't tell wedder you were burying a relative or friend."[41]

The violent strain in vaudeville reached a kind of culmination in the celebrated comedy routines of Weber and Fields. Both Lew Fields (whose real name was Moses Schoenfeld) and Joe Weber were Jews from the Lower East Side of New York. At the height of their fame in the 1890s, the pair was making an incredible $4,000 a week. Their Broadway theater was, according to the *Dramatic Mirror*, "the most popular music hall in America," and some of the top stars in the country, including Lillian Russell, were part of their troupe. They were the most famous two-man act in the history of vaudeville—and one of the roughest. A "double Dutch knockabout act" in vaudeville taxonomy, Weber and Fields were inspired by earlier "rough" acts in which performers traded "bumps," stage jargon for blows to the head and upper body. Their first professional performance was at the Chatham Museum on the Bowery in 1877, and they later worked for Harry Hill, who believed their raucous performances would appeal to the patrons of his famed establishment. "Scenes at a Boxing School" was one of their popular early sketches.[42]

In their act, Fields played Meyer and Weber played Mike; they mangled English and each other. In the slapstick manner of the day, their sketches concluded with Fields pummeling Weber. "All the public wanted to see was Fields knock the hell out of me," Weber recalled. Injuries were common, and the pair learned an important lesson in an 1885 Providence performance. Weber's skull protector slipped, and when Fields hit him over the head with a walking stick, blood spurted out. The crowd screamed with laughter; by the end of the act the theater was in an uproar, and the pair had to take an extra curtain call before Weber could receive medical attention. The harder Weber was hit, the more people laughed, and "when we bled audiences seemed to like us all the better," Fields remembered.[43]

In 1912 Weber and Fields wrote a newspaper article that summed up some of the lessons they learned performing in vaudeville for thirty-five years. It was entitled "Adventures in Human Nature" because they believed their decades on stage had given them insight into the popular mind. Audiences, they had discovered, took intense delight in seeing others hoodwinked, humiliated, and hurt. "As the chance of pain, the portion of physical misery, the proportion of tragedy becomes diminished . . . so does the proportion of laughter become less and less." This "may seem mean—anything you may care to call it;—but it is true." The one caveat was that the pain not be accompanied by a permanently crippling injury. Weber and Fields over the years learned exactly what audiences most enjoyed. At the top of the list, they determined, was "to see two friends fight." Second in pleasure was watching the underdog get the worst of it, especially in "a one-sided fight with the weaker man consistently losing." Human nature, they believed, required that we laugh at seeing a man beaten, "and the more often he is beaten the more we laugh." The pair became connoisseurs of cruelty and discovered that the loudest laughter came when someone was poked in the eye, when "a man choke[d] another man and shake[d] his head from side to side" and when a victim was kicked.[44]

As they learned what got the biggest audience response, their act evolved. It was always the bigger Fields who assaulted the five-four Weber. Weber was strangled, hit over the head, and had his eyes gouged. (Apparently it was Weber and Fields who made the poke in the eye a vaudeville staple. Two fingers got a bigger laugh than one finger they learned.) What elevated Weber and Fields above earlier knockabout acts was their clever dialogue, exquisite timing, and especially the brilliant conceit that the pair were not enemies but close friends. In one of their most popular early routines, "The Choking Sketch," Weber (Mike) asks Fields (Meyer) why he keeps attacking him.

"Why? Why? Because I *like* you! Mike when I look at you—I have such a—feeling that—oh, I can't express myself! Such a —oo—oo—oo—oo! (*Chokes him [Weber], then turns to the audience*) Why do I go with him? (*Pointing at Weber*) When I look at him my heart goes out to him. (*To Weber*) When you are away from me, I can't keep my mind off you. When you are with me I can't keep my

Lew Fields and Joe Weber. Photograph by Byron Studios, c. 1900. Billy Rose Theatre Division, The New York Public Library for the Performing Arts, Astor, Lenox, and Tilden Foundations.

hands off you. (*Chokes him*) But sometimes I feel that you do not return my affection. You do not feel—something that—oo—oo—oo—oo! (*Chokes him again, etc.*)"

On stage this would have been delivered with a "Dutch" accent. The sight of Fields strangling Weber, Weber's eyes popping out as they staggered around, Fields insisting all the while that "I luff you, Mike," proved irresistible to audiences. The homoerotic and the violent were bound together, and Mike and Meyer alternated between them capriciously in a way quite similar to an older style of male relationships. Weber and Fields's costumes reinforced this archaic quality: they wore outlandish outfits, loud baggy pants, and jackets several sizes too small. Their makeup was equally absurd, and they wore preposterously fake beards. This was the appearance favored by comedians decades earlier, but it was passé by the 1890s. The pair seem to have made a conscious decision to continue in the manner of classic Dutch acts. The dated features of their act likely made their mayhem more acceptable to audiences—it was clearly situated in the past.[45]

"THE 'GUY' IS INFERIOR TO YOU AND DESERVES EVERYTHING HE IS STUPID ENOUGH TO TAKE"

Laughable violence was also found in late nineteenth-century literature. Just as southwestern literature had situated disorder in the past and minstrelsy located it among blacks, a body of writing emerged that centered tumult on male children, on the "bad boy." A degree of unruliness had long been tolerated, even admired, among young men as a sign of spunk. One rather remarkable example of the indulgence boys received came from the pen of Lydia Maria Child who in 1853 wrote *Isaac T. Hopper: A True Life*, a biography of her Quaker friend who championed a wide variety of antebellum reform causes. She devotes considerable attention to Hopper's boyhood pranks. Here is what he did. He tied "the boughs of trees together in narrow paths, that people traveling in the dark might hit their heads against them." He sawed a footbridge almost in half, then said something "very impertinent" to the schoolmaster who chased him over the bridge, and when the bridge broke the schoolmaster only "with difficulty saved himself from drowning." Hopper threw gunpowder into the schoolhouse stove and the resulting explosion "did some injury to the master." But, Child cheerfully concluded, "there was no malice in his fun."[46]

Hopper's "pranks" seemed to have been regarded merely as evidence of high spirits and were taken as good jokes. With the increasing emphasis on decorous behavior, however, it was "self-conquest" that was becoming valued. Although admiration for unruly boys remained, moralists argued that literature for young people should be uplifting and present children who were models of Protestant virtue. Jacob Abbott, in his series of *Rollo* stories, the first of which was published in 1835, essentially created American juvenile fiction. Abbott, a Congregational minister and teacher, explained that the books were written "to awaken and cherish the spirit of humble and unobtrusive but heartfelt piety" in youth. In *Rollo in France* (1854), Rollo, traveling with friends of his parents, kept the Sabbath, even in roistering Paris. It was tempting to go sightseeing, but Rollo concludes that "it was not right" and would be "displeasing to God . . . to spend any part of the day which God had consecrated for his own service and to the spiritual improvement of the soul in ordinary . . . amusements." Instead Rollo spends Sunday afternoon reading the Bible to his little sister.[47]

Such impossibly good boys inspired a backlash, in part because of the suspicion that few real youths could take the saintly Rollo very seriously but also perhaps because of the growing fear that American men were becoming overly refined. Boys needed something that was more cultivated than dime novels but more robust than Sunday-school tales. Thomas Bailey Aldrich's bestselling *The Story of a Bad Boy* (1869) fit the bill, and its success, along with that of John Habberton's *Helen's Babies* in 1876, transformed bad-boy stories into a literary genre. Many of these bad boys were "bad" only in comparison to the angelic heroes that appeared in earlier children's fiction. The bad boy in Bailey's book, like others in this type of literature, gets into schoolyard fights, sets off firecrackers, and pulls some mild pranks. These boys are not really evil but simply headstrong, playful, and inquisitive; they are good at heart. The older idea that a propensity for mischief in boys was a sign of spirit, which had never entirely waned, revived.[48]

If most literary bad boys are merely mischievous, some are truly mean. "The Christmas Fireside" (1865), one of Mark Twain's earliest stories, turns the good boy tale completely on its head. It portrays a boy who, unlike the youths in didactic literature, not only does bad deeds but does not regret them and gets away with them. "Once he climbed up in Farmer Acorn's apple tree to steal apples, and the limb didn't break, and he didn't fall and break his arm . . . and repent and become good. Oh, no—he stole as many apples as he wanted, and came down all right, he was ready for the dog, too, and knocked him endways with a rock." The story concludes in Twain's characteristic cynicism: "He grew up, and married, and raised a large family, and brained them all with an axe one night, and got wealthy by all manner of cheating and rascality; and now he is the infernalest, wickedest scoundrel in his native village, and is universally respected, and belongs to the Legislature." Twain, of course, was to brilliantly develop the bad boy into a character of complexity and meaning in *Tom Sawyer* (1876) and *Huckleberry Finn* (1885).[49]

George W. Peck's famed bad boy, did not, unlike Twain's Huck, transcend the bad-boy genre, but Peck's fictional protagonist was more than a gentle riposte to priggish Rollos. "Hennery," the bad boy, is a real hellion. George Peck was a Wisconsin newspaperman and Democratic politician, a mayor of Milwaukee and two-term governor of Wisconsin. His bad boy tales began as newspaper sketches and were later expanded into a series of bad-boy books. The most popular was *Peck's Bad Boy and His Pa* (1883), which was to remain in print until the end of the next century. Its phenomenal popularity generated Peck's Bad Boy songs, Peck's Bad Boy plays, and even, two decades later, a Peck's Bad Boy comic strip. The setting of the stories is middle class; Peck realized that the trappings of respectability made the chaos that Hennery caused all the more disruptive. "The boy," as he is called, is no child, and the book does not seem to have been intended solely, or perhaps even primarily, for children. Hennery is finished with school and is working; in one story he is a "teller" in a livery stable: "When a man comes into hire a horse I have to go down to the saloon and tell the livery man."[50]

The central narrative of the book is the recounting of Hennery's practical jokes, one after another. "The boy" displays the true character of the prankster, as E. F. Bleiler explains in his introduction to a 1958 edition of the stories: "The 'guy' is inferior to you and deserves everything he is stupid enough to take." Once the conditions for playing a good prank materialize, Hennery cannot rest until the prank is accomplished. He puts castor oil in the maple syrup pitcher, kerosene in the vinegar jug, and pepper into the stove at Sunday school. He is "a terror to cats." "Dynamiting a Dog" in *Peck's Red Headed Boy* (1903) recalls the savage humor of southwestern literature. "A man had a dog he wanted killed" and hires some boys to do it. They decide "to get a stick of dynamite and blow the dog sky-high." The explosive is tied to the dog's tail, and after some anxious moments when the dog, a friendly creature, runs after them, it detonates. "Pieces of dog, blood [and] hair" were everywhere, and "nearly every boy was covered with blood."[51]

The most developed and important character in the stories, however, is not the boy, but Pa, who strains to live up to the tenets of middle-class propriety but never entirely pulls it off. After a few months of decorous behavior, Pa begins to exhibit the classic symptoms: drinking, betting on horse races, going to prizefights, and playing practical jokes. Peck admires Pa's failure, for respectability is a racket. In Peck, as in Twain, the bad-boy tale becomes a work of social criticism. Pranks become a weapon against gentility. Members of the church are pious hypocrites, and businessmen cheat customers whenever they can. In one memorable incident, Hennery soaks his father's handkerchief in liquor and folds a deck of cards into it before Pa goes to church. His father takes out the handkerchief while testifying at the service, the cards go flying into the air, and the smell of whiskey permeates the building. Pa is being punished, in Peck's view justly so, for his attempts to put on airs, to become a part of that sanctimonious fraud known as the middle class. He is better off being himself, a bibulous, disheveled, fun-loving dreamer.[52]

The bad boy and the Bowery Boy intersected in the 1890s in what became an enduring legacy of the jolly vein in American culture—the newspaper comic strip. Cartoons were nothing new—they had been appearing in newspapers and magazines throughout the nineteenth century—but what Ohio-born artist Richard Outcault drew for the Sunday *New York World* in 1895 was innovative: it was in color and appeared weekly. Outcault, like other early comic artists, was indebted to vaudeville humorists. Journalist Roy L. McCardell, writing in 1905, noted that "the knock-about comedians of the old-time music-halls might easily have posed for most of the pictures" printed in the Sunday comic supplements of newspapers. Outcault entitled his comic *Hogan's Alley*, after the location of "Maggie Murphy's Home," a popular song in Ned Harrigan's *Reilly and the Four Hundred*, which played on Broadway in 1890–91. Hogan's Alley was in New York City's tough Fourth Ward, and its inhabitants, a panoply of ethnic, racial, and social types, struggled, very much in the tradition of Harrigan's Mulligan plays, to get along with each other. The adults were coarse caricatures, but the tenement waifs that were really the focus of the cartoon were realistically drawn, inspired apparently by Jacob Riis's photographs.[53]

The newspapers in which *Hogan's Alley* appeared, Joseph Pulitzer's *New York World* and later William Randolph Hearst's *New York Journal*, were not genteel newspapers, and *Hogan's Alley* was not a genteel place. Prominently featured in the front of each cartoon was a child with a shaved head who was dressed in a yellow nightshirt and who commented on events in New York dialect—this was bad boy Mickey Dugan, the famous Yellow Kid. Outcault's original cartoon was a single tableau. Some were simply poignant depictions of slum children playing by organizing a tea party or staging their own circus, but in others, the youngsters mimicked public events such as political conventions and prizefights, giving Outcault a chance to remark on the news of the day. It was a cartoon about children but not a cartoon for children. Even after criticism forced Outcault to tone down the mayhem, he still infused brutality into his work. One scholar wrote that Outcault saw "comedy in violence and casual cruelty." Eyes are gouged, dogs kicked, and, in an Outcault trademark, people fall from tenement fire escapes. Blacks take an incredible pounding in early comics and *Hogan's Alley* was no exception: in Outcault's cartoon, African Americans are punched in the face, butted by billy goats, hit in the head with golf clubs, and have their hair pulled out.[54]

The Yellow Kid was a spectacular success and likely inspired the name "yellow journalism." Outcault was part of the famous group of newspapermen that Hearst in 1896 hired away from the *World* to the *Journal*, and for a while both papers ran versions of *Hogan's Alley*. In 1900 Outcault began drawing a new cartoon for the *New York Herald* about a black boy called *Poor Lil Mose*. (That name again!) Mose lasted for a little over a year, and in 1902 Outcault created his most popular comic strip, *Buster Brown.* It differs in a number of ways from *Poor Lil Mose,* but the name "Brown" perhaps creates a suggestion that Buster's unruliness is analogous with that of blacks. Buster is a bad boy, a very bad boy. Outcault realized, as Peck had before him, that placing the bad boy within a respectable, in Buster's case upper-class, household only multiplies the possibilities for comic destruction. Like Hennery, Buster was an unfettered prankster, and Outcault was given a full page to elaborate on his practical jokes. Before a formal dinner, Buster blacks up the faces of the portraits on the dining-room wall and pulls off the tablecloth sending the formally set china and silverware flying. No motive is given for Buster's pranks; they seem simply to stem from a love of destroying order and creating chaos. In one Sunday strip Outcault answered the question of what Buster had done during the rest of the week: "On Monday he painted the kitchen with stove blacking. Tuesday he accidentally set the house on fire. Wednesday he put kerosene in the soup. Thursday he put ink in the wash tub." Usually in the last panel, Buster apologizes, but often with a sardonic observation that seems intended for the strip's many adult readers. "Children are human. They don't become inhuman until they grow up," went one. Buster Brown was even more popular than the Yellow Kid, touching off a rage for Buster Brown plays, Buster Brown suits, and Buster Brown shoes.[55]

The second founding father of American comics was Rudolph Dirks who began drawing *The Katzenjammer Kids* in the *New York Journal* in 1897. "Katzenjammer" in German literally means the yowling of cats, or in slang, a hangover. The German-born Dirks, an accomplished painter, took the idea of the Katzenjammer Kids from *Max und Moritz,* a series of illustrated books by Wilhelm Busch, inspired in part by the Till Eulenspiegel tales, featuring two prank-playing boys that were wildly popular in Germany in the 1860s. Dirks also drew heavily on the bad-boy stereotype and on vaudeville "Dutch" humor. All the characters speak in German dialect. The agitated turbulence of the Kids, Hans and Fritz, plays comically against the popular stereotype of the stolid Dutchman. The plot is basically one prank per strip, mostly played on Mama or the Captain (her male companion).[56]

Hans and Fritz are a perfect match, so attuned to mischief that rarely is it necessary for them to plot a practical joke. Both instantly understand that a bear in a cage is to be let out of the cage. Even when they know they will be caught and disciplined, they play pranks—they can't help themselves. Usually, the strip ends with the boys crying as they are spanked. As with Buster Brown, however, the sheer delight they take in havoc outweighs the pain of punishment; typically they execute their pranks grinning fiendishly from ear to ear. Their love of pandemonium is palpable; for Christmas 1903 Hans and Fritz excitedly ask for a battleship and a tiger. The pair achieved popularity, Roy McCardell sarcastically explained, by "their habit of setting their dear old mother on fire, hitting her with clubs . . . [and] tying ropes across her path to trip her." Hans and Fritz are masters of devastation. As in the Mulligan plays, explosions often cap the action. The Kids are demolition experts, using fireworks, flash powder, gunpowder, gasoline, and dynamite. "'Is it powder Hans?' 'No, it is dynamite,'" Hans's practiced eye determines before the inevitable detonation in "The Katzenjammer Kids Explode a Ship" from 1902. "Mit dose kids, society iss nix!" blurts out the Inspector (a truant officer) in one strip. Writes cartoon historian Richard Marschall, "they live to destroy and reduce, and no characters in the comics or in all fiction take more undiluted delight in such mayhem." Sut Lovingood actually might have an edge here, but there is no doubt that anarchic violence has rarely been more fondly depicted.[57]

The Katzenjammer Kids was the longest running and probably the most popular American comic strip in history. In 1914 Dirks had a falling out with Hearst and went to the *World* where he continued to draw the strip under the title *The Captain and the Kids*. The *Journal*, which retained the copyright for the title *Katzenjammer Kids*, then hired another cartoonist to draw it. Even though the strips over the years became more constrained, the jolly thrust remained. In 1907 Dirks introduced Sandy the butcher boy into his version of the Katzenjammer Kids. Sandy is recognizably the type, perhaps the last of a long line of brawling butchers going back to Mose. Sandy talks tough in a Bowery dialect—"Don't gimme me no back-talk nieder"—and beats Fritz up.[58]

The ferocity of the early comics strips outraged many. Ralph Bergengren, writing in the *Atlantic Monthly*, was dismayed that "physical pain is the most glaringly omnipresent" of cartoon motifs. Much of what passes for humor in the supplements is merely "the crude brutality of human nature, mocking at grief and laughing boisterously at physical deformity." *Lippincott's Monthly Magazine* found the comics to be nothing less than "a national peril." Were someone to enter a home and "induce the young people to indulge in malicious practical jokes," that person would be thrown out of the house, but every Sunday parents let their children read cartoons, which almost invariably end with some poor victim "being maltreated, blown to pieces or battered to a jelly." Comics overturn any conception of right and wrong by appealing to "one of the basest traits in human nature—joy at another's misfortune." Cartoon scholars in later decades were not so much outraged by early comic strips as puzzled by them. As with southwestern writers like Henry Clay Lewis, commentators wondered what readers found amusing in this decimation. What exactly was funny about the funnies? Colton Waugh, in his history of comic strips, could only conclude that "it would seem that readers like to see simple, helpless people beaten, kicked, [and] cuffed around."[59]

Among the first commercial animated cartoon shorts was a Katzenjammer Kids adaptation, "Policy and Pie" (1918), and animation continued the unabashed mayhem that had characterized comic strips. It became, indeed, one of the most distinctive features of the new form of entertainment. Finding ways to "bludgeon someone on paper" was, according to Norman M. Klein in his history of cartoons, the formula for success for early animation artists. The first generation of cartoonists, virtually all of whom worked in New York City, learned not only from comic strips but from vaudeville. Dave Fleischer, who teamed with his brother Max on the popular *Out of the Inkwell* series and later *Betty Boop* and *Popeye*, attributed the comic timing of their cartoons in part to his watching Weber and Fields while working as a theater usher. Early cartoons displayed a strong partiality for jolly action; not only fighting and violence but also pranks and drinking were common themes.[60]

E. G. Lutz's landmark book *Animated Cartoons* (1920) explained so clearly and precisely how cartoons were made that almost anyone who could draw could produce them, including the young Walt Disney, who repeatedly checked the book out of the Kansas City public library. Lutz believed that the archetypal comic cartoon plot was a clash between two antagonists, "growing in violence." "It is indispensable, for the sake of an uninterrupted animation," that there be "a cumulative chain of actions, increasing in force and resultant misfortune." A man having his hat knocked off by a brick, "one of the most primitive of practical jokes," would be an ideal incident, humorous in both anticipation and execution. Disney learned the lesson well. The Mickey Mouse of *Steamboat Willy* (1928), the first cartoon made for synchronized sound, "was only partly civilized." Audiences used to the tamer Mickey of later decades would be surprised watching his early performances, advised *New York Times* writer Jesse Green. The primordial Mickey was "uninhibited, bare-chested, rough-and-ready to the point of sadism. . . . Like most cartoon characters of the period, he blithely trafficked in fistfights, drownings, [and] dismemberments."[61]

The fascination with jolly comportment in late nineteenth-century popular culture stands in juxtaposition to jolly fellowship's waning significance in society at large. Propriety had made significant progress. Self-control, not impulsiveness, now was beginning to seem natural. That jolly male behavior ebbed at the same time cultural mayhem thrived raises the question of whether the violence and

Radiating "dent" lines give emphasis to this bludgeon blow.

PLENTY OF MOVEMENT IS DEMANDED IN SCREEN PICTURES.

Examples of cartoon humor. From E. G. Lutz, *Animated Cartoons: How They Are Made, Their Origin and Development* (New York, 1920), 240, 224.

pranks found in books, stage productions, and cartoons played a role in curbing real social disorder. Could the psychological pleasure that men once received from actually drinking, fighting, and playing practical jokes be obtained to some degree by reading about and watching characters doing these things? Perhaps the brutal comedy on display in vaudeville and in the comic strips was part of the refinement of comportment. But it remains an open question whether cultural depictions of unruly conduct actually diminish real violence or only provide a rehearsal for it and perhaps even intensify it. There is no evidence that the ferocious treatment of blacks in popular culture led to less real violence being inflicted against African Americans. Indeed, jolly fellowship may have played a small but significant role in the post–Civil War wave of intimidation and violence against blacks.

In Pulaski, Tennessee, in the spring of 1866 a group of six men gathered to found a social club. All had been in the Confederate army, and four were lawyers. The association seemed to have been originally intended as a burlesque of fraternal orders like the Freemasons in which the members would wear fantastic costumes and the leaders would have preposterous titles. They chose for the club's name Ku Klux Klan. According to Allen W. Trelease, the Klan's historian, "all the evidence" indicates "that the Klan was designed purely for amusement and for some time after its founding it had no ulterior motive or effect." Membership was by invitation, and rejected members were given "the old snipe-hunting dodge" or stuffed into a barrel and rolled downhill. Trelease surmised that "it may be that the playing of practical jokes on each other broadened into playing them on outsiders, especially Negroes." Some commentators have expressed puzzlement how playing jokes could mutate so quickly into menace and coercion, but pranks in the nineteenth century were, as has been seen, often mean spirited, even vicious. The Klan's transformation into a white terrorist group was remarkably similar to the transformation of the Hounds in 1849 San Francisco from a company of men originally devoted to parading "in fantastic or ridiculous dresses" and committing "pranks of a character calculated to amuse the community" to the leaders of a vicious mob attack on Chileans and other foreigners, and it suggests how easily jolly fellowship could be turned to purposeful violence.[62]

If calculated motives could at times be found in the jolly fellows' pranks, may it also be that even obviously instrumental violence was sometimes infused with a love for disorder and senseless destruction for its own sake? W. J. Cash wrote in *The Mind of the South* (1941) that "I do not think it is true . . . that anybody was ever lynched in the land simply because the Southerners counted it capital fun." "Simply" is a key word here, because Cash believed what he called "the old frolic tendency" was, in fact, a key part of the gruesome "spectacle lynchings" of the late nineteenth and early twentieth centuries. Many observers have remarked on the carnival atmosphere that surrounded these events, and Cash noted the "disposition to revel in the most devilish and prolonged agonies," which seemed especially apparent in "Negro barbeques" in which victims were tortured, burned, and mutilated. Lynching was a complex phenomena that encompassed a wide range of motives: it terrorized and intimidated the black population, expressed white sexual fears, conveyed raw notions of justice, was an outlet for white economic frustration, and unified the white community in time of crisis. But is it not also possible to see lurking in the background the sheer elemental pleasure in total power, in inflicting pain on others, especially others of a different race, that has been seen so often in this book? If northern audiences could watch blacks being dismembered on stage, southern whites could enjoy the real thing.[63]

Central to the "old social order" of the early nineteenth century was the constant fighting among both individual men and groups of men. This type of essentially voluntary violence sharply diminished by the turn of the twentieth century. But as the Klan and lynching make obvious, violence remained central to the American experience. Although the connection between literary and theatrical representations of disorder and real violence remains unclear, the cultural importance of jolly fellowship was substantial. It exerted a powerful influence on American culture from its first appearance in minstrelsy and southwestern literature in the 1830s and 1840s to the comic strips and cartoons of the twentieth century.

Conclusion

"As I say, we ain't no New York City or Chicago, but we have pretty good times. Not as good, though, since Jim Kendall got killed. When he was alive, him and Hod Meyers used to keep this town in an uproar. I bet there was more a laughin' done here than any town its size in America," a barber tells a newcomer to town in the opening of Ring Lardner's widely anthologized 1925 short story "Haircut." The tale is set in an unnamed small town and told by "Whitey," the barber, as he cuts a customer's hair. Jim Kendall was the town's jolliest fellow, the prince of the barbershop crowd. Fired from work because he paid "more attention to playin' jokes than makin' sales," he hangs around the poolroom and barbershop, does odd jobs around town, and drinks. His coarse jests in barbershop badinage were unsurpassed. As were his pranks. "There wasn't nothin' in the way of gags Jim couldn't think up, when he put his mind to it." On the coldest day of the year Kendall sent word to Whitey that a man on a remote farm needed to be shaved for burial. When the barber got there, the supposed corpse opened the door. One of Kendall's favorite practical jokes was sending anonymous notes to random men with messages such as "ask your wife about the book agent that spent the afternoon last week." "Of course," Whitey explained, "he never knew what really come of none of these jokes, but he could picture what *probably* happened and that was enough." Kendall's favorite target was Paul Preston, a "half-wit" whom Kendall sent on ridiculous errands to the delight of "the gang."[1]

One person who is kind to Preston is Julie Gregg. College educated and single, she is infatuated with the town's handsome young doctor, Ralph Stairs. Knowing that Stairs is out of town, Kendall disguises his voice and, posing as the doctor, invites Julie to come over and talk. Kendall and the poolroom gang are hiding outside when Julie arrives. She rings the bell and calls out, "Is that you, Ralph?" at which point Kendall and his cohorts burst into laughter. "She pretty near fell downstairs and the whole gang chased after her[,] . . . all the way home hollerin' 'Is that you Ralph?'" Within a few days everyone in town has heard the story—including Paul Preston. A few days later Kendall invites Preston to go duck hunting, presumably to "play some joke on him, like pushin' him in the water." Preston accepts, and once they are out on the water, Kendall "gives the gun to Paul" and tells "him to try his luck. Paul hadn't never handled a gun and he was nervous. He was shakin' so hard that he couldn't control the gun. He let fire and Jim sunk back in the boat, dead. . . . It probably served Jim right, what he got. But we still miss him around here. He certainly was a card!"[2]

Lardner may not have intended his story as an allegory on jolly fellowship, but he clearly understood that Kendall was not simply a unique individual but represented a type of man and a set of attitudes shared by others. Jokers like Kendall were once a fixture in villages, towns, and cities throughout the country. "Practical unkind jokes" such as those played by Kendall and the gang were part of a broader pattern of comportment I have called jolly fellowship. Once, whenever men gathered, heavy drinking, gambling, fighting, and pranks could follow. It was a subculture of some coherence with its nicknames, its distinctive rituals, such as mock trials, and a characteristic ethic, the "two consciences," that united charity toward fellow group members with animosity and often violence toward outsiders. The antics of the jolly fellows in the early nineteenth century were regarded indulgently by the community, but the Second Great Awakening and the spread of middle-class values created, in Edward Jarvis's words, "a moral and intellectual epidemic" that turned public opinion against drinkers, fighters, and pranksters. It was an extended and contentious struggle, but in the end, jolly fellowship was, in most places, as reformers boasted in St. Johnsbury, Vermont, "forsaken or driven into a corner."[3]

Arch Bristow's question, quoted in the introduction, "Why have men quit fighting?" puzzled others as well. What was once routine became rare. It seemed to some almost a transformation in human nature. So successful were the forces of respectability that by the late nineteenth century concerns began to be voiced that moralists had been too successful: middle-class men had become docile. There was a growing confidence among reformers that restraint was now internalized, and so standards could be relaxed without fear that men would resort to two-fisted jolly conduct. This confidence proved justified. After prohibition laws were virtually all repealed in the twentieth century, alcohol consumption remained far below that of the 1820s and 1830s. Boxing was legalized, but individual male fighting continued to abate. The hallowed American institution of the barroom brawl all but vanished.[4]

Kendall's death, Lardner suggests, marked the end of an era. But if "Haircut" narrates a jolly fellow's physical demise, it also testifies to jolly fellowship's cultural endurance. The moral revolution of the early nineteenth century marginalized disorderly male behavior in most places, but jolly fellowship proved resilient and continued to thrive in male domains in cities and the West. The preservation of jolly fellowship in the lower wards of New York City was especially consequential. Manhattan's predominance in cultural production ensured the national significance of jolly themes. Jolly fellowship provided inspiration not only for fiction but for minstrelsy, vaudeville, and comic strips.

Even in the twentieth century, jolly motifs continued to echo through American culture. Hollywood honored the noble gambler, and animated cartoons gave new vitality to the jolly staple of comic violence. In Missouri-born journalist Herbert Asbury jolly fellowship found its historian. His first book, *The Gangs of New York* (1928), chronicled the city's lowlife in the nineteenth and early twentieth centuries. He followed up with a series of entertaining "informal histories" on urban vice districts: San Francisco in the *Barbary Coast* (1933), New Orleans in *The French Quarter* (1938), and Chicago in *Gem of the Prairie* (1940). In 1942 Asbury turned his attention to the virtually forgotten Pennsylvania oil rush in *The Golden Flood*. His history of gambling, *Sucker's Progress* (1938), is still useful. Asbury believed that his readers, who must surely have been overwhelmingly male, would find these subjects as fascinating as he did, and he was rewarded by strong sales.[5]

The significance of the jolly tradition in American popular culture should not obscure its impact on serious literature. The jolly cultural tradition and, perhaps even more importantly, milieus that resisted refinement provided a resource for those writing outside what George Santayana called "the genteel tradition." Kendall is only one of a long line of pranksters in American fiction going back to Sut Lovingood, and Lardner joins a list of writers including George Washington Harris, Mark Twain, and Edgar Lee Masters who drew on jolly fellows for fictional inspiration. Although it may be an exaggeration to suggest, as Ann Douglas does, that genteel nineteenth-century American culture became feminized, it is nevertheless true that women played a pivotal role in fostering respectability and exerted a significant influence on mainstream Victorian culture. Jolly fellowship was resolutely, resplendently masculine and had a vitality rarely matched in mainstream culture—"Gusto it certainly showed, even in its colder moments," Constance Rourke remarked. Its vigorous pugnacity combined with its bracing cynicism about the human condition could be a forceful alternative to polite, churchly, formal America.[6]

Ring Lardner seems to have had little doubt that Kendall's passing was "a good thing." The jolly tradition could be the wellspring of an impulsive generosity and a liberating vulgarity but also of a brutal sadism. I suspect that not too many of us today would spend much time lamenting the end of the era of drunken brawls and vicious pranks. Yes, Jarvis's "moral and intellectual epidemic" brought cruelties of its own. One of the most striking features of jolly fellowship was the consensus that pain inflicted on animals was funny. Here can be seen a change in mental attitude at its most deep seated: what was once comic now causes immediate revulsion. But may there not be greater inhumane treatment of animals today? Does not factory farming systematically inflict more suffering and on a far larger scale than the jolly fellows' haphazard and informal viciousness? It is veiled suffering as opposed to the direct, vivid, pain that was inflicted by jolly fellows. Still, although things like factory farming may complicate the idea that moral progress has been made, few today likely would join the barber in missing the Kendalls of the world. The "colder moments" Rourke refers to were, as D. H. Lawrence well understood, very cold indeed. Jolly fellowship exploited the weak for the benefit and amusement of the strong. People of color, lunatics, and cripples were degraded as a recreation.

The faces on the computer screen are of young men asleep or passed out, faces and bodies painted with magic markers, covered with mustard or shaving cream, chairs and other heavy objects piled on top of them. This is "drunk shaming," a tradition among college men, in which, according to the *Washington Post*, "an individual who has drunk himself into a stupor is decorated with markers, makeup, food and, occasionally, furniture." Jolly fellowship never quite disappeared. Condemned by moralists for decades, scorned by respectability, it remains with us yet, buried, ready to emerge at odd times and in idiosyncratic places. "The standard rule," one shamer told the *Post*, "is that if you fall asleep with your shoes on, you're fair game." Photos are taken and then posted on Internet Web sites devoted to the endeavor. "Drunk shaming is not new," the *Post* explained. It had been going on "perhaps for decades." In fact, it had been going on for centuries. Clearly there are differences. Today's drunk shamers lack the jolly fellows' distinctive viciousness. In the nineteenth century a victim's hair would be cut off and his clothes might be torn to shreds. Victims' faces are no longer literally blackened; today's adornments can be readily washed off. It is a joke, not an attack. Nevertheless the concept behind it is similar—embarrassing someone for the psychological pleasure of others. The Internet, indeed, allows anyone with a computer to locate enclaves in which attitudes the jolly fellows would have found familiar are on display. Witness the popularity of fighting Web sites. These feature mostly amateur videos of, as one Web site promises, "School Fights, Sport Fights, Street Fights," not to mention "Gang Fights," "Funny Fights," and "Brawls." There are practical joking sites as well.[7]

It has even been suggested that the late twentieth and early twenty-first centuries saw regression from civility. There has been a general breakdown of restraint, so the argument goes; gambling, swearing, violence, unbridled sex, and impulsive behavior are rampant. But any return to two-fisted jolly fellowship seems extremely unlikely. Norbert Elias argued that within a framework in which a high degree of automatic constraint has become second nature, a certain latitude is possible without danger of sliding into license. The touchstone for reformers in the nineteenth century was drinking, "the parent of almost all other vices in our country," one temperance advocate called it. Drinking was the foundation on which jolly fellowship was constructed, the prime rationale for male disorder, and as long as alcohol consumption remains as it does today, slightly over two gallons per person, less than a third of 1820s and 1830s levels, there appears scant likelihood of a return of the disorderly comportment of earlier decades. Despite the seemingly growing interest in male fighting in popular culture, there appears to be little evidence of an increase in actual fights.[8]

The search for answers to Arch Bristow's question "Why have men quit fighting?" has revealed a complicated story both about why men fought and why they quit fighting. "The old school of men," the raucous tavern regulars, who were such a conspicuous feature of life in the early nineteenth century have vanished. And Wilbur Cross was right; with their passing, "the old social order came to its end." Yet if jolly fellows disappeared, jolly fellowship never completely vanished. Even after the male milieus that sustained it in the nineteenth and early twentieth centuries lost their demographic and cultural distinctiveness, jolly fellowship remained, lurking around the edges of respectability, offering alternatives, attractive and abhorrent, to a more placid modern way of life.

Acknowledgments

It is a pleasure to thank people and organizations who have aided me in the preparation of this book. Three scholars commented on the entire manuscript. Tyler Anbinder not only gave it a close reading but also shared his knowledge of New York City history and provided me with several useful sources. I am extraordinarily grateful for his support and aid. Martin Bruegel, one of the finest American historians I know, helped me conceptualize the book's central arguments and see aspects of the issue that I had missed. Stuart Blumin was, as usual, very insightful and helpful in his remarks. I thank him. Andrew Zimmerman read several parts of the manuscript, made valuable suggestions, and encouraged me to develop my arguments more fully. Dewey Wallace's prodigious knowledge of American religious history deepened and clarified the argument of chapter 3. Looking back at Nick Salvatore's and Gerd Korman's incisive and detailed comments on the proposal for the book, I realize the finished product owes them a considerable debt. I also thank Peter Buckley for his comments on a paper that presented an early version of *Jolly Fellows.* Timothy Gilfoyle answered my questions about the flash press. I am grateful for the comments of Ronald J. Walters, the reader for the Johns Hopkins University Press. I owe a very special thanks to Robert J. Brugger of the Johns Hopkins University Press, who has been a supporter of this project throughout the embarrassingly long time it took me to write it. I am also grateful to my colleagues in the Department of History at the George Washington University for their friendship over the years. Conversations with Ed Berkowitz, Leo Ribuffo, Bill Becker, Dane Kennedy, Marcy Norton, and Andrew Zimmerman made this a better book.

Librarians at the Chicago Historical Society, the Milwaukee County Historical Society, the New Hampshire Historical Society, the Washington County (Ohio) Historical Society, and the State Historical Society of Wisconsin helpfully responded to my queries. I am deeply appreciative of the interlibrary loan staff at George Washington for fulfilling my many requests. Philippa and Richard Brown, historians of Waterville, New York, confirmed that sociologist John M.

Williams's village of "Blanktown" was indeed Waterville. I thank Kathy Hodges of the Idaho State Historical Society for background information on the "Snake War." I am grateful to Mark Haller for making available to me his unpublished paper on gambling and politics in nineteenth-century Chicago. The Pacific Security Scholarship at the Huntington Library enabled me to research the California portion of the book. Presentations of material at the Society for the Historians of the Early American Republic Conference, the General Society of Mechanics and Tradesmen, and the George Washington University Urban Studies Seminar helped clarify my views.

Onset of Moral Reform by Decade

1800–1810	Peterborough, New Hampshire; Charleston, South Carolina; Henderson County, Kentucky
1810–20	Norwich, New York
1820–30	Irasburgh, Vermont; Concord, Massachusetts; Sturbridge and Southbridge, Massachusetts; Bethel, Connecticut; state of New Jersey; Richmond, Virginia; Selma, Alabama
1830–40	Waldoboro, Maine; Hartford, Connecticut; Trumansburg, New York; Malborough, New York; Washington County, Pennsylvania; state of Kentucky; Marietta, Ohio; Harrison County, Ohio; state of Illinois; Warm Springs, Virginia; Newberry, South Carolina
1840–50	Waterville, New York; Reynoldsville, Pennsylvania; Lancaster, Ohio; Orange County, Virginia; Williamsburg County, South Carolina; Newton County, Mississippi; state of Mississippi

Sources:

1800–1810	Albert Smith, *History of the Town of Peterborough, Hillsborough, New Hampshire* (Boston, 1876); *Witness to Sorrow: The Antebellum Autobiography of William J. Grayson*, ed. Richard J. Calhoun (Columbia, S.C., 1990); Edmund L. Starling, *History of Henderson County, Kentucky* (1887; rpt., Evansville, Ill., 1965).
1810–20	Henry Clarke Wright, *Human Life: Illustrated in My Individual Experience as a Child, a Youth, and a Man* (Boston, 1849).
1820–30	"History of Irasburgh, to 1856," *Proceedings of the Vermont Historical Society*, n.s., 1 (1930): 99–118; Edward Jarvis, *Traditions and Reminiscences of Concord, Massachusetts, 1779–1878*, ed. Sarah Chapin (Amherst, Mass., 1993); George Davis, *Historical Sketch of Sturbridge and Southbridge* (West Brookfield, Mass., 1856); P. T. Barnum, *The Life of P. T. Barnum: Written by Himself* (1855; rpt., Urbana, Ill., 2000); Andrew D. Mellick Jr., *The Story of an Old Farm: Life in New Jersey in the Eighteenth Century* (Somerville, N.J., 1889); Samuel Mordecai, *Richmond in By-Gone Days* (1860; rpt., Richmond, Va., 1946); John Hardy, *Selma: Her Institutions and Her Men* (1879; rpt., Selma, Ala., 1957).
1830–40	Jasper Jacob Stahl, *History of Old Broad Bay and Waldoboro* (Portland, Me., 1956); Edward Thomas Day, *The Andrus Bindery: A History of the*

Shop, 1831–1838, ed. Newton C. Brainard (Hartford, Conn., 1940); *A History of Trumansburg* (n.p., 1890); Charles H. Cochrane, *The History of the Town of Malborough, Ulster County, New York* (Poughkeepsie, N.Y., 1887); John S. Van Voorhis, *The Old and New Monongahela* (1893; rpt., Baltimore, Md., 1974); *Solon Robinson, Pioneer and Agriculturalist*, ed. Herbert Anthony Kellar (Indianapolis, Ind., 1936); *Wanderings of a Vagabond: An Autobiography*, ed. John Morris (New York, 1873); William Cooper Howells, *Recollections of Life in Ohio from 1813 to 1840* (1895; rpt., Gainesville, Fla., 1963); Thomas Ford, *A History of Illinois: From Its Commencement as a State in 1818 to 1847* (1854; rpt., Urbana, Ill., 1995); John Belton O'Neall and John A. Chapman, *Annals of Newberry* (Newberry, S.C., 1892).

1840–50 John M. Williams, *An American Town: A Sociological Study* (New York, 1906); Ward C. Elliott, *History of Reynoldsville and Vicinity* (1894; rpt., Punxsutawney, Penn., 1922); John Sherman, *Recollections of Forty Years* (Chicago, 1895); W. W. Scott, *A History of Orange County, Virginia* (Richmond, Va., 1907); Samuel D. McGill, *Narrative of Reminiscences in Williamsburg County* (n.d.; rpt., Kingstree, S.C., 1952); A. J. Brown, *History of Newton County, Mississippi, from 1834 to 1894* (Jackson, Miss., 1894); Henry S. Foote, *A Casket of Reminiscences* (1874; rpt., New York, 1968).

APPENDIX B

Correlation of Selected Social Statistics, New York City, by Ward, 1855

	Child/man	Age	Proximity	Boardinghouses
Child/man				
Age	−.679			
Proximity	−.845	.902		
Boardinghouses	−.771	.657	.699	
Saloons	−.714	.732	.666	.775

Spearman rank-order correlation (all significant at .05 level)
N = 21 (Ward 12 was excluded, since it was north of the built-up area of the city.)
Child/man = Children 1–5 per men 20–45
Age = percentage of persons aged 20–45
Proximity = distance of ward center from city hall
Boardinghouses = percentage of total boardinghouses in ward
Saloons = number of licensed liquor establishments per person

Sources: Demographic statistics compiled from the *Census of the State of New York, 1855* (New York, 1855); boardinghouses from *Trow's New York City Directory for 1855* (New York, 1854), cited in Kenneth A. Scherzer, *The Unbounded Community: Neighborhood Life and Social Structure in New York City, 1830–1875* (Durham, N.C., 1992); licensed liquor establishments from *Manual of the Corporation of the City of New York for 1855*, ed. D. T. Valentine (New York, 1855). The actual statistics are in Richard B. Stott, *Workers in the Metropolis: Class, Ethnicity and Youth in Antebellum New York City* (Ithaca, 1990), 288.

Notes

INTRODUCTION

1. Arch Bristow, *Old Time Tales of Warren County [Pennsylvania]* (n.p., 1932), 271, 272.

2. Anson West, *History of Methodism in Alabama* (1893; rpt., Spartanburg, S.C., 1983), 568.

3. There are a considerable number of works on disorderly male behavior in nineteenth-century America. The most important include W. J. Rorabaugh, *The Alcoholic Republic: An American Tradition* (New York, 1979); Elliott J. Gorn, "'Gouge and Bite, Pull Hair and Scratch': The Social Significance of Fighting in the Southern Backcountry," *American Historical Review* 90 (1985): 18–43; Elliott J. Gorn, *The Manly Art: Bare-Knuckle Prize Fighting in America* (Ithaca, N.Y., 1986); Paul A. Gilje, *The Road to Mobocracy: Popular Disorder in New York City, 1763–1834* (Chapel Hill, N.C., 1987); Ted Ownby, *Subduing Satan: Religion, Recreation, and Manhood in the Rural South, 1865–1920* (Chapel Hill, N.C., 1990); Timothy J. Gilfoyle, *City of Eros: New York City, Prostitution, and the Commercialization of Sex, 1790–1920* (New York, 1992); Ann Fabian, *Card Sharps and Bucket Shops: Gambling in Nineteenth-Century America* (1990; rpt., New York, 1999); Michael Kaplan, "New York City Tavern Violence and the Creation of a Working-Class Male Identity," *Journal of the Early Republic* 15 (1995): 591–617; Amy S. Greenberg, *Cause for Alarm: The Volunteer Fire Department in the Nineteenth-Century City* (Princeton, N.J., 1998); and Edward E. Baptist, *Creating an Old South: Middle Florida's Plantation Frontier before the Civil War* (Chapel Hill, N.C., 2002).

4. The literature on constructions of manhood in nineteenth-century America is large; see Leonard Ellis, "Men Among Men: An Exploration of All-Male Relationships in Victorian America" (PhD diss., Columbia University, 1982); *Meanings for Manhood: Constructions of Masculinity in Victorian America*, ed. Mark C. Carnes and Clyde Griffen (Chicago, 1990); E. Anthony Rotundo, *American Manhood: Transformations in Masculinity from the Revolution to the Modern Era* (New York, 1993); Gail Bederman, *Manliness and Civilization: A Cultural History of Gender and Race in the United States, 1880–1917* (Chicago, 1995); Michael Kimmel, *Manhood in America: A Cultural History* (New York, 1996), and Bruce Dorsey, *Reforming Men and Women: Gender in the Antebellum City* (Ithaca, N.Y., 2002).

5. Edward Jarvis, *Traditions and Reminiscences of Concord, Massachusetts, 1779–1878*, ed. Sarah Chapin (Amherst, Mass., 1993), 185. There are a vast number of works that treat nineteenth-century reform. Those most relevant to the themes of this study include John Allen Krout, *The Origins of Prohibition* (New York, 1925); Whitney R. Cross, *The Burned-Over District: The Social and Intellectual History of Enthusiastic Religion in Western New York, 1800–1850* (Ithaca, N.Y., 1950); Paul Boyer, *Urban Masses and Moral Order in America, 1820–1920* (Cambridge, Mass., 1978); Ian R. Tyrrell, *Sobering Up: From Temperance to Prohibition in Antebellum America, 1800–1860* (Westport, Conn., 1979); Ted Ownby, *Subduing Satan;* Richard Bushman, *The Refinement of America: Persons, Houses, Cities* (New York, 1992); and Robert H. Abzug, *Cosmos Crumbling: American Reform and the Religious Imagination* (New York, 1994).

6. On the Bowery and the Bowery milieu, see Alvin F. Harlow, *Old Bowery Days: Chronicles of a Famous Street* (New York, 1931); Peter George Buckley, "To the Opera House: Culture and Society in New York City, 1820–1860" (PhD diss., State University of New York at Stony Brook, 1984), 295–409; Sean Wilentz, *Chants Democratic: New York City and the Rise of the American Working Class, 1788–1850* (New York, 1984), 257–71; and Christine Stansell, *City of Women: Sex and Class in New York, 1789–1860* (New York, 1986), 89–101.

7. The sesquicentennial of the gold rush saw the publication of a number of histories of the it and its significance in American history. The most significant are Malcolm J. Rohrbough, *Days of Gold: The California Gold Rush and the American Nation* (Berkeley, Calif., 1997); Susan Johnson, *Roaring Camp: The Social World of the California Gold Rush* (New York, 2000); and Brian Roberts, *American Alchemy: The California Gold Rush and Middle-Class Culture* (Chapel Hill, N.C., 2000). The phrase "New New York" is from Philip J. Ethington, *The Public City: The Political Construction of Urban Life in San Francisco, 1850–1900* (Cambridge, Eng., 1994), 50.

8. Turn-of-the-twentieth-century constructions of masculinity are discussed in Bederman, *Manliness and Civilization;* Kim Townsend, *Manhood at Harvard: William James and Others* (1996; rpt., Cambridge, Mass., 1998); Rotundo, *American Manhood;* and Kimmel, *Manhood in America.*

9. Edmund Wilson, *Patriotic Gore: Studies in the Literature of the American Civil War* (1962; New York, 1994), 509. Robert Darnton, foreword to Jacques-Louis Ménétra, *Journal of My Life*, ed. Daniel Roche, trans. Arthur Goldhammer (New York, 1986), xii.

10. Constance Rourke, *American Humor: A Study of National Character* (1931; rpt., Gainesville, Fla., n.d.), 297. D. H. Lawrence, *Studies in Classical American Literature* (1923; rpt., London, 1977), 68.

11. S. G. Goodrich, *Recollections of a Lifetime; or, Men and Things I Have Seen* (New York, 1857), 265. In addition to offering evaluations through comments in the notes, I indicate my assessment in the text with words and phrases such as "recalls," "claims," and "tells the story."

12. Census Bureau, *Population: 1790 to 1990*, www.census.gov/population/www/census data/files/table-4.pdf.

13. Mark Twain, *Life on the Mississippi* (1883; rpt., New York, 1986), 293.

CHAPTER 1. THE TAVERN CROWD

1. P. T. Barnum, *The Life of P. T. Barnum: Written by Himself* (1855; rpt., Urbana, Ill., 2000), 29.

2. Nathaniel Hawthorne, "Ethan Brand," in *The Portable Hawthorne,* ed. Malcolm Crowley (New York, 1969), 267. William Otter Sr., *History of My Own Times,* ed. Richard B. Stott (Ithaca, N.Y., 1995), 111. "Trade and Travel in Post-Revolutionary Virginia: A Diary of an Itinerant Peddler, 1807–1808," ed. Richard Beeman, *Virginia Magazine of History and Biography* 84 (1976): 176. Thomas Mooney, *Nine Years in America* (Dublin, Ire., 1850), 65. The *Oxford English Dictionary* (s.v. "fellow," "jolly") equates the terms: "*Good or jolly fellow:* agreeable or pleasant companion; usually one who is fond of feasting and good company, a convivialist."

3. Robert Baird, *Religion in the United States of America* (1844; rpt., New York, 1969), 222. Mechal Sobel, *Teach Me Dreams: The Search for Self in the Revolutionary Era* (Princeton, N.J., 2001), 138. Dixon Wecter, *When Johnny Comes Marching Home* (Cambridge, Mass., 1944), 60–72. Wecter believes that this picture of camp life, although exaggerated, contained some truth; see also Charles Knowles Bolton, *The Private Soldier under Washington* (1902; rpt., Port Washington, N.Y., 1964), 227–31.

4. Jonathan D. Sassi, *A Republic of Righteousness: The Public Christianity of the Post-Revolutionary New England Clergy* (New York, 2001), 54–57. *The Reminiscences of Neal Dow: Recollections of Eighty Years* (Portland, Me., 1898), 155. James Draper, *History of Spencer, Massachusetts, from Its Earliest Settlement to the Year 1860* (Worcester, Mass., n.d.), 76. William J. Grayson, *Witness to Sorrow: The Antebellum Autobiography of William J. Grayson,* ed. Richard J. Calhoun, (Columbia, S.C., 1990), 59; Grayson's autobiography was written in about 1862.

5. Although there are a number of studies on colonial taverns, less has been written on taverns in the early nineteenth century. See Kym S. Rice, *Early American Taverns: For the Entertainment of Friends and Strangers* (Chicago, 1983); Paton Yoder, *Taverns and Travelers: Inns of the Early Midwest* (Bloomington, Ind., 1969); and Karen Spitulnik, "The Inn Crowd: The American Inn, 1730–1830," *Pennsylvania Folklife* 2 (1972): 25–40. Sidney I. Pomerantz, *New York: An American City, 1783–1803* (1938; rpt., New York, 1965), 466. Yoder, *Taverns and Travelers,* 28. John T. Faris, *Old Roads Out of Philadelphia* (Philadelphia, 1917), 123; see also Stephen Jenkins, *Old Boston Post Roads* (New York, 1913). Fr. Simon Bruté, "Emmitsburg, 1823," manuscript, St. Joseph's Provincial House, Emmitsburg, Md.

6. On general stores, see Gerald Carson, *The Old Country Store* (New York, 1954). *Spirit of the Times,* 13 February 1847. Liquor sales: Christopher Clark, *The Roots of Rural Capitalism: Western Massachusetts, 1780–1860* (Ithaca, N.Y., 1990), 212, and Kenneth R. Wesson, "The Southern Country Store Revisited: A Test Case," *Alabama Historical Quarterly* 42 (1980): 164. Jasper Joseph Stahl, *History of Old Broad Bay and Waldoboro,* 2 vols. (Portland, Me., 1954), 2:241; this passage is apparently based on an unidentified memoir from the mid-1800s. Theophilus Eaton, *Review of New-York; or, Rambles through the City* (New York, 1814), 53–54.

7. Daniel Drake, *Pioneer Life in Kentucky, 1785–1800,* ed. Emmet Field Horine

(New York, 1948), 188. J. M. D. Burrows, *Fifty Years in Iowa: Being the Personal Reminiscences of J. M. D. Burrows* (1888; rpt., Chicago, 1942), 2; see also Irving S. Dix, "The Country Store," *Once Upon a Memory: The Upper Delaware,* 3 vols. (Equinmunk, Penn., 1987), 1:71–73.

8. Rice, *Early American Taverns,* 72–73, and Martin Bruegel, *Farm, Shop, Landing: The Rise of a Market Society in the Hudson Valley,* 1780–1860 (Durham, N.C., 2002), 32. Women's room: William Brown, *America: A Four Year's Residence in the United States and Canada* (Leeds, Eng., 1849), 14. Daniel R. Hundley believed that southern taverns "off the public highway" received a traveler "once in six months" (*Social Relations in Our Southern States,* ed. William J. Cooper [Baton Rouge, La., 1979], 232). Margaret Van Horn Dwight, *A Journey to Ohio in 1810 as Recorded in the Journal of Margaret Van Horn Dwight,* ed. Max Farrand (New Haven, Conn., 1941), 35, 26, 40.

9. W. J. Rorabaugh, *The Alcoholic Republic: An American Tradition* (New York, 1979), 16. Samuel Livingston French, *Reminiscences of Plymouth, Luzerne County, Penna.* (Plymouth, Penn., 1915), 41. Isaac Weld, *Travels through the United States of North America, and the Provinces of Upper and Lower Canada* (London, 1799), 109. *Missouri Republican,* 12 September 1825, quoted in Laurence A. Johnson, *Over the Counter and On the Shelf: Country Storekeeping in America, 1620–1920,* ed. Marcia Ray (Rutland, Vt., 1961), 35–36.

10. Peter Thompson, *Rum Punch and Revolution: Taverngoing and Public Life in Eighteenth-Century Philadelphia* (Philadelphia, 1999), 40–41. David W. Conroy, *In Public Houses: Drink and the Revolution of Authority in Colonial Massachusetts* (Chapel, Hill, N.C., 1995), 318–19. Walter B. Steven, *The Missouri Tavern* (Columbia, Mo., 1921), 271. Revolutionary veterans: Alice Morse Earle, *Stage-Coach and Tavern Days* (New York, 1900), 70; Gerald R. Baum, "Tavern Life in Upstate New York" (master's thesis, State University of New York at Oneonta, n.d.), 355; and Spitulnik, "The Inn Crowd," 33–34. James Alexander, *Early Charlottesville: Recollections of James Alexander, 1828–1874,* ed. Mary Rawlings (Charlottesville, Va., 1942), 68–69. Harry Ellsworth Cole, *Stagecoach and Tavern Tales of the Old Northwest,* ed. Louise Phelps Kellog (1930; rpt., Detroit, Mich., 1978), 286. Otter, *History of My Own Times.*

11. Rorabaugh, *The Alcoholic Republic,* offers a very thorough survey (61–93); the figures on per capita consumption are on 233, the 2004 average was 2.2 gallons. [Charles Knight?], *The British Mechanic's and Labourer's Hand Book* (London, 1840), 64–66; this emigrant guidebook gives a detailed account of American drinking habits. Henry Clarke Wright, *Human Life: Illustrated in My Individual Experience as a Child, a Youth, and a Man* (Boston, 1849), 107. *Advice Among Masters: The Ideal in Slave Management in the Old South,* ed. James O. Breeden (Westport, Conn., 1980), 250–51. Henry C. Levens and Nathaniel M. Drake, *A History of Cooper County, Missouri* (St. Louis, Mo., 1876), 192.

12. Rorabaugh, *The Alcoholic Republic,* 6–7. *The British Mechanic's and Labourer's Hand Book,* 19. Samuel D. McGill, *Narrative of Reminiscences in Williamsburg County* (n.d.; rpt., Kingstree, S.C., 1952), 45. M. L. Weems, *The Drunkard's Looking Glass,* 4th ed. (n.p., 1816), 4.

13. Arch Bristow, *Old Time Tales of Warren County [Pa.]* (n.p., 1932), 271. *Wanderings of a Vagabond: An Autobiography*, ed. John Morris (New York, 1873), 12. The Library of Congress attributes *Wanderings of a Vagabond* to "John O'Connor," who Herbert Asbury, in *Sucker's Progress: An Informal History of Gambling in America from the Colonies to Canfield* (1938; rpt., Montclair, N.J., 1969), 11, describes as "a novelist of the period." The author recalls growing up in Marietta, Ohio. The Marietta manuscript population census in 1830 shows a "John Morris" but no "John O'Connor." My guess: this is Morris's story as told to John O'Connor. Grayson, *Witness to Sorrow*, 65.

14. Elliott J. Gorn, "'Gouge and Bite, Pull Hair and Scratch': The Social Significance of Fighting in the Southern Backcountry," *American Historical Review* 90 (1985): 18–43. Almira Doty Stewart, quoted in Laurel Thatcher Ulrich, *The Age of Homespun: Objects and Stories in the Creation of an American Myth* (New York, 2001), 402. "Travel Diary of John and Sarah Heckewelder with Their 2-Year-Old Daughter Anna Salome from Cayahaga River to Bethlehem, Oct. 9 to Nov. 15, 1786," in *Thirty Thousand Miles with John Heckewelder*, ed. Paul A. W. Wallace (Pittsburgh, Penn., 1958), 215. Newell Leroy Sims, *A Hoosier Village: A Sociological Study* (1912; rpt., New York, 1968), 87; the village is called "Aton" in the book, but Sims's description makes it obvious it was Angola. Daniel Harmon Brush, *Growing Up with Southern Illinois, 1820 to 1860*, ed. Milo M. Quaife (Chicago, 1944), 57. William Johnson, *William Johnson's Natchez: The Ante-Bellum Diary of a Free Negro*, ed. William Ransom Hogan and Edwin Adam Davis (1951; rpt., Baton Rouge, La., 1979), 123 (4 June 1836) and 398 (13 August 1842). Lizzie R. Mitchell, *History of Pike County, Georgia, 1822–1932* (Spartanburg, S.C., 1980), 28.

15. Charles Comstock, *A History of South-Kingstown: With a Particular Description of the Hornet's Nest Company, and the Cats Let out of the Bag* (Newport, R.I., 1806), 20. James Flint, *Letters from America* (Edinburgh, 1822), vol. 9 of *Early Western Travels, 1748–1864*, ed. Reuben Gold Thwaites (Cleveland, Ohio, 1904–7), 87. George Haydock, *Incidents in the Life of George Haydock, Ex-Professional Wood Sawyer, of Hudson* (Hudson, N.Y., 1845), 4. Paul A. Gilje, *The Road to Mobocracy: Popular Disorder in New York City, 1763–1834* (Chapel Hill, N.C., 1987), 237–40. Michael Kaplan, "New York City Tavern Violence and the Creation of a Working-Class Male Identity," *Journal of the Early Republic* 15 (1995): 591–617. Otter, *History of My Own Times*, 50.

16. George G. Channing, *Early Recollections of Newport, R.I.* (Newport, R.I., 1868), 187–88. Alan Taylor, *William Cooper's Town: Power and Persuasion on the Frontier of Early America* (New York, 1995), 181. William Dean Howells, *A Boy's Town* (New York, 1890), 130. *The Confessions of Edward Isham: A Poor White Life in the Old South*, ed. Charles C. Bolton and Scott Culclasure (Athens, Ga., 1998), 6.

17. *Wanderings of a Vagabond*, 13. Charles Morrow Wilson, *The Magnificent Scufflers: Revealing the Great Days When America Wrestled the World* (Brattleboro, Vt., 1959), 26–42. Albert Smith, *History of the Town of Peterborough, Hillsborough County, New Hampshire* (Boston, 1876), 79. Edward T. Fairbanks, *The Town of St. Johnsbury, Vt.* (St. Johnsbury, Vt., 1914), 161. Bristow, *Old Time Tales*, 209. On the loose meaning of "boy," see Joseph F. Kett, *Rites of Passage: Adolescence in America, 1790 to the Present* (New York, 1977), 11–14, and E. Anthony Rotundo, *American Manhood: Trans-*

formations in Masculinity from the Revolution to the Modern Era (New York, 1993), 356. William Herndon and Jesse W. Weik, *Herndon's Life of Lincoln*, ed. Paul Angle (Cleveland, 1930), 70. Fortescue Cuming, *Sketches of a Tour in the Western Country* (Pittsburgh, Penn., 1810), vol. 4 of *Early Western Travels, 1748–1846*, 137.

18. Tom Parramore, "Gouging in North Carolina," *North Carolina Folklore Society* 22 (1974): 55–63. *Augusta Centinel*, quoted in *Raleigh Star*, 31 May 1810, quoted in Guion Griffis Johnson, *Ante-Bellum North Carolina* (Chapel Hill, N.C., 1937), 42. Ebenezer Hiram Stedman, *Bluegrass Craftsman: Being the Reminiscences of Ebenezer Hiram Stedman, 1808–1886*, ed. Francis L. S. Dugan and Jacqueline Bull (Lexington, Ky. 1959), 32, 33. *The Confessions of Edward Isham*, 11. Hawkins Taylor, quoted in Timothy R. Mahoney, *Provincial Lives: Middle Class Experience in the Antebellum Middle West* (Cambridge, Eng., 1999), 75. Samuel Rogers, quoted in Ellen Erslinger, *Citizens of Zion: The Social Origins of Camp Meeting Revivalism* (Knoxville, Ky., 1999), 99.

19. Gilje, *The Road to Mobocracy*. John F. Watson, *Annals of Philadelphia and Pennsylvania in the Olden Times*, 3 vols. (Philadelphia, 1845), 1:283. Thomas Robinson Hazard, *The Jonny-Cake Papers of "Shepard Tom"* (Boston, 1915), 4. Anne Kathleen Baker, *A History of Old Syracuse: 1654 to 1899* (Fayetteville, N.Y., 1937), 79.

20. *More New Hampshire Folk Tales*, ed. Mrs. Guy Spence (Plymouth, N.H., 1936), 46–47. French, *Reminiscences of Plymouth*, 4–5. *Thomas B. Searight's "The Old Pike": An Illustrated History of the National Road*, ed. Joseph E. Morse and R. Duff Green (Orange, Va., 1971). 15. Stephen Logan interview with John Nicolay, in *An Oral History of Abraham Lincoln: John Nicolay's Interviews and Essays* (Carbondale, Ill., 1996), 68 (quoted in Douglas L. Wilson, *Honor's Voice: The Transformation of Abraham Lincoln* [New York, 1998], 143). *Spirit of the Times*, 6 September 1845.

21. The most comprehensive, if sometimes exaggerated, history of American gambling is Herbert Asbury, *Sucker's Progress: An Informal History of Gambling in America from the Colonies to Canfield* (1938; rpt., Montclair, N.J., 1969). Less comprehensive but more analytical are John M. Findlay, *People of Chance: Gambling in American Society from Jamestown to Las Vegas* (New York, 1986); Ann Fabian, *Card Sharps and Bucket Shops: Gambling in Nineteenth-Century America* (1990; rpt., New York, 1999); and Jackson Lears, *Something for Nothing: Luck in America* (New York, 2003). *The British Mechanic's and Labourer's Hand Book*, 67. Faro: Asbury, *Sucker's Progress*, 3–19, and J. H. Green, *An Exposure of the Arts and Miseries of Gambling* (Cincinnati, Ohio, 1843). Ostensibly an exposé of gambling, Green's book is really a gambler's guidebook with detailed descriptions of faro and other games along with tips on how to win. J. H. Green, *A Report on Gambling in New York* (New York, 1851), 93. F. Vernon Aler, *Aler's History of Martinsburg and Berkeley County, West Virginia* (Hagerstown, Md., 1888), 253. Philip Tone, *Pioneer Life; or, Thirty Years a Hunter* (1854; rpt., Salem, N.H., 1899), 10, 11. Cole, *Stagecoach and Tavern Tales*, 122–23.

22. George Davis, *Historical Sketch of Sturbridge and Southbridge* (West Brookfield, Mass., 1856), 175. Smith, *History of the Town of Peterborough*, 82. D. Thompson, *History of the Town of Montpelier* (Montpelier, Vt., 1860), 129.

23. Weld, *Travels through North America*, 109. Edwin J. Scott, *Random Recollections of a Long Life, 1806–1876* (Columbia, S.C., 1884), 13. Timothy Flint, *Recollections of the Last Ten Years in the Valley of the Mississippi*, ed. George R. Brooks (Carbondale, Ill., 1968), 47. Yoder, *Taverns and Travelers*, 105. Alexander F. Pratt, "Reminiscences of Wisconsin," *First Annual Report and Collections of the State Historical Society of Wisconsin* (Madison, Wisc., 1855), 144–45.

24. The best history of billiards and its social milieu is Leonard Ellis, "Men Among Men: An Exploration of All-Male Relationships in Victorian America" (PhD diss., Columbia University, 1982), 61–125. Weld, *Travels through North America*, 109. *The Virginia Journals of Benjamin Henry Latrobe, 1795–1798*, 2 vols., ed. Edward C. Carter II et al. (New Haven, Conn., 1977), 2:327 (9 November 1797). Yoder, *Taverns and Travelers*, 117. *New York Clipper*, 9, 16, and 23 May 1868. Groceries: Tyler Anbinder, *Five Points: The Nineteenth-Century New York City Neighborhood That Invented Tap Dance, Stole Elections, and Became the World's Most Notorious Slum* (New York, 2001), 191–92.

25. On cockfighting in America, see J. W. Cooper, *Games Fowls, Their Origin and History* (West Chester, Penn., 1869) and George Ridley Scott, *History of Cockfighting* (London, n.d.). Buffalo: Brown, *America*, 15–16. Johnson, *Ante-Bellum North Carolina*, 180. Cooper, *Game Fowls*, 301–4. Cockpits: Melvin Adelman, A *Sporting Time: New York City and the Rise of Modern Athletics* (Urbana, Ill., 1986), 240–43; J. Thomas Scharf and Thompson Wescott, *History of Philadelphia, 1604–1884*, 3 vols. (Philadelphia, 1884), 2:941; Andrew O'Conor, *Forty Years with Fighting Cocks* (Goshen, N.Y., 1929), 118; and Dale A. Somers, *The Rise of Sports in New Orleans, 1850–1870* (Baton Rouge, La., 1972), 204–6.

26. Although it focuses mostly on thoroughbred racing, the best history of this period is John Hervey, *Racing in America, 1665–1865*, 2 vols. (New York, 1944). Richmond: *Racing in America*, 2:12–13. Watson, *Annals of Philadelphia*, 1:277–78. William Richter, "Slavery in Baton Rouge, 1820–1860," *Louisiana History* 10 (1969): 140. *Hillsborough Recorder*, 8 June 1825, quoted in Johnson, *Ante-Bellum North Carolina*, 99.

27. Edward Jarvis, *Traditions and Reminiscences of Concord, Massachusetts, 1779–1878*, ed. Sarah Chapin (Amherst, 1993), 101–2. Hazard, *The Jonny-Cake Papers*, 111. Harold E. Samson, *Tug Hill Country: Tales from the Big Woods* (Sylvan Beach, N.Y., 1971), 147–48. Grayson, *Witness to Sorrow*, 60.

28. Jarvis, *Traditions and Reminiscences of Concord*, 101–2. Comstock, *A History of South-Kingstown*. John S. Van Voorhis, *The Old and New Monongahela* (1893; rpt., Baltimore, Md., 1974), 45. W. Jerome Spence and David L. Spence, *A History of Hickman County, Tennessee* (1900; rpt., Easley, S.C., n.d.), 129. *The History of Waukesha County, Wisconsin* (Chicago, 1880), 689. The chapter "Practical Joking at Tavern Gatherings," in Cole, *Stagecoach and Tavern Tales*, 285–98, contains many other examples, mostly from the 1850s.

29. James D. Pinckney, *Reminiscences of Catskill* (Catskill, N.Y., 1868), 32. "From Turnbridge, Vermont to London, England—The Journal of James Guild, Peddler, Tinker, Schoolmaster, Portrait Painter, from 1818 to 1824," *Proceedings of the Vermont*

Historical Society, n.s., 5 (1937): 261–62. Thomas Lincoln Wall, *Clearfield County, Pennsylvania: Past and Present* (n.p., n.d.), 67. Weems, *The Drunkard's Looking Glass*, 5.

30. There are two works that contain information on the Hornet's Nest Company: Charles Comstock's 1806 *History of South-Kingstown* and Thomas Robinson Hazard's *The Jonny-Cake Papers of "Shepard Tom"* (first published in the *Providence Journal* between 1879 and 1881). Hazard relates the cat story with the same principals but different details from what Comstock gives in his pamphlet—for example, in Hazard the cat buyer becomes the representative of William Gray of Boston, the great East India merchant (183). Hazard's account also contains material not found in Comstock on Gardiner and others, some of whom Robinson knew growing up in Kingston. Hazard's version perhaps came from oral tradition, perhaps from a vaguely remembered reading of Comstock years earlier, or perhaps from both.

31. Barnum, *The Life of P. T. Barnum*, 55. Grayson, *Witness to Sorrow*, 60. Jarvis, *Traditions and Reminiscences of Concord*, 101. Seth Wyman, *Life and Adventures of Seth Wyman* (Manchester, N.H., 1843), 121–22; for other examples of laxatives and emetics, see Otter, *History of My Own Times*, 81–82; Samson, *Tug Hill Country*, 103–4; and Angus Murdoch, *Boom Copper: The Story of the First U. S. Mining Boom* (New York, 1943), 69–70. Jerome S. Buck, *Pioneer History of Milwaukee* (Milwaukee, Wisc., 1876), 123–24.

32. Otter, *History of My Own Times*, 81–82. Jarvis, *Traditions and Reminiscences of Concord*, 102. Carson, *The Old Country Store*, 225. "Turpentining": Carson, *The Old Country Store*, 225, and Kemp Battle, *History of the University of North Carolina*, 2 vols. (rpt., Spartanburg, S.C., 1974), 1:262.

33. Scharf and Thompson, *History of Philadelphia*, 2:985. *Western Citizen*, 10 December 1814, quoted in J. Winston Coleman, *Stage-Coach Days in the Bluegrass* (Louisville, Ky., 1935), 60–61. Henry Fearon, *Sketches of America* (London, 1819), 276–77.

34. John Beekman, quoted in James F. W. Johnston, *Notes on North America, Agricultural, Economical, and Social*, 2 vols. (Edinburgh, 1851), 2:270. Wilson Thompson, *The Autobiography of Elder Wilson Thompson: His Life, Travels, and Ministerial Labors* (1867; rpt., Conley, Ga., 1978), 92. Scott, *Random Recollections*, 13.

35. Daniel Drake, *Pioneer Life in Kentucky*, 192. Roy Zebelon Chamlee Jr., "The Sabbath Crusade: 1810–1920" (PhD diss., George Washington University, 1968). Stahl, *History of Old Broad Bay and Waldoboro*, 241. Drake, *Pioneer Life in Kentucky*, 190–91. Grayson, *Witness to Sorrow*, 27.

36. Comstock, *A History of South-Kingstown*, 8; this was actually a popular saying: see Sean Wilentz, *Chants Democratic: New York City and the Rise of the American Working Class, 1788–1850* (New York, 1984), 79. Heman Bangs, *The Autobiography and Journal of Heman Bangs* (New York, 1872), 19. Van Horn Dwight, *Journey to Ohio*, 48. Charles Augustus Murray, *Travels in North America during the Years 1834, 1835, and 1836* (London, 1839), 220; see also Thomas Hamilton, *Men and Manners in America* (Edinburgh, n.d.), 174, and James Dawson Burn, *Three Years Among the Working Classes in the United States during the War* (1865; rpt., New York, 1982), 69.

37. Comstock, *A History of South-Kingstown*, 20. Cornelius W. Larison, *Silvia Dubois: A Biografy of the Slav Who Whipt Her Mistres and Gand Her Fredom*, ed. Jared C. Lobdell (New York, 1988), 29. Larison was a spelling reformer; the quotations here are from this edition's translations into standard English. Prostitution: Timothy J. Gilfoyle, *City of Eros: New York City, Prostitution, and the Commercialization of Sex, 1790–1920* (New York, 1992), 48, 120, 122, and Clare A. Lyons, *Sex Among the Rabble: An Intimate History of Gender and Power in the Age of Revolution, Philadelphia, 1730–1830* (Chapel Hill, N.C., 2006), 101, 279–81. *New York Whip*, 12 February 1842.

38. Richard Godbeer, *Sexual Revolution in Early America* (Baltimore, Md., 2002), 260–61, 299–339. Lyons, *Sex Among the Rabble*, 183–307. *New York Post*, 26 December 1806. Otter, *History of My Own Times*, 44; the date is probably 1804. Gilje, *The Road to Mobocracy*, 236–41. Gilfoyle, *City of Eros*, 76–82. "Spree": Gilfoyle, *City of Eros*, 79–80; Michael Kaplan, "New York City Tavern Violence," 611–15; and Christine Stansell, *City of Women: Sex and Class in New York, 1789–1860* (New York, 1986), 96–99. Seth Wyman, *The Life and Adventures of Seth Wyman* (Manchester, N.H., 1843), 133.

39. Jean Martin Flynn, *The Militia in Antebellum South Carolina Society* (Spartanburg, S.C., 1991). Edmund L. Starling, *History of Henderson County, Kentucky* (1887; rpt., Evansville, Ill., 1965), 561. Jarvis, *Traditions and Reminiscences of Concord*, 165. Frederick J. Seaver, *Historical Sketches of Franklin County* (Albany, N.Y., 1918), 641. Starling, *History of Henderson County*, 561. John Langdon Silbey, *A History of the Town of Union, in the County of Lincoln, Maine* (Boston, 1851), 386. [Johnson Verplanck?], *"Our Travels, Statistical, Geographical, Mineorological, Geological, Historical, Political and Quizzical": A Knickerbocker Tour of New York State, 1822*, ed. Louis Leonard Tucker (Albany, N.Y., 1968), 46. Levens and Drake, *A History of Cooper County*, 139–40.

40. Seaver, *Historical Sketches of Franklin County*, 639. William E. Schermerhorn, *History of Burlington, New Jersey* (Burlington, N.J., 1927), 103–4. Starling, *History of Henderson County*, 561–67; quotations, 566.

41. On the unruliness of collegians in this period, see Steven J. Novack, *The Rights of Youth: American Colleges and Student Revolt, 1798–1815* (Cambridge, Mass., 1977); Burton J. Bledstein, *The Culture of Professionalism: The Middle Class and the Development of Higher Education in America* (New York, 1978), 228–36; and Kett, *Rites of Passage*, 51–59. Rodney Hessinger, *Seduced, Abandoned, and Reborn: Visions of Youth in Middle-Class America, 1780–1849* (Philadelphia, 2005), 77–78, 87–92. Lori Glover, *Southern Sons: Becoming Men in a New Nation* (Baltimore, Md., 2007), 61–62. Joseph Holt Ingraham, *Alice May and Bruising Bill* (Boston, 1845), 39. David A. Stameshkin, *The Town's College: Middlebury College, 1800–1915* (Middlebury, Vt., 1985), 107. Battle, *History of the University of North Carolina*, 1:261–62. Philip Alexander Bruce, *History of the University of Virginia, 1818–1919*, 5 vols. (New York, 1920–22), 2:277; 2:275–76.

42. Phillips Russell, *These Old Stone Walls* (Chapel Hill, N.C., 1972), 32. George Ticknor, *Life of William Hickling Prescott* (Boston, 1864), 18. Julian M. Sturtevant, *Julian M. Sturtevant: An Autobiography*, ed. J. M. Sturtevant Jr. (New York, 1896),

96–97. David. F. Allmendinger, *Paupers and Scholars: The Transformation of Student Life in Nineteenth-Century New England* (New York, 1975), 108. "One pitched fight a year": Henry D. Sheldon, *Student Life and Customs* (New York, 1901), 113. Lyman Hotchkiss Bagg, *Four Years at Yale* (New Haven, Conn., 1871), 504–5.

43. Robert F. Pace, *Halls of Honor: College Men in the Old South* (Baton Rouge, La., 2004), 82–83. Battle, *History of the University of North Carolina,* 1:578. Andrew Dickson White, *Autobiography of Andrew Dickson White* (New York, 1905), 20–21. Oscar Handlin, "Making Men of the Boys," in Bernard Bailyn et al., *Glimpses of the Harvard Past* (Cambridge, Mass., 1986), 53. Battle, *History of the University of North Carolina,* 1:577–78.

44. The drinking in early industrial workplaces has been extensively documented by labor historians. The classic article is Herbert Gutman, "Work, Culture and Society in Industrializing America," in *Work, Culture and Society in Industrializing America* (New York, 1977), 33–39. Wright, *Human Life,* 129. *Fincher's Trades' Review,* 27 January 1866.

45. Herbert Brokmeyer, *A Mechanic's Diary* (Washington, D.C., 1910), 12. David N. Johnson, *Sketches of Lynn* (1880; rpt., Westport, Conn., 1970), 54. Edward Thomas Day, *The Andrus Bindery: A History of the Shop,* 1831–1838, ed. Newton C. Brainard (Hartford, Conn., 1940), 34. James Campbell, *The Life and Sketches of James Campbell, Paper Maker* (Philadelphia, 1850), 14.

46. Wright, *Human Life,* 135. For other examples of workshop pranks, see Caleb Snug, "The Autobiography of Caleb Snug, of Snugtown, Carriage-Maker," *New York Coach-Makers' Magazine* 3 (1860): 25; W. H. Francis, *History of the Hatting Trade in Danbury, Conn.* (Danbury, Conn., 1860), 32; and Paul Fisher, *An Uncommon Gentry* (Columbia, Mo., 1952), 27–28 (printers). Johnson, *Sketches of Lynn,* 47.

47. John Mason Peck, *Forty Years of Pioneer Life: Memoir of John Mason Peck,* ed. Rufus Babcock (Philadelphia, 1864), 90.

48. Johnston, *Notes on North America,* 2:270. *Searight's "The Old Pike,"* 15. *Statistical Inquiry into the Condition of the People of Color of the City and Districts of Philadelphia* (Philadelphia, 1849), 40. Richard C. Wade, *Slavery in the Cities: The South, 1820–1860* (New York, 1964), 84–90, 146–60. Robert Russell, *North America; Its Agriculture and Climate* (Edinburgh, 1857), 158 (quoted in Johnson, *Ante-Bellum North Carolina,* 559). *Louisville Daily Democrat,* 17 March 1858, quoted in Wade, *Slavery in the Cities,* 86.

49. On slave drinking, see Eugene Genovese, *Roll, Jordan, Roll: The World the Slaves Made* (New York, 1974), 641–46. Sarah Fitzpatrick interview, in *Slave Testimony: Two Centuries of Letters, Speeches, Interviews, and Autobiographies,* ed. John W. Blassingame (Baton Rouge, La., 1977), 652. Abe C. Ravitz, "John Pierpont and the Slaves' Christmas," *Phylon* 21 (1960): 384–85 (quoted in Genovese, *Roll, Jordan, Roll,* 579). Frederick Douglass, *My Bondage and My Freedom,* ed. William L. Andrews (1855; rpt., Urbana, Ill., 1987), 156. Katie Rowe interview, in *The WPA Oklahoma Slave Narratives,* ed. T. Lindsay Baker and Julie Baker (Norman, Okla., 1996), 358. Allen Parker, *Recollections of Slavery Times* (Worcester, Mass., 1895), 65.

50. Larison, *Silvia Dubois,* 104, 32; this book contains Larison's own reminiscences

as well as his interviews with Dubois. Edward L. Ayers, *Vengeance and Justice: Crime and Punishment in the Nineteenth-Century American South* (Oxford, Eng., 1984), 133. Henry Bibb, *Narrative of the Life and Adventures of Henry Bibb* (1849), in *Puttin' On Ole Massa: the Slave Narratives of Henry Bibb, William Wells Brown and Solomon Northrup*, ed. Gilbert Osofsky (New York, 1969), 68. Larison, *Silvia Dubois*, 32. Grayson, *Witness to Sorrow*, 61. Bibb, *Narrative*, 68. *Five Black Lives: The Autobiographies of Venture Smith, James Mars, William Grimes, The Rev. G .W. Offley, James L. Smith* (Middletown, Conn., 1971), 136.

51. Fabian, *Card Shops and Bucket Shops*, 136–42. Green, A *Report on Gambling*, 90–92. *Statistical Inquiry into the Condition of the People of Color*, 40. Jeff Forret, *Race Relations at the Margins: Slaves and Poor Whites in the Antebellum Southern Countryside* (Baton Rouge, La., 2006), 56–62. William Attamore, "Journal of a Tour to North Carolina," *James Sprunt Historical Publications* 17 (1922): 17 (24 November 1787). John Thomas, *From Tennessee Slave to St. Louis Entrepreneur: The Autobiography of John Thomas*, ed. Loren Scheninger (Columbia, Mo., 1984), 66.

52. Lawrence W. Levine, *Black Culture and Black Consciousness: Afro-American Folk Thought From Slavery To Freedom* (New York, 1977), 102–20. Mrs. William Preston Johnson, "Two Negro Tales," *Journal of American Folklore* 9 (1896): 196–98 (quoted in Levine, *Black Culture and Black Consciousness*, 117). I discuss the white stereotype of the jolly black in chapter 6.

53. Snipe Hunting: *Lay My Burden Down: A Folk History of Slavery*, ed. Benjamin A. Botkin (Chicago, 1945), 57. On minstrelsy, see chapter 6 of this book.

CHAPTER 2. JOLLY FELLOWSHIP

1. Trial of Joseph Blakemore, 8 September 1731, the Proceedings of the Old Bailey, University of Sheffield, Sheffield, Eng., www.hrionline.ac.uk/oldbailey/html_units/1730s/t17310908–15.html. Blakemore acquitted of murder but found guilty of manslaughter.

2. Black servants: Alice Morse Earle, *Stage-Coach and Tavern Days* (New York, 1900), 90, 92. James F. W. Johnston, *Notes on North America, Agricultural, Economical, and Social*, 2 vols. (Edinburgh, 1851), 2:270. For a fascinating account that sheds light on black drinking places and dance cellars in early nineteenth-century New York and Philadelphia, see Shane White, "The Death of James Johnson," *American Quarterly* 51 (1999): 753-95, esp. 763–68. C. W. Larison, *Silvia Dubois: A Biografy of the Slav Who Whipt Her Mistres and Gand Her Fredom*, ed. Jared C. Lobdell (New York, 1988), 28–29.

3. Bruce Dorsey, *Reforming Men and Women: Gender in the Antebellum City* (Ithaca, N.Y., 2002), 101. Edward T. Fairbanks, *The Town of St. Johnsbury, Vt.* (St. Johnsbury, Vt., 1914), 159. *Lewis Miller, Sketches and Chronicles: The Reflections of a Nineteenth Century Pennsylvania German Folk Artist*, ed. Robert Turner (York, Penn., 1966). Samuel Mordecai, *Richmond in By-Gone Days* (1860; rpt., Richmond, Va., 1946), 263–65. William Otter Sr., *History of My Own Times*, ed. Richard B. Stott (Ithaca, N.Y., 1995), 74.

4. Gaius Leonard Halsey, *Reminiscences of Village Life and Panama and California from 1840 to 1850* (Unadilla, N.Y., 1902), quotation, 208. Information regarding Unadilla comes from Francis Whiting Halsey, *Pioneers of Unadilla Village* (Unadilla, N.Y., 1902); Shirley Boyce Goerlich, *At Rest in Unadilla, Otsego County, New York* (Sidney, N.Y., 1987); and U.S. Census Office, *Seventh Census of the United States, 1850*, manuscript, Unadilla Township, Otsego County, N.Y., microfilm, National Archives, Washington, D.C.

5. Charles Comstock, *A History of South-Kingstown: With a Particular Description of the Hornet's Nest Company, and the Cats Let out of the Bag* (Newport, R.I., 1806), 20–29. Caroline E. Robinson, *The Gardiners of Narragansett: Being a Genealogy of the Descendants of George Gardiner* (Providence, R.I., 1919), 141–42. Otter, *History of My Own Times*, 123–25. Gilbert: Tax List, 1818, Gettysburg Borough, Adams County, Adams County Historical Society, Gettysburg, Penn., and *History of Cumberland and Adams County, Pennsylvania*, 3 vols. (Chicago, 1886), 3:93, 3:145. *History of Waukesha County, Wisconsin* (Chicago, 1880), quotation, 689. *Raleigh Southern Weekly Post*, 27 March 1852, quoted in Guion Griffis Johnson, *Ante-Bellum North Carolina* (Chapel Hill, N.C., 1937), 99.

6. On Bailes, see Otter, *History of My Own Times*, 102 fn. 94. Daniel R. Hundley, *Social Relations in Our Southern States* (1860; rpt., Baton Rouge, La., 1979), 237–38.

7. Lawyers in politics: Glenn C. Altschuler and Stuart M. Blumin, *Rude Republic: Americans and Their Politics in the Nineteenth Century* (Princeton, N.J., 2000), 97–105. On the tavern's connection with law and politics, see Paton Yoder, *Taverns and Travelers: Inns of the Early Midwest* (Bloomington, Ind., 1969), 95–103, and Gerald R. Baum, "Tavern Life in Upstate New York" (master's thesis, State University of New York Oneonta, n.d.), 171–77, 356–58. Lee Burns, "The National Road in Indiana," *Indiana Historical Society Publications* 7 (1923): 232. Samuel Livingston French, *Reminiscences of Plymouth, Luzerne County, Penna.* (Plymouth, Penn., 1915), 17. Yoder, *Taverns and Travelers*, 100–101.

8. Richard J. Carwardine, *Evangelicals and Politics in Antebellum America* (New Haven, Conn., 1993), 216–17. Ian R. Tyrrell, *Sobering Up: From Temperance to Prohibition in Antebellum America, 1800–1860* (Westport, Conn., 1979), 109. Jed Dannenbaum, *Drink and Disorder: Temperance Reform in Cincinnati from the Washingtonian Revival to the WCTU* (Urbana, Ill., 1984), 146. *New York Tribune*, 21 December 1844, quoted in Lee Benson, *The Concept of Jacksonian Democracy: New York as a Test Case* (1961; rpt., New York, 1966), 198.

9. Michael Grossberg, "Institutionalizing Masculinity: The Law as a Masculine Profession," in *Meanings for Manhood: Constructions of Masculinity in Victorian America*, ed. Mark C. Carnes and Clyde Griffen (Chicago, 1990), 137–38. Edward Jarvis, *Traditions and Reminiscences of Concord, Massachusetts, 1779–1878*, ed. Sarah Chapin (Amherst, Mass. 1993), 102–3. Grindle Reynolds, "Memoir of Thomas Heald," in *Memoirs of the Members of the Social Circle in Concord*, 2nd ser. (Cambridge, Mass., 1888), 63–66. Charles Comstock, *A History of South-Kingstown*, 10, 9. Harry Ellsworth Cole, *Stagecoach and Tavern Tales of the Old Northwest*, ed. Louise Phelps Kellogg (Cleveland, 1930), 285.

10. On the mock trial in Europe, see Robert Darnton, "Workers Revolt: The Great Cat Massacre of the Rue Saint-Séverin," in *The Great Cat Massacre, and Other Episodes in French Cultural History* (New York, 1984), 77. John Dunlop, *Artificial and Compulsory Drinking Usages in the United Kingdom* (London, 1844), 121, 132, 145. Charles Townsend Harris, *Memories of Manhattan in the Sixties and Seventies* (New York, 1928), 32. Thomas Chamberlain, diary, 2 June 1835, New York Public Library, New York City. Henry Bushnell, *History of Granville, Licking County, Ohio* (Columbus, Ohio, 1889), 92–93. James S. Buck, *Pioneer History of Milwaukee* (Milwaukee, Wisc., 1876), 171–72. For another example, see Carolyn W. Baldwin, "The Dawn of the Republican Party in New Hampshire: Impressions from the Journal of Benjamin Gerrish, Jr. of Dover, January to March 1859," *Historical New Hampshire* 30 (1975): 32.

11. Comstock, *A History of South-Kingstown*, 6. *History of Waukesha County*, 651. Halsey, *The Pioneers of Unadilla Village*. P. T. Barnum, *The Life of P. T. Barnum: Written by Himself* (1855; rpt., Urbana, Ill., 2000), 49; Barnum himself was also a Universalist.

12. [Charles Knight?], *The British Mechanic's and Labourer's Hand Book* (London, 1840), 64–73; quotation, 65. Thomas L. Nichols, *Forty Years of American Life*, 2 vols. (London, 1864), 1:133. Otter, *History of My Own Times*. Michael Kaplan, "New York City Tavern Violence and the Creation of a Working-Class Male Identity," *Journal of the Early Republic* 15 (1995): 591–617. Paul A. Gilje, *The Road to Mobocracy: Popular Disorder in New York City, 1763–1834* (Chapel Hill, 1987), esp. 236–45.

13. Comstock, *A History of South-Kingstown*, 18. Barnum, *The Life of P. T. Barnum*, 28–141. Edwin J. Scott, *Random Recollections of a Long Life, 1806–1876* (Columbia, S.C., 1884), 88.

14. Jarvis, *Traditions and Reminiscences of Concord*, 102–3, 105.

15. David Ramsay, *Ramsay's History of South Carolina*, 2 vols. (1808; rpt., Newberry, S.C., 1858), 2:21. Fairbanks, *Town of St. Johnsbury*, 192. J. H. F. Claibourne, *Mississippi as a Province, Territory and State, with Biographical Notices of Eminent Citizens* (Jackson, Miss., 1880), 413–14 (quoted in William Johnson, *William Johnson's Natchez: The Ante-Bellum Diary of a Free Negro*, ed. William Ransom Hogan and Edwin Adam Davis [1951; rpt., Baton Rouge, 1979], 146 [16 November 1836]). *Pug's Visit to Mr. Punch* (Philadelphia, 1815), n.p.

16. *Wanderings of a Vagabond: An Autobiography*, ed. John Morris (New York, 1873), 13. Jonas Heinrich Gudehus, "Journey to America," in *Ebbe fer Alle-Ebber, Ebbes fer Dich/Something for Everyone, Something for You: Essays in Memoriam of Albert Franklin Buffington*, trans. Larry M. Neff (Breinigsville, Penn., 1980), 292–93. James Ross, *Life and Times of Elder Reuben Ross* (n.d., rpt., Nashville, 1977), 49. "Trade and Travel in Post-Revolutionary Virginia: A Diary of an Itinerant Peddler, 1807–1808," ed. Richard Beeman, *Virginia Magazine of History and Biography* 84 (1976): 178. John Langdon Silbey, *A History of the Town of Union, in the County of Lincoln, Maine* (Boston, 1851), 386. Ross, *Life and Times*, 49. Joanne B. Freeman, *Affairs of Honor: National Politics in the New Republic* (New Haven, Conn., 2001), 174.

17. *Bluegrass Craftsman: Being the Reminiscences of Ebenezer Hiram Stedman, 1808–1886*, ed. Francis L. S. Dugan and Jacqueline Bull (Lexington, Ky., 1959), 92. Barnum, *The Life of P. T. Barnum*, 90–91.

18. Drunkenness: John Allen Krout, *The Origins of Prohibition* (New York, 1925), 1–50; Krout notes that "in the middle Atlantic and Southern colonies the lawmakers frowned as fiercely upon intemperance as they did in New England" (28). Gambling: John M. Findlay, *People of Chance: Gambling in American Society from Jamestown to Las Vegas* (New York, 1986), 20–22; *The Development of the Law of Gambling, 1776–1976* (Washington, D.C., 1977); and Johnson, *Ante-Bellum North Carolina*, 185–87, 446–48. Michael Stephen Hindus, *Prison and Plantation: Crime, Justice, and Authority in Massachusetts and South Carolina, 1767–1878* (Chapel Hill, N.C., 1980). Tolerance of gambling: *The Development of the Law of Gambling*, 71, 175, 237–38, 252, 321, 383–84. "Personal grievances": Hindus, *Prison and Plantation*, 97; see also Edward E. Baptist, *Creating an Old South: Middle Florida's Plantation Frontier before the Civil War* (Chapel Hill, N.C., 2002), 231–32. Henry Fearon, *Sketches of America* (London, 1819), 276–77. Unlucky: Roger Lane, *Violent Death in the City: Suicide, Accident, and Murder in Nineteenth-Century Philadelphia* (Cambridge, Mass., 1979), 66.

19. Gilje, *The Road to Mobocracy*, 235–41; Gilje defines a "tavern riot" as involving "at least 15–20 persons for which there is no easily classifiable cause" (256). Paul O. Weinbaum, *Mobs and Demagogues: The New York Response to Collective Violence in the Early Nineteenth Century* (Ann Arbor, Mich., 1979), 35–68. Sheriff quoted in Stephen Nissenbaum, *The Battle for Christmas* (New York, 1996), 92.

20. On colonial American taverns, see Alice Morse Earle, *Stage-Coach and Tavern Days*; Kym S. Rice, *Early American Taverns: For Entertainment of Friends and Strangers* (Chicago, 1983); Carl Bridenbaugh, *Cities in the Wilderness: The First Century of Urban Life in America, 1625–1742* (1938; rpt., London, 1971), 427–34; Richard Gildrie, *The Profane, the Civil, and the Godly: The Reformation of Manners in Orthodox New England, 1679–1749* (University Park, Penn., 1994); 63–83; Bruce C. Daniels, *Puritans at Play: Leisure and Recreation in Colonial New England* (New York, 1995), 141–59; David W. Conroy, *In Public Houses: Drink and the Revolution of Authority in Colonial Massachusetts* (Chapel Hill, N.C., 1995); Peter Thompson, *Rum Punch and Revolution: Taverngoing and Public Life in Eighteenth-Century Philadelphia* (Philadelphia, 1999); Sharon V. Salinger, *Taverns and Drinking in Early America* (Baltimore, Md., 2002); Rhys Isaac, *The Transformation of Virginia, 1740–1790* (Chapel Hill, N.C., 1982), 94–98; and Allan Kulikoff, *Tobacco and Slaves: The Development of Southern Cultures in the Chesapeake, 1680–1800* (Chapel Hill, N.C., 1986), 221–26. Massachusetts Historical Society, *Collections of the Massachusetts Historical Society, 1792–1941*, 1st ser., 10 vols. (1792–1809), 6:226 (quoted in Bridenbaugh, *Cities in the Wilderness*, 272). On male fighting in colonial New England, see Anne S. Lombard, *Making Manhood: Growing Up Male in Colonial New England* (Cambridge, Mass., 2003), 120–45. Wenham: Gildrie, *The Profane, the Civil, and the Godly*, 75–76. James Freeman, notebook, 5 November 1764, quoted in Francis D. Cogliano, *No King, No Popery: Anti-Catholicism in Revolutionary New England* (Westport, Conn., 1995), 28.

Early American Taverns, 111–14. "Horse-play": Increase Mather, quoted in Gildrie, *Profane, the Civil, and the Godly,* 75.

21. Court Papers, Philadelphia City, 2, quoted in Bridenbaugh, *Cities in the Wilderness,* 390. On Philadelphia tavern brawls, see Thompson, *Rum Punch and Revolution,* 102–3. "Kicking, Scratching": Thomas Anburey, *Travels through the Interior Parts of America,* 2 vols. (London, 1789), 2:349 (quoted in Isaac, *Transformation of Virginia,* 95). Isaac, *Transformation of Virginia,* 95–98. Rice, *Early American Taverns,* 100–101. Elkanah Watson, *Men and Times of the Revolution* (New York, 1856), ed. Winslow C. Watson, 60. Thompson, *Rum Punch and Revolution,* 102. Carl Bridenbaugh, *Cities in Revolt: Urban Life in America, 1743–1776* (New York, 1955), 365. T. H. Breen, "Horses and Gentlemen: The Cultural Significance of Gambling Among the Gentry of Virginia," *William and Mary Quarterly,* 3rd series, 34 (1977): 239–57.

22. For the role of drinking places in England, see Peter Clark, *The English Alehouse: A Social History, 1200–1830* (London, 1983). Dice: John Ashton, *The History of Gambling in England* (1899; rpt., Detroit, Mich., 1968), 27. Clark, *English Alehouse,* 233–34. Chester: Joseph Strutt, *The Sports and Pastimes of the People of England* (1801; rpt., London, 1845), 277.

23. J. Carter Wood, *Violence and Crime in Nineteenth-Century England: The Shadow of Our Refinement* (London, 2004), 70–94, quotation, 73. Geoffrey Pearson, *Hooligan: A History of Respectable Fears* (New York, 1983), 188. "Tis no festival": David Underdown, *Revel, Riot and Rebellion: Popular Politics and Culture in England* (Oxford, Eng., 1987). 96. John Harlend and T. T. Wilkinson, *Lancashire Legends, Traditions, Pageants, Sports, &c.* (London, 1873), 145–47. Witney: George Laurence Gomme, *The Village Community* (London, n.d.), 240, 242. Dorothy George, *London Life in the Eighteenth Century* (1925; rpt., New York, 1965), 280. Roger B. Manning, *Village Revolts: Social Protests and Popular Disturbances in England, 1509–1640* (New York, 1988), 193–98. Max Beloff, *Public Order and Popular Disturbances, 1660–1714* (London, 1963), 21–22, 30–31. *West County Records,* quoted in Peter Clark, "The Alehouse and Alternative Society," in *Puritans and Revolutionaries: Essays Presented to Christopher Hill,* ed. Donald Pennington and Keith Thomas (Oxford, Eng., 1978), 58.

24. For the role of drinking places in early modern European society, see B. Ann Tlusty, *Bacchus and Civic Order: The Culture of Drink in Early Modern Germany* (Charlottesville, Va., 2001); Thomas Brennan, *Public Drinking and Popular Culture in Eighteenth-Century Paris* (Princeton, N.J., 1988); and *The World of the Tavern: Public Houses in Early Modern Europe,* ed. Beat Kümin and B. Ann Tlusty (Aldershot, Eng., 2002). Tlusty, *Bacchus and Civic Order,* 128–29. Arlette Farge, *Fragile Lives: Violence, Power and Solidarity in Eighteenth-Century Paris,* trans. Carol Shelton (Cambridge, Eng., 1993), 272. Robert Muchembled, *La violence au village: Sociabilité et comportements populaires en Artois du XVe au XVIIe siècle* (Paris, 1989), 100. Cynthia Maria Truant, *The Rights of Labor: Brotherhoods of Compagonnonage in Old and New Regime France* (Ithaca, N.Y., 1994). Archives départementales de la Haute-Garonne, 11 May 1730, Montpellier, quoted in Truant, *The Rights of Labor,* 117. Eva Lacour, "Faces of

Violence Revisited: A Topology of Violence in Early Modern Germany," *Journal of Social History* 34 (2000): 650. Hazard: Andrew Cowell, *At Play in the Tavern: Signs, Coins, and Bodies in the Middle Ages* (Ann Arbor, Mich., 1999), 82. "Countless tricks": Felix Platter, quoted in Fernand Braudel, *The Structures of Everyday Life: The Limits of the Possible*, trans. Sîan Reynolds (New York, 1979), 234.

25. Robert C. Davis, *The War of the Fists: Popular Culture and Public Violence in Late Renaissance Venice* (New York, 1994). Carolyn Conley, "The Agreeable Recreation of Fighting," *Journal of Social History* 33 (1999): 57–68. Patrick O'Donnell, *Irish Faction Fighters of the Nineteenth Century* (Dublin, Ire., 1975). William Carleton, *Traits and Stories of the Irish Peasantry* (London, 1867), 316 (quoted in Conley, "The Agreeable Recreation of Fighting," 57).

26. Norbert Elias, *The Civilizing Process: Sociogenetic and Psychogenetic Investigations*, rev. ed., trans. Edmund Jephcott, ed. Eric Dunning, Johan Goudsblom, and Stephen Mennell (Oxford, Eng., 2000). Lawrence Stone, "Interpersonal Violence in English Society, 1300–1980," *Past and Present* 101 (1983): 27. The European evidence is discussed in Stone, "Interpersonal Violence in English Society"; Manuel Eisner, "Modernization, Self-Control and Lethal Violence: The Long-term Dynamics of European Homicide Rates in Theoretical Perspective," *British Journal of Criminology* 41 (2001): 618–38; Ted Robert Gurr, "Homicide Trends in Violent Crime: A Critical Review of the Evidence," *Crime and Justice* 3 (1981): 295–353; and James A. Sharpe, "Crime in England: Long Time Trends and the Problem of Modernization," in *The Civilization of Crime: Violence in Town and Country Since the Middle Ages*, ed. Eric A. Johnson and Eric H. Monkkonen (Urbana, Ill., 1996), 17–34. Late medieval homicide rates: Eisner, "Modernization, Self-Control and Lethal Violence," 628–29. Pieter Spirenburg, "Knife Fighting and Popular Codes of Honor in Early Modern Amsterdam," in *Men and Violence: Gender, Honor and Rituals in Early Modern Europe and America*, ed. Pieter Spirenburg (Columbus, Ohio, 1998), 105–6. Eisner, "Modernization, Self-Control and Lethal Violence," 632. Robert B. Shoemaker, *The London Mob: Violence and Disorder in Eighteenth-Century England* (London, 2004), 171.

27. Randolph Roth, "Homicide in Early Modern England, 1549–1800: The Need for Quantitative Synthesis," *Crime, Histoire et Sociétés/Crime, History and Society* 5 (2000): 55–57. Eric H. Monkkonen, *Murder in New York City* (Berkeley, Calif., 2001), 11–13. The uncertainty about the eighteenth-century American homicide rate owes to the fact that most studies rely on convictions and executions, not homicides. Monkkonen, *Murder in New York City*, 155. Southern homicide rates in the nineteenth century range from fifteen to sixty per one hundred thousand; see H. V. Redfield, *Homicide, North and South* (Philadelphia, 1880); Hindus, *Prison and Plantation*; Fox Butterfield, *All God's Children: The Bosket Family and the American Tradition of Violence* (New York, 1995), 8–9; and Baptist, *Creating an Old South*, 233. On homicide rates in the American West, see chapter 7 of this book. Charles Morrow Wilson, *The Magnificent Scufflers: Revealing the Great Days when America Wrestled the World* (Brattleboro, Vt., 1959), 26–42. *Narrative of Charles T. Woodman, a Reformed Inebriate* (Boston, 1843), 43.

28. Elliott J. Gorn, "'Gouge and Bite, Pull Hair and Scratch': The Social Sig-

nificance of Fighting in the Southern Backcountry," *American Historical Review* 90 (1985): 18–43. Bill Cecil-Fronsman, *Common Whites: Class and Culture in Antebellum North Carolina* (Lexington, Ky., 1992), 170–76. Johnson, *William Johnson's Natchez*. Johnson, *Ante-Bellum North Carolina*, 42. Tom Parramore, "Gouging in North Carolina," *North Carolina Folklore Society* 22 (1974): 55–63. *Bluegrass Craftsman*, 32, 33. *The Confessions of Edward Isham: A Poor White Life in the Old South*, ed. Charles C. Bolton and Scott Culclasure (Athens, Ga., 1998), 11. Johnson, *William Johnson's Natchez*, 182 (28 June 1837).

29. G. W. Featherstonhaugh, *Excursion through the Slave States, from Washington on the Potomac to the Frontier of Mexico* (1844; rpt., New York, 1968), 166. Ross, *Life and Times*, 86. Bert Chapman, *"Hey Rube"* (Hollywood, Calif., 1933), 18. Lydia Maria Child, *Isaac T. Hopper: A True Life* (Boston, 1853), 8. Henry C. Brokmeyer, *A Mechanic's Diary* (Washington, D.C., 1910), 12. On the physiological effects of drinking, see William B. Taylor, *Drinking, Homicide, and Rebellion in Colonial Mexican Villages* (Stanford, Calif., 1979), 70–72.

30. There is a considerable literature on nineteenth-century male friendships; see Karen V. Hansen, "'Our Eyes Beheld Each Other': Masculinity and Intimate Friendships in Antebellum New England," in *Men's Friendships*, ed. Peter M. Nardi (Newberry Park, Calif., 1992), 25–58; E. Anthony Rotundo, *American Manhood: Transformations in Masculinity from the Revolution to the Modern Era* (New York, 1993), 75–91; Donald Yacovone, "'Surpassing the Love of Women': Victorian Manhood and the Language of Fraternal Love," in *A Shared Experience: Men, Women, and the History of Gender*, ed. Laura McCall and Donald Yacovone (New York, 1998), 195–222; Anya Jabour, "Male Friendship and Masculinity in the Early National South: William Wirt and His Friends," *Journal of the Early Republic* 20 (2000): 83-111; Caleb Crain, *American Sympathy: Men, Friendship, and Literature in the New Nation* (New Haven, 2001); Jonathan Ned Katz, *Love Stories: Sex between Men before Homosexuality* (Chicago, 2001); and Kenneth R. Bowling, *Peter Charles L'Enfant: Vision, Honor, and Male Friendship in the Early American Republic* (Washington, D.C., 2002). George Birmingham, letter to Henry Price, 7 March 1847, in "The Diary of Henry Edward Price," in *British Records Relating to America in Microform* (East Ardsley, Eng., 1963), 41. Price had saved this letter in his diary; it was discovered after his death. Ross, *Life and Times*, 86; "Unco happy" is Robert Burns's description of the result of Tam O'Shanter's market day drinking. *Bluegrass Craftsman*, 46, 47. Buck, *Pioneer History of Milwaukee*, 173.

31. John Ibson, *Picturing Men: A Century of Male Relationships in Everyday American Photography* (Chicago, 2006). David Deitcher, *Dear Friends: American Photographs of Men Together, 1840-1918* (New York, 2001). *New York Clipper*, 18 April 1857; italics in the original. David M. Halperin, *How to Do the History of Homosexuality* (Chicago, 2002), 118–21.

32. Elliott J. Gorn, *The Manly Art: Bare-Knuckle Prize Fighting in America* (Ithaca, N.Y., 1986), 142. Buck, *Pioneer History of Milwaukee*, 130–31. Owen Wister, *The Virginian: A Horseman of the Plains* (1902; rpt., Lincoln, Nebr., 1992), 16.

33. The attention men in the nineteenth century paid to physiognomy is discussed

in Amy S. Greenberg, "A Grey-Eyed Man: Character, Appearance, and Filibustering," *Journal of the Early Republic* 20 (2000): 673–99. John Corrigan, *Business of the Heart: Religion and Emotion in the Nineteenth Century* (Berkeley, Calif., 2002), 200. James M. Williams, *American Town: A Sociological Study* (New York, 1906), 40. Otter, *History of My Own Times*, 178, 184–85. Tyler Anbinder, *Five Points: The Nineteenth-Century New York City Neighborhood That Invented Tap Dance, Stole Elections, and Became the World's Most Notorious Slum* (New York, 2001), 165, 169–70; see also chapter 4 of this book. Williams, *American Town*, 60. Buck, *Pioneer History of Milwaukee*, 130. Jarvis, *Traditions and Reminiscences of Concord*, 105.

34. George H. White, "Yankee Lewis' Famous Hostelry in the Wilderness," *Michigan Pioneer and Historical Society Recollections* 36 (1896): 305. Williams, *American Town*, 203–5. Caroline Kirkland, *A New Home—Who'll Follow? Glimpses of Western Life* (1839; rpt., New Haven, Conn., 1965), 100. Yoder, *Taverns and Travelers*, 6–7, 33–34. William Herndon and Jesse W. Weik, *Herndon's Life of Lincoln*, ed. Paul Angle (Cleveland, 1930), 60.

35. Otter, *History of My Own Times*, 58–59; for another example, see Thomas Slaughter, *Bloody Dawn: The Christiana Riot and Racial Violence in the Antebellum North* (New York, 1991), 44–45.

36. Otter, *History of My Own Times*, 50, 58–59, 43; the 1806 riot is described and analyzed in Gilje, *The Road to Mobocracy*, 130–33. Peter Way, *Common Labor: Workers and the Digging of North American Canals, 1780–1860* (Cambridge, Eng., 1993), 194–97. Elias Pym Fordham, *Personal Narrative of Travels in Virginia, Maryland, Pennsylvania, Ohio, Indiana, Kentucky*, ed. Frederic Austin (Cleveland, Ohio, 1906), 129. Way, *Common Labor*, 179.

37. James D. Pinckney, *Reminiscences of Catskill* (Catskill, N.Y., 1862), 27–28. Robert Bailey, *The Life and Adventures of Robert Bailey* (Richmond, Va., 1832), 37–38. Scott, *Random Recollections*, 35, 49. Buck, *Pioneer History of Milwaukee*, 127.

38. Featherstonhaugh, *Excursion through the Slave States*, 99. Charles William Janson, *The Stranger in America, 1793–1806* (1807; rpt., New York, 1835), 310. Herndon and Weik, *Herndon's Life of Lincoln*, 41. This account is based on an interview with Green B. Taylor; see *Herndon's Informants: Letters, Interviews, and Statements about Abraham Lincoln*, ed. Douglas Wilson and Rodney O. Davis (Urbana, Ill., 1998), 130. Esther Sharp Sanderson, *County Scott and Its Mountain Folk* (Huntsville, Tenn., 1958), 62. Paul E. Johnson, *A Shopkeeper's Millennium: Society and Revivals in Rochester, New York, 1815–1817* (New York, 1978), 54. Albert Lombard, *The "High Private," with a Full and Exciting Account of the History of the New York Volunteers* (New York, 1848), 41. Susan G. Davis, *Parades and Power: Street Theater in Nineteenth-Century Philadelphia* (Berkeley, Calif., 1986), 39.

39. The literature on the biological bases of human behavior is vast; for a summary, see Steven Pinker, *The Blank Slate: The Modern Denial of Human Nature* (New York, 2002). David D. Gilmore, *Manhood in the Making: Cultural Concepts of Masculinity* (New Haven, Conn., 1990), quotations, 220, 10. See also David D. Courtwright, *Violent Land: Single Men and Social Disorder from the Frontier to the Inner City* (Cambridge, Mass., 1996), 9–25.

40. Charles Francis Adams, "Study of Church and Town Government," in *Three Episodes of Massachusetts History*, 2 vols. (1892; rpt., New York, 1965), 2:795. Horace Bushnell, *A Discourse on the Moral Tendencies and Results of Human History* (New York, 1843), 8. Elias, *Civilizing Process*; for a somewhat similar argument, see Phillipe Ariès, *Centuries of Childhood: A Social History of Family Life*, trans. Robert Baldick (New York, 1962). Robert Van Krieken, *Norbert Elias* (London, 1998), 153–56.

41. Anburey, *Travels through the Interior of America*, 2:349 (quoted in Isaac, *The Transformation of Virginia*, 95, 98). James B. Walker, *Incidents of Pioneer Life in the Early Settlements and Cities of the West* (Chicago, 1881), 42. Gudehus, "Journey to America," 293. Otter, *History of My Own Times*, 175.

42. On self-controlled manhood, see Gail Bederman, *Manliness and Civilization: A Cultural History of Gender and Race in the United States, 1880–1917* (Chicago, 1995), 10–12; E. Anthony Rotundo, *American Manhood*, 55; and chapter 3 of this book. William Otter, boatman John Habermehl, and former gambler John Morris (the last two discussed in the next chapter) are probably the closest thing there is to defenders of jolly fellowship.

43. Shoemaker, *The London Mob*, 154. "I am the man": Monkkonen, *Murder in New York City*, 73–75. New York Superior Court Minutes, 1811, quoted in Monkkonen, *Murder in New York City*, 74. Henry Benjamin Whipple, *Bishop Whipple's Southern Diary, 1843–1844*, ed. Lester B. Shippee (1937; rpt., New York, 1968), 25 (15 November 1843). Johnson, *William Johnson's Natchez*, 492 (29 August 1844). *Wanderings of a Vagabond*, 13. Maria Ward Brown, *The Life of Dan Rice* (Long Branch, N.J., 1901), 55.

44. Baptist, *Creating an Old South*, 133. Sanderson, *County Scott*, 62. Wiley Britton, *Pioneer Life in Southwest Missouri* (Kansas City, Mo., 1929), 307.

45. Baptist, *Creating an Old South*, 103–31. James Crouthamel, *James Watson Webb: A Biography* (Middletown, Conn., 1969), 71–79. On dueling, see Joanne B. Freedman, *Affairs of Honor: National Politics in the New Republic* (New Haven, Conn., 2001), 160–98; Bertram Wyatt-Brown, *Southern Honor: Ethics and Behavior in the Old South* (New York, 1982), 349–61; and Kenneth S. Greenberg, *Masters and Statesmen: The Political Culture of American Slavery* (Baltimore, Md., 1985), 23–41. Dickson D. Bruce Jr., *Violence and Culture in the Antebellum South* (Austin, Tex., 1979), 73–74. Baptist, *Creating an Old South*, 107. Johnson, *William Johnson's Natchez*.

46. Edward L. Ayers, *Vengeance and Justice: Crime and Punishment in the Nineteenth-Century American South* (Oxford, Eng., 1984), 132–33. *A Narrative of the Life and Labors of Rev. G. W. Offley* (Hartford, Conn., 1860), in *Five Black Lives: The Autobiographies of Venture Smith, James Mars, William Grimes, The Rev. G. W. Offley, James L. Smith* (Middletown, Conn., 1971), 136. Francis Comte de Castelnau, "Essay on Middle Florida, 1837–1838," trans. Arthur Seymour, *Florida Historical Quarterly* 26 (1948): 236 (quoted in Baptist, *Creating an Old South*, 204). Butterfield, *All God's Children*, 32.

47. Brown, *The Life of Dan Rice*, 92. John D. Cayton, *Early Bench and Bar of Illinois* (Chicago, 1893), 52–53 (quoted in Timothy R. Mahoney, *Provincial Lives:*

Middle-Class Experience in the Antebellum Midwest [Cambridge, Eng., 1999], 208).

48. On the charivari, see E. P. Thompson, "Rough Music," in *Customs in Common: Studies in Traditional Popular Culture* (New York, 1993), 467–531; on the charivari in colonial America, see *Riot and Revelry in Early America*, ed. William Pencak, Mathew Dennis, and Simon Newman (University Park, Penn., 2002).

49. On the social significance of nicknames, see David D. Gilmore, *Aggression and Community: Paradoxes of Andalusian Culture* (New Haven, Conn., 1987), 77–95, and Mahoney, *Provincial Lives*, 91–98. Edward Field, *The Colonial Tavern: A Glimpse of New England Town Life in the Seventeenth and Eighteenth Centuries* (Providence, R.I., 1897), 192–93. John Jay Janney, *John Jay Janney's Virginia: An American Farm Lad's Life in the Early Nineteenth Century*, ed. Asa Moore Janney and Werner L. Janney (McLean, Va., 1978), 78. J. M. Reid, *Sketches and Anecdotes of Old Settlers* (Keokuk, Iowa, 1877), 11. Mahoney, *Provincial Lives*, 92. Buck, *Pioneer History of Milwaukee*, 170. *John Jay Janney's Virginia*, 113. Mahoney, *Provincial Lives*, 92–94. Reid, *Sketches and Anecdotes*, 11–13.

50. Charles Fenno Hoffman, *A Winter in the West*, 2 vols. (1835; rpt., Ann Arbor, 1966), 2:30–31.

51. Jarvis, *Traditions and Reminiscences of Concord*, 104. Thomas Robinson Hazard, *The Jonny-Cake Papers of "Shepard Tom"* (Boston, 1915), 135. Hoffman, *A Winter in the West*, 2:221. William T. Thompson, *Major Jones' Scenes in Georgia* (1843; rpt., Upper Saddle River, N.J., 1969), 43. Scott, *Random Recollections*, 122.

52. On Banks's drinking, see Scott, *Random Recollections*, 122. Philip Hallie, *Cruelty*, rev. ed. (Middletown, Conn., 1982). *Bluegrass Craftsman*, 95. John M. Roberts, diary, 29 July 1853, quoted in *Buckeye Schoolmaster: A Chronicle of Midwestern Rural Life, 1853–1865*, ed. J. Merton England (Bowling Green, Ohio, 1996), 157.

53. Otter, *History of My Own Times*, 146–48, 99.

54. *Bluegrass Craftsman*, 91–92. Daniel Wickberg, *The Senses of Humor: Self and Laughter in Modern America* (Ithaca, N.Y., 1998), 47–72.

55. William McLaren, "Reminiscences of Pioneer Life in Illinois," quoted in John Mack Faragher, *Sugar Creek: Life on the Illinois Prairie* (New Haven, Conn., 1986), 153. Jon T. Coleman, *Vicious: Wolves and Men in America* (New Haven, Conn., 2004). Mrs. George A. Perkins, *Early Times on the Susquehanna* (Binghamton, N.Y., 1906), 181–85. James Fenimore Cooper, *The Pioneers* (1823; rpt., New York, 1991), 242–50, quotations, 246, 250.

56. Joseph Jackson, "Vauxhall Garden," *Pennsylvania Magazine of History and Biography* 67 (1933): 294–95. J. Thomas Scharf and Thompson Wescott, *History of Philadelphia, 1604–1884*, 3 vols. (Philadelphia, 1884), 2:598. *Niles' Weekly Register*, 11 September 1819. E. Merton Coulter, *College Life in the Old South* (New York, 1928), 95. S. Wilkeson, "Early Recollections of the West, Number 8: Channel of Trade—Western Boatmen," *American Pioneer* 2 (1843): 272.

57. Bill Buford, *Among the Thugs* (New York, 1992), 217, 218.

CHAPTER 3. REFORM

1. Edward Jarvis, *Traditions and Reminiscences of Concord, Massachusetts, 1779–1878*, ed. Sarah Chapin (Amherst, Mass., 1993), 185; brackets in the original.

2. George Davis, *Historical Sketch of Sturbridge and Southbridge* (West Brookline, Mass., 1856), 176. *Wanderings of a Vagabond: An Autobiography*, ed. John Morris (New York, 1873), 12, 17. Walter McElreath, *Walter McElreath: An Autobiography*, ed. Albert B. Saye (Macon, Ga., 1984), 45. William J. Grayson, *Witness to Sorrow: The Antebellum Autobiography of William J. Grayson*, ed. Richard F. Calhoun (Columbia, S.C., 1990), 65–66.

3. Henry Clarke Wright, *Human Life: Illustrated in My Individual Experience as a Child, a Youth, and a Man* (Boston, 1849), 143, 241.

4. Ted Ownby, *Subduing Satan: Religion, Recreation, and Manhood in the Rural South, 1865–1920* (Chapel Hill, 1990). Grayson, *Witness to Sorrow*, 67. Edmund L. Starling, *History of Henderson County, Kentucky* (1887; rpt., Evansville, Ill., 1965), 105–6. On the persistence of southern disorder, see chapter 9 of this book.

5. W. J. Rorabaugh, *The Alcoholic Republic: An American Tradition* (Oxford, Eng., 1979), 233.

6. Jarvis, *Traditions and Reminiscences of Concord*, 185. Robert H. Abzug, *Cosmos Crumbling: American Reform and the Religious Imagination* (New York, 1994), offers a convincing account of the moral reform crusade.

7. John Habermehl, *Life on Western Rivers* (Pittsburgh, Penn., 1901), 44, 36, 189.

8. Arrests: Roger Lane, "Urbanization and Criminal Violence in the Nineteenth Century: Massachusetts as a Test Case," in *The History of Violence in America*, ed. Hugh Davis Graham and Ted Robert Gurr (New York, 1969), 472–76, and Edward L. Ayers, *Vengeance and Justice: Crime and Punishment in the Nineteenth-Century American South* (New York, 1984), 74–87. *Wanderings of a Vagabond*, 13, 17.

9. *Wanderings of a Vagabond*, 17. Stephen Branch, *Address Delivered before the Providence Temperance Society, June 17, 1835* (Providence, R.I., 1835), 15. Mississippi's gallon law: Henry S. Foote, *A Casket of Reminiscences* (1874; rpt., New York, 1968), 264–71, and Christopher Waldrep, *Roots of Disorder: Race and Criminal Justice in the American South, 1817–1880* (Urbana, Ill., 1998), 42–43, quotation 42.

10. Norbert Elias, *The Civilizing Process: Sociogenic and Psychogenic Investigations*, rev. ed., trans. Edmund Jephcott, ed. Eric Dunning, Johan Goudsblom, and Stephen Mennell (Malden, Mass., 2000), esp. 303–12. Eric H. Monkkonen, "Homicide: Explaining American Exceptionalism," *American Historical Review* 111 (2006): 87–89, 91–92. *Ann Arbor (Mich.) State Journal*, 31 August 1836, quoted in John W. Quist, *Restless Visionaries: The Social Roots of Antebellum Reform in Alabama and Michigan* (Baton Rouge, La., 1998), 134.

11. The literature on this subject is large. For two comprehensive syntheses, see Charles Sellers, *The Market Revolution: Jacksonian America, 1815–1846* (New York, 1991), and Christopher Clark, *Social Change in America: From the Revolution to the Civil War* (Chicago, 2006).

12. Important works on early nineteenth-century rural development include Michael Merrill, "Cash is Good to Eat: Self-Sufficiency and Exchange in the Rural Economy of the United States," *Radical History Review* 4 (1977): 42-70; James A. Henretta, "Families and Farms: Mentalité in Pre-Industrial America," *William and Mary Quarterly*, 3rd ser., 35 (1978): 3-32; Christopher Clark, *The Roots of Rural Capitalism: Western Massachusetts, 1780-1860* (Ithaca, N.Y., 1990); Winifred Barr Rothenberg, *From Market-Places to a Market Economy: The Transformation of Rural Massachusetts, 1750-1850* (Chicago, 1992); and Martin Bruegel, *Farm, Shop, Landing: The Rise of a Market Society in the Hudson Valley, 1780–1860* (Durham, N.C., 2002). Kenneth Sokoloff and Georgia Villaflor, "The Market for Manufacturing Workers During Early Industrialization: The American Northeast 1820–1860," in *Strategic Factors in Nineteenth Century American Economic History: A Volume to Honor Robert W. Fogel*, ed. Claudia Goldin and Hugh Rockloff (Chicago, 1992), 29–62. Jackson Lears, *Something for Nothing: Luck in America* (New York, 2003), 58–60. Scott A. Sandage, *Born Losers: The History of Failure in America* (Cambridge, Mass., 2005), 11–12. Cooperation: Bruegel, *Farm, Shop, Landing*, 13–15, 19–23. Jarvis, *Traditions and Reminiscences of Concord*, 52.

13. Bruegel, *Farm, Shop, Landing*, 113–14. *Hudson Bee*, 15 March 1803, and *Catskill Recorder*, 18 January 1828, quoted in Bruegel, *Farm, Shop, Landing*, 92. Jarvis, *Tradition and Reminiscences of Concord*, 56. James M. Williams, *American Town: A Sociological Study* (New York, 1906), 203–5. Christoph Vetter, *Zwei Jahre in New-York* (Hof, Ger., 1849), 160. Caleb Crain, *American Sympathy: Men, Friendship and Literature in the New Nation* (New Haven, Conn., 2001), 149–51. John Corrigan, *Business of the Heart: Religion and Emotion in the Nineteenth Century* (Berkeley, Calif., 2002), 233–35. *New Englander* 16 (1858), quoted in Corrigan, *Business of the Heart*, 235.

14. Sandage, *Born Losers*. On Jarvis, see Gerald N. Grob, *Edward Jarvis and the Medical World of Nineteenth-Century America* (Knoxville, Tenn., 1978). Jarvis, *Traditions and Reminiscences of Concord*, 184, 188, 191, 57–69, 76–99. Jack Larkin, "From 'Country Mediocrity' to 'Rural Improvement': Transforming the Slovenly Countryside in Central Massachusetts, 1775–1840," 175–200, in *Everyday Life in the Early Republic*, ed. Catherine E. Hutchins (Winterhur, Del., 1994), 175–200. Brian Donahue, *The Great Meadow: Farmers and Land in Colonial Concord* (New Haven, Conn., 2004), 227–29. On the greater availability of consumer goods, see Bruegel, *Farm, Shop, Landing*, 159–86.

15. Rev. Joseph Doddridge, *Notes on the Settlement and Indian Wars of the Western Parts of Virginia and Maryland* (Wellsburgh, Va., 1824), 189, 191, 189.

16. Michael Zakim, "Sartorial Ideologies: From Homespun to Ready-Made," *American Historical Review* 106 (2001): 1553–86. Thomas Ford, *A History of Illinois: From Its Commencement as a State in 1818 to 1847* (1848; rpt., Urbana, Ill., 1995), 61. Alfred Henry Lewis, *Richard Croker* (New York, 1901), 44.

17. Stuart M. Blumin, *The Emergence of the Middle Class: Social Experience in the American City, 1760–1900* (Cambridge, Eng., 1989). Richard Bushman, *The Refinement of America: Persons, Houses, Cities* (New York, 1992), quotation, 19. John F. Kasson, *Rudeness and Civility: Manners in Nineteenth-Century Urban America* (Chapel

Hill, N.C., 1990). *Miscellanies by Henry Fielding Esq.*, vol. 1, ed. Henry Knight Miller (Middletown, Conn., 1972), 150 (quoted in Bushman, *Refinement of America*, 89).

18. P. W. Counts, quoted in John Belton O'Neall and John A. Chapman, *The Annals of Newberry* (Newberry, S.C., 1892), 554. Mark A. Noll, *America's God: From Jonathan Edwards to Abraham Lincoln* (New York, 2002), 203–6. Bennet Tyler, *The New England Revivals, as They Existed at the Close of Eighteenth and the Beginning of the Nineteenth Century* (1846; rpt., Wheaton, Ill., 1980). John B. Boles, *The Great Revival, 1787–1805* (Lexington, Ky., 1972). Paul K. Conkin, *Cane Ridge: America's Pentecost* (Madison, Wisc., 1990). Christine Heyrman, *Southern Cross: The Beginnings of the Bible Belt* (Chapel Hill, N.C., 1997). Joshua Bradley, *Accounts of Religious Revivals in the United States from 1815 to 1818* (1818; rpt., Wheaton, Ill., 1980). Whitney R. Cross, *The Burned-Over District: The Social and Intellectual History of Enthusiastic Religion in Western New York, 1800–1850* (Ithaca, N.Y., 1950). Kathryn Teresa Long, *The Revival of 1857–1858: Interpreting an American Religious Awakening* (New York, 1998).

19. William Brown, *America: A Four Years' Residence in the United States and Canada* (Leeds, Eng., 1849), 43. John Roberts, diary, 20 August 1857 and 5 April 1858, quoted in *Buckeye Schoolmaster: A Chronicle of Midwestern Rural Life, 1853–1865*, ed. J. Merton England (Bowling Green, Ohio, 1996), 133, 141.

20. *The Memoirs of Charles G. Finney: The Complete Restored Text*, ed. Garth M. Rosell and Richard A. G. Dupuis (Grand Rapids, Mich., 1976), 102; the original edition was published in 1876. Rev. George G. Smith, *The Life and Letters of James Osgood Andrew* (Nashville, Tenn., 1882), 79. William G. McLoughlin Jr., *Modern Revivalism: Charles Grandison Finney to Billy Graham* (New York, 1959), 58.

21. Bradley, *Accounts of Religious Revivals*, 194. Report of Joel T. Benedict to the Missionary Society of Connecticut, 1814, quoted in James H. Smith, *History of Chenango and Madison Counties, New York* (Syracuse, N.Y., 1880), 344. John D. Post, *The Last Great Subsistence Crisis in the Western World* (Baltimore, Md., 1977). Wright, *Human Life*, 142. C. R. Johnson, *History of the First One Hundred Years of the First Congregational Church in Norwich, New York, 1814–1914* (Norwich, N.Y., 1914), 26, 33–34. Lewis Perry, *Childhood, Marriage, and Reform: Henry Clark Wright, 1790–1870* (Chicago, 1980), 318. Wright, *Human Life*, 141–44.

22. Wright, *Human Life*, 148. Bradley, *Accounts of Religious Revivals*, 197. Wright, *Human Life*, 149. Bradley, *Accounts of Religious Revivals*, 197–98. Perry, *Childhood, Marriage, and Reform*, 99–104. Johnson, *History of the First One Hundred Years of the First Congregational Church of Norwich*, 12, 35.

23. Wright, *Human Life*, 147, 105. Henry Clarke Wright, letter to his father, 17 January 1817, quoted in Wright, *Human Life*, 150–51. Perry, *Childhood, Marriage, and Reform*, 99–104. Bradley, *Accounts of Religious Revivals*, 199, 201.

24. For the clerical establishment interpretation, see Charles I. Foster, *An Errand of Mercy: The Evangelical United Front, 1790–1873* (Chapel Hill, N.C., 1960); for a study emphasizing the role of businessmen, see Paul R. Johnson, *A Shopkeeper's Millennium: Society and Revivals in Rochester, New York, 1815–1837* (New York, 1978).

25. The "Finney revivals" and economic change are connected in Cross, *The*

Burned Over District; Johnson, *Shopkeeper's Millennium;* and Mary Ryan, *The Cradle of the Middle Class: The Family in Oneida County, New York, 1790–1865* (Cambridge, Eng., 1981). Curtis D. Johnson, *Islands of Holiness: Rural Religion in Upstate New York, 1790–1860* (Ithaca, N.Y., 1989), argues that economic interpretations are of limited use in understanding the revivals in Cortland County, New York.

26. Donald G. Mathews, *Religion in the Old South* (Chicago, 1977), 42–45. Richard M. Cameron, *The Rise of Methodism: A Source Book* (New York, 1954), 318–19. Jolly ministers: Charles Roy Keller, *The Second Great Awakening in Connecticut* (1942; rpt., n.p., 1968), 139–41; Heyrman, *Southern Cross,* 11–14; Bruce C. Daniels, *Puritans at Play: Leisure and Recreation in Colonial New England* (New York, 1995) 168; and Samuel Goodrich, *Recollections of a Lifetime; or, Men and Things I Have Seen,* 2 vols. (New York, 1857), 1:182, 1:185. "Licentiousness": Richard J. Carwardine, *Evangelicals and Politics in Antebellum America* (New Haven, Conn., 1993), 57. William Warren Sweet, "Churches as Moral Courts of the Frontier," *Church History* 2 (1933): 3–21. For examples of church courts admonishing men for fighting, see Heyrman, *Southern Cross,* 249, and William Warren Sweet, *The Presbyterians,* vol. 2 of *Religion on the American Frontier* (1936; rpt., New York, 1964), 442. Mathews, *Religion in the Old South,* 42. John Todd, *The Student's Manual,* rev. ed. (Northampton, Mass., 1854), 244.

27. "Extract of a Letter from a Missionary to a Friend in Rockbridge County," *Virginia Religious Magazine* 1 (1805): 233. David Ramsay, *Ramsay's History of South Carolina,* 2 vols. (1808; rpt., Newberry, S.C., 1858), 2:20–21.

28. E. Kirby, "Account of the Revival of Religion in Provincetown," *The Methodist Magazine* 3 (1820): 233. *A Narrative of the Revival of Religion in the County of Oneida* (Washington, D.C., 1827), 24. "From John Lewis, New Diggings, Wis.," *Home Missionary* 17 (1845): 275–76.

29. "A History of Irasburgh to 1856," *Proceedings of the Vermont Historical Society,* n.s., 1 (1930): 110. Albert Hopkins and Story Hebard, quoted in David F. Allmendinger, *Paupers and Scholars: The Transformation of Student Life in Nineteenth-Century New England* (New York, 1975), 119. *A Narrative of the Revival of Religion,* 22.

30. Wilson Thompson, *The Autobiography of Elder Wilson Thompson: His Life, Travels, and Ministerial Labors* (1876; rpt., Conley, Ga., 1978), 310. McLoughlin, *Modern Revivalism,* 58. Noll, *America's God,* 179–83.

31. Ann Douglas, *The Feminization of American Culture* (New York, 1977), 115–18. Heyrman, *Southern Cross,* 312. David W. Kling, *A Field of Divine Wonders: The New Divinity and Village Revivals in Northwestern Connecticut, 1792–1822* (University Park, Penn., 1992), 178. Terry Bilhartz, *Urban Religion and the Second Great Awakening* (Rutherford, N.J., 1986), 97, 26. Long, *The Revival of 1857–1858,* 69–71. Ryan, *The Cradle of the Middle Class,* 83–108.

32. Grayson, *Witness to Sorrow,* 67–72. Heyrman, *Southern Cross,* 235. *A History of Trumansburg* (n.p., 1890), 34.

33. Peter Cartwright, *Autobiography of Peter Cartwright,* ed. Charles L. Wallis (New York, 1956), 248, 71, 254, 248. James Finley, *Autobiography of Rev. James Finley,* ed. W. P. Strickland (Cincinnati, 1855), 253, and Rev. Alfred Brunson, *Western Pioneer: Incidents in the Life and Times of Alfred Brunson, A.M., D.D.* (Cincinnati, 1872),

284–85. Cartwright, *Autobiography of Peter Cartwright*, 213. Jacob Knapp, *Autobiography of Elder Jacob Knapp* (New York, 1868), 95–96.

34. Grayson, *Witness to Sorrow*, 70–71, 68. *Pittsburgh Gazette*, 26 August 1786, quoted in Marian Silveus, "Churches and Social Control on the Western Pennsylvania Frontier," *Western Pennsylvania Historical Magazine* 19 (1936): 124. "Extract of a Letter from a Missionary," 232.

35. Newell Leroy Sims, *A Hoosier Village: A Sociological Study* (1912; rpt., New York, 1968), 87, 145, 146, 147. Further information on Angola is found in Ira Ford et al., eds., *History of Northeast Indiana: LaGrange, Steuben, Noble and Dakota Counties*, 2 vols. (Chicago, 1920), 1:311–17.

36. Sims, *A Hoosier Village*, 147, 146, 100, 87, 46, 54.

37. Ibid., 170, 169.

38. Abzug, *Cosmos Crumbling*, 30–56. Lyman Beecher, *The Autobiography of Lyman Beecher*, 2 vols., ed. Barbara M. Cross (Cambridge, Mass., 1961), 1:179–80. Lyman Beecher, *Six Sermons on the Nature, Occasions, Signs and Evils and Remedy of Intemperance* (Boston, 1827).

39. Lyman Beecher, *A Reformation of Morals Practicable and Indispensable* (Andover, Mass., 1814).

40. Beecher, *A Reformation of Manners*, 17. Joel Bernard, "Original Themes of Voluntary Moralism: The Anglo-American Reformation of Manners," in *Moral Problems in American Life: New Perspectives on Cultural History*, ed. Karen Haltunen and Lewis Perry (Ithaca, N.Y., 1998), 15–39. Beecher, *A Reformation of Manners*, 17.

41. Keller, *The Second Great Awakening*, 141–53. Jonathan D. Sassi, *A Republic of Righteousness: The Public Christianity of Post-Revolutionary New England* (New York, 2000), 140–43. *Constitution of the Schenectady Society for the Promotion of Good Morals* (Schenectady, New York, 1814). *Constitution of the New Jersey Society for the Suppression of Vice and Immorality* (New Brunswick, N.J., 1818). J. Thomas Jable, "Aspects of Moral Reform in Early Nineteenth-Century Pennsylvania," *Pennsylvania Magazine of History and Biography* 102 (1978): 344–63. *Addresses of the Chillicothe Association for Promoting Morality and Good Order* (Chillicothe, Ohio, 1815). Richard C. Wade, *The Urban Frontier: Pioneer Life in Early Pittsburgh, Cincinnati, Lexington, Louisville, and St. Louis* (1959; rpt., Chicago, 1972), 123–24. John Allen Krout, *The Origins of Prohibition* (New York, 1925), 95. Guion Griffis Johnson, *Ante-Bellum North Carolina: A Social History* (Chapel Hill, N.C., 1937), 169. Daniel S. Dupre, *Transforming the Cotton Frontier: Madison County, Alabama, 1800–1840* (Baton Rouge, La., 1997), 156. "Andover South Parish Society for the Reformation of Morals," *Christian Spectator* 1 (1819): 663. *Schenectady Society for the Promotion of Good Morals*, 3. *New Jersey Society for the Suppression of Vice and Immorality*, 18.

42. *Christian Spectator* 1 (1819): 464. Rev. Lebbeus Armstrong, *The Temperance Reformation: Its History From the Organization of the First Temperance Society to Adoption of the Liquor Law of Maine, 1851*, 2nd ed. (New York, 1851), 79. James Campbell, *The Life and Sketches of James Campbell, Paper Maker* (Philadelphia, 1850), 19. Daniel Drake, *Pioneer Life in Kentucky, 1785–1800*, ed. Emmet Field Horine (New York, 1948), 192.

43. Ian R. Tyrrell, *Sobering Up: From Temperance to Prohibition in Antebellum America, 1800–1860* (Westport, Conn., 1979). Krout, *The Origins of Prohibition*. Jonathan Zimmerman, "Dethroning King Alcohol: The Washingtonians in Baltimore," *Maryland Historical Magazine* 87 (1992): 376–77, 384. 250,000: Jed Dannenbaum, *Drink and Disorder: Temperance Reform in Cincinnati from the Washingtonian Revival to the WCTU* (Urbana, Ill., 1984), 60. Tyrrell, *Sobering Up*, 252–309.

44. On temperance in the South, see Douglas W. Carlson, "Temperance in the Cotton Kingdom" (PhD diss., University of Illinois, 1982). Jeremiah Bell Jeter, *Recollections of a Long Life* (Richmond, Va., 1891), 34–35. C. C. Pearson and J. Edwin Hendricks, *Liquor and Anti-Liquor in Virginia, 1619–1919* (Durham, N.C., 1967), 54–92. James Benson Sellers, *The Prohibition Movement in Alabama, 1702 to 1943* (Chapel Hill, N.C., 1943), 23. Louisiana: *Richmond Compiler*, 1 March 1842, quoted in John Q. Anderson, "Drinking, Fighting and Fooling: Sidelights of the Social History of Antebellum Louisiana," *Louisiana History* 5 (1964): 33. On temperance in the Old Northwest, see Dannenbaum, *Drink and Disorder*; Tyrrell, *Sobering Up*, 242–44; Charles E. Carnap, "Temperance Movement and Legislation in Indiana," *Indiana Magazine of History* 12 (1920): 3–38; Joseph Schafer, "Prohibition in Early Wisconsin," *Wisconsin Magazine of History* 8 (1925): 281–99; Dan Elbert Clark, "The Beginnings of Liquor Legislation in Iowa," pt. 1, *Indiana Journal of History and Politics* 5 (1907): 193–212; and Dan Elbert Clark, "The Beginnings of Liquor Legislation in Iowa," pt. 2, *Indiana Journal of History and Politics* 6 (1908), 55–87. Dannenbaum, *Drink and Disorder*, 34. Floyd B. Streeter, "History of Prohibition Legislation in Michigan," *Michigan History Magazine* 2 (1918): 295.

45. Nancy F. Cott, "Passionless: An Interpretation of Victorian Sexual Ideology, 1790–1850," *Signs* 4 (1978): 219–36. Nancy Cott, *The Bonds of Womanhood: "Women's Sphere" in New England, 1780–1835* (New Haven, Conn., 1997). Lori D. Ginzberg, *Women and the Work of Benevolence: Morality, Politics and Class in the Nineteenth-Century United States* (New Haven, Conn., 1990) 13–19. Sara Josepha Hale, *Women's Record; Or Sketches of Distinguished Women From the Creation to A.D. 1854* (New York, 1855), xxxvi, xxxv. Douglas, *Feminization of American Culture*, 90–93. Bruce Dorsey, *Reforming Men and Women: Gender in the Antebellum City* (Ithaca, N.Y., 2002), 38–39. C. Dallett Hemphill, *Bowing to Necessities: A History of Manners in America, 1620–1860* (New York, 1999), 195.

46. Barbara Leslie Epstein, *The Politics of Domesticity: Women, Evangelism, and Temperance in Nineteenth-Century America* (Middletown, Conn., 1981). Krout, *The Origins of Prohibition*, 214–16. Tyrrell, *Sobering Up*, 67–68, 179–82. Ruth M. Alexander, "'We Are Engaged as a Band of Sisters': Class and Domesticity in the Washingtonian Temperance Movement," *Journal of American History* 75 (1988): 771–72. *Worcester County Cataract*, 9 August 1843, and *Norfolk Democrat*, 27 May and 15 July 1842, quoted in Tyrrell, *Sobering Up*, 181.

47. Sociologist David Martin in *Temples of Fire: The Explosion of Protestantism in Latin America* (Oxford, Eng., 1990), 181–82, notes that women understood that Protestantism promoted a form of personality that diminished machismo and domesticated men.

48. Tyrrell, *Sobering Up*, 87–115. Krout, *The Origins of Prohibition*, 182–220. Dorsey, *Reforming Men and Women*, 120–24. Keller, *The Second Great Awakening*, 136–37. Robert F. Pace, *Halls of Honor: College Men in the Old South* (Baton Rouge, La., 2004), 62. Philip Alexander Bruce, *History of the University of Virginia, 1818–1919*, 5 vols. (New York, 1920–22), 3:129–133. Scott C. Martin, *Killing Time: Leisure and Culture in Southeastern Pennsylvania, 1800–1850* (Pittsburgh, Penn., 1995), 92–93. On black temperance, see Donald Yacovone, "The Transformation of the Black Temperance Movement, 1827–1854: An Interpretation," *Journal of the Early Republic* 8 (1988): 281–97; Pearson and Hendricks, *Liquor and Anti-Liquor in Virginia*, 63; Krout, *The Origins of Prohibition*, 189–90; and Charles Tinsley Thrift, "The Operation of the American Home Missionary Society in the South, 1828–1861" (PhD diss., University of Chicago, 1936), 166–68. *Advice Among Masters: The Ideal in Slave Management in the Old South*, ed. James O. Breeden (Westport, Conn., 1980), 252–53.

49. T. S. Arthur, *Ten Nights in a Bar-Room* (1854, rpt., New York, n.d.). Frank Luther Mott, *Golden Multitudes: The Story of Best Sellers in the United States* (New York, 1947), 129–30. Gerald Bordman, *The Oxford Companion to the American Theater* (New York, 1984), 659. David S. Shields, "The Demonization of the Tavern," in *The Serpent in the Cup: Temperance in American Literature*, ed. David S. Reynolds and David Rosenthal (Amherst, Mass., 1997), 10–21. Arthur, *Ten Nights in a Bar-Room*, 51.

50. Judith N. McArthur, "Demon Rum on the Boards," *Journal of the Early Republic* 9 (1989): 537. Arthur, *Ten Nights in a Bar-Room*, 255–56.

51. Joseph Holdich, *The Life of Wilbur Fisk, D.D.* (New York, 1842), 207. *Temperance Recorder* 2, no. 5 (1833): n.p. On the importance of temperance as a political issue, see William E. Gienapp, *The Origins of the Republican Party, 1852–1856* (New York, 1987), 44–60.

52. Horace Greeley, *Recollections of a Busy Life* (New York, 1868), 101. Mark M. Pomeroy, *Journey of Life*, vol. 1 of *Reminiscences and Recollections* (New York, 1890), 65. Ebenezer Raymond Murray, letter to the American Home Missionary Society, 27 January 1831, quoted in Cross, *Burned-Over District*, 131. John S. Gilkeson, *Middle-Class Providence, 1920–1940* (Princeton, N.J., 1986), 33. William H. Bird to his secretaries, 28 February 1854, American Home Missionary Society papers, quoted in Clifford S. Griffin, *Their Brothers' Keepers: Moral Stewardship in the United States, 1880–1865* (New Brunswick, N.J., 1960), 116–17. Thrift, "The Operation of the American Home Missionary Society in the South," 177.

53. John Marsh, *Temperance Recollections* (New York, 1866), 59–64. *Spirit of Liberty*, 9 July 1842, quoted in Martin, *Killing Time*, 92. *Now and Then* 3 (1890): 21–29.

54. *Wanderings of a Vagabond*, 23. Rorabaugh, *The Alcoholic Republic*, 233. D. Griffiths Jr., *Two Years' Residence in the New Settlements of Ohio, North America* (1835; rpt., Ann Arbor, Mich., 1966), 130. Groceries: Martin Bruegel, "The Rise of a Market Society in the Rural Hudson Valley, 1780–1860" (PhD diss., Cornell University, 1994), 347–48; *Spirit of the Age and the Journal of Humanity*, 20 June 1833; and *Temperance Recorder* 2, no. 5 (1833): n.p. Thrift, "The Operation of the American Home Missionary Society in the South," 167. D. M. Bare, *Looking Eighty Years Back-*

ward and a History of Roaring Spring, Pa. (Findlay, Ohio, 1920), 62. Horace Greeley, *Recollections of a Busy Life*, 102.

55. *The Development of the Law of Gambling, 1776–1976* (Washington, D.C., 1977), 244–74, 308–28. Ann Fabian, *Card Sharps and Bucket Shops: Gambling in Nineteenth-Century America* (1991; rpt., New York, 1999), 26–31, 80. *Second Annual Report of the New York Association for the Suppression of Gambling* (New York, 1852), 16–17. Herbert Asbury, *Sucker's Progress: An Informal History of Gambling in America from the Colonies to Canfield* (1938; rpt., Montclair, N.J., 1969), 191–96.

56. *Memphis Appeal*, quoted in *Spirit of the Times*, 16 March 1844.

57. T. S. Arthur, *Advice to Young Men on Their Duties and Conduct in Life* (Boston, 1847), 117, 77. Michael Kimmel, *Manhood in America: A Cultural History* (New York, 1996), 44–50. Hemphill, *Bowing to Necessities*, 84–85. Elaine Franz Parsons, *Manhood Lost: Fallen Drunkards and Redeeming Women in the Nineteenth-Century United States* (Baltimore, Md., 2003), 64–66. Maria J. McIntosh, *Conquest and Self-Conquest; or, Which Makes the Hero?* (New York, 1843), 20–22, 31, 40–45.

58. John Todd, *The Young Man*, 2nd ed. (Northampton, Mass., 1845), 157. Frederick A. Flickhardt, "History of the Sons of Temperance," in *The Sons of Temperance Offering for 1851*, ed. T. S. Arthur (New York, 1850), 309. "System": Richard D. Brown, *Modernization: The Transformation of American Life 1600–1865* (Prospect Heights, Ill. 1976), 101–8, and Stuart M. Blumin, *The Emergence of the Middle Class*, 121–32. Rodney Hessinger, *Seduced, Abandoned, and Reborn: Visions of Youth in Middle-Class America, 1780–1850* (Philadelphia, 2005), 141–42. Dorsey, *Reforming Men and Women*, 106–7. Flickhardt, "History of the Sons of Temperance," 309. "Leads a sporting life": Mercantile Agency report in Ryan, *The Cradle of the Middle Class*, 141. "Too fond of a spree": credit report in Sandage, *Born Losers*, 151. Stuart M. Blumin, *The Urban Threshold: Growth and Change in a Nineteenth-Century American Community* (Chicago, 1976), 209.

59. Henry C. Noble, diary, 4 December 1831, quoted in Francis Whiting Halsey, *Pioneers of Unadilla Village* (Unadilla, N.Y., 1902), 167.

60. Henry Walter, "An Autobiography of an English Tramp from 1812 to 1888 Inclusive." I thank Professor Jane W. Torrey for permission to quote from this document.

61. Greeley, *Recollections of a Busy Life*, 102. "Men away from home": Habermehl, *Life on Western Rivers*, 188, and George Devol, *Forty Years a Gambler on the Mississippi* (1887; rpt., Bedford, Mass., n.d.), 148. William Otter Sr., *History of My Own Times*, ed. Richard B. Stott (Ithaca, N.Y., 1995).

62. "The Diary of an Apprentice Cabinetmaker: Edward Jenner Carpenter's 'Journal,' 1844–1845," ed. Christopher Clark, *Proceedings of the American Antiquarian Society* 98 (1988): 303–94, quotations, 330 (18 April 1844), 334 (13 May 1844).

63. Roberts, diary, 15 and 27 October 1858, quoted in *Buckeye Schoolmaster*, 157, 150. A similar ambivalence is found in the diary of the devout and temperate Virginia farmer Daniel W. Cobb, whose diary is printed in Daniel W. Crofts, *Old Southampton: Politics and Society in a Virginia County, 1834–1869* (Charlottesville, Va., 1982). Cobb was clearly fascinated by male mayhem—his diary contains detailed descriptions of duels and brawls. Crofts argues that the descriptions in the diary were

a way of sharing in the pleasures of such disorderly behavior while maintaining self control.

64. Edward T. Fairbanks, *The Town of St. Johnsbury, Vt.* (St. Johnsbury, Vt., 1914), 132.

65. Emmanuel Le Roy Ladurie, *The Peasants of Languedoc*, trans, John Day (Urbana, Ill., 1974), 307–9. On "civilizing spurts" see Elias, *Civilizing Process*, 157–58.

66. "Moral revolution": Anson West, *History of Methodism in Alabama* (1893; rpt., Spartanburg, S.C., 1983), 568.

67. William A. Alcott, *The Young Man's Guide* (Boston, 1836), 314. For the classic "evil city" argument, see Todd, *The Young Man*, 120–27. Calvin Colton, *History and Character of American Revivals of Religion* (London, 1832; rpt., New York, 1973), 18. Paul Boyer, *Urban Masses and Moral Order in America, 1820–1920* (Cambridge, Mass., 1978).

68. *Knickerbocker* 7 (1836): 537–39 (quoted in Bayrd Still, *Urban America: A History With Documents* [Boston, 1974], 195). *Evangelist and Religious Review*, 14 April 1859, quoted in Corrigan, *Business of the Heart*, 47. Charles I. Foster, "The Urban Missionary Movement," *Pennsylvania Magazine of History and Biography* 75 (1951): 47–65.

69. Timothy Dwight, *Travels in New England and New York*, 4 vols., ed. Barbara Miller Solomon (Cambridge, Mass., 1969), 2:162. Rush Welter, "The Frontier West as Image of American Society: Conservative Attitudes Before the Civil War," *Mississippi Valley Historical Review* 46 (1960): 593–614. Lyman Beecher, *A Plea for the West* (1835; rpt., New York, 1977), 11. James L. Batchelder, *The United States, the West, and the State of Ohio, as Missionary Fields* (Cincinnati, Ohio, 1848), 43. Foster, *An Errand of Mercy*, 192–206. Colin Brummitt Goodykoontz, *Home Missions on the American Frontier* (Caldwell, Ohio, 1939).

CHAPTER 4. NEW YORK

1. Horace Greeley, *Recollections of a Busy Life* (New York, 1868), 102.

2. *Wanderings of a Vagabond*, ed. John Morris (New York, 1873), 12. John Habermehl, *Life on Western Rivers* (Pittsburgh, Penn., 1901), 36.

3. Robert E. Park, "The City: Suggestions for the Investigation of Human Behavior in an Urban Environment," in Robert E. Park, Ernest W. Burgess and Roderick D. McKenzie, *The City* (1925; rpt., Chicago, 1967), 44–46.

4. Greeley, *Recollections of a Busy Life*, 102. Habermehl, *Life on Western Rivers*, 36. William Otter Sr., *History of My Own Times*, ed. Richard B. Stott (Ithaca, 1995), 179.

5. Robert E. Park, "The City," 44. Herbert Gutman, "Work, Culture and Society in Industrializing America, 1815–19191," in *Work, Culture and Society in Industrializing America: Essays in American Working-Class History* (New York, 1976), esp. 32–54.

6. Paul A. Gilje, *Liberty on the Waterfront: American Maritime Culture in the Age of Revolution* (Philadelphia, 2004). Kenneth A. Scherzer, *The Unbounded Community: Neighborhood Life and Social Structure in New York City, 1830–1875* (Durham,

N.C., 1992), 97–119. U.S. Census Office, *Seventh Census of the United States, 1850* (Washington, D.C., 1850), 88–91. A sample of the city's lower-ward boarders from the 1850 manuscript census showed that 80 percent were men, the great majority aged eighteen to thirty, nearly all single (U.S. Census Office, Seventh Census of the United States, 1850, Manuscript Population Schedules, Wards, Two, Four and Seven, New York City, National Archives, Washington, D.C.). The forty-five boardinghouses in the sample housed 698 individuals, 558 men and 140 women; of the men 535 were single. Most were skilled; unskilled workers usually could not afford to pay boardinghouse rents and lodged with private families. Howard Chudacoff, *The Age of the Bachelor: Creating an American Subculture* (Princeton, N.J., 1999). *New York Dissected by Walt Whitman*, ed. Emory Holloway and Ralph Adimain (New York, 1936), 96.

7. Wendy Gamber, *The Boarding-House in Nineteenth-America* (Baltimore, Md., 2007). "Wild oats": Fannie Benedict, "Boardinghouse Experience in New York," *Packard's Monthly*, n.s., 1 (1869): 103. Thomas Gunn, *The Physiology of New York Boardinghouses* (New York, 1857), 196, 202. G. W. Sheldon, "The Old Ship-Builders of New York," *Harper's New Monthly Magazine* 65 (1882): 234. Boardinghouse humor: Harry B. Weiss, "A Brief History of American Jest Books," *New York Public Library Bulletin* 47 (1943): 285, and Robert Toll, *Blacking Up: The Minstrel Show in Nineteenth-Century America* (New York, 1974), 181.

8. [Charles Knight?], *The British Mechanic's and Labourer's Hand Book* (London, 1840), 63. On the gendered geography of nineteenth-century cities, see Richard B. Stott, *Workers in the Metropolis: Class, Ethnicity, and Youth in Antebellum New York City* (Ithaca, N.Y., 1990), 204–11, 214–35, and Sarah Deutsch, *Women and the City: Gender, Space and Power in Boston, 1870–1940* (Oxford, Eng., 2000).

9. Alvin F. Harlow, *Old Bowery Days: Chronicles of a Famous Street* (New York, 1931), 174, 216. Sean Wilentz, *Chants Democratic: New York City and the Rise of the American Working Class, 1788–1850* (New York, 1984), 257–71. Cornelius Mathews, *A Pen-and-Ink Panorama of New-York City* (New York, 1853), 124. Junius Henri Browne, *The Great Metropolis: A Mirror of New York* (1869; rpt., New York, 1975), 128. *National Police Gazette*, 6 December 1879. George G. Foster, *New York in Slices: By an Experienced Carver* (New York, 1849), 121. Foster, *New York in Slices*, 120.

10. Francis McLean, "Bowery Amusements," in *University Settlement Society Report for the Year 1899* (New York, 1900), 14, 89–92. On excursions to the Bowery by nonworkers, see Charles H. Haswell, *Reminiscences of an Octogenarian in the City of New York* (New York, 1897), 354–55, and Browne, *The Great Metropolis*, 327. Christine Stansell, *City of Women: Sex and Class in New York, 1789–1860* (New York, 1986), 89–92. Timothy J. Gilfoyle, *City of Eros: New York City, Prostitution, and the Commercialization of Sex, 1790–1920* (New York, 1992), 31–33, 199–202. George G. Foster, *New York by Gas-Light, and Other Urban Sketches*, ed. Stuart M. Blumin (Ithaca, N.Y., 1990), 154–55. Claudia D. Johnson, "That Guilty Third Tier: Prostitution in Nineteenth-Century American Theaters," in *Victorian America*, ed. Daniel Walker Howe (Philadelphia, 1976), 111–20.

11. Mathews, *A Pen-and-Ink Panorama*, 127–29.

12. Roy L. McCardell, "When the Bowery was in Bloom," *Saturday Evening Post*,

19 December 1925, 87. Gabriel Furman, "The Customs, Amusements, Style of Living, and Manners of the People from the First Settlement to the Present Time," Ms. 2673, typescript, 303–5, New York Historical Society, New York City; Furman wrote this piece in about 1844. Paul A. Gilje, *The Road to Mobocracy: Popular Disorder in New York City, 1763–1834* (Chapel Hill, N.C., 1987), 256–60. Browne, *The Great Metropolis*, 131. On Bowery fighting, see also Cornelius W. Willemse, *A Cop Remembers* (New York, 1933), 35.

13. Emma Jones Lapansky, "South Street Philadelphia, 1762–1865: 'A Haven for Those Low in the World'" (PhD diss. University of Pennsylvania, 1975), 166–72. Harry Silcox, *Philadelphia Politics from the Bottom Up: The Life of Irishman William McMullen, 1824–1901* (Philadelphia, 1989), quotation, 34. George G. Foster, "Philadelphia in Slices," *New York Tribune*, 30 October 1848, reprinted in *Pennsylvania Magazine of History and Biography* 93 (1969): 47–48. David R. Johnson, *Policing the Urban Underworld: The Impact of Crime on the Development of the American Police, 1800–1887* (Philadelphia, 1979), 73–89.

14. Herbert Asbury, *Gem of the Prairie: An Informal History of the Chicago Underworld* (1940; rpt., DeKalb, Ill., 1986), 57, 58, 61–62, 122, 246–47, 276–319. Mark Haller, "Gambling, Politics, and Neighborhood Change in Chicago: The Civil War to World War I," unpublished paper; my thanks to Professor Haller for making this available to me. Asbury, *Gem of the Prairie*, 95–176. "Wide open": *Chicago Tribune*, 8 August 1907. Twenty gambling halls: Johnson, *Policing the Urban Underworld*, 160. On "the Store" and McDonald, see chapter 8 of this book. *National Police Gazette*, 17 April 1880. Asbury, *Gem of the Prairie*, 123–29, 242–319. "Drug stores, blacksmith shops": Charles Washburn, *Come into My Parlor: A Biography of the Aristocratic Everleigh Sisters of Chicago* (New York, 1943), 120.

15. *Dictionary of American Regional Usage*, ed. Frederic Gomes Cassidy (Cambridge, Mass., 1985), s.v. "bhoy." *I'm a B'hoy* (Philadelphia, n.d.), American Songs and Ballads, Rare Books and Special Collections, Library of Congress, Washington, D.C. (Spring Garden was incorporated into Philadelphia in 1854.) Foster, "Philadelphia in Slices," 35. William T. Thompson, *Major Jones' Sketches of Travel* (Philadelphia, 1848), 78 (quoted in Richard H. Thornton, *An American Glossary* [1912; rpt., New York, 1962], 58); Fell's Point is a Baltimore neighborhood. *St Louis Reveille*, 25 March 1847, reprinted in *Old Southwest Humor from the St. Louis Reveille, 1844–1850*, ed. Fritz Oehlschlaeger (Columbia, Mo., 1990), 45. *The Diaries of Peter Decker: Overland to California in 1849, and Life in the Mines, 1850–1851*, ed. Helen S. Giffen (Georgetown, Calif., 1966), 81.

16. William Duer, *Reminiscences of an Old Yorker* (New York, 1867), 31–32. Charles Dance, *Beulah Spa; or, The Two B'hoys* (New York, 1833). George C. D. Odell, *Annals of the New York Stage*, 15 vols. (New York, 1927–49), 4:28 and 5:274, 5:363, 5:448, 5:369, 5:561. Benjamin A. Baker, *A Glance at New York* (New York, 1857). Foster, *New York in Slices*, 43–47.

17. On the genesis of *A Glance at New York*, see David L. Rinear, "F. S. Chanfrau's Mose: The Rise and Fall of an Urban Folk-Hero," *Theatre Journal* 33 (1981): 199-212; *New York Clipper*, 6 April 1878; and Frank Chanfrau and Benjamin Baker

folders, Harvard Theatre Collection, Houghton Library, Harvard University, Cambridge, Mass. Peter G. Buckley, "On Urban Types: Comic and Social, from Egan to Mayhew," in *Cities and Markets: Studies in the Organization of Human Space*, ed. Rondo Cameron and Leo Schnore (Lanham, Md., 1997), 329–39. *A Glance at New York*, 15, 18, 20.

18. Odell, *Annals of the New York Stage*, 5:364. William K. Northall, *Before and Behind the Curtain* (New York, 1851), 91. *Union Jack*, 16 September 1848, quoted in Richard M. Dorson, "Mose, the Far-Famed and World Renowned," *American Literature* 15 (1943): 290, 293–97, 299; some of these were probably sketches rather than full-length plays. William Dean Howells, *Years of My Youth and Three Essays*, ed. David J. Nordloh (Bloomington, Ind., 1975), 32.

19. Jay Monaghan, *The Great Rascal: The Exploits of the Amazing Ned Buntline* (New York, 1951), 147–56, 168. Ned Buntline, *The Mysteries and Miseries of New York: A Story of Real Life* (New York, 1848). Mathews, *A Pen-and-Ink Panorama*, 138. Northall, *Before and Behind the Curtain*, 129.

20. On Foster's background and career, see Stuart M. Blumin, "George G. Foster and the Emerging Metropolis," in Foster, *New York by Gas-Light*, 1–63. Adrienne Segal, *The Image of the City in Popular Literature* (Port Washington, N.Y., 1981). Foster, *New York by Gas-Light*, 169. On Foster's taxonomy of New York society, see Stuart M. Blumin, "Exploring the New Metropolis: Perception, Depiction and Analysis in Mid-Nineteenth-Century New York," *Journal of Urban History* 11 (1984): 9–38.

21. Foster describes the b'hoy in *New York in Slices*, 43–46, and *New York by Gas-Light*, 169–77. Foster, *New York in Slices*, 45. Foster, *New York by Gas-Light*, 175–76.

22. Soaplocks: John M. Todd, *Sketches of the Life of John M. Todd (Sixty-two Years in a Barber Shop)* (Portland, Me., 1906), 300, and John Herbert Clairborne, *Seventy-five Years in Old Virginia* (New York, 1904), 26–27. Buckley, "On Urban Types." David M. Henkin, *City Reading: Written Words and Public Space in Antebellum New York* (New York, 1998), 101–35. Isabelle Lehuu, *Carnival on the Page: Popular Print Media in Antebellum America* (Chapel Hill, N.C., 2000), 36–58. *A Dictionary of Americanisms in Historical Principles*, 2 vols., ed. Mitford M. Mathews (Chicago, 1951), gives only New York citations for "g'hal."

23. Elliott J. Gorn, *The Manly Art: Bare-Knuckle Prize Fighting in America* (Ithaca, N.Y., 1986), 36–41. *The American Fistiana* (New York, 1873), 6–11.

24. *New York Herald*, 9 February 1849. On Sullivan's career, see *Life and Battles of Yankee Sullivan Embracing Full and Accurate Reports of His Fights* (Philadelphia, 1854); Ed James, *The Life and Battles of Yankee Sullivan* (New York, 1879), 3–15; *New York Clipper*, 5 July 1856; and Gorn, *The Manly Art*, 69–73.

25. James, *The Life and Battles of Yankee Sullivan*, 22. Gorn, *The Manly Art*, 73–97. Wallace Shugg, "'This Great Test of Man's Brutality': The Sullivan-Hyer Prizefight at Still Pond Heights, Maryland in 1849," *Maryland Historical Magazine* 95 (2000): 47–63.

26. *Harper's Weekly*, 22 October 1859. *New York Herald*, 6, 8, and 9 February 1849. *Philadelphia Public Ledger*, 9 February 1849. *Baltimore Sun*, 8 and 9 February 1849, quoted in Shugg, "'This Great Test of Man's Brutality,'" 53. Octavius Thorndike

Howe, *Argonauts of '49: History and Adventures of Emigrant Companies from Massachusetts, 1849–1850* (Cambridge, Mass., 1923), 127. The *Leonore* left Boston on 1 February, so its passengers did not know of Hyer's 7 February victory.

27. William Harding, *John C. Heenan of Troy, N.Y.* (New York, 1881), 6. *New York Herald*, 22 October 1858. Thomas Bigelow Paine, *Thomas Nast: His Period and His Pictures* (New York, 1904), 37. *New York Clipper*, 5 March 1860. On the Heenan-Sayers fight see Alan Lloyd, *The Great Prizefight* (New York, 1977), and Gorn, *The Manly Art*, 148–57. *Harper's Weekly*, 5 May 1860, 280–81. William Howard Russell, *My Diary North and South* (1863; rpt., New York, 1965), 14.

28. On the American-English sporting rivalry in the nineteenth century, see John Dizikes, *Sportsmen and Gamesmen* (Boston, 1981).

29. Harding, *John C. Heenan*, 6. *Life and Battles of Yankee Sullivan Embracing Full and Accurate Reports of His Fights*, 54. William L. Knapp, "*I Die a True American*": *The True Life of William Pool* (New York, 1855). *The American Fistiana*, 19.

30. *New York Clipper*, 5 July 1856. Owen Kildare, *My Mamie Rose: The Story of My Regeneration* (New York, 1903), 69. *Life and Battles of Yankee Sullivan Embracing Full and Accurate Reports of His Fights*, 16. Gribben's: *Wilkes' Spirit of the Times*, 18 May 1861. *New York Clipper*, 10 September 1857.

31. Herbert Asbury, *The French Quarter: An Informal History of the New Orleans Underworld* (1936; rpt., Garden City, N.Y., 1938), 212–18. On early New York gambling, see J. H. Green, *A Report on Gambling in New York* (New York, 1851), 54–68; Ann Fabian, *Card Sharps and Bucket Shops: Gambling in Nineteenth-Century America* (1990; rpt., New York, 1999), 38–46; and Herbert Asbury, *Sucker's Progress: An Informal History of Gambling in America from the Colonies to Canfield* (1938; rpt., Montclair, N.J., 1969), 165–76. Green, *A Report on Gambling in New York*, 69. For descriptions of fancy gambling in New York, see *New York Herald*, 10 April 1849; Foster, *New York by Gas-Light*, 107–9; "The Gambling-Houses of New York," *St. James' Magazine* 20 (1867): 252–53; and Ferdinand Longchamp, *Asmodeus in New-York* (New York, 1868), 131–36. "Rich young rakes": Foster, *New York by Gas-Light*, 108–9. "The Gambling-Houses of New York," 252.

32. On billiards in New York, see Green, *A Report on Gambling in New York*, 79–84; Foster, *New-York by Gas-Light*, 84–91; and *New York Clipper*, 9 and 16 May 1868, quotation, 16 May 1868.

33. William J. Snelling, *Exposé of the Vice of Gambling, as It Lately Existed in Massachusetts* (Boston, 1833), 30. *Wanderings of a Vagabond*, 233. Philadelphia: Asbury, *Sucker's Progress*, 127–28, and *Wanderings of a Vagabond*, 326–27. Washington: Asbury, *Sucker's Progress*, 127, 128, 134–46; *Wanderings of a Vagabond*, 140–41; *New York Times*, 26 November 1858; and Edward Winslow Martin, *Behind the Scenes in Washington* (n.p., 1873), 499–501. Asbury, *The French Quarter*, 218. Frank Soulé, John Gihon, and James Nisbet, *The Annals of San Francisco* (1855; rpt., Palo Alto, Calif., 1966), 452.

34. On Walsh, see Robert Ernst, "The One and Only Mike Walsh," *New-York Historical Society Quarterly* 26 (1952): 43–65; Wilentz, *Chants Democratic*, 327–35; Peter Adams, *The Bowery Boys: Street Corner Radicals and the Politics of Rebellion*

(Westport, Conn., 2005); and Gerald Leonard Cohen, *Origin of the Term "Shyster"—Supplementary Information* (Frankfort am Main, 1984). *New York Leader,* 19 March 1859. *New York Herald,* 18 March 1859.

35. Mike Walsh, *Sketches of the Speeches and Writings of Michael Walsh* (New York, 1843). *Subterranean,* 28 February 1846, 4 October 1845, and 10 January 1846. *New York Herald,* 18 March 1859.

36. Walsh, *Sketches,* 25, 11–12. "Fish-blooded calves": *Subterranean,* 27 September 1845. *New York Ledger,* 27 October 1860. Tyler Anbinder, *Five Points: The Nineteenth-Century New York City Neighborhood That Invented Tap Dance, Stole Elections, and Became the World's Most Notorious Slum* (New York, 2001), 156–58.

37. Seward: *New York Clipper,* 5 August 1854. *New York Whip,* 17 September 1842. Hyer: J. Fairfax McLaughlin, *The Life and Times of John Kelly, Tribune of the People* (New York, 1885), 147, and *New York Herald,* 18 and 19 March 1859. Ridgely: Arthur Quinn, *The Rivals: William Gwin, David Broderick, and the Birth of California* (New York, 1994), 43, and Marilynn Wood Hill, *Their Sisters' Keepers: Prostitution in New York City, 1830-1870* (Los Angeles, 1993), 157.

38. *Subterranean,* 12 September 1846.

39. Kenneth Holcomb Dunshee, *As You Pass By* (New York, 1952), 113. *New York Leader,* 17 March 1860. *New York Times,* 18 March 1859. *New York Leader,* 17 March 1860. McLaughlin, *The Life and Times of John Kelly,* 149. *New York Leader,* 17 March 1860.

40. "The Ghost of Mike Walsh" (New York, [1859]), American Songs and Ballads, Rare Books and Special Collections, Library of Congress, Washington, D.C. *New York Leader,* 31 March 1860. *New York Clipper,* 27 February 1869. Maunsell Field, "A Catcher of Gossip," *Harper's New Monthly Magazine* 48 (1874): 113.

41. *New York Tribune,* 14 January 1885. The 14 January 1885 obituary of Rynders in the *New York Times* defined a sporting man as "a gambler, a turfman, and sundry other things which are supposed to ostracize a man from good society." Edward Van Every, *Sins of New York as "Exposed" by the "Police Gazette"* (New York, 1930), 14. I discuss the connections between minstrels and the sporting fraternity in chapter 6.

42. *New York Whip,* 2 September 1842, refers to Philadelphia gamblers as "sporting men." Later in the century, the term "sporting man" had the connotation of someone who patronized prostitutes, but the context of this article, entitled "Sporting Men," makes clear that at that time it referred solely to gamblers. John M. Findlay, *People of Chance: Gambling in American Society from Jamestown to Las Vegas* (New York, 1986), 44–78.

43. This information on Rynders is drawn from obituaries in the *New York Times,* 14 January 1885, the *New York Tribune,* 14 January 1885, the *New York Herald,* 14 January 1885, the *New York Clipper,* 24 January 1885, and from Michael Kaplan, "The World of the B'hoys: Urban Violence and the Political Culture of Antebellum New York City, 1825–1860" (PhD diss., New York University, 1996), 113–32. "Lithe, dark, handsome": Thomas L. Nichols, *Forty Years of American Life,* 2 vols. (London, 1864), 1:159. *New York Times,* 14 January 1885.

44. *New York Clipper,* 24 January 1885. *New York Herald,* 12 July 1849 and 17 Janu-

ary 1850. On Rynders's involvement in horse racing, see *Wilkes' Spirit of the Times,* 12 February 1870 and 17 January 1885, and Melvin L. Adelman, *A Sporting Time: New York City and the Rise of Modern Athletics, 1820–1870* (Urbana, Ill., 1986), 72. *New York Times,* 14 January 1885. Arena: Ned James, "Rynders and His Sporting Confreres," *New York Clipper,* 24 January 1885. *National Police Gazette,* 24 January 1846, and Gilfoyle, *City of Eros,* 88.

45. *New York Herald,* 14 January 1885. *New York Leader,* 19 March 1859. The fullest history of the early Empire Club is George B. Wooldridge's account in the *New York Leader,* 3 September 1859. Matthew Breen, *Thirty Years of New York Politics Up-to-Date* (New York, 1899), 303. *New York Herald,* 14 January 1885. Nichols, *Forty Years of American Life,* 150.

46. *New York Leader,* 3 September 1859. J. Frank Kernan, *Reminiscences of the Old Fire Laddies and Volunteer Fire Departments of New York and Brooklyn* (New York, 1885), 52–54. *New York Tribune,* 1 November 1844. Wheaton Lane, *Commodore Vanderbilt: An Epic of the Steam Age* (New York, 1942), 83. Hershel Parker, vol. 1 of *Herman Melville: A Biography* (Baltimore, Md., 1996), 333. *New York Times,* 14 January 1885. Astor Place: Peter G. Buckley, "To the Opera House: Culture and Society in New York City, 1820–1860" (PhD diss. State University of New York at Stony Brook, 1984), 62–75; Kaplan, "The World of the B'hoys," 152–167; and Monaghan, *The Great Rascal,* 171–81. Ably defended by John Van Buren, Rynders was acquitted of all charges stemming from the riot; the transcript of the trial was printed in the *New York Herald,* 16 and 17 January 1850.

47. Jacques Le Goff, "Licit and Illicit Trades in the Medieval West," in *Time, Work, and Culture in the Middle Ages* (Chicago, 1980), 58–70. *New York Tribune,* 8 November 1845. Thomas Mooney, *Nine Years in America* (Dublin, Ire., 1850), 145. Thomas F. De Voe, *The Market Book: A History of the Public Markets of the City of New York* (1862; rpt., New York, 1970), 434–35. "Kills for Keyser": Harlow, *Old Bowery Days,* 148–49, and Nichols, *Forty Years of American Life,* 1:157.

48. Baker, *A Glance at New York,* 10. De Voe, *The Market Book,* 389. *New York Clipper,* 6 December 1873. Gilje, *The Road to Mobocracy,* 243–45.

49. Peter Gammie, "Pugilists and Politicians in Antebellum New York: The Life of Tom Hyer," *New York History* 45 (1994): 270–71. Gilfoyle, *City of Eros,* 85, 328. Ed James, *Life and Battles of Tom Hyer* (New York, 1879), 1. *New York Clipper,* 9 July 1864.

50. *New York Whip,* 3 September 1842. Gorn, *The Manly Art,* 142. *New York Clipper,* 9 July 1864. "Slim-waisted": Charles Townsend Harris, *Memories of Manhattan in the Sixties and Seventies* (New York, 1928), 53. Rynders: *New York Clipper,* 24 January 1885. Dennis Tilden Lynch, *"Boss" Tweed* (New York, 1939), 33. McLaughlin, *The Life and Times of John Kelly,* 17. On the importance of physical size and strength in New York politics in this era, see Anbinder, *Five Points,* 165, 169–70.

51. Charles P. Duane, *Against the Vigilantes: The Recollections of Dutch Charley Duane,* ed. John Bossenecker (Norman, Okla., 1999), 74. James, *Life and Battles of Tom Hyer,* 20. *National Police Gazette,* 23 June 1883. Odell, *Annals of the New York Stage,* 451. Gammie, "Pugilists and Politicians," 284. *New York Clipper,* 9 July 1864. *New York Tribune,* 17 April 1849. Union Club: William Harding, "American Prize-

Ring," *National Police Gazette,* 11 September 1880, and James, "Rynders and His Sporting Confreres," *New York Clipper,* 24 January 1885.

52. On Morrissey, see chapter 8. *The Life and Battles of John Morrissey* (New York, n.d.), 6–7, 11–12. *New York Times,* 15 September 1854. On Poole, see *Life of William Poole, With a True Account of the Terrible Affray in Which He Received His Death Wound* (New York, 1855); Knapp, *"I Die a True American,"* and *New York Times,* 9 March 1855. James, *Life and Battles of Tom Hyer,* 22–23. *New York Herald,* 12 March 1855. *National Police Gazette,* 23 June 1883.

53. Amos Dock fight: *New York Tribune,* 28 July 1854; *New York Herald,* 28 July 1854; and *New York Clipper,* 5 August 1854. The *Clipper* prints several letters giving conflicting accounts of the battle. *"Rough and Tumble"; or, The Amos Dock Fight between Poole and Morrissey* (New York, [1854]), American Songs and Ballads, Rare Books and Special Collections, Library of Congress, Washington, D.C.

54. *Life of William Poole,* 52. *New York Clipper,* 5 August 1854. The supporters of both men included both Irish and non-Irish. The diversity of Morrissey's gang is found in an article reprinted from the *New York Herald* in *Life of William Poole,* 82–83, and in the *New York Times,* 21 June 1888. Hyer in 1852 had counted Yankee Sullivan among his allies; *New York Tribune,* 10 March 1855. Hyer's closest comrade was Charley Duane. Duane was, like Morrissey, a Tipperary-born Catholic (John Bossenecker, "The Violent Life of Charles Duane," in *Against the Vigilantes,* 7–9). "Standard bearer": Knapp, *"I Die a True American,"* 10. Poole's shooting and its background and aftermath are described and analyzed in Elliott J. Gorn, "'Good-Bye, Boys, I Die a True American': Homicide, Nativism and Working-Class Culture in Antebellum New York City," *Journal of American History* 74 (1987): 388–409.

55. *New York Times* quoted in *Life of William Poole,* 61. *National Police Gazette,* 23 October 1880.210 Charles Haswell, *Reminiscences of an Octogenarian,* 498. *New York Herald,* 12 March 1855.

56. Alexander Gardiner, *Canfield: The True Story of America's Greatest Gambler* (Garden City, N.Y., 1930), 47. Green, *A Report on Gambling in New York,* 60. James, *Life and Battles of Tom Hyer,* 23–24. Gorn, *The Manly Art,* 123–24. William L. Riordan, *Plunkitt of Tammany Hall* (1905; rpt., New York, 1991), 86. Joseph Mitchell, "McSorley's Wonderful Saloon," in Joseph Mitchell, *Up in the Old Hotel, and Other Stories* (New York, 1993), 7.

57. *New York Herald,* 18 and 19 March 1859. *Porter's Spirit of the Times,* 26 March 1859; this obituary was written by George Wilkes. *Life of William Poole* reprints the inquest proceedings.

58. *New York Herald,* 19 March 1859. The inquest makes clear that there was nothing unusual about Walsh's late-night drinking on the day he died. Cohen, *Origin of the Term "Shyster,"* 46, 81.

CHAPTER 5. THE GOLD RUSH

1. Kimball Webster, *The Gold Seekers of '49: Being a Personal Narrative of the Overland Trail and Adventures in California and Oregon from 1840 to 1854* (Man-

chester, N.H., 1917), 126–27. Robert Bonner was the author of *The Temperance Harp: A Collection of Songs Suitable for Washingtonian and Other Total Abstinence Societies* (Northampton, Mass., 1842) and other temperance works. Bonner's career is described in Elinor Wilson, *James Beckwourth: Black Mountain Man and War Chief of the Crows* (Norman, Okla., 1972), 137–46.

2. The original title of Francis Parkman's *Oregon Trail* in *Knickerbocker* magazine was "The Oregon Trail; or, A Summer's Journey Out of Bounds." Francis Parkman, *The Oregon Trail*, ed. David Levine (New York, 1982). Sarah Royce, *A Frontier Lady: Recollections of the Gold Rush and Early California*, ed. Ralph Henry Gabriel (New Haven, Conn., 1932), 109.

3. M. Fairchild, letter to John C. Brigham, 20 May 1831, American Bible Society archives, New York, N.Y. (quoted in Clifford S. Griffin, *Their Brother's Keepers: Moral Stewardship in the United States, 1800–1865* [New Brunswick, N.J., 1960], 59). American Tract Society, *Annual Report* 31 (1856): 181–82 (quoted in Griffin, *Their Brother's Keepers*, 59). Isaac Debman, 26 January 1826, quoted in William Warren Sweet, "The Churches as Moral Courts of the Frontier," *Church History* 2 (1933): 8.

4. Robert W. Johannsen, *To the Halls of the Montezumas: The Mexican War in the American Imagination* (New York, 1985). Flags: Andrew Bell, *Men and Things in America* (London, 1838), 31. Amy S. Greenberg, *Manifest Manhood and the Antebellum American Empire* (Cambridge, Eng., 2005), notes the connections between what she calls "martial manhood" and the war. *New York Weekly Tribune*, 27 June 1846, quoted in Paul Foos, *A Short Offhand Killing Affair: Soldiers and Social Conflict During the Mexican-American War* (Chapel Hill, N.C., 2002), 51.

5. James McCaffrey, *Army of Manifest Destiny: The American Soldier in the Mexican War, 1846–1848* (New York, 1992), 36–37. *Niles' National Register*, 25 July 1846. J. Jacob Oswandel, *Notes of the Mexican War* (Philadelphia, 1885), 20. John R. Kenly, *Memoirs of a Maryland Volunteer* (Philadelphia, 1873), 77, 23. *Louisville Journal*, 29 June 1846, quoted in *Niles' National Register*, 25 July 1846.

6. I discuss male behavior on riverboats in chapter 7. Kenly, *Memoirs of a Maryland Volunteer*, 34, 27. Jonathan Drake Stevenson, *Memorial and Petition of Col. J. D. Stevenson* (San Francisco, 1886), 16a, 17. Albert Lombard, *The "High Private," with a Full and Exciting Account of the History of the New York Volunteers* (New York, 1848), 41–47. Francis D. Clark, *The First Regiment of the New York Volunteers* (New York, 1882), 63–64. John Henry Hollingsworth, *The Journal of Lieutenant John Henry Hollingsworth of the First New York Volunteers* (San Francisco, 1923), 5 (8 November 1846), 19 (24 January 1847). "Old Dan Tucker": Joshua H. Vincent, notebook, 8 November 1846, California Historical Society, quoted in Donald C. Biggs, *Conquer and Colonize: Stevenson's Regiment and California* (San Rafael, Calif., 1977), 77. John Henry Hollingsworth, *Journal of Lieutenant John Henry Hollingsworth*, 9 (28 November 1846).

7. Franklin Smith, *The Mexican War Journals of Captain Franklin Smith*, ed. Joseph E. Chance (Jackson, Miss., 1991), 66–67 (quoted in Richard Bruce Winders, *Mr. Polk's Army: The American Military Experience in the Mexican War* [College Station, Tex., 1997], 85). Kenly, *Memoirs of a Maryland Volunteer*, 47. Winders, *Mr. Polk's*

Army, 86–87. George Winston Smith and Charles Judah, *Chronicles of the Gringos: The U. S. Army in the Mexican War, 1846–1848* (Albuquerque, N.Mex., 1968), 287–89. McCaffrey, *Army of Manifest Destiny*, 118–19.

8. Laurie F. Maffly-Kipp, *Religion and Society in Frontier California* (New Haven, Conn., 1994), esp. 1–3, 50–54. *Home Missionary* 21, no. 11 (March 1849): 252 (quoted in Maffly- Kipp, *Religion and Society in Frontier California*, 50). George Shepard and S. L. Caldwell, *Addresses of the Reverends Professors George Shepard and S. L. Caldwell to the California Pioneers from Bangor, Maine* (Bangor, Me., 1849), 5 (quoted in Maffly-Kipp, *Religion and Society in Frontier California*, 57).

9. Stuart A. McLean, "Opposition to the California Gold Rush: The Sentimental Argument, 1849–1853," in *American Renaissance and the American West*, ed. Christopher Durer et al. (Laramie, Wyo., 1982), 92–93. George R. Graham, "Going around the Horn, the Direct Road to Fortune," *Graham's American Monthly Magazine* 34 (1849): 331–32. "Editors' Table," *Godey's Magazine and Lady's Book* 38 (1849): 294. Maffly-Kipp, *Religion and Society in Frontier California*, 64–74.

10. Barry L. Dutka, "New York Discovers Gold in California: How the Press Fanned the Flames of Gold Mania," *California Historical Society Quarterly* 53 (1984): 313–20, 341. Ralph Bieber, "California Gold Mania," *Mississippi Valley Historical Review* 35 (1948): 3–28. My figure of two hundred thousand men passing through California is simply a guess based on the population of California and records of those who traveled there by way of the Oregon Trail and of those who arrived in San Francisco by ship. Webster, *The Gold Seekers of '49*, 104.

11. U.S. Census Office, *Seventh Census of the United States, 1850, Statistics* (Washington, D.C., 1853), xxxvi–xxxvii, 966–83. Albert L. Hurtado, *Indian Survival on the California Frontier* (New Haven, Conn., 1990), 1; by the end of the 1850s the Indian population is estimated to have been thirty thousand. Eliza W. Farnham, *California, In-Doors and Out* (New York, 1856), 155.

12. J. D. Borthwick, *Three Years in California* (Edinburgh, 1857), 32. *New York Herald*, 11 January 1849. Ships' passengers lists giving occupation that I examined were those of the *North Bend* (from Boston in 1849) and the *Robert Browne* (from New York in 1849) listed in *California Gold Rush Voyages, 1848–1849: Three Original Narratives*, ed. John Pomfret (San Marino, Calif., 1954), and that of the *Capiapo* (Panama to San Francisco, 1849) given in "Numbers of Passengers on Board the Brig Capiapo Bound to San Francisco," in William Penn Abrams, diary, Bancroft Library, University of California, Berkeley. The total occupational distribution was: skilled and semiskilled manual workers, 153; nonmanual workers, 66; farmers, 54; unskilled workers, 7. John D. Unruh, *The Plains Across: The Overland Migrants and the Trans-Mississippi West, 1840–1860* (Urbana, Ill., 1979).

13. Elizabeth Margo, *Taming the Forty-niner* (New York, 1955), 9. Louise A. K. S. Clappe, *The Shirley Letters: Being Letters Written in 1851–1852 from the California Mines* (Salt Lake City, Nev., n.d.), 44 (30 September 1851).

14. Charles D. Ferguson, *The Experiences of a Forty-niner during Thirty-four Years' Residence in California and Australia*, ed. Frederick T. Wallace (Cleveland, Ohio, 1888), 9. Thomas Wylly, "Reminiscences of a Trip to California and Back in 1849

and 1851," typescript, Bancroft Library, University of California, Berkeley. Malcolm J. Rohrbough, *Days of Gold: The California Gold Rush and the American Nation* (Berkeley, Calif., 1997), 186–88.

15. On pre-gold-rush female opposition to leaving settled regions to migrate west, see Joan E. Cashin, *A Family Venture: Men and Women on the Southern Frontier* (Baltimore, Md., 1991), 44–49, and John Mack Faragher, *Men and Women on the Overland Trail* (New Haven, Conn., 1979), 163–68. On female opposition to the gold rush, see Rohrbough, *Days of Gold*, 35–39. William Crosby to Lucy D. Taube, 12 May 1852, University of Kentucky Library, Lexington, Kentucky, (quoted in Rohrbough, *Days of Gold*, 37).

16. Charles A. Kirkpatrick, journal, 7 May and 23 June 1849, Bancroft Library, University of California, Berkeley. Rohrbough, *Days of Gold*, 33–39. Gaius Leonard Halsey, *Reminiscences of Village Life and of Panama and California from 1840 to 1850* (Unadilla, N.Y., 1902), 208, 250. Gaius Leonard Halsey, "Gold Rush Diary, 1849," and Gaius Leonard Halsey, letter to Julia Halsey, 12 October 1849, New York State Historical Association, Cooperstown, N.Y. Halsey and Mead were the only two of the Col. Williams's seven regulars who went west, and Halsey's and Mead's party included at least four other Unadillans.

17. The 150th anniversary of the rush saw the publication of several new histories. The most significant are Rohrbough, *Days of Gold*; Susan Johnson, *Roaring Camp: The Social World of the California Gold Rush* (New York, 2000); and Brian Roberts, *American Alchemy: The California Gold Rush and Middle-Class Culture* (Chapel Hill, N.C., 2000). Benjamin Butler Harris, "'Crumbs of '49,'" 2 pts., 1:12, 1:31, Huntington Library, San Marino, Calif. "Petrel," no. 7, 26, in William H. De Costa, "Journal of the Passage of the Ship *Duxbury* to San Francisco," Huntington Library, San Marino, Calif.

18. William Taylor, *California Life Illustrated* (New York, 1858), 204. J. H. Avery, *The Land of Ophir, Ideal and Real* (New York, 1853), 9.

19. C. W. Haskins, *The Argonauts of California* (New York, 1890), 73. Ferguson, *The Experiences of a Forty-niner*, 153–54.

20. David Goodman, *Gold Seeking: Victoria and California in the 1850s* (Stanford, Calif., 1994). Jeremy Mouat, "After California: Later Gold Rushes of the Pacific Basin," in *Riches for All: The California Gold Rush and the World*, ed. Kenneth N. Owens (Lincoln, Nebr., 2002), 268–73. *Household Words*, 22 May 1852, quoted in Goodman, *Gold Seeking*, 65. Goodman, *Gold Seeking*, 71–77, 162–66. Pierre Berton, *The Klondike Fever: The Life and Death of the Last Great Gold Rush* (New York, 1958), 158–65, 318–24. Maffly-Kipp, *Religion and Society in Frontier California*, 152–67. Roberts, *American Alchemy*, 221–23.

21. "Mining Life in California," *Harper's Weekly*, 3 October 1857, 633. William Swain, letter to his mother, 15 April 1850, quoted in J. S. Holliday, *The World Rushed In: The California Gold Rush Experience* (New York, 1981), 363.

22. Hinton R. Helper, *The Land of Gold* (Baltimore, Md., 1855), 118.

23. Nathan Blanchard, journal, 82 (26 October 1854), 92 (28 November 1855), 101 (3 May 1857), Huntington Library, San Marino, Calif.

24. Borthwick, *Three Years in California*, 117. William Redmond Ryan, *Personal Adventures in Upper and Lower California*, 2 vols. (1850–51; rpt., New York, 1973) 2:26–27. Mrs. Mallie Stafford, *The March of Empire through Decades* (San Francisco, 1884), 81. Haskins, *The Argonauts of California*, 124. Borthwick, *Three Years in California*, 332.

25. John Doble, *John Doble's Journal and Letters from the Mines: Mokelumne Hill, Jackson, Volcano and San Francisco, 1861–1865*, ed. Charles L. Camp (Denver, 1962), 4. Haskins, The *Argonauts of California*, 170. George Hunter, *Reminiscences of an Old Timer* (San Francisco, 1887). Pringle Shaw, *Ramblings in California* (Toronto, n.d.), 177.

26. Helper, *The Land of Gold*, 109. Taylor, *California Life Illustrated*, 285. Kirkpatrick, journal, 27 October 1849. Sherlock Bristol, *The Pioneer Preacher*, ed. Dewey Wallace (Urbana, Ill., 1989), 91.

27. James H. Carson, "Early Recollections of the Mines," in *Bright Gem of the Western Seas: California, 1846–1852*, ed. Peter Browning (Lafayette, Calif., 1991), 10. Phineas Underwood Blunt, journal, 1 November 1849, microfilm, Bancroft Library, University of California, Berkeley. *Two Diaries of Peter Decker: Overland to California in 1849, and Life in the Mines, 1850–1851*, ed. Helen S. Griffen (Georgetown, Calif., 1966), 251 (13 January 1851). The Mexican gambling game of monte was played with a forty-eight-card deck. Edward Washington McIlhany, *Recollections of a '49er* (Kansas City, Mo., 1908), 100–101.

28. Hubert Howe Bancroft, *California Inter Pocula* (San Francisco, 1888), 673. *California Inter Pocula* is the best source on gold-rush drinking; the Latin translates as "California between drinks." Frank Marryat, *Mountains and Molehills; or, Recollections of a Burnt Journal* (1855; rpt., Stanford, Calif., 1952), 37. Matthew Gilbert Upton, "Etchings in El Dorado; or, the Wags and Waggeries of the Argonauts of '49," n.p., Huntington Library, San Marino, Calif. Bancroft, *California Inter Pocula*, 674. Clappe, *The Shirley Letters*, 91, 92 (27 January 1852).

29. Alonzo Hubbard, diary, vol. 1, 4 July 1852, Huntington Library, San Marino, Calif. Clappe, *The Shirley Letters*, 144 (5 July 1852). Alonzo Delano, *Old Block's Sketch Book* (1855; rpt., Santa Ana, Calif., 1947), 38. Harris, "'Crumbs of '49,'" 2:20.

30. The "Southern Mines" are on the tributaries of the San Joaquin River. Roger D. McGrath, "A Violent Birth: Disorder, Crime and Law Enforcement, 1849–1890," in *Taming the Elephant: Politics, Government and Law in Pioneer California*, ed. John F. Burns and Richard Orsi (Berkeley, Calif., 2003), 41–42. Letter from an unidentified miner to his wife in Salem, May 1850, Huntington Library, San Marino, Calif. On high gold-rush homicide rates, see Randolph Roth, "Guns, Murder, and Probability: How Can We Decide Which Figures to Trust?" *Reviews in American History* 35 (2007): 166–75. John Boessnecker, *Gold Dust and Gunsmoke: Tales of Gold Rush Outlaws, Gunfighters, Lawmen, and Vigilantes* (New York, 1999), 353; on 323–25 he gives homicide rates for other gold-rush locales—in the mines in the 1850s most are in the range of 75–125 per 100,000. Clare V. McKanna Jr., in *Race and Homicide in Nineteenth-Century California* (Reno, Nev., 2002) 103, calculates the homicide rate in Tuolumne County in the 1850s as 95 per 100,000. Kevin J. Mullen, *Dangerous*

Strangers: Minority Newcomers and Criminal Violence, 1850–2000 (New York, 2005), 15. Edward E. Baptist, *Creating an Old South: Middle Florida's Plantation Frontier before the Civil War* (Chapel Hill, N.C., 2002), 256. On California dueling, see Bancroft, *California Inter Pocula*, 748–84; Boessnecker, *Gold Dust and Gunsmoke*, 204–24; and Philip J. Ethington, *The Public City: The Political Construction of Urban Life in San Francisco, 1850–1900* (Cambridge, Eng., 1994), 80–83. Bancroft, *California Inter Pocula*, 743, 757, 760–61.

31. James Warren Wood, journal, 4 August 1850, Huntington Library, San Marino, Calif. Wylly, "Reminiscences of a Trip to California," n.p. Frank Soulé, John Gijon, and James Nisbet, *The Annals of San Francisco* (1855; rpt., Palo Alto, Calif., 1966), 248. William Kelly, *A Stroll through the Diggings of California* (London, 1852), 57.

32. Johnson, *Roaring Camp*, 180–83. C. Grant Loomis, "The Captive B'ar in California Amusements," *Western Folklore* 7 (1948): 336–41. Borthwick, *Three Years in California*, 289–98.

33. Haskins, *The Argonauts of California*, 71. William T. Russell, "Cusps," 190, typescript, Bancroft Library, University of California, Berkeley. Clappe, *The Shirley Letters*, 94 (27 January 1852). Edward F. O'Day, *An Appreciation of James Wood Coffroth* (San Francisco, 1926), 15. Upton, "Etchings in El Dorado," n.p.

34. Warren Sadler, journal, 25 September 1850, Bancroft Library, University of California, Berkeley. [Julius H. Pratt?], "California: Anecdotes of the Mines," *Century Magazine* 42 (1891): 270.

35. Gustavus Swansey, journal, 7 November 1852 and 11 September 1853, Huntington Library, San Marino, Calif. Reminiscences of John De Laittre, 118, microfilmed typescript, Bancroft Library, University of California, Berkeley. Clappe, *The Shirley Letters*, 182 (4 September 1852).

36. William M'Collum, *California as I Saw It* (1850; rpt., Los Gatos, Calif., 1960), 160. On the limits of "fellow feeling," see Johnson, *Roaring Camp*, 127–30. McIlhany, *Recollections of a '49er*, 105. Hunter, *Reminiscences of an Old Timer*, 32–33.

37. Johnson, *Roaring Camp*, 185–234. Charles Howard Shinn, *Mining Camps: A Study in American Frontier Government* (New York, 1885). Friedrich Gerstäcker, *Scenes of Life in California*, trans. George Cossgrave (San Francisco, 1940), 37–66. Rudolph M. Lapp, *Blacks in the California Gold Rush* (New Haven, Conn., 1977). Borthwick, *Three Years in California*, 164, 165.

38. Clappe, *The Shirley letters*, 142 (5 July 1852). Shaw, *Ramblings in California*, 17. Clappe, *The Shirley Letters*, 148, 150 (4 August 1852). John Hovey, "Historical Account of the Troubles between the Chileans and American Miners in the Calaveras Mining District, Commencing December 6, 1849 and Ending January 4, 1850," n.p., Huntington Library, San Marino, Calif. On the "Chilean War," see Johnson, *Roaring Camp*, 196–208, and Jay Monaghan, *Chile, Peru and the California Gold Rush of 1849* (Berkeley, Calif., 1973), 243–48. Gunter Barth, *Bitter Strength: A History of the Chinese in the United States, 1850–1870* (Cambridge, Mass., 1964), 129–35. Johnson, *Roaring Camp*, 242–51.

39. James H. Carson, "Tulare Plains" (1852), in *Bright Gem of the Western Seas*, 75–76. Charles Ross Parke, *Dreams to Dust: A Diary of the California Gold Rush*,

1849–1850, ed. James E. David (Lincoln, Nebr., 1989), 89 (1 January 1850). Russell, "Cusps," 86. J. M. Letts, *California Illustrated: Including a Description of the Panama and Nicaragua Routes* (New York, 1852), 112. *San Francisco Alta California*, 2 June 1849, reprinted in *Exterminate Them! Written Accounts of the Murder, Rape, and Enslavement of Native Americans during the California Gold Rush*, ed. Clifford E. Trafzer and John R. Hyer (East Lansing, Mich., 1999), 114.

40. Halsey, *Reminiscences of Village Life and of Panama and California*, 223. "Mose in California": *New York Herald*, 13 and 14 February 1849. George R. MacMinn, *Theater of the Golden Era in California* (Caldwell, Idaho, 1941), 163–65. *San Francisco Alta California*, 17 April and 28 June 1850. Edward Ely, *The Wanderings of Edward Ely*, ed. Anthony and Alison Sirna (New York, 1954), 155 (18 October 1851). Wood, journal, 24 February 1850.

41. The "Petrel," and its short-lived rival the "Shark," are both in De Costa, "Journal of the Passage of the Ship *Duxbury* to San Francisco." William H. De Costa, "Journal of a Voyage to San Francisco, 1849," Huntington Library, San Marino, Calif., identifies many of the allusions in the "Petrel" and makes clear that De Costa was the principal author. On the " Petrel," see Roberts, *American Alchemy*, 105–12; quotation, 105. The "Petrel," nos. 2, 6; cf. Benjamin A. Baker, *A Glance at New York* (New York, 1857), 22, 32.

42. Biggs, *Conquer and Colonize*. Stevenson, *Memorial and Petition of Col. J. D. Stevenson*, 13–14. *New York Herald*, 8 July 1846. *Subterranean*, 18 July 1846. Foos, *A Short Offhand Killing Affair*, 74–78. *New York Tribune*, 21 August 1846. Walter Murray, "Narrative of a California Volunteer with Stevenson's Regiment," in *Publications of the Society of California Pioneers for the Year 1941* (San Francisco, 1941), 13. Frederick Stanhope Hill, "To California before the Gold Rush," in James Lynch, *With Stevenson to California* (1896; rpt., Oakland, Calif., 1951), 48–50.

43. Biggs, *Conquer and Colonize*, 118. *Californian*, 15 September 1847, quoted in Kevin J. Mullen, *Let Justice Be Done: Crime and Politics in Early San Francisco* (Reno, Nev. 1989), 29. Hubert Howe Bancroft, *Popular Tribunals*, 2 vols. (San Francisco, 1887), 1:78.

44. On the Hounds and the 16 July riot, see Soulé, Gijon, and Nisbet, *The Annals of San Francisco*, 553–61, and Bancroft, *Popular Tribunals*, 1:76–102. The origin and significance of the name "Hounds" is not known for certain. "Parading": *San Francisco Alta California*, 2 August 1849. "Help themselves": Daniel Knower, *The Adventures of a Forty-niner* (1894; rpt., Ashland, Calif., 1971), 52. "Under the pretense": John Williamson Palmer, "Pioneer Days in San Francisco," *Century Illustrated Monthly Magazine* 45 (1892): 554. "Whip and drive": *San Francisco Alta California*, 2 August 1849.

45. *Spirit of the Times*, 18 November 1854. Soulé, Gijon, and Nisbet, *The Annals of San Francisco*, 647. *Wilkes' Spirit of the Times*, 5 May 1860. Ethington, *The Public City*, 50.

46. David A. Williams, *David C. Broderick: A Political Portrait* (San Marino, Calif., 1969), 5–10. James O'Meara, *Broderick and Gwin* (San Francisco, 1881), 1–12. "Bravest fighters": J. Frank Kernan, *Reminiscences of the Old Fire Laddies and Volunteer Fire Departments of New York and Brooklyn* (New York, 1885), 114. J. Fairfax

McLaughlin, *The Life and Times of John Kelly, Tribune of the People* (New York, 1885), 24. "Instinctive fondness": O'Meara, *Broderick and Gwin*, 14. On Broderick's good manners and erudition, see George Wilkes, "David C. Broderick," *Wilkes' Spirit of the Times*, 22 October 1859. John W. Forney, *Anecdotes of Public Men* (New York, 1874), 23–24. Matthew Breen, *Thirty Years of New York Politics Up-to-Date* (New York, 1899), 305–6. A list of the founding members of the Spartan Association is printed in the *New York Leader*, 27 October 1860. Williams, *David C. Broderick*, 15. O'Meara, *Broderick and Gwin*, 12.

47. *New York Tribune*, 2 November 1846. *New York Herald*, 4 November 1846. "Aristocratic portion of Tammany Hall": O'Meara, *Broderick and Gwin*, 20–21. Wilkes, "David C. Broderick." Williams, *David C. Broderick*, 17–27.

48. *San Francisco Alta California*, 28 June 1850. Wilkes, "David C. Broderick." Edgar A. Adams, "Various California Private Mints, 1849–1855," *American Journal of Numismatics* 65 (1911): 175–77. Williams, *David C. Broderick*, 43–55. On Broderick's organization, see Roger W. Lotchin, *San Francisco, 1846–1856: From Hamlet to City* (1974; rpt., Lincoln, Nebr., 1979), 217–22. O'Meara, *Broderick and Gwin*, 69. *San Francisco Alta California*, 26 July 1853, quoted in R. A. Burchell, *The San Francisco Irish, 1848–1880* (Berkeley, Calif., 1980), 126.

49. Lois Foster Rodecap, "Tom Maguire, Napoleon of the Stage," *California Historical Society Quarterly* 20 (1941): 289–314, and *California Historical Society Quarterly* 21 (1942): 39–74, 141–82, 239–75, is the best source on Maguire's life. On Maguire in New York, see Rodecap, "Tom Maguire, Napoleon of the Stage," pt. 1, 290–93. *New York Leader*, 10 March 1860. On Maguire's early California career, see *New York Clipper*, 15 February 1862. "Testimony of Thomas Maguire," in *In the Matter of the Last Will and Testament of David Broderick, Deceased* (San Francisco, 1860), 78. Pauline Jacobson, *City of the Golden Fifties* (Berkeley, Calif., 1941), 263. *New York Clipper*, 25 January 1896. *New York Journal*, 21 January 1896, clipping in Thomas Maguire folder, Harvard Theatre Collection, Cambridge, Mass.

50. Bancroft, *Popular Tribunals*, 2:605. William B. Seecrest, "There Once Was a Badman Named Mulligan," *Real West* 27 (1984): 14–25. Head butting: John Myers Myers, *San Francisco's Reign of Terror* (Garden City, N.Y., 1966), 74.

51. On Fallon, see Kevin J. Mullen, "Malachi Fallon: San Francisco's First Police Chief," *California Historical Society Quarterly* 62 (1983): 100–105, and Augustine Costello, *Our Firemen: A History of the New York Fire Departments* (New York, 1887), 174, 507. On Scannell, see Jacobson, *City of the Golden Fifties*, 53–56, quotation, 53; Costello, *Our Firemen*, 435–36; Lotchin, *San Francisco, 1846–1856*, 221; and Bancroft, *Popular Tribunals*, 2:597–601. John Bossenecker, "The Violent Life of Charles Duane," in Charles P. Duane, *Against the Vigilantes: The Recollections of Dutch Charley Duane*, ed. John Bossenecker (Norman, Okla., 1999), quotation, 42.

52. *The American Fistiana* (New York, 1873), 23. Enos Christman, *The Letters and Journal of a Forty-niner*, ed. Florence Morrow Christman (New York, 1930), 110 (22 February 1850). Sullivan: *New York Times*, 30 June 1856, and Boessnecker, *Gold Dust and Gunsmoke*, 168–70. Lilly: Foos, *A Short Offhand Killing Affair*, 117–19; Duane, *Against the Vigilantes*, 202; and Bancroft, *Popular Tribunals*, 2:6–8, 2:280–81. "Beauti-

fully formed": *Saturday Evening Post*, 23 May 1857. *A Year of Mud and Gold: San Francisco in Letters and Diaries, 1849–1850*, ed. William Benemann (Lincoln, Nebr., 1999), 92. "'Sporting' generally": *New York Times*, 5 November 1857. "Lots of acquaintances": *New York Sun*, 6 May 1878, clipping in "Scrapbook on New York City Politics, 1875–1878," New York Public Library, New York City. *New York Times*, 2 May 1878. Hyer: Duane, *Against the Vigilantes*, 75–77. Ed James, *The Life and Battles of John C. Heenan, the Hero of Farnborough* (New York, 1879), 2.

53. On Wilkes's life and career, see Alexander Saxton, "George Wilkes: Mutations of Artisan Radicalism," in *The Rise and Fall of the White Republic: Class Politics and Mass Culture in Nineteenth-Century America* (London, 1990), 205–22; a more critical perspective is found in *The Answer of John F. Chamberlain to the Complaint of George Wilkes* (New York, 1873), and in Wilkes's obituary in the *New York Clipper*, 3 October 1885. Robert Ernst, "The One and Only Mike Walsh," *New-York Historical Society Quarterly* 36 (1952): 49. *New York Clipper*, 3 October 1885. *Wilkes' Spirit of the Times*, 10 September 1859. *National Police Gazette*, 24 July 1852.

54. *Pacific News*, 1 February 1851. Williams, *David C. Broderick*.

55. "6th Ward Irish": Jonas Winchester to Ebenezer, 31 May 1850, in Jonas Winchester papers, quoted in Lotchin, *San Francisco, 1846–1856*, 224. *San Francisco Evening Bulletin*, 12 October 1855, quoted in Ethington, *The Public City*, 120. The literature on the 1856 vigilantes is vast. The most convincing account is in Ethington, *The Public City*, 86–169. Broderick's relation to the 1856 vigilante movement is examined in Robert M. Senkewicz, *Vigilantes in Gold Rush San Francisco* (Stanford, Calif., 1985), 159–88. Scannell: Bancroft, *Popular Tribunals*, 2:185–92, 2:446. Thomas Maguire to the executive committee, 28 June 1856, quoted in Ethington, *The Public City*, 159. Expulsions: *San Francisco Alta California*, 6 and 10 June 1856, and Bancroft, *Popular Tribunals*, 2:272–82. Sullivan: *San Francisco Alta California*, 1 and 2 June 1856.

56. Williams, *David C. Broderick*, 156, 205–40. Arthur Quinn, *The Rivals: William Gwin, David Broderick and the Birth of California* (New York, 1994).

57. I discuss the New York–West connection in later years in chapter 7.

58. Taylor, *California Life Illustrated*, 205. Greeley, *Recollections of a Busy Life* (New York, 1868), 102. "Old Forty-nine," *Hutching's California Magazine* 1 (1856): 70.

59. Richard Hale, *Log of a Forty-niner*, ed. Carolyn Hale Russ (Boston, 1923), 60 (quoted in Roberts, *American Alchemy*, 264). J. H. Green, *A Report on Gambling in New York* (New York, 1851), 16. *The Wanderings of a Vagabond: An Autobiography*, ed. John Morris (New York, 1873), 184.

CHAPTER 6. CULTURAL CONNECTIONS

1. James K. Kennard Jr., "Who Are Our National Poets?" *Knickerbocker* 26 (1845): 335.

2. Elliott J. Gorn, *The Manly Art: Bare-Knuckle Prize Fighting in America* (Ithaca, N.Y., 1986), 136. Thomas Robinson Hazard, *The Jonny-Cake Papers of "Shepard Tom"*

(Boston, 1915), 112–18. *Hanover Spectator*, 14 March 1883. John T. Reily, *Conewago: A Collection of Catholic Local History* (Martinsburg, W.Va., 1885), 170.

3. Edmund Wilson, *Patriotic Gore: Studies in the Literature of the American Civil War* (1962; rpt., New York, 1994), 509. P. T. Barnum, *The Life of P. T. Barnum: Written by Himself* (1855; rpt., Urbana, Ill., 2000), 1–2, 30–35.

4. Barnum, *The Life of P. T. Barnum*, 148–76. James W. Cook, *The Arts of Deception: Playing with Fraud in the Age of Barnum* (Cambridge, Mass., 2001), 3–12.

5. Fred Fedler, *Media Hoaxes* (Ames, Iowa, 1989). Richard Adams Locke, *The Moon Hoax; or, A Discovery That the Moon Has a Vast Population of Human Beings* (1859; rpt., Boston, 1975), 31, 38. *New York Leader*, 25 August 1860. Fedler, *Media Hoaxes*, 34–50.

6. William H. Robertson, *The History of Thoroughbred Racing in America* (Englewood Cliffs, N.J., 1964), 33–65. John Hervey, *Racing in America, 1665–1865*, 2 vols. (New York, 1944), 2:71–173. On Porter and the founding and early *Spirit of the Times*, see Francis Brinley, *Life of William T. Porter* (1860; rpt., New York, 1970), 3–36; Norris W. Yates, *William T. Porter and the "Spirit of the Times": A Study of the Big Bear School of Humor* (Baton Rouge, La., 1957), 3–36; and John Dizikes, *Sportsmen and Gamesmen* (Boston, 1981), 47–55. *Spirit of the Times*, 10 December 1831 and 3 March and 19 May 1832. Brinley, *Life of William T. Porter*, 63.

7. The *Spirit* building was at 1 Barclay Street, Monteverde's at No. 5, and Henry Colton's gambling hall, perhaps the most lavish in the nation, was No. 8 (*Doggett's New York City Directory for 1851* [New York, 1850]). Monteverde's: George C. Foster, *New York by Gas-Light, and Other Urban Sketches*, ed. Stuart M. Blumin (1850; rpt., Ithaca, N.Y., 1990), 88; *New York Leader*, 2 April 1859; *New York Clipper*, 30 June 1868; and Yates, *William T. Porter and the "Spirit of the Times,"* 4. Poe and Melville: Hershel Parker, vol. 1 of *Herman Melville: A Biography* (Baltimore, Md., 1996), 570–71. On Herne, see Herbert Asbury, *Sucker's Progress: An Informal History of Gambling in America from the Colonies to Canfield* (1938; rpt., Montclair, N.J., 1969), 173–15.

8. James Kirke Paulding, *The Lion of the West* (Stanford, Calif., 1954), 54.

9. *Tall Tales of Davy Crockett: The Second Series of Crockett Almanacs, 1839–1841*, ed. Michael A. Lofaro (Knoxville, Tenn., 1987). Carroll Smith-Rosenberg, "Davy Crockett as Trickster: Pornography, Liminality, and Symbolic Inversion in Victorian America," in *Disorderly Conduct: Visions of Gender in Victorian America* (New York, 1985), 90–108. *Ben Hardin's Crockett Almanac: 1842* (Baltimore, Md., 1841), n.p. *Crockett's Yaller Flower Almanac* (New York, 1836), 20. *Crockett Almanac* (Philadelphia, 1849), n.p.

10. Kenneth S. Lynn, *Mark Twain and Southwestern Humor* (Boston, 1959), 62–71. Franklin J. Meine, introduction to *Tall Tales of the Southwest: An Anthology of Southern and Southwestern Humor, 1830–1860* (New York, 1930), xvii. Augustus Baldwin Longstreet, *Georgia Scenes* (1835; rpt., Nashville, Tenn., 1992), xxii.

11. Yates, *William T. Porter and the "Spirit of the Times,"* 89–189. Dizikes, *Sportsmen and Gamesmen*, 60–62. *New York Clipper*, 30 January 1869 and 4 November 1882. *Centennial Newspaper Exhibition, 1876* (New York, 1876), 186–87.

12. *Porter's Spirit of the Times*, 24 July 1858. *The Big Bear of Arkansas, and Other Tales*, ed. William T. Porter (Philadelphia, 1845), vii.

13. For an example of such *Spirit*-like stories set outside the South, see Cornelius Mathews, "The Merry-Makers, Exploit No. 1," in *The Motley Book: A Series of Tales and Sketches of American Life* (1838; rpt., New York, 1840), which stages the action in upstate New York (141–51); on the relationship of such stories to *Spirit*-style literature see, Allen F. Stein, *Cornelius Mathews* (New York, 1974), 70–71. Yates, *William T. Porter and the "Spirit of the Times,"* 136.

14. Constance Rourke, *American Humor: A Study in National Character* (1931; rpt., Tallahassee, Fla., 1986), 69. "Barclay Street Guards" pranks: Yates, *William T. Porter and the "Spirit of the Times,"* 144. *Spirit of the Times*, 20 June 1846, 13 February and 17 April 1847, and 1 January 1848. *Trumpet Blast of Freedom*, in *Spirit of the Times*, 23 February 1850 and 3 May 1851.

15. *Spirit of the Times*, 18 July 1846. Johnson Jones Hooper, *Adventures of Captain Simon Suggs, Late of the Tallapoosa Volunteers* (1858; rpt., Tuscaloosa, Ala., 1993), 31–32. *Spirit of the Times*, 29 May 1852. William T. Thompson, *Major Jones' Scenes in Georgia* (1843; rpt., Upper Saddle River, N.J., 1969), 136–60.

16. Lynn, *Mark Twain and Southwestern Humor*, 46–99. Lawrence Frederick Kohl, *The Politics of Individualism: Parties and American Character in the Jacksonian Era* (New York, 1989), 70.

17. Joseph G. Baldwin, *The Flush Times of Mississippi and Alabama: A Series of Sketches* (1853; rpt., Baton Rouge, La., 1987), 91, 84, 84–85, 88–89. In "Davy Crockett as Trickster," Carroll Smith-Rosenberg notes how the Crockett myth inverts social norms.

18. Lynn, *Mark Twain and Southwestern Humor*, 46–99. Constance Rourke, *American Humor*, 60–70. Longstreet, *Georgia Scenes*, 9, 64. Thompson, *Major Jones' Scenes of Georgia*, 39. Baldwin, *The Flush Times of Mississippi and Alabama*, 192, 1.

19. The large literature on Prentiss attests to his stature among southern men. See, in addition to Baldwin, *The Flush Times of Mississippi and Alabama*, 197–222, T. B. Thorpe, "Reminiscences of Seargent S. Prentiss," *American Whig Review* 15 (1851): 236–50; George Lewis Prentiss, *A Memoir of S. S. Prentiss*, 2 vols. (New York, 1879); Joseph D. Shields, *The Life and Times of Seargent Smith Prentiss* (Philadelphia, 1883); and Dallas C. Dickey, *Seargent S. Prentiss: Whig Orator of the Old South* (1945; rpt., Gloucester, Mass., 1970), 392–94. For the folkloric Prentiss, see *Weekly Jackson Southron*, 30 August 1850, reproduced in *Humor of the Old South*, ed. Arthur Palmer Hudson (New York, 1936) 187–92; Henry S. Foote, *A Casket of Reminiscences* (1874; rpt., New York, 1968), 428–36; *American Wit and Humor* (New York, 1859), 10; and Baldwin, *The Flush Times of Mississippi and Alabama*, 209, 218–19, 222, 220.

20. Dickey, *Seargent S. Prentiss*, 389–92. Baldwin, *The Flush Times of Mississippi and Alabama*, 218–19.

21. Henry Clay Lewis, *Odd Leaves from the Life of a Louisiana Swamp Doctor* (1850; rpt., Baton Rouge, La., 1997).

22. Lewis, *Odd Leaves*, 59–64. Lynn, *Mark Twain and Southwestern Humor*, 104.

23. Donald Day, "The Life of George Washington Harris," in *Sut Lovingood's*

Nat'ral Born Yarnspinner: Essays on George Washington Harris, ed. James E. Canon and M. Thomas Inge (Tuscaloosa, Ala., 1996), 33–61. Wilson, *Patriotic Gore*, 509.

24. F. O. Matthiessen, *American Renaissance: Art and Expression in the Age of Emerson and Whitman* (London, 1941), 637. George Washington Harris, *Sut Lovingood Yarns: A Facsimile of the 1867 Dick and Fitzgerald Edition*, ed. M. Thomas Inge (New York, 1987), 172, 246.

25. Sut at a camp meeting: Harris, *Sut Lovingood Yarns*. Milton Rickels, "The Imagery of George Washington Harris," in *The Frontier Humorists: Critical Views*, ed. M. Thomas Inge (Hamden, Conn., 1975), 158. "I hearn a noise": George Washington Harris, "Sut Lovingood at Bull's Gap," in *High Times and Hard Times: Sketches and Tales by George Washington Harris*, ed. M. Thomas Inge (Knoxville, Tenn., 1967), 150. M. Thomas Inge, "Sut Lovingood's Yarns" in *High Times and Hard Times*, 110–11.

26. Milton Rickels, *George Washington Harris* (New York, 1965), 84. Harris, *Sut Lovingood Yarns*, 210–15.

27. Harris, *Sut Lovingood Yarns*, 216–26.

28. John Thomas, *From Tennessee Slave to St. Louis Entrepreneur: The Autobiography of John Thomas*, ed. Loren Schweninger (Columbia, Mo., 1984), 49. Molly Niederlander Ramshaw, "Jump, Jim Crow! A Biographical Sketch of Thomas D. Rice," *Theatre Annual* 17 (1960): 36–47. Dale Cockrell, *Demons of Disorder: Early Blackface Minstrels and Their World* (Cambridge, Eng., 1997), 62–66. W. T. Lhamon Jr., *Raising Cain: Black Face Performance from Jim Crow to Hip Hop* (Cambridge, Mass., 1998), 1–55, 157–72. See also Shane White, "The Death of James Johnson," *American Quarterly* 51 (1999): 769–70.

29. *New York Herald*, 12 April 1875. White: Langdon W. Moore, *Langdon W. Moore: His Own Story of His Eventful Life* (Boston, 1893), 33.

30. John J. Jennings, *Theatrical and Circus Life* (St. Louis, Mo., 1882), 371–72. Ralph Keeler, "Three Years as a Negro Minstrel," *Atlantic Monthly* 24 (1869): 79. On minstrels' love for pranks, see *New York Clipper*, 25 December 1915. "Joking on the stage": *New York Clipper*, 11 June 1864. *Seen and Heard* (Philadelphia) quoted in Edward LeRoy Rice, *Monarchs of Minstrelsy, from Daddy Rice to Date* (New York, 1911), 98–100; this account dates the hoax to 1877, but Bryant and Seymour died in 1875. Neilson's first American tour was in 1872. On the generosity of sporting men, see chapter 8 of this book. On the benefit for Dan Bryant, see *New York Clipper*, 1 and 8 May 1875.

31. Robert C. Toll, *Blacking Up: The Minstrel Show in Nineteenth-Century America* (London, 1974), 32. On the origin of the Virginia Minstrels, see *New York Clipper*, 13 April 1878; *New York Clipper*, 13 March 1880; and Hans Nathan, *Dan Emmett and the Rise of Early Negro Minstrelsy* (Norman, Okla., 1962), 113–19. "Astounding success": Charles White, "Negro Minstrelsy," *New York Clipper*, 29 April 1860. *Boston Evening Transcript*, 8 May 1843, quoted in Nathan, *Dan Emmett*, 120.

32. On Wooldridge, see Cockrell, *Demons of Disorder*, 130–35. J. Frank Kernan, *Reminiscences of the Old Fire Laddies and Volunteer Fire Departments of New York and Brooklyn* (New York, 1885), 487. House of Novelty: *New York Leader*, 26 January 1861. *New York Whip*, 9 July 1842 ("crim cons" is the abbreviation of "criminal con-

versation," i.e., adultery.) "Clever Fellows": Ned James, "Rynders and His Sporting Confreres," *New York Clipper,* 24 January 1885, and *New York Leader,* 3 March 1860, which is Wooldridge's own account of the episode. Wooldridge's own account of the Catherine Street meeting, quoted in the *New York Clipper,* 13 April 1878, is in the first person, but whether he was actually there or was describing what others told him is uncertain. Wooldridge's column, Old Sports of New York, began running in the *New York Leader* on 27 August 1859; Wooldridge is identified as the author in, among other places, the *New York Clipper,* 24 January 1885.

33. On Rice, see Maria Ward Brown, *The Life of Dan Rice* (Long Branch, N.J., 1901), quotation, 54; John C. Kunzog, *The One-Horse Show: The Life and Times of Dan Rice, Circus Jester and Philanthropist* (Jamestown, N.Y., 1962); Eric Lowell Engdahl, "A Biographic and Critical Study of the Life and Works of Dan Rice: The American Circus Clown, 1823–1900" (PhD diss., UCLA, 1990); and David Carlyon, *Dan Rice: The Most Famous Man You've Never Heard Of* (New York, 2001). Prizefight: undated clipping from the *Philadelphia Times* and unidentified clipping, both in the Dan Rice folder, Harvard Theatre Collection, Houghton Library, Harvard University, Cambridge, Mass.

34. For examples of "Jordan is a Hard Road to Travel," see Mrs. D. B. Bates, *Incidents on Land and Water; or, Four Years on the Pacific Coast* (Boston, 1857), 18, and George Hunter, *Reminiscences of an Old Timer* (San Francisco, 1887), 69. "Appeared to surpass New York": Richard Moody, *Ned Harrigan: From Corlear's Hook to Herald Square* (Chicago, 1980), 18. On the theater and minstrelsy in gold-rush California, see George R. MacMinn, *The Theaters of the Golden Era in California* (Caldwell, Idaho, 1941), 421–45, and Constance Rourke, *Troupers of the Gold Coast; or, The Rise of Lotta Crabtree* (New York, 1928). On the San Francisco Minstrels, see *New York Clipper,* 5 April 1879; Toll, *Blacking Up,* 151–54; and MacMinn, *Theaters of the Golden Era in California,* 421–26.

35. Toll, *Blacking Up,* 25–64, 40, 41, 36.

36. J. J. Trux, "Negro Minstrelsy—Ancient and Modern," *Putnam's Monthly Magazine* 3(1855): 75.

37. On the meaning of minstrelsy, see Nathan, *Dan Emmett;* Toll, *Blacking Up;* Alexander Saxton, "Blackface Minstrelsy," in *The Rise and Fall of the White Republic: Class Politics and Mass Culture in Nineteenth-Century America* (London, 1990), 165–81; David Roediger, "Black Skins, White Masks: Minstrelsy and White Working Class Formation in the Antebellum United States," in *The Wages of Whiteness: Race and the Making of the American Working Class* (London, 1991), 115–27; Eric Lott, *Love and Theft: Blackface Minstrelsy and the American Working Class* (New York, 1993); Cockrell, *Demons of Disorder;* and William J. Mahar, *Behind the Burnt Cork Mask: Early Blackface Minstrelsy and Antebellum American Popular Culture* (Urbana, Ill., 1999).

38. Mahar, *Behind the Burnt Cork Mask,* 55, 42. "Lubly Fan Will You Cum Out To Night?" (Boston, 1844), in *Series of Old American Songs: Reproduced in Facsimile from Original or Early Editions,* ed. S. Foster Damon (Providence, R.I., 1936), no. 39. "Old Dan Tucker" (New York, 1843), reproduced in Cockrell, *Demons of Disorder,*

140. "Dandy Jim From Caroline" (New York, 1843), in *Series of Old American Songs*, no. 34.

39. *The "Guzzlin' Jim" Songster* (New York, 1871), 24–25. *Bryant's Songs and Programmes for One Year*, ed. William L. Hobbs (New York, 1861), 20. *The Negro Singer's Own Book* (Philadelphia, [1846]), 30.

40. "The Original Jim Crow" (New York, c. 1832), reproduced in W. T. Lhamon Jr., *Jump Jim Crow: Lost Plays, Lyrics, and Street Prose of the First Atlantic Popular Culture* (Cambridge, Mass., 2003), 95–98. "Tell Me Josey Whar You Been" (Boston, 1841), in *Series of Old American Songs*, no. 29.

41. "Old Dan Tucker," *The Celebrated Negro Melodies as Sung by the Virginia Minstrels* (Boston, 1843), reproduced in Nathan, *Dan Emmett*, 454–56.

42. C. W. Haskins, *The Argonauts of California* (New York, 1890), 61. The "Petrel," no. 5, 18, in De Costa, "Journal of the Passage of the Ship *Duxbury* to San Francisco," William H. Huntington Library, San Marino, Calif. Trux, "Negro Minstrelsy," 75. Cornelius Mathews, *A Pen-and-Ink Panorama of New-York City* (New York, 1853), 90. *Folk Song U.S.A.*, ed. Alan Lomax (1947; rpt., New York, 1975), 112–13, 132–33; and *American Folk Ballads: Tunes and Songs as Sung by Pete Seeger* (New York, 1961), 52. Frazier-Patterson Band, "Old Dan Tucker," *Altamont: Black String Band Music*, Rounder Records, audiocassette C-0238. *Remembering Slavery: African Americans Talk about Their Personal Experiences of Slavery*, ed. Ira Berlin, Marc Favreau, and Steven F. Miller (New York, 1998), 182.

43. I provide more evidence on the vicarious pleasure white audiences took in seeing violence inflicted on blacks in chapter 9. John W. Smith, "The Quack Doctor," in *This Grotesque Essence: Plays from the American Minstrel Stage*, ed. Gary D. Engle (Baton Rouge, La., 1978), 33, 34.

44. *Literary World*, 7 July 1849. *The Harp of a Thousand Strings*, ed. S. Avery (New York, 1858). George Kummer, "Who Wrote 'The Harp of a Thousand Strings?'" in *The Frontier Humorists*, 219–29. Mahar, *Behind the Burnt Cork Mask*, 80–85. "Bressed Am Dem Dat 'Spects Nuttin', Kaze Day Aint a Gwine to Git Nuttin!" reproduced in Nathan, *Dan Emmett*, 410–12.

45. For the history of the troupe, see "Col. T. Allston Brown's Early History of Negro Minstrelsy: Its Rise and Progress in the United States," in *Burnt Cork and Tambourines* (n.p., n.d.), 132–51; Nathan, *Dan Emmett*, 227–30; there is also information in the Dan Bryant folder in the Harvard Theatre Collection, Houghton Library, Harvard University, Cambridge, Mass., and in obituaries of Jerry Bryant in the *New York Clipper*, 20 April 1860, and of Dan Bryant in the *New York Herald*, 12 April 1875, *New York Clipper*, 24 April 1875, *New York World*, 11 April 1875, and *New York Times*, 11 April 1875. *New York Clipper*, 12 September and 8 August 1857. Nathan, *Dan Emmett*, 231.

46. *New York Herald*, 12 April 1875. William Harding, *John C. Heenan of Troy, N.Y.* (New York, 1881), 15, 33. *New York Herald*, 12 April 1875. Ed James, *Life and Battles of Tom Hyer* (New York, 1879), 24. *Wilkes' Spirit of the Times*, 18 December 1869 and 1 October 1870. *New York Clipper*, 1 and 8 May 1875.

47. *Bryant's Songs and Programmes for One Year*, 3. Nathan, *Dan Emmett*, 229. *Bryant's Essence of Ole Virginny* (New York, 1859), 26–27. *New York Clipper*, 9 June 1860.

48. *Boston Daily Transcript*, 25 March 1840, quoted in Nathan, *Dan Emmett*, 241. *Knickerbocker* 32 (1848): 181. "Letter from Mr. William Patterson Himself," in *Big Bear of Arkansas*, 115. "Jones' Fight," *Spirit of the Times*, 25 January 1840. *Big Bear of Arkansas*, 32–41. See also *New York Flash*, 3 September 1842, and "Billy Patterson and His Celebrated Rival the Georgia Major," in *A Quarter Race in Kentucky, and Other Tales*, ed. William T. Porter (Philadelphia, 1846), 107–9. "Who Struck Billy Patterson?" Bryant's Minstrels playbill, 21 January 1862, Dan Bryant folder, Harvard Theatre Collection, Houghton Library, Harvard University, Cambridge, Mass. The "Shark," 18 July 1849, in De Costa, "Journal of the Passage of the Ship *Duxbury* to San Francisco." *San Francisco Alta California*, 16 August 1849. Nathan, *Dan Emmett*, 295. "Billy Patterson," reproduced in Nathan, *Dan Emmett*, 374–77.

49. "White faces": Keeler, "Three Years a Negro Minstrel," 77.

50. "Ill-Count McGinnis": *This Grotesque Essence*, 14, 80. *Bryant's Songs and Programmes for One Year*, 142–43. "Ould Ireland's the place for a frolic" and "Finnegan's Wake": *Bryant's New Songster* (New York, n.d.), 65, 24. "Conny O'Ryan": *Christy's New Songster and Black Joker*, ed. E. Byron Christy and William E. Christy (New York, 1868), 25. David Grimsted, *Melodrama Unveiled: American Theater and Culture, 1800–1850* (Berkeley, Calif., 1968), 190. "Tuscaloosa Sam": *Tony Pastor's Comic Songster* (New York, n.d.), 45–46.

51. "Mose": *New York Clipper*, 6 April 1878. Charles White, *The Hop of Fashion; or, The Bon-Ton Soiree* (New York, n.d.). "The Ticket Taker," in *This Grotesque Essence*, 78–84. "Hop of Fashion," Bryant's Minstrels playbill, 17 August 1858, Harvard Theatre Collection, Houghton Library, Harvard University, Cambridge, Mass. *Bryant's Songs and Programmes for One Year*, 604. "Wake up, Jake," Nineteenth-century copyright deposits, vol. 30 (1848), Music Division, Library of Congress, Washington, D.C. Jon Newsome, "The Music," liner notes for *Where Home Is: Life in Nineteenth-Century Cincinnati*, New World Records, NW251. The "Challenge Dance" sketch is printed in *This Grotesque Essence*, 14–20.

52. M. M. Bakhtin, *The Dialogic Imagination*, ed. Michael Holquist, trans. Caryl Emerson and Michael Holquist (Austin, Tex., 1981), 61–63. Ann Douglas, *The Feminization of American Culture* (New York, 1977). Nicholas E. Tawa, *Sweet Songs for Gentle Americans: The Parlor Song in America, 179–1860* (Bowling Green, Ohio, 1980). Jon F. Finson, *Voices That Are Gone* (New York, 1994), 3–42.

53. *Bryant's "Put Me in My Little Bed" Songster* (New York, 1870), 4, 9. *Tony Pastors' Great Sensation Songster* (New York, n.d.), 42–43. *Gus Williams' Olympic Songster* (New York, 1857), 13. *George Christy's Essence of Old Kentucky* (New York, 186?), 1. *Captain Jinks of the Horse Marines Songster* (New York, 1868), 26.

54. George Wakeman, "Grotesque Songs," *Galaxy* 4 (1867): 789–96; Wakeman was the coauthor of the famed 1863 *Miscegenation* hoax. *Tony Pastor's 201 Bowery Songster* (New York, n.d.), 55.

55. Saxton, "Blackface Minstrelsy," 172, 171.

CHAPTER 7. WILD EAST AND WILD WEST

1. John White, *Sketches from America* (London, 1870), 261–62. William E. Webb, "Air Towns and Their Inhabitants," *Harper's Magazine* 51 (1875): 828–35.

2. Robert Service, *The Shooting of Dan McGrew, and Other Poems* (New York, 1993), 13; "Men That Don't Fit In" was first published in 1907.

3. Stewart W. Holbrook, *Holy Old Mackinaw: A Natural History of the American Lumberjack*, 2nd ed. (New York, 1956). Walter W. Wyckoff, *The Workers: An Experiment in Reality: The East* (New York, 1905), 254–55 (quoted in Holbrook, *Holy Old Mackinaw*, 135).

4. John S. Springer, *Forest Life and Forest Trees: Comprising Winter Camp Life among the Loggers, and Wild-Wood Adventure* (New York, 1851), 151–52. Holbrook, *Holy Old Mackinaw*, 14–18. James M. Mundy, *Hard Times, Hard Men: Maine and the Irish, 1830–1860* (Scarborough, Me., 1990), 34–36, 103–14, 126–27. Henry D. Sheldon, *Student Life and Customs* (New York, 1901), 113.

5. John W. Fitzmaurice, *"The Shanty Boy"; or, Life in a Lumber Camp* (1889; rpt., Upper Saddle River, N.J., 1970), 174–75, 177. Jeremy W. Kilar, *Michigan's Lumbertowns: Lumber Men, and Laborers in Saginaw, Bay City and Muskegon, 1870–1905* (Detroit, Mich., 1990), 72. Holbrook, *Holy Old Mackinaw*, 119–20. John Moore, *John Moore* (n.p., 1901), 56.

6. Parker Owen, quoted in Kilar, *Michigan's Lumbertowns*, 126. On Silver Jack Driscoll, see Fitzmaurice, *"The Shanty Boy,"* 119–20. Frank P. Bohn, quoted in Holbrook, *Holy Old Mackinaw*, 115. Kilar, *Michigan's Lumbertowns*, 126–27 92.

7. Blake McKelvey, "Rochester and the Canal," *Rochester History* 55 (1949): 10–11. George E. Condon, *Stars in the Water: The Story of the Erie Canal* (Garden City, N.Y., 1975), 130–32. Carol Sheriff, *The Artificial River: The Erie Canal and the Paradox of Progress, 1817–1862* (New York, 1996), 147. H. P. Marsh, *Rochester and Its Early Canal Days* (Rochester, N.Y., 1914), 12, 32, 13. Ronald Shaw, *Erie Water West: A History of the Erie Canal, 1792–1854* (Lexington, Ky., 1966), 221–22. Watervliet: Harry Sinclair Drago, *Canal Days in America: The History and Romance of Old Towpaths and Waterways* (New York, 1972), 284. Buffalo: Condon, *Stars in the Water*, 256–63. Vernon Leslie, *Canal Town: Honesdale, 1850–1875* (Honesdale, Penn., 1983), 2–3, 9, 69, 71. *Honesdale Republic*, 29 March 1866, quoted in Leslie, *Canal Town*, 69. Leslie, *Canal Town*, 152.

8. Herbert Asbury, *The Golden Flood: An Informal History of America's First Oil Field* (New York, 1942). John W. Forney, quoted in John J. McLaurin, *Sketches in Crude Oil* (1902; rpt., Westport, Conn., 1976), 117. *New York Herald*, 30 July 1865. S. P. Irvin, *The Oil Bubble* (Franklin, Penn., 1865), 148–49 (quoted in Asbury, *The Golden Flood*, 225). McLaurin, *Sketches in Crude Oil*, 184. Charles C. Leonard, *The History of Pithole* (Pithole, Penn., 1867), 83. *Pithole Daily Record*, 14 October 1865, quoted in Asbury, *The Golden Flood*, 208. William Culp Darrah, *Pithole, the Vanished City: A Story of the Early Days of the Petroleum Industry* (n.p., 1972), 200.

9. Petroleum Centre: McLaurin, *Sketches in Crude Oil*, 132. "One thousand dollars a throw": this seems very unlikely. The dazzling image of the high-rolling gambler

routinely led the press to exaggerate gambling winnings; see chapter 8 of this book. *Titusville Herald,* 30 November 1865, quoted in Asbury, *The Golden Flood,* 210. George Trainor, *The Life and Adventures of Ben Hogan, the Wickedest Man in the World* (n.p., 1878), 66. Asbury, *The Golden Flood,* 224–25.

10. Dale A. Somers, *The Rise of Sports in New Orleans, 1850–1900* (Baton Rouge, La., 1972), 7–14. Dennis C. Rousey, *Policing the Southern City: New Orleans, 1805–1889* (Baton Rouge, La., 1996), 46–48. Albert A. Fossier, *New Orleans: The Glamour Period, 1800–1840* (New Orleans, La., 1957), 381–90, 463–64; quotation, 383. Henry Fearon, *Sketches of America,* 3rd ed. (London, 1819), 273. Herbert Asbury, *Sucker's Progress: An Informal History of Gambling in America from the Colonies to Canfield* (1938; rpt., Montclair, N.J., 1969), 109–23. Herbert Asbury, *The French Quarter: An Informal History of the New Orleans Underworld* (Garden City, N.Y., 1938). *Wanderings of a Vagabond,* ed. John Morris (New York, 1873), 221–23. Somers, *The Rise of Sports in New Orleans,* 53–61, 159–91.

11. Christopher Morris, *Becoming Southern: The Evolution of a Way of Life in Warren County and Vicksburg, Mississippi, 1770–1860* (New York, 1995). H. S. Fulkerson, *Random Recollections of Early Days in Mississippi* (Vicksburg, Miss., 1885), 96. Ann Fabian, *Card Sharps and Bucket Shops: Gambling in Nineteenth-Century America* (1990; rpt., New York, 1999), 31–34. *Niles' Weekly Register,* 1 August 1835. "Potent spirit of old rye": *Wanderings of a Vagabond,* 341. James Lal Penick, *The Great Western Land Pirate: John A. Murrell in Legend and History* (Columbia, Mo., 1981). *Wanderings of a Vagabond,* 345–46.

12. Henry Ker, *Travels through the Western Interior of the United States, 1808–1816* (Elizabeth, N.J., 1816), 41 (quoted in D. Clayton James, *Antebellum Natchez* [Baton Rouge, La., 1969], 169). Edith Wyatt Moore, *Natchez-Under-the-Hill* (Natchez, Miss., 1958). Joe Cowell, *Thirty Years Passed among the Players in England and America* (New York, 1844), 95. *William Johnson's Natchez: The Ante-Bellum Diary of a Free Negro,* 2 vols., ed. William Ransom Hogan and Edwin Adam Davis (1951; rpt., Baton Rouge, La., 1993). Scott Holzer, "Brawling on the Bluff: Working Class Culture and Politics in Antebellum Memphis" (PhD diss., University of Mississippi, 1995), 176–210. Mason Peck, *Forty Years of Pioneer Life: Memoir of Mason Peck, D.D.,* ed. Rufus Babcock (1864; rpt., Carbondale, Ill., 1965), 87.

13. Louis C. Hunter, *Steamboats on the Western Rivers: An Economic and Technological History* (Cambridge, Mass., 1949), 391. Michael Allen, *Western Rivermen, 1762–1861: Ohio and Mississippi Boatmen and the Myth of the Alligator Horse* (Baton Rouge, La., 1990).

14. Allen, *Western Rivermen.* S. Wilkeson, "Early Recollections of the West—Western Boatmen," *American Pioneer* 2 (1843): 273. "Jack": George Forman, "The Life and Ancestry of Geo. Forman of Stratford-Ontario," typescript, Western History Research Center, University of Wyoming, Laramie (quoted in Allen, *Western Rivermen,* 181). T. B. Thorpe, "Reminiscences of the Mississippi," *Harper's New Monthly Magazine* 12 (1855): 30. George W. Brown, *Old Times in Oildom* (Oil City, Penn., 1911), 97. Wilkeson, "Early Recollections of the West," 272.

15. *Half Horse, Half Alligator: The Growth of the Mike Fink Legend,* ed. Walter

Blair and Franklin J. Meine (Chicago, 1956). "Symmetry of an Apollo": Morgan Neville, "The Last of the Boatmen," in *Half Horse, Half Alligator,* 52. Ben Casseday, *The History of Louisville, from Its Earliest Settlement until the Year 1852* (Louisville, Ky., 1852), 73–75. *Spirit of the Times,* 9 November 1844 and 22 March 1851; *New York Clipper,* 6 August 1859. Robert Darnton, foreword to Jacques-Louis Ménétra, *Journal of My Life,* ed. Daniel Roche, trans. Arthur Goldhammer (New York, 1986), xii. Timothy Flint, "Mike Fink: The Last of the Boatmen," in *Half Horse, Half Alligator,* 60.

16. *Wanderings of a Vagabond,* 419. John Habermehl, *Life on Western Rivers* (Pittsburgh, Penn., 1901), quotations, 168, 81. J. R. Talbot, *Turf, Cards, and Temperance; or, Reminiscences in a Checkered Life* (Bristol, R.I., 1882), 84. Thomas C. Buchanan, *Black Life on the Mississippi: Slaves, Free Blacks, and the Western Steamboat World* (Chapel Hill, N.C., 2004), 75–76.

17. Hunter, *Steamboats on the Western Rivers,* 393–94. G. W. Featherstonhaugh, *Excursion through the Slave States, from Washington on the Potomac to the Frontier of Mexico* (1844; rpt., New York, 1968), 137. Habermehl, *Life on Western Rivers,* 36. *Wanderings of a Vagabond,* 422–23. Peter Cartwright, *Autobiography of Peter Cartwright,* ed. Charles L. Wallis (New York, 1956), 190. Unidentified quotation in Hunter, *Steamboats on the Western Rivers,* 461.

18. William Main Doerflinger, *Shantymen and Shantyboys: Songs of the Sailor and Lumbermen* (New York, 1951), 411–12. Habermehl, *Life on Western Rivers,* 46. Thomas Hamilton, *Men and Manners in America* (Edinburgh, n.d.), 174. "On steamboats there is no Sunday": Habermehl, *Life on Western Rivers,* 166. George H. Devol, *Forty Years a Gambler on the Mississippi* (1887; rpt., Bedford, Mass., n.d.), 242.

19. Devol, *Forty Years a Gambler,* 235. *New York Clipper,* 10 April 1870. Herman Melville, *The Confidence-Man: His Masquerade,* ed. Stephen Matterson (London, 1990).

20. Sol Smith, *Theatrical Management in the West and South for Thirty Years* (1868; rpt., New York, 1968), 182. Devol, *Forty Years a Gambler,* 73.

21. On the not so wild West, see, for example, Gilbert C. Fite, *The Farmers' Frontier, 1865–1900* (New York, 1966), and Dean L. May, *Three Frontiers: Land and Society in the American West, 1850–1900* (Cambridge, Eng., 1994). Population estimates come from *The New Encyclopedia of the American West,* ed. Howard Lamar (New Haven, Conn., 1998). Watson Parker, *Deadwood: The Golden Years* (Lincoln, Nebr., 1981), 131–32. Estelline Bennett, *Old Deadwood Days* (New York, 1928), 7.

22. Robert R. Dykstra, *The Cattle Towns: A Social History of the Kansas Cattle Trading Centers Abilene, Ellsworth, Wichita, Dodge City and Caldwell, 1867–1885* (New York, 1976), 246–48. David T. Courtwright, *Violent Land: Single Men and Social Disorder from the Frontier to the Inner City* (Cambridge, Mass., 1996), 56–58. Anne M. Butler, *Daughters of Joy, Sisters of Mercy: Prostitutes in the American West, 1865–1890* (Urbana, Ill., 1985). Marion S. Goldman, *Gold Diggers and Silver Miners: Prostitution and Social Life on the Comstock Lode* (Ann Arbor, Mich., 1981), 25–26. Stephen Crane, "The Bride Comes to Yellow Sky," in *The Red Badge of Courage, and Other Stories* (New York, 1991), 257–73. Wilbur F. Sanders, "The Story of George Ives," in John X. Beidler, *X. Beidler: Vigilante,* ed. Helen Fitzgerald Sanders (Norman, Okla., 1957), 58.

23. Anne Ellis, *The Life of an Ordinary Woman* (1929; rpt., New York, 1973), 66. George Kohrs, *An Autobiography* (Deer Lodge, Mont., 1977), 7. Robert K. DeArment, *Knights of the Green Cloth: The Saga of Frontier Gamblers* (Norman, Okla., 1982). Frank F. Bell, *Gladiators of Glittering Gulch* (Helena, Mont., 1985), 19–43. "Jesse James," reproduced in Norm Cohen, *Long Steel Rail: The Railroad in American Folksong* (Urbana, Ill., 1981), 97–99. Clark Secrest, *Hell's Belles: Prostitution, Vice, and Crime in Early Denver*, rev. ed. (Boulder, Colo., 2002), 272. Nolie Mumey, *Creede: History of a Colorado Silver Mining Town* (Denver, Colo., 1949), 135–42. William R. Collier and Edwin V. Westrate, *The Reign of Soapy Smith* (Garden City, N.Y., 1953).

24. John J. Callison, *Bill Jones of Paradise Valley* (Kingfisher, Okla., 1914), 43. *New York Clipper*, 25 July 1868. *Denver Daily Tribune*, 21 September 1878, quoted in Duane A. Smith, *Rocky Mountain Mining Camps: The Urban Frontier* (Bloomington, Ind., 1967), 233. Philip Ashton Rollins, *The Cowboy: An Unconventional History of Civilization on the Old-Time Cattle Range* (1936; rpt., Norman, Okla., 1979). John D. Young, *John D. Young and the Colorado Gold Rush*, ed. Dwight L. Smith (Chicago, 1969), 139, 141.

25. A. K. McClure, *Three Thousand Miles through the Rocky Mountains* (Philadelphia, 1869), 212. George Herenden, letter to his sister, 4 March 1878, quoted in Elliott West, *The Saloon on the Rocky Mountain Mining Frontier* (Lincoln, Nebr., 1979), 60. Libeus Barney, *Letters of the Pike's Peak Gold Rush: Early-Day Letters by Libeus Barney, Reprinted from the "Bennington Banner," Vermont, 1859–1860* (San Jose, Calif., 1959), 40, 74–76. See also Vardis Fisher and Opal Laurel Holmes, *Gold Rushes and Mining Camps of the Early American West* (Caldwell, Idaho, 1968), 109, and Evelyn A. Schlatter, "Drag's a Life: Women, Gender, and Cross-Dressing in the Ninteenth-Century West," in *Writing the Range: Race, Class and Culture in the Women's West*, ed. Elizabeth Jameson and Susan Armitage (Norman, Okla., 1997), 334–45.

26. Noah Smithwick, *The Evolution of a State; or, Recollections of Old Texas Days* (1900; rpt., Austin, Tex., 1968), 75. John Lockhardt, "Reminiscences of the Old Town of Washington," reprinted in Mrs. Joanne Lockhardt Wallis, *Sixty Years on the Brazos: The Life and Letters of Dr. John Washington Lockhardt, 1824–1890* (1930; rpt., New York, 1966), 41. White, *Sketches from America*, 263. *Dodge City Globe*, 18 March 1879, quoted in Dykstra, *The Cattle Towns*, 242.

27. W. J. Rorabaugh, *The Alcoholic Republic: An American Tradition* (New York, 1979), 232. Eliot Lord, *Comstock Mining and Miners* (1883; rpt., Berkeley, Calif., 1959), 377.

28. Frank Richard Prassel, *The Western Peace Officer: A Legacy of Law and Order* (Norman, Okla., 1972). Alexander Taylor Rankin, letter to Mrs. Kelly, 10 August 1860, reproduced in *Alexander Taylor Rankin (1803–1885): His Diary and Letters*, ed. Nolie Mumey (Boulder, Colo., 1966), 90. D. Freeman, *Midnight and Noonday; or, Incidental History of Southern Kansas and Indian Territory* (1892; rpt., Sumter County, Kans., 1976), 290. See also Robert Marr Wright, *Dodge City: The Cowboy Capital and the Great Southwest in the Days of the Wild Indian, the Buffalo, the Cowboys, Dance Halls, Gambling Halls, and Bad Men* (1913; rpt., New York, 1975), 170. Gary L. Cunningham, "Chance, Culture and Compulsion: The Gambling Games of the Kansas

Cattle Towns," *Nevada Historical Society Quarterly* 28 (1982): 256. Dykstra, *The Cattle Towns*, 130–31, 243–53. Horace V. Redfield, *Homicide, North and South* (Philadelphia, 1880), 72. Dykstra, *The Cattle Towns*, 128–31.

29. John Henry Cady, quoted in West, *The Saloon on the Rocky Mountain Mining Frontier*, 2. Mrs. M. M. Mathews, *Ten Years in Nevada* (Buffalo, N.Y., 1880), 187. M. W. Warner, *Warner's History of Dakota County, Nebraska* (Lyons, Nebr., 1893), 355. Craig Miner, *West of Wichita: Settling the High Plains of Kansas, 1865–1890* (Lawrence, Kans., 1986), 98. Ellis, *The Life of an Ordinary Woman*, 195.

30. George Hand, *Whiskey, Six Guns and Red-Light Ladies: George Hand's Saloon Diary, Tucson, 1875–1878*, ed. Neil B. Carmony (Silver City, N.M., 1994), 174 (7 March 1878), 41 (7 March 1875), and 51 (9 June 1875).

31. *Boise News*, 5 March 1864, quoted in Fisher and Holmes, *Gold Rushes and Mining Camps of the Early West*, 189. Agnes Morley Cleaveland, *No Life for a Lady* (Boston, 1941), 176. E. H. Saltiel and George Barnett, *History and Business Directory of Cheyenne* (1868; rpt., New Haven, Conn., 1975), 17. On boxing in western mining towns, see Ball, *Gladiators of Glittering Gulch*; *New York Clipper*, 13 May 1865, 22 May 1875, and 21 April 1883; West, *The Saloon on the Rocky Mountain Mining Frontier*, 85–87; Odie B. Faulk, *Dodge City: The Most Western Town of All* (New York, 1977), 136–37; and Parker, *Deadwood*, 184.

32. Rolf Johnson, *Happy as a Big Sunflower: Adventures in the West, 1876–1890*, ed. Richard E. Jensen (Lincoln, Nebr., 2000), 41 (2 March 1877). W. W. Mills, *Forty Years at El Paso, 1858–1898* (El Paso, Tex., 1962), 9. E. C. Abbott and Helena Huntington Smith, *We Pointed Them North: Recollections of a Cowpuncher* (New York, 1939), 247. *Galveston News*, 1878, quoted in Redfield, *Homicide, North And South*, 69. *Idaho Lore*, ed. Vardis Fisher (Caldwell, Idaho, 1939), 28–29.

33. David T. Courtwright calculates the homicide rate to have been 105 per 100,000 in Leadville in 1880 and at least 50 in the cattle towns (*Violent Land*, 82, 96–97). Clare V. McKanna Jr., in *Homicide, Race, and Justice in the American West, 1880–1920* (Tucson, Ariz., 1997), estimates the murder rate in Abilene, Kansas, at its height as a cattle town to have been 87.6 per 100,000 (162). Roger McGrath puts the homicide rate in the mining town of Aurora, Nevada, 1861–65, at 64 per 100,000 and in Bodie, California, 1878–82, at 116 (*Gunfighters, Highwaymen and Vigilantes: Violence on the Frontier* [Berkeley, Calif., 1984], 254). Eric H. Monkkonen found yearly rates of 100 to 300 in Los Angeles in the 1840s and 1850s ("Homicide in Los Angeles, 1827–2002," *Journal of Interdisciplinary History* 36 [2005]: 170–71). McKanna's study of murder in Arizona from 1870 to 1880 found a homicide rate of 34 per 100,000 in Las Animas and 70 in Gila counties (*Homicide, Race, and Justice in the American West*, 26). Western historians have long debated how violent the West really was. Robert R. Dykstra argues that it has been exaggerated ("Violence, Gender and Methodology in the 'New' Western History," *Reviews in American History* 27 [1999]: 79–86). He is correct to emphasize that fatal affrays were never an everyday occurrence, but I find convincing Roger D. McGrath and Randolph Roth's argument that the homicide rate was higher, and in many western places much higher, than elsewhere in the United States; see McGrath, *Gunfighters, Highwaymen and Vigilantes*, 261–71, and

Randolph Roth, "Guns, Murder, and Probability: How Can We Decide Which Figures to Trust?" *Reviews in American History* 35 (2007): 166–75. In *Race and Homicide in Nineteenth-Century California* (Reno, Nev., 2002), Clare McKanna Jr. notes that in 1860 there were more homicides in Tuolomne County, California, than in Vermont, Maine, New Hampshire, and Connecticut combined (105). McKanna, *Homicide, Race and Justice in the American West,* 27. McGrath, *Gunfighters, Highwaymen and Vigilantes,* xi.

34. Bennett, *Old Deadwood Days,* 142. William Larimer Jr., letter to his wife, February 1859, in *The Reminiscences of General Larimer and His Son William H. H. Larimer,* ed. Herman S. Davis (Lancaster, Penn., 1918), 168. Richard B. Hughes, *Pioneer Years in the Black Hills* (Glendale, Calif., 1957), 109. Watson Parker, *Gold in the Black Hills* (Norman, Okla., 1966), 151. See also *Wilkes' Spirit of the Times,* 14 May 1878. Smith, *Rocky Mountain Mining Camps,* 223. *Dodge City Globe,* 2 September 1878, quoted in C. Robert Haywood, *Cowtown Lawyers: Dodge City and Its Attorneys, 1876–1886* (Norman, Okla., 1988), 73.

35. Mari Sandoz, *Old Jules* (1935; rpt., Lincoln, Nebr., 1962), 41. "Endless practical jokes": Cleaveland, *No Life for a Lady,* 177. Shirley Zupan and Harry J. Owens, *Red Lodge: Saga of a Western Area* (Billings, Mont., 1979), 241. Mock gunfights: *Dodge City Times,* 21 April 1877, quoted in Nyle H. Miller and Joseph W. Snell, *Why the West Was Wild: A Contemporary Look at the Antics of Some Highly Publicized Kansas Cowtown Personalities* (Topeka, Kans., 1963), 21–22, and Daniel Ellis Conner, *A Confederate in the Colorado Gold Fields,* ed. Donald J. Berthong and Odessa Davenport (Norman, Okla., 1970), 121–22. *Colorado City (Tex.) Clipper,* 11 April 1885, quoted in Henry Allen Smith, *The Compleat Practical Joker* (1953; rpt., New York, 1980), 41. *Dodge City Times,* 29 September 1877, quoted in Faulk, *Dodge City,* 146. Larry Barsness, *Gold Camp: Alder Gulch and Virginia City, Montana* (New York, 1962), 96.

36. Albert W. Thompson, *They Were Open Range Days: Annals of a Western Frontier* (Denver, Colo., 1946), 33–34. *Texas Narratives,* vol. 5 of *The American Slave: A Composite Autobiography,* ed. George P. Rawick (Westport, Conn., 1972), 3:207. Mark Twain, *Roughing It,* ed. Harriet Elinor Smith and Edgar M. Branch (Berkeley, Calif., 1995), 221–27, 631–32. Smith and Branch conclude that "Nevada tradition and internal evidence suggest that the mock trial . . . actually took place" (632); see also Mark Twain, *The Great Landslide Case,* ed. Frederick Anderson and Edgar M. Branch (Berkeley, Calif., 1972), 9–27.

37. Paul M. Angle, *"Here I Have Lived": A History of Lincoln's Springfield, 1821–1865* (Springfield, Ill., 1935), 106–8. McClure, *Three Thousand Miles through the Rocky Mountains,* 410–11. Edwin C. Torrey, *Early Days in Dakota* (n.p., 1925), 275–77. "'Rip-snortin' gymnasium": *Virginia City Daily Union,* 29 January 1864, quoted in *Mark Twain of the Enterprise: Newspaper Articles and Other Documents, 1862–1864,* ed. Henry Nash Smith (Berkeley, Calif., 1957), 145. Richard G. Lillard, "Studies in Washoe Journalism and Humor" (PhD diss., University of Iowa, 1943), 11, quoted in *Mark Twain of the Enterprise,* 100–101. Alfred Doten attended a session of the Third House in Carson City in 1901; see *The Journals of Alfred Doten, 1849–1903,* 3 vols., ed. Walter Van Tilburg Clark (Reno, 1973), 3:2098 (15 March 1901). *Mark Twain of the*

Enterprise, 103. James Knox Polk Miller, *The Road to Virginia City: The Diary of James Knox Polk Miller*, ed. Andrew F. Rolle (Norman, Okla., 1960), 97–98 (9 January 1866). *San Francisco Alta California*, 18 April 1850.

38. Carlyle Channing Davis, *Olden Times in Colorado* (Los Angeles, 1916), 294. McClure, *Ten Thousand Miles through the Rocky Mountains*, 210. Edmund F. Hartshorn, *Sequel to "Experiences of a Boy"* (Newark, N.J., 1911), 10–11. Richard A. Van Ormon, *A Room for the Night: Hotels of the Old West* (Bloomington, Ind., 1966), 3–17. Thomas J. Noel, *The City and the Saloon: Denver, 1858–1916* (Denver, Colo., 1996), 17. West, *The Saloon on the Rocky Mountain Mining Frontier*, 50, 63–64. Mathews, *Ten Years in Nevada*, 192, 172, 173.

39. *Dodge City Times*, 13 April 1878, quoted in Miller and Snell, *Why the West Was Wild*, 303. Baylis John Fletcher, *Up the Trail in '79*, ed. Wayne Gard (Norman, Okla., 1966), 63. Noel, *The City and the Saloon*, 26. Fred Hart, *The Sazerac Lying Club: A Nevada Book* (San Francisco, 1878), 210. *History of Denver*, ed. Jerome S. Smiley (Denver, 1901), 471–73. Noel, *The City and the Saloon*, 28. Roy. T. Wortman, "Denver's Anti-Chinese Riot, 1880," *Colorado Magazine* 42 (1965): 275–91.

40. McClure, *Three Thousand Miles through the Rocky Mountains*, 42. Parker, *Deadwood*, 52. Jerry Bryan, *An Illinois Gold Hunter in the Black Hills*, ed. Clyde C. Walton (Springfield, Ill., 1960), 35 (2 August 1876). William T. Ballou, "Adventures of William T. Ballou," Bancroft Library, University of California, Berkeley, 6. Ballou's story is confirmed in the *Boise News*, 30 July 1864, which gives the number killed as 36 (Ballou estimated 120). Gregory Michno, *Deadliest Indian War in the West: The Snake Conflict, 1864–1868* (Caldwell, Idaho, 2007), 66. The background of this engagement in the "Snake War" is found in "Fort Boise," *Idaho State Historical Society Reference Series* 365 (1965): 1–2. I would like to thank Kathy Hodges of the Idaho State Historical Society for providing me with information on this event.

41. Isabella L. Bird, *A Lady's Life in the Rocky Mountains* (1879; rpt., London, 1982), 213. Rollins, *The Cowboy*, 83. Johnson, *Happy as a Big Sunflower*, 160 (7 June 1879). West, *The Saloon on the Rocky Mountain Mining Frontier*, 68, 66.

42. Callison, *Bill Jones*, 44. Miller and Snell, *Why the West Was Wild*, reprints articles from Dodge papers that suggest the high level of violence in Dodge City. Wright, *Dodge City*, 248, 207.

43. Callison, *Bill Jones*, 45. *Dodge City Times*, 21 April 1877, reproduced in Miller and Snell, *Why the West Was Wild*, 21. Wright, *Dodge City*, 223–37, quotation, 227. Robert C. Haywood, "'No Less a Man': Blacks in Cow Town Dodge City, 1876–1886," *Western Historical Quarterly* 19 (1988): 165. *Dodge City Globe*, 9 September 1876, reproduced in Miller and Snell, *Why the West Was Wild*, 157.

44. Wright, *Dodge City*, 242–45. "'Hokey-pokey' . . . carbon disulphide, or 'high life,' . . . when put on an animal . . . drives it into a frenzy": Bob Kennon and Ramon F. Adams, *From the Pecos to the Powder: A Cowboy's Autobiography* (Norman, Okla., 1965), 81.

45. Steven R. Frady, *Red Shirts and Leather Helmets: Volunteer Fire Fighting on the Comstock Lode* (Reno, Nev., 1984), 83. George D. Lyman, *The Saga of the Comstock Lode: Boom Days in Virginia City* (New York, 1934), 119–22. Samuel P. Davis,

"The Lawless Element," in *History of Nevada*, 2 vols., ed. Samuel P. Davis (Reno, Nev., 1913), 2:249–58, 2:269–71. Effie Mona Mack, *Mark Twain in Nevada* (New York, 1947), 195–98. Twain, *Roughing It*, 308–17, 668–71. William B. Seecrest, "There Once Was a Badman Named Mulligan," *Real West* 27 (1984): 14–25. *New York Times*, 10 July 1858 and 21 November 1860. *Wanderings of a Vagabond*, 324–27. *San Francisco Alta California*, 8 July 1865. Twain, *Roughing It*, 323, 673.

46. *San Francisco Alta California*, 23 May 1867, reproduced in *Mark Twain's Travels with Mr. Brown*, ed. Franklin Walker and G. Ezra Dane (New York, 1940), 224; my thanks to Peter Buckley for calling this to my attention. *Mark Twain of the Enterprise*, 66. Melvin Schoberlin, *From Candles to Footlights: A Biography of the Pike's Peak Theatre, 1859–1876* (Denver, Colo., 1941), 52. Margaret G. Watson, *Silver Theater: Amusements of the Mining Frontier in Early Nevada, 1850–1864* (Glendale, Calif., 1964), 201. The song can be found in *Johnson's Original California Songs*, 2nd California edition (San Francisco, 1860), 19–20; references in the song make clear it was set in New York City. *Journals of Alfred Doten*, 3:1143 (18–26 November 1871); Doten was from Massachusetts. *Mark Twain of the Enterprise*, 73–75. *Journals of Alfred Doten*, 1:785 (16 June 1864). Cleaveland, *No Life for a Lady*, 187–88.

47. The information on Masterson's life and career is from Robert K. DeArment, *Bat Masterson: The Man and the Legend* (Norman, Okla., 1979); George G. Thompson, *Bat Masterson: The Dodge City Years* (Topeka, Kans., 1943); and Miller and Snell, *Why the West Was Wild*, 315–449. I discuss Masterson's practical joking in chapter 8. Wright, *Dodge City*, 299.

48. DeArment, *Bat Masterson*, 218–19. Michael T. Isenberg, *John L. Sullivan and His America* (Urbana, Ill., 1988), 271–74. *New York Clipper*, 13 July 1889. *National Police Gazette*, 8 August 1889. Miller and Snell, *Why the West Was Wild*, 436. Thompson, *Bat Masterson*, 45. Clark Secrest, *Hell's Belles*, 143–47. DeArment, *Bat Masterson*, 339–63.

49. *Dictionary of American Biography*, s.v. "Alfred Henry Lewis." *The Wolfville Yarns of Alfred Henry Lewis*, ed. Rolfe and John Humphries (Kent, Ohio, 1968). Flournoy D. Manzo, "Alfred Henry Lewis: Western Storyteller," *Arizona and the West* 10 (1968): 5–24.

50. DeArment, *Bat Masterson*, 373–97. W. B. Masterson, *Famous Gunfighters of the Western Frontier*, ed. Jack DeMattos (Monroe, Wash., 1982). Jack DeMattos, *Masterson and Roosevelt* (College Station, Tex., 1984). Edwin P. Hoyt, *A Gentleman of Broadway* (Boston, 1964). Patricia Ward D'Itri, *Damon Runyon* (Boston, 1982). Jimmy Breslin, *Damon Runyon* (New York, 1991). Breslin, *Damon Runyon*, 46–50, 83–84. DeArment, *Bat Masterson*, 386–87. Deputy marshal: *New York Times*, 7 February 1905. *New York Times*, 27 October 1921. Damon Runyon, "The Idyll of Miss Sarah Brown," in Damon Runyon, *Guys and Dolls* (New York, 1993), 17–24.

CHAPTER 8. SPORTING MEN

1. *Chicago Tribune*, 2 March 1883. "Bag of wind": *Chicago Tribune*, 2 March 1883; in sporting parlance a "dunghill" was a gamecock that would not fight. "Dirty dog": *New York Times*, 2 March 1883.

2. Most newspapers gave more coverage to Elliott's killing than to the Earp-Clanton affray in Tombstone; see the *Atlanta Constitution, Boston Globe, Detroit Free Press, New Orleans Picayune,* and *San Francisco Chronicle,* 27 or 28 October 1881 and 2 March 1883. *New York Times,* 8 March 1883. "Principal cities": *National Police Gazette,* 24 March 1883. *New York Times,* 8 March 1883. *New York Clipper,* 17 March 1883. "Nearly all classes of society": *New York Clipper,* 17 March 1883. *National Police Gazette,* 24 March 1883.

3. Numbers of sports: David R. Johnson, *Policing the Urban Underworld: The Impact of Crime on the Development of the American Police, 1800–1887* (Philadelphia, 1979), 160, and Thomas N. Doutney, *Thomas N. Doutney: His Life—Struggle and Triumphs* (Battle Creek, Mich., 1893), 144.

4. J. R. Talbot, *Turf, Cards and Temperance; or, Reminiscences in a Checkered Life* (Bristol, R.I., 1882), 75. Ed James, *The Life and Battles of Yankee Sullivan* (New York, 1880), 21, 11. "Opinions": *New York Clipper,* 29 January 1859. Tyler Anbinder, *Five Points: The Nineteenth-Century New York City Neighborhood That Invented Tap Dance, Stole Elections, and Became the World's Most Notorious Slum* (New York, 2001), 201–6.

5. McMullen: Henry C. Silcox, *Philadelphia Politics from the Bottom Up: The Life of Irishman William McMullen, 1824–1901* (Philadelphia, 1989); David Johnson, "Crime Patterns in Philadelphia," in *The People of Philadelphia: A History of Ethnic Groups and Lower Class Life,* ed. Allen F. Davis and Mark H. Haller (Philadelphia, 1973), 103–5; and Andrew H. Nelly, "The Violent Volunteers: A Study of the Volunteer Fire Department of Philadelphia, 1736–1871" (PhD diss., University of Pennsylvania, 1959), 70–73. Pendleton: Benjamin Perley Poore, *Perley's Reminiscences of Sixty Years in the National Metropolis* (1886; rpt., New York, 1971), 43–48, and Herbert Asbury, *Sucker's Progress: An Informal History of Gambling in America from the Colonies to Canfield* (1938; rpt., Montclair, N.J., 1969), 141–46. Thomas A. Martin, *Atlanta and Its Builders: A Comprehensive History of the Gate City of the South* (n.p., 1902), 46. Works Progress Administration, *Atlanta: A City of the Modern South* (New York, 1942), 14. *New Orleans Times,* 11 May 1870, quoted in Dale A. Somers, *The Rise of Sports in New Orleans, 1850–1890* (Baton Rouge, La., 1972), 56. *American Fistiana* (New York, 1873), 9. Herbert Asbury, *The French Quarter: An Informal History of the New Orleans Underworld* (Garden City, N.Y., 1938), 288–89. *Wanderings of a Vagabond: An Autobiography,* ed. John Morris (New York, 1873), 222.

6. Ned James, "Rynders and His Sporting Confreres," *New York Clipper,* 25 January 1885. Albert Lombard, *The "High Private," with a Full and Exciting Account of the History of the New York Volunteers* (New York, 1848), 8. *New York Illustrated News,* 5 May 1860. Lilly: Paul Foos, *A Short Offhand Killing Affair: Soldiers and Social Conflict During the Mexican-American War* (Chapel Hill, N.C., 2002), 117–19. McCleester: *New York Clipper,* 17 November 1860. Mulligan: William B. Seecrest, "There Once Was a Badman Named Mulligan," *Real West* 27 (1984): 14. Scannell: Augustine Costello, *Our Firemen: A History of the New York Fire Departments, Volunteer and Paid* (1887; rpt., New York, 1997), 435–36. *Wanderings of a Vagabond,* 316. Lombard, *The "High Private,"* 9, 40. "The Rowdy Gang": John Kreitzer, journal, 9 December 1846,

quoted in George Winston Smith and Charles Judah, *Chronicles of the Gringos: The U. S. Army in the Mexican War, 1846–1848* (Albuquerque, N.M., 1968), 46. Randy W. Hackenburg, *Pennsylvania in the War With Mexico* (Shippensburg, Penn., 1992), 123, 125. Silcox, *Philadelphia Politics from the Bottom Up*, 39–42.

7. *Wanderings of a Vagabond*, 427. J. Frank Kernan, *Reminiscences of the Old Fire Laddies and Volunteer Fire Departments of New York and Brooklyn* (New York, 1885), 153.

8. On filibustering in this era, see Charles Henry Brown, *Agents of Manifest Destiny: The Lives and Times of the Filibusters* (Chapel Hill, N.C., 1980); Amy S. Greenberg, *Manifest Manhood and the Antebellum American Empire* (Cambridge, Eng., 2005); and Robert E. May, *Manifest Destiny's Underworld: Filibustering in Antebellum America* (Chapel Hill, N.C., 2002). *Wilkes' Spirit of the Time*, 5 May 1860. "Pillage": James Carson Jamison, *With Walker in Nicaragua; or, Reminiscences of an Officer in the American Phalanx* (Columbia, Mo., 1909), 12. Robert E. May, "Filibustering in the Age of Manifest Destiny: The United States Army as Cultural Mirror," *Journal of American History* 78 (1991): 857–86. Greenberg, *Manifest Manhood*, 12, 168–69. Joseph G. Baldwin, *The Flush Times of Alabama and Mississippi* (1853; Baton Rouge, La., 1987), 84. Daniel R. Hundley believed that the "Southern bully" (his term for jolly fellow) "as a last resort turns filibuster" and "seeks by plundering and pillaging a helpless people . . . to bury in the excitement of adventure" a life of dissipation and gambling (*Social Relations in Our Southern States*, ed. William J. Cooper [Baton Rouge, La., 1979], 248).

9. Brown, *Agents of Manifest Destiny*, 157. Hubert Howe Bancroft, *History of California*, 7 vols. (1884–90; rpt., Santa Barbara, Calif., 1970), 6:603. Horace Bell, *Reminiscences of a Ranger; or, Early Times in Southern California* (1881; rpt., Santa Barbara, Calif., 1927), 215.

10. Brown, *Agents of Manifest Destiny*, 170–73. Albert Z. Carr, *The World and William Walker* (New York, 1963), 74–78. Walker's Baja California filibuster is recounted in Frank Soulé, John Gihon, and James Nisbet, *The Annals of San Francisco* (New York, 1855), 475–81; Bancroft, *History of California*, 6:593–98; William O. Scroggs, *Filibusters and Financiers: The Story of William Walker and His Associates* (1916; rpt., New York, 1969), 31–50; and Brown, *Agents of Manifest Destiny*, 194–209.

11. Amy S. Greenberg, "A Gray-Eyed Man: Character, Appearance and Filibustering," *Journal of the Early Republic* 20 (2000): 673–99. "Insignificant looking person": "A Letter from a Young Washingtonian," John Hill Wheeler Collection, Library of Congress, Washington, D.C., quoted in Greenberg, "A Gray-Eyed Man," 697. *New Orleans Delta*, 27 July 1857, quoted in Greenberg, "A Gray-Eyed Man," 680. Hubert Howe Bancroft, *History of Central America*, 3 vols. (San Francisco, 1883–87), 3:329.

12. Scroggs, *Filibusters and Financiers*, 67–70. Brown, *Agents of Manifest Destiny*, 216–18. William Walker, *The War in Nicaragua* (Mobile, Ala., 1860), narrates the expedition clearly and, scholars agree, relatively accurately. Miners: William V. Wells, *Walker's Expedition to Nicaragua: A History of the Central American War* (New York, 1856), 85–86.

13. *Wanderings of a Vagabond,* 184. On the authorship of this book, see chapter 1, note 13. "Great friend": Scroggs, *Filibusters and Financiers,* 333. *New York Times,* 10 May and 22 December 1856. *New York Tribune,* 22 December 1856, identifies Walker's leading city supporters; see also Wells, *Walker's Expedition to Nicaragua,* 226–27. *Bryant's Essence of Ole Virginny* (New York, 1859), 53. Seth Phelps, letter to Elisha Whittlesey, 16 May 1856, quoted in May, *Manifest Destiny's Underworld,* 131. For further evidence that sporting types were featured among Walker's supporters, see Roger W. Lotchin, *San Francisco, 1846–1856: From Hamlet to City* (1974; rpt., Lincoln, Nebr., 1979), 220; Joe Taylor, *Joe Taylor: Barnstormer* (New York, 1913), 14–15; Asbury, *The French Quarter,* 186–96; Alvin F. Harlow, *Old Bowery Days: Chronicles of a Famous Street* (New York, 1931), 230; and Scroggs, *Filibusters and Financiers,* 115–32. Mulligan: *New York Times,* 25 December 1856. Lilly: *New York Times,* 5 November 1857, and Hubert Howe Bancroft, *Popular Tribunals,* 2 vols. (San Francisco, 1887), 2:601–2.

14. Greenberg, *Manifest Manhood,* 29. Scroggs, *Filibusters and Financiers,* 300–305. Jamison, *With Walker in Nicaragua,* 63. *Star of the West: New York Tribune,* 30 January 1856. Jamison, *With Walker in Nicaragua,* 118, 112, 122.

15. *New York Times,* 16 January 1861. William O. Stoddard, *Inside the White House in War Times: Memoirs and Reports of Lincoln's Secretary,* ed. Michael Burlingame (Lincoln, Nebr., 2000), 35. *New York Clipper,* 27 April 1861. *Wanderings of a Vagabond,* 316–17.

16. Fire Zouaves: *New York Clipper,* 27 April 1861, and *Wilkes' Spirit of the Times,* 1 June 1861 and 4 January 1862. Izzy Lazarus: *New York Tribune,* 22 October 1858, and *New York Clipper,* 6 August 1853. Sixth New York: *New York Clipper,* 27 April and 4 May 1861; Harlow, *Old Bowery Days,* 345–46; Kernan, *Reminiscences of the Old Fire Laddies,* 152; and Gouverneur Morris, *History of a Volunteer Regiment* (New York, 1891), 22, 25. Mulligan: *New York Clipper,* 27 April 1861; *San Francisco Alta California,* 8 July 1865; and Seecrest, "There Once Was a Badman Named Mulligan," unidentified quotation, 23. Silcox, *Philadelphia Politics from the Bottom Up,* 56–59. *New York Clipper,* 21 September 1861, 14 June 1862, and 4 July 1863. *Wanderings of a Vagabond,* 316. William Howard Russell, *Pictures of Southern Life, Social, Political, and Military* (New York, 1861), 84, 85. George H. Devol, *Forty Years a Gambler on the Mississippi* (1887; rpt., Bedford, Mass., n.d.), 116–19.

17. Bell Wiley, *The Life of Billy Yank: The Common Soldier of the Union* (1952; rpt., Baton Rouge, 1978), 253. John W. DeForest, quoted in Wiley, *The Life of Billy Yank,* 252. Dixon Wecter, *When Johnny Comes Marching Home* (Boston, 1944), 219. Mason Long, *Life of Mason Long, the Converted Gambler,* 5th ed. (Fort Wayne, Ind., 1888), 43.

18. Gaines M. Foster, *Moral Reconstruction: Christian Lobbyists and Federal Legislation of Morality, 1865–1920* (Chapel Hill, N.C., 2002), 30, 78, 80, 224–25. *Wanderings of a Vagabond,* 184. Edward Winslow Martin, *Behind the Scenes in Washington* (n.p., 1873), 499–501.

19. *New York Tribune,* 22 October 1858.

20. On Queen and the early *Clipper,* see his obituary and related stories in the

New York Clipper, 28 October and 4 November 1882. Elliott: *New York Clipper*, 25 February 1882. James: *National Police Gazette*, 31 July 1880. *New York Leader*, 13 August 1859.

21. Elliott J. Gorn, *The Manly Art: Bare-Knuckle Prize Fighting in America* (Ithaca, N.Y., 1986), 164–78. *New York Clipper*, 10 April 1870.

22. On Fox's *Gazette*, see Edward Van Every, *Sins of New York as "Exposed" by the "Police Gazette"* (1930; rpt., New York, 1972), 145–299; Dan Schiller, *Objectivity and the News: The Public and the Rise of Commercial Journalism* (Philadelphia, 1981); Frank Luther Mott, *A History of American Magazines, 1850–1865* (Cambridge, Mass., 1957), 325–37; Elliott J. Gorn, "The Wicked World: The *National Police Gazette* and Gilded-Age America," *Media Studies Journal* 6 (1992): 1–15; and Howard P. Chudacoff, *The Age of the Bachelor: Creating an American Subculture* (Princeton, N.J., 1999), 187–210. *New York Times*, 15 November 1922. Harry Sinclair Drago, *Canal Days in America: The History and Romance of Old Towpaths and Waterways* (New York, 1972), 286–87. Van Every, *Sins of New York*, 158–60.

23. Michael T. Isenberg, *John L. Sullivan and His America* (1988; rpt., Urbana, Ill., 1994). *New York Clipper*, 18 February 1882. On Sullivan's extraordinary fame, see Isenberg, *John L. Sullivan*, 206–13. Unidentified newspaper clipping, quoted in Gorn, *The Manly Art*, 207.

24. Mackeever: Van Every, *Sins of New York*, 183–85. Allen: *National Police Gazette*, 15 December 1883.

25. Mott, *History of American Magazines*, 330–35. Van Every, *Sins of New York*, 160. John Rickards Betts, "Sporting Journalism in Nineteenth-Century America," *American Quarterly* 5 (1953): 39–57.

26. *National Police Gazette*, 18 February 1882. *New York Clipper*, 11 February 1882.

27. Nyle H. Miller and Joseph W. Snell, *Why the West Was Wild: A Contemporary Look at the Antics of Some Highly Publicized Kansas Cowtown Personalities* (Topeka, Kans., 1963), reprints relevant documents and newspaper articles, 519–63; see also William R. Cox, *Luke Short and His Era* (Garden City, N.Y., 1961), 89–150.

28. This list of nicknames is taken from *Wanderings of a Vagabond*; Talbot, *Turf, Cards, and Temperance*; and Harry Brolaski, *Easy Money: Being the Experiences of a Reformed Gambler* (Cleveland, Ohio, 1911). Harry Dodge, *The Autobiography of an Old Sport* (Syracuse, N.Y., 1885), 98.

29. *New York Clipper*, 20 May 1865. Joseph F. Hess, *The Autobiography of Joseph F. Hess, the Converted Prizefighter* (Rochester, N.Y., 1888), 33. *Poker Stories*, ed. J. F. B. Lillard (London, 1896), 58. *Baltimore American*, 4 May 1902.

30. Long, *Life of Mason Long*, 138. "Gamblers are called 'knights of the green cloth'" (*New York Slang Dictionary*, in *A Dictionary of Slang, Jargon and Cant*, 2 vols., ed. Albert Barrère and Charles G. Leland [n.p., 1889–90], 1:225). The term presumably refers to a faro layout.

31. Estelline Bennett, *Old Deadwood Days* (New York, 1928), 146. Poore, *Perley's Reminiscences*, 46. "The Female Sports of New York by One of Them" began running in the *National Police Gazette* on 24 March 1883. *Kansas City Times*, n.d., reprinted in

New York Clipper, 14 October 1876. Robert K. DeArment, *Knights of the Green Cloth: The Saga of Frontier Gamblers* (Norman, Okla., 1982), 269–72.

32. Wolf Mankowitz, *Mazeppa: The Lives, Loves and Legends of Adah Isaacs Menken* (London, 1982). Renée Sentilles, *Performing Menken: Adah Isaacs Menken and the Birth of American Celebrity* (Cambridge, Eng., 2003). Mankowitz's assertion that the *Clipper's* Ned James was a notorious former English lawyer and MP is incorrect—that was a different Ned James; see *New York Times*, 7 March 1882, and *National Police Gazette*, 31 July 1880. Ed James, *Biography of Adah Isaacs Menken* (New York, 1881), 6. George D. Lyman, *The Saga of the Comstock Lode: Boom Days in Virginia City* (New York, 1934), 280–81. Sentilles, *Performing Menken*, 190–97. David S. Reynolds, *Walt Whitman's America: A Cultural Biography* (New York, 1995), 376–78.

33. Bennett, *Old Deadwood Days*, 146. DeArment, *Knights of the Green Cloth*, 172–73. Rynders: *National Police Gazette*, 24 January 1846. Lilly: Thomas Reid, journal, 7 October 1849, quoted in *A Year of Mud and Gold and San Francisco in Letters and Diaries*, ed. William Benemann (Lincoln, Nebr., 1999), 92. *The Answer of John F. Chamberlain to the Complaint of George Wilkes* (New York, 1873). [John Chamberlain], *Marcus Cicero Stanley* (New York, 1877), 14. Helen Lefkowitz Horowitz, *Rereading Sex: Battles over Sexual Knowledge and Suppression in Nineteenth-Century America* (New York, 2002), 168. Mulligan: *National Police Gazette*, 15 May 1880. William E. Harding, *John Morrissey: His Life, Battles, and Wrangles* (New York, 1881), 11. Timothy J. Gilfoyle, *City of Eros: New York City, Prostitution, and Commercialization of Sex, 1790–1920* (New York, 1992), 73. Marilynn Wood Hill, *Their Sisters' Keepers: Prostitution in New York City, 1830-1870* (Los Angeles, 1993), 15. Harrison: *New York Tribune*, 13 August 1877, and, Gilfoyle, *City of Eros*, 71.

34. *New York Tribune*, 14 January 1885. Bennett, *Old Deadwood Days*, 150. The 1870 census of Virginia City showed nine of the twenty-six non-Chinese gamblers to be married (U.S. Census Office, Ninth Census of the United States, 1870, manuscript, Virginia City, County of Storey, State of Nevada, National Archives, Washington, D.C.) *San Francisco Alta California*, 4 June 1856, and *New York Times*, 30 June 1856.

35. *National Police Gazette*, 15 May 1880. W. B. "Bat" Masterson, "Doc Holliday," reprinted in *Famous Gunfighters of the Western Frontier*, ed. Jack DeMattos (Monroe, Wash., 1982), 80. Morrissey, Wilkes, and Earp were all married. *San Francisco Alta California*, 8 June 1856. *New York Clipper*, 8 November 1873.

36. Long, *Life of Mason Long*, 188.

37. Hess, *The Autobiography of Joseph F. Hess*, 17. Talbot, *Turf, Cards, and Temperance*, 25. *New York Tribune*, 13 August 1877. The huge gambling winnings reported in the press are likely exaggerated, perhaps greatly so; see the *New York Times*, 26 November 1858.

38. Gorn, *The Manly Art*, 173–74. Devol, *Forty Years a Gambler*, 86. R. G. Williams, *Thrilling Experience of the Welsh Evangelist R. G. Williams* (Chicago, 1896), quotation, 51. *New York Clipper*, 27 September 1873.

39. Louis Megargee, "John Chamberlain," *New York Herald*, 26 August 1896. Casey Tefertiller, *Wyatt Earp: The Life behind the Legend* (New York, 1997), 30–31. Robert K. DeArment, *Bat Masterson: The Man and the Legend* (Norman, Okla., 1979), 141–47,

236–38. Robert Marr Wright, *Dodge City: The Cowboy Capital and the Great Southwest in the Days of the Wild Indian, the Buffalo, the Cowboys, Dance Halls, Gambling Halls, and Bad Men* (1931; rpt., New York, 1975), 212–13. *Ford County Globe*, 17 February 1880, reprinted in Miller and Snell, *Why the West Was Wild*, 406–7.

40. W. W. Mills, *Forty Years at El Paso, 1858–1898* (El Paso, Tex., 1962), 22. Long, *Life of Mason Long*, 138. D. S. Tuttle, *Reminiscences of a Missionary Bishop* (New York, 1906), 192.

41. Jackson Lears, *Something for Nothing: Luck in America* (New York, 2003), 268–70. William Jerome and Jean Schwartz, "The Gambling Man" (1902) Rare Book, Manuscript, and Special Collections Library, Duke University, Durham, N.C., http://scriptorium.lib.duke .edu/sheetmusic/n/n03/n0307. *Baltimore Sun*, 14 May 1902. J. H. Green, A *Report on Gambling on New York* (New York, 1851), 58. *New York Times*, 26 November 1858. Devol, *Forty Years a Gambler*, 73. DeArment, *Knights of the Green Cloth*, 178. *New York Herald*, 2 May 1878. *Baltimore Sun*, 14 May 1902.

42. Long, *Life of Mason Long*, 53. *Wanderings of a Vagabond*, 380. Frank Tarbeaux, *The Autobiography of Frank Tarbeaux as Told to Donald Henderson Clarke* (New York, 1930), 103. Devol, *Forty Years a Gambler*, quotation, 89. Lears, *Something for Nothing*, 121–24.

43. Sarah Watts, *Rough Rider in the White House: Theodore Roosevelt and the Politics of Desire* (Chicago, 2003), 27. *Baltimore Sun*, 6 May 1902. *Chicago Record-Herald*, 10 August 1907. *Denver Times*, 16 September 1900, quoted in DeArment, *Bat Masterson*, 354.

44. Talbot, *Turf, Cards, and Temperance*, 75.

45. The information on Morrissey's life in this and the following paragraphs is taken from Harding, *John Morrissey*; Ed James, *The Life and Battles of John Morrissey* (New York, n.d.); *Life of John Morrissey: The Irish Boy Who Fought His Way to Fame and Fortune* (New York, 1878); *New York Times*, 2 May 1878; *New York Herald*, 2 May 1878; *New York Tribune*, 2 May 1878; *New York Sun*, 2 May 1878; and *New York Clipper*, 11 May 1878. Jack Kofoed's *Brandy for Heroes: A Biography of the Honorable John Morrissey* (New York, 1938) is entertaining but fictionalized and inaccurate.

46. "Any fighters?": *New York Herald*, 2 May 1878.

47. Talbot, *Turf, Cards, and Temperance*, 74. Harding, *John Morrissey*, 15.

48. Talbot, *Turf, Cards, and Temperance*, 74–75. *New York Herald*, 2 May 1878. Wheaton Lane, *Commodore Vanderbilt: An Epic of the Steam Age* (New York, 1942), 199. George Waller, *Saratoga: Saga of an Impious Era* (Englewood Cliffs, N.J., 1966), 119–227. David Black, *The King of Fifth Avenue: The Fortunes of August Belmont* (New York, 1981), 283–88. *New York Clipper*, 25 August 1866.

49. Waller, *Saratoga*, 119–40. Edward Hotaling, *They're Off: Horse Racing at Saratoga* (Syracuse, N.Y., 1995), 42–59. *Wilkes' Spirit of the Times*, 17 August 1863. *New York Clipper*, 13 August 1864. Jon Sternglass, *First Resorts: Pursuing Pleasure at Saratoga Springs, Newport, and Coney Island* (Baltimore, Md., 2001), 147–53. *New York Times*, 2 May 1878. Baker: Hotaling, *They're Off*, 89, and DeArment, *Knights of the Green Cloth*, 153–54.

50. Shoulder hitter: Matthew Hale Smith, *Sunshine and Shadow in New York*

(Hartford, Conn., 1868), 398–401, and Talbot, *Turf, Cards, and Temperance*, 74. *New York Clipper*, 3 November 1866. "Disturbing presence": *New York Times*, 2 May 1878. Evidence of Morrissey's prominence in politics is found in "Scrapbook on New York City Politics, 1875–1878," New York Public Library, New York City.

51. *New York Clipper*, 25 August 1866. *Life of John Morrissey*. *New York Times*, 2 and 3 May 1878; Morrissey's opposition to Tweed surely was primarily responsible for the paper's approving attitude. *Ballads and Sea Songs of Newfoundland*, ed. Elisabeth Bristol Greenleaf (Cambridge, Mass., 1933), 175. Charles F. Finger, *Frontier Ballads Heard and Gathered* (New York, 1927), 44–47. Gorn, *The Manly Art*, 122–23.

52. On Hill's background and career, see the obituaries in the *New York Tribune*, 28 August 1896, and the *New York Times*, 28 August 1896, and in the *National Police Gazette*, 12 September 1896. *San Francisco Alta California*, 6 June 1867, reprinted in *Mark Twain's Travels with Mr. Brown*, ed. Franklin Walker and G. Ezra Dane (New York, 1940), 270–74.

53. Smith, *Sunshine and Shadow in New York*, 436. James L. Ford, *Forty-Odd Years in the Literary Shop* (New York, 1921), 197–99. "Ablaze with light," "little disturbances": *National Police Gazette*, 22 November 1879. *New York Times*, 28 August 1896. Van Every, *Sins of New York*, 199–206. Female sparring: *New York Clipper*, 9 April 1881. Isenberg, *John L. Sullivan*, 4–5, 102–3. *New York Times*, 28 January 1896. Gilfoyle, *City of Eros*, 27. Charles Townsend Harris, *Memories of Manhattan in the Sixties and Seventies* (New York, 1928), 30–31. Van Every, *Sins of New York*, 202.

54. *The Night Side of New York: A Picture of the Great Metropolis after Nightfall* (New York, 1866), 81–84. Smith, *Sunshine and Shadow in New York*, 435–45. James D. McCabe, *New York by Sunshine and Gaslight* (New York, 1882), 612–15. J. W. Buel, *Metropolitan Life Unveiled; or, The Mysteries and Miseries of America's Great Cities* (St. Louis, Mo., 1882), 53–54. Samuel A. Mackeever, *Glimpses of Gotham and City Characters*, 7th ed. (New York, 1881), 59–60; this is a reprint of the 22 November 1879 *National Police Gazette* article. *Harry Hill's Greatest Songster* (New York, 1882), 3; this publication seems to have been sold at Hill's to men wanting a souvenir of their visit. *New York Times*, 30 September 1887 and 28 August 1896.

55. *National Police Gazette*, 14 May 1887. "Gambling king": *Chicago Record-Herald*, 10 August 1907. On McDonald, see Van Every, *Sins of New York*, 234–50; Herbert Asbury, *Gem of the Prairie: An Informal History of the Chicago Underworld* (1940; rpt., DeKalb, Ill., 1986), 142–54; Richard C. Lindburg, *To Serve and Collect: Chicago Politics and Political Corruption from the Lager Beer Riot to the Summerdale Scandal* (New York, 1991), 90–99; David R. Johnson, "A Sinful Business: The Origins of Gambling Syndicates in the United States, 1840–1887," in *Police and Society*, ed. David H. Bayley (Beverly Hills, Calif., 1977), 24–27; and Emmett Dedmon, *Fabulous Chicago*, enlarged ed. (New York, 1981), 138–41. *Chicago Tribune*, 8 August 1907. *Chicago Inter-Ocean*, 10 August 1907. *Chicago Tribune*, 8 August 1907. Claudius O. Johnson, *Carter Henry Harrison I: Political Leader* (Chicago, 1928), 185–88. Donald L. Miller, *City of the Century: The Epic of Chicago and the Making of America* (New York, 1996), 437–52. On Slater, see *Baltimore Sun*, 4 May 1902; *Baltimore American*, 4 May 1902; *Washington Post*, 23 February 1908; *Wanderings of a Vagabond*, 189–97; and Asbury,

Sucker's Progress, 405–7, 412–13. *Baltimore Sun*, 4 May 1902. *New York World*, 12 September [1870?], quoted in *Wanderings of a Vagabond*, 190. *Baltimore American*, 4 May 1902. On Chase, see DeArment, *Knights of the Green Cloth*, 161–78; Forbes Parkhill, *The Wildest of the West*, 3rd ed. (Denver, Colo., 1957), 64–69, 72; Clark Secrest, *Hell's Belles: Prostitution, Vice, and Crime in Early Denver*, rev. ed. (Boulder, Colo., 2002), 86–89, 101, 143, 170–71; and Scott Dial, *The Saloons of Denver* (Ft. Collins, Colo., 1973), 28–29, 37–39, 40–41, 61–66. *Denver Rocky Mountain News*, 28 September 1921.

56. Howard R. Rabinowicz, *Race Relations in the Urban South, 1865–1890* (Urbana, Ill., 1980), 243–46. *New York Clipper*, 13 August 1864.

57. *Wanderings of a Vagabond*, 367. Kenneth Kusmer, *A Ghetto Takes Shape: Black Cleveland, 1870–1930* (Urbana, Ill., 1976), 146–47. *Detroit Plaindealer*, 13 February 1891, quoted in David M. Katzman, *Before the Ghetto: Black Detroit in the Nineteenth Century* (Urbana, Ill., 1973), 173. Wendell P. Dabney, *Cincinnati's Colored Citizens: Historical, Sociological, and Biographical* (1926; rpt., New York, 1970), 180, 191. Jeffrey S. Adler, *First in Violence, Deepest in Dirt: Homicide in Chicago, 1875–1920* (Cambridge, Mass., 2006), 127. Roger Lane, *William Dorsey's Pennsylvania and Ours: On the Past and Future of the Black City in America* (New York, 1991), 16–17, 322.

58. Owen Kildare, *My Mamie Rose: The Story of My Regeneration* (New York, 1903), 79. Malinda Jenkins, *Gambler's Wife: The Life of Malinda Jenkins*, ed. Jesse Lilenthal (1933; rpt., Lincoln, Nebr., 1998). Charles Spencer Tate, *Pickway: A True Narrative* (Chicago, 1905).

59. Robert Bailey, *The Life and Adventures of Robert Bailey* (Richmond, Va., 1832). John Kenny Williams, *Vogues in Villainy: Crime and Authority in Antebellum South Carolina* (Columbia, S.C., 1959), 47–48. T. S. Arthur, *Ten Nights in a Bar-Room* (New York, n.d.), 25, 49.

60. George F. Stewart, *Bret Harte: Argonaut and Exile* (Boston, 1931), esp. 47–52. Bret Harte, "The Outcasts of Poker Flat," in *Selected Stories and Sketches*, ed. David Wyatt (Oxford, Eng., 1995), 18–28.

61. Harte, "The Outcasts of Poker Flat," 20.

62. The sporting man as southern man was not the reality. Of the twenty-six non-Chinese gamblers in Virginia City in 1870, only eight were from the South; six were from New York State (U.S. Census Office, Ninth Census of the United States, 1870, manuscript, Virginia City, County of Storey, State of Nevada, National Archives, Washington, D.C.).

63. Michael Denning, *Mechanic Accents: Dime Novels and Working-Class Culture in America* (New York, 1987). Albert Johansen, *The House of Beadle and Adams and Its Dime and Nickel Novels*, 3 vols. (Norman, Okla., 1950–62), 1:9. Edward Willett, *Flush Fred, the Mississippi Sport* (New York, 1884). Edward Willett, *Flush Fred the River Sharp; or, Hearts for Stakes* (New York, 1888), quotations, 2, 3. Joseph E. Badger, *Dainty Lance, the Boy Sport; or, The Bank Breaker's Decoy Duck* (New York, 1880). C. E. Tripp, *Ace High the Frisco Detective; or, The Girl Sport's Double Game* (New York, 1893). Howard Holmes, *Captain Coldgrip, the Sport Detective; or, The*

New York Spotter in Colorado (New York, 1886). Albert W. Aiken, *Doc Grip, the Sporting Detective; or, The Vendetta of Death* (New York, 1886).

64. Alfred Henry Lewis, *Wolfville* (New York, 1897), 108. Stephen Crane, "The Blue Hotel," in *The Red Badge of Courage, and Other Stories* (New York, 1991), 309. Edna Ferber, *Showboat* (New York, 1926), 185.

65. Bret Harte, "The Argonauts of '49," in *Selected Stories and Sketches*, 268–69.

66. *The "Guzzlin' Jim" Songster* (New York, 1871), 24–25. *Manhattan Melodrama*, MGM, 1934. Granville Stuart, *Forty Years on the Frontier*, 2 vols. (Cleveland, Ohio, 1925), 1:219 (26 August 1862).

67. *San Francisco Alta California*, 8 and 9 July 1865.

CHAPTER 9. CONTINUITIES AND COMPLEXITIES

1. Wilbur Cross, *A Connecticut Yankee: An Autobiography* (New Haven, Conn., 1943), 28–29, 27, 36, 56.

2. On the "women's crusade," see T. A. H. Brown, *A Full Description of the Origins and Progress of the New Plan of Labor by Women*, in Jane E. Stebbins, *Fifty Years History of the Temperance Cause* (Cincinnati, Ohio, 1874), 319–490; Eliza "Mother" Stewart, *Memories of the Crusade* (1889; rpt., New York, 1972); and Jack S. Blocker, *"Give to the Wind Thy Fears": The Women's Temperance Crusade, 1873–1874* (Westport, Conn., 1985). Stewart, *Memories of the Crusade*, 377. Lori D. Ginzberg notes the shift in postwar moral reform in *Women and the Work of Benevolence: Morality, Politics, and Class in the 19th-Century United States* (New Haven, Conn., 1990), 198–200.

3. Brown, *A Full Description*, 341. Edgar M. Baldwin, *The Making of a Township: Being an Account of the Early Settlement and Subsequent Development of Fairmont Township, Grant County, Indiana, 1829 to 1917* (1917; rpt., Evansville, Ind., 1979), 159–60. Catherine Gilbert Murdock, *Domesticating Drink: Women, Men, and Alcohol in America, 1870–1940* (Baltimore, Md., 1998), 20–41. Ruth Bordin, *Women and Temperance: The Quest for Power and Liberty, 1873–1900* (New Brunswick, N.J., 1990).

4. Robert Smith Bader, *Prohibition in Kansas: A History* (Lawrence, Kans., 1986), 60, 105. Herbert Asbury, *The Great Illusion: An Informal History of Prohibition* (Garden City, N.Y., 1950), 90–93. Paul E. Isaac, *Prohibition and Politics: Turbulent Decades in Tennessee, 1885–1920* (Knoxville, Tenn., 1965), 56, 10–11. Leonard Scott Blakey, *The Sale of Liquor in the South: The History of the Development of a Normal Social Restraint in Southern Commonwealths* (1912; rpt., New York, 1969), 13–15, 29–40.

5. *The Development of the Law of Gambling* (Washington, D.C., 1977), 93–94. Richard O'Connor, *Courtroom Warrior: The Combative Career of William Travers Jerome* (Boston, 1963), 83–114. *The Development of the Law of Gambling*, 103, 275–76, 280–81. Robert K. DeArment, *Knights of the Green Cloth: The Saga of Frontier Gamblers* (Norman, Okla., 1982), 389–93. Barton Wood Currie, "The Transformation of the Southwest through the Legal Abolition of Gambling," *The Century*, n.s., 53 (1908): 905–10. David Pietrusza, *Rothstein: The Life, Times, and Murder of the Criminal Genius Who Fixed the 1919 World Series* (New York, 2003).

6. *New York Clipper*, 22 October 1870. *New York Times*, 13 August 1873 and 8 June 1882.

7. James Turner, *Reckoning with the Beast: Animals, Pain, and Humanity in the Victorian Mind* (Baltimore, Md., 1980), xi. Katherine Grier, *Pets in America: A History* (Chapel Hill, N.C., 2006), 127–81. Bernard Oreste Orsi, "The Quality of Mercy: Organized Animal Protection in the United States, 1866–1930" (PhD diss., American University, 2002), 25–37. C. C. Buel, "Henry Bergh and His Work," *Scribner's Monthly* 42 (1879): 872.

8. Zulma Steele, *Angel in Top Hat* (New York, 1942), 141–49. Turner, *Reckoning with the Beast*, 52. Oliver Dyer, "Some Results of the 'Wickedest Man' Article," *Packard's Monthly* 1 (1869): 161–62. *New York Times*, 23 November 1870. Steele, *Angel in Top Hat*, 148–76. "Colorado correspondent": Steele, *Angel in Top Hat*, 105.

9. George Ade, *The Old-Time Saloon: Not Wet—Not Dry, Just History* (New York, 1931), 157. Newell Leroy Sims, *A Hoosier Village: A Sociological Study* (1912; rpt., New York, 1968), 46. Sims, *A Hoosier Village*, 54.

10. Don Marquis, *Son of the Puritans* (New York, 1939), 85. Lynn Lee, *Don Marquis* (Boston, 1981), 89, notes that "Hazleton," the village in this novel, is "obviously" Marquis's hometown of Walnut, Illinois. Sims, *A Hoosier Village*, 106.

11. Cross, *A Connecticut Yankee*, 27–43. Fred C. Holmes, *Side Roads: Excursions into Wisconsin's Past* (Madison, Wisc., 1949), 55–56. Cross, *A Connecticut Yankee*, 28–29, 36. Charles Morrow Wilson, *Backwoods America* (Chapel Hill, N.C., 1933), 23. Cross, *A Connecticut Yankee*, 54, 56.

12. Ted Ownby, *Subduing Satan: Religion, Recreation, and Manhood in the Rural South, 1865–1920* (Chapel Hill, N.C., 1990). Walter McElreath, *Walter McElreath: An Autobiography*, ed. Albert B. Saye (Mercer, Ga., 1984), 45. Robert Watson Winston, *It's a Far Cry* (New York, 1937), 48, 52.

13. Horace V. Redfield, *Homicide, North and South* (Philadelphia, 1880), 35, 17, 74, 55. Edward L. Ayers, *Vengeance and Justice: Crime and Punishment in the Nineteenth-Century American South* (New York, 1984). Ayers, *Vengeance and Justice*, 234. *Nashville Colored Republican*, 31 May 1874, quoted in Howard N. Rabinowicz, *Race Relations in the Urban South, 1865–1890* (Urbana, Ill. 1980), 246.

14. McElreath, *Walter McElreath*, 45, 44. Ownby, *Subduing Satan*. Chester Sullivan, *Sullivan's Hollow* (Jackson, Miss., 1978), 36, 50.

15. U.S. Census Office, *Twelfth Census of the United States, 1900, Population, Part 1* (Washington, D.C., 1901), 64. U.S. Census Office, *Tenth Census of the United States, 1880, Statistics of the Population of the United States* (Washington, D.C., 1883), 378. U.S. Census Office, *Twelfth Census of the United States, 1900, Statistics of Population* (Washington, D. C., 1901), xcii.

16. *Legislative History: Arizona, 1864–1912* (1926), quoted in *The Development of the Law of Gambling*, 390. Gilman Ostrander, *The Prohibition Movement in California* (Berkeley, Calif., 1957), 70. Richard Denny Parker, *Historical Recollections of Robertson County, Texas* (Salado, Tex., 1955), 83. William Willard Howard, "Modern Leadville," *Harper's Weekly*, 1 December 1888, 928.

17. David Deitcher, *Dear Friends: American Photographs of Men Together, 1840–*

1918 (New York, 2001). John K. Kasson, *Rudeness and Civility: Manners in Nineteenth-Century Urban America* (New York, 1990), 185–93. John Habermehl, *Life on Western Rivers* (Pittsburgh, Penn., 1901), 46. "Lager Beer," *Scientific American*, n.s., 1 (1859): 35. For evidence of the spread of lager, see Samuel Mordecai, *Richmond in By-Gone Days* (1860; rpt., Richmond, Va., 1946), 246, and Holmes, *Side Roads*, 63–64. W. J. Rorabaugh, *The Alcoholic Republic: An American Tradition* (New York, 1979), 233. F. W. Salem, *Beer, Its History and Economic Value as a National Beverage* (1880; rpt., New York, 1972), 91. Holmes, *Side Roads*, 59. Cassandra Tate, *Cigarette Wars: The Triumph of "The Little White Slaver"* (New York, 1999), 20, 24–25. Richard Kluger, *Ashes to Ashes: America's Hundred-Year Cigarette War, the Public Health, and the Unabashed Triumph of Philip Morris* (New York, 1996). Richard J. Butler and Joseph Driscoll, *Dock Walloper: The Story of "Big Dick" Butler* (New York, 1933), 29.

18. Butler and Driscoll, *Dock Walloper*, 205. Richard M. Dorson, *Bloodstoppers and Bearwalkers: Folk Traditions of the Upper Peninsula* (Cambridge, Mass., 1952), 187, 190.

19. Anthony Channell Hilfer, *The Revolt from the Village, 1915–1930* (Chapel Hill, N.C., 1969), 5–24. Page Smith, *As a City on a Hill: The Town in American History* (1966; rpt., Cambridge, Mass., 1973), 261–66. Carl Van Doren, "Contemporary American Novelists—The Revolt from the Village: 1920," *Nation* 113 (1921): 407.

20. Edgar Lee Masters, "Father Malloy," *Commmonweal*, 14 December 1927, quoted in John E. Hallwas, introduction to Edgar Lee Masters's *Spoon River Anthology: An Annotated Edition*, ed. John E. Hallwas (Urbana, Ill., 1992), 9. Edgar Lee Masters, *Across Spoon River: An Autobiography* (1936; rpt., New York, 1969), 94, 29, 81, 82. Herbert K. Russell, *Edgar Lee Masters: A Biography* (Urbana, Ill., 2001), 19–21. "Those who want to live": Masters, quoted in *St. Louis Post-Dispatch*, 29 March 1918; see *Spoon River Anthology*, 395.

21. The notes to the poems in Hallwas's annotated edition of the *Spoon River Anthology* identify the real Lewistown people that the poems' characters were based on; most of the identifications were made by Masters himself in later years. Masters, *Spoon River Anthology*, 180, 155, 221, 194.

22. Masters, *Spoon River Anthology*, 340, 128, 337, 100.

23. Willa Cather, *My Ántonia* (1918; rpt., Boston, 1961), 219. Thomas B. Spear, *Chicago Dreaming: Midwesterners and the City, 1871–1919* (Chicago, 2005). Christine Stansell, *American Moderns: Bohemian New York and the Creation of a New Century* (New York, 2000), 44–55.

24. The literature on masculinity in the late nineteenth century is large. Among the most important studies are Gail Bederman, *Manliness and Civilization: A Cultural History of Gender and Race in the United States, 1880–1917* (Chicago, 1995); Kim Townsend, *Manhood at Harvard: William James and Others* (1996; rpt., Cambridge, Mass., 1998); E. Anthony Rotundo, *American Manhood: Transformations in Masculinity from the Revolution to the Modern Era* (New York, 1993), 232–46; and Michael Kimmel, *Manhood in America: A Cultural History* (New York, 1996), 117–41. Ann Douglas, *The Feminization of American Culture* (New York, 1977). Henry Childs Merwin, "On Being Civilized Too Much," *Atlantic Monthly* 79 (1897): 839, 840.

25. John Higham, "The Reorientation of American Culture in the 1890s," in *Writing American History: Essays in Modern Scholarship* (Bloomington, Ind., 1970), 79, 86. Sports: Jackson Lears, *No Place of Grace: Antimodernism and the Transformation of American Culture* (New York, 1981), 107–8; Elliott J. Gorn, *The Manly Art: Bare-Knuckle Prize Fighting in America* (Ithaca, N.Y., 1986), 179–206; Harvey Green, *Fit for America: Health, Fitness, Sport and American Society* (New York, 1986), 181–215; Rotundo, *American Manhood,* 239–44; and Clifford Putney, *Muscular Christianity: Manhood and Sports in Protestant America, 1880–1920* (Cambridge, Eng., 2001). Norbert Elias sees the rise of sport as a critical spurt in the civilizing process, but in America the sports boom of the late nineteenth century seems to have been associated with what Elias calls a "de-civilizing" spurt; see *The Norbert Elias Reader: A Biographical Selection,* ed. Johan Goudsblom and Stephen Mennell (Oxford, Eng., 1998), 98, 214. *New York Clipper,* 8 November 1879.

26. Gorn, *The Manly Art,* 185–206. Duffield Osborne, "A Defense of Pugilism," *North American Review* 146 (1888): 433, 435. Marshall Stillman, *Mike Donovan: The Making of a Man* (New York, 1918), 120–21. Gorn, *The Manly Art,* 197–99.

27. *National Police Gazette,* 24 November 1888. Townsend, *Manhood at Harvard,* 111–12. John Sayle Watterson, *College Football: History, Spectacle, Controversy* (Baltimore, Md., 2000), 26–63. Heisman, quoted in Wiley Lee Umphlett, *Creating the Big Game: John W. Heisman and the Invention of American Football* (Westport, Conn., 1992), 22, 87–90. *National Police Gazette,* 24 November 1888. J. William White and Horatio C. Wood, "Intercollegiate Football," *North American Review* 158 (1894): 108.

28. Theodore Roosevelt, "The Value of Athletic Training," *Harper's Weekly,* 23 December 1893, 1236. Michael Collins, *That Damned Cowboy: Theodore Roosevelt and the American West, 1883–1898* (New York, 1989). Sarah Watts, *Rough Rider in the White House: Theodore Roosevelt and the Politics of Desire* (Chicago, 2003), 141–61. Roderick Nash, *Wilderness and the American Mind,* rev. ed. (New Haven, Conn., 1967), 149–53. "Vigorous manliness": Theodore Roosevelt, quoted in Nash, *Wilderness and the American Mind,* 150. Theodore Roosevelt, *Ranch Life and Hunting Trail* (1888; rpt., New York, 1966), epigraph. G. Edward White, *The Eastern Establishment and the Western Experience: The West of Frederic Remington, Theodore Roosevelt, and Owen Wister* (New Haven, Conn., 1968), 60–67, 79–93.

29. John F. Kasson, *Houdini, Tarzan, and the Perfect Man: The White Male Body and the Challenge of Modernity of America* (New York, 2001), 21–76. Gorn, *The Manly Art,* 195–97. Watts, *Rough Rider in the White House,* 44. Edmund Morris, *The Rise of Theodore Roosevelt* (New York, 1979), 90–91. Michael T. Isenberg, *John L. Sullivan and His America* (Urbana, Ill., 1988), 346, 360–61. Roosevelt, "The Value of Athletic Training," 1236. *New York Times,* 10 October 1905. "Mollycoddles": Theodore Roosevelt, quoted in Townsend, *Manhood at Harvard,* 110. Watterson, *College Football,* 64, 66.

30. Blocker, *"Give to the Wind Thy Fears,"* 89–90, 182. Brown, *A Full Description,* 435–73, quotations, 435. Jed Dannenbaum, *Drink and Disorder: Temperance Reform in Cincinnati from the Washingtonian Revival to the WCTU* (Urbana, Ill., 1984), 216–18.

31. James M. Williams, *An American Town: A Sociological Study* (New York, 1906), 188. The town is called "Blankville" in the book, and I would like to thank Richard and Philippa Brown of the Waterville Historical Society for confirming the identification of Waterville as "Blankville."

32. Williams, *An American Town*, 132–50.

33. Murdock, *Domesticating Drink*, 52–69. Cross, A *Connecticut Yankee*, 42–43. Masters, *Across Spoon River*, 82.

34. Jesse C. Burt Jr., "The Savor of Old-Time Southern Railroading," *Railway and Locomotive Historical Society Bulletin* 84 (1951): 38–39, quoted in Walter Licht, *Working for the Railroad: The Organization of Work in the Nineteenth Century* (Princeton, N.J., 1983), 238; see also Paul Michel Taillon, "'What We Want is Good, Sober Men:' Masculinity, Respectability, and Temperance in the Railroad Brotherhoods, c. 1870–1910," *Journal of Social History* 36 (2002): 319–38.

35. *New York Herald-Tribune*, 12 June 1934. *New York Times*, 12 June 1934. Gerald Bordman, *Oxford Companion of the American Theater* (New York, 1984), 151. Herbert G. Goldman, *American National Biography*, s.v. "Maggie Cline." James G. Geller, *Famous Songs and Their Stories* (Garden City, N.Y., 1940), 116–17. J. W. Kelly, "Throw Him Down, McCloskey" (New York, 1930), Music Division, Library of Congress, Washington, D.C.

36. James H. Dormon, "Shaping the Popular Image of Post-Reconstruction American Blacks: The 'Coon Song' Phenomenon of the Gilded Age," *American Quarterly* 40 (1988): 450–71. William L. Van Deburg, *Hoodlums: Black Villains and Social Bandits in American Life* (Chicago, 2004), 108–17. Lawrence Levine, *Black Culture and Black Consciousness: African American Folk Thought from Slavery to Freedom* (New York, 1977), 407–20. Cecil Brown, *Stagolee Shot Billy* (Cambridge, Mass., 2003), 106–9. Geller, *Famous Songs*, 97–98. Charles E. Trevathan, *May Irwin's "Bully" Song* (Boston, 1896), Music Division, Library of Congress, Washington, D.C. May Irwin, "The Bully," 1907: *"Dear Old Golden Rule Days,"* Archeophone Records 9008, compact disc. The words to Irwin's 1907 recording differ slightly from the published sheet music; the quotations are from the sheet music. "Bully of the Town": *Folklore: From the Working Folk of America*, ed. Tristram Potter Coffin and Hennig Cohen (Garden City, N.Y., 1974), 91–92.

37. Dormon, "Shaping the Popular Image of Post-Reconstruction American Blacks," 450–71. Charles E. Trevathan, *May Irwin's "Bully" Song*, reproduced in *New York Journal*, 12 April 1896.

38. "In fact there is no distinctive Bowery Boy any more" noted the *National Police Gazette* on 2 April 1879. Richard Moody, *Ned Harrigan: From Corlear's Hook to Herald Square* (Chicago, 1980). *New York Times*, 7 June 1911.

39. Moody, *Ned Harrigan*.

40. Richard Moody, introduction to Edward Harrigan, *The Mulligan Guard Ball*, in *Drama from the American Theater*, 1762–1909, ed. Richard L. Moody (Cleveland, Ohio, 1966), 550. Moody, *Ned Harrigan*, 95. Harrigan, *The Mulligan Guard Ball*, 562.

41. Moody, *Ned Harrigan*, 124.

42. The information on the career of Weber and Fields comes from Felix Isman, *Weber and Fields: Their Tribulations, Triumphs and Their Associates* (New York, 1924), and Armond Fields and L. Marc Fields, *From the Bowery to Broadway: Lew Fields and the Roots of American Popular Theater* (New York, 1993).

43. Gilbert Douglas, *American Vaudeville: Its Life and Times* (1940; rpt., New York, 1963), 77. Fields and Fields, *From the Bowery to Broadway*, 69.

44. Joe Weber and Lew Fields, "Adventures in Human Nature," *Chicago Record Herald*, 23 June 1912, Sunday magazine, 7, 17. See also Brett Paige, *Writing for Vaudeville* (Springfield, Mass., 1915), 103–4.

45. "Choking Sketch," reproduced in Isman, *Weber and Fields*, opposite 180. Fields and Fields, *From the Bowery to Broadway*, 521–22.

46. Lydia Maria Child, *Isaac T. Hopper: A True Life* (Boston, 1853), 8–10. The background of this work is explained in Carolyn L. Karcher, *The First Woman of the Republic: A Cultural Biography of Lydia Maria Child* (Durham, N.C., 1994), 370–73.

47. Anne Trensky, "The Bad Boy in Nineteenth-Century American Fiction," *Georgia Review* 27 (1973): 503–17. Gail Schumnk Murray, *American Children's Literature and the Construction of Childhood* (New York, 1998), 39–41, 54–57, 72–75. Jacob Abbott, quoted in Bernard Wishy, *The Child and the Republic: The Dawn of Modern American Child Nurture* (Philadelphia, 1968), 59. Jacob Abbott, *Rollo in Paris* (Boston, 1854), 101.

48. Thomas Bailey Aldrich, *The Story of a Bad Boy* (1869; rpt., Hanover, N.H., 1990). [John Habberton], *Helen's Babies* (Boston, 1876). Trensky, "The Bad Boy in Nineteenth-Century American Fiction," 503–17.

49. Mark Twain, "The Christmas Fireside," in *Early Tales and Sketches*, vol. 15 of *The Works of Mark Twain*, ed. Robert H. Hirst (Berkeley, Calif., 1981), 405–10.

50. Charles F. Pidgin and Charles Blacke, *Peck's Bad Boy Songs* (Boston, 1884). Don Gifford, *American Comic Strip Collections, 1884–1939: The Evolutionary Era* (Boston, 1990), 20, 234. George W. Peck, *Peck's Bad Boy and His Pa* (1883; rpt., New York, 1958), quotation, 234.

51. E. F. Bleiler, introduction to Peck, *Peck's Bad Boy and His Pa*. Peck, *Peck's Bad Boy and His Pa*. George W. Peck, *Peck's Red-Headed Boy* (New York, 1901), 199–201; this story, which seems to be taken from Peck's newspaper column, is unrelated to the plot of the book.

52. Peck, *Peck's Bad Boy and His Pa*, 60–61.

53. Roy L. McCardell, "Opper, Outcault and Company: The Comic Supplement and the Men Who Make It," *Everybody's Magazine* 30 (1905): 772, 768. Richard Marschall, *America's Great Comic Strip Artists* (New York, 1989), 22. Max Morath et al., "Maggie Murphy's Home," in *Don't Give the Name a Bad Place: Types and Stereotypes in American Musical Theater, 1870–1900*, New World Records, NW265. Bill Blackbeard, *R. F. Outcault's Yellow Kid: A Celebration of the Kid who Started the Comics* (Northampton, Mass., 1995).

54. Early Yellow Kid cartoons are reproduced in Blackbeard, *R. F. Outcault's Yellow Kid*. Colton Waugh, *The Comics* (1947; rpt., Jackson, Miss., 1994), 7. Marschall,

America's Great Comic Strip Artists, 27–28. "Casual cruelty": Robert C. Harvey, *American National Biography*, s.v. "Richard Outcault."

55. Alan Havig, "Richard Outcault's 'Poor Lil' Mose': Variations on the Black Stereotype in American Comic Art," *Journal of American Culture* 11 (1988): 33–41. Waugh, *The Comics*, 8. *New York Herald*, 4 January 1903 and 6 March 1904.

56. Marschall, *America's Great Comic Strip Artists*, 42.

57. *New York American and Journal*, 6 December 1903. Marschall, *America's Great Comic Strip Artists*, 49. McCardell, "Opper, Outcault and Company," 765. "The Katzenjammer Kids Explode a Ship," reproduced in Marschall, *America's Great Comic Strip Artists*, 44. "Mit dose kids": Irving Howe, "Notes on Mass Culture," in *Arguing Comics: Literary Masters on a Popular Medium*, ed. Jeet Heer and Kent Worcester (Jackson, Miss., 2004), 49. Marschall, *America's Great Comic Strip Artists*, 49.

58. *Encyclopedia of American Comics*, ed. Ron Goulart (New York, 1990), 68, 212, 220. On the Bowery stereotype in this era, see Alvin F. Harlow, *Old Bowery Days: The Chronicle of a Famous Street* (New York, 1931), 419–30. Rudolph Dirks, *The Katzenjammer Kids: Early Strips in Full Color* (New York, 1974), 26–28.

59. Ralph Bergengren, "The Humor of the Color Supplement," *Atlantic Monthly* 98 (1906): 272, 270. Herman Scheffauer, "The Comic Supplement," *Lippincott's Monthly Magazine* 83 (1909): 382. Waugh, *The Comics*, 37.

60. "Policy and Pie," reproduced in *Origins of American Animation, 1900–1921* (Washington, D. C., 1993), videocassette. Norman M. Klein, *Seven Minutes: The Life and Death of the American Animated Cartoon* (London, 1993), 42, 20.

61. E. G. Lutz, *Animated Cartoons: How They Are Made, Their Origin and Development* (New York, 1920), 226, 238–39. Donald Crafton, *Before Mickey: The Animated Film, 1898–1928* (Cambridge, Mass., 1982), 200. Klein, *Seven Minutes*, 42–43. Jesse Green, "Can Disney Build a Better Mouse?" *New York Times*, 18 April 2004.

62. Allen W. Trelease, *White Terror: The Ku Klux Klan Conspiracy and Southern Reconstruction* (1971; rpt., Baton Rouge, La., 1995), 5. J. C. Lester and D. L. Wilson, *Ku Klux Klan: Its Origin, Growth, and Disbandment* (1884; rpt., New York, 1905), 22. Stanley F. Horn, *Invisible Empire: The Story of the Ku Klux Klan* (Boston, 1939), 18. On the "Hounds" episode, see chapter 5 of this book.

63. W. J. Cash, *The Mind of the South* (1941; rpt., New York, 1961), 125. On lynching, see Grace Elizabeth Hale, *Making Whiteness: The Culture of Segregation in the South, 1890–1940* (New York, 1998), 199–223; W. Fitzhugh Brundage, *Lynching in the New South: Georgia and Virginia, 1880–1930* (Urbana, Ill., 1993); and Neil R. McMillen, *Dark Journey: Black Mississippians in the Age of Jim Crow* (Urbana, Ill., 1990), 224–53.

CONCLUSION

1. Ring Lardner, "Haircut," in Lardner, *The Best Short Stories: 25 Stories from America's Foremost Humorist* (1957, rpt., New York, 1988), 23, 27, 30, 24, 27.

2. Lardner, "Haircut," in *The Best Short Stories*, 31–33.

3. For another Lardner story about practical joking, see "The Maysville Minstrel,"

in *The Best Short Stories,* 1–9. Edward Jarvis, *Traditions and Reminiscences of Concord, Massachusetts, 1779–1878,* ed. Sarah Chapin (Amherst, Mass., 1993), 185. Edward T. Fairbanks, *The Town of St. Johnsbury, Vt.* (St. Johnsbury, Vt., 1914), 132.

4. Fox Butterfield, "Barroom's Decline Underlies a Drop in Adult Killings," *New York Times,* 19 August 1996.

5. Herbert Asbury, *The Gangs of New York: An Informal History of the Underworld* (Garden City, N.Y., 1928). Herbert Asbury, *The Barbary Coast: An Informal History of the San Francisco Underworld* (Garden City, N.Y., 1933). Herbert Asbury, *The French Quarter: An Informal History of the New Orleans Underworld* (1936; rpt., Garden City, N.Y., 1938). Herbert Asbury, *Gem of the Prairie: An Informal History of the Chicago Underworld* (1940; rpt., DeKalb, Ill., 1986). Herbert Asbury, *The Golden Flood: An Informal History of America's First Oil Field* (New York, 1942). Herbert Asbury, *Sucker's Progress: An Informal History of Gambling in America from the Colonies to Canfield* (1938; rpt., Montclair, N.J., 1969), 165–76.

6. George Santayana, "The Genteel Tradition in American Philosophy," in *The Genteel Tradition: Nine Essays by George Santayana* (Cambridge, Mass., 1967), 38–54. Ann Douglas, *The Feminization of American Culture* (New York, 1977). Leo Marx, "The Uncivil Response of American Writers to Civil Religion in America," in *American Civil Religion,* ed. Russell E. Richey and Donald G. Jones (New York, 1974), 222–51. Constance Rourke, *American Humor: A Study of National Character* (1931; rpt., Gainesville, Fla., n.d.), 202.

7. Libby Copeland, "Sleeping It Off? Shmile for The Birdy!" *Washington Post,* 16 January 2005. Paul Farhi, "On the Web, Punch and Click: Amateur Fight Videos Are Proliferating Online," *Washington Post,* 22 June 2006. "Explosive Fight Videos," www .explosivefightvideos .com.

8. See for example, John Burnham, *Bad Habits: Drinking, Smoking, Taking Drugs, Gambling, Sexual Misbehavior, and Swearing in American History* (New York, 1993), and Gertrude Himmelfarb, *The De-Moralization of Society: From Victorian Virtues to Modern Values* (New York, 1995); for a critique, see Peter N. Stearns, *Battleground of Desire: The Struggle for Self-Control in Modern America* (New York, 1999). Norbert Elias, *The Civilizing Process: Sociogenetic and Psychogenetic Investigations,* 2nd rev. ed., trans. Edmund Jephcott, ed. Eric Dunning, Johan Goudsblom, and Stephen Mennell (Oxford, Eng., 2000), 157–58.

Index